On Red Earth Walking

On Red Earth Walking

The Pilbara Aboriginal Strike,
Western Australia 1946–1949

Anne Scrimgeour

On Red Earth Walking: The Pilbara Aboriginal Strike, Western Australia 1946–1949
© Copyright 2023 Anne Scrimgeour
Anne Scrimgeour asserts her right to be known as the author of this work.

All rights reserved. Apart from any uses permitted by Australia's *Copyright Act 1968*, no part of this book may be reproduced by any process without prior written permission from the copyright owner. Inquiries should be directed to the publisher.

First published 2020
This edition published 2023

Published by Monash University Publishing
Matheson Library Annexe
40 Exhibition Walk
Monash University
Clayton, Victoria 3800, Australia
www.publishing.monash.edu

Monash University Publishing brings to the world publications which advance the best traditions of humane and enlightened thought.

Monash University Publishing titles pass through a rigorous process of independent peer review.

ISBN: 9781922633965 (paperback)
ISBN: 9781925835694 (pdf)
ISBN: 9781925835700 (epub)

Cover image design by David Morgan; photo by Eugenie Knox.

Internal design by Les Thomas.

A catalogue record for this book is available from the National Library of Australia.

Scan the QR Code to view some of Anne Scrimgeour's photographs relating to *On Red Earth Walking*.
Aboriginal and Torres Strait Islander readers, please note that the selected images may contain images of deceased persons.

Contents

About the Author viii
Acknowledgements ix
Acronyms xi
Maps xii
Timeline, Late 1942 to Late 1949 xiv

1   *Marrngu* 1
2   'For the Better Care and Protection' 8
3   'They Were the Boss for Us' 22
4   'Here We Were Real Australians and They Discriminated
    Against Us': The Significance of the War 43
5   'McLeod Gave Us Hint and We Took It Up':
    The Movement Begins, 1943–45 67
6   'It Now Appears to Be Pretty General, This Striking Business':
    October 1945 – April 1946 100
7   'Tangled Versions': May Day 1946 118
8   'McLeod's Insidious Anti Fascist Communistic Activities':
    Responses, May–June 1946 131
9   'We Got Power Behind Us': Southern Support,
    May–June 1946 146
10 'All Got To Be in One': Race-Time Demonstrations,
    July–August 1946 171
11 'Unfortunately C of E into the Bargain': The Arrest of Peter Hodge,
    August 1946 186
12 'Start Rolling Up Swag, We Off': Walking Off,
    August–December 1946 196
13 'Far Too Strong and Cheeky': December 1946 – February 1947 217
14 'God Help the Blackfellow': Suppressing Dissent 241

15 'The Hide and the Audacity to Employ Full-Blooded Natives on the Jetty': The Politics of Racial Solidarity on the Port Hedland Waterfront, 1947...............................255

16 'No Iron Curtain': The High Court Appeals, March 1947..........271

17 'The Situation Is Ripe for a Complete Reorientation of Official Thinking': Ross McDonald and Aboriginal Autonomy, April 1947..281

18 'The Feeling Locally Is Very Strong Against the Strikers': The Strike and Settler Fear, April–August 1947 300

19 'The Natives Are Now Taking the Attitude They Can Camp Anywhere They Like': Contested Ground, 1947 309

20 'The Proposal Was a Sound One in Principle': Jack Gribble and 'Control and Supervision' of the Strikers, June – December 1947 324

21 'Imagine the Propaganda this Native Will Instil on the Younger Natives': Schooling, 1948 341

22 'The Best Brains Available': The Bateman Report and Restructure of the Department of Native Affairs, 1948.....................362

23 'Our School House Will Remain Until Bomb Blow It Apart': Late 1948 – Early 1949......................................372

24 'Plenty of Police and Plenty of Jails': Civil Disobedience, March–May 1949 389

25 'And Justice and Common Sense Would Prevail': April–July 1949..417

26 'How Politics Enter into This': The Seamen's Union Ban, July 1949 440

27 'In Their Struggle for Self Determination': The End of the Strike, September 1949–1950..452

Appendix A: Cathedral Chronicle 465
Appendix B: Jack Gribble..476
Character List..483
Bibliography 487
Index...495

Muwarr nyungu yarntarnarnajanaku karlijikupa kurntalku, jamujiku, kaparlijiku marrnguku kararr strikejarrinyilpiyi yirrku.

And also:

For Mark, Ellie, Leila, David and all the rest of my family, for the love, support and stem cells that have brought me through my year of leukaemia.

About the Author

Dr. Anne Scrimgeour worked with Pilbara Aboriginal people over many years and undertook extensive research into their history. She worked with Monty Hale on his bilingual autobiography, *Kurlumarniny: We Come from the Desert*, and published articles on the Pilbara strike and the Aboriginal cooperative movement that developed from the strike.

Acknowledgements

This book has been a long time in the making, and many people have contributed to its creation.

Thanks are due, first and foremost, to the *marrngu* men and women who sat with me in the early 1990s to record their memories and experiences on tape.

The Nyangumarta oral history recordings that are a key primary source for this book were transcribed and translated into English by Barbara Hale and Mark Clendon. Barbara's friendship, her patient assistance over many years in liaising with the Aboriginal community and the contribution she has made through her linguistic expertise have been invaluable.

I'd like also to acknowledge the generosity of Euan Bucknall and his son Rowyn, who accommodated my family for two months in 2007 while we undertook the transcription and translation of the oral history tapes. Euan also made his shed available as a workspace. The transcription and translation work could not have been accomplished without their hospitality, for which I thank them.

I am also indebted to John and Gwen Bucknall, who have, over many years, generously shared their extensive knowledge of the Pilbara Aboriginal community and its history.

Katrin and John Wilson have also significantly contributed to the creation of this book. I thank them for their abundant generosity, for the many hours they spent sharing their remarkable experiences and knowledge, for reading and responding to the manuscript, for the enthusiasm and encouragement they provided, and for their warm and welcoming hospitality and friendship.

I would also like to thank Victoria Haskins for her interest and her insights, Jan Richardson for her enthusiastic responses to my work, Jen Panucci for her interest and for reading and responding to the manuscript, and more recently Bain Attwood for his encouragement and assistance in many ways. In addition, I would like to thank Mark Chambers for his help.

David Morgan provided the cover image, for which I thank him.

I am also grateful to Ann Cornish and Sara Davies for giving me permission to use the remarkable letters of their parents and grandparents, Benja and Reg Sherlock.

Funding was provided by the Australian Institute of Aboriginal and Torres Strait Islander Studies for early research for this book in the State Records Office of Western Australia and for the transcription and translation of oral history recordings. The Western Australian History Foundation provided funding for research in the eastern states. I am also grateful to the State Library of Western Australia for assisting my research through a Battye Memorial Fellowship.

Throughout the research and writing of this book, my husband Mark Clendon has been a constant support, always believing in the value of this research, encouraging me when I felt discouraged, and being prepared to live frugally when family finances were tight and I talked of getting a proper paying job. He also provided practical help, reading and commenting on my work, and advising me on linguistic matters. I also thank my beautiful daughters, Ellie and Leila, for all the love, hugs and puttanesca, without which this book would probably not have been written.

Acronyms

ACP	Australian Communist Party
AFL	Anti-Fascist League
AIATSIS	Australian Institute of Aboriginal and Torres Strait Islander Studies
ALP	Australian Labor Party
ASIO	Australian Security Intelligence Organisation
AWU	Australian Workers' Union
CDNR	Committee for Defence of Native Rights
DE	Department of Education
DNA	Department of Native Affairs
NAA	National Archives of Australia
NLA	National Library of Australia
RAAF	Royal Australian Air Force
SLV	State Library of Victoria
SLWA	State Library of Western Australia
SROWA	State Records Office, Western Australia
UNO	United Nations Organisation
UWA	University of Western Australia
VDC	Volunteer Defence Corp

Maps

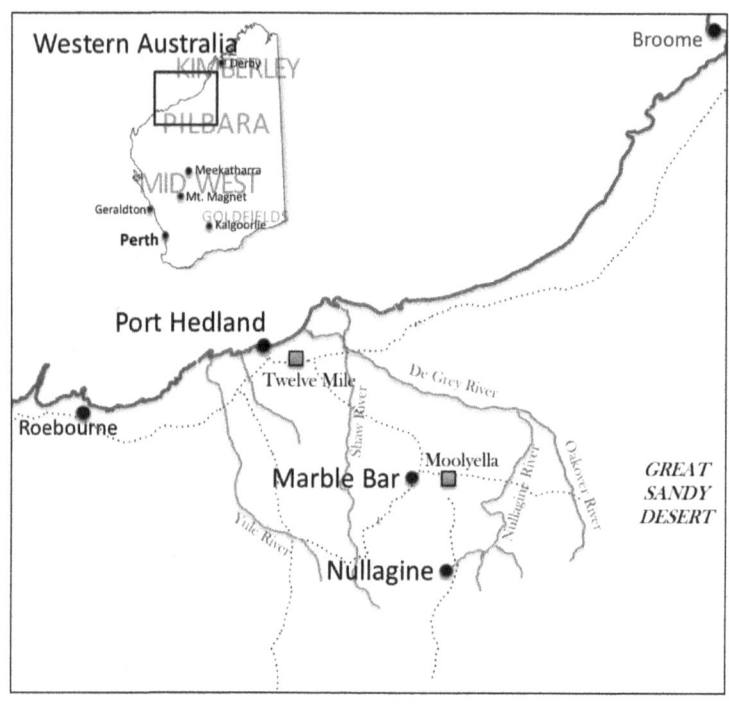

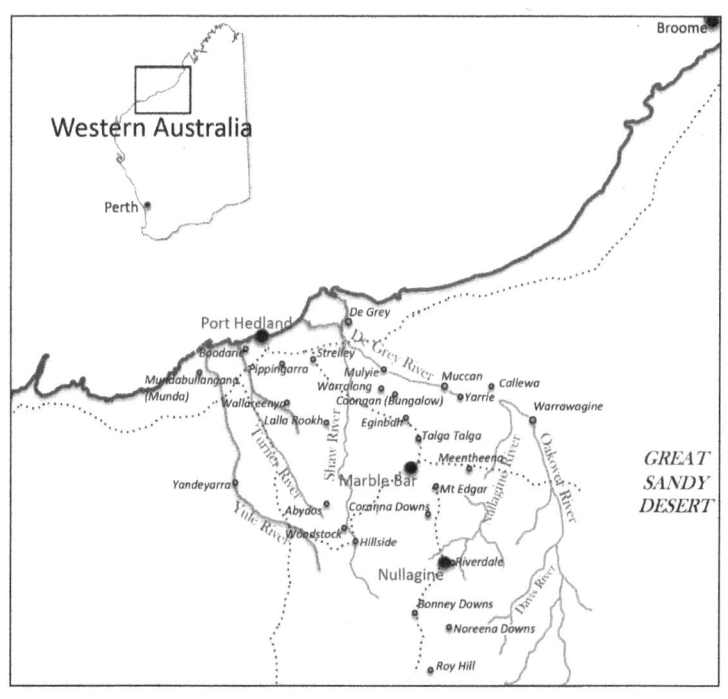

Timeline, Late 1942 to Late 1949

November 1942	Members of the Port Hedland Euralian community protest against the pass system.
April–June 1943	Euralian Association protests against work permit regulations in Port Hedland.
June 1943	McLeod advocates the Euralians' cause in Perth.
27 July 1943	Public meeting of the Port Hedland branch of the Anti-Fascist League.
October 1943	McLeod begins working on Bonney Downs Station with Kitchener. Strike discussions begin.
1944	Strike idea discussed by *marrngu*, with McLeod and among themselves. McLeod outlines plans to Elkin.
6 November 1944	McLeod successfully appeals Department of Native Affairs (DNA) decision regarding his eligibility to hold a permit to employ Aboriginal people.
23-24 July 1945	Race-time meetings in Port Hedland.
September 1945	WWII ends.
July–December 1945	Strike organisers move around stations. Probable timing of Skull Springs meeting.
Late 1945	Dooley begins working with McLeod and Kitchener.
April 1946	Dooley and McKenna visit stations in preparation for a strike on 1 May.
	McLeod visits Perth to garner support.
26 April 1946	Workers on De Grey station strike for higher wages. Awarded 5/- increase for the duration of the shearing.
30 April 1946	McLeod alerts the government to impending strike.
	Some early strikers granted temporary wage rises.
	Unsuccessful strike attempt at Warrawagine Station.

Timeline, Late 1942 to Late 1949

1 May 1946	Aboriginal people in the Port Hedland and Marble Bar region refuse to work. Most return to their jobs under police pressure.
7 May 1946	McKenna arrested.
8 May 1946	McKenna sentenced to three-month prison term.
9 May 1946	Dooley arrested.
10-15 May 1946	O'Neill and Fletcher visit stations to warn workers to stay at their jobs.
17 May 1946	Dooley sentenced to three-month prison term. McLeod arrested.
19 May 1946	200 people on the Perth Esplanade call for the release of Clancy, Dooley and McLeod.
25 May 1946	McLeod remanded on bail until 21 June.
28 May 1946	Protest meeting held in the Perth Town Hall. Committee for Defence of Native Rights (CDNR) formed.
13 June 1946	CDNR appeals to the United Nations for the right of Aboriginal workers to strike.
13-14 June 1946	McLeod addresses meetings in Perth and Fremantle.
21 June 1946	McLeod convicted and fined.
25 June 1946	McKenna and Dooley released before serving their full sentences.
25 July 1946	*Marrngu* defy a police order to camp out of town during Port Hedland races.
30 July 1946	*Marrngu* refuse to return to stations after the races.
2 August 1946	*Marrngu* demonstrate over ration coupons. McLeod arrested but released on good behaviour bond. Strikers march into Port Hedland in protest.
5 August 1946	Strikers set up camp at the Twelve Mile and Moolyella.
13 August 1946	Hodge visits Port Hedland. He and McLeod arrested.
15 August 1946	McKenna, Dooley and McLeod granted leave to appeal convictions.

23 August 1946	McLeod sentenced to 3 months imprisonment. Sentence held over awaiting outcome of appeal.
Second half 1946	More *marrngu* leave stations to join strike camps.
30 September – 1 October 1946	Carbine's protest at Warrawagine.
November 1946	Appeals by McLeod, McKenna and Dooley fail in the WA Supreme Court.
December 1946	Dorothy Hewett and Lloyd Davies visit strikers.
December 1946	Mackay leads a breakaway group of strikers.
2 January 1947	Mackay's breakaway group seized by McKenna and other strikers.
21 January 1947	Dispute over employment of 4 strikers on Port Hedland wharf.
1 February 1947	McKenna and other strikers receive prison sentences for taking breakaway group from Marble Bar.
4 March 1947	Hodge appeal upheld by the High Court of Australia. McLeod's appeal accordingly upheld by the Western Australian Supreme Court.
15 March 1947	WA Labor Government defeated by the Liberal Party.
1 April 1947	McDonald becomes WA Minister for Native Affairs.
5 April 1947	Mason attempts to negotiate with strikers at the Twelve Mile.
7 April 1947	Mt Magnet protest.
13 April 1947	Commissioner Bray retires.
17 April 1947	McBeath and O'Neill attempt to negotiate with strikers at the Twelve Mile.
21 April 1947	Boodari fire.
23 May 1947	McKenna and 3 other strikers fined for trespassing on Strelley Station.
June 1947	Bateman report submitted.

Timeline, Late 1942 to Late 1949

9 July 1947	Union dispute over the employment of Ronald Thompson as a wharf labourer.
24 September 1947	Mitchell sentenced to 7 days imprisonment for threatening to escalate the strike.
25 September 1947	Gribble arrives in Port Hedland as special officer with the Department.
December 1947	Gribble's appointment terminated.
Early 1948	Twelve Mile strike camp declines. Moolyella becomes the main strike camp.
May 1948	McLeod again proposes that the WA government make an abandoned station available to *marrngu* for their own community use.
June 1948	DNA recommends the establishment of a Department of Education school at Moolyella.
July 1948	McLeod becomes more directly involved with the strikers.
August 1948	Middleton appointed Commissioner of Native Affairs.
October 1948	Bryan submits written proposal for a Catholic mission on the abandoned White Springs Station.
November 1948	McLeod argues against proposals for a school at Moolyella in favour a school on an Aboriginal owned and operated station.
December 1948	DNA declares the Twelve Mile a 'forbidden settlement' for Aboriginal people.
23 January 1949	Strikers given one month to tear down their dwellings and leave the Twelve Mile.
13 February 1949	Order for strikers to leave the Twelve Mile is rescinded after *marrngu* threaten to escalate strike action.
14 March 1949	Strikers remove Cocky from Corunna Downs Station.
25 March 1949	13 strikers receive prison sentences for entering Corunna Downs to remove workers. Strikers promise to fill the jails in protest.

4 April 1949	Middleton plans to send convicted men to Cosmo Newbery.
14 April 1949	33 men arrested for removing workers from Warrawagine Station.
21 April 1949	32 strikers receive prison sentences.
27 April – 1 May 1949	Middleton in Port Hedland to investigate the situation.
28 April 1949	Fremantle Branch of the Seamen's Union threatens to ban wool shipments from the Pilbara if strikers are not released.
20 June 1949	Ten more strikers arrested for removing workers from Noreena Downs. DNA acts to prevent further convictions.
28 June 1949	Fremantle branch of Seamen's Union institutes wool ban.
30 June 1949	Elliott-Smith flies to Port Hedland to try to contain the situation.
5 July 1949	Elliott-Smith reaches an agreement with the strikers, granting concessions in return for an undertaking to cease protest action.
6 July 1949	Cases against 10 strikers dismissed in Marble Bar court.
16–18 July 1949	Seamen on the SS *Kybra* refuse to load wool in Port Hedland.
17 July 1949	Elliott-Smith wires agreement to a wage scale.
August 1949	WA government backs away from Elliott-Smith's agreement.
8–12 September 1949	400 *marrngu* hold meetings near Marble Bar to debate whether to adhere to their agreement with Elliott-Smith or to remain independent.
Second half 1949	Some *marrngu* return to employment while others begin prospecting.

Chapter 1

Marrngu

In the years following the Second World War, colonised peoples throughout the world took action to achieve greater independence though processes of decolonisation. This is the story of a localised decolonising movement that took place immediately after the war in a region of Australia's north-west, where Aboriginal labour on vast sheep and cattle stations was central to a system of colonial domination and accommodation. Because of the close links between their colonised status and the labour they provided for an economically important and politically powerful industry, the action taken by Aboriginal people, beginning in 1946, to gain greater autonomy and dignity in their lives involved withholding their labour in a prolonged strike. Walking away from pastoral stations and other workplaces, for the next three years Aboriginal people formed self-supporting communities and, with southern activists providing essential support, successfully resisted pastoralist, police and government pressure to return to work. They would, through their action, achieve significant economic, social and political change. This is the story of their struggle.

The region of Western Australia's north where the strike took place is the traditional country of Ngarla-, Nyamal-, Nyiyaparli- and Kariyarra-speaking people. It is harsh, hot, semi-arid country, where spiky spinifex grass and areas of low scrub cover the red earth between low, rugged hills. In the 1860s, Europeans began arriving in the area to establish vast sheep and cattle stations along the Yule and De Grey river systems, which flow in the summer months, when cyclonic activity brings heavy rains, and which dry into strings of pools and waterholes for the rest of the year. By the time of the strike, local Aboriginal people, called *marrngu* in the Nyangumarta language, had served as a labour force on stations for decades. As early as 1879, for example, all of the 18,000 sheep on the large coastal station of Mundabullangana were shepherded by *marrngu*, and a newspaper report stated in 1883 that on De Grey Station, which ran 40,000 sheep and 6000 head of cattle, all the work was 'done by natives, sheep shearing, washing wool, fencing, tank making, bullock and horse driving, in fact all the work required on and about the station'.[1] Women

---

1   *Australian Town and Country Journal*, 7 April 1883, p. 26.

as well as men worked for the settlers, providing domestic services as well as stock work. With the discovery of gold in the 1880s, Aboriginal people also worked for miners, providing domestic and other services in the mining camps. By 1946, generations of *marrngu* had lived alongside and worked for the settler community throughout the Pilbara's Riverline Country.

Among those who took part in the strike were men and women with a less extensive history of labour and settler contact. These were speakers of Nyangumarta, Mangarla, Warnman and the Western Desert Language, who had travelled into the Riverline Country from the Great Sandy Desert to the south and east in a population movement that was probably accelerated by severe drought in 1923 and 1924. Movements of Aboriginal populations are often referred to as 'drift', suggesting 'movement devoid of agency',[2] but *marrngu* speak of a long period of discussion and deliberation before families made the decision to migrate. Ginger Bob (Palyakulayi), a Mangarla speaker who made the journey with his parents in the 1920s, said:

> Our people were all talking and discussing something with each other. We set out walking toward the west. And it was for good, then, we set out for the west and we weren't coming back. They talked with each other about what they were doing; some stayed and some were going to go west. 'Alright, you lot go on, we might come along behind you'. Some people went on ahead, they set out and came in from the east, travelling on foot.[3]

In speaking of the decision to migrate, *marrngu* cite both push and pull factors as motivating forces. Settler intrusions into the Great Sandy Desert, particularly with the creation of the Canning Stock Route in 1910, had led to violent encounters, including a punitive expedition that settlers carried out in 1911 in retaliation for the spearing of three drovers. The family of Snowy Jittermarra (Maruntu), who spoke the Western Desert dialect, Kartujarra, travelled in to the small Riverline town of Nullagine after Snowy's grandfather was shot,[4] and Solomon Cocky (Ngalyarrkiny), born in the desert in 1912, came in to Noreena Downs Station with his family as a child after his father

---

2 Tim Rowse, *White Flour, White Power: From Rations to Citizenship in Central Australia*, Cambridge University Press, Cambridge, New York and Melbourne, 1998, p. 33.
3 Ginger Bob (Palyakulayi), recorded by Anne Scrimgeour, 5 October 1993, translated from Nyangumarta by Barbara Hale and Mark Clendon, AIATSIS collection, soundfile 'Palyakulayi 4'.
4 Snowy Jittermarra (Maruntu), recorded by Anne Scrimgeour, 5 August 1993, author's collection.

had been shot in the shoulder near the rabbit-proof fence.[5] Mac Gardiner (Pirntilkampanyaja), whose mother spoke the Western Desert dialect of Manyjilyjara, and whose father spoke Warnman, was also born in about 1912 at a waterhole called Kinyu, incorporated into Canning Stock Route as Well 35.[6] He spoke of his family's fear of settler violence in the desert:

> We started to get frightened because of what we were hearing, namely that they were killing *marrngu* people. We used to see them coming down from the north with cattle, down the road that went past Kinyu and Kunawariji.[7] When we were camped [near a well] we would run away in fright, and stay out there in fear. Then they'd look around ... and make sure the way was clear. As they travelled, the people who lived around the wells out there in the east would call out to us to come over to their camps. But we were all afraid from what they told us they had heard, that *walypila* were killing everybody, we were frightened because of that.[8]

However, *marrngu* have tended to speak of the desire for flour, tea, sugar and tobacco, rather than the fear of violence, as the motivating force behind the decision to migrate. Harry Wandarri, a Nyangumarta man, said he came in because his father wanted 'white man's tobacco'.[9] Some *marrngu* had been introduced to these commodities by drovers travelling on the Canning Stock Route, while others spoke of being given the new foods and tobacco by *marrngu* travelling out to the desert from station country, apparently with the intention of encouraging desert dwellers to come in. Jack Paanju, a Warnman speaker, told Norman Tindale in 1953 that *marrngu* had 'come out into the desert bringing sugar: and the desire for more of it brought them in'.[10] According to Mac Gardiner, people working at Barramine, a station on the margins of the

---

5 Solomon Cocky, recorded by Anne Scrimgeour, 15 May 1991, author's collection. Solomon said that he was born in the year that the SS *Koombana* sank.
6 Mac Gardiner (Pirntilkampanyaja), recorded by Anne Scrimgeour, 29 September 1993, author's collection.
7 The Canning Stock Route.
8 Mac Gardiner (Pirntilkampanyaja), recorded by Anne Scrimgeour, 5 August 1993, translated from Nyangumarta by Barbara Hale and Mark Clendon, AIATSIS collection, soundfile 'Pirntilkampanyaja 1'. The term *'walypila'* or 'whitefellas' refers to Europeans.
9 Norman Tindale, journal, 11 May 1953, p. 299, 'University of Adelaide and University of California Anthropological Expedition, 1952–1954', South Australian Museum, AA 338/1/19/1.
10 Tindale, journal, 21 May 1953, p. 285.

desert, had been 'breaking us in'. They had travelled all through the desert, Mac said, introducing people to a form of tobacco superior to the bush tobacco that grew in the hills. 'This other tobacco better than you battle [for] amongst the hills', they would say. '"Tobacco here, stick tobacco". They bring all people in, all of us'.[11] 'No people there, all went towards this way', Mac said. 'Follow the food, and the flour, sugar, we follow that one, come this way'.[12]

Some who travelled to station country did not intend to remain permanently. Billy Thomas's Mangarla-speaking father wanted to return to the desert after working for some time at Barramine Station, but he was prevented from doing so by the police because his labour was required. 'We looked after all the horses', Billy (Pitpit) said:

> [W]e mustered the sheep, we fixed all the fences, we chopped wood and graded the roads ... People wanted to go back to their own countries, but the *walypila* prevented them because of all the work they were doing. They were working all the time. If anyone went back the bosses went out looking for them and brought them back. They would go out after them on horseback and bring them back.[13]

When *marrngu* failed to return to their desert country, family members followed to find out what had become of them and were themselves put to work:

> When they went looking for them, they were all taken as well, and held to work. Some *walypila* took them to mine for gold, while others went to Pinturiji, near Jirrpayinya, where they worked repairing the rabbit-proof fence, looking after horses, mending fences, chopping wood and running around doing other things as well. Now *marrngu* people lived permanently on the stations and couldn't go back.
>
> Some people did go back: from Nullagine (Yirrangkaji) they went east out to Skull Springs (Wantilurr). The police rode out to Wantilurr after them and brought them back under guard. 'You can't go back', they

---

11   Gardiner (Pirntilkampanyaja), recorded by Anne Scrimgeour, 29 September 1993, author's collection. Tim Rowse records a similar account (*White Flour, White Power*, p. 65).

12   Gardiner (Pirntilkampanyaja), recorded by Anne Scrimgeour, 29 September 1993, author's collection.

13   Billy Thomas (Pitpit), recorded by Anne Scrimgeour, 6 October 1993, translated from Nyangumarta by Barbara Hale and Mark Clendon, AIATSIS collection, soundfile 'Pitpit 1'.

said, 'you've got to work, you've got work to do. What do you want to go back there for?' And now there was nobody left out there, they had all departed and couldn't get back. They always wanted to go back, but they were living here now. The station bosses would tell the police about any *marrngu* people [who absconded].[14]

Other *marrngu* made the decision to move into station country permanently. Ginger Bob travelled in as a child with his Mangarla-speaking parents and younger brother. 'Our parents told people, "We've brought our two boys in here" when we'd met up with others', suggesting that the journey was made to provide opportunities for the rising generation.[15]
In contrast to Billy Thomas's account of people being prevented from returning to the desert, some *marrngu* spoke of being repeatedly driven away when they tried to camp close to station country to learn what they could of European ways. One desert man said that the men of his group had agreed that it was no longer possible for them to return to their former way of life and had decided to learn what they could of station life. They made many attempts to do so before they succeeded.[16] Harry Wandarri told Norman Tindale that his family group had been hunted away when they first approached Warrawagine Station, but that they did not go far before returning.

Some of the people who went on strike in 1946 were the children of desert migrants, while many had themselves undertaken the long journey and made the profound changes involved in the transition from a hunter-gather economy to life in the settler-dominated Riverline region. They remembered living as children at the desert waterholes of their home country, the long journey they had made with their families, and their eventual arrival at the rabbit-proof fence, a fence constructed in the early years of the twentieth century to prevent the spread of rabbits from the eastern states. This fence, 1800 kilometres long, stood like a boundary between the familiar world the desert people had always known and the unfamiliar world they were about to enter, blocking their passage to the west until they found a way to clamber over it, coming thereby into a new world full of new animals and new and surprising things.

---

14 Thomas (Pitpit), by Anne Scrimgeour, 6 October 1993, AIATSIS collection, soundfile 'Pitpit 1'.
15 Ginger Bob (Palyakulayi), recorded by Anne Scrimgeour, 30 September 1993, translated from Nyangumarta by Barbara Hale and Mark Clendon, AIATSIS collection, soundfile 'Palyakulayi 1'.
16 John Wilson, 'Authority and Leadership' in a "New Style" Aboriginal Community', Masters Thesis, University of Western Australia, 1961, p. 36.

Mac Gardiner (Pirntilkampanyja) was about twelve years old when he made the journey into station country in the mid-1920s. As an old man, he laughed to remember the fear with which he and his brother had looked down from a sandhill at their first glimpse of station buildings and at the owner-manager of Barramine Station, Herbert Barker. Cigarette smoke issuing from Barker's mouth appeared to the frightened boys to be evidence of his ferocity:

> Get up in that big sandhill, and we seen the house, we had to run back that way, trying to go back, run back.
>
> 'Wai, wai wait! *Palama* now!' He tell us, 'That's a house now'.
>
> ...
>
> '*Wayi*, sit down'. We sit down and have a good look ... Not too sure. Barker, he was smoking cigarette. Oh, we see'm, oh, Christ, he getting cheeky[17] now!
>
> We want to run away. He got smoke coming out! We want to go back. 'Oh, he getting cheeky now!' Well, turn around and run away, right back. 'Oh, he getting *kuli*![18] See'm? Smoke coming out'.[19]

New arrivals from the desert spent some time on the edge of station country, becoming accustomed to the new sights and learning from local people the things they needed to know to survive in this new environment. When they felt confident to do so, they moved on to the outlying stations of Warrawagine, Barramine and, further to the south, Balfour Downs. Some remained on these outlying stations, settling in the large 'native camps' in the dry creek beds in the vicinity of station homesteads. Mac Gardiner settled on Warrawagine Station, learning the skills needed to engage in station work there. Other *marrngu* moved on after a period of time, travelling further into the Riverline Country to reunite with relatives on other stations, or joining the community of Aboriginal miners who made a living gouging alluvial tin at the Moolyella tin field near Marble Bar, which served as a further staging post for some in the process of adjustment and acclimatising to a new social and economic environment.

It was an environment in which two societies existed side by side: the settler social and economic realm, in which *marrngu* remained marginal and which

---

17   Hostile, aggressive.
18   Angry, aggressive.
19   Gardiner (Pirntilkampanyaja), recorded by Anne Scrimgeour, 5 August 1993, author's collection.

they learned to navigate with care and servility; and the social, cultural and religious world of the local Aboriginal community, into which the new arrivals were incorporated through existing family relationships and congruent kinship structures. When Ginger Bob, a Mangarla speaker who travelled from the desert as a child, approached the time of his initiation, the classificatory older brother who took him under his wing and made arrangements for his initiation was a local Nyamal man, Clancy McKenna (Warntupungkarna).[20] The new arrivals were introduced to the ceremonial life of the traditional owners of the Riverline country and instructed in its ritual, while the strength of the cultural practice and knowledge they brought from the desert impressed the local people, revitalising and invigorating the cultural and religious life of the local community.[21] Adapting culturally to life in the new environment, the new arrivals joined a *marrngu* community accustomed to making the cultural adaptations necessary for the ongoing incorporation of new arrivals from the desert. It seems likely that these cultural adjustments, made both by those arriving from the desert and by those incorporating the new arrivals into their social and religious life, resulted in a dynamic Aboriginal culture accustomed to adaptation and change, which would serve as the bedrock of Aboriginal industrial and political action in the 1940s.

---

20 Ginger Bob (Palyakulayi), recorded by Anne Scrimgeour, 12 December 1993, translated from Nyangumarta by Barbara Hale and Mark Clendon, AIATSIS collection, soundfile 'Palyakulayi 18'.
21 John Wilson, 'Authority and Leadership', pp. 34–35, 37, 38.

Chapter 2

'For the Better Care and Protection'

European settlers, arriving to establish sheep stations along the ephemeral De Grey and Yule river systems from the 1860s, secured and retained both the land and the labour of the local people through violence. *Marrngu* who later went on strike spoke of mass killings perpetrated in the decades following the arrival of the Europeans. These events included the killing of over fifty people fishing in a stream, and an incident in which a much larger group was driven into tidal swamps and shot.[1] Following the spearing of a *walypila* on a desert station, *marrngu* were rounded up and forced to build a circular pyre upon which over eighty people were burned.[2] 'In coast side, very near all bin shot down', Snowy Jittermarra said:

> They shooting all the people, when the white fella coming from – from Perth anyhow, coming this way. They bin shoot all the people all along in this beach. This country bin full of, full of people, from De Grey up the river and right down to desert ... All them fellas get shot down.[3]

An 1886 newspaper reported that since Aboriginal people on De Grey had been 'taught a lesson they have never forgotten', they were now 'the most useful in the district',[4] and pastoralists (or 'squatters') in other parts of the north felt that similar treatment in other areas could have a similarly positive result. 'I think if the government would allow the settlers to give the natives a good dressing down, as was done at the De Grey a few years ago', one squatter said in 1882, 'it would effectively put a stop to sheep stealing'.[5]

Ngarla, Nyamal, Nyiyaparli and Kariyarra people were forcibly recruited as divers for a pearling industry operated by the European newcomers as a profitable sideline while highly profitable pastoral ventures became established.

---

1   John Wilson, 'Authority and Leadership', p. 35, note 16.
2   John Wilson, 'Authority and Leadership', p. 35, note 16.
3   Jittermarra (Maruntu), recorded by Anne Scrimgeour, 5 August 1993, author's collection.
4   *West Australian*, 6 March 1886, p. 5.
5   *Herald* (Fremantle), 9 December 1882, p. 2.

Aboriginal workers, both station workers and those blackbirded into the pearling industry, reported severe beatings and depravation.[6] The brutal flogging that led to the death of six *marrngu* workers at Bendhu Station in 1897 is probably only unusual in that it came to the attention of authorities, and the young perpetrators were charged. Although overt violence was playing less of a role in pastoralist control of Aboriginal labour by the 1940s, the threat of physical violence remained constant for Aboriginal people.

In theory, pastoralist power over Aboriginal people was curtailed by the Department of Native Affairs (DNA). Western Australia had been granted self-government in 1890 subject to conditions arising from Imperial Government concerns over allegations of gross abuse of Indigenous people in Western Australia and the unsatisfactory treatment of Indigenous people in other self-governing colonies. In order to ensure that Western Australian Aboriginal people were afforded some measure of protection from settler self-interest, the Imperial Government stipulated, as a condition under which self-government was granted, that £5000 or 1 per cent of consolidated revenue be set aside annually for expenditure on the education and welfare of Aboriginal people, and that this provision must be included in the new Constitution. To further protect Aboriginal people from settler self-interest, the Imperial Government stipulated that these funds be administered by a Protection Board answerable to the governor rather than to colonial Parliament. This provision was enshrined in 1889 as section 70 of the Constitution.

While the colonial government agreed to its inclusion as the price of responsible government, it acted quickly to have section 70 cancelled once self-government had been granted. After some years of agitation by the colonial government, the necessary Royal consent for section 70's repeal was received in 1897.[7] The Aborigines Protection Board was replaced by an Aborigines Department under colonial government control, which received

---

6   Margaret Allen, 'The Brothers Up North and the Sisters Down South: The Mackay Family and the Frontier', *Hecate*, vol 27, no. 2, 2001, pp. 7–31.

7   See a special edition of *Studies in Western Australian History* (edited by Jane Lydon and Ann Curthoys, *Governing Western Australian Aboriginal People: Section 70 of WA's 1889 Constitution*, vol. 30, 2016) for articles relating to the history of section 70. Also see Peter W. Johnston, 'The Repeals of Section 70 of the Western Australian Constitution Act 1889: Aborigines and Governmental Breach of Trust', *Western Australian Law Review*, vol. 19, 1989, pp. 318–351; Ann Curthoys and Jeremy Martens, 'Serious Collisions: Settlers, Indigenous People and Imperial Policy in Western Australia and Natal', *Journal of Australian Colonial History*, vol. 15, 2013, pp. 122–144; Neville Green, 'From Princes to Paupers: The Struggle for Control of Aborigines in Western Australia 1887–1898', *Early Days: Journal of the West Australian Historical Society*, vol.11, no. 4, 1998, pp. 446–462.

nothing like the funding stipulated in section 70. Legislation was passed in 1905 'for the better care and protection of the Native Inhabitants of Western Australia', and, after various name changes, the department responsible for protecting Western Australian Aboriginal people from abuse and exploitation, especially from pastoral interests in the north, became the Department of Native Affairs in 1936.

Protective legislation, known by the time of the strike as the *Native Administration Act 1936*, contained restrictive provisions designed to protect Aboriginal people by controlling all aspects of their lives. The legislation severely impacted the lives of Aboriginal people, particularly those living in the south of the state. It also included provisions designed to enable the Department to maintain some level of control over Aboriginal employment. Employers could only engage Aboriginal workers under a permit issued by the Department through local 'Protectors of Natives' who were, in most instances, local police officers. Permits could stipulate conditions of employment and could be cancelled if conditions were not met.

In addition to work permits issued to employers, the Act set out regulations for employment agreements between employers and Aboriginal workers, but agreements were not mandatory and were rarely used. A senior officer of the Department of Native Affairs wrote in 1947 that he had 'not seen an agreement effected between a native and an employer' in five years in the role.[8] Although southern supporters of the strike would point to section 26 of the Act as placing unacceptable restraints on Aboriginal workers, such regulations only applied under labour agreements.[9] Apart from the compulsory requirement to obtain employment permits, squatters were, to a large degree, able to avoid departmental interference in pastoral labour relations. They depended instead on an alternative informal system of governance that controlled Aboriginal people as effectively as protective legislation controlled people in the south, but which vested power in pastoralists' hands.[10]

At the core of this system of governance was the provision of rations to Aboriginal people in return for labour. As Nettelbeck and Foster have shown, ration distribution was 'an effective means of Aboriginal pacification, surveillance, and reward' that became an institutionalised tool of governance

---

8   C. L. McBeath, Acting Commissioner of Native Affairs to Ross McDonald, 9 April 1947, p. 3, SROWA 1947/0305/84.
9   This point is further discussed in Chapter 3.
10 Writing of Pilbara district, John Wilson has noted that prior to the strike there was less government intervention in the lives of Aboriginal people there than there was in the south of the state. 'Authority and Leadership', p. 22.

on the Australian frontier.[11] Along with violence, rations had been used in northern pastoral areas to make land available for sheep and cattle by bringing groups of Aboriginal people into the vicinity of station homesteads. To receive rations – consisting primarily of tobacco, tea and sugar, flour or bread, and meat – Aboriginal people were required to camp in designated 'native camps' close to station homesteads, often in the dry bed of a nearby creek or river, leaving the country free for pastoral activity while simultaneously creating a pool of labour for the stations. Pastoral stations, and the relationship between squatters and Aboriginal station residents, became key sites of colonial governance.

A powerful pastoral lobby and strong pastoral representation in the state's Parliament ensured that pastoralists maintained control of Aboriginal labour relations. Parliamentarians of all persuasions stressed the importance of Aboriginal pastoral labour to the state. In discussing the possibility of the Commonwealth government taking control of Aboriginal affairs under the *Commonwealth Powers Act* of 1943, for example, Country Party member of the Legislative Assembly Charles Baxter asked the house:

> Has any consideration been given in the Federal sphere to the usefulness of the natives of this State to our great pastoral industry? ... It is very difficult now for the pastoralists to carry on with the native labour that is available to them, and I say to the people of this State, and not to pastoralists alone, that if authority is given to the Commonwealth Government to control the aboriginals it will render useless a race which has been, and can be, of considerable use to Western Australia. It will render the position of the pastoral industry impossible inasmuch as those engaged in that industry will not have labour available from the native race.[12]

The importance of Aboriginal labour to the pastoral industry was a powerful reason for limiting government interference in a pastoral labour system that was working effectively from the settler's point of view. The system was justified by subverting the concept of 'protection'. The imperative to ensure protection from exploitation and abuse was itself exploited, reframed through racist understandings to an insistence that Aboriginal people needed protection from their own impulsive and instinctive behaviour through mechanisms of

---

11 Amanda Nettelbeck and Robert Foster, 'Food and Governance on the Frontiers of Colonial Australia and Canada's North West Territories', *Aboriginal History*, vol. 36, 2012, pp. 21–41.
12 Charles Baxter, Parliamentary Debates (Hansard), Western Australia: Legislative Council, 23 March 1943, p. 2925.

control. Claiming to 'know the natives', squatters identified pastoral labour arrangements as the most effective mechanism for providing protective control. In 1952, Liberal Party member of the Western Australian Legislative Council Les Craig, a pastoralist with interests in Pilbara stations, explained the need for control:

> I and my brothers have a station, the whole of which is run by natives or half-castes ... But these natives have been brought up on the station under strict supervision ... Under strict supervision – and only under strict supervision – such natives do well, but they are not capable of having responsibilities placed upon them unless they are under control. The problem on a station is not a serious one because the natives are continuously under control from childhood.
>
> ... The native is instinctively a child of nature. What he wants to do he does, irrespective of whether it is right or wrong. Many of them cannot distinguish between right and wrong but do something simply because they want to do it. It is the inherited urge.[13]

This recasting of the concept of 'protection' from an imperative to impose limits on settler power to a perceived need to impose control over Aboriginal people served as an effective antidote to perceptions that entrusting the protection of Aboriginal people to a sector of society most dependent on their labour was like putting a fox in charge of the chicken coop.

In a contradiction of concurrent claims that Aboriginal labour was essential to the industry's survival, pastoralists sought to further obscure the self-serving nature of this arrangement by claiming that they tolerated Aboriginal residence on pastoral leases out of charity rather than a need for their labour. They argued that while Aboriginal people were well served by an arrangement that provided them with 'station homes where they were fed and nursed and had an easy-going life that appealed to them', the cost and inconvenience of feeding and caring for station communities placed a heavy burden on stations.[14] They argued that costs outweighed the return they received from the occasional unskilled and inefficient labour of a few Aboriginal workers. However, a closer examination of the situation in the Pilbara in the 1940s indicates that Aboriginal labour was not as costly or as inefficient as squatters claimed.

---

13 L. Craig, Parliamentary Debates (Hansard), Western Australia: Legislative Council, 11 November 1952, p. 1960.
14 Jenny Hardie, *Nor'Westers of the Pilbara Breed*, Hesperian Press, Canberra, 1988, p. 181.

At the time of the strike, accusations that Aboriginal people were exploited by the pastoral industry were countered by the argument that Aboriginal labour was not cheap because large numbers of non-working people were supported in return for the labour of a few. 'It has become part of the tradition of the North-West for the squatter to provide food and clothes for the entire family of his employees', an article in the *West Australian* newspaper pointed out, 'not only wives and children, but also indigent uncles, aunts and other relatives'.[15] Minister for the North West Bob Coverley fielded criticism of conditions in the North West in 1946 by asserting that Aboriginal labour was expensive, and that 'out of 90 natives on a station, only 15 or 20 would be effective workers, the remainder being dependents whom pastoralists were obliged to maintain'.[16] Drawing on information provided by Port Hedland's Catholic priest, Father Edward Bryan, Geraldton's Catholic newspaper, the *Cathedral Chronicle*, provided a similar example of the high number of dependents supported in proportion to the number of workers. In return for the occasional services 'of an unskilled man who has to be constantly superintended', and the service of one of his wives 'who does a little housework', a station would pay £1 per week for the man and 5/- for his wife', the *Cathedral Chronicle* claimed, as well as supplying clothing, food and tobacco for seven adults, including the man and both his wives, his parents and the parents of at least one of his wives; and his children would also be fed and clothed.[17]

The claim that food, clothing and tobacco were provided in addition to 30/- for each working couple exaggerated the costs incurred by stations, however. Some *marrngu* workers in the district did receive some form of payment, ranging from 5/- to, on rare occasions, as much as 50/-. However, even the highest paid Aboriginal workers received wages below federal award rates, being excluded from the award. Many men and almost all women were unpaid. Cranky (Kujupurra) and Mac Gardiner both worked on Warrawagine Station without pay, while Bruce Wandarri, who worked there as a blacksmith, was paid 12/- a week, out of which he bought his own tobacco and clothing, and clothing for his children. Another man, Billy, with long experience as overseer on Coongan Station, was paid 17/-, from which he had to buy his own clothing and tobacco.

Items considered essential by *marrngu* were excluded from the ration. According to Cranky, sugar was not included in the ration at Warrawagine but

---

15 *West Australian*, 27 June 1946, 'Native Question, Problems in Pilbara', SROWA 1945/0800/200.
16 *Westralian Worker*, 23 August 1946, p. 11.
17 *Cathedral Chronicle*, September 1946, p. 1.

had to be purchased.[18] Clothing was rarely supplied to non-working people. Deductions could be made from wages to cover the cost of clothing and other essentials, and this was cited by strike leaders Dooley Binbin (Winyirin or Yurlpuly) and Clancy McKenna (Warntupungkarna) as factors contributing to Aboriginal dissatisfaction with their pastoral labour conditions. Dooley[19] stated in a court hearing: 'We thought we having too much deducted from wages'.[20] According to one of the strikers, Sam Coppin, they were in debt 'all year round. Never get off the debt, all the time. That's the way, keep us there all the time. Man want to go away, he get the police, fetch him back, because you owe too much to the station'.[21] In 1951, the mining cooperative established by *marrngu* in the wake of the strike paid a £50 debt to the Corunna Downs Station store to enable the release of Aboriginal workers to join the cooperative.[22]

The suggestion that several children were supported for each male worker is not borne out in the statistics. The number of children on pastoral stations was extremely low, at only one child to every five adults. In November 1946, for example, there were 146 adults at the Twelve Mile strike camp near Port Hedland, but only thirty children. In 1952, there were 554 Aboriginal men and women involved in the Pilbara mining cooperative, with only 109 children between them. Twenty-five children were living on stations at the time with 220 adults.[23] The claim that stations fed and clothed children while also paying their parents is also unfounded. Bruce Wandarri, who was unusual in having four young children, had to purchase clothing for them from the 12/- per week he received for his work as a blacksmith.

The large number of non-working adults supposedly supported by stations is also not borne out in the records. Dave Pullen, a newly-appointed Native Affairs officer, reported in 1949 that although he 'had been led to believe that the stations were, great-heartedly, maintaining hundreds of aged and

---

18 Cranky (Kujupurra), recorded by Anne Scrimgeour, June 1993, translated from Nyanguamarta by Barbara Hale and Mark Clendon, AIATSIS collection, soundfile 'Kujupurra 3'.
19 The surname 'Binbin' as part of Dooley's *walypila* name was rarely used during the 1940s and 1950s. Accordingly, in this book he is referred to simply as 'Dooley'.
20 High Court appeal, D. W. McLeod v. G. R. Richards, NAA A10074 1947/8, 9, 10.
21 Sam Coppin, in Heather Williams and David Noakes, *How the West Was Lost: The Story of the 1946 Aboriginal Pastoral Workers' Strike*, directed by David Noakes, Friends Film Productions and Market Street Films Ltd, Perth, 1987, DVD.
22 Don McLeod, Statement to Committee Investigating Native Labour, p. 20, March 1952, SROWA 1952/0830 v1/106.
23 Frank Gare to Chairman, Committee of Enquiry, SROWA 1952/0830 v1/173.

indigent people', his first patrol in the Kimberley 'debunked this ... idea rather completely'. He found only seventy-two aged and indigent people spread over twelve Kimberley stations, and when he suggested that they could be shifted to a ration camp if stations found it too burdensome to maintain them, he was 'perturbedly informed that, actually, these old people <u>weren't</u> such a burden and that they were a valuable connecting link between the active workers and the station'.[24] More than half the adults living on Kimberley stations visited by Pullen in 1949 provided labour.[25] Although statistics for the Pilbara before the strike are not available, it is likely that the situation there was similar to that in the Kimberley. Even then, not all non-working people were rationed. Cranky (Kujupurra) said that on Warrawagine Station he and other workers would eat only a portion of the bread and meat that they received at mealtimes, keeping the rest to take back to camp for the old people.[26]

On stations where rations were supplied to people classed as 'indigent', these people were often required to undertake some labour in exchange, even though they were not considered employees, as correspondence between the Department of Native Affairs and the manager of Mulyie Station on the Pilbara's De Grey River in 1938 illustrates. The Department, at that time under the commissionership of A. O. Neville, insisted that the station should pay the cost of train fares for two older station residents who had to travel to Port Hedland for medical treatment: a man, Peebo, and a woman called Waterlily. Although the local doctor, having seen Waterlily cleaning boots and carrying buckets of hot water for the homestead, testified that she worked on the station, the station manager insisted that she was not employed, and that the work that she and Peebo did was 'for their own good and happiness' rather than being of benefit to the station. He believed that this was 'the ideal help that the country can give the native'.[27] He described Waterlily as 'a good old thing'. 'She suffers from varicose veins', he said:

> and at times she is crippled with them. She looks on this as home and likes to do a little now and then but is a free agent and comes and goes as she pleases. What better can she have – food, clothing and a home. I can do no more if the Department insists on us paying her train fares

---

24 Dave Pullen, District Officer, West Kimberley District, Annual Report, September 1949, SROWA 1949/0722 (underlining in original).
25 Dave Pullen, Annual Report, September 1949, p. 7, SROWA 1949/0722.
26 Cranky (Kujupurra), recorded by Anne Scrimgeour, June 1993, AIATSIS collection, soundfile 'Kujupurra 3'.
27 Manager of Mulyie to Francis Illingworth Bray, 4 June 1939, SROWA 1937/0432/21.

and other expenses. Please ask them to provide for her and I'll see she does no work for us although she will be disappointed if she is told to go back to camp.[28]

'When one gets run into all sorts of other expenses', he complained, 'it makes one feel that what one does to help the native is not appreciated'.[29] According to this understanding, the charitable support that stations provided for women like Waterlily involved, in addition to the provision of 'food, clothing and a home', allowing her to do some 'small menial work' about the station homestead.

The assertion that Aboriginal labour was costly and inefficient also rested on a general disparagement of Aboriginal workers as lazy and incompetent. A report in the *West Australian* in 1934 noted that pastoralists in the De Grey River region expressed a high level of annoyance with Aboriginal workers, referring frequently to the 'cheeky nigger' or the 'lazy nuisance'.[30] 'Through no fault of their own they lack that initiative which is required of any worker', the *Cathedral Chronicle* explained. '[E]xcepting as stockmen, they are unskilled in every other branch of work. And for this reason they require the constant supervision of an overseer'.[31] But a third layer of contradiction to conflicting claims that Aboriginal labour was indispensable on the one hand, but more costly and inefficient than it was worth on the other, was noted by Frank Gare, an officer of the Department of Native Affairs in the 1950s. In an oral history recording made in 1999, Gare said:

> Most of the station people you talk to, the employers, spoke very well of their stockmen. They usually had criticism in a general way of Aborigines in general, but they usually said, 'Oh, but I've got good men here, they're good stockmen. I couldn't do without them'. It was rather an odd attitude that their employees were well above the average. But if you went to each station in turn they all had the same idea'.[32]

A belief in the ineptitude of Aboriginal labour was so deeply held by pastoralists that it persisted, despite the evidence to the contrary in their own experience with Aboriginal workers.

---

28 Manager of Mulyie to managing director of the De Grey River Pastoral Company, enclosed with letter from the managing director of Mulyie to Bray, 15 September 1939, SROWA 1937/0432/25.
29 Manager of Mulyie to Bray, 4 June 1939, SROWA 1937/0432/21.
30 *West Australian*, 23 August 1934, p. 21.
31 *Cathedral Chronicle*, March 1947, p. 1.
32 Frank Ellis Gare, interviewed by W. J. E. Bannister, Bringing Them Home Oral History Project, 1999, http://nla.gov.au/nla.oh-vn1379490.

If the labour of Aboriginal men was considered of little value, the work undertaken by Aboriginal women was not even classed as labour. Aboriginal domestic workers were frequently portrayed as laughably incompetent and more trouble than they were worth. In 1945, an article in a Western Australian newspaper declared that, although domestic labour was plentiful in the state's Kimberley region and in the Northern Territory, housewives there 'have as much trouble with their servants as city housewives have without them. Reason is that the household help up north comprises gins, and they take a lot of watching'. The article referred to 'the hard work involved in training gins to be clean, to do what they are told'.[33] In referring to Aboriginal women's domestic service in her history of the Pilbara published in 1981, Jenny Hardie, who married into a pastoralist family in the 1960s, referred to Aboriginal women drifting up to the homestead each day, 'to be taught by "the missus" the finer arts of domesticity'.[34] Her description suggests that the 'missus' provided a service by teaching Aboriginal women the domestic skills they lacked. This depiction of domestic workers, called 'housegirls', as forever under tuition, cast in the role of children to benevolent white women, effectively rendered their labour invisible. When squatters and their supporters spoke of the high cost of Aboriginal labour relative to the value of the services they received in return, women were often numbered among the dependents of male workers, despite the fact that some did 'a little housework' in the homestead.

The image of women 'drifting up to the homestead' for a few hours each day and doing 'a little housework' conflicts with Aboriginal women's memories of hard work, long days and a strict routine regulated by the ringing of bells. According to Caroline Jula (Jula), her working day as a housegirl at Warrawagine Station began before sunrise. 'We go early, for light'm kitchen', she said:

> We light'm kitchen, we cook'm anything for breakfast, for boys and girls and all whitefellas too.[35] We do'm cooking, after we make'm bell ring for breakfast, for boys and girl coming, get'm … Sweep'm. Make a bed, for whitefellas in the house … Set the table for dinner, and after finish we wash the dishes and after dinner we going back to the camp, river … We going river, in the camp, we wait for that bell now. 'E ring a bell, for everybody, we coming in … And three o'clock we coming back, do

---

33 *Daily News*, 8 January 1945, p. 10. The use of the term 'gin' for an Aboriginal woman was common before the mid-twentieth century, but is now considered offensive.
34 Hardie, *Nor'Westers*, p. 181.
35 'Boys and girls': Aboriginal English terms for Aboriginal men and women.

the work again. Give'm cup of tea, you know, whitefellas, I give'm cup of tea, and water'm garden, afternoon. And suppertime, night-time, get a supper, have'm supper, and after tea we go do the work, they just feed'm whitefellas, you know.[36]

After washing the dishes, the women would return to camp in the creek at about seven o'clock, ready for an early rise the next morning. When women withdrew their labour in 1946, the importance of domestic labour to the effective operation of pastoral stations became apparent, as we shall see.

A further feature of squatter constructions of Aboriginal labour as expensive and inefficient was the assertion that many stations rationed more workers than were needed for much of the year to ensure that a sufficient workforce was available during the busier months. This, again, was highlighted as an example of squatter philanthropy. Owen Coppin, owner of Yarrie Station on the Pilbara's De Grey River, argued in 1946, for example, that 'the majority of native employers carry 50 per cent of employees as "passengers" for nine months of the year rather than see natives who have been born and bred on the properties wandering about destitute and homeless'.[37] While seasonal fluctuations in labour needs would have been the same if non-Aboriginal labour had been used, the complaint also overlooked the constant provision of Aboriginal domestic labour. Moreover, *marrngu* were sent away for a holiday, called *pingkayi*,[38] during the low season, and particularly during the wet summer months when station work was difficult. This practice enabled *marrngu* to maintain religious and cultural practices and connections with Country, and to maintain family and wider social networks across station communities, but many resented the way they were simply turned out during slack periods to leave the station on foot, in the same way that horses had their shoes removed and were turned out into a paddock.[39]

Claims that Aboriginal station residence was tolerated out of a kind of sentimental solicitude for displaced and helpless people sit uncomfortably with squatters' concurrent insistence that Aboriginal labour was essential for their industry's survival. Nevertheless, such claims served to counter attempts

---

36 Caroline Jula (Jula), recorded by Anne Scrimgeour, 13 August 1991, author's collection.
37 Coppin, letter to the editor, *West Australian*, 5 May 1946, p. 3.
38 The term entered the English lexicon in the north as 'pink-eye', or 'pinki'.
39 Jittermarra (Maruntu), recorded by Anne Scrimgeour, 5 August 1993, author's collection.

by the Department of Native Affairs to regulate labour relations. Despite claiming that Aboriginal labour was indispensable, pastoralists consistently warned the Department that their benevolence had its limits, and that if the cost or inconvenience of supporting dependent station communities became too great, they would have no choice but to let pragmatism override sentiment and cease using Aboriginal labour altogether. The managing director of the prosperous De Grey River Pastoral Company, which owned Mulyie Station, warned the Department in 1939 that it could not afford to continue caring for 'non-working' people like Waterlily and Peebo if its relationship with the recipients of its charity were to be regulated by an unappreciative Department as a labour relationship. If pressed to pay transport costs for such people, they would have no alternative but to 'discontinue feeding and clothing these and other indigent natives and not allow them to do any small menial work whatsoever. Under such circumstances we would have to look to your Department to provide for them in every way'.[40]

'A lot of stations feed dependents so as to get one or two that are of any use', A. E. (Ted) Richardson of Pippingarra Station reminded the Department in 1946:

> and it appears that if regulations are too severe they will be compelled to discontinue, employing only the ones that can earn what is paid and given to them as the cost of production will be more than the industry can afford.[41]

Owen Coppin, of Yarrie Station, warned that:

> any arbitration which aims at placing natives on a parity with white employees must envisage a wholesale replacement of natives by white labour, with the resultant shifting of the bulk of the native population to reserves and encampments, where they will be the charge of a benevolent Government, subsisting on a soul-destroying dole, contributed by the already over-burdened taxpayer.[42]

This threat and repeated reminders that the burden of housing and feeding a large Aboriginal population would fall to the Department if pastoralists

---

40   Managing director, De Grey River Pastoral Co., to Bray, 15 September 1939, SROWA 1937/0432/24.
41   Richardson to Bray, 24 June 1946 (incorrectly dated 1945), p. 2, SROWA 1946/0799/12.
42   Coppin, letter to the editor, *West Australian*, 5 May 1946, p. 3.

decided that they were, after all, more trouble than they were worth, hung like Damocles' sword over the head of the underfunded Department.

In the years leading up to the strike, the Department's reluctance to disrupt pastoral labour arrangements was strengthened by the state Labor government's appointment in 1939 of Aubrey Augustus Michael (Bob) Coverley as the Minister for the North West with responsibility for Aboriginal affairs. Since first winning the seat of Kimberley for the Labor Party in 1924, Coverley had made no secret of his belief that settler interests in the north should take priority over Aboriginal interests. Criticising what he called the 'stupid system of protecting the aborigines to the detriment of the settlers as a whole', he argued that Aboriginal reserves hindered white settlement, and called for reserve land to be thrown open for selection.[43] He complained that Western Australia's restrictive *Aborigines Act 1905* 'provided protection for the blacks, [but] no protection at all for the whites'.[44] He was also vocal in his opposition to any government interference in the free use of Aboriginal labour by northern pastoralists and other settlers. The unregulated use of labour was not only essential for the settlement and development of the north, he argued, but would ensure that taxpayers were not burdened with the expense of keeping a 'useless race'.[45]

Peter Biskup writes in his history of Aboriginal administration in Western Australia that the decision of the newly-elected Labor government to give Coverley responsibility for Native Affairs in 1939 was 'little short of a sell-out by the administration to the pastoralists'.[46] The Commissioner of Native Affairs while Coverley held the Native Affairs portfolio was Francis Illingworth Bray, described by Biskup as 'a public servant personified'.[47] Unlike his predecessor, A. O. Neville, and his successor, the proactive and forthright S. G. Middleton, Bray had no vision for changing the status of Aboriginal people in the state but sought rather to maintain the status quo. As a result, the priorities of the

---

43   Quoted in Peter Biskup, *Not Slaves, Not Citizens: The Aboriginal Problem in Western Australia 1898–1954*, University of Queensland Press, St. Lucia, 1973, p. 186; Coverley, evidence given to the Moseley Commission, *West Australian*, 28 March 1934, p. 8.

44   Coverley, evidence given to the Moseley Commission, *West Australian*, 28 March 1934, p. 8.

45   Coverley, Parliamentary Debates (Hansard), Western Australia: Legislative Assembly, 12 December 1929, p. 2163; 3 December 1936, pp. 2380–2381; Coverley, evidence given to the Moseley Commission, *West Australian*, 28 March 1934, p. 8.

46   Biskup, *Not Slaves*, pp. 177–178.

47   Biskup, *Not Slaves*, p. 180.

Department tended to be determined by the overtly pro-pastoralist Coverley,[48] whose contention that getting Aboriginal people to work was the best that could be done for them conveniently coincided with the needs of squatters and pearlers in his electorate. During Coverley's eight-year term as minister, the position of the Department could be summed up by his statement that 'natives were good workers when correctly handled'.[49]

---

48   Biskup, *Not Slaves*, p. 180.
49   *Daily News*, 4 March 1944, p. 7.

Chapter 3

'They Were the Boss for Us'

In place of formal agreements regulated by the Department of Native Affairs, a system of control was in place in the northern regions of Western Australia that was consistent with squatters' self-representation as caregivers to a dispossessed and helpless race. The overt violence with which pastoralists had originally secured and retained Aboriginal labour had, by the 1940s, been replaced with a complex relationship in which loyalty and paternal benevolence overlay a continuing undercurrent of intimidation and denigration. Central to this relationship was pastoralist control over Aboriginal access to rations and country, but this was augmented by the use of the police to ensure Aboriginal compliance with pastoral labour needs. In the hierarchical social system of northern pastoral regions, squatter authority was backed by local police officers who accepted responsibility for keeping Aboriginal people under control, and who prided themselves on knowing 'how to handle the natives'. They supported pastoralist control over Aboriginal labour, visiting stations on their patrols and reporting on the behaviour of workers. Constable McMahon reported in 1940, for example, that the manager of Strelley Station near Port Hedland had no complaints and that 'his natives were giving satisfaction'.[1] 'On control issues', Ann McGrath writes, 'settlers and police cooperated closely'.[2]

While resenting and avoiding government regulation of Aboriginal labour, pastoralists called on the Department to support the police in ensuring that mechanisms for controlling Aboriginal people were instituted. The Department acted to some extent as an extension of the Police Department to ensure that Aboriginal labour remained compliant and that informal mechanisms of control remained in place. Native Affairs officers were often ex-policemen with frontier experience, usually in the Kimberley, where, charged with the task of making Aboriginal country available to settlers, they had forceful and often violent interactions with Aboriginal

---

1   McMahon, police patrol report, 29 October 1940, SROWA 1943/0099 v7.
2   Ann McGrath, *Born in the Cattle: Aborigines in Cattle Country*, Allen and Unwin, Sydney, London and Boston, 1987, p. 119.

people.³ The roles of police and Native Affairs officers converged. Police officers were appointed as 'Protectors of Natives' and vested with extensive responsibility and authority over Aboriginal people. Pastoralists supported the practice of giving the role of protector to police officers because, as a Pilbara pastoralist and politician argued in Parliament in 1936, it enabled protectors 'to exercise a certain amount of restraint' over Aboriginal people, 'by virtue of being police'.⁴

As late as the 1940s, Aboriginal people could be arrested on minor charges and transported in chains and, as their protectors were also the police, they received little legal protection. Ron and Catherine Berndt found, in a survey of Aboriginal pastoral labour in regions to the Pilbara's north and north-east in the mid-1940s, that 'the image of police officials represented to Aborigines ... arrests, neck-chaining or wrist-chaining of prisoners and witnesses, physical violence, and the forcible return of runaways to station employment'.⁵

Prevailing squatter attitudes in the Pilbara, including the role that police played in maintaining control over Aboriginal people, are portrayed in *The Green Stick*, a pro-pastoralist novel about the strike and cooperative movement written by Pilbara station owner James Doughty and published in 1960. 'A policeman's job in a district like this is mainly concerned with the niggers', a policeman, Henderson, says in the novel:

> Whites don't give any trouble beyond the occasional pub brawl – nothing criminal. Coons don't give much trouble either, if you know how to handle 'em. And that's one thing I thought I did know. I always believed I knew how to handle niggers.⁶

The fictional policeman, modelled on the Marble Bar policeman Gordon Marshall, regrets changing attitudes in the 1950s. 'There's nearly always a nigger in the cells these days', he complains. 'At one time they'd never have got near the place, I'd have given 'em what was coming to them without worrying

---

3   These men had inherited a culture of policing the Kimberley, described by Chris Owen in *Every Mother's Son is Guilty: Policing the Kimberley Frontier of Western Australia 1882–1905*, University of Western Australia Publishing, Crawley, 2016. See also Mary Anne Jebb, *Blood, Sweat and Welfare: A History of White Bosses and Aboriginal Pastoral Workers*, University of Western Australia Publishing, Crawley, 2002.
4   Frank Welsh, Parliamentary Debates (Hansard), Western Australia: Legislative Council, 3 December 1936, p. 2384.
5   Ronald M. Berndt and Catherine H. Berndt, *End of an Era: Aboriginal Labour in the Northern Territory*, Australian Institute of Aboriginal Studies, Canberra, 1987, p. 8.
6   James Doughty, *The Green Stick*, Collins, London, 1960, p. 142.

about a magistrate'.[7] Having no access to education, *marrngu* had no access to information about their legal rights, and no reason to believe that the power exercised by the pastoralists and the police was not absolute.

Informal systems were used to ensure that workers stayed at their places of employment. Supporters of the strike were critical of restrictions imposed on Aboriginal workers by section 26 of the *Native Administration Act*, which stated that:

> Any native who without reasonable cause, shall neglect or refuse to enter upon or commence his service, or shall absent himself from his service, or shall refuse or neglect to work in the capacity in which he has been engaged, or shall desert or quit his work without the consent of his employer, or shall commit any other breach of his agreement, shall be guilty of an offence against this Act.

However, section 26 only applied as a condition of the rarely used employment agreements. Its punitive restrictions, therefore, could not be legally applied to Aboriginal pastoral workers in the Pilbara who were not employed under such agreements. Rather, an informal system was in place which gave pastoralists control over the movement of Aboriginal labour without the need to comply with conditions that formal agreements imposed on employers. Edward Holthouse, who owned Muccan Station on the Pilbara's De Grey River, referred to an 'unwritten law' that no-one would employ Aboriginal workers from another station. Although unwritten, it was 'rigidly enforced and assisted by the police', he wrote, and it ensured that 'absconding natives' had nowhere to go.[8]

This unwritten law was imposed as rigidly as if it had legal basis. Pastoralists came to assume that they had a legal right to force *marrngu* to remain on their station of employment, an assumption no doubt strengthened during the Second World War by departmental instructions that Aboriginal pastoral labour was to be retained for service to a wool industry that was vital to the war effort. 'It's the policemen's job to see that blackfellers stay where they're put', the protagonist in *The Green Stick* says. 'If one of mine cleared out, and I was too busy to chase after him myself, I'd just notify Henderson, and Henderson would get him back for me ... It's the law'.[9] Peter Coppin (Kangkushot) recalled that 'those days, police and station owners work together. Anyone run away bang

---

7   Doughty, *The Green Stick*, p. 143.
8   Edward Holthouse, *One Life's Journey*, Hesperian Press, Carlisle, 1987, p. 19.
9   Doughty, *The Green Stick*, p. 126.

him in jail, ring up the boss and say I got your boy in jail. What about come and pick him up'.[10] In 1943, for example, Constable McRae was contacted by the owner-manager of Wallal Station, north-east of Port Hedland, and advised that 'one of his natives named Tommy had become slightly out of hand and had two days previously left his employ'. McRae agreed to locate and return the absconding worker.[11]

The lack of freedom to move between stations was resented by Aboriginal workers and cited as a major cause of dissatisfaction that gave rise to the strike. 'If people pulled out from one station to another station', Peter Coppin said, 'the boss would ring and get the other boss to send them back. Can't keep him there. All that sort of thing was going on'.[12] According to a police report written in the second year of the strike, the strikers' 'main complaint, with the exception of conditions, pay, etc., was that, if they were employed by one station, and after a while, they desired to go to another station, the manager of that station, would not employ them, because they belonged to another station'.[13] 'Whose niggers are they?', a character asks in *The Green Stick*.[14]

Police coercion was also used to ensure that Aboriginal workers returned to stations when their labour was required after the holiday time, or *pingkayi*. In 1944, after several stations complained that Aboriginal workers had failed to return from the holiday allowed for the Port Hedland races week, Constable Les Fletcher visited Mundabullangana (Munda) Station, where initiation ceremonies were taking place. After moving 'freely amongst natives', making people aware of his presence and instructing them to return to their stations when ceremonies were over, he saw 'several parties of natives started for their homestations' when the proceedings were over two days later.[15]

Marrngu resented the pastoralist's use of police coercion in this way. According to Billy Thomas:

> When we'd go on holiday from the station, we'd go on foot. Then on the day they wanted us back, maybe after a couple of weeks, we'd be

---

10 Peter Coppin (Kangkushot), interview recorded by Bill Bunbury for Radio National's 'Hindsight' series *It's Not the Money It's the Land,* December 2000, cited in Tim Bunbury, *It's Not the Money It's the Land: Aboriginal Stockmen and the Equal Wages Case,* Fremantle Arts Centre Press, North Fremantle, 2002, p. 45.
11 McRae, police patrol report, 1 December 1943, SROWA 1939/1777 v7.
12 Jolly Read and Peter Coppin, *Kangkushot: The Life of Nyamal Lawman Peter Coppin,* Aboriginal Studies Press, Canberra, 1999, p. 60.
13 Keith Weaver, police patrol report, 5 October 1947, SROWA 1946/2538 v8.
14 Doughty, *The Green Stick,* p. 34.
15 Les Fletcher, police patrol report, 1 October 1944, SROWA 1939/1777 v7.

expected to walk back to work. If anyone stayed away for longer than two weeks, they'd send the police out after us, and the police would hunt us back to work on the station. So then we'd go back on foot. They got sick of all this kind of thing.[16]

Aboriginal people exchanged their labour for continued access to country through residence on pastoral leases. McGrath argues that 'being allowed to remain or travel on what was often their tribal territory, and to continue much of their traditional life', was one of the most important concessions gained by Aboriginal people in their relationship with pastoralists.[17] Thalia Anthony agrees, writing that 'the loyalty of the worker, demonstrated through ongoing labour services, is bestowed in return for access to land'.[18] Station-supplied rations were supplemented by weekend food-gathering activities at local waterholes, remembered as a significant part of childhood by *marrngu* who grew up on Pilbara stations. Some forms of station labour gave workers greater access to country than others; those engaging in stockwork or fencing, for example, combined station work with hunting and food gathering to supplement station rations. Station labour also provided Aboriginal people with access to pastoral leases for ceremonial purposes during *pingkayi*.

Pastoralists' continuing control over access to country, however, was an important feature of an effective system of control. Pastoralist Edward Holthouse described the arrangement as 'emerging from the days of slave trading to one of control of nomadic natives who otherwise would be wandering at large on these large pastoral properties'.[19] Aboriginal use of country was entirely at the discretion of leaseholders, who used the police to shift *marrngu* from their property. In 1943, for example, a policeman moved a group of about thirty Aboriginal people from a Pilbara pastoral lease after the manager complained that 'their tucker was getting short and they were starting to make a nuisance of themselves, and that while they remained there he could

---

16 Billy Thomas (Pitpit), addressing school children on a field trip to Wantilurr (Skull Springs), recorded by Anne Scrimgeour, 21 September 1992, translated from Nyangumarta by Barbara Hale and Mark Clendon, AIATSIS collection, soundfile 'Pitpit Talking to Kids'.
17 McGrath, *Born in the Cattle*, p. 105.
18 Thalia Anthony, 'Labour Relations on Northern Cattle Stations: Feudal Exploration and Accommodation', University of Sydney Law School, Legal Studies Research Paper 07/43, 2007, p. 120.
19 Holthouse, *One Life*, p. 20.

get no good out of his own Station Natives. He would like them shifted on'.[20] Conflicts over access to pastoral leases would be an ongoing feature of the strike.

In the aftermath of the violence of colonial occupation, the threat of physical violence remained a constant presence for Aboriginal people. Pastoralists maintained discipline through sanctions including physical punishment.[21] Mac Gardiner remembered Les Miller, manager at Warrawagine Station, handcuffing young men suspected of stealing vegetables from the garden, and beating them with his belt, and Caroline Jula remembered Miller's wife, Edith, giving her a hiding for fighting when she was a young domestic servant, or 'housegirl'.[22] 'Never let a blackfeller down in the way of a promise', an experienced pastoralist advises in *The Green Stick*. 'If you promise him a tin of jam, give him a tin of jam; and if you promise him a hiding, give him a good one ... You've got to treat him same as you would a horse, or a dog, or a child. Gentle but firm'.[23] This accepted wisdom was part of the pastoralist code on 'how to handle natives'. Edith Miller made a very similar statement in explaining why her husband, Les, was considered a good boss. 'They all said the boss was a "proper good fella"', she said, 'because if he "promised 'em holiday, he'd give 'em holiday", and if he promised, "me hiding, he give us hiding"'.[24]

Repeated displays of violence by the police served to maintain settler dominance over Aboriginal people.[25] The practice of shooting their dogs to reduce numbers, usually carried out by the police in response to complaints made by pastoralists, was central to this program of intimidation. Dog culls were routinely carried out without warning in dawn raids on *marrngu* camps, which, given the history of violence in pastoral areas, must have been terrifying for the Aboriginal people involved. Although Aboriginal men were legally entitled to own one dog each (Aboriginal women were not permitted to own any), the police had no way of ascertaining the number of men in a camp before carrying out the raid. A newly-recruited police officer, Edgar Morrow, described his first dawn dog cull in Broome in the early 1920s. In response

---

20 McMahon, police patrol report, 29 October 1940, SROWA 1943/0099 v7.
21 McGrath, *Born in the Cattle*, pp. 107–108.
22 Gardiner (Pirntilkampanyaja), recorded by Anne Scrimgeour, 29 September 1993, author's collection; Jula, recorded by Anne Scrimgeour, 13 August 1991, author's collection.
23 Doughty, *The Green Stick*, p. 68.
24 Edith Miller, interviewed by Ronda Jamieson, 1982, transcript, p. 87, SLWA OH506.
25 McGrath, *Born in the Cattle*, p. 120.

to a complaint 'concerning destruction of fowls by native dogs', Morrow was instructed:

> to go to the camp and destroy all the dogs I could find. With a sinking heart I made my way out on horseback before daybreak. As I waited for the light to improve before making my final rush into the sleeping camp, I wondered where was the picturesqueness of this particular setting. To wait in concealment for a chance to shoot a sleeping dog was not only unsporting – it seemed sordid and mean.
>
> A touch of the spur in Bushman's ribs sent him hurtling into the camp. He had done his job before and knew what was wanted. My first shot caused a wild scramble of naked natives and yelping dogs into the swamp. But one large yellow beast tore inland whining and snapping at his bleeding side. My lead bullet had torn a hole from which he would soon die. Backward and forward I galloped through the scattered shelters shooting wherever I saw a dog. Very soon it was all over and I dismounted to inspect the deserted camps, and to put any suffering animal out of its misery.[26]

While Morrow described with distaste a task he felt to be cowardly, raids such as these often seem to have had no other purpose than to create fear in Aboriginal people. In October 1943, for example, Constable McRae found two young *marrngu* women alone at a remote Pilbara station outcamp, presumably the sexual partners of the absent station worker who lived there. At dawn the following morning, he writes, he 'revealed my identity to the gins, destroyed their two dogs and moved on at 6 am'.[27] Aboriginal people felt powerless to respond to such actions. Monty Hale (Minyjun) recalled a dawn raid on his family's camp at Moolyella, near Marble Bar, in the 1930s. 'We just sat down quietly', he wrote, 'and when the police went back we cried for all those dogs'.[28]

Through such actions, settler society reasserted and restated its domination of Aboriginal people, achieved through violence, and made the threat of violence against *marrngu* themselves a constant presence. 'The *possibility* of violence', Rowse writes, 'underlay all transactions'.[29] As McGrath notes, 'Whites realised

---

26 E. Morrow, *The Law Provides*, Herbert Jenkins Ltd, London, 1937, facsimile edition, Hesperian Press, Carlisle, 1984, p. 33.
27 McRae, police patrol report, 27 October 1944, SROWA 1943/0099 v7.
28 Monty Hale, 'Early Memories', *Mikurrunya*, vol. 6, no. 2, 1984, cited in John Bucknall, 'Jacob Oberdoo (Minyjun) c. 1920s – 1989 (First Draft)', unpublished paper, p. 3.
29 Rowse, *White Flour, White Power*, p. 64 (emphasis in original).

they could only maintain their dominant position by perpetuating the fear of the gun which had been such an effective control in the past'.[30] Action taken by *marrngu* in 1951 to oppose the police dog culls would be effective in bringing an end to the practice of dawn raids throughout the state.

Marrngu were not entirely powerless in their relationship with pastoralists prior to the strike; workers did sometimes refuse to obey orders they believed to be unreasonable. When Molly Williams (Kulyu) was a young woman at Ettrick, an outcamp of Mulyie Station, her husband refused to bring in some horses during the midday heat, saying he would do so later in the afternoon. Ordered to roll his swag and leave, he and Molly walked to the head station of Mulyie, where the manager told him to take no notice of the outstation boss and employed him as a musterer.[31] Workers could also respond to unfair treatment by going bush at a time when their labour was needed. In 1940 the manager of Bungalow (or Coongan) Station was reluctant to shoot troublesome dogs during the shearing because he feared that his workers would 'clear out' and leave him shorthanded. Once the shearing was over, however, he made a complaint to the police, who killed the dogs in a dawn raid on the camp.[32] Nevertheless, Aboriginal people had very little room to manoeuvre within the relationship; it was, as Michael Hess claims, a matter of 'bargaining at the margins'.[33]

Although the threat of violence and imprisonment underpinned the relationship between pastoralists and Aboriginal workers, the decision of the Bungalow (Coongan) Station manager to have dogs killed by the police, rather than killing them himself, hints at other factors at play in the relationship, beyond simply the imposition of power through intimidation and violence. Snowy Jittermarra (Maruntu) suggested this in an account of the use of police to return workers to stations:

> When the time come [to return to the stations], sometime we might [be] running late, well, we see the policeman coming. 'Hey, there's a policeman coming'. All the boys there, how many people belong to the Noreena or Bonney Downs, he sort them out, police gotta sort them out. And when you ready to go, you better go in the time ... Well, we

---

30 McGrath, *Born in the Cattle*, p. 106.
31 Molly Williams (Kulyu), recorded by Anne Scrimgeour, 13 August 1991, author's collection.
32 McMahon, police patrol report, 3 July 1940, SROWA 1943/0099 v7.
33 Michael Hess, 'Black and Red: The Pilbara Pastoral Workers' Strike, 1946', *Aboriginal History*, vol. 18, no. 1, 1994, p. 66.

see the policeman coming, push us back to the station ... And squatter was happy: 'Oh, you come back?' Never say anything. Next day, never going to give us spell, just after we bin walk from Nullagine to Noreena and we got to start straight away ... doesn't matter how tired. And that's the way we are.[34]

Snowy's statement 'Never say anything' suggests that the collusion between pastoralists and the police was known but not explicitly acknowledged. Gillian Cowlishaw has noted the 'apparently contradictory and uneven practices, from extreme racial violence to a sentimental form of solicitude' that characterised race relations in pastoral areas.[35] Constructions of Aboriginal people as childlike underpinned a paternalistic benevolence that masked the coercive nature of labour relations. Pastoralists adopted a parental role, disciplining when they deemed it necessary, but also nurturing and guiding men and women who were, they believed, incapable of caring for themselves. Edith Miller claims to have played a mothering role to over 100 Aboriginal people at Warrawagine Station:

> And I had to look after these natives, be doctor, nurse, friend, and patch up any marital problems they had. And that was where I really got to know the natives, and realised what a likeable people they were. They were very childlike, and needed someone to help them with their problems. It's all very well for the people to say we were too paternal with them, but you had to be, because they were like children.[36]

'With its promised protection and a concern for the servant's welfare', McGrath writes, 'paternalism played a central role in the control pastoralists wielded over Aboriginal people'.[37] Paradoxically, a component of the paternalistic relationship that existed on stations was the illusion that stations protected their workers from violence. Monty Hale's family, newly arrived in the pastoral regions from the Great Sandy Desert, first took up station residence and employment after police shot their dogs in a dawn raid at the Moolyella tin field. Their shift to Mt Edgar Station, where the squatter spoke Nyamal and was considered 'a reasonable boss', was a direct result of the killing of

---

34   Jittermarra (Maruntu), recorded by Anne Scrimgeour, 5 August 1993, author's collection.

35   Gillian Cowlishaw, *Rednecks, Eggheads and Blackfellas: A Study of Racial Power and Intimacy in Australia*, Allen and Unwin, St Leonards, 1999, p. 138.

36   Edith Miller, interviewed by Jamieson, 1982, transcript, p. 51, SLWA OH506.

37   McGrath, *Born in the Cattle*, p. 121.

their dogs, according to John Bucknall.[38] Without dogs, it was more difficult to live by hunting, but their move to Mt Edgar was also motivated by the perception that station residence offered a degree of protection from violent acts of this nature.

The duplicitous nature of the relationship between pastoralists and workers on pastoral stations is exemplified by the fact that while pastoralists initiated police action against *marrngu*, they also provided protection from such action. Pastoralists were able to maintain an image of paternal benevolence by calling on the police to undertake the harsher aspects of control, in much the same way that Christopher Casby, in Dickens' *Little Dorrit,* plays the benevolent patriarch to the impoverished residents of Bleeding Heart Yard, while calling on his rent collector, Pancks, to squeeze them hard for rent.

Squatters also sometimes played a protective role in relation to the removal of Aboriginal children. In accordance with departmental policy of biological absorption, children of mixed descent, and particularly girls, were removed from their communities to institutions, in a social engineering scheme designed to curtail the growth of a large mixed-race population. It was intended that a gradual, generational dilution of Aboriginality could be achieved by ensuring that girls who were removed from their families only gave birth to children fathered by white men, either within marriage or otherwise. Pastoralists were required to notify the Department of Native Affairs of any mixed-descent child on their stations, under threat of being denied employment permits. Some pastoralists complied. Molly Williams' older brother, Peter Braeside, was removed from Coongan Station after the owner, Vivian Robinson, alerted the Department to his presence. 'Just call him', Molly said, 'and put him, chuck him in the car and take him away. Mummy went to Port Hedland, she trying to stop'm, no, he said he gotta go to school'.[39]

In 1939, Constable Gordon Marshall of Marble Bar drove out to Warrawagine Station to remove three young girls. 'I drove my car as fast as I could right into the homestead yard', he wrote:

> and pulled up between the kitchen and butchers shop at 4 pm ... Amy or Yimmy was located on verandah of the butchers shop and Lena in the native camp 80 yards away. There were over 30 natives at the butchers shop when I took these children and they made an awful fuss.[40]

---

38 Bucknall, 'Jacob Oberdoo', p. 3.
39 Molly Williams (Kulyu), tape 1, recorded 13 August 1991, author's collection.
40 Marshall to Bray, 2 August 1940, p. 2, SROWA 1939/1226/24.

Marrngu were told that children who were removed were being sent away for schooling. 'They all wanted to know what they took them away for', Mac Gardiner said. '"Oh, they'll learn to read and write, and come back. They'll help you then, once they've learned to read and write". We waited for their children, but they'd gone for good'.[41]

The removal of children was an issue raised as a grievance by *marrngu* during the strike. Striker Tommy Sampie wrote in 1947 that *marrngu* 'told [Constable] Mason that quite a lot of children had been sent up Moore River, taken away from their mothers, and have never been heard of. We all just waking up to the Government laws against us'.[42] While child removals continued throughout other parts of Western Australia, the militancy of *marrngu* during and following the strike brought an end to child removals in that area. Their pre-strike experiences of child removal would have an impact on the education of their children, however. Although literacy was highly valued by *marrngu* and schooling for their children was one of the principal aims of the strike movement, parents were extremely cautious about any educational arrangement that involved their children being separated from their community, such as the school the Department attempted to establish at the White Springs Mission in the early 1950s.

The protective nature of the pastoralists' relationship with Aboriginal people was sometimes played out in relation to child removals. While some pastoralists alerted police to the presence of children of mixed parentage on their properties, others attempted to prevent such removals. On the occasion in 1939 when Marshall removed Amy and Lena from Warrawagine Station, Les and Edith Miller tried to disguise the identity of a third girl, Polly, who was being trained to work in their home as a domestic servant. Their action in doing so brought them into conflict with the police and the Department. 'I consider the action of the Millers very low in endeavouring to hide these children', Marshall wrote in a report, underlining the sentence to emphasise his frustration.[43] Although Polly was removed as far as Port Hedland, the Millers successfully arranged for her return to Warrawagine by 'adopting' her,

---

41 Gardiner (Pirntilkampanyaja), recorded by Anne Scrimgeour, 5 August 1993, AIATSIS collection, soundfile 'Pirntilkampanyaja 15'.

42 Tommy Sampie to Committee for Defence of Native Rights, 'A First Hand Report on Police Persecution of Aborigines', undated [1947], SROWA 1943/0621/31. Although Sampie's name is often spelt 'Sampey' or 'Sampi', he spelt his name 'Sampie', and his niece, Sheila, agrees that this is the correct spelling.

43 Marshall to Bray, 30 January 1940, p. 8, SROWA 1939/1226/10 (underline in original).

and she continued to work as their domestic servant, remaining with them when they shifted to De Grey Station.[44]

Pastoralists also obstructed departmental attempts to remove children by warning *marrngu* when visits from the police or other 'Protectors of Natives' were imminent. When Maggie Ginger (Nyirrarlpi) was a child on Muccan Station on the De Grey River, her family would be alerted by the owner whenever the policeman was due to arrive, and Maggie and other children would be hidden by their families at a waterhole to the west of the homestead, while the squatter led the police to search in the opposite direction.[45] Such actions served to strengthen the bond between *marrngu* and pastoralists.

The sense of loyalty and obligation engendered by the apparent protection provided by their labour relationship with pastoralists in a hostile and threatening environment 'welded master and servant into a continuing contract with complex reciprocal obligations', according to McGrath.[46] A newly-appointed departmental officer to the Kimberley in 1949 was surprised by 'the extreme loyalty of a native to his boss', which he thought had 'almost the quality of the absurd loyalty between a much cuffed dog and his master'.[47] It was through personal relationships based on loyalty, Thalia Anthony claims, together with Indigenous identification with, and sense of loyalty to, a particular station and area of country, that pastoralists maintained control of Aboriginal labour.[48] Aboriginal dependence on station-supplied rations, created by the non-payment or inadequate payment of station workers, was not essential to the relationship, but served to strengthen the ties that bound *marrngu* to their station bosses. These personal bonds, severely tested in 1946 when *marrngu* asked for more adequate reward for their labour, were to have a profound impact on the nature and duration of the strike.

Composed of such contradictory features as coercive solicitude and protective intimidation, pastoralist–*marrngu* interactions were further complicated by relationships of intimacy, warmth and affection on the one hand and marked social distance on the other. Strict rules of social conduct, framed in terms of knowing 'how to handle the natives', ensured that racialised social boundaries

---

44   Edith Miller, interviewed by Jamieson, 1928, transcript, p. 60, 81, SLWA OH506.
45   Maggie Ginger (Nyirrarlpi), recorded by Anne Scrimgeour, 15 June 1993, AIATSIS collection, soundfile 'Nyirrarlpi 27'.
46   McGrath, *Born in the Cattle*, p. 121.
47   Dave Pullen, Annual Report, September 1949, p. 7, SROWA 1949/0722.
48   Thalia Anthony, 'Criminal Justice and Transgression on Northern Australian Cattle Stations', in Ingereth Macfarlane and Mark Hannah (eds.), *Transgressions: Critical Australian Indigenous Histories*, Aboriginal History Monograph 16, ANU E press, 2007.

remained in place. 'Well we never mix with them, that's the trouble', Peter Coppin said. 'We don't like to be with them. Maybe we don't like each other. They don't like us and we don't like them, sort of thing'.[49] A Kimberley pastoralist also remembered the social distance that existed in the 1940s. 'You never spoke, you know', he said:

> The only time was when you gave an order sometimes. He wouldn't talk to you unless he had to come up and tell you something. In those days in the stock camp, a blackfella wouldn't come up and talk or anything like that.[50]

The use of a restricted code when talking to Aboriginal people, such as one may use when talking to very young children, also worked to mark social boundaries. Although *walypila* and *marrngu* worked together on stations, it was believed that familiarity would breed contempt and undermine settler authority. Kimberley pastoralist Michael Durack explained:

> The man in this country who goes in for talking to the black, exchanging ideas with him, asking him if he is satisfied with his lot and treating him literally as his 'black brother', receives no respect from the native in exchange. If he is a station manager or a stockman with black boys under him he will soon find that he has lost his influence in the camp. He will be laughed at behind his back. His orders will be disregarded. He will likely be told to do the job himself. If there is any real ill-feeling between the races, perhaps even blows exchanged, it will invariably be found to be in the case where a white man has acted with the black on a more equal footing.[51]

'They always had to be kept in their place', a Kimberley pastoralist's wife told the *Daily News* in 1945. 'A man was a "no good boss" if he laughed or talked with them'.[52]

While pastoralists argued that Aboriginal people themselves desired social separation, John Wilson found otherwise. *Marrngu* he spoke to in 1959 and 1960 expressed resentment at the social distance that existed between themselves and the squatters. They remembered pastoralists from the early

---

49   Read and Coppin, *Kangkushot*, p. 15.
50   Jebb, *Blood, Sweat and Welfare*, p. 199.
51   Quoted in Paul Hasluck, *Shades of Darkness: Aboriginal Affairs 1925–1965*, Melbourne University Press, Carlton, 1988, p. 59.
52   *Daily News*, 8 January 1945, p. 10, 'Maids Plentiful But Troublesome in North'.

decades of the century with some nostalgia, despite the overt violence of earlier interactions, because social distance had not then been so pronounced. 'They were sometimes rough', one elder told John Wilson, 'but they were good old daddies. You could talk to them, not like some of these young fellows who've taken over'.[53]

Codes of social interaction defined by race were complicated by the presence of people of mixed descent. In *The Green Stick*, the protagonist is uncomfortable at this blurring of racial lines:

> So far as labour went he'd always preferred the full-bloods. You knew what you didn't know about full-bloods, but with half-castes you either under- or over-estimated them. And it was harder to draw a line. With the dinkum blackfeller there was no need to draw a line. The line was already drawn, and he could see it as clearly as you could. So long as neither of you over-stepped the line everything went smoothly.[54]

The racialised hierarchy of pastoral stations was understood in spatial terms, as lines that should not be crossed. Social lines of demarcation were maintained by physical boundaries, creating what Gillian Cowlishaw calls 'spaces for races'.[55] Imaginary lines drawn in the red Pilbara sand ensured that Aboriginal people remained physically, socially and economically on the periphery of the settler world. Lines of exclusion around towns and other settler social spaces could only be crossed by *marrngu* in their role as servants. On some stations, Aboriginal men were not allowed within the vicinity of the homestead. In 1991, Cranky stood on the driveway at some distance from the Warrawagine homestead and told me that this was where he and other Aboriginal workers had stood to receive their orders each morning.[56] It was the point beyond which they were, under normal circumstances, not permitted to pass. Constable Marshall wrote in 1946 that at Warrawagine 'the male natives are forbidden at all times within a reasonable distance of the White peoples' quarters, & they have no reason whatever to go there'.[57] Lines of demarcation along gendered as well as racial lines, served to facilitate sexual relationships between white men and black women.[58]

---

53   Quoted in John Wilson, 'Authority and Leadership', p. 36.
54   Doughty, *The Green Stick*, p. 68.
55   Cowlishaw, *Rednecks, Eggheads and Blackfellas*, p. 59.
56   Cranky (Kujupurra), recorded by Anne Scrimgeour at Warrawagine, 1991, author's collection.
57   Marshall, police patrol report, 4 October 1946, 1946/2538 v8.
58   This is further discussed in Chapter 14.

Aboriginal people on stations lived and ate in designated areas separate from management and other workers. Such spaces came to represent social or even evolutionary status in the settler imagination. When pastoralists spoke of Aboriginal people living 'in the river', they referred not only to the physical location of station 'native camps', but also to a figurative location on an evolutionary scale. People of mixed descent were seen to occupy an intermediate position in this social and evolutionary hierarchy. When the 'half-caste' couple Rory and Bidgie McPhee moved into a two-roomed hut located between the homestead and the 'native camp' on Warrawagine, the Millers spoke of having taken them 'out of the river', in a social elevation which placed them in a midway position in the racialised hierarchy of the station.[59] Such elevation required the agency of whites; it was the Millers who raised the McPhees by taking them 'out of the river'.

Strict social separation gave rise to the existence of two distinct social worlds in pastoral regions. The tenet 'Don't interfere with their tribal life' was part of the pastoralist code on 'how to handle the natives'. When *marrngu* left the stations during *pingkayi* to visit family and participate in social and cultural activities, they were said to be responding to an instinctive primal urge to 'go bush', their social and cultural life imagined as a primitive realm of chaos and disorder unmoderated by culture, intellect or civilisation. The 'bush', or 'down the river', was imagined both as a physical area away from station homesteads and a space of primitivity to which *marrngu* were drawn through a primal urge, from which they would return dirty, dishevelled and hungry – relieved, it seemed, to return to the order of station life and the regularity of station rations. 'They'd go walkabout down the river', Edith Miller said. 'And if you met one of those housegirls down the river you wouldn't believe it was the same girl, because they wouldn't bath or change their dress or anything, they looked absolutely filthy ... They were always quite pleased to come back'.[60] 'The call of the wild is too strong for the native', the owner of Pilbara's Warralong Station and National Party politician Frank Welsh explained in the Legislative Council in 1944. 'He will "go bush" at times no matter how civilised he has become'.[61] The rich and continuing social, cultural and religious life of Aboriginal people was hidden from pastoralists, who knew the Aboriginal people who lived and worked beside them only in their roles as 'stockboys', 'house gins' and the dependent recipients of station rations.

---

59 Edith Miller, interviewed by Jamieson, 1982, transcript, p. 72, SLWA OH506.
60 Edith Miller, interviewed by Jamieson, 1982, transcript, p. 81, SLWA OH506.
61 Frank Welsh, Parliamentary Debates (Hansard), Western Australia: Legislative Council, 25 October 1944, p. 1329.

Yet, paradoxically, interactions between squatters and *marrngu* included relationships of intimacy and affection. Sexual intimacy between white men and Aboriginal women was a common feature of station life. Through the children born of such unions, Aboriginal and squatter families were linked by kinship. Even when there was no actual family connection, mutual dependence gave the relationship between *marrngu* and pastoralists a familial quality. *Marrngu* often regarded individual pastoralists as something like kin, incorporating them into kinship networks with existing structures of entitlement and obligation. A particular affection was felt for squatters who had spent some of their childhood growing up on stations. *Marrngu* remembered fondly the *walypila* children they had cared for and taken out bush on Sundays. Maggie Ginger remembered her family taking Lang Coppin, the young son of the owner of Yarrie Station, to a local waterhole on weekends and teaching him to hunt, fish and speak Nyangumarta. 'That's the way now we bin learn'm little boy, Yarrie, Lang, Nyangumarta we bin learn'm, we bin take'm all way, cook'm everything, cook'm bungarra, he learning Nyangumarta, full Nyangumarta he talk'.[62] *Marrngu* spoke of having grown such children up.

In childhood, there was nothing of the marked social distance that characterised adult *marrngu–walypila* relationships. *Marrngu* remembered their non-Aboriginal playmates warmly. Cranky laughed to remember the mischief he had made at Warrawagine with the Miller's son, Peter, his *yarlpu*;[63] and Caroline Jula spoke of her friendship with Peter's sister, Patsy. Children spoke a shared language. Frank (Bidge) Welsh, the son of the politician who spoke of 'the call of the wild', spent his early years playing with Aboriginal children at Warralong Station, speaking their language, he said, more than he spoke English. 'It was all I could virtually speak', he said.[64] Social distance was established when he was sent to school in Perth. Asked what language he had spoken with his playmates as a child, Bidge Welsh replied, 'Oh I don't know, the Warralong group, I don't know what they were. Nyamal or something. But I've forgotten most of it now'.[65]

Nevertheless, within structures of power inequality and established rules of social interaction that existed in pastoral regions, there was room for genuine and long-lasting friendships, especially among people who had grown up together. Peter Coppin said that he and Bidge Welsh remained friends into

---

62 Maggie Ginger (Nyirrarlpi), recorded by Anne Scrimgeour, 13 May 1993, author's collection. *Bungarra* is a commonly used Western Australian term for a goanna.
63 Someone of the same age that one grew up with.
64 Frank (Bidge) Welsh, interviewed by Anne Bloemen, 1995, SLWA OH2689/42.
65 Welsh, interviewed by Bloemen, SLWA OH2689/42.

adulthood, and Peter Miller was well-liked by *marrngu* because he did not forget his childhood friendships.[66] 'He's a whitefella, my friend', Cranky said in 1993. 'We're the same age. I see him there in Hedland all the time, getting old-fella like me'.[67] Memoirs and biographies of men and women who grew up in pastoralist families, such as Judith Drake-Brockman and Mary and Elizabeth Durack, provide further examples of affectionate relationships that developed within the master–servant relationship on stations.[68] Reg and Benja Sherlock's daughter, Ann, who lived on Strelley and Abydos Stations as a child in the 1940s, has maintained a warm and ongoing friendship with *marrngu* families.[69]

Despite being treated like children in need of paternalistic care, *marrngu* appreciated pastoralist benevolence. Social distance was resented, but acts of kindness were appreciated and remembered, despite an underpinning sentiment of condescension. Although Edith Miller treated Aboriginal men and women like children, she was remembered with respect. Decades after the strike, a *walypila* who referred to Edith Miller in mildly disparaging terms received a gentle rebuke from Sambo Bina (Yawarta-bloke), who said that Mrs Miller had been good to them. He remembered her sitting on the verandah at Warrawagine with her sewing machine. 'Mrs Miller always saw that we had proper trousers, and if we didn't, we would line up at her sewing machine on the verandah and she would fix them up for us'.[70] Miller had an affectionate, if maternalistic, friendship with Bidgie, the woman she 'took out of the river', which continued well after Miller left the Pilbara.[71] Nevertheless, relationships of friendship and intimacy were, as Deborah Bird Rose writes, 'always framed by the structure and practice of power'.[72]

---

66   Katrin Wilson, 'The Allocation of Sex Roles in Social and Economic Affairs in a "New Style" Australian Aboriginal Community, Pindan, Western Australia', Master of Science Thesis, University of Western Australia, 1961, p. 172.

67   Cranky (Kujupurra), pers. comm., Mijijimaya, 1993.

68   Judith Drake-Brockman, *Wongi Wongi,* Hesperian Press, Victoria Park, 2001; Brenda Niall, *True North: The Story of Mary and Elizabeth Durack,* Text Publishing Company, Melbourne, 2013.

69   Ann Cornish, email to author, 28 June 2014.

70   John Bucknall, 'Commentary to Extracts Taken from Letters Authored by Reg and Benja Sherlock', unpublished paper, 2010, p. 20.

71   Edith Miller, interviewed by Jamieson, 1982, transcript, pp. 71–72, SLWA OH506.

72   Deborah Bird Rose, *Hidden Histories: Black Stories from Victoria River Downs, Humbert River and Wave Hill Stations,* Aboriginal Studies Press, Canberra, 1991, p. 210.

This was the material that made up labour relations in pastoral areas. Denigration and social distance, together with coercion and intimidation exerted principally through the agency of the police, formed the weft of the fabric of labour relations, woven together with protection, benevolence, loyalty and attachment. Labour relations were underpinned by personal bonds of duty and entitlement that resembled the roles, responsibilities and obligations of Aboriginal kinship structures. Yet *marrngu* chafed at the inequality of the arrangement. When they went on strike in May 1946, they did not seek to fracture the relationship, but to engage with the pastoral industry on more equitable terms. They felt that their labour was not adequately recognised or rewarded. Rations provided by stations as a central component of the relationship varied from station to station, but many *marrngu* complained of the paucity and poor quality of the rations provided. 'We only get little bit of bread, and meat, stink, you know, and old tea', Caroline Jula said. 'Everyone bin get'm, for dinner. In the hand, no plate, nothing'.[73] 'Prison clothes, prison tucker. We can only buy'm everything prison', Molly Williams said. The way portions were carefully measured out appeared overly-parsimonious to *marrngu*. 'And we only get a ration, sugar, in a small bag, but not big one, only little one. Tea, tobacco, soap. That's the lot, that's our ration'.[74]

Cranky described mealtimes at Warrawagine:

> We used to go up [to the kitchen] with quart-pots, billy cans and fruit tins in our hands to get our tea.
>
> We'd go up and the cook gave us tea in a bucket. It wasn't nice tea, it was just tea without sugar; if we wanted sugar in it, we had to buy our own. When they rang the bell for us, we would take our pannikins and billy cans, and the old people would go as well. Some people had quart-pots and others that didn't had to use fruit tins.[75]

While non-Aboriginal workers were given their food on plates and ate at tables, *marrngu* received bread and meat in the hand and ate it outside 'on the woodheap'. This mealtime segregation was a frequently mentioned grievance. 'We'd take the food to the woodheap and eat there', Cranky said. 'In winter we would light a fire there, and eat beside the fire. We used to divide it up and take half of the bread and half of the meat and give it to our parents'.

---

73 Jula, recorded by Anne Scrimgeour, 13 August 1991, author's collection.
74 Molly Williams (Kulyu), recorded 13 August 1991, author's collection.
75 Cranky (Kujupurra), recorded by Anne Scrimgeour, June 1993, AIATSIS collection, soundfile 'Kujupurra 3'.

Rations included provisions distributed on Sundays. 'No wages', Caroline Jula said. 'Only soap and tobacco and needle and cotton, that's all, and one bar soap, that's all, one bar of soap, no any more'. At Warrawagine, women were provided with one dress per year, and had to use old flour bags to make other clothing when this wore out. 'And you keep'm this dress and all this right up to Christmas', Caroline said. 'We keep'm that dress. You know that bag, white bag from bag flour? We mend'm [i.e. sew] that one, you know, we cut'm up half, make'm dress'.[76]

The lack of adequate shelter was another complaint.[77] 'No good we camping in the rubbish heap, we're camping in the river', Snowy Jittermarra (Maruntu) said:

> When the rain come we got to run back to shearing shed, we got to camp amongst the sheep when it's shearing time, you know? Some camp in the saddle room, some camp in the shearing shed, some old people they still in the river, putting some sort of iron or canvas, just enough to keep him bit dry but still they get wet through.[78]

They knew their labour was important to the pastoral industry and felt entitled in return to adequate food and clothing, reasonable accommodation and some level of monetary reward. ''Cause whitefellas are giving us pretty low', Billy Thomas (Pitpit) said. 'We're doing more work than whitefellas. He's sitting down there and writing that *he's* doing that, but we're doing that, not him. We don't get paid for that. We live on rough tucker and never treat us proper way'.[79]

Marrngu also resented the coercive nature of the relationship and the use of the police to restrict their freedom of movement. They resented being turned out of the station when their labour was not required, and being harassed by the police to return when they were needed again, even while ceremonies were still underway. They resented their powerlessness and the humiliation they suffered at the hands of pastoralists and the police. They could do nothing but obey when pastoralists walked down to the station camp when they were singing at night and told them to 'shut up and go to sleep'.

---

76   Jula, recorded by Anne Scrimgeour, 13 August 1991, author's collection.
77   Monty Hale, *Kurlumarniny: We Come from the Desert*, Aboriginal Studies Press, Canberra, 2012, p. 23.
78   Snowy Jittermarra (Maruntu), recorded by Anne Scrimgeour, 5 August 1993, author's collection.
79   Thomas, Billy (Pitpit), recorded by Anne Scrimgeour, 6 October 1993, author's collection.

Billy Thomas remembered one occasion in Nullagine in particular, when a big group were singing:

> The policeman come along, 'what you fellas' making all this noise? Can't you go to bed? Too much noise, I can't even sleep'. Well people can't help, can't put up for it, they just got to go away. They were frightened of the policeman, because they might go to jail. They were the boss for us. Always, you know, frightened of them. Treat us like animal.[80]

Marrngu had no option but to bend to these indignities. Despite chafing under the humiliation of such encounters and the inequality of their labour relationship with pastoralists, fear of police violence and incarceration prevented them from taking action to improve their situation. Discussing reasons for the strike, Billy Thomas said:

> We got to give the people some right, [and] they'll be ready for everything. That's what we're doing, because squatter always growl, growl, growl all the time. These days you can't see people do that [i.e. it was different back then], because we were really frightened, we might get a hiding or go in jail or something like that.[81]

To fail to be adequately subservient was to be regarded as a 'cheeky nigger', inviting physical punishment or arrest. Denied education, *marrngu* had no access to knowledge of their legal rights, and their treatment at the hands of the police gave them no reason to believe that settler power over their lives was not absolute. They could only respond with the sort of strategies that James C. Scott calls 'the weapons of the weak' – stealing vegetables from station gardens, for example, or 'going bush' for a while when their labour was required. Pastoralist complaints about the inefficiency of Aboriginal labour and the need for constant supervision may also have been a result of *marrngu* dissatisfaction with the inadequate reward they received for their labour.

Nevertheless, *marrngu* were anxious to find a way to address their grievances and set their relationship with pastoralists on a more just and equal footing. 'We'd already done enough of that for them', Billy Thomas said. 'For a long time we'd been letting them treat us how they liked'.[82] Snowy Jittermarra

---

80 Billy Thomas (Pitpit), in Williams and Noakes, *How the West Was Lost*.
81 Thomas (Pitpit), recorded 6 October 1993, author's collection.
82 Thomas (Pitpit), recorded by Anne Scrimgeour, 21 September 1992, AIATSIS collection, soundfile 'Pitpit Talking to Kids'.

claimed that people had been unhappy with their situation for a long time, and that people of his father's generation sought means to improve it. 'All the old people bin make up their mind, "How we going to help ourself?"'[83]

As it turned out, events that took place during the Second World War were to offer a way forward.

---

83 Jittermarra (Maruntu), recorded by Anne Scrimgeour, 5 August 1993, author's collection.

Chapter 4

'Here We Were Real Australians and They Discriminated Against Us'

The Significance of the War

The strike took place within a year of the end of the Second World War. Historians have argued that changes brought about by the war played a catalytic role in the development of Aboriginal activism, by creating an awareness that social and economic oppression was not inevitable and that alternatives were indeed possible. It has been claimed that greater employment opportunities at better rates of pay, both within the Army and in jobs vacated by white workers, gave Aboriginal people a taste of award wages and decent working conditions and led to their rejection of oppressive pre-war labour conditions. The war also, it is argued, brought them into contact with soldiers and other military personnel from areas outside the northern pastoral regions who were not imbued with the northern culture of racial denigration and segregation. Such contacts, it is claimed, opened Aboriginal eyes to new ideas of racial equality, providing the spark that, in the Pilbara, led Aboriginal people to take action to change the circumstances of their lives. Lloyd Davies, for example, makes a direct link between wartime conditions and the strike:

> The war years 1939 to 1945 produced many changes. There was an acute shortage of labor everywhere which gave the Aborigines (and particularly the mixed race workers) a greater bargaining power. After the Japanese attack tens of thousands of soldiers were sent to remote parts of the country and made contact with and befriended the local Aborigines. The soldiers in particular spread ... subversive ideas ... These factors brought to combustion point the anger which had been smouldering in Aboriginal communities for many years and created conditions to

enable them to achieve the demands which they had been making over
years for better wages and living and working conditions.[1]

Similarly, Deborah Wilson claims that, 'for a short and exciting time', the war transformed 'some Aboriginal people into high-value workers, with parity, maybe equality' with white workers.[2] The Pilbara strike arose, she argues, from 'the impact of war', when 'fair army wages and conditions became catalysts bolstering Aboriginal workers to make a bold and defiant stand'.[3]

However, a closer examination of conditions for Aboriginal workers in the Pilbara during the war exposes flaws in this argument. Aboriginal pastoral workers in the Pilbara did not experience labour situations on a par with white workers during the war. The continued production of wool was vital to the war effort, and the exodus of white workers from the pastoral industry placed additional pressure on Aboriginal workers, hardening existing mechanisms for ensuring that their labour was available to the pastoral industry. Despite the deployment of large numbers of soldiers to Port Hedland from 1942, and the construction of a secret airbase at Corunna Downs Station which brought a further influx of servicemen into the region, little interaction was permitted between local Aboriginal people and military personnel. Aboriginal people were not employed in the construction of the airbase or in its operation. Only a few 'light-skinned' Aboriginal people from the region were recruited into the services.[4] I have found no evidence that any Aboriginal person involved in the strike was employed by the Army, or that they were able to obtain alternative labour at higher rates of pay, or that pay rates increased as a result of wartime labour shortages.

Also questionable is the argument that the Aboriginal demands for change were inspired by contact with servicemen bringing new ideas and new ways of relating to Aboriginal people. Since very few *marrngu* were employed by the Army or the air force, they had little opportunity for interaction. Measures were put in place to prevent servicemen mixing with Aboriginal people, arising largely from an obsessive anxiety to prevent sexual interactions between servicemen and Aboriginal women. Moreover, there is no reason to suppose that servicemen were less racist than other groups of people that *marrngu*

---

1   Lloyd Davies, 'Protecting Natives? The Law and the 1946 Aboriginal Pastoral Worker's Strike', *Papers in Labour History*, vol. 1, 1988, p. 33.
2   Deborah Wilson, *Different White People: Radical Activism for Aboriginal Rights 1946–1972*, University of Western Australia Publishing, Crawley, 2015, p. 40.
3   Deborah Wilson, *Different White People*, p. 42.
4   Rose Nowers, interviewed by Jenny Hardie, undated, SLWA OH2701/5.

met. While pastoralists adopted a rigid code of behaviour in their dealing with Aboriginal people, *marrngu* also had contact with *walypila* who were not part of the pastoral community, such as miners. Miners did not mix socially with pastoralists, and while many were no doubt racist in their dealings with *marrngu*, others were not.[5] John Wilson writes, for example, that 'with the European miners came new ideas'.[6] Ginger Bob (Palyakulayi) tells of meeting some miners at the Lalla Rookh gold mine prior to the strike, when he was a young man travelling with his classificatory brother, Clancy McKenna (Warntupungkarna), a Nyamal man who would later take a leading role in the strike. 'We saw their camp, where the *walypila* were staying', Ginger said:

> Those *walypila* were generous, they would give you things, and weren't mean. Those *walypila* from that time were good ... Indeed, two *walypila* called out to us, 'Come on over; g'day, g'day'. We stopped and had a talk with them. They gave Clancy some money, because some of the *walypila* knew him, that brother of mine. They gave us good food, and we all sat together, not separately. They looked after us well there, and when they gave us food we all ate together; we sat facing each other; those *walypila* were generous. After we'd had dinner with them that evening, he thanked them. I had no idea what to do, but he knew *walypila*. I was awkward, and didn't say anything.[7]

Such accounts suggest that ideas and attitudes introduced by servicemen during the war may not have been as novel as some writers have suggested, nor as influential in creating the imperative for change.

In arguing this, I am not suggesting that wartime changes were unimportant in creating the conditions that led to the strike. The crucial change, however, was not the creation of temporary conditions of equal pay and equal status for Aboriginal people, but the imposition of discriminatory wartime restriction. It was the erection of additional barriers on the grounds of race that was important in creating, if indirectly, an impetus for the strike, rather than any temporary dismantling of such barriers.

At the same time as this hardening in the treatment of Aboriginal people was taking place, there was an opposing shift in thinking in the broader Australian population towards more liberal ideas of human rights and equality.

---

5   Welsh, interviewed by Bloemen, SLWA OH2689/42.
6   John Wilson, 'Authority and Leadership', p. 26.
7   Ginger Bob (Palyakulayi), recorded by Anne Scrimgeour, 12 December 1993, AIATSIS collection, soundfile 'Palyakulayi 18'.

These opposing shifts – the increased imposition of racially based restrictions on the one hand, and the emergence of ideas of human equality and human rights on the other – were important in creating preconditions for the events of 1946 and beyond, not because of their direct impact on the Aboriginal people who conducted the strike, but because of their impact on the non-Aboriginal organiser, Don McLeod.

Donald William McLeod was born in 1908 in Western Australia's Mid West regional town of Meekatharra, where his father, William Henry McLeod, owned the Queen of the Hill Gold Mine. When Don was two years old, his father sold the gold mine and shifted his family to the coastal Mid West town of Geraldton, where he invested in a row of shops and bought a cottage for his large family.[8] When Don was four, his mother died following the birth of her ninth child. A week later, young Donald sparked a large-scale search when he wandered away from a Methodist picnic and became lost. The two events were so closely linked in his memory that he later believed that they had happened on the same day. 'Why I don't know, but [my mother] chose to die on the day of our Sunday school picnic', he wrote.[9] It is an indication of his toughness that when he was found miles away from the picnic ground after being lost for thirty hours, the four-year-old was quite nonplussed, unaware that he was lost, and stated that he was walking back to the picnic to get dinner and a drink.[10] McLeod remembered the Methodist minister loudly preaching, 'Come rejoice with me for that which was lost is found'.[11]

Following his mother's death, young Donald and his brothers were sent to board at the Presentation Convent at Greenough, twenty-five kilometres to the south of Geraldton. Don hated his time there. 'They tried to belt Roman Catholicism up my backside with a strap', he said.[12] 'And the only thing they taught me was to be a rebel. And never to submit to intolerant authority'.[13] He was there for six years, until he turned ten, when he moved back to Geraldton to attend the local public school in the care of an aunt.[14] He left school early,

---

8   Zoe Smithson, 'Some McLeods, Mainly Donald', SLWA PR14514/MCL/1.
9   McLeod, draft autobiography, chapter 1, p. 2, Marchant Trust Collection, UWA MS118 series 1 file 13.
10 *Geraldton Guardian*, 14 September 1912, p. 3.
11 Quoted in McLeod, draft autobiography, chapter 1, p. 2, Marchant Trust Collection, UWA MS118 series 1 file 13.
12 McLeod, interviewed by David Carlton, 24 December 1996, transcript, p. 2, SLWA OH2739.
13 McLeod, draft autobiography, chapter 1, p. 2, Marchant Trust Collection, UWA MS118 series 1 file 13.
14 Donald McLeod, interviewed by Chris Jeffery, 1977, SLWA OH331.

and spent his early adult years engaging in manual work in various parts of the state, including agricultural labour, roadwork, kangaroo shooting, wheat bag lumping and mining, sometimes on his own and sometimes with his father.[15] Following his father's death from a stroke in the bush in 1932 while prospecting for gold in the southern Pilbara, McLeod established the Silversheen white asbestos mine at Meilga Station in the Ashburton district, 500 kilometres south of Port Hedland.

In later years, McLeod consistently identified the beginning of his interest in Aboriginal issues with a chance discussion he had at the Silversheen mine with Alec Fenton, a director of the British Belting and Asbestos Company, who visited Australia in 1936 to source white asbestos. Fenton wondered why better use was not being made of Aboriginal labour, particularly in mining. 'They are very intelligent people', he said to McLeod. 'It surprises me that you don't make better use of them'.[16] He told McLeod that he had met an Aboriginal man on Roy Hill Station, an intelligent patriarch who reminded him very much of his own grandfather, although better looking. He believed that Aboriginal people were much more able than they were given credit for, and deserved better treatment.[17]

McLeod held mainstream views at the time regarding Aboriginal capabilities, and he brushed off Fenton's remarks. 'I said, well, blackfellers like living in the open and the squatters fed them, and they'd be a charge on the state if they didn't feed them – just the normal thing that people had to say about blackfellers, because I knew no better'.[18] Nevertheless, Fenton's remarks planted a seed in McLeod's mind that would serve as a catalyst in shifting his thinking from the widely accepted racist understandings of Aboriginal difference, to consider social, political and economic causes of Aboriginal disadvantage.[19] McLeod would continue to correspond with Fenton for many years.[20]

After forfeiting the Silversheen mine in 1939, McLeod began working further north, in the Nullagine area.[21] The seed planted by Fenton's comments began to grow when he was well sinking on Roy Hill Station, probably in

---

15 E. C. Lutze, 'Donald McLeod Before Skull Springs: The Origins of His Radicalism', BA (Honours) Thesis, University of Western Australia, 1984, p. 33.
16 McLeod, interviewed by Carlton, 1996, transcript, p. 3, SLWA OH2739.
17 McLeod, interviewed by Jeffery.
18 McLeod, interviewed by Jeffery.
19 Lutze, 'Donald McLeod Before Skull Springs', p. 2.
20 For example, McLeod to Fenton, 16 October 1959, SLWA 1568A/9/92–4.
21 *South Western Advertiser*, 22 September 1939, p. 6.

1942, with the help of an Aboriginal man named Kitchener. A Nyiyaparli speaker a few years McLeod's senior, Kitchener had begun working on Ethel Creek Station as a child, becoming known as an exceptionally good station hand,[22] having outstanding skills as a stockman, blacksmith, saddle-maker and mechanic.[23] He began working on Roy Hill Station in 1941.[24] Despite his abilities, which impressed McLeod, he was unpaid. McLeod came to know him as a friend. Although not involved in the strike itself, Kitchener was to play an important part in instigating the strike movement and also in raising McLeod's awareness of the humanity of Aboriginal people and the conditions under which they lived on stations.

At Roy Hill, McLeod also came to know an Aboriginal man of mixed descent, Edgar Lockyer. Both McLeod and Lockyer were dismissed from Roy Hill after disputes with the manager, leaving without receiving pay that was due to them. According to McLeod, Lockyer's equipment and semi-trailer were retained by the station, allegedly to cover his debts. Angry and frustrated at the power wielded by pastoralists and by his and Lockyer's inability to obtain fair recompense for their labour, McLeod shifted further north and took a job laying pipes at the Comet Gold Mine, near the small town of Marble Bar which served as a service centre for pastoralists and miners in the region.[25]

McLeod's increasing awareness of Aboriginal people and the conditions under which they lived, gained through his experiences in the North, found expression in a rising current of thought taking place in Australia throughout the 1940s. New understandings of the nature of Aboriginality, from prevailing assumptions of inherent biological inferiority to understandings of the social and cultural basis of human difference, were taking hold. The war strengthened this shift, propelled in part by Aboriginal war service and increased contact between Aboriginal and non-Aboriginal Australians. Ideological opposition to fascism saw a groundswell of interest in liberal ideas, which further strengthened a liberalisation of attitudes towards Aboriginal people. The Anti-Fascist League (AFL), founded by Edward (Bill) Beeby in 1940, at a time when the Australian Communist Party (ACP) was banned, was attracting widespread

---

22 McMahon to Bray, 14 October 1943, SROWA 1943/0685/25.
23 McLeod, draft autobiography, chapter 1, p. 13, Marchant Trust Collection, UWA MS118 series 1 file 13.
24 McMahon to Bray, 14 October 1943, SROWA 1943/0685/25.
25 McLeod, draft autobiography, chapter 2, p. 5, Marchant Trust Collection, UWA MS118 series 1 file 8.

interest throughout Western Australia.[26] League activities were conducted through weekly radio broadcasts on human rights and civil liberties issues presented by Beeby and other socialists. These broadcasts served as a focus for discussion in branches established throughout Western Australia during the war years.[27] ACP member Joan Williams said that people flocked to the Anti-Fascist League in the early years of the war. In 1943, there were 2700 members involved in seventy-two branches, which held weekly meetings across the state.[28] A League member 'well remember[ed] the organised listeners' groups that gathered around wirelesses each Sunday evening to hear Bill Beeby speak' and 'marvelled at his knowledge and words of wisdom'.[29] Aboriginal issues were included in these broadcasts and discussions, with talks given by anthropologist Fred Rose, for example.[30] While working at the Comet Gold Mine near Marble Bar, McLeod became involved in the Marble Bar branch of the League, taking on the role of secretary, and also joined a discussion group at the Comet mine. He said that the Marble Bar branch had resolved 'by every means' to 'endeavour to assist the coloured people in their attempt to gain equality both social and economic and political'.[31]

While McLeod was thinking about and discussing ideas of Aboriginal social, economic and politic equality in Marble Bar, 200 kilometres away the issue was being confronted in a practical way. In Port Hedland, a community of people of mixed European and Aboriginal descent had achieved a degree of equality in the town. Some, including the prominent Clarke and Dann families, had come to Port Hedland from the Beagle Bay Mission in the Kimberley. Proud of their mixed heritage, they referred to themselves as Coloured or Euralian. In 1934, Lawrence (Pop) Clarke established the Euralian Association to provide social activities and to give the community a voice in

---

26 Bobbie Oliver and W. S. Latter, 'Spooks, Spies and Subversives! The Wartime Security Service', in Jenny Gregory (ed), *On the Homefront: Western Australia and World War II*, University of Western Australia Press, Nedlands, 1996, pp. 180–181. Beeby and his wife Ida established the Patch Theatre in Perth in 1938.
27 The Manifesto, Plan and Constitution of The Anti-Fascist League of Western Australia, SLWA PR14951/1. Socialists involved in this movement, who presented broadcasts, included John Solosy and Harry Leighton. Justina Williams, *Anger and Love*, Fremantle Arts Centre Press, South Fremantle, 1993, p. 94.
28 *Bruce Rock Post and Corrigin and Narembeen Guardian*, 5 August 1943.
29 Roma Gilchrist, 'The Story of the Modern Women's Club 1938–1958', SLWA 3255A/17.
30 Peter Monteath and Valerie Munt, *Red Professor: The Cold War life of Fred Rose*, Wakefield Press, Mile End, 2015, p. 76. Rose was in Perth between April 1942 and June 1943.
31 McLeod to Bray, 27 June 1943, pp. 5–6, SROWA 1943/0685/8–9.

their struggle for decent housing, education, employment and equal status with the non-Aboriginal community. His daughter Helena, who started the Coolbaroo Club in Perth as a similar organisation, remembered her father 'going around talking his head off about improving our lot'. She described the Euralian Association as having 'no outside influence, no church creating – just us folks, the coloured people themselves'.[32]

Many in the Euralian community were active Catholics with a close relationship with the local priest, Father Edward Bryan. 'We practically ran the church for him in those days', Pop Clarke's daughter, Rose Nowers, said, 'because we were the greater majority of Catholics ... we being the coloured'.[33] In 1941, coloured children made up the majority of students at the local public school, and Minister for the North West Bob Coverley received complaints from the parents of non-Aboriginal children and requests for segregation within the school and the provision of separate toilets.[34] Although Coverley found the Euralian children to be tidy and clean, he nevertheless recommended the provision of segregated toilets. Before these could be constructed, however, white residents of the town were evacuated under threat of a Japanese invasion, the school was closed and in 1942 a school for coloured children was opened in the town by Presentation Convent nuns.[35]

Despite the push for segregation in the state school in 1941, the community had achieved a degree of acceptance within Port Hedland. Some had Australian Workers' Union (AWU) membership and were employed on the wharf and on the railway line that joined Port Hedland to the inland town of Marble Bar. While most lived apart from the non-Aboriginal population in an area known as the One Mile, Pop Clarke had purchased a house in town for his family and, with house prices falling during the war, others followed suit, much to the consternation of the Department of Native Affairs. Although the Department found no legal impediment to 'halfcastes' purchasing land in town, John Bisley, officer in charge of the Native Hospital and the Department's representative in the town, strongly advised the Port Hedland Road Board, the body holding local government authority, against allowing this breaking down of racialised spatial boundaries. 'The Road Board secretary had been warned for years past', Bisley wrote, 'what the result will be if they allow them to settle in the town proper'. The secretary of the Port Hedland Road

---

32   Quoted in Steven Kinnane, *Shadow Lines*, Fremantle Arts Centre Press, Fremantle, 2003, p. 336.
33   Nowers, interviewed by Hardie, SLWA OH2701/5.
34   Various documents, SROWA 1941/0763.
35   Various documents, SROWA 1941/0763.

Board replied that 'the position today is that a half caste can be chairman of the Roads Board'.³⁶ This may have overstated the situation, but does give an indication of the level of acceptance that Euralians had won. 'I told him that it would be useless to try and shoulder the blame on to the Department after the war', Bisley grumbled.³⁷ His opposition to the breaking down of racial segregation in the town is interesting in the light of the radical changes that were to take place in departmental policy over the coming decade: by 1951, the tables would be reversed, as the Department sought to implement policies of assimilation.

In early 1942, non-Aboriginal civilians were evacuated from Port Hedland under the threat of invasion by the Japanese. At a meeting in Port Hedland in early February, Len Taplin, the leader of the local battalion of the Volunteer Defence Corp (VDC), called on the Euralian community to assist in the war effort, arguing that their cooperation would go a long way towards breaking down racial prejudice in the town.³⁸ The community needed no urging – 'We were very patriotic', Pop Clarke's daughter, Rose Nowers, said.³⁹ The enlistment of non-Aboriginal men into the armed forces, together with the evacuation of non-Aboriginal residents from the town following the bombing of Broome in March, led to labour shortages that the Euralian community were more than willing to alleviate. They undertook essential work, including unloading munitions and supplies at the wharf. McLeod would later speak of the contribution the Euralians made to the war effort in Port Hedland. 'Called on by the leaders of the VDC to assist the war effort', he told a meeting in Perth in 1946, 'the half-castes responded wholeheartedly. One in particular spent 5 days and nights taking munitions down the coast'.⁴⁰ On 30 July, Port Hedland was also bombed.

The war brought increased opportunities for employment and housing for the Euralian community, but fears that Aboriginal people in the north could pose a security threat led to the imposition of new racially based restrictions. Military personnel were deployed to carry out surveillance operations designed to detect subversive activities in northern Aboriginal communities. Early in 1942, the Department's newly-appointed northern inspector, Laurence (Laurie) O'Neill, was recruited as a lieutenant in 101 North Australia Field Security

---

36 Bisley to Bray, 30 November 1942, SROWA 1942/0919/34.
37 Bisley to Bray, 30 November 1942, SROWA 1942/0919/34.
38 McLeod, draft autobiography, chapter 2, p. 4, Marchant Trust Collection, UWA MS118 series 1 file 8.
39 Nowers, interviewed by Hardie, SLWA OH2701/5.
40 *Workers' Star*, 21 June 1946, p. 2, 'Fremantle Backing for Native Rights Struggle'.

for precisely this reason.[41] A decade's experience in 'handling the natives' as a Kimberley policeman made him, Francis Bray wrote, ideally suited 'for investigation on native matters as affecting the defense of the state'.[42] Cecil Kelly, who served with O'Neill in 101 Security Section, recalled: 'The bloody blacks that's what we watched mostly, keep an eye on the blacks, because if anything had have happened, well the blacks would have more or less been the first to join the Japs … There was plenty of 5th column, right through the north'.[43] In Port Hedland, John Bisley noted similar suspicions. 'The military authorities are not keen on the coloured people being on the coast in any number these times', he wrote. 'There is no secret about it the majority openly state that if the Japs come they would get a better deal than they have had in the past (the Jap diver has certainly done his propaganda job well with the half-castes)'.[44]

Certainly, the possibility that their situation could be improved if the Australian forces were defeated by the Japanese was an idea not lost on many Aboriginal people throughout the north. 'To tell you the truth, we often all talked amongst ourselves about the Japanese', Marble Bar resident Jack McPhee (Wanamurraganya) admitted:

> Over the years there'd been good relationships between the Aboriginal people and the Afghans and Chinese, so we wondered if the Japanese would be as easy to get on with. Some of the tribal people thought that everyone from that part of the world was the same, so they thought the Japanese would be as good to them as what the Chinese had been. Either way, they figured the Japanese wouldn't be as bad as the Aussies.[45]

For the Clarkes, however, the idea that they were anything other than patriotic Australians was unthinkable. They put their shoulders to the wheel in support of the war effort, and bitterly resented the discrimination they suffered when their young men stepped forward to enlist for military service. Although the Lockyer brothers were accepted, the Clarkes were rejected, apparently

---

41   Major Gibson to Bray, telegram, 19 March 1942, SROWA 1941/1107/66.
42   Bray to Under Secretary for the North-West, 27 March 1942, SROWA 1941/1107/72.
43   Quoted in Peter J. Bridge, *Fighting the Kimberley: The Three Australian Corps Kimberley Guerilla Warfare Group 1942–1943*, Hesperian Press, Carlisle, 2011, p. 309.
44   Bisley to Bray, 30 June 1942, p. 2, SROWA 1942/0919/6.
45   Quoted in Sally Morgan, *Wanamurraganya: The Story of Jack McPhee*, Fremantle Arts Centre Press, Fremantle, 1989, p. 146.

because of their darker skin colour.[46] 'Here we were real Australians', Rose Nowers said, 'and they discriminated against, left us with a very bitter feeling for many years'.[47] The war brought into sharp relief the reality that, in spite of the level of social and economic inclusion achieved and a strong identity as 'real Australians', Euralians continued to be regarded as outsiders requiring increased control and surveillance as wartime security measures.

While the authorities worried about the threat of Aboriginal people forming a fifth column in the event of an invasion, a more immediate concern was the likelihood of sexual misconduct in towns like Port Hedland, where large numbers of young soldiers were deployed in June 1942. Army authorities urged the Department of Native Affairs to shift all 'half-castes' away from Port Hedland to Coballana Pool, some forty-five kilometres inland, to prevent sexual contact between soldiers and Aboriginal women.[48] The Department lacked the resources to comply with such a request, however, and the Army instead issued orders to the troops prohibiting interaction with Aboriginal women, while Bisley and the local police constable, Charles Chipperfield, did what they could to prevent fraternisation. Bisley felt sure they were 'going to have some trouble with the women and the soldiers', as 'the female half castes both married and single' had gone 'soldier mad'.[49] In an effort to keep one young couple of lovers apart, he arranged to have the soldier stationed out of town, but reported in October that the soldier had returned to town and that his girlfriend had confessed to Bisley's wife that she could not keep away from him.

On receipt of this report, the Commissioner for Native Affairs, Francis Bray, decided that the time had come to take firm action. Concerned that continued intercourse between the soldiers and Aboriginal women would lead Army authorities to order the evacuation of all Aboriginal people from the town, he proclaimed Port Hedland a prohibited area, making it illegal for any Aboriginal person to be within a three-mile radius of the post office unless holding a 'native pass'. Such passes were to be issued only to people who did not associate with soldiers and who were considered to be of good conduct.[50] Anyone not qualifying for a pass was to be ordered out of town

---

46   A memorial to the five Lockyer brothers has been erected at Whim Creek. See https://monumentaustralia.org.au/themes/people/military/display/61239-lockyer-brothers-memorial.
47   Nowers, interviewed by Hardie, SLWA OH2701/5.
48   Gibson to Bray, telegram, 15 June 1942, SROWA 1942/0919/9.
49   Bray to Gibson, 17 June 1942, SROWA 1942/0919/12; Bisley to Bray, 30 June 1942, SROWA 1942/0919/5–7.
50   Bray to Bisley, 2 October 1942, SROWA 1942/0919/20; Bray to Coverley, 12 October 1942, SROWA 1942/0919/23; Bray to Bisley, 4 November 1942, SROWA

to find employment on stations, where labour was in short supply. Bray instructed Bisley to work with the police to rigidly enforce the prohibited area proclamation.[51]

Perhaps taking their cue from Bray's call for rigid enforcement, Bisley and Police Constable Chipperfield's announcement of the Prohibited Area proclamation to the Euralian community in November 1942, and the issuing of 'native passes', was carried out in a tactless and officious manner.[52] For people like the Clarkes, doing their bit for the war effort on the Port Hedland wharf and already smarting at being debarred from enlistment because of the colour of their skin, the issue of 'native passes' added insult to injury. 'All these men worked on the wharf all this time', Rose Nowers said, 'and all of a sudden they had to have special passes and yellow tickets'.[53] At a meeting of the Euralian Association, it was decided that no-one should accept a pass. Bisley reported that there was 'a considerable amount of trouble from the "Euralian Society" and the Clarke family' over the proclamation of the prohibited zone and the issuing of the pass cards.[54] Pop Clarke and his sons made a fire on the town jetty and burned their passes in a public display of defiance.[55] Rose Nowers remembered sitting on the verandah of their home when Constable Chipperfield arrived looking for her father and brothers, Vince and Jerry, to charge them with burning their passes, 'and we ended up having a most beautiful row', she said. 'He told me that what they were going to do was eventually shift us all out to 4 Mile and that's where we would have to live for the duration of the war'. Rose replied that if they wanted to do that sort of thing they would have to physically carry them out.[56]

The threat of evacuation to the Four Mile Well was effective in achieving reluctant acquiescence to the system, however, and Bisley and Chipperfield wisely refrained from ensuring that people carried the passes. Bisley wrote in December that things were 'now working smoothly and everyone concerned now realizes the benefit they are gaining through Port Hedland being declared a Prohibited Area'.[57] McLeod wrote a few months later that the purpose of this measure was understood and 'less resistance is held against it but it is

---

1942/0919/33.
51 Bray to Bisley, 4 November 1942, SROWA 1942/0919/33.
52 McLeod to Bray, 27 June 1943, SROWA 1943/0685/4–9.
53 Nowers, interviewed by Hardie, SLWA OH2701/5.
54 Bisley to Bray, 22 December 1942, p. 1, SROWA 1942/0919/36.
55 Nowers, interviewed by Hardie, SLWA OH2701/5.
56 Nowers, interviewed by Hardie, SLWA OH2701/5.
57 Bisley to Bray, 22 December 1942, p. 2, SROWA 1942/0919/37.

considered unnecessary and discriminatory'.[58] According to Rose Nowers, the regulation 'caused a lot of bad feeling, a lot of ill feeling'.[59]

The pass system, however, did not put an end to Army concerns that invading Japanese forces could find willing allies in an oppressed Aboriginal population with invaluable knowledge of the country. While pressure to evacuate all Aboriginal people from Port Hedland in June 1942 had been resisted as impracticable by the Department, renewed calls for evacuation were made in early 1943, this time for the removal of 'nomadic, unemployed, aged and infirm natives from the North-West coastal areas from Carnarvon to Derby and a distance inland of approx. 100 miles'.[60] Pressure for the evacuation came principally from the North-West Battalion of the VDC, which had promised greater acceptance of the Euralian community, and which included 'the greater majority of the [non-Aboriginal] population of the North-West'. The influence of pastoralists in this proposal is indicated by calls made unanimously at a meeting of VDC members that:

> (i) All aged, infirm and nomad natives, including unemployed, be moved <u>at once</u> back from the coast to points at least 100 to 150 miles
>
> (ii) All working natives, that is, Station natives, be registered on the Station at which they are employed and not be allowed to move from this Station without a permit from the Station owner or manager.[61]

Bray again insisted that evacuation was logistically impossible and could achieve no good purpose. Nevertheless, the Army presented the Department with a written proposal for the establishment of six internment camps for non-working Aboriginal people, with the 'control, rationing and discipline of natives in camps' to be carried out by the Department.[62] That the proposal was designed to protect valuable labour resources for the pastoral industry is indicated by Brigadier Hoad's argument that:

> if inland feeding centres are established now, natives who are in employment at the present time could be sent there in the case of enemy invasion, and their chance of being available after the war for

---

58   McLeod to Bray, 27 June 1943, p. 2, SROWA 1943/0685/5.
59   Nowers, interviewed by Hardie, SLWA OH2701/5.
60   Major Ednie Brown to Bray, 14 January 1943, SROWA 1943/0102/1.
61   Brigadier Hoad to Bray, 24 March 1943, p. 1, SROWA 1943/0102/9 (underlining in original).
62   Draft Plan for the Evacuation of Natives from North-West Coastal Areas to Controlled Camping Areas Inland, SROWA 1943/0102/9.

labour in the NORTH-WEST would then be much brighter. If these feeding stations are not established now, or at a future date, then if there is an invasion, there is every chance that practically all natives would be liquidated by the enemy before they left these shores. The labour problem after the war would then be most difficult.[63]

The proposal was rejected by both Bray and the Commissioner of Police, who thought that the only way it could be carried out 'would be for the Army to establish internment camps with armed guards and for the natives concerned to be interned, otherwise the idea of holding them would be futile'.[64] Bray was also concerned that such an evacuation would descend into a 'nigger hunt', as he claimed had happened in the Mid West when the Army had attempted to deal with Aboriginal people there. He warned Brigadier Hoad that he would be forced to take legal action if such 'crudeness' in the Army's handling of Aboriginal people was repeated.[65] Bray's accusation that previous actions by the Army suggested that 'nigger hunting' was a real possibility raises questions about assumptions concerning the positive nature of Aboriginal interactions with servicemen during the war.

The proposal to establish camps away from the coast was never implemented, but while it remained in abeyance, the Department, anxious to ensure that nothing took place that might cause the idea to be resurrected, imposed an increased level of surveillance and control over the activities, movement and employment of Port Hedland's Euralian community. Section 18(1) of the *Native Administration Act 1936* enabled the Department to control the employment of Aboriginal people through the issuing of work permits to employers, but the legislation specifically excluded 'any male person over twenty-one years of age who is of half blood or less than half blood descent from the original full blood inhabitants of Australia or from their full blood descendants, where such a person does not live after the manner of the original full blood inhabitants or their full blood descendants'.

Work permits had not been required to employ members of Port Hedland's Euralian community for many years. However, with increased wartime security concerns and a desire to ensure that Aboriginal labour was employed where it was most needed, the work permit system became more rigidly enforced. In April 1943, Constable Chipperfield informed Alfred Bonham, officer in charge of both the Port Hedland to Marble Bar railway and the Port Hedland

---

63   Brigadier Hoad to Bray, 24 March 1943, p. 2, SROWA 1943/0102/8.
64   Commissioner of Police to Bray, 7 April 1943, SROWA 1943/0102/12.
65   Bray to Hoad, 10 April 1943, p. 3, SROWA 1943/0102/16.

wharf, that he needed to obtain permits from the Department of Native Affairs to continue to employ the Euralian men providing essential labour in both workplaces. When the workers were informed of this, they were outraged. 'The men themselves object to this procedure, and say it is classing them as natives', Bonham wrote.[66]

Chipperfield also confronted Euralian Association member Jack Coffin, threatening imprisonment if he continued to work for the Main Roads Department without a permit.[67] His threat had no legal basis – it was the employer, not the worker, who was obliged to obtain a permit – and may have been prompted by the departmental directive to prioritise the labour needs of the pastoral industry by directing workers to station employment. Coffin refused to work under these conditions and resigned. Other members of the Euralian community also announced that they would not work under permit.[68] In early May, Commissioner Bray wrote:

> From information which has reached me it is evident that there is a widespread intention on the part of the local half-castes to defy authority and the local measures of control. In view of this, firm action is necessary to meet their attitude, especially as it concerns the local military situation.[69]

Don McLeod took up the cause of the Euralian community at this time, jumping boots and all into political activism for Aboriginal rights issues that would continue until the end of his life and to the end of the century. In an autobiography written in 1955 with Leslie Marchant, he said he was invited by Edgar Lockyer to a 'big half-caste meeting' in Port Hedland.[70] While the timing of this is unclear, it seems most likely that it was a meeting held to

---

66   Bonham to Deputy Secretary of Railways, 29 April 1943, SROWA 1943/0441/1.
67   McLeod, pamphlet entitled 'Tyranny Within the Law', SROWA 1943/0460/5–6; Biskup, *Not Slaves*, p. 213. Biskup assumes that this was Yarrie Jack Coppin (Ngarlkapangu), brother of Sam Coppin and Peter Coppin (Kangkushot). However, Jack Coffin was of a different family. His family had owned Redcliffs Station, which they struggled to retain following the death of his father. After working for some time mining gold at Tambora, he had shifted into Port Hedland and was a member of the Port Hedland branch of the Anti-Fascist League in 1943. Bill Day, 'Coffin Family of Redcliffs Station, Pilbara, Western Australia', http://www.drbilldayanthropologist.com/resources/CoffinFamilyHistory.pdf,
68   Bonham to Deputy Secretary of Railways, 29 April 1943, SROWA 1943/0441/1.
69   Commissioner Bray to Deputy Secretary of Railways, 6 May 1943, SROWA 1943/0441/3.
70   McLeod, draft autobiography, chapter 2, p. 34, Marchant Trust Collection, UWA MS118 series 1 file 8.

formulate a response to the imposition of permit regulations. In late May or early June, McLeod travelled to Perth to give voice to Euralian community grievances through Anti-Fascist League broadcasts and discussions with Commissioner Bray.[71] He also raised the issue of the increased restrictions placed on the freedom of movement of Aboriginal pastoral workers arising from Bray's wartime directive that they not be permitted to seek employment outside the pastoral industry.[72]

McLeod's advocacy for the rights of the Euralian community in 1943 has prompted historians to overstate his role in Port Hedland's wartime protests. Robert Hall, for example, claims that McLeod 'performed a catalytic role in the encouragement of Aboriginal radicalism in the Port Hedland district. He organised strikes and protests in response to the pass system imposed upon Port Hedland Aborigines'.[73] There is no evidence that he played an active or organisational role in the protests, however. Reports made to Bray about the protests in late 1942 over the issue of passes would certainly have made reference to McLeod had he been in any way involved, especially given his Anti-Fascist League associations, and it is unlikely that he would have been accepted into the VDC in April 1943 had he been involved in this unrest. And given the Euralian community's activism over this issue, there is no reason to suppose that they required McLeod's encouragement or guidance a few months later, when they staged further protests over work permits. Again, local officials would not have failed to mention McLeod's involvement in reports to the Department had there been any involvement to report. In fact, it appears that McLeod's emergence as an Aboriginal rights activist was inspired by the radicalism of the Port Hedland Euralian community rather than the other way around, their wartime protests serving as a practical expression of ideas circulating through Anti-Fascist League broadcasts and discussions.

While there is no evidence that McLeod was involved in any form of political activity prior to June 1943, this situation changed dramatically with his visit to Perth. He made contact with Bill Beeby and contributed material for his radio program. During June, Beeby's anti-fascist radio broadcasts aired the issue of the restrictive wartime treatment of the Euralian community along with other Aboriginal issues. Beeby also launched an appeal for literature for

---

71 McLeod to Bray, 27 June 1943, p. 1, SROWA 1943/0685/4.
72 Chipperfield to Inspector Read, 1 July 1943, p. 1, SROWA 1943/0685/1.
73 Robert A. Hall, *The Black Diggers: Aborigines and Torres Strait Islanders in the Second World War*, Aboriginal Studies Press, Canberra, 1997 (electronic edition), p. 128.

the Port Hedland Euralian community.[74] McLeod began writing articles for the *Fremantle Districts Sentinel*, the mouthpiece of the Anti-Fascist League. His first article, appearing on 1 July 1943 and entitled 'Democracy – Reality or Lip Service', may have been written while he was in Perth. Since racial difference had social rather than biological causes, he argued, 'claims that one race, one nation, or one class, have the God-given right to rule' were groundless.[75] A later long article, entitled 'Tyranny Within the Law' with reference to John Locke's statement 'where ever law ends, Tyranny begins', specifically discussed the injustices suffered by the Port Hedland Euralian people under discriminatory wartime restrictions.[76]

McLeod's visit to Perth in June 1943 marked, as well, the beginning of a scheme to acquire land to enable Aboriginal people to establish independent communities and agricultural enterprises. While in Perth he applied to the Lands Department to lease 28,000 acres of land in the Pilbara, which he later said was to be for 'the benefit of natives'. The application was unsuccessful, as the land was insufficient to provide reasonable livelihood.[77]

Through Beeby, McLeod met communists and other left-wing activists, including the anthropologist Fred Rose, during that visit to Perth.[78] He met and began corresponding with the communist writer Katharine Susannah Prichard, who was an associate of Beeby's, and also with the writer Mary Durack, and through them he was put in touch with a wider network of activists beyond Western Australia, including Tom Wright, the federal president of the Sheet Metal Workers' Union. Through them, he was introduced to Communist Party policy on Aborigines, particularly Wright's 1939 pamphlet 'New Deal for the Aborigines'. He found a community of left-wing activists in Perth, particularly those associated with the Communist Party, who were keen to engage in Aboriginal issues but who felt out of touch with conditions in the remote north of the state, where they believed the problem was most critical. They welcomed McLeod as a valuable contact who, as a long-time resident of the north, could have an important role to play in putting them in touch with Aboriginal conditions and issues in the north.

It was probably on this trip to Perth that McLeod learned something of the brutal history of the treatment of Aboriginal people in Western Australia.

---

74 Bray to Commissioner of Police, 3 July 1943, SROWA 1943/0685/12; Clarke to Beeby, 2 July 1943, published in the *Fremantle Districts Sentinel*, 15 July 1943, p. 2.
75 *Fremantle Districts Sentinel*, 1 July 1943, p. 3.
76 SROWA 1943/0460/5–6.
77 G. L. Needham to Bray, 20 April 1944, SROWA 1944/0394/4.
78 Monteath and Munt, *Red Professor*, p. 76.

Either from the contacts he made there, or, as he claimed, through his own research in the State Library, he learned of the undertaking, made when self-government was granted in 1889, to set aside £5000 or 1 per cent of gross revenue for the benefit of the Aboriginal people of the state, enshrined as section 70 of the Western Australian Constitution. He also learned of the government's manoeuvrings to have these provisions repealed once self-government had been achieved. He saw this as a gross betrayal of Aboriginal people, engineered by greedy men who would be made rich through the theft of Aboriginal land and the exploitation of their labour. He later described it as 'the deliberate rape of a splendid people', and believed he had found the key to understanding the current status of Aboriginal people as an exploited and impoverished underclass.[79]

When McLeod returned by boat to Port Hedland at the end of June 1943, he had a network of left-wing and activist contacts, a new understanding of the historical background to the situation of Aboriginal people in Western Australia, a head full of ideas about how the situation might be addressed and an armload of 'pamphlets, books, etc., of an educational and political nature for distribution amongst the half-castes ... at Port Hedland'.[80] According to the *Sentinel*, this was 'an example of socialist endeavour in action'.[81]

By the time McLeod disembarked at Port Hedland, unrest over the issue of work permits had subsided. I can find little information about the protest undertaken by the Euralian community at this time, but the situation seems to have been unsettled for some weeks: Bray wrote on 6 May of the 'widespread intention on the part of the local half-castes to defy authority', and it was not until mid-June that Chipperfield was able to report that the situation was now satisfactory.[82] The Department had issued permits to the Department of Railways and other employers, and Euralian workers were no longer refusing to work under permit. In August, Bray told the Deputy Director of Security for Western Australia that 'firm action was taken and nothing further has been heard of the matter'.[83] Just what 'firm action' was taken is not clear, but with military authorities pushing for the evacuation of Aboriginal people from the coast, the Department would certainly have been anxious to contain the

---

79 McLeod to Brian Fitzpatrick, 28 March 1956, Papers of Jessie Street, NLA 2683/10/70.
80 *Fremantle Districts Sentinel*, 1 July 1943, p. 2.
81 *Fremantle Districts Sentinel*, 1 July 1943, p. 2.
82 Chipperfield to Bray, 15 June 1943, SROWA 1943/0460/3.
83 Bray to the Deputy Director of Security for WA, Perth, 12 August 1943, SROWA 1943/0796/15–16.

unrest as quickly as possible. Threats of imprisonment or large-scale evacuation from the town were no doubt used to pressure the men to continue working.

However, the protest was to a degree successful in bringing about a relaxation of the Department's hardline approach to permit regulations. Chipperfield recommended that the 'better class natives' like the Clarkes apply to the Department for exemption from the provisions of the Act, believing that this would 'do away with any future bother with them'.[84] Such exemptions were, however, available only to the few who, like the Clarkes, had secured houses in the town, while those living at the One Mile remained subject to work permit regulations, and the issue remained a source of discontentment.

The Euralian community therefore welcomed the interest shown by the Anti-Fascist League in their cause. They held a number of meetings with McLeod on his return, and on 2 July Pop Clarke wrote to Beeby, thanking him for his favourable broadcast 'regarding the Euralians' and requesting Euralian Association affiliation with the League.[85] Edgar Lockyer and McLeod formed a branch of the AFL in Port Hedland, made up principally of members of the Euralian community, and plans were made to hold a meeting during the weekend of the Port Hedland races to discuss their grievances with Commissioner Bray, Minister Bob Coverley and their local Member of Parliament, Bill Hegney, all of whom were invited to attend.[86] McLeod, who was closely involved in these arrangements, hoped that 'a representative deputation of employers and prominent towns people' would also attend the meeting.[87]

The Department was concerned about the links being developed between Aboriginal people and the Anti-Fascist League. Military intelligence authorities were alerted. Major Colin Ednie Brown, of the secretive Services Reconnaissance Department, received a copy of McLeod's long letter inviting Bray to the Port Hedland AFL meeting and setting out the Euralian community's grievances.[88] Ednie Brown also received a copy of Chipperfield's report on McLeod's activities in Port Hedland following his trip to Perth. 'I have had a long conversation with this man regarding the aims of the League and its benefits', Chipperfield wrote:

---

84 Chipperfield to Bray, 15 June 1943, SROWA 1943/0460/3.
85 The letter was published in the *Fremantle Districts Sentinel*, 15 July 1943, p. 2.
86 Chipperfield to Inspector Read, 1 July 1943, SROWA 1943/0685/1–2.
87 McLeod to Bray, 27 June 1943, p. 1, SROWA 1943/0685/4.
88 McLeod to Bray, 27 June 1943, SROWA 1943/0685/4–9.

and find that he is more or less interesting himself in the uplift of the native generally, or, as he terms it, equality for all the oppressed peoples of the earth. His contention, and it is the gospel that he is preaching, is that all peoples, irrespective of creed, class or colour, should enjoy equality of rights and that a common law should be made applicable to all ...

Obviously, if this man is to be permitted to preach his gospel far and wide, it is going to cause discontent among the natives, and a lot of trouble can be expected from them in the future, whenever the provisions of the Native Administration Act are applied to them.[89]

The Deputy Director of Security in Western Australia sought further information on the Euralian Association.[90]

Bray also alerted the Commissioner of Police to the fact that Aboriginal issues had been discussed in Beeby's AFL broadcasts during June, and that a further appeal had been made for literature for northern Aboriginal communities. Bray was concerned that this could include 'literature or correspondence of a disruptive nature to the happiness and welfare of the natives'. 'I believe it has been suggested that the organization of branches of the Anti-Fascist League amongst the natives would improve their circumstances and status in post-war reconstruction', he wrote. 'Reasonable efforts along these lines are not objectionable, but the natives are easily influenced and possibly many of them would become susceptible to undesirable doctrines'.[91] In response, the Police Department investigated the level of influence that Anti-Fascist League broadcasts might be having within Aboriginal communities in the north. Police officers in most northern centres reported, however, that no Aboriginal people listened to the broadcasts, few having access to radios, and that anti-fascist teaching was having no impact on Aboriginal people in their districts. Port Hedland's Constable Chipperfield, on the other hand, reported that he 'definitely consider[ed] that these broadcasts [were] having a derrogatory [sic] effect on the natives'. While few had radios, broadcasts were published in pamphlet form and sent to branches and discussed at meetings.[92] Constable Gordon Marshall in Marble Bar believed that in his district, also,

---

89 Chipperfield to Inspector Read, 1 July 1943, SROWA 1943/0685/1.
90 Deputy Director of Security for Western Australia to Bray, 4 August 1943, SROWA 1943/0796/14; Bray to the Deputy Director of Security, 12 August 1943, SROWA 1943/0796/15–16.
91 Bray to Commissioner of Police, 3 July 1943, SROWA 1943/0685/12.
92 Chipperfield to Inspector Coppinger, 10 August 1943, SROWA 1943/0685/20–21.

Aboriginal people were being adversely influenced by the League. 'I am sure that McLeod and his undesirable followers are influencing the half-castes of this district of whom there are quite a number now, to become white men and white women and have white people's rights, by becoming exempt from the Native Administration Act', he wrote:

> This in itself is doing these people harm as not all of them and in fact very few, would live the white man's way for very long, and in my opinion these people would be far happier if allowed to live their own life without being influenced by Messrs. Beeby, McLeod and their followers.[93]

On 27 July 1943, while investigations into the effect of Beeby's broadcasts were being carried out, the public meeting of the Port Hedland branch of the Anti-Fascist League was held in the Port Hedland Mechanics Institute hall to discuss the 'unexpected and strict enforcement of the Regulations under the Native Affairs Dept' despite promises made on 9 February 1942 that racial prejudice would cease in the district if Euralians supported the war effort.[94] Questions relating to qualification for exemption from the Act, particularly regarding housing, were also on the agenda. By holding the meeting at the end of the annual Port Hedland race weekend, organisers hoped to attract station people, both *walypila* and *marrngu*, who were in town for the races.

The meeting was disappointing, however. Although Bray and Coverley had been invited to discuss these issues, neither was present. Neither was Bill Beeby. The meeting was convened by McLeod and well attended, although most of those who attended were members of the Euralian community.[95] McLeod later said that two resolutions were unanimously adopted, the first being that, because of promises made in early 1942, 'the half caste people in the Hedland district should be accepted at once as equal citizens'. The second unanimously accepted resolution, according to McLeod's later account, was that 'an inquiry should be undertaken to see how best their less fortunate relations, the full-blooded people employed in the pastoral industry could be assisted'.[96]

However, other accounts suggest that these resolutions had less support than McLeod claimed. A military intelligence officer in the audience reported that the meeting failed in its object of 'obtaining support for improved conditions

---

93 Marshall to Coppinger, 3 September 1943, SROWA 1943/0685/22–23.
94 Chipperfield to Coppinger, 10 August 1943, p. 2, SROWA 1943/0685/21.
95 Chipperfield to Coppinger, 10 August 1943, p. 2, SROWA 1943/0685/21.
96 McLeod, draft autobiography, chapter 2, p. 6, Marchant Trust Collection, UWA MS118 series 1 file 8.

for half-castes', and that had it 'been convened other than under the heading of the Anti-Fascist League, support would have been in favour of the half-castes having more equal rights'.[97] Constable Chipperfield, who also attended, believed that McLeod was 'prepared to advise the natives against the authority of those who control their interest', but that the meeting showed that he had little support from the Euralian community.[98] Helena Clarke also indicates that the Euralians did not throw their support behind McLeod's call for action to be taken to address the conditions of Aboriginal people on stations. Her father was supportive in principle, she said, but believed that action needed to be taken by the people concerned, not by others. He believed in Aboriginal control of Aboriginal matters.[99]

The Euralian Association came under strong pressure to dissociate itself from the Anti-Fascist League. A few days after the meeting of 27 July, McLeod raised the question of conditions and treatment of 'the half-castes resident in the town' at a meeting held in Port Hedland by William (Bill) Hegney, the Labor Member for Pilbara in the Western Australian Legislative Assembly and a member of the state executive of the AWU. Hegney replied that nothing could be done while they associated themselves with the anti-fascists, and he accused McLeod of exploiting them. At an AWU meeting held a few days after this, the anti-communist Hegney warned Euralian AWU members that if they continued to associate with the Anti-Fascist League they would lose the support of the AWU and the Labor Party.[100] Pressure also came from the local Catholic priest, Edward Bryan, who had a close relationship with the Euralian community. Chipperfield reported shortly after the public meeting that Bryan was 'endeavouring to persuade the half-castes to abandon the League, and as he holds quite a sway over the natives, it is anticipated that this will be brought about'.[101]

Nevertheless, affiliation with the AFL proved to be a successful strategy on the part of the Euralian Association. Aware that resentment at the rigid imposition of work permit regulations had led the Euralian community to seek the support of the left, authorities acted to prevent further radicalisation by addressing core grievances. It was an example of the positive impact of anti-communism in the movement for Aboriginal rights, which Lachlan

---

97 Major Ednie Brown to Bray, 11 August 1943, SROWA 1943/0685/14.
98 Chipperfield to Coppinger, 10 August 1943, SROWA 1943/0685/20–21.
99 Cited in Kinnane, *Shadow Lines*, p. 337.
100 Bisley to Bray, 30 July 1943, SROWA 1943/0685/13.
101 Chipperfield to Coppinger, 10 August 1943, SROWA 1943/0685/20–21.

Clohesy has noted.[102] Bill Hegney recommended to the Department that a more lenient approach be taken over the issue, and submitted a list of names of people that he considered 'should be dealt with sympathetically under the permit regulations'. Hegney was Catholic, and it seems likely that the list was compiled by Father Bryan, who knew the Euralian community well. Hegney advised Bray to 'instruct the Local Protector that such persons were not required to work under permit regulations'.[103] Rose Nowers remembered that the permit system was a regulation made and not carried out: it was 'just broken like that'.[104] The Euralians had won the battle.

McLeod believed that the Port Hedland protests and the establishment of an AFL branch with mainly Aboriginal membership were contributing factors in Coverley's decision to introduce the Native (Citizenship Rights) Bill into Parliament the following year.[105] The Bill was passed at the end of 1944, enabling Aboriginal people to apply for a Certificate of Citizenship, which offered greater rights than the Certificate of Exemption to people who could show that they had adopted 'the manner and habits of civilized life'. The increasing radicalism of the Port Hedland Euralians and similar communities, chafing under the restrictive measures of the *Native Administration Act*, was a potential threat to the system of controls that ensured the continued availability of compliant Aboriginal labour in the pastoral north. It was hoped, perhaps, that by providing Euralians with citizenship rights, widespread agitation for change in northern pastoral regions could be averted. It was, however, a measure instituted too late to prevent the inspirational role that the Euralians' wartime activism played in McLeod's radicalisation, and the ripple effect that this would create throughout the Pilbara over the next few years.

McLeod had little involvement with the Euralian community affairs following the public meeting of 27 July. Despite the bad feeling engendered by the rigid enforcement of work permit regulations, the more lenient approach adopted by the Department on Hegney's recommendation eased tensions within the Euralian community to some extent. Advice from the strongly anti-communist Father Bryan may also have been influential in the Euralians'

---

102   Lachlan Clohesy, 'Fighting the Enemy Within: Anti-communism and Aboriginal Affairs', *History Australia*, vol. 8, no. 2, 2011, pp. 128–152.
103   Bray to Coverley, 17 September 1943, SROWA 1943/0796/23.
104   Nowers, interviewed by Hardie, SLWA OH2701/5.
105   *Workers' Star*, 21 June 1946, p. 2, 'Fremantle Backing for Native Rights Struggle'. McLeod believed that Bryan influenced Coverley and Hegney to introduce legislation to make it possible for Aboriginal individuals to achieve citizenship rights. McLeod, draft autobiography, chapter 2, p. 9, Marchant Trust Collection, UWA MS118 series 1 file 8.

decision to distance themselves from McLeod's enthusiastic campaigning. More important, however, is the observation made by Pop Clarke's daughter, Helena, that her father believed that Aboriginal matters should be in the hands of Aboriginal people.[106] The Euralians neither wanted nor needed someone from outside their community to fight their battles for them.

Security concerns also played a role in curbing McLeod's Port Hedland activities. While working at the Comet Gold Mine, he had done some prospecting on his own account and found sufficient gold to enable him to purchase a Ford V8 three-ton truck. In the middle months of 1943, he was using this to undertake cartage contracts, carting gravel and water to the Corunna Downs RAAF base and running a weekly service delivering fuel and stores to the base from the railhead at Meekatharra.[107] In September, two months after the public meeting in Port Hedland, the RAAF debarred him from entrance to any aerodrome or RAAF establishment, and he was no longer able to continue his work there.[108] Instead, he went back down to the Nullagine area and took on fencing and well-sinking work for his friends Doug and Thora Gallop on Bonney Downs Station, renewing his contact with Kitchener and coming into contact with other *marrngu* station workers. Still fired with a zeal sparked by the activism of the Euralian community in Port Hedland, he began discussions that would lead to the development of the strike movement.

---

106 Cited in Kinnane, *Shadow Lines*, p. 337.
107 McLeod, draft autobiography, chapter 3, p. 3, Marchant Trust Collection, MS118 series 1 file 13, and chapter 2, p. 13, series 1 file 13.
108 Sub-area Security Officer, Royal Australian Airforce, AOH, Adelaide, to Deputy Director of Security, SA, 8 March 1944, 'McLeod, Donald [alleged communist connected with aborigines in Western Australia]', NAA D1918 S3008.

Chapter 5

'McLeod Gave Us Hint and We Took It Up'

The Movement Begins, 1943–45

Mirta wanyjarnija milpanya? Paliny wanyjarningulu?
Pinakarrikinyinganinyi pajukarrinyinganaku paliny nyungu.

How did Mirta get here? Where did he come from? He listened to us, and sympathised.[1]

According to most accounts written since 1970, the strike movement had its genesis at a place known to Aboriginal people as Wantilurr, and to *walypila* as Skull Springs. The story has the quality of a legend. In 1942, when McLeod was working as a fencing and well-sinking contractor on stations near Nullagine, he was invited by *marrngu* to attend a Law meeting at Skull Springs on the Davis River, a tributary of the Oakover River to the east of Nullagine.[2] The meeting had taken five years to organise, and it had taken five years for McLeod to become convinced that they had a safe place to meet. It was attended by Aboriginal Lawmen from all over the state, speaking twenty-four languages and requiring sixteen interpreters to ensure successful communication. The Lawmen discussed their grievances with McLeod and asked him to assist them in formulating a plan to address their situation of economic and social disadvantage. It took six weeks to hammer out the details of action to be

---

1 Ginger Bob (Palyakulayi), recorded by Anne Scrimgeour, 8 December 1993, translated from Nyangumarta by Barbara Hale and Mark Clendon, AIATSIS collection, soundfile 'Palyakulayi 9'.
2 In Law meetings senior Aboriginal people (usually men) come together, often from a wide geographical area, to plan and conduct religious and ceremonial activities over a number of days or weeks. Lawmen are men who have achieved a high level of religious knowledge, expertise and authority.

taken, and the Lawmen selected Dooley to organise the strike, with a second organiser to be selected by Dooley and McLeod.[3]

It is difficult to authenticate this narrative. There is, understandably, no documentary evidence of the Skull Springs meeting. McLeod's account of what took place at Skull Springs is the sole source of later written retellings of the meeting and its significance, and there is no record of McLeod ever speaking or writing about it prior to 1959. Draft copies of an autobiography he wrote with Leslie Marchant in 1955 include detailed discussion of his life before 1946 and of the development of his interest in Aboriginal issues, but no mention at all is made of the Skull Springs meeting.[4] During the strike and during the 1950s, McLeod consistently claimed that his involvement in the strike movement had begun in July 1945 when he was approached by a deputation of Aboriginal people in Port Hedland, who asked him to be their representative and spokesman. In 1956, for example, he told the historian Brian Fitzpatrick:

> I became interested in the Native Question about 1937 and after some study of the question took some public action in the interests of less coloured people in Pt Hedland during probably 1942 and was later asked to act as the representative of the present group of people in September 1945.[5]

I have found no evidence that McLeod spoke or wrote about Skull Springs prior to 1959, when he told anthropology students John and Katrin Wilson, in 'a matter-of-fact' way, that he had attended a meeting there.[6]

In addition to the time gap between the event and its retelling, the facts surrounding the Law meeting remain elusive because of the lack of corroborating evidence to support McLeod's account. While *marrngu* accounts of the strike do make reference to Skull Springs as a highly significant event

---

3   Raymond J. T. Butler, 'Education, the State and the Indigenous Minority: A Case Study from Western Australia', Master of Education Thesis, Murdoch University, 1985; Submission by the Nomads Group of Aborigines to the Federal Cabinet, Commonwealth of Australia, 1973, p. 6, NAA A4252, 49; D. W. McLeod, *How the West Was Lost: The Native Question in the Development of Western Australia*, Don McLeod, Port Hedland, 1984, p. 40–41; Don McLeod, interviewed by John Clements, 1975, SLWA OH4005/3; McLeod, interviewed by Jeffery, SLWA OH331.
4   McLeod, draft autobiography, Marchant Trust Collection, UWA MS118 series 1.
5   McLeod to Brian Fitzpatrick, 28 June 1956, Papers of Jessie Street, NLA 2683/10/70. See also McLeod to Secretary, Aboriginal Australian Fellowship, Sydney, 21 February 1957, SLWA 1568A/1/62–73.
6   John and Katrin Wilson, email to author, 13 October 2016.

in the development of the movement, I have found no accounts provided by anyone who actually attended the meeting, other than McLeod. No mention of Skull Springs was made by Dooley Binbin and other *marrngu* when they outlined the history of the strike to the Wilsons at Pilgangoora in 1959.[7] Nor is there any reference to this apparently highly significant meeting in Donald Stuart's work *Yandy*, which he published in 1959 after living and working with the group in 1952 and 1953, and after being introduced by *marrngu* to aspects of Aboriginal Law.[8] Graham Alcorn, the editor of the Communist Party newspaper the *Workers' Star*, who communicated extensively with McLeod prior to and in the early period of the strike, also makes no reference to Skull Springs in notes he made for Max Brown's version of the strike, *The Black Eureka*.[9] Brown worked with the group in 1953, at the same time as Stuart, but did not produce his important account of the strike until 1976.[10] Significantly, this account does refer to the meeting at Skull Springs, as do nearly all accounts of the strike written after 1970.

McLeod's belated description of Skull Springs, unsupported by other first-person accounts and having an epic and mythological quality, needs to be treated with caution by historians. Historical uncertainties include discrepancies over its timing. Central to McLeod's post-1960 accounts of the process by which he became involved in the strike movement is his claim that the Law meeting on the Davis River took place in 1942, predating his activism in the Port Hedland protests against wartime restrictions, and five years after he had been stimulated into thinking about what he called 'the Native Question' by comments made to him by the English asbestos dealer, Alec Fenton. According to McLeod's account, it was at this time that Aboriginal people began to ask him why they had so little freedom in their own country. 'Having had my attention drawn to them', he said:

> I got to know them a bit and they approached me and finally when they got to know me better and asked me what they could do to get out of the mess that they were in and I said, 'What mess is that?' and they said, 'Well we can't leave our work, we're tied here, and we don't get

---

7   John and Katrin Wilson, email to author, 13 October 2016. The Wilsons made notes of the account provided by *marrngu* at Pilgangoora: Dooley Binbin et al., 'History of the '46 Strike', as told to John Wilson by Dooley and the men of Pilgangoora. However, I have been unable to locate a copy of this.
8   Donald Stuart, *Yandy*, Georgian House, Melbourne, 1959.
9   Graham Alcorn, 'The Struggle of the Pilbara Station Hands for Decent Living Standards and Human Rights', with forward and notes by Max Brown.
10 Max Brown, *The Black Eureka*, Australasian Book Society, Sydney, 1976.

any wages for what we're doing, and we can't leave. [We don't know why] the policeman take us back and this is our country and yet we have to work here for this bloke, how does this come about?' I said 'I don't know but I'll find out'.[11]

To find out why, McLeod says, he visited the State Library of Western Australia in Perth. There he found disturbing evidence of atrocities committed against Aboriginal people during the early years of colonial occupation, and of the colonial government's betrayal of Aboriginal people in repealing section 70 of the Constitution. 'I found out how they'd been robbed by the state', McLeod said:

> Well, having found out what their problem was and passed it on to them, I left it with them. And they nattered it over and some time later they come back on it and said, 'Well now how we going to get out of it?', and I said 'There's only one way to get out of it, the same as everyone else got to get out of a situation like this – you've got to organise yourselves, and so long as you can get solidarity right throughout the state, and all the blackfellers understand the position and what they've got to do, and you stick together and back up that argument, well you must win'. And they said, 'Well if we can organise the whole state, well will you guide us and show us how to go about it?' And not thinking they'd be able to do it, of course, I was silly enough to promise that I would.[12]

As McLeod would tell the story in later decades, five years of discussion and planning, following the revelation of the broken promise of section 70, culminated eventually in Aboriginal people from a wide area of the country coming together at Skull Springs to formulate a strategy to address their disadvantage. He would emphasise his reluctance to become involved, and the insistent entreaties that eventually drew him into the affair. 'For five years they were at me and at me and at me', he said:

> and I did the research and found out what the position was and I was so bloody ashamed I didn't like to talk to them any more. Anyhow finally they shanghaied me and took me out to a place called Skull Springs ... Some bloke Kitchener from Roy Hill, Ethel Creek, he'd battled very hard to get me in because he worked with me for a while ... Kitchener

---

11   McLeod, interviewed by Jeffery, SLWA OH331.
12   McLeod, interviewed by Clements, tape 1, SLWA OH4005/3.

> knew if they could get me on their side I'd be worth having. And he battled and battled and battled to get me to listen to these old people and I wouldn't have a bar of it, I wanted to make a million, two or three million. I said, 'Wait till I've made the money, then I can be useful to you. I'm no use to you while I'm broke'. Bruce Wandarri said, 'We can't afford to lose you, you've got to do this'.
>
> Well I'd have been a louse, you know, here these people couldn't read and write, they couldn't talk English. Some could talk English with difficulty. If you wouldn't do what they wanted, you really would be a louse. So in the finish I buckled in.[13]

He said that at Skull Springs, 'they gave me a crash course in native law and I gave them the way the state had fiddled with their estate and what they were entitled to and ... what they'd have to do to recover it'.[14] 'They wanted to get this 1 per cent of gross revenue they'd found out about'.[15]

In 1975, he also told John Clements that he had been instructed at the meeting to acquire land to enable Aboriginal people to establish themselves as an enclave within Western Australia:

> I had to get hold of about 12 million acres of pastoral lease, Mundabullangana in the west, down behind Nullagine in the south and up to De Grey in the north and as time went by we'd buy all the stations between. Now on these places we would establish the blackfellers and take advantage of western technology, and as they were able to support themselves so we'd draw more and more people in from the desert. At that time there were eight thousand people in the desert and they would establish themselves in their own country and they'd buy the land remaining inside this horseshoe piece of land, and they'd invite in amongst them sympathetic whites and so forth so they'd have an integrated colony, and enclave in Western Australia, and the transition would be orderly and smooth.[16]

Whether or not McLeod was actually instructed to work towards this goal at Skull Springs, it was a vision that he would maintain for many years, and that *marrngu* would, by 1953, have made significant steps towards achieving.

---

13 McLeod, interviewed by Carlton, 1996, transcript, p. 8, SLWA 2739.
14 McLeod, interviewed by Jeffery, SLWA OH331.
15 McLeod, interviewed by Carlton, 1996, transcript, p. 8, SLWA 2739.
16 McLeod, interviewed by Clements, tape 2, SLWA OH4005/3.

A central feature of McLeod's account is the authority within Aboriginal Law that was conferred upon him by the senior Lawmen at the Skull Springs meeting. 'They gave me a position in the law above any lawman', he said. 'Since blackfellers take some time to do the consensus, in the event of needing to take a quick decision, if I took any decision then everybody would stick to that'.[17] Any decision he made would 'be binding upon all the communities represented at this meeting', and complicated mechanisms were established to maintain communication lines between different groups so that the results of negotiations would be known to everyone as soon as possible.[18] In order to give him the status required, he was given 150 square miles of land around Nullagine, 'so that I could approach the state government as an equal'.[19] 'My title to these lands was crystallised in wooden objects carved out of living trees taken from the boundary of the estate', he wrote, 'the story of my ownership being carved into these objects'.[20]

In later decades, this narrative of being unwillingly drawn into the strike movement and instructed by senior Lawmen from all over Western Australia to take action to address Aboriginal grievances became the cornerstone of McLeod's claim to have authority to speak and act on behalf of Aboriginal people. Diverted from his own life goals ('I wanted to make a million') and drawn into the affair through his own basic human decency ('you really would be a louse') only after years of urgent and insistent appeals from *marrngu*, he claimed an authority derived not from his role as an activist but as one who had been chosen for this task. He had not sought involvement or authority, he claimed, but authority had been bestowed upon him nevertheless. This construction of events only makes sense if, as he claimed, the Skull Springs meeting predated his involvement in the 1943 Euralian wartime protests in Port Hedland, and if he became involved in their activism as a result of instructions he had received at Skull Springs.

Yet the claim that Skull Springs took place in 1942 is problematic. Evidence that it probably happened later is significant in assisting us to disentangle the events leading up to the strike from McLeod's contribution to the construction of his own legendary status. While McLeod claimed that his involvement in the strike movement began in discussion with Aboriginal people in the Fortescue district in 1937 or earlier, it appears instead to have been a more

---

17   McLeod, interviewed by Jeffery, tape 1.
18   McLeod, *How the West Was Lost*, p. 41.
19   McLeod, interviewed by Jeffery, tape 1.
20   McLeod, *How the West Was Lost*, p. 41.

localised movement, developing within a shorter timeframe than his account suggests.

This is not to suggest that McLeod's version of this history was necessarily deliberately fabricated. Repeatedly urged by interested people in later years to provide details of the strike and the events leading up to it, he could talk for hours but had, by his own admission, a very poor memory for dates and the sequence of events. The sequence of events in the autobiography he wrote with Leslie Marchant in 1955 is jumbled and contradictory. 'I haven't got the dates nor is my memory good enough to remember the routine that went into our early struggle', he told the non-Aboriginal activist Ian Spalding in 1959 when asked to sketch out a history of the movement. 'I can remember the incidents when my mind is jogged but a lot is now faded in the haze of time'.[21] His dates and sequencing of events tend, as a result, to be inaccurate.

Documentary evidence of his involvement in Aboriginal issues begins in June 1943, when his advocacy for the rights of the Port Hedland Euralian community first brought him to the attention of authorities. In September, when he was debarred from entry to the RAAF airbase at Corunna Downs, he began working on Bonney Downs Station as a well sinker and fencing contractor, and in October he applied to the Department for a permit to employ his old friend Kitchener as a woodcutter. This was his first application for permission to use Aboriginal labour. Police Constable McMahon at Nullagine wrote that McLeod was not well known to him, although he had been a labourer about the Nullagine and Marble Bar districts for a considerable time.[22] It seems unlikely that McLeod would not have come to police or departmental attention prior to this if he had been working, travelling or associating with Aboriginal people in the district to any extent. Interactions between settlers and *marrngu*, other than as bosses and workers, were looked on with suspicion and did not go unnoticed. In 1952, a pastoralist stated, 'I noticed McLeod about seven years ago talking to natives, an unusual thing for a white man. I asked him his idea in talking so often to the natives'.[23]

Constable McMahon recommended against granting a permit on the grounds of McLeod's involvement in Anti-Fascist League branches in Marble Bar and Port Hedland, and the fact that he had, of late, 'interested himself very much in the Native Question'. 'McLeod, himself, informed me that he has been warned off all Aerodromes, so this shows the class of person

---

21 McLeod to Spalding, 14 January 1959, SLWA 1568A/8/36–37.
22 McMahon to Bray, 14 October 1943, SROWA 1943/0685/25.
23 Edmund John Jeffries, Statement to Committee Investigating Native Labour, 1952, p. 7, SROWA 1952/0830/133.

he really is', McMahon wrote.[24] Bray agreed that McLeod should not be allowed to employ Aboriginal people but, in refusing the application, cited as his reason a directive of the Australian Government's wartime Manpower Directorate, which ordered that all Aboriginal pastoral labour must be retained on stations.[25]

McLeod therefore applied to the General Director of Manpower, this time requesting permission to employ 'three boys' for repair work on stations. Although the use of the word 'boy' to refer to Aboriginal men had wide currency, McLeod never used it after this time, and may have deliberately done so when writing to Manpower to allay fears that he had any interest in Aboriginal people other than as menial labourers. Although he wrote that three workers would be sufficient, he applied for a general permit to employ ten, 'owing to the difficulty of keeping the same boys for any length of time, they get the wanderlust and move off at the most unexpected times'.[26] Bray advised Manpower against supporting McLeod's appeal. 'In my opinion the Anti-Fascist people are Communists in principle', Bray argued, 'and since McLeod has been prohibited from entering aerodromes or Air Force Installations, I am not satisfied that he is a desirable person to employ natives, and propose to stand on this decision'.[27] Manpower accordingly declined to interfere in the Department's decision.

Both the Police and the Native Affairs departments were anxious to prevent McLeod from associating with Aboriginal people but, apart from denying him a work permit, there was little they could do. They hoped that some further action, beyond prohibiting his employment on RAAF bases, could be taken under wartime security regulations 'to restrain the activities of the AFL and particularly those of the Man McLEOD'.[28] The Commissioner of Police recommended that efforts be made to restrain McLeod, and sent copies of reports of McLeod's activities to the Deputy Director of Security.[29]

McLeod persisted in his effort to obtain a permit to employ Aboriginal workers, however. Bonney Downs Station was part-owned and managed by his

---

24   McMahon to Bray, 14 October 1943, SROWA 1943/0685/25.
25   Bray to McLeod, 4 November 1943, SROWA 1943/0685/26.
26   McLeod to Deputy-Director General of Manpower, 10 January 1944, SROWA 1944/0162/1.
27   Bray to the Deputy Director General of Manpower, 28 January 1944, SROWA 1944/0162/3; Deputy Director of Manpower to McLeod, 3 February 1944, 1944/0162/5.
28   Bray to Commissioner of Police, D. Hunter, 22 October 1943, SROWA 1943/0685/24, capitalised in the original.
29   Hunter to Bray, 18 October 1943, SROWA 1943/0685/23.

friends Doug and Thora Gallop, and in March 1944 Doug Gallop confirmed that the work McLeod was undertaking was essential to the running of the station, with two wells and twenty-five or more miles of fencing needed. To complete this work, Gallop said, McLeod needed to provide his own Aboriginal labour, as all station workers were fully engaged.[30] In light of this, the Department reluctantly granted permission for McLeod to employ three workers, on condition that they were not withdrawn from other stations, and that they be employed only on Bonney Downs.[31]

During much of 1944, therefore, McLeod had a permit to employ three Aboriginal workers, working with them mainly in well sinking and fencing on Bonney Downs Station. Along with Kitchener, he worked with two men named Alec and Mick. According to *marrngu* oral history accounts, the strike movement had its beginnings in discussions between McLeod and three classificatory brothers of the *Milangka* subsection, who were working together sinking wells and erecting windmills on Bonney Downs Station. These discussions, conducted over a considerable period, led eventually to the strike idea being discussed with Lawmen at Skull Springs.

During 1944, Clancy McKenna (Warntupungkarna), a key player in the strike movement, became involved in these discussions. The son of a white pastoralist and a Nyamal woman, he had greater fluency in English than many *marrngu*, and earned higher wages than most. However, he resented the fact that he was paid lower wages for doing the same work as well as, or better than, a *walypila* worker. Employed as a truck driver at Marble Bar at a wage of £6 per week, he had demanded the award rate of over £7, and overtime at award rates. When his wage demands were refused on the ground that, because he was Aboriginal, he was not allowed to cart liquor without a white offsider, he resigned.[32] Jack McPhee (Wanamurraganya) described him as 'a thinking man'. 'He wasn't the kind of person to go along with you unless it made real good sense to him', he said.[33]

McKenna seems to have begun discussions with McLeod while employed carting goods between Marble Bar and the Blue Spec mine, passing regularly through Nullagine where McLeod was sinking a well. McPhee remembered that McKenna was 'very impressed with Don McLeod'. 'Don McLeod thought black people should be treated the same as whites', he said, 'and I think it was

---

30 McMahon to Bray, 6 March 1944, SROWA 1944/0162/9–12.
31 Bray to McMahon, 21 March 1944, SROWA 1944/0162/13.
32 O'Neill to Bray, 5 November 1945, p. 3, SROWA 1945/0800/34.
33 Quoted in Morgan, *Wanamurraganya*, p. 165.

he who started Clancy thinking that something could be done, and that you didn't just keep putting up with bad treatment'. He remembered McKenna saying, 'Sour bread and kangaroo, old tea and no pay, that's not right Jack. Now you take my mob, there were thirty of us working on the station and only three of us getting paid, and then it wasn't much'.[34]

Oral history accounts indicate that *marrngu* had been discussing the injustices of their work and living conditions for many years before they began discussions with McLeod. 'The feeling among the Aborigine people was building up everywhere', Peter Coppin said. 'But there was nothing we could do, you know. People got to feeling that we not getting a fair go and at the same time we don't know how to start. We didn't know what to do'.[35] Since even minor transgressions met with severe repercussions, including beatings, imprisonment and indefinite exile from the region, there was no reason for *marrngu* to believe that they would not be killed if they took a stand. The fear of being shot was very real. Snowy Jittermarra claimed that people of his father's generation had been unhappy with their conditions and wondered, 'How we going to help ourself?' Although they talked about taking some sort of action to alter their situation, he said, there was no-one who could help them. Later, however, 'all the old people put together, and mention about this Don McLeod':

> 'Hey, Don McLeod is a good man. Can we try that man give him a talking up?'
>
> 'Mmm, alright'.
>
> ...
>
> 'What about we talk about it and put together and make some sort of [action]?' My father was talking to everybody now, and we start. Some, two or three fella bin working, my father's brothers, all the brothers anyhow, bin working with the Don McLeod, good well sinker, sinking well, all around Noreena boundary and Nullagine, they was putting up the windmill there. They keep talking. 'Can you help us?'
>
> ...
>
> Alright, all that problem now, we start working on that one now. And Don McLeod say, 'By God, we're going to be in trouble!'

---

34 Quoted in Morgan, *Wanamurraganya*, p. 162.
35 Read and Coppin, *Kangkushot*, p. 60.

'Oh well, we're all going to be in trouble, we'll help you and we'll stick together and help you'.

'Alright'.

He did.[36]

Billy Thomas also claimed that *marrngu* had been discussing their grievances and searching for a way to gain greater control over their lives, well before McLeod's involvement:

> Those days now, when we were kids, those old people who have now passed away could see what was going on, and they used to meet up and talk about it, from the south and from the north. They used to talk about what they were doing to us. 'We're working hard for them and they're not giving us any money. They don't put us in houses, we have to camp outside. We leave home and go off to work, but they don't give us good food. We have to eat outside.'
>
> The old man Ngarnka (Don McLeod), when he was a working man, he went around working as a well sinker, really, or a miner. He was living and working at the last place there, in Bonney Downs, and he was digging the Wallareenya well. He had with him all those *Milangka* men, my classificatory fathers, who had come from Noreena Downs in the east, and from Bonney Downs in the west. They were digging that well on the Bonney Downs boundary. They lived there, and after a while they became confident enough to talk to him, and they talked together about how this had come about. They talked to each other about how the *walypila* used to treat them in the old days. And when we were kids, even recently, how they were still treating us even then, we who were coming along after them.[37]

McLeod was able to provide the information they needed to address the injustice they suffered, by informing them that they did have legal rights, limited though these were, and that authorities needed to abide by the law in their dealings with *marrngu*. 'You see I've found out some things Jack', McKenna told McPhee: 'white people can't kill us these days, that's too much,

---

36 Jittermarra (Maruntu), recorded by Anne Scrimgeour, 5 August 1993, author's collection.
37 Thomas (Pitpit), recorded by Anne Scrimgeour, 21 September 1992, AIATSIS collection, soundfile 'Pitpit Talking to Kids'. *Ngarnka*, or *Ngarnkawaru* (bearded one), along with *Mirta* (old man), were names used by *marrngu* to refer to McLeod.

all they can do is try and frighten us, tell lies about us and put us in gaol'. McLeod also told *marrngu* that, as their labour was essential to an important industry, striking could be an effective way to address their situation. It was not illegal for them to take strike action, he said. 'I remember Clancy telling me', McPhee said, '"Striking is the only way, we don't want to be treated like dogs anymore"'.[38]

Although he played down his role in instigating the strike, McLeod clearly took an active role in sowing the seeds of the strike idea. Among a disempowered Aboriginal population seeking a way 'to help ourself', his ideas found fertile soil. Ideas discussed at Bonney Downs and around Nullagine between McLeod, his *Milangka* co-workers and Clancy McKenna during 1944 were raised by *marrngu* at a number of large meetings at Nullagine, Moolyella and Marble Bar. Kitchener was active in 'spreading the word about better things to come'.[39] Secular meetings held in conjunction with religious ceremonies and Law gatherings provided opportunities for discussion to take place.

As well as talking to *marrngu* about their conditions and possible means for addressing their disadvantage, McLeod was politically active on a number of other fronts at this time. Late in 1943, he stood as the Progressive Labor candidate for the state seat of Pilbara, losing the election on 20 November 1943 to the Labor candidate, Bill Hegney.[40] He was also corresponding with people outside the Pilbara who were interested in Aboriginal issues, and beginning to inform a network of campaigners about his activities. In March 1944, he urged the Anti-Fascist League to affiliate with the Communist Party which, he said, was 'the only People's Party in this State today who constantly and actively champions the people's cause vigorously and aggressively', and by July he was writing to Ernie Thornton, national secretary of the Federated Ironworker's Association, describing himself as 'a Party member undisclosed'.[41] McLeod also corresponded with Mary Durack, who wrote to him in October 1944, 'I am very interested in all you have to say of your struggle for the half castes etc in your district'. Durack passed some of his information on 'to those down here who are interesting themselves in the

---

38 Quoted in Morgan, *Wanamurraganya*, p. 162.
39 Shane Ostenfeld, 'The Pilbara Dispute', BA (Honours) Thesis, University of Sydney, 1991, p. 27. Ostenfeld cites Dooley Binbin et al., 'History of the '46 Strike', as told to John Wilson by Dooley and the men of Pilgangoora, p. 3, as his source for this.
40 *West Australian*, 22 October 1943, p. 1; McLeod, draft autobiography, chapter 2, pp. 15–18, Marchant Trust Collection, UWA MS118 series 1 file 8.
41 McLeod, letter to the editor, *Fremantle Districts Sentinel*, 4 May 1944, p. 2; second quotation cited in Hess, 'Black and Red', p. 69.

question'.⁴² Through Durack, he was put in touch with A. P. Elkin, Professor of Anthropology at Sydney University, with whom he began an energetic correspondence from August 1944.⁴³

He was probably also writing to author and Communist Party member Katharine Susannah Prichard at this time. Joan Williams remembered that, for some time prior to 1946, McLeod had 'been writing voluminous letters in his terrible scrawl to Katharine Susannah Prichard, debating the way forward for Aborigines' and 'seeking advice, and Katharine brought those letters and discussed them with Graham Alcorn, in particular'.⁴⁴ Alcorn was editor of the communist newspaper the *Workers' Star* and took on the Aboriginal portfolio within the state branch of the ACP. These Communist Party connections were to become vital during the early months of the strike. Information on McLeod's activities was already spreading outside Western Australia. Valentine Leeper, of the Victorian Aboriginal Group, questioned Bray about the government preventing McLeod from leasing land 'for the benefit of natives'.⁴⁵ McLeod was also distributing literature from the Progressive Bookshop.⁴⁶ Although he claimed to have become involved in the strike movement under duress, it is clear that he was politically engaged and active in establishing political connections.

By August 1944, McLeod was writing to A. P. Elkin of a scheme for 1500 Pilbara Aboriginal people to acquire 5 million acres of pastoral lease country on which to establish their independence, progressively absorbing further people from the desert. 'The natives in this district are organising themselves', he wrote:

> and discussing the best methods of struggle to achieve their rights. Their ultimate aim is to secure a block of ground (they have some 5,000,000 acres in view) on which and a few smaller blocks they can maintain themselves entirely by agriculture (irrigation) and grazing. They hope to be able to have their people educated in their own language and in

---

42   Mary Miller [Durack] to McLeod, 2 October 1944, McLeod ASIO file, vol. 2, NAA A6119, 3306, p.1

43   McLeod to Elkin, 21 August 1944, A. P. Elkin Papers, University of Sydney Archives, box 71, folder 189.

44   Joan Williams, writing as Justina Williams, *Anger and Love*, p. 127; Joan Williams, interviewed by Susan Hartley, interviews with members of the WA Communist Party, 1997, SLWA OH3989.

45   Leeper to Bray, 27 March 1944, SROWA 1944/0394/1.

46   Section Officer C to Senior Section Officer B, 14 May 1959, McLeod ASIO file, vol. 2, NAA A6119, 3306, p. 69.

English have their own people trained as Doctors teachers and scientists and to control their own affairs without interference from outside and gradually to absorb the bush man (their block abuts on to wild country) and together raise their living standards until they can reach equality with all comers. They realise that this task is a big one especially as it seems that not only will they have to depend on their own efforts but that all sorts of difficulties will be put in their way by vested interests through the gov[ernment]. However they maintain that it is better to go down in struggle than to be exterminated by disease neglect and exploitation. Of course they do not speak in this language they merely say they have been held too low too long.[47]

Corresponding closely with the platform of the Communist Party of Australia, this was a scheme McLeod had been discussing, he told Elkin, 'with the more intelligent natives' for over twelve months.[48] As a beginning, he applied in October 1944 under the Western Australian *Mining Act 1904* for a 'Miners Homestead Lease', to be known as 'D-Day', about ten kilometres south of Nullagine, to serve as a training ground.[49] 'We hope to grow vegetable and fruit and poultry and eggs etc.', he told Elkin, to experiment with tropical agriculture and irrigation, 'and to finally build up a reserve of food so that at the appointed time the whole fifteen hundred will come over and set down for at least six months'.[50] Although the D-Day scheme did not proceed, McLeod continued to seek suitable land to serve as a base for what he called 'my experiment', 'the programme I have laid out' and also 'the scheme I have put up for advancement of our native peoples or more properly to the scheme to which they themselves look for real advancement'.[51]

McLeod's scheme 'for advancement of our native people' overlapped a vision of the Pilbara transformed through intensive agriculture. The Pilbara's environment, as well as its people, was being exploited by a powerful few, he believed. The wealth created by the pastoral industry was lost to the region, spent in the south by wealthy pastoralists instead of being reinvested in

---

47 McLeod to Elkin, 21 August 1944, A. P. Elkin Papers, University of Sydney Archives, box 71, folder 189.
48 McLeod to Elkin, 18 October 1944, A. P. Elkin Papers, University of Sydney Archives, box 71, folder 189.
49 *Northern Times*, 13 October 1944, p. 2.
50 McLeod to Elkin, 18 October 1944, A. P. Elkin Papers, University of Sydney Archives, box 71, folder 189.
51 McLeod to Elkin, 20 October and 10 November 1944, A. P. Elkin Papers, University of Sydney Archives, box 76, file 262 and box 71, file 189.

developing and regenerating the district. The result of this exploitation was the impoverishment and destruction of the Aboriginal people who provided pastoral labour, and the impoverishment and destruction of the land through overstocking. In an article published in the *Workers' Star* in June 1945 entitled 'How Private Enterprise Has Stifled the North West', he called for government funding to develop the region's resources to their full potential. With its rich deposits of silver lead, iron ore, copper and asbestos, several hundred square miles of auriferous country, untouched fishing grounds, and a rise and fall tide from twenty-five to thirty feet offering a potential source of power, he believed the area could support a population of half a million people if its resources were fully developed. During 1945, the Nullagine Progress Association provided a forum for his ideas, and he looked forward to the planned formation of a broad-based organisation to formulate strategies for post-war development of the region. He hoped that this organisation would enable some of his ideas to be put into place, including the setting up of a Regional Development Council to investigate possibilities for future productivity, build roads, open up mineral deposits and plan new modern towns. His vision of a populated, prosperous and productive North West went hand in hand with his vision for the emancipation of Aboriginal people, and was one he continued to hold before him throughout his involvement in the strike movement.

Although granted a provisional permit to employ three men on Bonney Downs, McLeod appealed against the Department's decision that he was 'not a fit and proper person' to employ Aboriginal people. His appeal was heard in November 1944 by magistrate and government medical officer Dr Harold Dicks, who found in his favour,[52] and the Department had no choice but to grant him a general permit, which was issued in January 1945.[53] Bray blamed the outcome of McLeod's appeal on a lack of support from pastoralists for the Department's attempt to curtail his activities. He wrote that at that time, 'the Department was alone in its objections to McLeod'.[54]

The general permit to employ Aboriginal people enabled McLeod to associate more freely and travel about with *marrngu* during 1945. He was, nevertheless, still prevented by section 39 of the *Native Administration Act* from visiting Aboriginal camps or speaking with groups. One way to overcome this difficulty was to obtain a departmental appointment as a Protector of

---

52   Clerk of Courts, Marble Bar, to Bray, 7 November 1944, SROWA 1944/0162/24.
53   Bray to Commissioner of Police, 24 November 1944, SROWA 1944/0162/25.
54   Bray to O'Neill, 22 August 1945, SROWA 1945/0800/25.

Natives. He and McKenna made plans to discuss the strike idea with *marrngu* when they gathered in Port Hedland for the annual race meeting in July 1945, and to suggest that a request be made to the Department for McLeod to be appointed a Protector.[55] At a ceremonial Law meeting at Marble Bar early in 1945, McKenna spoke of his discussions with McLeod and told everyone present to spread the word that McLeod wanted to hold a meeting at the Port Hedland Four Mile camp during the race weekend.[56] When McKenna met with McLeod prior to the races to let him know that arrangements were in place for a meeting, McLeod suggested that a delegation of *marrngu* approach him to formally request his attendance.[57]

On the Monday of the race weekend, 23 July 1945, while most people in Port Hedland gathered for the second day of horse races, a deputation of six men, including McKenna, Roy Mackay, Tommy from Nullagine and Ronnie Captain from Mundabullangana Station, approached McLeod as suggested, and asked him to accompany them to a meeting.[58] In claiming that his attendance at the meeting at the invitation of this deputation was his point of entry into the movement, McLeod sought to protect himself from prosecution for breaches of sections of the *Native Administration Act*, and also to legitimise his request for recognition as the chosen representative of Aboriginal people. He feigned surprise at the invitation. 'As a matter of fact', he wrote to Commissioner Bray, 'I was greatly intrigued that I should be picked out by these people to watch over their interests for it is not uncomplimentary to me as you will agree'.[59]

McLeod met with a group of *marrngu* men that morning, and they discussed plans for organising a strike for the following year. Plans for a scheme to acquire land to establish their own pastoral and agricultural enterprises were also discussed. Leaders were selected to organise the strike. According to John Wilson, McKenna, Kitchener and Mick from Pippingarra nominated themselves for the committee, and Ronnie Captain, Teddy Allen from De Grey and Tommy Clarke from Mulyie were chosen. Yarrie Jack Coppin (Ngarlkapangu) was appointed to represent Warrawagine, and two other

---

55 McKenna, High Court appeal, D. W. McLeod v. G. R. Richards, NAA A10074 1946/8, 9, 10, p. 24.
56 Katrin Wilson, 'The Allocation of Sex Roles', p. 49.
57 McKenna, High Court appeal, D. W. McLeod v. G. R. Richards, NAA A10074 1946/8, 9, 10 p. 24.
58 McLeod, High Court appeal, D. W. McLeod v. G. R. Richards, NAA A10074 1946/8, 9, 10 p. 42.
59 McLeod to Bray, 23 July 1945, p. 2, SROWA 1945/0800/2.

men, Rory McPhee and Tommy of Eginbah Station, were self-nominated.[60] Another account identifies Sam Mitchell, Teddy Allen, Tommy Clarke, McKenna, and Tommy and Jimmy Woodman as leaders selected at this time. It was decided that these ideas should be further discussed at a larger meeting that afternoon.

Following these discussions, McLeod returned to town and asked Constable Fletcher, as Protector of Natives, to accompany him to the meeting at the Four Mile. While the ostensible reason for this request was to legalise McLeod's attendance at the meeting under the *Native Administration Act*, it was also a strategic move on McLeod's part. It ensured that a government official was present when Aboriginal people at the meeting indicated their wish for McLeod to represent them and act as their spokesman. McLeod told Fletcher that *marrngu* had formulated a scheme to start a self-supporting settlement of their own and had asked him to handle their affairs.

Fletcher was unable to attend that day, but agreed to be present at a meeting the following day. McLeod returned to the Four Mile and spoke at a gathering of people there. He then wrote to Commissioner Bray, informing him that he had learned at the meeting that:

> at a discussion the previous evening it had unanomously [*sic*] been decided to ask me to act as an inspector to look after the conditions of their employment and so on.
>
> I explained that the matter of appointing inspectors was a job for your dept. [and] they agreed that this was so but that they felt they were entitled to have some say in this matter for they felt that their treatment at times left much to be desired and they had no one in whom they could trust to place their troubles and if I would take the job they would know that when need arose I could be depended on to support them and explain their privileges to them and watch over their interests generally.[61]

The following morning, Tuesday 24 July, as racegoers began leaving Port Hedland for their stations and mining camps, *marrngu* workers remained at the Four Mile instead of returning by train to their stations that day as expected.[62] Fletcher arrived at the Four Mile prior to the arranged meeting

---

60 John Wilson, 'Authority and Leadership', p. 50.
61 McLeod to Bray, 23 July 1945, SROWA 1945/0800/1–2.
62 Fletcher to Bray, 10 August 1945, p. 4, SROWA 1945/0800/16; Greene to Hegney, 7 August 1945, SROWA 1945/0800/10.

time to discuss matters with *marrngu* before McLeod's arrival. The meeting got underway without McLeod, and Fletcher 'questioned the natives regarding their scheme'. McKenna told him of their idea:

> to start a settlement on some country of which McLeod knew near Nullagine, to produce poultry eggs and fresh vegetables for sale to the Blue Speck [*sic*] mine, this settlement to provide a home for indigent natives, and furnish them with an independent means of livelihood. McLeod was to be superintendent, of course, with all the administrative and financial responsibility.[63]

'Of course', Fletcher wrote, 'I realized that this scheme had never emanated from any native, and that McLeod had engineered the whole thing, with Clancy as his field officer among the natives'. He urged those present to deal with the Department and not McLeod, but McKenna insisted that McLeod 'was a man who had always helped the natives and he was their choice. They felt better at having someone of their own selection to act on their behalf'.[64]

No mention was made of the planned strike in Fletcher's presence, with discussion that day focused solely on plans for acquiring land and establishing an independent Aboriginal settlement. One idea discussed at that time was that of renting crown land at Horse Creek, south of Skull Springs on the Davis River, and mustering 'cleanskin' cattle there to form the basis of their own pastoral enterprise. When McLeod arrived, he joined in the discussion, painting, Fletcher wrote, 'a beautiful picture of the future through intense agriculture etc and the independence of the natives with their own town complete with schools and other social services'.[65] In reply to Fletcher's argument that a settlement in the Nullagine area would not suit Port Hedland or coastal people, McLeod suggested that one of the recently abandoned stations on the Turner River could be taken up and re-established by *marrngu*. He suggested that Abydos Station, which had a nice homestead near a permanent pool of water, would be ideal. Fletcher wrote to Bray that the 'question of finance was brushed aside by copious discourse on rehabilitation schemes etc and unlimited assistance from the Government'.[66]

---

63   Fletcher to Bray, 10 August 1945, pp. 1–2, SROWA 1945/0800/13–14.
64   Fletcher to Bray, 10 August 1945, p. 2, SROWA 1945/0800/14.
65   Fletcher to Bray, 10 August 1945, pp. 2–3, SROWA 1945/0800/14–15.
66   Fletcher to Bray, 10 August 1945, p. 3, SROWA 1945/0800/15.

While McLeod and McKenna were the main speakers, Roy Mackay and Kitchener were vocal in expressing enthusiasm for the scheme.[67] A skilled station hand who worked at Mundabullangana Station, Roy Mackay had not previously met McLeod. Although Fletcher advised *marrngu* to hold on to their money, McKenna took a collection as the beginning of a fund towards their settlement scheme, and £14/6/3 was obtained. Fletcher 'remonstrated with them for being misled' by someone like McLeod.[68] He reported that he regarded McLeod 'as a dangerous man among the natives'.[69]

McLeod reported on the Four Mile meeting in a letter to Bray, asking for Abydos Station to be made available as a settlement for Aboriginal people dislocated by the closure of stations, 'it being understood that I would superintend this work and help establish their permanent establishment'. He presented it as a scheme that originated from *marrngu*, writing that he was 'favourably impressed with the proposition' and was 'inclined to consider favourably a proposition put up by your dept along these lines'.[70]

It was a risky step for McLeod to take to draw the Department's attention to himself in this way and to seek official sanction for his involvement with Aboriginal people, particularly given that he had acted illegally in holding discussions with *marrngu* prior to the meeting with Fletcher. Although the Department rejected out of hand his request for appointment as a Protector, Fletcher's attendance at the Four Mile meeting was an informal recognition of his role, enabling the strike movement to gain a foothold. Two years later, the Acting Commissioner of Native Affairs described Fletcher's attendance at the meeting as a 'major blunder'.[71]

In the weeks following the race-time meeting, pastoralists expressed alarm at reports they were hearing from their workers about a proposed strike that was to take place the following May unless wages of £3 a week were paid. The local branch of the Pastoralists Association urged its head office in Perth to take action on the matter, and Fletcher began making inquiries among station workers about the truth of the rumours.[72] Pastoralists accused McLeod of causing unrest, and urged the Commissioner and the local Member of Parliament, Bill Hegney, to take action. 'That Communist Chap, McLeod, has been trying to stir up trouble among station natives',

---

67   Fletcher to Bray, 10 August 1945, p. 3, SROWA 1945/0800/15.
68   Fletcher to Bray, 10 August 1945, p. 4, SROWA 1945/0800/16.
69   Fletcher to Bray, 10 August 1945, p. 6, SROWA 1945/0800/17.
70   McLeod to Bray, 24 July 1945, p. 3, SROWA 1945/0800/6.
71   McBeath to Ross McDonald, 9 April 1947, p. 1, SROWA 1947/0305/82.
72   Fletcher to Bray, 10 August 1945, p. 5, SROWA 1945/0800/17.

Harry Greene of Talga Talga Station, who was chairman of the Marble Bar Road Board, wrote. 'Although he is discredited by most white Residents he can easily cause a deal of descension [sic] amongst the natives'.[73]

There were verbal altercations between McLeod and pastoralists. McLeod complained to Bray that Greene had made 'very heated and blustering' accusations that he was inciting natives to refuse employment. Greene had warned him that he would rue his actions, he wrote. Feigning ignorance of the proposed strike, he told Bray that he had approached Fletcher 'to see if he could enlighten me on the matter' and had been told that workers on one of the stations refused to work until they received higher wages. McLeod denied giving any such instructions, arguing that it would have been poor policy to do so, as he was trying to get the proposal to establish a settlement underway.[74]

Some *marrngu* were eager to begin strike action immediately. At Warralong Station, just after the race week meetings, *marrngu* refused to work unless higher wages were paid.[75] McLeod, however, cautioned against premature action.[76] They first needed to organise themselves, he said, and should act only when all workers were prepared to make a united stand. He advised *marrngu* to focus on obtaining their own land as an economic base before conducting a strike; according to McKenna, he said that 'when they had built the place up they would have a strike and be independent'.[77] He also insisted that it was important not to strike while the war was on. Not only was there an increased threat of prosecution under Australia's wartime emergency regulations if they took action during the war, but they could prejudice their cause if they withdrew their labour from an industry that was essential to the war effort.[78] McLeod also needed time to organise support in the south, which was to be vital to the success of the strike.

The end of the war was close at hand, however. Two weeks after the Four Mile meeting, Hiroshima was bombed. On the same day, Bray wrote to McLeod, rejecting his offer to act as honorary inspector and to develop Abydos Station as an Aboriginal settlement.[79]

---

73 Greene to Hegney, 7 August 1945, SROWA 1945/0800/10.
74 McLeod to Bray, 26 July 1945, p. 1, SROWA 1945/0800/7.
75 McLeod, High Court appeal, D. W. McLeod v. G. R. Richards, NAA A10074 1946/8, 9, 10, p. 43.
76 Kitchener, High Court appeal, D. W. McLeod v. G. R. Richards, NAA A10074 1946/8, 9, 10, p. 30.
77 *West Australian*, 21 June 1946, p. 6.
78 John Wilson, 'Authority and Leadership', p. 41.
79 Bray to McLeod, 6 August 1945, SROWA 1945/0800/10.

Immediately following the race weekend, McLeod flew to the tiny abandoned copper mining town of Whim Creek, 120 kilometres south-east of Port Hedland, to attend a large meeting organised to formulate plans to develop the North West and stimulate its recovery from seven years of drought and wartime conditions. The purpose of the Whim Creek convention, attended by politicians and a large number of people from a wide area of the North West, was to establish an organisation that could represent regional interests and present a united front to government to ensure that the region was not overlooked in Australia's post-war development. McLeod looked forward to the establishment of a new broad-based organisation that would bring about radical change, wresting economic control from the hands of the squattocracy to enable the implementation of progressive ideas for the regeneration of the Pilbara. He saw himself as vitally involved in this process. For some time, he had worked with the Nullagine Progress Association to formulate proposals, including the establishment of Regional Development Councils, to present to the meeting.

He was given no opportunity to do so, however. While the convention was attended by a broad cross-section of the community, pastoralists dominated its agenda through the appointment of Harry Greene of Talga Talga Station as chairman, and proposals and motions that were not in accordance with pastoral interests were ignored. The North-West and Kimberley Advancement Association which was established at the Whim Creek meeting had a strong pastoralist bias. In the following months, branches were set up in regional centres from Carnarvon through to Wyndham, with Harry Greene, who was no friend of McLeod's, elected president of the central executive. 'We never got a chance', McLeod said.[80]

Hoping still to be able to influence the organisation at a local level, McLeod attempted to form a branch at Marble Bar, and invited all local organisations to a convention there on 22 and 23 September 1945 to discuss the outcome of the conference, and to make further plans for the area's development.[81] The Port Hedland Euralian Association, invited to represent the interests of coloured people, declined to attend. The reason for this is unclear. Laurie O'Neill of the Department of Native Affairs wrote with some satisfaction that 'although they were at one time supporters of McLeod, Father Bryan informs me that they are now definitely against him so much so that they

---

80 McLeod, draft autobiography, chapter 3, p. 8, Marchant Trust Collection, UWA MS118 series 1 file 13.
81 *West Australian*, 5 September 1945, p. 4.

refused his invitation to attend his proposed convention at Marble Bar as delegates representing the coloured population'.[82]

If the Euralian Association really was 'definitely against' McLeod, as O'Neill believed, there had been a falling out in the previous six months, for in March 1945 Pop Clarke been writing to McLeod as a friend. 'Don we know you are working side by side with us', he wrote. As well as expressing his reservations at the benefits to be gained for Aboriginal people from Western Australia's new Citizenship Rights Bill, Clarke had written about the significant improvements being instituted for Aboriginal workers by the new management at Indee Station, where his son Vince had been working.[83] Plans for a general strike that would impact progressive managers such as the McWhirters at Indee may have led the Euralians to distance themselves from McLeod's activism. Certainly, their pro-pastoralist priest, Father Bryan, believed that Aboriginal station workers had more to lose than to gain from strike action and was active in working to convince his coloured parishioners that McLeod's methods were dangerously communistic and antithetical to their genuine advancement.

The Marble Bar convention was attended by representatives of the local road board, the Nullagine Road Board, Comet Gold Mines Ltd, the Comet Gold Mines branch of the AWU, the Pastoralists Association, the Marble Bar and Nullagine branches of the Country Women's Association and the Nullagine Progress Association, but if McLeod hoped to establish a local broad-based organisation to undertake development projects that did not necessarily coincide with the pastoral interests, he was quickly disillusioned. With pastoralists suspicious of his motives and anxious to prevent him using such an organisation as a vehicle for his activities, the meeting moved immediately to block him. A motion raised at the meeting proposed that:

> any suggestions for the advancement of the North-West ... should be submitted to the committee of the North-West Advancement Association for its consideration, and that any effort by any person or organisation not made through the committee would not have the support of the represented organisations.

McLeod attempted unsuccessfully to oppose the motion, and was effectively silenced.[84] Although he later claimed that his role in the formation of the

---

82 O'Neill to Bray, 5 November 1945, p. 4, SROWA 1945/0800/35.
83 L. W. Clarke to McLeod, 21 March 1945, A. P. Elkin Papers, University of Sydney Archives, box 76, file 262.
84 *West Australian*, 24 September 1945, p. 4.

Association had 'established his standing in the community', O'Neill wrote that he had 'no standing in the community but has a small following among poor class whites'.[85] Far from becoming a vehicle for achieving the regeneration of the north that McLeod envisaged, the Association became a conservative voice of the North West establishment, calling for taxation relief for pastoralists and businesses in the north and for improved conditions for the settler community, including the exclusion of Aboriginal children from mainstream schools.[86] A year after its establishment, it called on the Western Australian Government to take action to oppose the strike.[87]

If *walypila* interest in McLeod's ideas for regenerating the Pilbara was quickly extinguished by a pastoral elite concerned to protect its own interests, his ideas took hold among a powerless and disaffected Aboriginal population. In the months following the Four Mile meetings, the ideas discussed at the race-time meeting spread around the scattered Pilbara stations. While McLeod returned to Bonney Downs Station, *marrngu* organisers travelled throughout the region, collecting funds towards acquiring a station property and discussing the strike idea with station communities.[88] Ron Captain and McKenna travelled around the Port Hedland area, 'moving about from place to place', Fletcher wrote, 'and keeping the natives down this end in more or less a ferment'.[89] Ron Captain was, like McKenna, clearly dissatisfied with conditions of pastoral employment for Aboriginal people. The previous year he had threatened to leave his job on Munda Station and take other Aboriginal workers with him. Native Affairs Inspector Laurie O'Neill had warned him against such action, telling him he was free to leave if he wished, but that he must not interfere with others. Captain had left the station.[90]

Dougal Cornish, a large man possibly of Afghan descent who was also known as Big Dougal, may also have been involved in collecting funds and spreading the word in the Marble Bar area. His job as a truck driver for A. J. Thompson in Marble Bar took him to many of the stations in the region, providing the opportunity to discuss the plan with *marrngu* communities in that area, while Kitchener collected funds further south in the Nullagine area.[91]

---

85 McLeod, interviewed by Clements, SLWA OH4005/3; O'Neill to Bray, 5 November 1945, SROWA 1945/0800/33.
86 *Northern Times*, 17 October 1947, p. 5.
87 'Advancement Assn' to Bray, telegram, 6 May 1946, SROWA 1945/0800/63.
88 Fletcher to Bray, 15 October 1945, p. 1, SROWA 1945/0800/26.
89 Fletcher to Bray, 15 October 1945, p. 2, SROWA 1945/0800/27.
90 O'Neill to Bray, 5 November 1945, p. 2, SROWA 1945/0800/33.
91 Fletcher to Bray, 15 October 1945, p. 2, SROWA 1945/0800/27.

Fletcher attempted to counter the influence of McKenna and Captain in his police district, patrolling the stations and 'firmly convincing' *marrngu*, he wrote, 'that a strike was not a good idea.' But, he added, I 'found that when I returned to the same station some time later, one of these men had been around and talked them over again to their way of thinking'. To prevent the strike idea achieving greater momentum, he urged the Department to take firm action, recommending that the four men be removed from the district under ministerial warrant.[92] The Department's power to remove Aboriginal people to an institution in another part of the state for an indefinite period was an effective weapon in preventing Aboriginal people from reacting against restrictive government policies and settler practices. Repeated calls for strike leaders to be removed from the district under section 12 of the *Native Administration Act 1936* would be made by pastoralists, police and DNA officers during the course of the strike.

Commissioner Bray instructed Native Affairs Inspector Laurie O'Neill to carry out a tour of the region to assess the situation.[93] O'Neill, who was again working as Travelling Inspector for the northern region of Western Australia after two years in the military, was less concerned than Fletcher. He had a poor estimation of the capacity of Aboriginal people to organise coordinated action such as a strike and had faith in the strength and effectiveness of the mechanisms of settler control. As a Kimberley policeman in the 1930s, he had told author Ion Idriess that Kimberley settlers could be grateful 'that the abos lack co-operation because of their tribal intrigues and jealousies ... Otherwise no white men could live in this country'.[94] It was unlikely that *marrngu* would be capable of coordinating strike action over a wide area, he thought, and he advised against removing the agitators, believing that this could exacerbate the situation by playing into McLeod's hands. 'There is no doubt that a strike at that time would be a serious blow to the pastoralists', he wrote, but he was 'convinced that there is not sufficient organization amongst the natives for them to act simultaneously'.[95] Given this belief, he found McLeod's activities laughable rather than dangerous, and considered him 'a well meaning crank'.[96]

---

92 Fletcher to Bray, 15 October 1945, p. 4, SROWA 1945/0800/29.
93 Bray to O'Neill, 22 August 1945, SROWA 1945/0800/25.
94 Quoted in Ion Idriess, *Over the Range: Sunshine and Shadow in the Kimberleys*, Angus and Robertson, Sydney, 1937, p. 22.
95 O'Neill to Bray, 5 November 1945, p. 2, SROWA 1945/0800/33.
96 O'Neill to Bray, 26 May 1946, p. 1, SROWA 1945/0800/143.

'McLeod Gave Us Hint and We Took It Up'

The belief that Aboriginal people lacked organisational capacity severely affected the ability of pastoralists, police and the Department to respond effectively to rumours of a strike, and to the strike itself. Yet arranging events involving participants from a widespread area was routine for *marrngu*. Some time prior to becoming involved in the strike movement, Clancy McKenna (Warntupungkarna), for example, had been responsible for arranging the initiation of his young classificatory brother Ginger Bob (Palyakulayi). As with the organisation of the strike, McKenna made initial arrangements for Ginger Bob's initiation in Port Hedland during race week. Following the races, he and Ginger took the train to Carlindi Station. 'He let everyone know at De Grey, Mulyie and Warralong Stations', Ginger said:

> He sent a telegram to let everyone know at Marble Bar, Moolyella and Nullagine. He let all my *karnku*[97] relations know. And the next morning he and two others took me to the west. They took me to Tabba Tabba Station, but there was hardly anybody there, and we only got two or three people. From there we went to Strelley, but there were no *marrngu* there and we went on. We arrived at De Grey Station where Nyamal and Southern Ngarla people were living, but they were all very busy working and we didn't get anybody. So my boss [Clancy] said, 'We'll go on to Mulyie Station'. He took me there and we stayed with Nyamal people there. We could understand the Nyamal mob when they spoke, he knew Nyamal and he knew those people. We stayed in the camp there, and in the morning went north to Pardoo Station where we got a few people and took them back to Mulyie. The next morning he said, 'That's that; let's go on to Warralong Station'. Two of the Mulyie people joined us. We waited at Warralong for Kangku [Peter Coppin], and some others. Warralong people already knew what was happening and were ready for our arrival. 'Here they come now', they said. 'Sure enough, this is what the message was about'. We spent one night there, and in the morning we went east to Kurlumpurrnya, or Coongan Station, which is the other name for Kurlumpurrnya. There was no-one there so we continued on eastwards to Eginbah Station, where one of my other brothers arrived to take me on to Yarrie. From there we went to Moolyella, but there was no-one there. The people from Nullagine and the stations were

---

97 *Karnku*: people of the initiate's parents' generation representing two of the four skin groupings, as a generational moiety.

already camped at Yukurlukurlunya, near Marble Bar, waiting for us at the ceremonial ground there. A lot of people were there.[98]

This was a part of the cultural and social life of Pilbara Aboriginal people that was invisible to *walypila* – even, and perhaps especially, to men like Laurie O'Neill, with a reputation for 'knowing the natives'. *Walypila*, who knew Aboriginal people only as workers or as the dependent recipients of station rations, were simply unaware of the network of social and family relationships, and practices developed in the maintenance of a continuing religious and cultural life, which *marrngu* would draw on to organise the strike. 'We had always said that they could never be conscripted or got together in a crowd', pastoralist Edith Miller said, 'but there we are, we were wrong, they were'.[99]

Despite concerns that a strike could significantly damage the pastoral industry, squatters were sufficiently complacent to feel that no concerted action was needed to forestall industrial action, beyond calling for McLeod to be prosecuted. Most were confident that the mechanisms in place to ensure Aboriginal compliance with settler control could be called into play to effectively prevent a strike. Not everyone was so complacent, however. Reg Sherlock, manager of Strelley Station near Port Hedland, urged the chairman of the local branch of the Pastoralists Association to hold a meeting to formulate a response, but the chairman thought this unnecessary. When the strike did take place, Sherlock wrote, 'We have ourselves to blame for not having got together during the last ten months, for we were forewarned ... I'm apparently the only one who was convinced that the natives meant business'.[100]

The natives did mean business. Widely discussed by Aboriginal people in Pilbara station and mining communities during the second half of 1945, the ideas raised at the Four Mile meeting were taken up for further discussion at a number of meetings held during *pingkayi* time in the summer of 1945–46. Whether these talks focused mainly on the plan to work together to buy their own land or whether the strike idea was the principal topic of discussion is not clear. The two ideas seemed to go hand in hand, however. Certainly, strike plans took shape during this period, with a strike date set now set, on McLeod's suggestion, for 1 May 1946, May Day. Discussions no doubt included intense debate, as some *marrngu* were opposed to the strike and

---

98   Ginger Bob (Palyakulayi), recorded by Anne Scrimgeour, 12 December 1993, AIATSIS collection, soundfile 'Palyakulayi 18'
99   Edith Miller, interviewed by Jamieson, 1982, transcript, p. 108, SLWA OH506.
100 Reg Sherlock to Kitty, 15 May 1946, Sherlock family personal collection.

never took part in the action. For others, the idea must have aroused great anxiety; it was no small thing to challenge settler authority in this way. A meeting held at the Nullagine One Mile reserve just before Christmas 1945, where people had gathered for initiation ceremonies, seems to have been important in the decision to go ahead with the strike. McLeod was invited to speak.[101] It was probably at this meeting that McKenna introduced McLeod to Dooley, a Nyangumarta man also known as Winyirin or Yurlpuly, who had spent his early years in the desert. Dooley had not been involved in the movement up to this time and had not been present at the race-time meetings, but was sent to Nullagine from Marble Bar by *marrngu* to find out what was going on. McLeod, thinking in union terms, saw him as a delegate. After the Nullagine meeting, Dooley joined McLeod at Bonney Downs. He was to become a key organiser in the weeks leading up to the strike and a principal leader of the strike.

It seems likely that one of the events at which the strike idea was discussed at this time was the Law meeting that McLeod was invited to attend on the Davis River at Wantilurr, or Skull Springs. Despite its name, Skull Springs is a beautiful, wooded area of waterholes shaded by papery-barked cajuput trees, an oasis in the spinifex. McLeod was in the area at the time, working with three Aboriginal men, cutting cajuput wood for the Blue Spec mine. *Marrngu* accounts of the Skull Springs meeting describe it as the culmination of a long period of discussion between McLeod and his *marrngu* co-workers on Bonney Downs. McLeod was working on the construction of a windmill at Nullagine in October 1944, and when this was complete, Billy Thomas (Pitpit) said, the men continued discussing the strike for a long time, at Deep Well and at Wallareenya, Bonney Downs and Noreena Downs, before eventually taking the matter to a meeting at Skull Springs.[102]

Accounts given by McLeod also suggest that the meeting took place in late 1945. He had a permit to employ Aboriginal people during 1945 and was waiting for parts for his boring plant when he went to Skull Springs with three men. 'I couldn't get parts', he said, 'the war wasn't long finished'.[103] When the boring plant broke down, he worked at repairing mills, with Dooley helping him. He also spoke of the Skull Springs meeting taking place about the time of the formation of the North-West and Kimberley Advancement

---

101   Jackson, High Court appeal, D. W. McLeod v. G. R. Richards, NAA A10074 1946/8, 9, 10, p. 32.
102   Stan J. Wightman, police report, 17 October 1944, SROWA 1944/0162/20–22; *Mikurrunya*, Strelley community newsletter, vol. 18, no. 1, May 1996, p. 5.
103   McLeod, interviewed by Carlton, 1996, transcript, p. 10, SLWA OH2739.

Association, and of his relationship with Thora Gallop, of Bonney Downs Station, following the death of her husband in March 1945. After talking of Skull Springs, McLeod said that:

> When I came back in 1942 I had a girl, a part-owner of Bonney Downs as my secretary so I had an introduction to the squatters, and they found it hard to accept. [*laughs*] Well you never heard so much squawking in all – bloody hell you wouldn't believe it. Oh bloody awful.[104]

Native Affairs Inspector O'Neill wrote in November 1945 of a 'persistent rumour' that McLeod would marry Thora Gallop, and thought it would be 'interesting to note the reactions of McLeod when he becomes a Pastoralist himself'.[105] *Marrngu* also remembered McLeod's relationship with Thora Gallop as something more than a friendship, saying that he could have become a pastoralist.[106] McLeod's linking of the Skull Springs meeting with his relationship with Thora Gallop lends weight to my suggestion that it took place at the end of 1945. This later timing is also more consistent with McLeod's claim that Dooley was nominated as an organiser by the Lawmen at Skull Springs.

The apparent contradiction between evidence of McLeod's activism and *marrngu* claims that they urged him to support them in the strike can be explained by the fact that the impetus for strike action became *marrngu*-driven in the wake of the Four Mile meetings. As McKenna said in a court statement, 'McLeod gave us hint about the strike and we took it up'.[107] While McLeod had been active in creating the spark of the strike movement, urging *marrngu* to consider strike action as a means of gaining greater control over their lives, *marrngu* had taken the spark of his ideas to set the spinifex alight. Taken up, discussed and spread throughout the *marrngu* community, the strike idea had become their own. 'I told McLeod all boys were going on strike', Dooley said. 'All boys talk about strike since Hedland races'.[108]

Before risking arrest, imprisonment and exile by taking strike action, *marrngu* needed to be sure that McLeod's word could be trusted, and that he was willing to provide the necessary advice and assistance. At Christmas

---

104 McLeod, interviewed by Carlton, 1996, transcript, p. 11, SLWA OH2739.
105 O'Neill to Bray, 5 November 1945, SROWA 1945/0800/33–35.
106 John and Katrin Wilson, interviewed by the author, 13 November 2014.
107 McKenna, High Court appeal, D. W. McLeod v. G. R. Richards, NAA A10074 1946/8, 9, 10, p. 28.
108 Dooley (Dooley Binbin) (Winyirin or Yurlpuly), High Court appeal, D. W. McLeod v. G. R. Richards, NAA A10074 1946/8, 9, 10, p. 23.

1945, they asked him if he was still willing to take on the role of Protector.[109] Before committing himself to involvement, McLeod needed to be sure that *marrngu* had the necessary numbers and determination for a strike to succeed. In an account of the strike given to school children on a trip to Skull Springs in 1992, Billy Thomas said:

> Alright, you know, now we're coming to 1946, the strike. Before the strike they were talking about all this. 'Where's a quiet place where we can have a meeting?' Well, they said, 'Let's go out to Wantilurr'. So all those old people who have since passed away came out here, to talk about going on strike. I was living with them, I was working at Riverdale at the time, working for the old man Jim Allsop. They came through Kurlkuny, they travelled along the stock route. They came all the way down that way to the south. They followed that road through Milpiyina all the way here. There were lots of people here. We didn't know what they were talking about; we were too young at the time. They discussed the situation and they chose the old man McLeod right at these springs ... They told him, 'You'll have to help us'.
>
> 'I'm a whitefella', he said. 'I know about the law. If I do that I'll have to go to jail, possibly for a long time'.
>
> 'We'll support you. We're urging you to do it', they told him.
>
> I wasn't there myself, I was too young.[110]

This later timing of the Skull Springs meeting demythologises McLeod's involvement in the movement. His involvement was not that of someone who, diverted from his own life priorities, was surprised to have been 'picked out by these people to watch over their interests'.[111] Instead, we see someone who worked actively to convince *marrngu* that settler authority was not absolute, that within a non-Aboriginal legal system stacked against Aboriginal people there was room to manoeuvre to challenge settler authority, and that industrial action could be, in his words, 'a useful weapon'.[112]

---

109 McLeod, High Court appeal, D. W. McLeod v. G. R. Richards, NAA A10074 1946/8, 9, 10, p. 43.
110 Thomas (Pitpit), recorded by Anne Scrimgeour, 21 September 1992, AIATSIS collection, soundfile 'Pitpit Talking to Kids'.
111 McLeod to Bray, 23 July 1945, SROWA 1945/0800/1–3.
112 McLeod, High Court appeal, D. W. McLeod v. G. R. Richards, NAA A10074 1946/8, 9, 10, p. 43.

The discrepancy between his account of this Law meeting as the genesis of the strike movement, and the evidence of his activism for two years before he and three *marrngu* workers set off in his Ford V8 to cut cajuput wood from the Davis River, alert us to the need to treat with some caution other aspects of his Skull Springs narrative. Rather than a meeting planned over five years to formulate a strategy to address *marrngu* social and economic disadvantage, John Wilson believes that it was probably a large ceremonial meeting to which McLeod was invited, possibly a component of one of the 'revivalist' ceremonies common at the time. Discussions about the strike may have taken place during secular meetings often conducted prior to the main ceremony, rather than being the principal reason for the gathering.[113]

We should also treat with caution McLeod's claim to have received status and authority within Aboriginal Law, embodied in land and wooden objects, from the Lawmen at Skull Springs. Accepting this account on face value, some writers have extended these claims to construct narratives of their own. Deborah Wilson claims incorrectly that McLeod was 'a fully initiated man'.[114] Eddy Lutze also refers to McLeod being initiated into Aboriginal Law at Skull Springs, although he may have used this term to refer to his introduction to Aboriginal Law at that time rather than to formal initiation.[115]

Others have drawn on McLeod's narrative to speculate on connections between the strike and religious 'travelling cults' which were active at that time. 'Strongly suspect[ing]' that the Skull Springs meeting was a gathering for the transmission of the *Kuranggara* cult to the Pilbara, Tony Swain is intrigued by apparent connections between the strike movement and a travelling cult, *Julurru*, which, according to anthropologist Barbara Glowczewski, had been dreamed in the Pilbara by a man called Coffin. Given the involvement of Jack Coffin in the threatened Port Hedland strike of 1943 and the leadership role that Peter Coppin (or Coffin) played in the later strike movement, Swain incorrectly assumes, as Biskup does, that they were brothers, and wonders at these connections – two brothers, two strikes and a religious movement dreamed by one of them.[116] More intriguingly still, for Swain, the *Julurru* myth concludes with the mythic figures of two brothers entering the ground at a sacred place near Abydos Station, and near Yandeyarra Station, purchased

---

113 John and Katrin Wilson, email to author, 13 October 2016.
114 Quoted in http://www.abc.net.au/news/2015-08-31/don-mcleod-different-white-people-and-the-pilbara-strike/6737248 (no longer available).
115 Lutze, 'Donald McLeod Before Skull Springs', p. 5.
116 Tony Swain, *A Place for Strangers*, Cambridge University Press, Cambridge, 1993; Biskup, *Not Slaves*, p. 213.

'MCLEOD GAVE US HINT AND WE TOOK IT UP'

by the strikers in 1951 and managed, Swain writes, 'by none other than Peter Coffin (Coppin)'.[117]

Other writers have drawn on Swain's conjectures to assume that the strike was a manifestation of a religious movement through which McLeod derived his authority. 'McLeod and his followers were to exercise considerable influence on neighbouring groups', Martin Preaud noted in his PhD thesis, 'through the transmission of the *Juluru* towards the north and their anti-colonial ideology'.[118] Stephen Muecke takes the connection further, conflating *Kurunggara* and *Julurru*, and portraying McLeod as a leader installed through the power of an Aboriginal cult movement. '*Kurunggara* was ... reformist', he wrote:

> terrifying in its evocation of power, capable of replacing old traditions. It installed new leaders among the various Pilbara mobs, including Don McLeod. In him two kinds of power collided, whitefella power from the South ... and Aboriginal power from the North in the form of a rapidly spreading cult that taught by performative enaction that, from the blackfella point of view too, things could change.[119]

While Aboriginal Law, woven into the fabric of *marrngu* life, inevitably played a role in action taken by Aboriginal people to change the circumstances of their lives, shaping the organisation that developed as a result, there is no evidence to support the contention that the strike was the manifestation of a religious movement. McLeod had little involvement in Law business, holding himself at a respectful distance from an aspect of *marrngu* life for which he had high regard and which he believed should be preserved from an inquisitive *walypila* gaze. 'I have never captured more than a brief glimpse of what their cultural heritage meant to the people', he told historian Brian Fitzpatrick a decade after the strike began, 'but it is clearly sustaining and wholy [*sic*] satisfying and some aspects of it touchingly beautiful'.[120]

Whatever authority was granted him at Skull Springs, it is likely that the major significance of McLeod's attendance at the meeting was his exposure to the richness, beauty and sustaining power of Aboriginal Law. Given

---

117 Swain, *A Place for Strangers*, p. 258.
118 Martin Preaud, 'Country, Law and Culture', PhD Thesis, James Cook University, 2009. p. 51.
119 Stephen Muecke, 'Don McLeod's Law: The Genesis of the Aboriginal Concept of the Strike', in Russell West-Pavlov and Jennifer Wawrzinek', *Frontier Skirmishes, Literary and Cultural Debates in Australia after 1992*, Winter Verlag, Heidelberg, 2010, p. 78.
120 McLeod to Brian Fitzpatrick, 28 March 1956, p. 4, Papers of Jessie Street, NLA 2683/10/73.

widespread perceptions of Aboriginal culture as a realm of chaos in contrast to civilisation's order, the formality and dignity he witnessed at the Skull Springs meeting was eye-opening. He later spoke of:

> all the protocol and status – you know, same as you'd get in any parliament, nobody would speak to anybody inferior to himself, a bloke would come in from some other place and he'd stand and send in his credentials and when they'd identified him, well then a bloke of equal standing would go out and invite him in and they'd exchange presents, and these would be split up amongst his followers and the big exchange would be split up among – all the pomp of a group of nations coming together, a little united nations in fact went on.[121]

The world McLeod entered on the Davis River was a reversal of the social order of the *walypila* world in which *marrngu* lived at the margins, dominated and excluded by social and spatial lines drawn in the red sand. At the beautiful, wooded waterhole of Skull Springs, McLeod was the outsider, but he found himself accepted with a warm hospitality that moved him profoundly. Perhaps he, too, felt socially excluded in the non-Aboriginal world, snubbed by the pastoral community when he tried to establish organisations for the development of the Pilbara, dismissed as having 'no standing in the community' beyond 'a small following among poor class whites',[122] his attempt to take a leadership role in developing the region blocked by the actions of the powerful elite. Although he laughed in the telling, he may also have felt keenly the pastoralists' scorn at the possibility of his marrying Thora Gallop and becoming a pastoralist himself: 'Well you never heard so much squawking in all – bloody hell you wouldn't believe it. Oh bloody awful'.[123] When he told John and Katrin Wilson about Skull Springs in 1959, it was the welcoming warmth he experienced that he spoke of, rather than any authority granted him there.[124]

At a time when Aboriginal Law and culture were viewed as impediments to the 'advancement' of Aboriginal people by most advocates for reform, the strength and maturity of the cultural practices that McLeod witnessed at Skull Springs gave him an appreciation of the bedrock on which *marrngu* action for change would be founded. Through attendance at ceremonies such as this, he became aware of the existence of a network of family and social

---

121 McLeod, interviewed by Clements, tape 2, SLWA OH4005/3.
122 O'Neill to Bray, 5 November 1945, SROWA 1945/0800/33.
123 McLeod, interviewed by Carlton, 1996, transcript, p. 11, SLWA OH2739.
124 John and Katrin Wilson, email to author, 13 October 2016.

relationships, and of an organisational structure that would be vital to the strike movement. While the maintenance of Aboriginal religious and social life was a key feature of CPA policy for 'full-bloods', he found evidence here of the viability of this approach, enabling him to reject assimilationist assumptions about the fundamental requirements for change and to work effectively with *marrngu* over the following years.

Chapter 6

'It Now Appears to Be Pretty General, This Striking Business'

October 1945 – April 1946

Marrngu discussed the idea of a strike at meetings throughout the second half of 1945 and in the early weeks of 1946. While Dooley, working with McLeod at Bonney Downs Station, took a crash course in strike organisation, police and officers of the Department of Native Affairs did what they could to curtail the activities of organisers. The Department accepted O'Neill's advice concerning the capacity of Aboriginal people to organise coordinated action, but the challenge to settler authority mounted by McKenna, Captain, Kitchener and Cornish could not be ignored. The Department was concerned to ensure that they be given a clear message that agitation would not be tolerated. Constable Les Fletcher of Port Hedland was sufficiently concerned by their activities to urge for ministerial approval for their removal to Moola Bulla, a government Aboriginal settlement and cattle station in the east Kimberley.[1] Laurie O'Neill, however, the Department's sole Travelling Inspector for the vast region of the state north of the twenty-sixth parallel, who travelled to the Port Hedland–Marble Bar area to look into the situation in late October 1945, insisted that such a measure could be usefully employed later, in the unlikely event that some form of strike action was attempted. Holding firmly to his belief that Aboriginal people lacked the capacity to organise, he assured the Department that 'it is only on the few stations where there are agitators that anything would even be attempted, and that could easily [be] stopped by the removal of the agitators at the time'.[2]

While recommending against the immediate use of ministerial warrants to remove strike organisers to another part of the state, O'Neill was quite willing to use the *threat* of removal to curtail the activities of strike organisers.

---

1   Fletcher to Bray, 15 October 1945, p. 4, SROWA 1945/0800/29.
2   O'Neill to Bray, 5 November 1945, p. 2, SROWA 1945/0800/33.

On a patrol carried out in October 1945 to investigate unrest in the area, he warned Ronnie Captain that 'as long as he was working for his living and behaving himself he would not be interfered with but otherwise consideration would be given to removing him from the district'. He also warned Clancy McKenna that if he 'interfered with the employment of other natives ... he would be likely to be removed from the district'.[3] Constable Fletcher also threatened McKenna with legal action if he continued collecting funds to purchase land.[4] Bray later wrote that 'for some months the natives were warned against the mischievous propaganda of Communist McLeod. This general warning was made throughout the district, but particular care was taken to warn Clancy McKenna specifically because he was a channel for McLeod's insidious propaganda'.[5]

These threats were apparently effective. McKenna later said that he had 'got windy'.[6] He told McLeod that he had been warned by Fletcher not to continue collecting funds to purchase land. McLeod said that they would 'bust it up with a strike and see how we get on'.[7] Under threat of removal to an institution, McKenna agreed to take a job sinking a bore at Marble Bar, where Constable Gordon Marshall could keep an eye on him. O'Neill reported at the end of October that conditions appeared 'very satisfactory' in Marble Bar, and that Constable Marshall was not 'very worried just at present regarding McLeod although he states that he believes matters to be somewhat different at Nullagine'.[8] Marshall had McKenna 'under observation' and stated that 'he is not now giving any trouble'.[9] McKenna introduced Dooley to McLeod at this time, possibly to take over the organisational work that he himself was now unable to carry out. Dougal Cornish had been banned from Marble Bar and ordered to work at Warralong Station for illegal drinking. Losing his trucking job as a consequence, Cornish was no longer able to continue collecting funds and spreading the strike idea.[10] Captain also seems to have stopped actively organising by the end of 1945,

---

3   O'Neill to Bray, 5 November 1945, p. 3, SROWA 1945/0800/34.
4   McKenna, High Court appeal, D. W. McLeod v. G. R. Richards, NAA A10074 1946/8, 9, 10, p. 25.
5   Bray to Acting Minister and Premier Wise, 27 May 1946, SROWA 1945/0800/111.
6   The Nyangumarta term *wirnti*, meaning 'afraid'.
7   McKenna, High Court appeal, D. W. McLeod v. G. R. Richards, NAA A10074 1946/8, 9, 10, p. 25.
8   O'Neill to Bray, 29 October 1945, SROWA 1945/0800/32.
9   O'Neill to Bray, 5 November 1945, p. 3, SROWA 1945/0800/34.
10 Marshall, police patrol report, 2 May 1946, SROWA 1943/0099 v7.

under pressure from Fletcher and O'Neill, moving to Moolyella near Marble Bar to work tin.

While McKenna worked on the bore in Marble Bar under the watchful eye of Constable Marshall, Dooley, Kitchener and McLeod did fencing and repair work on Bonney Downs Station, and by March 1946 were prospecting at Taylor's Creek, near Nullagine.[11] Despite the meetings and the discussions taking place during *pingkayi* time, threats made by the police and O'Neill had effectively curtailed the activities of strike organisers. Visiting Marble Bar with Thora Gallop, McLeod spoke to McKenna and found that active organisation had stalled under pressure from the authorities.[12] McKenna was 'supposed to be going around', Dooley said, 'but was too busy'.[13] A further request from McLeod to Commissioner Bray urging his appointment as honorary Inspector of Natives was rejected in early March.[14] According to Katrin Wilson, McLeod was pessimistic.[15] Despite widespread interest in the movement, it seemed to have lost momentum through the withdrawal of its leadership by the early months of 1946, and there seemed little reason to believe that Aboriginal workers would be sufficiently organised to take coordinated action on 1 May.

With McLeod due to travel to Perth in April for the annual state conference of the Communist Party, Dooley stepped up as a strike organiser. Sent from Marble Bar to Bonney Downs in late 1945, he had been given a crash course in strike organisation by McLeod and Kitchener, and by April he felt ready to mount the barricades – indeed, according to people who knew him in later years, he remained on the barricades all his life, forever running strikes.[16] 'We had all made up our minds to strike', he told a court hearing. 'We all going to follow Don McLeod'.[17] Although Dooley assured McLeod that 'all boys [said] they were going to set down', McLeod insisted that there was no point taking any action unless everyone sat down together. Dooley pointed out that

---

11 Dooley, High Court appeal, D. W. McLeod v. G. R. Richards, NAA A10074 1947/8, 9, 10, p. 20.

12 McKenna, High Court Appeal, D. W. McLeod v. G. R. Richards, NAA A10074 1946/8, 9, 10, p. 26.

13 Dooley, High Court appeal, D. W. McLeod v. G. R. Richards, NAA A10074 1946/8, 9, 10, p. 20.

14 Bray to McLeod, 5 March 1946, SROWA 1945/0800/43.

15 Katrin Wilson, 'The Allocation of Sex Roles', p. 51.

16 John and Katrin Wilson, recorded by Anne Scrimgeour, Fremantle, 25 May 2016, author's collection.

17 Dooley, High Court appeal, D. W. McLeod v. G. R. Richards, NAA A10074 1946/8, 9, 10, p. 24.

if they were all going to 'set down' on the same day, they needed some way of knowing the date.

In response, McLeod gave Dooley a letter to take into Ken Duncan of Hansen's Store in Marble Bar, introducing Dooley and asking if he would mind 'drafting him up a map to show him number of days to 1st May'.[18] According to Stuart in his novelised account of the strike, *Yandy*, McLeod wrote the letter on baking powder labels with a piece of lead cut from a bullet. He told Dooley to collect money from *marrngu* if they had it, but not to worry if they did not, and to give the money to George Turner in Port Hedland.[19] He gave Dooley a second letter of introduction to take to Turner.

Dooley took the mail truck to Marble Bar, where Ken Duncan made him a calendar, described later by O'Neill as 'a crude drawing of a calendar showing the date on which the strike is to commence and which carries a crude representation of the Red Star'.[20] Duncan showed Dooley how to mark off each day until 1 May. Dooley held a meeting at the Marble Bar reserve, attended by Aboriginal men who were permitted to live at the town reserve, either because they were employed in the town or because they qualified for government rations. He told them that the strike was going ahead.[21] What were they going to do, he asked them – go for Don McLeod, or go the other way? They were for the McLeod side, they said.[22] Dooley told them to stop work on 1 May and showed them how to use the calendars. McKenna also attended the meeting and agreed to return to organisational work and to collect funds, despite the threat of removal to an institution. Over the following weeks, both he and Dooley worked to ensure that employees across a number of stations and other workplaces were prepared to take strike action on 1 May.

The campaign undertaken by McKenna and Dooley at this time, and the delivery of calendars to stations across hundreds of miles of Pilbara country, has become an emblematic feature of the strike narrative. It was, however, the culmination of many months of discussions. Most of the men that Dooley and McKenna addressed were already aware of the strike plan, at least in general terms. In this final stage of the campaign, Dooley and McKenna attempted

---

18 Duncan, High Court appeal, D. W. McLeod v. G. R. Richards, NAA A10074 1946/8, 9, 10, p. 36.

19 Dooley, High Court appeal, D. W. McLeod v. G. R. Richards, NAA A10074 1946/8, 9, 10, p. 20.

20 O'Neill to Bray, 9 May 1946, SROWA 1945/0800/70.

21 Dooley, High Court appeal, D. W. McLeod v. G. R. Richards, NAA A10074 1946/8, 9, 10, p. 21.

22 Paddy Northover, High Court appeal, D. W. McLeod v. G. R. Richards, NAA A10074 1946/8, 9, 10, p. 34.

to gauge the extent of support for the strike, and to make sure that those who were willing to strike knew what they needed to do and when to do it. May Day, the day selected for the strike at McLeod's suggestion, coincided with the beginning of the shearing season, and it was hoped that a complete withdrawal of Aboriginal labour at this crucial time of the year would severely affect pastoral operations and force pastoralists to take seriously the strikers' demands for increased wages, better working conditions and the right to choose their own Protector. The message that McKenna and Dooley took to the stations was that on 1 May everyone was to remain in camp and refuse to work until they received a message from McLeod indicating that their demands had been agreed to. The strike was expected to last ten to fourteen days.[23] McKenna and Dooley visited only a few stations at this stage, with the message spread to other communities by *marrngu* they encountered along the way.

Following his meeting with McKenna and other Marble Bar residents, Dooley took the train to Eginbah Station and spoke to several men there, including Jimmy Woodman of Lalla Rookh Station. As Woodman did not feel confident about knowing when to strike, Dooley drew up a duplicate calendar for him to take back to his station community. At Eginbah, Dooley also spoke to men from Warrawagine and gave them the message to pass on to the Warrawagine workers. Rory McPhee said he would know the date and did not need a calendar.

Dooley then went on by train to Bungalow (Coongan) Station where he spoke to Billy Bungalow, who also said he would know the day and did not need a calendar. At nearby Warralong Station, Dougal Cornish, too, knew the date and did not need a calendar. However, the Warralong workers indicated that they did not wish to participate in the strike. 'All say all frightened – don't think to strike', Dooley said.[24] This reticence is interesting, given Constable Fletcher's report that Cornish was one of the agitators spreading news of the strike following the Four Mile meetings the previous year. Over the coming years, Cornish was to have an ambivalent relationship with the movement, sometimes participating even at a leadership level and at other times taking an actively oppositional stance. It may be that Fletcher was mistaken in his belief that Cornish had been one of the agitators the previous year, but it may also be that threats of exile under ministerial warrant had been effective in

---

23   McKenna, court statement, McLeod Donald William v. Richards George Ronald, NAA A10078 1946/13 Part 2, p. 26.

24   Dooley, High Court appeal, D. W. McLeod v. G. R. Richards, NAA A10074 1946/8, 9, 10, p. 21.

warning him against continuing involvement in the strike. Ordered to work at Warralong and already under a cloud for illegal drinking, he may have been reluctant to draw further attention to himself.[25]

From Warralong, Dooley took the train into Port Hedland and gave McLeod's letter of introduction to George Turner, foreman of the Public Works Department. Turner arranged a lift for him on a truck due to go out to Munda and Boodarie Stations on 24 April, a week before the planned strike. Dooley spoke to workers at both stations and 'gave them word and show[ed them the] paper'. He collected £6/10/- and an assurance from Roy Mackay that they would 'set down' on 1 May.[26] Most agreed to join in and donated £1.[27] Dooley took the funds back to George Turner to hold until McLeod's return from Perth, keeping 30/- for himself for expenses. Returning to Marble Bar on the train, he met Massey of Boodarie Station and Ernie Mitchell (Putungaja) from Tabba Tabba Station, who would both become important strikers and leaders of the movement throughout the 1950s. Massey took the message to Strelley Station, leaving a copy of the calendar with Wambi Ball before returning to Pippingarra. Mitchell did not need a calendar, and returned to Tabba Tabba with the message that everyone should stop work on 1 May.[28] 'Yurlpuly [Dooley] went around with calendars', Billy Thomas (Pitpit) told schoolchildren in 1992. 'He went right around to all the stations out there, and they all agreed to finish. They would all go on strike on the same day, from everywhere. From the Port Hedland district right up to Marble Bar and Nullagine, everyone would stop'.[29]

Meanwhile, McKenna took the message to Carlindi, De Grey and Pardoo Stations, travelling to Carlindi by train. At Carlindi, the men said they had 'no money chuck in – sorry [they would] like to do it'. On De Grey Station, on the coast east of Port Hedland, workers told McKenna that they were ready to strike.[30]

---

25 Marshall, police report, p. 11, SROWA 1943/0099 v7.
26 Dooley, High Court appeal, D. W. McLeod v. G. R. Richards, NAA A10074 1946/8, 9, 10, p. 21, Mackay, p. 33.
27 Dooley, High Court appeal, D. W. McLeod v. G. R. Richards, NAA A10074 1946/8, 9, 10, p. 21.
28 Dooley, High Court appeal, D. W. McLeod v. G. R. Richards, NAA A10074 1946/8, 9, 10, p. 21.
29 Thomas (Pitpit), recorded by Anne Scrimgeour, 21 September 1992, AIATSIS collection, soundfile 'Pitpit Talking to Kids'.
30 McKenna, High Court appeal, D. W. McLeod v. G. R. Richards, NAA A10074 1946/8, 9, 10, pp. 26–27.

While McKenna and Dooley campaigned in the north, McLeod flew south to Perth, with the twofold purpose of negotiating with the Department for an appointment as honorary Inspector of Natives and mobilising the public support that would be vital to the success of any action taken by Aboriginal people. He still hoped at this time that the threat of a strike would force the Department to approve his appointment as an honorary Inspector of Natives. He promised Kitchener, who saw him off on the plane, to keep him informed of the success of his negotiations, and said that if they did not get all they wanted they should 'sit down'.[31]

In seeking public support for the strike, McLeod drew on the network of contacts he had made since his visit to Perth in June 1943, particularly in the labour movement and the Australian Communist Party. He had joined the ACP, and had connections within the party's Western Australian branch, whose systems for disseminating information included regular radio broadcasts, weekly public open-air meetings and a weekly newspaper, the *Workers' Star*.[32] These were to prove particularly important in publicising the strike and galvanising essential public support. The Party's platform for Aboriginal reform coincided closely with McLeod's ideas, and the Western Australian branch was looking for ways to implement its program and eager to take up the cause. One member, Joan Williams, said that the branch, looking to involve itself in the issue of the exploitation of Aboriginal labour in the pastoral industry, could not believe its luck when McLeod had begun corresponding with Katharine Susannah Prichard.[33] McLeod was invited to attend the annual state Party conference as a consultative delegate, and the Party school in Perth. According to Graham Alcorn, he gave an address to the conference and received unanimous support for his activities in the Pilbara.[34]

McLeod campaigned actively during the few weeks he spent in Perth. Poet, author and Communist Party member Dorothy Hewett remembered meeting this 'astonishing man' who arrived from Port Hedland 'in his ill-fitting blue suit, to astound us all with his arguments and grasp of Marxist theory. Late at night in the Alcorns' Cottesloe flat we listened spellbound to McLeod's stories

---

31   Kitchener, High Court appeal, D. W. McLeod v. G. R. Richards, NAA A10074 1947/8, 9, 10, p. 30.
32   Just when he became a member is unclear. He described himself as 'a party member undisclosed' in 1944, and he was certainly a member when he visited Perth in March 1946. Alcorn, 'The Struggle of the Pilbara Station Hands'.
33   Joan Williams, not dated, cited in Hess, 'Black and Red', p. 70.
34   Alcorn, 'The Struggle of the Pilbara Station Hands', p. 13.

and plans for an Aboriginal Nor'-West'.[35] 'McLeod told us of the Aborigines' poor pay, the squalid camps on the stations, the plundering of issue rations by some station owners', Joan Williams remembered:

> 'The influential whites up there hate me', he said. 'They call me a violent trouble-maker. They're out to get me. I have to step carefully, hide my movements'. Since they called him a commo, he might as well be one, he added.[36]

'And here he is', Hewett wrote, 'bearded, intense, with deep-set eyes hidden under a protruding brow, sitting by the Alcorns' fire in "The Kremlin" calling on us to take up the cause and send revolutionary cadres to the Pilbara. We felt as if we were on trial'.[37]

Following the conference, McLeod attended a month-long class on Marxist theory conducted by J. B. Miles, General Secretary of the ACP, at Perth's London Court.[38] Joan Williams remembered his attendance at the study group. He was shy, she remembered, and spoke in a low voice, but with passion:

> Small and wiry, blue eyes blazing above a black beard, his passion contrasting with the deliberation of 'JB' whose words came in a Scottish burr between long puffs on his beloved pipe. He gave high praise to McLeod but seemed to dismiss Dorothy Hewett and myself as middle-class enthusiasts.[39]

Although McLeod later dismissed his association with the Communist Party as no more than a pragmatic strategy to generate support for the strike movement, his knowledge of Marxist theory, which elicited high praise from Miles, suggests that his involvement was ideological as well as tactical. On at least one occasion he openly identified as a communist, even when such a disclosure did not assist his cause. Arguing in 1947 against the assumption that the strike was communist-driven, McLeod wrote, 'Although I personally am a communist, one swallow does not make a summer'.[40]

---

35 Dorothy Hewett, preface to Brown, *The Black Eureka*.
36 Joan Williams, *Anger and Love*, p. 127.
37 Dorothy Hewett, *Wild Card, an Autobiography, 1923–1958*, McPhee Gribble, South Yarra, Vic., 1990, p. 123. "The Kremlin" was name given by communists to Graham and June Alcorn's home in the Perth suburb of Cottesloe.
38 Alcorn, 'The Struggle of the Pilbara Station Hands', p. 13.
39 Joan Williams, *Anger and Love*, p. 127.
40 *Cathedral Chronicle*, March 1947, p. 6.

On 7 and 14 April, McLeod spoke at open-air meetings on the Perth Esplanade, addressing those gathered on 'the reason for the present situation of the natives in the North-West and how their conditions could be alleviated'. Following his first Esplanade talk, which included 'a brief outline of native culture with illustrations of folk songs', 'questions were thick and fast', according to the *Workers' Star*, 'proof of a great degree of interest from the large crowd gathered on the Perth Esplanade last Sunday afternoon to hear Don McLeod from Nullagine speak on Native Affairs'.[41] He also spoke on 'the impact of White settlement on Native culture' to a gathering at the Modern Women's Club, established by Prichard in 1938 as an organisation in which women were free to 'discuss any subject that concerned them'. Prichard later wrote that 'The Club always sponsored the interests of Aborigines' and that 'Don McLeod's appeal for the Aborigines who left the stations in the May Day strike was made at the Modern Women's Club'.[42]

While in Perth, McLeod wrote again to Commissioner Bray urging the Department to respect the wishes of Aboriginal people, as expressed at the Four Mile meeting the previous year, by appointing him Inspector of Natives in an honorary capacity. He requested an interview to discuss the matter personally. At one stage during his time in Perth, he planned to bring a delegation of Aboriginal people from the Pilbara to meet Bray to add weight to his demands, and wired Kitchener to take the first available flight down. Kitchener later told a court hearing that he did not go as he had no money.[43] McKenna also said in a court statement that McLeod had 'arranged for Dep. to Perth – but no funds'.[44] McLeod presumably expected that Kitchener would access funds held by Ken Duncan in Marble Bar.

Bray, however, refused to meet McLeod, repeating his earlier assertion that the Department already had a capable and qualified inspector in 'Mr. L. O'Neill', who carried out his duties with the assistance of local protectors, and that the appointment of McLeod as honorary inspector was therefore superfluous.[45] McLeod sent a second wire to Kitchener advising him 'not to

---

41 *Workers' Star*, 5 April 1946, p. 1, and 12 April 1946, p. 1.
42 Katharine Susannah Prichard, Notes on the Modern Women's Club, p. 3, SLWA 3255A/19.
43 Kitchener, High Court appeal, D. W. McLeod v. G. R. Richards, NAA A10074 1947/8, 9, 10, p. 30.
44 Kitchener, High Court appeal, D. W. McLeod v. G. R. Richards, NAA A10074 1947/8, 9, 10, p. 30.
45 Bray to McLeod, 11 April 1946, SROWA 1945/0800/45.

bother'.[46] On 25 April, as McLeod prepared to return north, the *Workers' Star* reported that 'the Native Affairs Department has denied aboriginal station hands in the north-west the fundamental right of workers throughout the world – the right to organise'.[47]

By the time McLeod returned to Port Hedland at the end of April, sporadic strike action had already begun. On the large coastal station of De Grey, at the mouth of the De Grey River, workers decided to strike before 1 May, when mustering would be underway and workers would be spread throughout the property. Opponents of the strike later referred to this as evidence that *marrngu* had no idea what a strike was all about, but the decision to make their demand before the muster began was not unreasonable. On the morning of 26 April they told Les Miller, who had shifted from Warrawagine Station to take over the management of De Grey, that they would not undertake the muster unless they were all paid 'thirty bob' a week. Fletcher reported that Miller was in 'an awkward situation on account of the proximity of shearing operations and was forced to agree to their demands for £1.10.0 per week, but stipulating that it was only during the mustering and shearing'. According to Miller, the workers accepted the pay increase in lieu of bonuses, such as clothing, which were usually given when shearing finished. In a letter to the editor of the *Northern Times* newspaper, he downplayed the event as simply a reasonable request for wages, which any of his employees had a right to make, claiming that 'there was never any indication of a strike, or threatened strike, amongst the natives here'.[48] He was clearly more alarmed by the demand than this letter suggests, however, and he rang Fletcher to inform him of what had taken place, threatening 'that immediately after shearing, he will perform a very severe culling out and will only retain working natives who are more or less reliable'.[49] The threat that non-productive, or less productive, workers would be evicted from stations if *marrngu* made demands for pay increases was one that would be widely made by pastoralists in response to the strike, in line with pastoralist claims that they supported unproductive Aboriginal people as an act of charity.

Workers on Pippingarra Station, on the coast just to the west of Port Hedland, also demanded higher wages when they threatened strike action on 30 April. To prevent disruption to the shearing, the owner-manager, A. E. (Ted) Richardson, like Miller at De Grey, agreed to pay an additional 5/- per week

---

46 Kitchener, High Court appeal, D. W. McLeod v. G. R. Richards, NAA A10074 1947/8, 9, 10, p. 30.
47 *Workers' Star*, 25 April 1946, p. 5.
48 Miller, letter to the editor, *Northern Times*, 15 May 1946, SROWA 1945/0800/118.
49 Fletcher to Bray, 2 May 1946, SROWA 1945/0800/56.

during the shearing, with other arrangements to be made when the shearing was over. Workers agreed to this arrangement and returned to work.[50]

Importantly, women also demanded wages at this time. Edith Miller remembered Lily Spree and other women approaching her for wages at De Grey Station. 'The women weren't paid then', she said:

> and they held us up over that, and I sympathized with them. They came to me first and said, 'I want you to tell boss' – this was Lily – 'I want you to tell boss we want wages', and I said, 'No good me telling boss, you blokes got to tell him, you got to tell him why you wantum wages'. 'Oh we want 'um, oh want to buy 'um'. 'What you want to buy 'um because you get dresses given you'. '[We] want to buy 'um self'.[51]

Miller said she discussed it with her husband, and £1 per week was made to the women, although this seems to have applied only to Lily Spree and one other woman who were working as domestic servants.[52] The request and the concession made by station management, although trivialised by Miller, is highly significant. Preparations for the strike had been made largely by men, and the basic rate of 30/- demanded by *marrngu* when they stopped work was generally understood to be applicable to male workers. Yet women also worked on stations, mainly as domestic workers and usually unpaid, and their labour was often essential to the running of the station. Although apparently excluded from plans for the strike, they were to be active participants. The withdrawal of their domestic labour would be severely felt, and this would be reflected in improved wages for women.

On 30 April, workers at Mundabullangana (Munda) Station, on the coast to the west of Port Hedland, told the manager, Rob Lukis, that they were 'pulling out' and refused to go to their jobs. While Roy Mackay and Mick Lee, described by Fletcher as 'the disturbing elements',[53] went into Port Hedland to confer with McLeod, Lukis gave the others half an hour to think the matter over, warning them that if they did not return to work they would be removed from the station.[54] He rang Constable Fletcher, informing him of what had taken place and asking him to tell Mackay, 'the troublemaker', that he was

---

50 Fletcher to Bray, 2 May 1946, SROWA 1945/0800/56.
51 Edith Miller, interviewed by Jamieson, 1982, transcript, p. 63, SLWA OH506.
52 Katrin Wilson, 'The Allocation of Sex Roles', p. 76.
53 Fletcher to Bray, 2 May 1946, p. 1, SROWA 1945/0800/56.
54 O'Neill, statement for McLeod trial, SROWA 1945/0800/134.

not to return to Munda, as he would not be tolerated within the boundary fence. 'And any other native who would not work would be treated likewise'.[55]

While the strikers intended to remain on the station, they were now told that if they did not work they would be ordered to leave and threatened that their eviction would enforced by the police. The threat was effective, and most workers returned to their jobs, with only Mackay, Lee and Mackay's wife, Nancy, still refusing to work.[56] Several days later, Lukis acted on his threat, calling on Fletcher to remove the three strikers from the property, together with nine other non-working *marrngu*, including a family with four young children displaced by the closure of Yandeyarra Station some months previously.

Pastoralist control over Aboriginal residence on pastoral leases was a central feature of the colonial relationship in northern pastoral areas, and a key means by which settlers gained access to Aboriginal labour. Residence on pastoral leases was contingent upon a willingness to undertake whatever labour was required, and squatter authority in this regard was consistently supported by police action. It was entirely consistent with common practice that Fletcher should undertake the removal of Aboriginal people from Munda at Lukis's request, transporting the women and children some eighty miles to the Twelve Mile camp near Port Hedland and ordering the men to walk.

Until their eviction, non-working *marrngu* and those made homeless through the closure of stations like Yandeyarra the previous year had been provided with rations by the management at Munda Station under a feudalistic system that was now coming under pressure from Aboriginal demands for increased wages. The eviction of these non-workers from the station property signalled a breaking down of this relationship. It was a message to *marrngu* that if they were no longer prepared to fulfil their part of the arrangement by providing low-paid or unpaid labour, then pastoralists were no longer willing to ration their non-working relations. It was an action that declared that any attempt to commercialise Aboriginal labour was a breach of the rationing relationship, putting at risk paternalistic pastoralist tolerance of Aboriginal community residence on pastoral leases. Les Miller's threat to 'perform a very severe culling out' after the shearing was a similar signal to *marrngu* and the Department that pastoralists' tolerance of station community residence was contingent on the continued availability of compliant Aboriginal labour.

---

55   Fletcher to Bray, 2 May 1946, p. 2, SROWA 1945/0800/57.
56   Fletcher to Bray, 2 May 1946, p. 1, SROWA 1945/0800/56; O'Neill, statement for McLeod trial, 24 May 1946, p. 2, SROWA 1945/0800/134. Nancy was the daughter of Kundjing.

Aboriginal workers on stations further inland also began strike action before 1 May. At Warrawagine, the large sheep and cattle station on the Nullagine River on the edge of the Great Sandy Desert, *marrngu* were working in two separate teams, one engaged in a cattle muster and the other preparing for the shearing twenty miles from the Warrawagine homestead at the shearing shed at Sheep Camp (Pintunya). Cranky was one of the cattlemen carrying out a muster near the Braeside outstation with the *walypila* overseer, Billy Sheppard, when they received word about the strike.

'We made our way back with the cattle to Warrawagine', Cranky said:

> 'We'll go on strike', I said, 'we'll stay in the camp and talk it over'.
>
> '*Yu*', everybody agreed.
>
> The people over in the west [at Sheep Camp] also discussed the matter.[57]

On the morning of 29 April, none of the Aboriginal workers at the Warrawagine homestead area proceeded to their usual occupation, instead shifting to the meathouse where they were permitted to shelter during rain. No-one brought horses into the yard to begin the day's work. Some of the men went up to the homestead to see Bill Sheppard:

> 'Has anybody put the horses in the yard?' Sheppard asked.
>
> We said, 'No, nobody went to get the horses'.
>
> 'Oh yeah? What's wrong?'
>
> 'Well, today we're finishing off'.
>
> That was 1946.
>
> 'Ah, who gave you fellas a hand? Did somebody give you a hand?'
>
> 'No, we just made up our minds to stop, because we've no home, we camp in the river ... '
>
> 'Ah, yeah? Somebody must have given you a hand'.
>
> 'No, we just made up our mind, because we get low wages and rubbish tucker in the woodheap'.
>
> And so that was that. The boss said, 'Well, you wait. I'll get the police'.

---

57 Cranky (Kujupurra), recorded by Anne Scrimgeour, June 1993, AIATSIS collection, soundfile 'Kujupurra 3'.

We said, 'Yeah, you can get the police. We're not working. We're waiting for the police'.

So we left them, and went and got our swags. We rolled up our swags, our blankets, and shifted to the other side of the road crossing ... We made camp there, about two miles from the homestead.[58]

Cranky emphasised that all *marrngu* at Warrawagine at that time moved out to this camp, including the women and girls who worked as domestic servants in the house and the old people and children who usually remained in their camp in the dry bed of the Nullagine River during the day. 'Nothing in the house', he said, 'nothing in the river, all the old people, we took him over there'.[59]

About twenty miles from the homestead, at the station's shearing shed at Sheep Camp, called Pintunya by *marrngu*, Aboriginal sheep workers also stopped work that morning. Shearing operations were underway there under the oversight of G. A. (Jim) Lewis, who had taken over the management of Warrawagine from Les Miller. Aboriginal musterers, working under the supervision of a *marrngu* man, Yarrie Jack Coppin (Ngarlkapangu), were engaged in bringing in sheep for shearing. Crow Yougarla (Yakalya) was one of those who stopped work that day. Although he worked for the neighbouring station of Yarrie, he was assisting with the Warrawagine sheep muster and was at the mustering camp near Pintunya:

> Monday, everyone, Monday, all got to be strike. So we, everyone, all the musterers too, get them horses in the morning, saddle up, everyone, we went Sheep Camp, all the musterers all stop. And squatter-bloke, Jim Lewis, he there: 'What happened?'
>
> 'We striking off, finish. We're not working, all the Warrawagine mob. And Sheep Camp mob same again'.
>
> He was mustering the cattle then, he had a mob of cattle in the yard [at] Warrawagine Station. And this mob he had a mob of sheep in the yard.
>
> 'No, we're not going back. We're finished'.[60]

---

58   Cranky (Kujupurra), recorded by Anne Scrimgeour, June 1993, AIATSIS collection, soundfile 'Kujupurra 3'.

59   Cranky (Kujupurra), recorded by Anne Scrimgeour at Warrawagine, 1991, author's collection.

60   Crow Yougarla (Yakalya), recorded by Anne Scrimgeour, 21 August 1991, author's collection.

Lewis responded by sacking all the strikers. While the operation of the station was dependent on the labour of Aboriginal people, pastoralist control was premised on a fundamental denial of this fact, and Lewis refused to undermine his authority by entering into negotiation. Instead, he adopted the usual strategy of calling on the police to ensure the continued compliance of his Aboriginal workers.

As there was no telephone at Sheep Camp, he sent an urgent message to nearby Callewa Station to call on the Marble Bar policeman, Gordon Marshall, to visit the station to force the workers to return to their jobs.[61] Marshall took the news very seriously. He laid the blame for the unrest squarely on McLeod's shoulders and was critical of the failure of the Department of Native Affairs to take earlier action to prosecute him. 'Donald Wm. McLeod has been dabbling in native matters for some time', he wrote, '& must be classed a Communist'.[62] Like Fletcher, he believed that a wage increase for Aboriginal workers would result in mass evictions. 'A great expense is going to be thrown upon the Government, in feeding & clothing unemployed natives', he wrote. 'I considered it my duty as protector of natives, to endeavour to keep the natives on the right track by strongly advising them not to strike'.[63] As the pastoralist Doughty wrote in his novel *The Green Stick*, 'It's the policemen's job to see that blackfellers stay where they're put'.[64]

'Alright, next day, the policeman's coming, Mr Marshall', Crow said. Marshall left Marble Bar at 4 am on 30 April, taking six hours to make the journey of 100 miles over poor roads to the Warrawagine shearing shed at Pintunya. Seven *marrngu* had stopped work there, and Marshall spoke to them in the presence of Lewis. According to Crow, Marshall told them that he had already been to the Warrawagine homestead and had persuaded the domestic workers and cattlemen to return to work:

> And that same morning we see that Mr Marshall he come to Sheep Camp.
>
> 'No, we're not working'.
>
> '... All the Warrawagine is all working, cattle camp mob. All working'.
>
> ...

---

61   Marshall, police patrol report, 30 April 1946, SROWA 1943/0099 v7.
62   Marshall, police patrol report, 30 April 1946, SROWA 1943/0099 v7.
63   Marshall, police patrol report, 30 April 1946, SROWA 1943/0099 v7.
64   Doughty, *The Green Stick*, p. 126.

'But we all, all gotta be in one, all gotta finish. Not working'.

'No, no, you fellas got to work. You'll be in serious trouble'.

'No, we're alright. We'll go that'.[65]

Yarrie Jack Coppin joined Marshall and Lewis in urging the strikers to return to their jobs.[66] Under this pressure, and believing that strikers at the homestead had already returned to work, *marrngu* at Sheep Camp agreed to continue with the muster. 'Without any difficulty at all these 7 boys, stated they were prepared to start work again, & Mr. Lewis agreed to start them', Marshall wrote. 'Yarrie Jack spoke good advice to them in my presence'.[67] 'We had a big argument', Crow said. 'We went back to work'.[68]

Having averted strike action at Pintunya, Marshall and Yarrie Jack went on to the homestead, and then with Billy Sheppard went to speak to the *marrngu* who had made camp about two miles away. Rather than walking to where the strikers were camped, Marshall sent Yarrie Jack to tell the strikers that he wanted to speak with them. 'We stayed there until the policeman came, with a half-caste bloke, *Milangka*', Cranky said. '"A policeman's coming. Get up!"'[69] It was an assertion of Marshall's authority that *marrngu* found difficult to disregard, although they were aware that complying with the demand weakened their position. Cranky recalled that they said to one another, 'He should have come up over there but never mind we'll go and see'm'.[70]

'I spoke to the 20 natives concerned', Marshall wrote:

> They like the other 7 were in the dark, and willingly offered to go back to work – they were given their jobs back, – no force or threats of any kind were brought to bear – However, I did warn them, that if any one of them tried to make another stop work, they would get into serious bother.[71]

---

65 Yougarla (Yakalya), recorded by Anne Scrimgeour, 21 August 1991, author's collection.
66 Marshall, police patrol report, 30 April 1946, SROWA 1943/0099 v7.
67 Marshall, police patrol report, 30 April 1946, SROWA 1943/0099 v7.
68 Yougarla (Yakalya), recorded by Anne Scrimgeour, 21 August 1991, author's collection.
69 Cranky (Kujupurra), recorded by Anne Scrimgeour, June 1993, AIATSIS collection, soundfile 'Kujupurra 3'. *Milangka* is Yarrie Jack Coppin (Ngarlkapangu), referred to by his section name.
70 Cranky (Kujupurra), recorded by Anne Scrimgeour, June 1993, AIATSIS collection, soundfile 'Kujupurra 3'.
71 Marshall, police patrol report, 30 April 1946, 1943/0099 v7.

Marrngu accounts contradict Marshall's report. According to Cranky, Marshall threatened them with arrest if they refused to return to work, tipping a bag of chains onto the ground:

> 'Are you fellas going back to work?' Marshall asked.
>
> 'No, we're not working. We're finishing off'.
>
> 'Alright. Well, you want this one?' he asked, tipping chains out of the bag and showing them to us.
>
> 'You fellas want this?'
>
> 'It's up to you'. That was the end of that. He put the chains back again.[72]

The chains were a powerful reminder of the power wielded by the police to arrest, incarcerate and exile Aboriginal people, and their display in these circumstances was a clear threat. 'We didn't know much English', another Warrawagine worker, Mac Gardiner, remembered. 'They tried to bluff us into going back. We didn't know much English and they stopped us from saying anything, to make us go back.'[73]

In addition to the threatening display of chains, Marshall was able to weaken the resolve of *marrngu* at the Warrawagine homestead by informing them that their co-workers at Sheep Camp had returned to their jobs. 'The policeman told us, "All that lot have gone back to work"', Cranky said.[74] They felt let down by the sheep musterers. 'If them fellas would have been hard, we would have been hard, but all them fellas come back and so we come back, all the job back'.[75]

'We couldn't get out of it, nothing', Mac Gardiner said. 'Police want us station'.[76]

'Feeling satisfied that all would be well at Warrawagine', Marshall travelled back towards Marble Bar, visiting Callewa Station, where he found that *marrngu* were not planning to strike (and where, indeed, *marrngu* never did

---

72 Cranky (Kujupurra), recorded by Anne Scrimgeour, June 1993, AIATSIS collection, soundfile 'Kujupurra 3'.

73 Gardiner (Pirntilkampanyaja), recorded by Anne Scrimgeour, 5 August 1993, AIATSIS collection, sound file 'Pirntilkampanyaja 18'.

74 Cranky (Kujupurra), recorded by Anne Scrimgeour, June 1993, AIATSIS collection, soundfile 'Kujupurra 3'.

75 Cranky (Kujupurra), recorded by Anne Scrimgeour at Warrawagine, 1991, author's collection.

76 Gardiner (Pirntilkampanyaja), recorded by Anne Scrimgeour, 29 September 1993, author's collection.

strike), and Yarrie Station, where *marrngu* told him that although they knew about the proposed strike, they 'were quite prepared to carry on & see what happens'. From Yarrie, he spoke by telephone to the manager of Coongan Station, who had been told by his Aboriginal workers that they were going to strike. 'As it now appeared to be pretty general, this striking business', he wrote, 'I decided to patrol all stations on this route'.[77]

Such was the situation when dawn broke on May Day, 1 May 1946, the day marked with a crude red star on the calendars that Dooley had made and distributed. Laurie O'Neill, comfortable in his conviction that Aboriginal people lacked the ability to organise coordinated action and that the troublemakers' activities had been effectively curbed, was away from the area at Fitzroy Crossing in the east Kimberley. At Warrawagine homestead, workers woke to proceed to their jobs as usual – cooking, cleaning the homestead, watering the gardens, fencing, chopping wood, working the cattle – disappointed that their attempted strike action had been so quickly suppressed by the police.

At the shearing shed at Pintunya, too, and in the sheep mustering camp, workers woke to carry on with their work. At nearby Yarrie Station, Gordon Marshall, now aware that widespread strike action was planned for that day, rose early in preparation for a tour of stations along the De Grey River to make sure that no such action took place. At Munda Station, only Roy Mackay, Nancy and Mick Lee remained defiantly in camp, while other *marrngu* prepared to go about their jobs. On De Grey, workers had won their wage increase for the shearing and woke to the morning of 1 May in mustering camps and at the station homestead. In Port Hedland, Constable Les Fletcher was on the alert, aware that, despite O'Neill's assurances, widespread strike action was planned that day throughout the district.

---

77   Marshall, police patrol report, 30 April 1946, SROWA 1943/0099 v7.

Chapter 7

'Tangled Versions'

May Day 1946

Despite the fact that the strike movement had its origins around Nullagine, stations in that region did not take part in the May Day action. Kitchener had been the principal Aboriginal instigator and had actively campaigned and collected funds in the Nullagine area following the race-time meeting the previous year, but does not seem to have undertaken the sort of organisational work in the Nullagine area that Dooley and McKenna carried out further north. Threats of arrest and removal from the district had apparently been successful in dissuading him from further involvement. From discussions with McLeod, he had understood that the action they were planning was legal within *walypila* law – and indeed it was not illegal to take strike action – but he had been successfully convinced otherwise. While O'Neill had failed to contact him during his patrol of the area in late 1945, Kitchener had probably come under some pressure from Constable Rowe of Nullagine to cease his activities. He certainly came under pressure from the new manager of Bonney Downs Station, a Mr Allan, who had taken over management of the station in April 1946, when its part-owner, Thora Gallop, purchased the Five Mile Store in the tiny town of Nullagine and moved there with her young daughter. Constable Rowe reported that Allan had 'had a thorough talk with Kitchener on various aspects of communism and explained the general workings of this type of agitator, which appeared to satisfy the native'.[1] McLeod said that Kitchener refused to participate, 'as he feared that it was against the white man's law'.[2] Rowe believed that 'this native might settle down' if he could be kept away from McLeod, but with Thora Gallop living in Nullagine, this seemed unlikely; it was anticipated that McLeod would live in Nullagine also. It is also possible that Kitchener's involvement in the movement had

---

1   Rowe to Bray, 9 May 1946, SROWA 1945/0800/74.
2   McLeod, draft autobiography, chapter 1, p. 9, Marchant Trust Collection, UWA MS118 series 1 file 13.

been motivated by enthusiasm for the project to acquire land rather than by the idea of going on strike, although, certainly, McLeod had been speaking to him about striking since they first began working together on Bonney Downs Station in 1943.[3]

In 'native camps' on stations across the Marble Bar and Port Hedland region, there was a widespread, although not universal, intention to participate in the May Day strike action. It was not, however, the well-coordinated walk-off of 800 Aboriginal people, carried out with 'near clock-work precision', that many writers claim.[4] Rather, the action that took place on or around 1 May was hesitant, poorly coordinated and far from unanimous. Nor did *marrngu* plan to walk off stations that day. Some *marrngu* did leave their workplaces at this time, shifting to Moolyella and the Twelve Mile, where large strike camps would later be established. Most did not do so voluntarily, however, but were evicted from towns and stations for striking. Neither were they all workers: they included nine non-working men, women and children evicted from Munda Station as a result of the strike action that workers had taken there. By the end of the first week of May, only about thirty *marrngu* had left their workplaces, and only one station, Indee, was experiencing labour shortages as a result of the strike.[5]

Nevertheless, a significant proportion of Pilbara Aboriginal people did participate, attempted to participate or intended to participate in the action planned for 1 May. Discussions about the strike had been taking place since early 1944 and more actively since the 1945 race-time meeting, and Aboriginal station communities knew that a strike was planned for the beginning of the shearing season on 1 May 1946. There was uncertainty, however, even among those who supported the strike idea, about just what was required for their participation. Instructions carried by Dooley and McKenna and spread by word of mouth were for all *marrngu* to refuse to work from 1 May onwards,

---

3   Kitchener, High Court appeal, D. W. McLeod v. G. R. Richards, NAA A10074 1947/8, 9, 10, p. 31.

4   Deborah Wilson, *Different White People*, p. 52. Reference to 800 Aboriginal people walking away from stations on 1 May include Provisional Committee for Defence of Native Rights, circular, 23 May 1946. McLeod also claimed that 800 walked off on 1 May: for example, McLeod to Ron Hurd, Secretary of the Fremantle Branch of the Seamen's Union, 14 April 1949, SLWA 5121A. See also Wikipedia, '1946 Pilbara Strike', *Wikipedia the Free Encyclopedia,* http://en.wikipedia.org/wiki/1946_Pilbara_strike; Patsy Adam Smith, *No Tribesman,* Rigby, Adelaide, 1971, p. 44.

5   The thirty included nine people evicted from Marble Bar on 3 May for striking, three workers and nine non-working people evicted from Munda Station, two workers who shifted to the Twelve Mile from Pippingarra Station, and eight people evicted from Indee Station for demanding higher wages.

remaining in their camps until they received word that negotiations carried out by McLeod were successful. McLeod believed that such action at a critical time of the year, when all available labour was required for shearing operations, would cripple pastoral operations to such an extent that the Department would be forced to agree to his appointment as an Inspector of Natives. Such an appointment would enable him to work effectively to improve the status of Aboriginal people, put in place the scheme for establishing a settlement to develop agricultural and pastoral enterprises, and achieve improvements in their living and working conditions on stations.

The plan was extremely difficult for *marrngu* to adhere to, however. While many were determined to do whatever was required to address the unequal and coercive nature of the pastoral labour arrangement, the complex nature of their relationship with pastoralists, with its familial ties of duty, entitlement and reciprocity, made sustained refusal to assist with pastoral operations extremely difficult, especially while they remained on the stations. Approaching their station bosses to announce, 'We're not working today' was difficult enough, but the expectation that small *marrngu* communities could maintain this stance for days on end, without a clear set of demands or the power to negotiate, was unrealistic. Required to withhold their labour to give McLeod a lever to negotiate on their behalf, they found their bosses' questions, 'What's the matter?' and 'Why aren't you working?', difficult to answer. Some strikers, like those at Warrawagine, responded by listing their grievances – 'We just made up our minds to stop, because we've no home, we camp in the river ... we get low wages and rubbish tucker in the woodheap' – while others told employers that they were striking 'for Don McLeod'.[6] 'They could not give me any reasons for ceasing work other than that they had been told to do so', O'Neill wrote.[7] This did little to counter the accusation, made by pastoralists, the police and O'Neill, that they were being manipulated by McLeod for his own ends, and it weakened the strikers' position when they came under pressure from their bosses and the authorities to return to work.

The action was further weakened by a lack of clarity about just what the strike was about. As well as the instruction to refuse to work until notified, many had also understood that their main demand was a universal minimum wage of 30/- per week. According to ACP member Joan Williams, the 30/- wage demand had been made on the advice of Graham Alcorn, editor of

---

6   Cranky (Kujupurra), recorded by Anne Scrimgeour, June 1993, AIATSIS collection, soundfile 'Kujupurra 3'; Tommy Dodd, High Court appeal, D. W. McLeod v. G. R. Richards, NAA A10074 1946/8, 9, 10, p. 31.

7   O'Neill, statement for McLeod's trial, 24 May 1946, p. 1, SROWA 1945/0800/135.

the Communist Party newspaper, the *Workers' Star*. In correspondence with McLeod, Alcorn had 'said that if the strikers were to get support from unions they should have definite demands, such as thirty shillings a week for stockmen, so that their exploitation would be clearly understood'.[8] By framing the action in these terms, the strikers would be able to mobilise essential support for the movement from left-wing organisations and trade unions.[9]

The 30/- demand was problematic, however. Wages and conditions for Aboriginal workers on stations and other workplaces across the region varied widely. Stations on the desert fringe with a high proportion of newly-arrived desert migrants tended to have larger resident communities and were less likely to make monetary payments. On stations closer to Port Hedland, wages were higher. Some workers already received wages in excess of 30/- per week. On stations where wages were close to 30/-, and where it was customary to provide a bonus, either monetary or in kind, as an incentive during or following the shearing, the demand for 30/- was too low. The decision of workers at De Grey and Pippingarra Stations to accept the 5/- wage increase for the duration of the shearing threatened to undermine the wider strike action.

While *marrngu* continued to identify a basic wage of 30/- per week as their principal demand, and while the Communist Party consistently cited this as the strikers' core demand, McLeod had, by 1 May, shifted away from this demand as too low, and too easily granted, to enable the strike to achieve significant or lasting results. On 30 April, therefore, when he notified the Western Australian Government of the impending strike, he identified the right to organise and to elect their own representatives as the strikers' principal demands. In a telegram to Premier Frank Wise, he wrote:

I AM ASKED TO ADVISE YOU THAT FOLLOWING SPARODIC STRIKE ACTION A GENERAL STRIKE NATIVE WORKERS WILL OPEN MAY FIRST STRIKE DEMANDS YOUR GOVERNMENT RECOGNISE THEIR RIGHT TO ORGANISE AND APPOINT A REPRESENTATIVE DELAYED SETTLEMENT WILL WIDEN TROUBLE AREA AND DISLOCATE SHEARING OPERATIONS I AM ASKED TO HANDLE NEGOTIATIONS FOR STRIKERS RECOMMEND

---

8   Joan Williams, *Anger and Love*, p. 127.
9   Minoru Hokari has argued that this was also the case for the Gurindji walk-offs from Wave Hill twenty years later. ('From Wattie Creek to Wattie Creek: An Oral History Approach to the Gurindji Walk-Off', *Aboriginal History*, vol. 24, 2000, p. 113).

ACCEPTANCE MODERATE DEMANDS ENABLE
SHEARING PROCEED HAVE WRITTEN ADVISE.[10]

He followed the telegram with a letter, drafted in Perth, with copies forwarded to the Commissioner of Native Affairs, Francis Bray, and widely distributed to newspapers, politicians, unions and other organisations, which also stated that 'the demands of the strikers are that their right to organise be accepted by your Government and their right to appoint a representative be given effect to'.[11]

On 1 May, workers on Strelley Station, fifty kilometres east of Port Hedland, and on Tabba Tabba Station further to the south, refused to work, but were uncertain about how they should proceed. Should they return to work if their demand for 30/- per week was granted, or should they continue to remain in camp until they heard from McLeod, even if wage increases were granted? Some workers, such as Ernie Mitchell (Putungaja) of Tabba Tabba Station, already received 50/- per week. They decided to discuss the situation with McLeod in Port Hedland to clarify their position, and told station management – Reg Sherlock on Strelley Station and Alan Crawford on Tabba Tabba – that they would not return to work until they had spoken to McLeod. Sherlock and Crawford contacted Constable Les Fletcher in Port Hedland, who advised them to accede to the strikers' wishes and bring representatives from each station into town, calling first at the police station so that he, Fletcher, could talk to them.

When Ernie Mitchell and another man from Tabba Tabba, and Wambi Ball and Robin from Strelley Station, arrived in Port Hedland on 2 May, they refused to see Fletcher before speaking to McLeod. According to Fletcher, they wanted to know from McLeod what his instructions were now that they had stopped work. Fletcher intruded on their discussion and asked McLeod what the strikers' demands were. Although we only have Fletcher's account of the discussion that took place, there seems to have been some disagreement between McLeod and Wambi Ball about what demands should be made. McLeod insisted that he was not interested in wages, as these were a domestic matter between workers and management on stations, but that 'the natives were unanimous in their desire to better themselves and had appointed him as their representative', and were striking because the Commissioner had refused them the right do so.[12] It was the right to elect their own representative that

---

10 McLeod to Premier Wise, telegram, 30 April 1946, SROWA 1946/150.
11 McLeod to Wise, 30 April 1946, p. 1, SROWA 1946/150/46.
12 Fletcher to Bray, 2 May 1946, p. 3, SROWA 1945/0800/58

was the core demand. According to Fletcher, McLeod 'told the boys that that was what they were being organised for'.[13] Fletcher denied that Bray had refused them this right, stating that he had simply refused to accept McLeod as that representative.

Wambi Ball, however, stated that they had definitely understood from strike organisers that they should demand 30/- per week. Despite McLeod's insistence that representation was the main issue, the Tabba Tabba and Strelley workers decided to negotiate a wage increase. Fletcher believed that 'the boys did not appear to understand the representative idea'.[14] These two competing objectives were to be a source of conflict within the strike movement over the coming months, with some strikers viewing increased wages and working conditions on stations as the primary goal, while others wanted to hold out for greater autonomy.

Following their discussion with McLeod, the Tabba Tabba and Strelley men talked the matter over with their employers in Fletcher's presence and agreed to return to work for a temporary wage increase of 5/- per week. This was to be paid 'during the shearing only', Fletcher wrote, 'with a review when shearing was completed, and the boys were content with that arrangement'.[15] On Tabba Tabba, as on De Grey, the temporary wage increase was to be paid in lieu of bonuses usually given when the shearing was complete, and on Strelley Station an extra 5/- was usually paid during the shearing, so Aboriginal workers gained little from the temporary wage increases.[16] Strelley manager Reg Sherlock wrote that his station was no worse off for this concession.[17] The agreement appeared to be something of a sleight of hand on the part of station managers and seemed to confirm the authorities' belief that *marrngu* did 'not understand and [had] no value for money'.[18] However, it enabled *marrngu* to put off taking strike action until after the shearing. While it made sense from a strategic point of view to strike when labour was most needed, a sense of loyalty to stations and squatter bosses made this the most difficult time for *marrngu* to refuse to work. Many were reluctant to let their stations down at this critical time. The agreement with Alan Crawford of Tabba Tabba, for example, enabled Ernie Mitchell to see

---

13 Fletcher to Bray, 2 May 1946, p. 3, SROWA 1945/0800/58
14 Fletcher to Bray, 2 May 1946, p. 4, SROWA 1945/0800/59.
15 Fletcher to Bray, 2 May 1946, p. 4, SROWA 1945/0800/59.
16 O'Neill, statement for McLeod trial, 24 May 1946, p. 1, SROWA 1945/0800/135
17 Reg Sherlock to Kitty, 15 May 1946, Sherlock family personal collection.
18 Coverley, 'Notes of Deputation from the State Executive, Australian Labour Party', 2 July 1946, SROWA 1945/0800/269.

out the shearing before leaving the station to join the small community of strikers at the Twelve Mile, near Port Hedland.

This willingness to compromise weakened the May Day action. The success of the strategy was contingent on widespread coordinated stoppages, but circumstances on stations varied, and *marrngu* adapted the action to their own situation. At De Grey, as we have seen, *marrngu* decided to strike before the muster began, and at Carlindi Station, on the East Strelley River, workers decided to put off striking until the owner-manager, Don McGregor, returned from Perth, where he was having medical treatment.[19]

The difficulty of coordinating action across widely dispersed workplaces further contributed to the failure of the action planned for that day. Not all those who needed Dooley's rough hand-drawn calendars had received them, nor did the calendars always prove an effective tool for determining the right day to strike. While workers on Munda and Warrawagine Stations stopped work early, other station communities were still waiting for the message to begin the strike as May Day came and went, and many who intended to take part in the action found themselves confronted by Constable Gordon Marshall even before they had downed tools.

The patrol carried out by Marshall during the first two days of May played a significant role in suppressing the May Day strike. *Marrngu* at Coongan (or Bungalow) Station on the De Grey River had been visited by Dooley some weeks previously and were prepared to strike. On 30 April, they notified the manager, Neville Flight-Smith, of their intention. Flight-Smith persuaded them to hold off their stop-work action until Marshall's arrival the following morning. Marshall spent 'a good deal of time' talking to *marrngu*, including a man called Billy Bungalow, a strong supporter of the strike. Marshall described him as 'a strong McLeod man'.[20] When Marshall told them that Flight-Smith was a good boss, Billy Bungalow retorted, 'If he is such a good boss, you work for him'.[21]

Nevertheless, Marshall managed to persuade them not to strike. 'These like the other natives, said that McLeod had told them to stop work, & await word from him', Marshall wrote.[22] Although in reporting on his patrol he portrayed his interaction with strikers as friendly discussion and advice, it is likely that he used intimidation and threats of arrest, backed up if necessary

---

19   O'Neill, statement for McLeod trial, 24 May 1946, p. 2, SROWA 1945/0800/134.
20   Marshall to Bray, 1 June 1946, p. 1, SROWA 1945/0800/170.
21   In Williams and Noakes, *How the West was Lost*.
22   Marshall, police patrol journal, 1 May 1946, SROWA 1943/0099 v7.

by a display of the bag of chains that had been successfully used the previous day to convince *marrngu* at Warrawagine to return to work. Equally powerful was Marshall's insistence that the strike was not proceeding on any of the stations he had visited on his patrol.

Workers at Eginbah and Mulyie Stations intended to strike, but were waiting to be notified of the right day to do so. Both station communities were visited by Marshall on 1 May and persuaded not to engage in any strike action.[23] O'Neill reported that Mulyie workers were unsure about whether or not to take part in the strike and were dissuaded from doing so by Marshall's visit.[24] At Nimingarra Station, also, workers intended to strike but had not done so when Marshall visited on the afternoon of 1 May. They too were persuaded by Marshall that the strike was not going ahead and that there would be consequences if they did not continue working. At Muccan station on the De Grey River, Marshall found people particularly determined to resist intimidation. He described them as 'very touchy' and 'strongly McLeod's way'. Nevertheless, they had not been aware that the strike had started and were still working when Marshall arrived to speak to them on 2 May. They gave him 'a good hearing', he wrote, and decided to follow his advice and continue working.[25] Marshall believed his patrol of stations had been successful in 'setting the natives' minds at ease'.[26] 'I am quite satisfied that had I not got out early and made this patrol amongst these people', he wrote:

> they would have all followed the Warrawagine natives and gone on strike, and this would have been a very bad smash, as the natives would never have got their jobs back again, or if any it would only have been the pick boys of each place - this would have thrown a large number onto the Government to keep, as some of these people could not live in the bush and on bush tucker.[27]

'Pastoralists were very thankful for this patrol', Marshall wrote, '& I feel sure that it will have a good effect on the native generally'.[28]

Many station communities needed no such persuasion. At both Callewa and Hillside Stations, *marrngu* had no interest in the strike and no intention

---

23 Marshall to Bray, 1 June 1946, p. 2, SROWA 1945/0800/171.
24 O'Neill, statement for McLeod trial, 24 May 1946, SROWA 1945/0800/13.
25 Marshall to Bray, 1 June 1946, p. 2, SROWA 1945/0800/171.
26 Marshall, letter accompanying travel voucher, SROWA 1945/0800/167.
27 Marshall to Bray, 1 June 1946, p. 4, SROWA 1945/0800/173.
28 Marshall to Bray, 1 June 1946, p. 2, SROWA 1945/0800/171.

of being part of the action. Willie Lockyer of Hillside Station stated that he had been telling McLeod for years that he was on the wrong track.[29] *Marrngu* at Boodarie Station, near Port Hedland, also chose not to strike, despite having been visited by both Dooley and McKenna, and despite telling Dooley that they would join in.[30] On stations where the general consensus was to take part in the action, some individuals had personal reasons for not being involved. Although most workers on Eginbah Station were prepared to strike, for example, Clancy McKenna's stepfather, Murphy Ball, who had five small children to support, told the manager, 'I can't go on strike boss, I got too many kids to go bush!'[31]

Other station communities were sufficiently uncertain about the advisability of striking that they were easily persuaded to keep working. At Lalla Rookh Station, *marrngu* had the calendar that Dooley had drawn up for Jimmy Woodman, and on 1 May they told owner-manager Edmund Jeffries that they would not work. After discussing the matter with Jeffries, however, they decided to wait and see what happened on other stations. The fear of repercussions if only a few workers took such action was clearly at play here.[32]

Marrngu at Warralong Station were also wary of taking part. Dooley had visited the station the previous month, and had found that people there were fearful and not inclined to join in.[33] Their reticence is interesting, given that Dougal Cornish, who had been an early agitator for the strike, was working at Warralong, along with Peter Coppin (Kangkushot), who later played a prominent role in the strike and who would become a leader of the movement in the 1950s and beyond. When Marshall visited the station on 1 May, *marrngu* had not stopped work, and he reported, after speaking to them, that he was sure they would not stop now.[34]

Strike action was not limited to workers on stations. Some town workers and miners also struck on 1 May. Dooley was in Marble Bar that day and, with his encouragement, men and women employed in the hotel, at the garage, and as domestic servants in private homes, including Marshall's, stayed at the town reserve instead of proceeding to their jobs. Tommy Dodd, Jackson and

---

29 Marshall to Bray, 1 June 1946, p. 3, SROWA 1945/0800/172.
30 O'Neill's statement for McLeod trial, 24 May 1946, p. 1, SROWA 1945/0800/135.
31 Marshall, police patrol journal, 1 May 1946, 1943/0099 v7.
32 O'Neill's statement for McLeod trial, 24 May 1946, p. 2, SROWA 1945/0800/134.
33 Dooley, High Court appeal, D. W. McLeod v. G. R. Richards, NAA A10074 1946/8, 9, 10, p. 21.
34 Marshall, police patrol report, 1 May 1946, SROWA 1943/0099 v7.

Paddy Northover informed the owner of the Ironclad Hotel that they were going on strike – not against their bosses, they said, but 'for Don McLeod'.[35] When Marshall returned from his successful patrol of stations in the area in the late afternoon of 2 May, he found the strike underway there. 'Every native employed in and about Marble Bar, were on strike', he wrote, 'and were sitting down in the town natives camp' together with six strikers who had walked into town from nearby Limestone Station.[36]

Just as Aboriginal residence on pastoral properties was conditional on compliance with settler labour demands, residence on the Marble Bar native reserve was restricted to people employed in the town, indigents on government rations and people receiving medical attention. Restriction of movement and residence was central to the controls exercised over Aboriginal people. By striking, *marrngu* forfeited their right to live in Marble Bar. 'At 7 pm. I lined all the unemployed natives up & spoke to them', Marshall wrote:

> & warned them that any that were not at work in the morning, to take their swags & walk out of the town, as the town camp is only for ration natives, sick natives attending hospital & casual visitors.

Under pressure from Marshall, and with Dooley having left for Limestone Station, the strikers agreed to return to their jobs. The following morning, the Limestone workers returned to their station. When the Marble Bar workers reported for work, however, their employers refused to reinstate them, and all but one were sacked. Now unemployed, they were ordered by Marshall to leave town and to support themselves gouging alluvial tin at Moolyella, twelve miles away. They included the parents of Molly Williams, who worked for Marshall without pay, looking after goats.[37] 'Although they did not much work', Minister Bob Coverley said, 'they would have had a home for the rest of their lives, but now they are forced to draw rations from the Government'.[38] 'This position was a sad one for the native', Marshall wrote. 'The employers of these natives that stuck, will not employ them again'.[39] It was a punitive

---

35 Tommy Dodd, High Court appeal, D. W. McLeod v. G. R. Richards, p. 31, NAA A10074 1946/8, 9, 10, p. 31.
36 Marshall to Bray, 1 June 1946, p. 1, SROWA 1945/0800/170.
37 Molly Williams (Kulyu), tape 1, recorded 13 August 1991, author's collection; Coverley, 'Notes of Deputation from the State Executive', Australian Labour Party, 2 July 1946, p. 4, SROWA 1945/0800/272.
38 Coverley, 'Notes of Deputation from the State Executive', Australian Labour Party, 2 July 1946, p. 4, SROWA 1945/0800/272.
39 Marshall to Bray, 1 June 1946, p. 3, SROWA 1945/0800/172.

response intended to send a message to *marrngu* that their labour was not essential and that such challenges to settler authority would not be tolerated.

Learning that those deported to Moolyella had no money or food, Dooley drew on strike funds held by Ken Duncan at Hansen's Store to purchase a supply of tobacco.[40] These domestic workers formed a nucleus of what would later become a large strike camp at Moolyella.

With stop-work activities taking place in isolated pockets over a wide geographic area, it was difficult for organisers to know just how the strike was progressing. On the moonless night of 1 May, McKenna and McLeod met in secret on the beach at Port Hedland to exchange news. McLeod was eager to know if the strike was going ahead as planned. McKenna had little information to give him; the strike was strong, he said, but not everyone had struck. McLeod assured him that they had strong support from people in the south. 'Don't worry', he said, 'we got power behind us'. He told McKenna that he expected the strike to last four days or a week, depending on how things developed in Perth. They agreed to hold a further meeting on the beach 'behind Sue's' in Port Hedland two nights later to assess the situation and decide on further steps that needed to be taken.[41]

The 'power' behind them, the southern support essential to the success of the strike, needed to be kept informed of events, but at this early stage McLeod had little factual information to give. Nevertheless, he wired the *Daily News* in Perth, informing them that 'seven hundred to a thousand' were involved in 'a natives' strike' and that the wool industry was paralysed, with five sheds 'being hung up'.[42] It was a gross overstatement of the actual situation. The *Daily News* contacted Bray for confirmation. This was the first information that the Department had received that the strike threatened by McLeod in his telegram of 30 April had actually taken place. Bray wondered what course of action could be taken. McLeod was 'a dangerous type of man, and an Anti-Fascist', he told his minister, Coverley, 'but it would appear that his activities are not unlawful, even though they are of a mischievous nature'.[43] The following day he wired Travelling Inspector O'Neill in Fitzroy Crossing, instructing him to proceed without delay to the Port Hedland area.[44]

---

40   Dooley, High Court appeal, D. W. McLeod v. G. R. Richards, NAA A10074 1946/8, 9, 10, p. 22.

41   McKenna, High Court appeal, D. W. McLeod v. G. R. Richards, NAA A10074 1946/8, 9, 10, p. 27.

42   Cited in Bray to Coverley, 2 May 1946, p. 1, SROWA 1945/0800/49.

43   Bray to Coverley, 2 May 1946, p. 1, SROWA 1945/0800/49.

44   Bray to O'Neill, telegram, 3 May 1946, SROWA 1945/0800/46.

Sporadic strike action continued through the first week of May. Although little action took place further south in the Nullagine region, workers on Roy Hill Station south of Nullagine stopped work on 6 May, demanding higher wages. They were told by the manager that they could either leave the station or continue working, but that no wage increase would be paid. Workers had returned to their jobs by the time Constable Rowe of Nullagine arrived, at the manager's request, to warn them against 'these Communistic teachings'.[45] In the Port Hedland area, Wallareenya Station workers stopped work on 4 May, returning to their jobs following a visit from Fletcher and an agreement that an increase of 5/- a week would be paid for the duration of the shearing.[46]

Perhaps encouraged by this outcome, eight *marrngu* stopped work a few days later at the nearby Indee Station, where shearing was underway. The manager refused to grant an increase 'as a matter of principle', preferring to carry on shorthanded and risk a reduced wool clip rather than to bow to demands he considered unreasonable.[47] According to a letter written to McLeod by Euralian Association secretary Pop Clarke a year earlier, the McWhirters of Indee Station had instituted significant improvements in accommodation, food and pay for Aboriginal workers when they took over management of the station, and resentment at their workers' decision to strike in spite of these improvements may have been behind their decision to evict.[48] The workers and their families left the station, shifting to the Twelve Mile camp near Port Hedland, where they joined *marrngu* evicted a few days earlier from Munda Station, forming the nucleus of a second strike camp that would be established there some weeks later.[49] On the banks of the Petermarer Creek, the Twelve Mile had been an Army camp during the war, and a well sunk there by the Army provided a supply of water.

Bray approved of the decision to remove to the Twelve Mile anyone who refused to work. 'This action will have a good influence on the native situation generally', he wrote.[50] Exemplifying the use of rations as a means of control and surveillance over Aboriginal people, the government rationed displaced workers 'to prevent them from travelling from station to station causing

---

45 Rowe to Bray, 9 May 1946, SROWA 1945/0800/74–75.
46 O'Neill, statement for McLeod trial, 24 May 1946, p. 2, SROWA 1945/0800/134.
47 O'Neill to Bray, 9 May 1946, SROWA 1945/0800/70.
48 L. W. Clarke to McLeod, 21 March 1945, A. P. Elkin Papers, University of Sydney Archives, box 76, file 262.
49 O'Neill to Bray, 26 May 1946, SROWA 1945/0800/144.
50 Bray to O'Neill, 14 May 1946, SROWA 1945/0800/68.

dissent amongst working natives'.[51] 'The natives will need to remain at the Twelve-Mile', Bray wrote, 'and this means that we shall at least know where they are, and be able to take prompt action should they attempt to leave the Twelve-Mile and travel from station to station for the purpose of causing dissent among working natives'.[52]

By the end of the first week in May, the authorities felt confident that order had been effectively re-established in the area and certainly felt under no pressure to negotiate with McLeod. No reply was given to his letter of 30 April. 'There is reason to believe that the trouble is clearing up', Bray wrote hopefully.[53] 'The Police Protectors in the affected districts have handled the matter very well indeed, and firmly too, and I am indebted to them for their thoughtful services'.[54]

---

51 O'Neill to Bray, 9 May 1946, SROWA 1945/0800/70–71.
52 Bray to O'Neill, 14 May 1946, SROWA 1945/0800/68.
53 Bray to Wise, 7 May 1946, SROWA 1945/0800/61.
54 Bray to O'Neill, 14 May 1946, SROWA 1945/0800/68.

Chapter 8

'McLeod's Insidious Anti Fascist Communistic Activities'

Responses, May–June 1946

By the end of the first week of May, the situation in the Pilbara had, to a large extent, returned to normal. On all stations except Indee, the shearing was proceeding largely unaffected, with *marrngu* carrying out their allotted tasks as usual. Nevertheless, the Department of Native Affairs came under pressure to show its colours in the affair. Its attempted intervention in pastoral labour relations through the permit system had been resented by many pastoralists, and there was some suspicion that its failure to take effective action to prevent the unrest arose from a sympathy with *marrngu* demands for improved wages and conditions. Constable Marshall expressed such a suspicion when first alerted to strike action on 30 April. 'I thought long ago that the Department of Native Affairs, had sufficient evidence to prosecute McLeod in some way or another', he wrote, 'but it appears to me that the Dept of Native Affairs are a little afraid of McLeod's backers, or are in favour with his views – in having natives wages increased etc'.[1]

The North-West and Kimberley Advancement Association, which, a year earlier, McLeod had hoped would become a vehicle for implementing his ideas for regenerating the Pilbara, demanded to know the Department's position on the situation. On 6 May, Bray received a telegram from the Association:

IN VIEW STRONG FEELINGS ENGENDERED THROUGH NATIVE STRIKE THIS ASSOCIATION WOULD APPRECIATE ADVISE REGARDING DEPARTMENTS ATTITUDE ON MATTER STOP NATIVE GUARDED FROM EXPLOITATION BY DEPARTMENT AND PRESENT SITUATION APPARENTLY CAUSED BY AGITATORS WITH ULTERIOR MOTIVES DOES

---

1   Marshall, police report, 30 April 1946, SROWA 1943/0099 v7.

NOT APPEAR POSSIBLY BENEFICIAL IN LONG RUN TO EITHER NATIVES OR PASTORALISTS.[2]

Both the Advancement Association and the Pastoralists Association pressured the government and the Department to take action to prevent any further destabilisation of Aboriginal labour. Bill Hegney, Member for Pilbara in the state Labor government and now state president of the AWU, added his voice to calls for the Department to take action. 'Pastoralists are anxious that some action be taken to prevent McLeod from disturbing the natives', he wrote.[3]

The Department was quick to reassure the pastoral lobby that it opposed the strike and that action was being taken to re-establish control. It believed that a resurgence of unrest could best be prevented by working in concert with the Police Department to establish sufficient evidence of McLeod's role in instigating the strike and so secure a conviction and a significant prison sentence. With McLeod out of the picture, it believed, the cause of the problem would be removed and order permanently restored. To achieve this, the Department's Travelling Inspector for the vast northern region, Laurie O'Neill, who was in Fitzroy Crossing at the beginning of May, was wired with urgent instructions:

PROCEED FIRST PLANE PORT HEDLAND NATIVE LABOUR SITUATION NOW VERY DISTURBED AND STRIKES TAKING PLACE BECAUSE OF MCLEOD'S INSIDIOUS ANTI FASCIST COMMUNISTIC ACTIVITIES COOPERATE WITH POLICE IN ANY POSSIBLE FIRM ACTION AGAINST MCLEOD BUT MAY NOW BE POSSIBLE TO OBTAIN EVIDENCE BREACH SECTION 39 FOR BEING ON PLACE WHERE NATIVES CONGREGATED PRESS FOR FULL TERM IMPRISONMENT HAVE ARRANGED PLANE JOURNEY[4]

Underpinning the Department's focus on securing a prosecution against McLeod as the solution to the disturbance was an assumption that Aboriginal people were incapable of engaging in organised political activity of this nature. In 1946, the Department and the Western Australian government still maintained a profoundly racist understanding of human difference, holding onto assumptions of the inherent biological inferiority of Aboriginal

---

2 'Advancement Assn' to Bray, telegram, 6 May 1946, SROWA 1945/0800/63.
3 Hegney to Premier, Frank Wise, 17 May 1946, SROWA 1946/150/46.
4 Bray to O'Neill, telegram, 3 May 1946, SROWA 1945/0800/46.

people against a tide of change that would radically alter policy in Aboriginal affairs by the end of the decade. Hugh Leslie, a Country Party Member of the Legislative Assembly, for example, recommended at this time a policy of complete segregation of Aboriginal people from the rest of the community. 'The native only reaches a stage of mental inferiority and experiences a feeling of antagonism to the white man when he is brought into contact with whites who impress that outlook upon him', he wrote. 'The difficulty arises when he is amongst the whites and gets the idea that he is as good as the white man. When he realises that he is, intellectually, backward, that is when his spirit of antagonism against the white man comes forward'.[5]

Aboriginal people were assumed to have limited intellectual facilities that restricted their capacity for rational thought. Fifteen years earlier, Native Inspector Laurie O'Neill, then a policeman in the Kimberley, had told the author Ion Idriess that 'the stone-age man' was 'chained to the primitive by a mental chain that he will never break; he seems to have been born a million years ago with a brain that could not expand as the rest of humanity developed'.[6] Instinct and impulse, it was believed, governed Aboriginal actions to a greater degree than rational thought. 'The natives are not of stable mental capacity as compared with whites', Commissioner Bray wrote in 1944, 'and they are not equipped educationally to resist the allurements put forth by Communists and Anti-Fascists, the latter being "horses of the same colour"'.[7] The *West Australian* of 4 May 1946 drew on information from Bray to report on the strike under the headline 'Easy Prey for Malcontents':

> A few malcontents are responsible for the trouble, which has an outside inspiration for the creation of unrest. Ordinarily the natives are well-behaved and are happy in the work which is given to them, but they are led easily and they are easy prey for the malcontents who are natives of bad character.[8]

Meanwhile, at least one of those 'malcontents' was continuing to keep the strike idea alive. On the night of 3 May, McKenna and McLeod, both fearful, met with a group of *marrngu* men, including Togo, Darby, Reggie and Angus, on the Port Hedland beach 'behind Sue's', as planned. It was

---

5   Hugh Alan Leslie, Parliamentary Debates (Hansard), Western Australia: Legislative Assembly, 14 November 1946, p. 1977.
6   Quoted in Idriess, *Over the Range*, p. 25.
7   Bray to Coverley, 2 October 1944, SROWA 1944/0077/10.
8   Bray, media statement, 3 May 1946, SROWA 1945/0800/52.

now clear that the May Day strike was failing, and McLeod told McKenna to continue working to encourage *marrngu* to keep the strike going. They decided to invite representatives from all stations in the region to a meeting at the Twelve Mile on 25 May to regroup, look at what had taken place on the various stations and plan next steps. They hoped the meeting would enable them to 'to clarify reports of strike progress and straighten out tangled versions'.[9] McKenna began immediately, meeting with men from Wallal and Mandora Stations on the coast north of Port Hedland who were camped at the Two Mile, informing them of the meeting and encouraging them to join the strike. Tommy Nangananga (Manapurtja), a Mangarla speaker who worked in Port Hedland as a police tracker, also attended the meeting at the Two Mile.

Over the next few days, McKenna moved around, spreading word in the Port Hedland region about the meeting and arranging for delegates to attend. He planned to leave Port Hedland on 8 May to take the message to Marble Bar and stations further afield, but O'Neill arrived from Fitzroy Crossing and put a stop to his activities. O'Neill placed him under arrest in Port Hedland on the night of 7 May, charged with breaching section 47 of the *Native Administration Act*, a section designed to prevent employers from poaching labour from other stations. It allowed for the prosecution of anyone 'who entices or persuades a native to leave any lawful service without the consent of a protector'.

O'Neill had previously advised against arresting McKenna and Dooley, fearing they could be held up as martyrs by McLeod. 'I was a little doubtful of the advisability of proceeding against natives under Sec. 47', he wrote, 'but it was very necessary to take some action against McKenna and Dooley and I could see no other means of doing so'.[10]

> It is realized that McKenna is only the mouthpiece of Don McLeod but he is responsible for other natives leaving their employment ... Some method of detaining McKenna was urgently necessary as he was continuing the agitation for a strike.[11]

It was also hoped that the arrests of McKenna and Dooley would provide a salutary lesson to other *marrngu*. Fletcher wrote a week later that there

---

9   McKenna, High Court appeal, D. W. McLeod v. G. R. Richards, NAA A10074 1946/8, 9, 10, p. 27.

10   O'Neill to Bray, 9 May 1946, p. 2, SROWA 1945/0800/71.

11   O'Neill to Bray, 9 May 1946, p. 1, SROWA 1945/0800/70.

was still 'an undercurrent of unrest amongst the natives', but that 'this was gradually subsiding as news of the arrest of the organisers spread'.[12]

The morning after his arrest, Clancy McKenna was brought before two local Justices of the Peace in the Port Hedland Police Court, convicted and sentenced to three months' imprisonment.[13] One of the Justices of the Peace, F. A. Leeds, belonged to a pastoralist family and was acting secretary of the local branch of the Pastoralists Association. Although it was O'Neill's role as an officer of the Department to defend Aboriginal prisoners in court, he was clearly actively involved in the decision to prosecute McKenna, who effectively received no defence at all. Bray was pleased to hear of McKenna's prosecution, writing to O'Neill that 'as this native had been previously warned by yourself and Constable Fletcher, but persisted in his insidious influence and created unrest with the natives, there was no alternative to his conviction under Section 47'.[14] Dooley was arrested at Moolyella the following day and held in the Marble Bar police cells awaiting a court hearing on the same charge.

With local Justices of the Peace sympathetic to the need to keep Aboriginal labour under control, and the prisoners only nominally represented by O'Neill, securing convictions for McKenna and Dooley was easily achieved. But as these men were believed to be acting under instruction from McLeod, their prosecution could only be a temporary solution to the unrest while the real troublemaker was continuing his agitation behind the scenes. The situation could only really be brought under control, it was believed, by removing McLeod through the imposition of a lengthy prison sentence. There was no evidence, however, that McLeod had broken any law. The Department had hoped for some time to find a way to prosecute him, but had been advised by the Crown Law Department that his actions were not unlawful.[15] Authorities had no doubt that he had met with groups of *marrngu* in breach of section 39 of the *Native Administration Act*, but the covert nature of his activities made this difficult to prove.[16] O'Neill believed, however, that sufficient evidence could be obtained to prove that he had enticed Aboriginal workers from their employment and to charge him with a breach of section 47, as McKenna and

---

12   Fletcher, police patrol report, 19 May 1946, SROWA 1939/1777 v7.

13   O'Neill to Bray, 9 May 1946, p. 1, SROWA 1945/0800/70.

14   Bray to O'Neill, 14 May 1946, SROWA 1945/0800/72.

15   Bray to Coverley, 2 May 1946, SROWA, p. 1, 1945/0800/49.

16   Section 39 reads: 'It shall not be lawful for any person, other than a superintendent or protector, or a person acting under the direction of a superintendent, or under a written permit of a protector, without lawful excuse, to enter or remain or be within or upon any place where natives are camped or where any natives may be congregated or in the course of travelling in pursuance of any native custom.

Dooley had been. 'No doubt he will be severely dealt with by local Justices in view of the sentence awarded McKenna', O'Neill wrote, 'but as there will probably be an appeal the evidence will need to be strong'.[17] One of the principal aims in arresting McKenna and Dooley was to pressure them to provide evidence that could be successfully used to prosecute McLeod.

After the conviction of McKenna and the arrest of Dooley, O'Neill and Fletcher undertook a joint patrol of stations affected by the strike to assess the level of unrest on stations and to warn *marrngu* not to engage in any further strike action. The patrol was also an opportunity to gather evidence that could be used in the case against Dooley and that could be later used to secure a conviction against McLeod. O'Neill's inclusion in the patrol may also have been to assure pastoralists, suspicious of departmental sympathy for the strike, that the Department was taking firm action to quell unrest. Although shearing was going ahead normally on all stations except Indee, and although many of the stations had already been visited by Marshall, this joint patrol by a policeman and by a Native Affairs officer who was also an ex-policeman was an expression of the strength of settler authority, signalling to *marrngu* that their action in the attempted strike was taken very seriously. *Marrngu* were warned against taking any further action of this kind. At Carlindi, for example, where *marrngu* were awaiting the return of the manager before taking strike action, O'Neill and Fletcher 'warned the natives not to cease work'.[18]

O'Neill and Fletcher felt that this patrol provided evidence to support their contention that Aboriginal people had acted in a disturbed and irrational manner when they attempted to strike. The uncertainty, anxiety and differing understandings of the action planned for 1 May were proof, they claimed, that *marrngu* had been incited to strike without reason or comprehension. O'Neill reported that none of *marrngu* he spoke to had any idea of what the strike was about. 'On neither Strelley or Tabba Stations', he wrote, 'did I see a native who understood what the word "strike" meant other than that it meant to cease work, they could not give me any reasons for ceasing work other than that they had been told to do so'.[19] They were quite satisfied with their conditions, he wrote, and intended to continue working. As Gillian Cowlishaw notes,

---

'Any person, save as aforesaid, who, without lawful excuse, the proof whereof shall lie upon him, is found in or within five chains of any such camp shall be guilty of an offence against this Act; but no person shall be prosecuted for an offence under this section except by the direction of a protector.'

17   O'Neill to Bray, 9 May 1946, p. 2, SROWA 1945/0800/71.
18   O'Neill, patrol journal, 11 May 1946, SROWA 1945/0800/127.
19   O'Neill, statement for McLeod trial, 24 May 1946, SROWA 1945/0800/135.

Aboriginal people were 'construed as victims of their desires, rather than in command of their actions ... No recognition or legitimacy was accorded to Aborigines' purposes'.[20] 'I believe that the natives made no decision at all', Fletcher wrote, 'McLeod having made their decision for them and they just follow his lead blindly'.[21] The authorities were prepared to believe that Aboriginal people across the Port Hedland and Marble Bar districts had decided to stand before their bosses and refuse to work just because someone had told them to, even though they knew such action could result in arrest, imprisonment or removal under ministerial warrant. It was consistent with racist assumptions about Aboriginal capacity for rational thought that such an explanation was found sufficient.

Marrngu seem to have been prepared to play along with this expectation. Lined up before the triumvirate of settler authority – the pastoralist, the policeman and the Native Affairs officer – there is little wonder that *marrngu* put on a show of slow-witted befuddlement and ignorance, assuring their inquisitors that they would not be misled into taking such action in the future. With vastly unequal power relations in northern pastoral areas, *marrngu* would sometimes demonstrate submission to authority by playing the 'dumb blackfellow'. In doing so, they avoided the arbitrary violence frequently perpetrated against anyone considered to be insufficiently submissive – 'a cheeky nigger'. A few years previously, a young police constable, Bill Mason, had beaten an Aboriginal man unconscious in the Kimberley for giving false information about his station of residence and for being 'cheeky'. The incident was brought to the attention of the authorities only because the extremely violent assault was carried out in the presence of oil workers from outside the Kimberley. Mason had suffered no disciplinary action as a result of the assault. While the police asserted that he had acted under 'extreme provocation', the only provocation seems to have been a failure on the part of his victim to demonstrate a suitable degree of submissiveness. None of the witnesses who made the complaint identified any other provocation.[22]

In the context of slavery in the southern states of America, displays of submissive obedience have been termed 'samboism'. The term was first used by Stanley Elkins in 1959, who believed it was evidence that slaves had been damaged psychologically by their enslavement.[23] Other writers, however, have

---

20 Cowlishaw, *Rednecks, Eggheads and Blackfellas*, pp. 61–62.
21 Fletcher to Bray, 19 August 1946, SROWA 1946/0799/41.
22 Various documents, SROWA 1940/0324.
23 Stanley Elkins, *Slavery: A Problem in American Institutional and Intellectual Life*, University of Chicago Press, Chicago, 1959.

argued that samboism was a strategy adopted for self-preservation. 'Sambo was in fact a guise', Bertram Wyatt-Brown writes, 'adopted and cast aside as needed'. '"I *wish* to be thought servile", says the sambo, in effect, not, "I *am* servile"'.[24] 'Proper slavish behaviour' included the shuffling of feet, hunched shoulders, downcast eyes and aimless gesturing of hand and body.[25]

There is evidence that *marrngu* used this strategy to resist pressure from authorities throughout the course of the strike. Police and Native Affairs officials would make repeated attempts to convince *marrngu* that their behaviour was against their own best interests, and again and again they believed they were making an impression on the strikers and progress towards ending the strike. As late as 1950, when the strike movement had entered a new phase and *marrngu* were reorganising themselves as a cooperative mining company, a Native Affairs officer encountered the same strategy from one of the leaders, Ernie Mitchell. When Mitchell explained something of the group's organisation to the officer, including the fact that McLeod handled the proceeds of the group's mining efforts, the officer challenged him:

> Asked what would happen if McLeod caught the next plane, he scratched his head. Asked what would happen if McLeod died he didn't know. Ernie is a staunch McLeodite and it will take a lot to sway him. Yet that he was a little impressed was evident because he asked if he could go and get McLeod and would I put the same questions to him.[26]

This scratching of the head, the pretended bewilderment, was, I suggest, a 'dumb blackfellow' performance which *marrngu* adopted to avoid engaging with anyone who spoke to them in a condescending or patronising manner. Interestingly, John and Katrin Wilson, who undertook anthropological research with the group in 1959–60, witnessed a similar performance when a gem buyer used simplified language in speaking to Ernie Mitchell and Peter Coppin. By 1960, these men had many years' experience as leaders of the mining cooperative, and both were shareholders and directors of an Aboriginal mining company, Pindan Pty Ltd, with Mitchell being Managing Director. Mitchell was also a director of a syndicate company, Simdan, and the principal liaison between Pindan and the outside world, engaging on a daily basis with

---

24   Bertram Wyatt-Brown, 'The Mask of Obedience: Male Slave Psychology in the Old South', *The American Historical Review*, vol. 93, no. 5, 1988, p. 1245 (emphasis in original).
25   Wyatt-Brown, 'Mask of Obedience', p. 1242.
26   N. P. Hawke, patrol report no. 2 of 1950/51, 2 April 1950 to 8 September 1950, SROWA 1950/0741/11–13.

non-Aboriginal people on many different levels.[27] 'Both of these guys were very switched on', Katrin Wilson said. The Wilsons therefore watched with some amazement when, approached by the gem buyer, 'they immediately, without any apparent arrangement between them, became dumb blackfellas'. They exhibited much of the body language that Wyatt-Brown had identified as 'proper slavish behaviour', looking down, rubbing their toes in the sand, mumbling, 'Ooh, I dunno'. 'He treated them like idiots, so they behaved like idiots', Katrin said. When the buyer looked away, the men made hand signals to one another, resuming their role-playing when he turned back.[28]

Ernie Mitchell was working at Tabba Tabba Station in mid-May 1946 when O'Neill and Fletcher undertook their patrol of stations. Having consulted with McLeod on 1 May, and having made an agreement with pastoralist Alan Crawford to continue working at an increased rate of pay for the duration of the shearing, Mitchell probably acted as spokesman for other Tabba Tabba workers during the officers' visit. One can imagine him and his co-workers, when sternly lectured and threatened by O'Neill, feigning ignorance and confusion, assuring him that they now understood that McLeod had misled them and that they would not be so foolish as to listen to such talk in future. 'After listening to Const. Fletcher and myself', O'Neill wrote, Tabba Tabba workers 'stated their intention of continuing work ... Like the Strelley natives, the [Tabba Tabba] crowd were satisfied that McLeod was causing trouble for them'.[29] Despite such assurances, however, Mitchell and another man named Paddy only stayed at Tabba Tabba to assist with the shearing. They left when the shearing was completed, joining the small community that had been displaced by the strike at the Twelve Mile. Since Mitchell was relatively well paid as a highly skilled station worker on a weekly wage of £2/10/-, and had no dispute with station management, his decision to leave Tabba Tabba to join the independent community at the Twelve Mile provides evidence that assurances of compliance with settler authority made during the joint patrol were merely a 'mask of obedience'.[30] Even so, O'Neill still chose to portray Mitchell as reacting to outside stimulus when he left the station, rather than as acting rationally. 'There is

---

27   Katrin Wilson, 'The Allocation of Sex Roles', p. 188. Simdan was a syndicate company formed in 1959 to exploit a manganese deposit as a joint project of Alfred J. Sims Pty Ltd. and the Aboriginal company, Pindan.
28   John and Katrin Wilson, recorded by Anne Scrimgeour, Fremantle, 25 May 2016, author's collection.
29   O'Neill, patrol journal, 11 May 1946, p. 1, SROWA 1945/0800/127.
30   Wyatt-Brown, 'Mask of Obedience'.

no doubt that indirectly the recent strike is the cause of Mitchell leaving station employment', O'Neill wrote, 'as it caused him to become unsettled and discontented'.[31]

The belief that Aboriginal people did not know what they were doing when they refused to work was widely accepted, underpinned by a poor estimation of their ability to understand concepts beyond their immediate lived experiences. The Member for Pilbara in the state's Labor government, Bill Hegney, wrote that 'needless to say the bulk of them did not know what they were leaving work for'.[32] O'Neill maintained his opinion that Aboriginal people were not capable of conducting a strike. 'I have had very many years experience amongst natives', he wrote, 'and I know that the strike organized for the 1st of May could not have originated from the natives themselves'. After talking to many Aboriginal people, he was confident that none had any understanding of the meaning of the word 'strike'.[33]

Certainly, *marrngu* held differing ideas about the objectives of the strike and the process by which those objectives might be achieved. Later usage of the word 'strike' in Aboriginal dialects of English suggests that it came to have a meaning for *marrngu* that differed from its Standard English meaning. In 1991, for example, Molly Williams used the term in referring to the split that took place in 1959, when a faction of the Aboriginal cooperative, led by Ernie Mitchell and Peter Coppin, broke away from a faction led by McLeod. 'Peter Coffin[34] and my son-in-law [Ernie Mitchell]', she said, 'bin start strike off him, leave this Old Man [McLeod]'.[35] Claims by *marrngu* in the 1980s and 1990s to be still on strike further suggests that it carried a different meaning in Aboriginal English.[36] But if *marrngu* purposes in refusing to work did not neatly correspond to O'Neill's understanding of the concept of a strike, it does not follow that their actions were a blind and uncomprehending response to McLeod's meddling interference in Aboriginal affairs.

Constable Gordon Marshall of Marble Bar also insisted that 'these people do not know what they are doing'. Among the strikers in Marble Bar on 1 May were six workers who were already receiving the demanded pay rate of 30/- a week. Marshall argued that their participation in a strike for 30/- a week was

---

31 O'Neill to Bray, 5 July 1946, SROWA 1945/0800/246.
32 Hegney to Wise, 17 May 1946, SROWA 1946/150/46.
33 O'Neill, statement for McLeod trial, 24 May 1946, p. 3, SROWA1945/0800/133.
34 The surnames 'Coppin' and 'Coffin' are used interchangeably.
35 Molly Williams (Kulyu), tape 1, recorded 13 August 1991, author's collection.
36 Hokari has also noted that the word had a different meaning in Gurindji Creole to its Standard English meaning. 'From Wattie Creek to Wattie Creek', p. 108.

clear evidence that they were acting without understanding.[37] However, 30/- was demanded as a basic wage rate for all (male) Aboriginal workers, and it is not inconsistent with the concept of a strike for all workers to down tools to achieve this. Nor is it inconsistent for all workers to come out in a show of solidarity. One of the Marble Bar men, Tommy Dodd, stated in court, 'I went on strike because I cant scab on others ... All wanted 30/- that why strike'.[38] These men also indicated that they wanted McLeod to represent them, stating that they were striking 'for Don McLeod'.

Marshall also referred to the participation in the strike of an old miner with his own prospecting area as evidence that *marrngu* had no understanding of what they were doing. However, *marrngu* probably joined the strike in the hope that, by doing so, they could achieve a greater degree of control over their lives. According to Jack McPhee, it was very difficult for Aboriginal prospectors to get a fair price for their mineral, many being paid in tea, sugar or tobacco at well below the true value of the mineral exchanged. Prospectors may well have joined the strike movement in the hope that this situation could be improved.

Nevertheless, throughout the course of the strike and beyond, the story of the miner going on strike against himself, and of the worker on 30/- a week striking for 30/- a week, would be laughingly repeated to portray Aboriginal strikers as rather pitiful and ludicrous puppets in someone else's game. Bray cited these two incidents to show 'the absurd but tragic aspects of using the natives so wretchedly'.[39] A short monthly report on McLeod by the Australian Security Intelligence Organisation (ASIO) stated that 'in many cases native boys earning £2/- per week went on strike for thirty shillings, which proves they do not understand the reasons for the strike'.[40] 'There was one native at Marble Bar who had a bit of a gold mine on his own, and he went on strike on himself', pastoralist Edith Miller said with a laugh in 1982, adding, 'But it was pitiful, really pitiful'.[41]

Over the following months, the Department repeated the assertion that 'investigation discloses that the station blacks do not understand McLeod's propaganda' to argue that no genuine grievances had motivated the strike.

---

37   Marshall, police patrol journal, 2 May 1946, SROWA 1943/0099 v7.
38   Tommy Dodd, High Court appeal, D. W. McLeod v. G. R. Richards, NAA A10074 1946/8, 9, 10, p. 31.
39   Bray to Coverley, 6 June 1946, SROWA 1945/0800/174.
40   ASIO monthly report for September, Donald William McLeod, vol. 1, NAA A6126, 1188.
41   Edith Miller, interviewed by Jamieson, 1982, transcript, p. 100, SLWA OH506.

It was frequently stated that Aboriginal people lived happy and carefree lives on stations. 'Never do we see a happier form of humanity than among the natives on a well-run station', northern pastoralist and Member of the Legislative Council Leslie Craig said. 'They laugh from morning till night'.[42] Only the mischievous interference of troublemakers like McLeod and his ilk threatened to destroy their peaceful contentment. The low standard of their living conditions was not the result of pastoralist parsimony but of their own backwardness. 'The natives are not sufficiently advanced to appreciate white conditions', Commissioner Bray wrote.[43] 'Nowadays, the employers are earnestly interested in looking after their native workers and their welfare', he insisted, and if satisfactory conditions were not being provided, 'the natives [were] responsible for this, due to their leanings to native standards'.[44] O'Neill agreed that *marrngu* had no genuine grievances and nothing to gain by going on strike. 'The average station native was contented and happy until influenced by [McLeod] and his agitations', he wrote. 'They were well fed and clothed and had enough money for their immediate needs. The average station native has no desire for housing conditions other than camping conditions and neither would he use sanitary conveniences if they were provided.'[45] Nor, apparently, were Aboriginal people sufficiently advanced to appreciate the payment of wages. 'They gamble, too', Bray wrote, 'and, in view of this, I doubt whether any monetary increases would help them much'.[46] The old argument that stations could not afford to pay wages because of the large number of non-working relations supported by stations was again called into play. 'McLeod, by his unprincipled doctrine, may have obtained some slight increases for some natives', Bray wrote:

> but his actions have caused unhappiness and unemployment to others because of their lack of ability and the fact that they have too many dependents for the Stations to employ them. This is unfortunate, as the natives like their work. They are carefree and happy with it, but you can rest assured that their interests will be watched and action will

---

42 L. Craig, Parliamentary Debates (Hansard), Western Australia: Legislative Council, 11 November 1952, p. 1961.
43 Bray to Wise, 27 May 1946, SROWA 1945/0800/111–112.
44 Bray to Doig, Secretary, Premier's Department, 22 May 1946, SROWA 1945/0800/92.
45 O'Neill to Bray, 7 June 1946, SROWA 1945/0800/37–36.
46 Bray to Acting Minister and Premier, Wise, 27 May 1946, SROWA 1945/0800/111–112.

be taken to see that they do not suffer the consequences of McLeod's action which are unpalatable to the great majority of civilized people.[47]

As innocent dupes in McLeod's power game, it was thought that *marrngu* needed protection from such manipulation. Pastoralists were 'not at all vindictive' towards Aboriginal workers who had threatened to strike, O'Neill wrote, but blamed 'the propaganda of McLeod and his assistants'.[48] Constable Rowe of Nullagine ordered all Aboriginal people from the surrounding mining camps to move onto the Nullagine reserve, reporting to Bray that 'in view of the bad effects of whites when they have more or less free access to natives', he took this action in an 'endeavour to remove them from bad influences to where they may be more easily protected'.[49] Bray replied, 'I will doubtless communicate with you later on as to what action can be taken to protect the natives from such a disturbing influence as McLeod'.[50] One strategy that Bray considered was to prevent McLeod coming into contact with Aboriginal people by denying work permits to any station that was willing to employ him.[51]

While Fletcher and O'Neill undertook their patrol, Dooley was held in the Marble Bar police lockup. According to Donald Stuart, who wrote a novelised account of the strike in *Yandy*, he was kept in chains for the five days he was held there.[52] *Marrngu* oral history accounts of being held in chains in the Marble Bar lockup three years later suggests that this was probably the case.[53] On 14 May, when Fletcher and O'Neill returned from patrol, Dooley was transferred to Port Hedland to attend court, transported in chains in an RAAF truck.[54] He was tried on 16 May and convicted for the same offence as McKenna, receiving a three-month sentence.[55]

With Dooley and McKenna safely out of the way, attention turned to securing a conviction of the real troublemaker. There was strong political pressure for a successful prosecution of McLeod. Pastoralists 'hoped he would be put inside and that that event would impress the natives'.[56] Hegney wrote to

---

47   Bray to Secretary, Industrial Union of Workers, 26 June 1946, p. 2, SROWA 1945/0800/199.
48   O'Neill to Bray, 9 May 1946, p. 1, SROWA 1945/0800/70.
49   Rowe to Bray, 9 May 1946, p. 2, SROWA 1945/0800/75.
50   Bray to Rowe, 14 May 1946, SROWA 1945/0800/76.
51   Bray to Wise, 14 May 1946, SROWA 1945/0800/73.
52   Stuart, *Yandy*, 1959, p. 66.
53   Williams and Noakes, *How the West Was Lost*.
54   Marshall, police patrol journal, 14 May 1946, SROWA 1943/0099 v7.
55   O'Neill to Bray, telegram, 17 May 1946, SROWA 1945/0800/78.
56   Benja Sherlock to Kitty, 21 June 1946, Sherlock family private collection.

Premier Wise, 'I understand McLeod has been charged for an offence under the native administration act. Successful prosecutions are the most effective way of preventing his causing further trouble among the natives'.[57] Bray was pleased to hear of McKenna's conviction, but wrote to O'Neill that:

> I would prefer the conviction of McLeod himself, and should be glad if you would exert every possible effort to secure his conviction under Section 39 for being on a place where natives are congregated, or for a breach of Section 47 for persuading natives to leave their employment.
>
> Judging by the events to date, I feel that the necessary evidence will be forthcoming from the natives to secure McLeod's conviction for either of the offences mentioned, and would be glad indeed to hear of your success along these lines, and of McLeod's conviction with the maximum term of imprisonment.[58]

'I want to attach all the blame in this unnecessary disturbance where it belongs', Premier Wise wrote.[59]

To ensure a prosecution that would stick, the Police Department sent Detective Sergeant G. R. (Ron) Richards of the Perth police to the Pilbara to carry out investigations. The day after Dooley's hearing, police searched McLeod's hotel room in Port Hedland, removing literature, private papers and correspondence, including Communist Party material and the notes of the Marxist Study class he had attended in April.[60] He was arrested and held in the police cells in Port Hedland. Charged with three counts of breach of section 47, he was remanded in custody, with his trial set for 24 May. To prevent communication between the three strike organisers, McKenna and Dooley were shifted to Marble Bar to serve their sentences, transported by mail plane under escort by O'Neill.[61] Detective Sergeant Richards and O'Neill toured the Marble Bar and Nullagine district to pursue further investigations and pick up witnesses for McLeod's trial.

Commissioner Bray thanked O'Neill, Fletcher and 'the other Protectors who have worked so well in circumventing McLeod's actions ... for their firmness in keeping the matter so well in hand'.[62] 'An attempt was made to

---

57 Hegney to Wise, 17 May 1946, SROWA 1946/150/46.
58 Bray to O'Neill, 14 May 1946, SROWA 1945/0800/72.
59 Wise to Bray, 4 June 1946, SROWA 1946/150/46.
60 *Workers' Star*, 7 June 1946, p. 2, 'McLeod Grilled for Three Hours Before Arrest'.
61 Marshall, police patrol journal, 14 May 1946, SROWA 1943/0099 v7.
62 Bray to O'Neill, 14 May 1946, SROWA 1945/0800/68.

paralyse the industry', he wrote, 'but firm action was taken and the strike did not succeed'.[63] Meanwhile, *marrngu* continued to provide the labour needed for shearing operations to proceed. 'The season has been a good one', Fletcher wrote on 19 May, 'and stock looks well. Few stations have yet completed shearing, but preliminary reports are that results are up to expectation'.[64] Nevertheless, O'Neill felt that things had not yet quite returned to normal. 'Work is continuing on all stations in the Pilbarra district', he wrote, 'but I feel that there is still an undercurrent of unrest on most Stations, McLeod has been discredited but the natives are still not quite sure of the position in many instances as they are unable to grasp the significance of his arrest and it will take some time for readjustment'.[65] The continuing rumble of dissatisfaction should, perhaps, have been a hint to the authorities that the May Day strike was something other than a mindless response to McLeod's agitation.

The conviction of McKenna and Dooley and the arrest of McLeod had not, it seems, succeeded in restoring peaceful contentment to the Aboriginal community, as the authorities had hoped. While dissatisfaction continued to rumble in the Pilbara, the arrests ignited a storm of protest in the south of the state that took authorities by surprise.

---

63 Bray to Wise, 27 May 1946, p. 1, SROWA 1945/0800/111.
64 Fletcher, patrol report, 19 May 1946, SROWA 1939/1777 v7.
65 O'Neill to Bray, 26 May 1946, SROWA 1945/0800/143–145.

Chapter 9

'We Got Power Behind Us'

Southern Support, May–June 1946

There was little indication during the first two weeks of May of much southern interest in Pilbara events. The weekly newspaper of the Western Australian branch of the Australian Communist Party, the *Workers' Star*, carried a small article on the strike on page 6 of its issue of 3 May, and two days later marchers in the annual May Day parade carried a banner reading 'Support Native Strikers'.[1] By the middle of May, however, letters to the premier from women's organisations and trade unions – written in response to McLeod's widely circularised letter to Premier Wise of 30 April and appealing for the right of Aboriginal workers to organise and select their own representatives – signalled the first rumblings of a growing public reaction. The premier dismissed these appeals. Southern organisations without knowledge of northern conditions, he replied, should leave matters in the hands of the departmental officers with expertise in native affairs, who were handling matters in the natives' best interests.[2]

The imprisonment of McKenna and Dooley, and McLeod's arrest, however, sparked a vigorous and broad-based response in the south. Individuals, church groups, unions and various women's organisations came together to protest the imprisonment of strike leaders and to call for the strikers' demands to be met. Although a wide range of organisations and individuals joined the protests, the Western Australian branch of the Australian Communist Party was particularly active in igniting interest and outrage. ACP members Katharine Susannah Prichard and Graham Alcorn had been corresponding with McLeod for some time, and interest and a readiness to respond to northern activism had been generated during his visit to Perth the previous month. Having a printing press, a weekly open-air forum on the banks of the Swan River at

---

1 *Workers' Star*, 10 May 1946, p. 1.
2 Wise to the Women's Christian Temperance Union, 17 May 1946, SROWA 1945/0800/88.

the Esplanade Reserve, and a weekly newspaper, the ACP had the capacity to act quickly to disseminate information and advertise protest action. The Party's platform for Aboriginal reform coincided closely with McLeod's, but members also believed that the struggle for Aboriginal justice should be undertaken by Aboriginal people themselves. 'We couldn't do it for them', ACP member Joan Williams said. 'We could help them and do what we could in the White community to promote understanding', but, she said, the initiative and leadership had to come from Aboriginal people themselves.[3] A campaign to support the Pilbara strike was, therefore, eagerly embraced by communists. Here was a fight for justice initiated, according to McLeod's account, entirely by Aboriginal people along lines consistent with the ACP's own program. And it needed their support. ACP member Edith Conochie remembered feeling 'very strongly involved' in the strike campaign.[4] 'That really hit me', communist poet and writer Dorothy Hewett said of the strike. 'I felt that emotionally'.[5]

The campaign began at the ACP's regular open-air meeting on the Perth Esplanade on Sunday 19 May, three days after the conviction of Dooley and the arrest of McLeod. While Police Constable Gordon Marshall, Travelling Inspector Laurie O'Neill and Detective Sergeant Ron Richards visited *marrngu* at the Moolyella tin field to gather evidence to ensure a successful conviction at McLeod's forthcoming trial, 200 people on the Perth Esplanade called on the Minister for Justice, Emil Nulsen, 'to revoke the sentences and free the imprisoned strike leaders, and to secure the withdrawal of the charges laid against Mr. D McLeod at Port Hedland, and his release from custody'. The imprisonment of strike leaders McKenna and Dooley was 'victimisation of the most brutal kind, incompatible with Australian Democracy', they stated. 'That the sentences were carried out under the administration of the State Labor Government is, we consider, a slurr [sic] on the labour movement'.[6]

The next day – while, 1500 kilometres to the north, O'Neill, Marshall and Richards interviewed Thora Gallop and Kitchener in Nullagine and Bonney Downs – the ACP produced a pamphlet setting out 'the natives' side of the case, compiled from material sent to the *Workers' Star* newspaper by Mr. Don

---

3   Joan Williams, interviewed by Hartley, SLWA OH3989.
4   Enid Conochie, interviews with members of the WA Communist Party, interviewed by Susan Hartley, SLWA OH 3989.
5   Dorothy Hewett, interviews with members of the WA Communist Party, interviewed by Susan Hartley, tape 2, SLWA OH 3989.
6   Leah Healy, Secretary, WA State Committee, ACP, to Nulsen, 20 May 1946, SROWA 1945/0800/110.

McLeod'.[7] This was circulated to unions, churches and women's organisations with an accompanying letter from Alec Jolly, calling on concerned citizens to protest the imprisonment of strike leaders. A medical doctor, Alexander Thomas Hicks Jolly had gained firsthand experience of the unequal treatment of Aboriginal people when he worked as the Western Australian Public Health Department's medical officer in Broome in the early 1940s. During this time, he had alerted the Department of Native Affairs to the need for an eight-bed ward for Aboriginal people in the town, but his request had been ignored. Instead, a separate morgue for Aboriginal people had been built at the request of the local settler community, so that Aboriginal bodies would not be held in the same place as *walypila* bodies.[8] While in Broome, Jolly had formed a close friendship with anthropologist Frederick (Fred) Rose, with whom he co-authored a number of academic anthropological articles. In 1946 Jolly was thirty-six years old and worked in a medical practice in the Perth suburb of Midland Junction, was also a member of the ACP, and was a close friend of Katharine Susannah Prichard. 'I have taken it upon myself as one who is deeply interested in the welfare of the natives', he wrote in his circular letter, 'to convene a meeting of citizens to discuss what action can be taken to bring the facts before the public and correct what I consider to be a miscarriage of justice'. Aware that the matter was urgent, with McLeod due to be tried on 24 May, he called a meeting for the following evening, 21 May.[9]

The pamphlet produced and circulated by the ACP presented McLeod's version of the strike, including the inaccurate but often-repeated statement that '800 native workers came out on strike on 1 May', and that 'on 20 stations only four people remained at work'. It also reproduced McLeod's claim that he had first become involved in strike plans during the Port Hedland races the previous year, when about 400 Aboriginal people had approached him to ask if he would act on their behalf as an honorary Inspector to police Native Administration regulations.[10] While on one hand the authorities portrayed McLeod as the instigator of the strike and *marrngu* as confused and passive

---

7   Leah Healy, Secretary, WA State Committee, ACP, to Nulsen, 20 May 1946, SROWA 1945/0800/110.
8   *Sunday Times*, 28 July 1946, 'Middle Course in Native Affairs', SROWA 1946/0895/7.
9   Jolly, circular letter, 20 May 1946, SROWA 1945/0800/156.
10 'An appeal to Democratic Citizens. Events in the Struggle of North West Aboriginal station hands to better their conditions. Compiled from reports sent to the *Workers' Star* newspaper by Mr. D. McLeod, Port Hedland', 20 May 1946. SROWA 1945/0800/155.

pawns, in this version of events *marrngu* had acted on their own initiative and it was McLeod who was passive, only becoming involved in response to requests for assistance, but having no organising or directive role. In fact, the truth lay between these polar understandings. McLeod was clearly active in agitating for and organising the strike, but nothing could have come of this without the activism and determination of *marrngu*.

At the meeting convened by Alec Jolly the following night, a Provisional Committee for Defence of Native Rights was constituted to take immediate action on a number of fronts, with Anglican minister Rev. H. V. P. (Peter) Hodge taking on the role of secretary. It was decided that a public meeting of protest would be held in the Perth Town Hall the following week to protest against 'the unjust and arbitrary treatment' of Clancy and Dooley, and to elect a permanent committee to support the strike.[11] All local organisations and unions were circularised about the meeting, and 10,000 leaflets written by Katharine Susannah Prichard were printed.[12] The Provisional Committee also decided to provide legal support for the imprisoned strike leaders, and if necessary to take their cases to the highest courts in the country. To provide immediate legal defence for McLeod, the committee engaged a lawyer, Fred Curran, who flew to Port Hedland to attend McLeod's hearing in the police court a few days later.[13]

Held in the police lockup in Port Hedland, McLeod kept in touch with *marrngu* and supporters in the south by passing and receiving messages through Tommy Nangkanangka (Manapurtja), who worked for the police as a 'police boy' or tracker. According to John Wilson, Nangkanangka ran a twice-daily mail service for McLeod.[14] John Bucknall remembered McLeod speaking of this 'on numerous occasions' in later years, 'as it obviously appealed to his anti-establishment sense of humour that Police Boy (tracker) Tommy was working for the strikers right under the nose of the authorities'.[15] On 22 May, McLeod wrote to Premier Wise to say that, although he had been instructed to invite him to a meeting at the Port Hedland Twelve Mile on 25 May, the meeting was now unlikely to go ahead as he, Dooley and McKenna were imprisoned. The purpose of the planned meeting, he wrote,

---

11   Hodge, Secretary, Committee for Defence of Native Rights, circular letter, 23 May 1946, SROWA 1946/150/46.
12   Katharine Susannah Prichard, pamphlet, issued by Rev. P. Hodge, Secretary, Provisional Committee for the Defence of Native Rights, SROWA 1945/0800/117.
13   Bray to Wise, 30 May 1946, SROWA 1945/0800/142.
14   John Wilson, 'Authority and Leadership', pp. 60–62.
15   Bucknall, 'Commentary to Extracts'.

was to discuss the rights of Aboriginal people to organise and appoint their own representative, the payment of a minimum wage of 30/- per week, and the enforcement of Regulation 81A to C of the *Native Administration Act*, which stipulated that employers must provide substantial food, drinking and bathing water and accommodation for Aboriginal workers, including 'sanitary convenience'. The meeting had also been proposed to discuss the right of native representatives to enter all workplaces to ensure that the regulations were complied with. Now that the meeting was not going ahead, McLeod wished to register:

> a vigerous [sic] protest against the action of the police in arresting Clancy Doolie [sic] and myself in connection with this matter, as such action is not in accord with the principles which have been the basis of progress in Aust. And on behalf of the native workers demand that a Royal Commission be appointed to enquire thoroughly into and report on application and policing of acts and regulations of the Native Affairs Dept which represent under present conditions a distortion of the original intentions and a grave injustice to the people concerned.[16]

A letter he wrote to Peter Hodge the following next day was reprinted in the *Workers' Star*:

> Although I had no misgivings that ultimately freedom-loving people would actively take up the very just case of native workers, it is heartening to have news of your timely intervention.
>
> Let me congratulate your committee on its initiative and prompt action, and although I am happy to know you have secured legal assistance to fight my case, let me suggest that at your meeting on Tuesday you give serious thought, if this has not already been done, to setting up a permanent and vigilant organisation established on a broad basis to secure for WA natives their rightful heritage of which they have been deprived.
>
> So that by moral and other assistance they may regain their simple human dignity and we can hope that, at some future date, they may take their place beside us as equal citizens and with us, help to build, to our mutual advantage, the future state of Australia, free from want, fear, aggression and intellectual domination.

---

16   McLeod to Wise, 22 May 1946, SROWA 1945/0800/114.

Again let me thank you and your committee and wish you a very real success at your public meeting on Tuesday.[17]

As McLeod wrote this, O'Neill and Ron Richards were travelling back from their patrol of stations with evidence for his trial scheduled for the following day, and, as O'Neill wired Bray, 'FEELING CONFIDENT CASES AGAINST MCLEOD'.[18] Along with other evidence for the McLeod trial, they brought Kitchener from Bonney Downs and Tommy Dodd and Jackson from Moolyella as witnesses. However, at the hearing the following morning, lawyer Fred Curran applied for the case to be adjourned and for McLeod to be remanded to 21 June. Bail was granted on a personal surety of £50, and £50 for each of the three charges.[19] McLeod did not have access to £200, and remained in the lockup for a few more days until Graham Alcorn's brother, Wilson, who was working at the Comet mine near Marble Bar, stood surety and he was released.[20] Kitchener, Dodd and Jackson were shifted from the Lock hospital, where they had been held to stop them communicating with McLeod, to the police lockup, where they were held until the date of the trial.[21]

With Curran's engagement as McLeod's defence counsel, O'Neill lost some of his confidence in the outcome of the trial. He urged Bray to also engage Counsel 'to watch the Department's interests', as he was 'convinced that the conviction or otherwise of McLeod is vital to future native welfare and the policy of the Dept. as well as to the future of the pastoral industry in the North West'.[22] Wise approved this recommendation, and the Department engaged KC Leonard Seaton to handle the case.[23] O'Neill was instructed to proceed to Perth to 'talk over matters' in preparation for the trial.[24] The Department felt that its case could be won on the basis of O'Neill's finding that Aboriginal people had no understanding of what they were doing when they went on strike.[25]

Meanwhile, the campaign to have the men released went ahead. In the days leading up to the Town Hall protest meeting, the provisional Committee

---

17 *Workers' Star*, 31 May 1946, p. 1, 'He Writes from Jail'.
18 O'Neill to Bray, telegram, 22 May 1946, SROWA 1945/0800/91.
19 *West Australian*, 25 May 1946, p. 13.
20 Joan Williams, notes for documentary, SLWA 5425A/62.
21 O'Neill to Bray, 26 May 1946, p. 2, SROWA 1945/0800/144.
22 O'Neill to Bray, 26 May 1946, p. 1, SROWA 1945/0800/143.
23 Bray, note, 5 June 1946, 1945/0800/146.
24 Bray to O'Neill, telegram, 27 May 1946, SROWA 1945/0800/109.
25 Wise, reminder, SROWA 1945/0800/146.

for the Defence of Native Rights (CDNR) posted advertisements in the *West Australian* reading, 'Persecution – Nor'west Natives. Protest against Tyranny', and had a short article on the meeting included in the *Daily News*.[26] On the night of 28 May, there were heavy storms, traffic difficulties and a blackout, but between 300 and 400 people made their way to the Perth Town Hall, including Deputy Commissioner of Native Affairs Charles Lewis (Lew) McBeath, who made a record of proceedings for the Department.[27] Detective Sergeant Ron Richards, recently returned from Port Hedland, also attended, anticipating that the meeting could provide further evidence in the case against McLeod.[28]

Alec Jolly opened the meeting, reading telegrams and letters of support from Western Australian and interstate unions and the Port Hedland branch of the AWU. Speakers representing a broad range of organisations – including unions, the Women's Christian Temperance Union and the Women's National Missionary Council – then addressed the gathering. Speakers included Peter Hodge, Tommy Nyinda Bropho of the Nyoongar community of the state's south-west, and Katharine Susannah Prichard representing the Modern Women's Club. The most forceful speaker, according to McBeath, was Graham Alcorn, representing the ACP, who likened McKenna, Dooley and McLeod to diggers who had fought and died for a similar cause at the Eureka Stockade.[29]

Following addresses by these speakers, the meeting elected a permanent committee. The Very Rev. Robert Henry Moore, the Anglican Dean of Perth, was elected as patron. Jolly was elected president, Gilbert Foxcroft of the Society of Friends and McLeod vice-presidents, and the Anglican minister Peter Hodge secretary.[30] Other members of the committee included Aboriginal activist Tommy Nyinda Bropho, broadcaster and peace and women's rights campaigner Irene Greenwood, and an Aboriginal woman, Mary Morden, who had been at the centre of protest action two years previously, when she refused to shift from Bayswater to a designated camping area and was removed by the Department of Native Affairs to the Moore River settlement as a result.[31]

---

26 *West Australian*, 24 May 1946, SROWA 1946/150; 27 May 1946, SROWA 1945/0800/115; *Daily News*, 27 May 1946, SROWA 1945/0800/116.
27 McBeath to Bray, 29 May 1946, SROWA 1946/0895/1.
28 O'Neill to Bray, 26 May 1946, SROWA 1945/0800/143.
29 McBeath to Bray, 29 May 1946, SROWA 1946/0895/1.
30 E. H. H. Hall, Parliamentary Debates (Hansard), Western Australia: Legislative Council, 6 August 1946, p. 105; *Workers' Star*, 31 May 1946, p. 1, 'Native Persecution Denounced'.
31 *Daily News*, 10 October 1944, p. 10.

Three motions were put forward and discussed at the meeting. The first of these supported the strikers' demands as outlined by McLeod in his letter to Wise. The demand for a minimum wage of 30/- per week aroused some debate. Was it appropriate, it was asked, to support a wage demand below the basic wage? Would it not be better to demand the basic wage for all Aboriginal workers? Another voice suggested that a demand of at least £2 or £2/10/- was more reasonable than 30/-. The original resolution, however, was passed by the meeting without amendment. Alcorn later defended the 30/- demand in an article in the *Workers' Star*, arguing that a minimum wage of 30/- a week was a demand around which all Aboriginal workers could mobilise, and which could 'be realised quickly as shown by the number of station owners who granted it'. Once this demand and the right to organise was achieved, he argued, Aboriginal workers could be relied upon to push for further wage increases.[32]

The Town Hall meeting also called for the administration of the state's Aboriginal people to be handed over to Commonwealth government control. This was a suggestion that accompanied almost every call for Aboriginal reform in Western Australia during the 1940s, both from within state Parliament and from activists concerned at the level of pastoralist control of Aboriginal policy in the state.

The meeting also undertook to 'seek all means' to secure the release of McKenna and Dooley by campaigning for their release within Western Australia, throughout Australia and internationally. As a first step, it was decided that the newly-elected committee should immediately wait on Premier Wise and Minister for Justice Nulsen to request the immediate release of McKenna and Dooley and for proceedings against McLeod to be dropped. The meeting also resolved to contact for support all trade unions and organisations in Australia, and international organisations including, if necessary, the United Nations Organisation (UNO), which had been established the previous year.

By the middle of May, the first trickle of letters of protest to the state Labor government had become a deluge. While Bob Coverley, the Minister for the North West who held the Native Affairs portfolio, was away on sick leave, Premier Frank Wise received a flurry of letters from individuals and organisations within the state and nationally, calling for strike demands to be conceded and the imprisoned leaders released. 'I feel also that the imprisonment of two of the strike leaders is not only not justified', one individual wrote:

---

32   *Workers' Star*, 7 June 1946, p. 6.

but the fact that they were imprisoned is sharply reminiscent of Hitlerite Germany.

The persecution of Don McLeod for assisting the aboriginal workers is also most repugnant to any decent minded Australian, and I am sure that the great majority of people are in sympathy with him.[33]

Writers included academics, federal politicians, Western Australian and interstate unions and women's organisations.[34] 'I have no knowledge of the merits or demerits of the Committee's view', Kim Beazley (Snr), the Member for Fremantle in the Federal Parliament, wrote to Coverley, 'but I do know that they are spreading the view that the strike was justified, and that the committee is campaigning against what they regard as a rigid and narrow interpretation of the 47th section of the W. A. Native Administration Act'.[35] Wise continued to insist that southern critics ignorant of conditions in the north should leave matters in the capable and experienced hands of Native Affairs officers, and defended the state's *Native Administration Act* as 'the best Act of the Commonwealth in connection with the administration of Native Affairs'.[36] 'I am afraid there is grave danger of your Executive not understanding all the import of McLeod's requests', he told the Women's Christian Temperance Union, assuring their members that 'all the matters affecting the welfare of the natives are being carefully watched by the Department of Native Affairs'.[37] He replied to criticism from the Western Australian Nurses Association and the Shop Assistants' and Warehouse Employees' Union by insisting that 'the methods adopted by McLeod are not in the best interests of Western Australian aborigines'.[38] The Nurses Association was not prepared to accept his assurances, asking what steps

---

33   J. C. Seman to Wise, 23 May 1946, SROWA 1945/0800/151.
34   Victoria–Riverina branch of Australian Workers' Union, Melbourne, to Wise, 30 May 1946, SROWA 1945/0800/181a; Secretary K & B Section AWU, Boulder, 30 May 1946, SROWA 1945/0800/182a; Secretary of Australian Coal and Shale Employees' Federation Union of Workers, WA Branch, to Doig, Under Secretary to Premier, 14 May 1946, SROWA 1945/0800/101; Women's Christian Temperance Union of WA to Wise, 16 May 1946, SROWA 1945/0800/87.
35   Kim Beazley (Snr) to Coverley, 29 May 1946, SROWA 1945/0800/130a.
36   Wise to General Secretary, Australian Railways Union, Sydney, 23 May 1946, SROWA 1945/0800/107.
37   Wise to Women's Christian Temperance Union, 17 May 1946, SROWA 1945/0800/88.
38   West Australian Shop Assistants' and Warehouse Employees' Union to Wise, 21 May 1946, SROWA 1945/0800/90; Western Australian Nurses Assn to Wise, 24 May 1946, SROWA 1945/0800/119.

the government had taken to achieve economic and social equality for Aboriginal people, and why McLeod's methods were not considered to be in their best interests.[39] Unions were particularly concerned that prison sentences were imposed under a state Labor government, and urged the government to take steps to have the men released. 'There is no doubt', wrote the Western Australian Management Committee of the Amalgamated Society of Carpenters and Joiners, 'that the Aboriginal workers' labour has been exploited by station owners and others, over the past years, and the organising of these workers is overdue'.[40] It was with some relief, no doubt, that Wise handed the matter over to Coverley on his return from illness in early June.

On Sunday 2 June, the weekend after the Town Hall meeting, Graham Alcorn and his wife Joy kept the ball rolling by addressing listeners on the Perth Esplanade on the subject of 'Native Rights'.[41] The *Workers' Star* was now publishing accounts of the strike in every issue, 'printing Don McLeod's dispatches from the Nor'-West as if they came from the revolutionary front', according to Dorothy Hewett, who, along with Graham Alcorn, converted McLeod's letters into articles.[42] The national ACP newspaper, the *Tribune*, took up and retold many of the *Workers' Star*'s accounts. Interstate Aboriginal organisations looked to the strike as the beginning of a new era. Speaking 'on behalf of 10,000 Aborigines represented by the Aboriginal League of NSW', the League's secretary Bert Groves, expressed:

> heartiest congratulations to Mr. Don McLeod and Mr. Clancy for their victory in the recent Aboriginal strike in West Australia ... The Aboriginal people were determined to fight for justice and for a new deal, and they looked on the West Australian co-operation of Unions and Aborigines as the beginning of a new era in all States when the inhuman conditions of the past would be ended.[43]

The Committee for Defence of Native Rights also took the issue to an international stage. On 13 June, an appeal was made to the General Secretary of the recently-established United Nations Organisation in New York calling on the UNO:

---

39   WA Nurses Association to Wise, 30 May 1946, SROWA 1945/0800/176.
40   State Management Committee, Amalgamated Society of Carpenters and Joiners of Australia to Wise, 20 May 1946, SROWA 1945/0800/96.
41   *Workers' Star*, 31 May 1946, p. 6.
42   Hewett, *Wild Card*, p. 123.
43   *Tribune*, 4 June 1946, p. 5.

to stand behind us in our demands on behalf of Australian Aboriginals generally, and in particular, to the elementary justice necessary to free Dooley and McKenna and save McLeod from a similar fate. We claim that the right to organize is a primary right of free men and its violation is against all the principles fought for by the United Nations.[44]

Copies of the UNO appeal were forwarded to Wise and Coverley; to Australia's representative on the UNO, Paul Hasluck; to Prime Minister Ben Chifley; and to other state and federal ministers, including Federal External Affairs Minister H. V. Evatt. The World Federation of Trade Unions received a copy of the UNO appeal, and the issue was also made known to the London-based Anti-Slavery Society, the League of Coloured Peoples, and the National Council for Civil Liberties in London. The passionate activist, writer and educationalist Mary Montgomery Bennet wrote from London, expressing support for the campaign. While working with Aboriginal people in Western Australia during the 1930s, mainly at the Mt Margaret Mission near Laverton, Bennett had fought vigorously for Aboriginal justice. Now living in London and active in the Anti-Slavery Society, she wrote to Alec Jolly in support of the strike. 'I hope so much that the Trade Unions will take the matter up and go through with it', she wrote. 'The thing is to sweep all these atrocious serf conditions away now. Of course the Native and Aboriginal Departments are Labour Bureaus with powers of Hitler'.[45] During the course of the strike she kept the Anti-Slavery Society informed on developments in the Pilbara.

McLeod, now out on bail, travelled to Perth to add his voice to the campaign. 'Propaganda that the natives are sub-normal or deficient has been out for years', he told the *Workers' Star*. 'The impression has been given that the station owners are doing them a good turn by employing them. In actual fact the natives carry the stations on their backs'.[46] The Committee for Defence of Native Rights arranged for him to give public talks in the Assembly Hall in Perth on 13 June and in Fremantle's Victoria Hall the following evening, advertised under the heading, 'Why Dooley and Clancy McKenna Are in Gaol. Aborigines Fight for Better Life. Nor'Wester D. W. McLeod Will Give the Facts'.[47] In Fremantle, addressing a 'small but very enthusiastic protest

---

44 Committee for Defence of Native rights to the Secretary-General of UNO, New York, 13 June 1946, SROWA 1945/0800/223.
45 Quoted in *Workers' Star*, 2 August 1946, p. 5.
46 *Workers' Star*, 7 June 1946, p. 2.
47 *West Australian*, 12 June 1946, SROWA 1945/0800/177.

meeting', he spoke of the high culture of Aboriginal people and about their struggle for better conditions. 'There has always been a savage struggle on the part of the pastoralists to keep the conditions down', he said, 'but the natives have also consistently struggled and gradually gained cash wages instead of payment in kind'. Tommy Bropho also spoke at the Fremantle meeting and received an enthusiastic response from the audience. 'We were good enough to stand beside your husbands, sons and brothers in this, and World War I', he said, 'then we are good enough to ask for our liberty now to live as white man lives. We ask to be united as one people under one Government.' Another Nyoongar man, Mr Morrison, also spoke.[48]

McLeod also hoped to address the Australian Labor Party (ALP) Metropolitan Council while he was in Perth, but his old adversary, Member for Pilbara Bill Hegney, opposed his request on the ground that McLeod had stood against his Labor candidacy in the 1943 state election.[49] Nevertheless, the Council did respond to the CDNR's campaign by calling for amendments to the *Native Administration Act 1936* to allow Aborigines to organise, and for strike leaders to be released. On 18 June, a deputation of the ALP Metropolitan Council met the Minister for Justice, Emil Nulsen, to argue that it was 'bad tactics on the part of the Labour Movement' to imprison men who were 'only trying to better the conditions of their fellow men'. It was 'hard that the law under a Labor Government finds it necessary to chastise these men so severely'. Nulsen had a greater genuine interest in Aboriginal issues than most Western Australian politicians and a sympathy for their claim for greater justice. He agreed that Aboriginal people had been exploited. He told the deputation that he understood the position very clearly and would have the case thoroughly examined.[50]

While the ALP Metropolitan Council met with Nulsen, McLeod and his defence counsel, Fred Curran, were on their way up to Port Hedland for McLeod's trial. There was by now a high level of interest in the case, generated in part by the CDNR's campaign. Arriving in Port Hedland, McLeod found letters of support from Mary Bennett in London, and from Tom Wright, federal president of the Sheet Metal Workers' Union and author of 'New Deal for Aborigines'.[51] The *Sunday Times* reported that 'Leading Perth lawyers, police and Govt. officials' were flying to Port Hedland 'for the case

---

48 *Workers' Star*, 21 June 1946, p. 2, 'Fremantle Backing for Native Rights Struggle'.
49 *Workers' Star*, 14 June 1946, p. 1, 'Free Natives!'.
50 Deputation notes, 18 June 1946, SROWA 1945/0800/193.
51 *Northern Times*, 21 June 1946, p. 15; Joan Williams, notes for documentary, SLWA 5425A/62.

against bearded Nor-Wester Donald McLeod on a charge under the Native Administration Act',[52] while a reporter from the *West Australian* travelled to Port Hedland to cover the hearing. The *Daily News* noted the 'intense local interest' in the case.[53]

Pastoralists from across the Port Hedland and Marble Bar districts travelled into town to attend the hearing in the hope that McLeod would be given a lengthy sentence and their labour problems put to rest. A meeting of the Pastoralists Association meeting was planned to coincide with the court case, in part to plan a strategy to restore control.[54] O'Neill travelled to Port Hedland from the north, making an overland journey from Fitzroy Crossing.[55] McKenna and Dooley were conveyed by train from Marble Bar to act as witnesses, joining Kitchener, Jackson and Tommy Dodd, who had been held at the police station since McLeod's release the previous month.[56] The small Port Hedland courthouse needed to be reorganised to accommodate the large number of witnesses called to give evidence, and when the hearing began on the afternoon of Thursday 20 June, the room was full to overflowing, those unable to find a seat having to listen from outside.[57] Resident Magistrate Maurice Harwood heard charges brought against McLeod of having counselled Dooley and McKenna to persuade Aboriginal people to leave their lawful service without the consent of the Protector (two counts), and of attempting to persuade Aboriginal people to leave their lawful service to attend the meeting planned for 25 May.

As the first witness, Dooley told the court of his discussions with McLeod when they worked together earlier in the year, of McLeod telling him 'to go round and tell the boys to strike', and of Ken Duncan giving him a calendar with seven weeks and three days on it, with the last day marked 'May 1'. He spoke of his meeting with McKenna and others at Marble Bar, of visiting stations to prepare workers to strike, of the strike that took place in Marble Bar, and of his arrest and sentence. Examined by Curran, he said that he was appealing the sentence, and that the men all wanted 30/- a week. McKenna spoke of discussions about buying a property that had taken place at the time of the Port Hedland races the previous year.

---

52 *Sunday Times*, 16 June 1946, SROWA 1945/0800/177.
53 *Daily News*, 21 June 1946, p. 10.
54 Benja Sherlock to Kitty, 21 June 1946, Sherlock family private collection.
55 O'Neill to Commissioner, 15 June 1946, SROWA 1941/1107/188.
56 Stuart, *Yandy*, 1959, p. 71; O'Neill to Bray, 26 May 1946, p. 2, SROWA 1945/0800/144.
57 *Daily News*, 20 June 1946, p. 10.

McLeod had told him they could build the place up and be independent, he said, and only later did they talk about striking. He told the court of the stations he had visited and of his meeting with McLeod on 1 May, when McLeod told him not to be afraid as they had power behind them. When asked who had first spoken about a strike, he said that McLeod had given them a hint, and they thought it was a good idea. In reply to Curran, he said that Aboriginal people were dissatisfied and wanted McLeod to represent them so they could get justice.[58]

The hearing was continued that evening. Kitchener also gave evidence about the 1945 Four Mile meeting, the discussions at Bonney Downs and the messages McLeod had sent him by telegram from Perth. Nick (or Mick) Doogiebee, who was working at Munda Station at the time of the strike, told of Dooley's visit there with the calendar in April. Tommy Dodd, who had worked at Marble Bar's Ironclad Hotel, told of the meeting with Dooley and McKenna four or five weeks before the strike, and of how, on the morning of the strike, he and other workers had informed their boss that they were going to strike. Asked by Seaton why he went on strike when he already earned 30/- a week, he replied that he did not want to scab on his mates. According to a report published in the *Workers' Star*, this reply brought 'a hearty applause from the crowded court'.[59] Jackson recalled that he had first heard about the plan to strike when McLeod spoke at a 'corroboree meeting' at Nullagine before Christmas 1945. Roy McKay and George Lockyer were also examined as witnesses that evening, and Paddy Northover, who had also worked at the Ironclad Hotel, was examined when the hearing resumed the following morning. George Turner told the court that Dooley had asked him to hold money collected from stations, and Ken Duncan said that Dooley had brought him a letter from McLeod, asking him to draft up a calendar showing the number of days to 1 May. George Miles, manager of the Ironclad Hotel, said that on the morning of 1 May, Aboriginal workers had told him they were going to strike 'because all other blackfellows were and they could not scab on them'.

Laurie O'Neill spoke about his role in inspecting conditions for Aboriginal workers and stated that conditions were satisfactory to his department. Asked by Curran about accommodation, he said that some workers had houses, but 'the majority would not live in a house if you gave it to them'.[60] They had suitable

---

58 High Court appeal, D. W. McLeod v. G. R. Richards, NAA A10074 1946/8, 9, 10.
59 *Workers' Star*, 28 June 1946, p. 1.
60 *West Australian*, 22 June 1946, p. 12.

accommodation, he said. Constable Fletcher was asked about the meeting he attended at the Port Hedland Four Mile the previous year, and Detective Sergeant Ron Richards gave evidence of his investigations.

During the afternoon, McLeod took the stand and gave his account of events leading up to the strike. He was asked to explain items of evidence that had been removed from his hotel room by Richards in early May. The court made much of handwritten notes that included the statement that:

> each and every one of these natives are potential communists. In Pilbarra alone we could recruit up to a thousand members of the party. It is our duty as Communists to relieve these people from their unhappy lot.[61]

McLeod later claimed that the statement had not been his own idea but had been made by a speaker at the Communist Party convention in April. He had simply made notes of the talk. In his court hearing, however, he stated that he had made the notes in preparation for an article. It is likely that the idea of 1000 potential communists was an argument he had used, or planned to use, to solicit Party support, Graham Alcorn suggests.[62] Communist Party member Joan Williams thought this not unlikely: '[H]e sometimes got carried away', she wrote.[63]

Final questioning at the trial focused on attempts to organise a meeting of delegates from each station on 25 May to discuss the outcome of the 1 May action. Addressing the court on the case, Curran argued that the labour conditions imposed on Aboriginal people under the *Native Administration Act 1936* contravened the *British Slavery Abolition Act* of 1833 and probably had no constitutional basis, as self-government had been achieved with the understanding that the new colony should not pass laws repugnant to the laws of British justice.[64]

Magistrate Harwood reserved his decision until the evening, and when court resumed after the tea break, according to the *Daily News*, there was a rush for seats, with dozens having to stand outside. Refraining from addressing the question of the Act's validity, Harwood found McLeod guilty of breaching

---

61 *West Australian*, 22 June 1946, p. 12.
62 Alcorn, 'The Struggle of the Pilbara Station Hands', p. 7.
63 Joan Williams, notes for documentary, SLWA 5425A/62.
64 Committee for the Defence of Native Rights, circular (undated), 'Aborigines are being exploited in the North-West', SROWA 1946/0895 (unnumbered).

section 47 of the *Native Administration Act* on all three counts, fining him a total of £50, with £15/12/2 costs for each charge.[65]

It was a hefty fine, but not the prison sentence that had been widely anticipated, even by McLeod himself, who had written to A. P. Elkin at the time of his arrest that 'my usefulness on their behalf will be impaired in the next three months as I too expect to get a term under section 47'.[66] Pastoralists who had not attended the trial were eager to learn the outcome. 'Reg went to the siding tonight to ring and see how the McLeod court case went today', Benja Sherlock, of Strelley Station, wrote:

> [He] heard that the brute has got off with a fine of fifty pounds and forty-six pounds costs. You will see all about it in the West, as there is a reporter up here. Everyone hoped he would be put inside and that that event would impress the natives. Goodness knows what their reaction will be now.[67]

Despite the disappointment of pastoralists, Bray congratulated O'Neill on his success in securing the conviction, which Coverley described as a setback to the communists.[68]

Evidence that the southern protest campaign had ruffled the feathers of the state Labor government came on the Monday following McLeod's hearing. Minister for Justice Emil Nulsen had received a deputation from the ALP Metropolitan Council a few days previously and, in view of the national and international attention given to Dooley's and McKenna's sentences, recommended that the men 'be released forthwith'. Coverley agreed that the men had 'been suitably punished'. Following a flurry of interdepartmental memorandums and telegrams, Lieutenant Governor James Mitchell had, by the end of the day, approved their early release and Constable Fletcher at Port Hedland had been informed of the decision by telegram.[69] McKenna

---

65 *Daily News*, 22 June 1946, p. 23; McBeath to McDonald, 9 April 1947, p. 3, SROWA 1947/0305/84.
66 McLeod to Elkin, 15 May 1946, A. P. Elkin Papers, University of Sydney Archives, box 76, file 262.
67 Benja Sherlock to Kitty, 21 June 1946, Sherlock family private collection.
68 Bray to O'Neill, 26 June 1946, SROWA 1945/0800/191; Coverley to Town Clerk, Collie, and Secretary Eastern Goldfields District Council of ALP, 17 July 1946, SROWA 1945/0800/246–249.
69 Bray to Coverley, 24 June 1946, SROWA 1945/0800/186; Nulsen to Mitchell, Under-Secretary for Law to McKillop, D/Controller General of Prisons; Coverley to Nulsen, 24 June 1946, SROWA 1945/0800/211; McKillop to Fletcher, telegram, 24 June 1946, SROWA 1945/0800/210.

and Dooley, now back in Marble Bar after the hearing, were surprised to find a few days later that they were free, despite having served only half of their three-month sentences.[70] Their early release significantly assisted the strike movement, enabling their participation and leadership in the effective action undertaken by *marrngu* in Port Hedland at the end of July.

Campaigners in Perth celebrated the men's release as a victory, the *Workers' Star* carrying a front-page spread under the headline 'Natives Freed'. 'This is a direct result of the pressure of unions and the people', the lead article stated:

> roused to anger by the injustice of the arrest and its violation of the fundamental right of every worker to organise to better his conditions ... The release of the two natives amounts to an admission by the Government of the injustice of their arrest, conviction and sentence.[71]

The CDNR immediately began preparing to appeal their convictions to clear their names.

The speed at which authorities acted to have the men released after McLeod's trial was clearly the result of the strong public pressure that had been brought to bear, including the appeal to the UNO and the criticism of the Labor Government's sanction of the imprisonment of strike leaders. The Department, however, was anxious to counter claims that the extension of clemency was the result of public pressure. 'The recommendation was not due to any pressure from any outside organization', Bray insisted, 'but simply because I considered the subsequent attitude and statements of the natives indicated that they were deserving of the exercise of leniency in respect to the remainder of their sentence'.[72] Yet continued harsh punitive treatment of Aboriginal people in other parts of the state make Bray's claim questionable. The following year, as we shall see, an Aboriginal man, Walter Cameron, received a two-month jail sentence for loitering in the Mid West town of Mt Magnet and, following his sentence, he was removed to the notorious government settlement at Moore River. Despite the minor nature of his offence, no consideration was given to remission of this harsh sentence.

Following McLeod's conviction, the Department launched a campaign to counter criticism of its responses to the strike. O'Neill was concerned that nothing was being put out to correct the 'incorrect propaganda ... being

---

70   Stuart, *Yandy*, 1959, p. 74.
71   *Workers' Star*, 28 June 1946.
72   Bray to O'Neill, 26 June 1946, SROWA 1945/0800/190.

used to work up public opinion'.[73] In the lead-up to the court case and in the expectation that McLeod would receive a prison sentence, Wise instructed Coverley 'to prepare, very carefully, a statement which could, if you wish, have Cabinet endorsement and which would be ready for issuing to the public at the appropriate moment'.[74] 'I think many minds are agitated as to whether justice is being done', he later wrote to Coverley:

> and as to whether the natives should be allowed to do this or do that. There are thousands of people who have no knowledge of the conditions or circumstances, nor do they know of what is being done. I think the time for such a statement is very appropriate and perhaps, without directly attacking it, it could be an effective means of silencing some of the Communistic activity.[75]

While the *Workers' Star* published articles critical of the treatment of Aboriginal people in the north, the government's and pastoralists' line was run by the *West Australian* newspaper, whose chairman of directors was pastoralist Langlois Lefroy. Following McLeod's trial, it carried a long article presenting the pastoralists' and the Department's version of the situation, written by a journalist who had travelled to Port Hedland to cover the hearing. It was Native Affairs administrators and employers of native labour who really understood the situation, the article claimed, not people in the south, whose misrepresentation impacted negatively on 'the inarticulate natives', who had become victims of ignorant southern interference. Noting the mutual dependence of pastoralists and Aboriginal workers, the article re-presented pastoralist claims that, in return for a small amount of labour from a few workers, stations supported large numbers of dependents who would otherwise be forced to turn to the government for subsistence, a practice they could not afford to continue if forced to pay a minimum wage. Inevitably, the article finished with 'some amusing incidents' connected with the strike, rolling out the stories of the old prospector who went on strike against himself and the 'native' earning 'fifty bob' who struck for 'thirty bob'. 'Perhaps the best story' was the decision by De Grey workers to strike before 1 May as 'they would be too busy mustering on that day!' The attempt by Aboriginal people to take strike action was made

---

73   O'Neill to Bray, 26 May 1946, p. 1, SROWA 1945/0800/143.
74   Wise to Coverley, 12 June 1946, SROWA 1945/0800/219.
75   Wise to Coverley, 19 July 1946, SROWA 1946/150/46.

to seem particularly farcical in light of the care and solicitude of pastoralists who maintained them and their many dependents.[76]

While, week after week, the *Workers' Star* listed organisations and quoted from correspondence condemning the Labor government's responses to the strike, the *West Australian* diligently reported the few expressions of support for the Department's position. Although many local government authorities had written to Wise and Coverley condemning the imprisonment of McKenna and Dooley, the *West Australian* reported on the 'scathing criticism of the Committee for the Defence of Native Rights' vented by a councillor of the Collie Shire Council in the state's south-west. These people were 'cranks', the councillor said, and 'if we agree to give them our support we will be placing ourselves on their level'. The Council did not, however, support this councillor's strong condemnation and wrote to the CDNR for more information on the issue.[77] The *West Australian* also reported on a decision made by a councillor of the North Fremantle Municipal Council, shortly after McLeod's trial, not to support the CDNR's protest because 'he thought that a certain section of the community was seeking notoriety at the expense of the aborigines'.[78]

The 'certain section of the community' that the councillor was loath to bolster by condemning the imprisonment of strikers was the ACP. If any doubts had previously existed about McLeod's political colours, these were dispelled by the disclosure in court of his handwritten reference to 1000 potential communists. 'This man ... is trying to communise the natives', James Mann, Country Party Member for Beverley in the Legislative Assembly, told Parliament. McLeod had been called a communist since 1943, initially because of his Anti-Fascist League affiliation, but largely because of the ideas he expressed. A departmental officer in the Kimberley noted in 1949 that 'any white man who mentions wages in the vicinity of a station is branded a Communist'.[79] Whether his links with communism were through Party membership, ideology or association, in the eyes of pastoralists, police and Native Affairs officials, there was no question that he was a communist; his advocacy for the rights of Aboriginal people alone made him so. Most pastoralists would have agreed with Reg Sherlock's description of him as 'a communist so-and-so and so-and-so, and then some', without needing to know whether or not he was a member of

---

76   *West Australian*, 27 June 1946, SROWA 1945/0800/200.
77   *West Australian*, 10 July 1946 'Native "Strikers"', SROWA 1946/150/46.
78   *West Australian*, 28 June 1946, 'Native Rights', SROWA 1946/0895/5.
79   Dave Pullen, patrol report, 9 August 1949, SROWA 1949/0456.

the ACP.⁸⁰ Police and Native Affairs reports consistently referred to 'Donald William McLeod, the Communist leader of the strike', 'the Communist, D. W. McLeod', or to 'the noted Communist, Donald William McLeod'.⁸¹ He was identified as a communist even in reports that had nothing to do with the strike: a police report into the search for a missing man referred to assistance provided by 'D. W. McLeod (Communist)'.⁸² The label would continue to be used long after he ceased to be associated with the ACP and when he was, in fact, openly critical of it. 'Although he is not officially connected with the Communist Party', a Native Affairs official stated in 1949, 'he has imbibed its doctrine and certainly preaches it'.⁸³

At the time of his involvement in the activism of the Port Hedland Euralians in 1943, McLeod had been considered an agent of the Anti-Fascist League, but since then it had been assumed that he was acting alone in his 'insidious communistic' activities among station people. The central role played by the ACP in the campaign for McKenna and Dooley's release, however, seemed to add new meaning to his communist label, convincing authorities that the strike had been instigated by the Communist Party for its own ends, with McLeod acting as its local agent. Labor Member for Pilbara Bill Hegney had flagged this possibility when he advised Premier Wise to ignore McLeod's letter of 30 April, which gave notice of impending strike action. 'Although his letter is headed "Port Hedland"', Hegney wrote, 'I am of opinion it was drafted and typed in the Perth Headquarters of the Communist Party – whose agent he is in Pilbara district'.⁸⁴

This suspicion seemed to be confirmed when initial calls on the public to protest the imprisonment of McKenna and Dooley came from a known communist, Alec Jolly, whose appeal was accompanied by a statement drawn from *Workers' Star* reports. Premier Wise instructed Commissioner Bray to try to ascertain 'which of the persons associated with McLeod are Communists – (a) on their own account, or (b) not prepared to come into the open'.⁸⁵ Commissioner Bray characterised the broad-based expression of public protest demonstrated at the well-attended Town Hall meeting of 28 May as simply

---

80 Reg Sherlock to Kitty, 15 May 1946, Sherlock family personal collection.
81 Marshall, police patrol report, 1 August 1948, SROWA 1946/2538 v8; McBeath to Secretary, State Housing Commission, 12 October 1948, SROWA1943/0621/82; Chipper, police patrol journal, 21 June 1949, SROWA 1946/2538 v8.
82 Chipper, police patrol journal, SROWA 1946/2538 v8.
83 Elliott-Smith to Middleton, 2 March 1950, SROWA 1949/0454/109–111.
84 Hegney to Wise, 17 May 1946, SROWA 1946/150/46.
85 Wise to Bray, 5 June 1946, SROWA 1946/150/46, and 1945/0800/158.

a Communist Party stunt. It was 'staged by the Communist Party', he said, and was well attended because 'most Communists would have to attend as a duty'. Although speakers represented a variety of organisations, many, such as the Tramways Union representative, were known to be communists.[86]

Wise, Coverley and Bray answered the flood of letters of protest they received during May and June, giving full accounts of the government and departmental view of the situation to individuals and organisations deemed to be supportive of the government position, but 'very scant attention' to letters received from those with 'affiliations similar to those to which Mr. McLeod belongs'. Suspicious of communist intrigues, they were reluctant to provide information even to inquiries that appear to have been genuine requests for clarification of the situation. A. C. Fox, Professor of Philosophy at the University of Western Australia, for example, wrote to Wise about a letter he had received from Alec Jolly, which enclosed a statement on the strike and a copy of a letter, dated 30 April, that Jolly had received from McLeod. Fox wrote that if the information contained in the statement and McLeod's letter was substantially correct, the action taken against McKenna, Dooley and McLeod 'warrants condemnation'. He was, however, not prepared to accept the information on face value, and asked for clarification from the Department.[87] While Bray could have welcomed the opportunity to correct inaccurate statements, he was suspicious. 'It seems to me that there is guile in Professor Fox's inquiry', he wrote:

> He acknowledges the possession of correspondence by Dr. Jolly and D. W. McLeod. These men are Communists. They suffer from the distemper of Communism, and their correspondence is sufficiently condemnatory of their methods and aims, yet Professor Fox requests information from the Premier. If this were supplied, I fear it would reach Dr. Jolly and MacLeod [sic] and their Communist friends.

He suggested, therefore, that Wise response to Fox as he responded to other writers suspected of having communistic sympathies.[88] Wise's response to such inquiries and criticisms was typically a brief dismissive statement that 'there is very much in the agitation and in the action taken that does not meet the eye. The whole thing is being stimulated by persons suspected of being

---

86   Bray to Wise, 30 May 1946, SROWA 1945/0800/142.
87   Fox to Wise, 27 May 1946, SROWA 1945/0800/162.
88   Bray to Secretary Doig, Premier's office, 29 May 1946, SROWA 1945/0800/121.

Communists and whose methods could not possibly meet with the approval of those who understand the problems'.[89]

A persistent belief that communist protesters had a dangerous and subversive agenda would seriously undermine the broader movement for Aboriginal rights in Australia over the following two decades. Communists would play a vital role in the movement, injecting vigorous support and introducing theoretical frameworks that provided important alternatives to assimilationist and paternalistic assumptions and solutions. Their active participation was a double-edged sword, however. Through the lens of post-war, anti-communist paranoia, entire campaigns became tainted by 'the distemper of communism'. The involvement of communists caused support for Aboriginal activists to be regarded as manipulation, campaigning as subversion, and organisations as communist fronts. As David McKnight notes in his history of ASIO, 'It was as if Marxism was a foreign disease whose carriers infected everyone and every organisation with whom they come in contact'.[90]

The prominent participation of non-communists in the CDNR, including the Anglican Dean of Perth, Robert Moore, Anglican minister Peter Hodge and May Vallance of the Women's Christian Temperance Union, did nothing to diminish the perception that it was a communist organisation. Their willingness to work with communists robbed these participants of any authority and robbed their expressions of concern over the treatment of strikers of any credibility. Bray referred to them as 'dupes or marionettes', enlisted by the communists 'for the purpose of Communist propaganda'.[91] Aboriginal participants in the support campaign were also portrayed as unwitting dupes of communist manipulation. Coverley wrote that the communists 'organised meetings and spread propaganda to influence public opinion, and even inveigled some native well-wishers into their meshes'.[92]

CDNR members tried to counter representations of their organisation as a communist front. The *Sunday Times* newspaper received letters from prominent members of the CDNR – including its patron, Dean Moore; May Vallance, who was one of three trustees; vice-president Gilbert Foxcroft of the Society of Friends; the young communist law student Lloyd Davies; and secretary Peter Hodge – refuting the claim that the CDNR was 'Communist directed and

---

89   Wise to Malloch Brothers, 22 May 1946, SROWA 1945/0800/95.
90   David McKnight, *Australia's Spies and their Secrets*, Allen and Unwin, St Leonards, 1994, p. 110.
91   Bray to Wise, 30 May 1946, SROWA 1945/0800/142.
92   Coverley to the Town Clerk, Collie, and Secretary, Eastern Goldfields District Council of the ALP, Kalgoorlie, 17 July 1946, p. 2, SROWA 1945/0800/247.

controlled'. Not all the letters were published, but the *Sunday Times* quoted from one under the heading 'Protest At "Red" Label'. The letter argued that the label was both 'quite incorrect and extremely harmful to this just cause':

> It is unfair to those people on the committee who are not led like sheep by any party.
>
> It is equally unfair to those who are Communists. It is unfair to the many people who have supported us, and it is most unfair to those for whom we struggle – the natives themselves.
>
> We do not deny that there are Communists on the Committee. These people, despite the fact that they make valuable contributions to the work, have no desire, opportunity, or power to exert more influence than other members.[93]

Moore countered attacks from other quarters at this time. On 7 July 1946, Robert Menzies, then federal Liberal Leader of the Opposition, spoke in a radio broadcast of his astonishment at 'the success with which revolutionary communism had wooed and won the support of not a few ardent Christians, including some of the clergy'. Since communism's intention was the revolutionary overthrow of the existing order, he argued, it could have nothing but hostility towards religion, and particularly Christianity.[94] Right-wing newspapers agreed, one quipping that a '"Right Rev." who is actually a "Left Rev," [was] a nice rosy plum to display in the Red basket'.[95] Although Menzies did not refer specifically to the CDNR, Moore refuted his criticism, arguing that, in fact, too few clergymen spoke up about social problems. He was quoted as saying that 'those of the clergy who deeply considered the matter had good grounds for their discontent with the present order, and that some of them thought that Communism was nearer to a Christian system of organised society than the present system'.[96]

If Coverley and Bray had given any credence to the CDNR's adamant denial that it was communist-driven – and it is not likely that they had – Moore's bravely principled statement, reported on the front page of the *Daily News*, that it was better to be considered a bit pink than to remain silent, would have wiped away any doubts about the CDNR's colours.[97] Coverley continued to

---
93   *Sunday Times*, 30 June 1946, p. 13, 'Protest At "Red" Label'.
94   Quoted in the *Argus* (Melbourne), 8 July 1946, p. 4.
95   *Voice* (Hobart), 13 July 1946, p. 1.
96   *Geraldton Guardian and Express*, 11 July 1946, p. 5.
97   *Daily News*, 10 July 1946, p. 1.

claim with confidence that 'the Communists are working through a subterfuge body known as the "Committee for Defence of Native Rights" and set up by themselves'.[98]

The characterisation of the CDNR as a communist subterfuge body limited its impact as a political lobby group. Coverley and Wise refused to meet deputations from the organisation, for example.[99] John Wilson believes that the perception of communist control caused church bodies to withdraw from active support.[100] Lloyd Davies, who was involved in setting up the CDNR, also claims that anti-communism undermined southern support for the strike, but in a different way. He argues that in 'the wave of anti-communist hysteria' being whipped up in Australia at that time, non-communists in the CDNR sought to avoid embarrassment by asking communists to withdraw. According to Davies, the withdrawal of the communist members left the organisation 'without a number of its most energetic workers', and it became ineffective.[101]

In mid-1947, under the name the 'Native Rights League' and with Joy Alcorn as secretary after Peter Hodge had shifted to Adelaide, the organisation continued to give some campaign support for the strike. By 1949, however, now as the Native Rights and Welfare League and with Joy Alcorn no longer involved, it took on a more local welfare focus, particularly in supporting Aboriginal people in the Perth suburb of Bassendean to obtain adequate housing. Graham Alcorn wrote that the tendency of 'middle-class delegates' to devote their energies to this kind of work was 'commendable enough', but that it diverted energy from the main issue. 'We could not get them to see that success in the Pilbara would open up perspectives for all Aboriginal and mixed-race people throughout Australia', he wrote.[102]

By 1950, the Native Rights and Welfare League was expressing support for the Department's increasingly assimilationist approach and congratulating the new Commissioner for his 'efforts to uplift the natives'.[103] The focus and energies of the ACP, too, according to Alcorn, shifted to other issues during the course of the strike. 'It must have seemed to Don up there that we were

---

98 Coverley to the Town Clerk, Collie, and Secretary, Eastern Goldfields District Council of the ALP, Kalgoorlie,17 July 1946, p. 2, SROWA 1945/0800/247.
99 *West Australian*, 11 July 1946, p. 12.
100 John Wilson, 'Authority and Leadership', pp. 60–62.
101 Davies, 'Protecting Natives', p. 39.
102 Alcorn, 'The Struggle of the Pilbara Station Hands', p. 3.
103 M. Cope, president, Native Rights and Welfare League, to Commissioner Middleton, 24 April 1950, SROWA 1946/0895/28–29.

failing badly', he wrote.[104] Referring to McLeod's disaffection with the ACP by the end of the 1940s, Dorothy Hewett also felt that the ACP had failed to adequately respond to the strike. 'What he wanted the communists to do in that winter of 1946 they were totally unable to deliver', she wrote.[105]

Despite this sense that communists had failed to live up to expectations in their support for the strike, the southern campaign, spearheaded by the CDNR with the support of the ACP, did play a vital role in enabling Aboriginal people to take effective action in the months following the unsuccessful strike of 1 May. The practice of responding to Aboriginal protest action swiftly and severely by imprisoning protesters and removing instigators from the district remained a key feature of departmental control throughout the 1940s. Without legal representation and the high level of public interest and scrutiny created by the southern campaign, there can be no doubt that strike leaders would have been removed permanently to institutions in other parts of the state, and McLeod imprisoned. As we shall see, successful judicial appeals mounted by the CDNR were to have important consequences for the strike movement. Although the CDNR was dismissed as a communist front organisation, the national and international criticism it generated successfully prevented authorities from responding to the strike with the punitive severity that continued to characterise settler responses to Aboriginal dissent more generally. The early release of Clancy McKenna and Dooley is evidence of this. In late July, when *marrngu* took successful group action to challenge settler authority, McKenna and Dooley were free to participate as leaders, and the visibility created by the CDNR's campaign effectively ensured that authorities responded with unaccustomed restraint.

---

104 Alcorn, 'The Struggle of the Pilbara Station Hands', p. 8.
105 Hewett, *Wild Card*, pp. 123–124.

Chapter 10

'All Got To Be in One'

Race-Time Demonstrations, July–August 1946

In the Pilbara, most *marrngu* continued working on stations throughout May and June 1946, but authorities were increasingly aware that station communities were not settling down to contented employment as expected. O'Neill wrote of 'an undercurrent of unrest' that continued to rumble below the surface.[1] Some pastoralists had threatened to expel non-productive workers when the shearing ended, and Constable Fletcher suspected that the number of ex-station people living at the Twelve Mile was likely to 'increase a little as those moved off stations where they caused trouble drift in'.[2] There was also anxiety about how workers who had been granted wage increases for the duration of the shearing would respond when wages were returned to pre-strike levels. On De Grey Station, the matter seemed to be settled to the satisfaction of pastoralists when the shearing ended and *marrngu* realised that temporary wage increases granted to some workers, in lieu of clothing and blankets provided to everybody when the shearing ended, actually disadvantaged workers on lower pay. As the nights turned cold in the middle of May, these workers decided to forego their extra wages so that everyone could receive the extra clothing and blankets that they did not have the funds to purchase.[3]

Marrngu on other stations left when the shearing ended. Ernie Mitchell and Paddy saw out the shearing on Tabba Tabba Station before leaving to join the small community at the Twelve Mile in early July. O'Neill could see no reason for them to leave, writing that he thought that Paddy had 'just decided to leave his employment and that he wouldn't work any more even if he had to live on lizards'.[4] Muccan Station also lost workers when the shearing ended, even though no temporary wage increase had been granted there. Paddy Yabarla

---

1   O'Neill to Bray, 26 May 1946, p. 1, SROWA 1945/0800/143.
2   Fletcher to Bray, 21 May 1946, SROWA 1946/0799/4.
3   O'Neill, patrol journal, 15 May 1946, SROWA 1945/0800/125.
4   O'Neill to Bray, 26 May 1946, p. 3, SROWA 1945/0800/145.

and seven other *marrngu* left Muccan when the shearing ended, joining the small community at Moolyella.[5]

When Pippingarra Station finished shearing in early June, A. E. (Ted) Richardson decided not to reduce wages until after McLeod's trial. With McLeod behind bars, he believed, there was less likelihood of trouble when wages were reduced. When he did reduce wages in mid-July, four of six workers left to join the Twelve Mile community.[6] Strelley Station also continued to pay wages at the higher rate beyond the end of the shearing. Unseasonably heavy rain in early July caused flooding just as shearing came to an end, and workers were needed for urgent repairs to fences and windmills.[7] 'We feel that we are living on the edge of a volcano', the manager's wife, Benja Sherlock, wrote to her sister. She dreaded the time that wages would be reduced, 'and we are quite likely to be without a soul on the place barring ourselves':

> Everyone roundabout has agreed to stand firm, and only if they will, with a united front we could see this business through. It is not so bad for those stations who have some white staff, but Reg will be utterly alone if they pull out from Strelley.
>
> It looks like the writing is on the wall as far as native staff goes, and we are just at the beginning of things. Goodness knows where it will all end.[8]

To establish a united front to deal with these walk-offs, pastoralists planned to meet at Warralong Station on 21 July, the weekend before the Port Hedland races, but unseasonably heavy rainfall had made roads unpassable, and the meeting was postponed.[9]

With his reputed knowledge of 'the native mind', O'Neill thought that one reason the situation remained unsettled was the 'confusing effect' created by the provision of government rations to *marrngu* at the Twelve Mile. He believed that the existence of a community that was receiving food without being required to work was 'a fairly attractive proposition to the native mind', preventing workers from settling to their employment as before.[10] He hoped to

---

5   J. C. Leete, of Muccan Station, to Marshall, 21 November 1946, SROWA 1943/0621/17.
6   Benja Sherlock to Kitty, 7 July 1946, Sherlock private family collection.
7   O'Neill to Bray, 16 July 1946, SROWA 1945/0800/274.
8   Benja Sherlock to Kitty, 7 July 1946, Sherlock private family collection.
9   Benja Sherlock to Kitty, 7 July 1946, Sherlock private family collection.
10 O'Neill to Bray, 26 May 1946, p. 3, SROWA 1945/0800/145.

remedy this disturbing influence by placing Twelve Mile people in employment, but, although the Department continued to claim that Aboriginal workers were 'very hazy as to the aspects of wages and living conditions',[11] he found that *marrngu* were very clear in their wage demands.

Although the manager of Indee Station, Don McWhirter, initially refused to re-employ workers who had gone on strike in early May, he agreed to employ Gordon and Joan Snowball at a combined wage of 25/- per week without keep, but with clothing supplied for Joan and their two children. The Snowballs rejected this offer as too low, however, and joined the community at the Twelve Mile. Later, O'Neill persuaded McWhirter to re-employ workers he had dismissed in May, and arranged for former employees to be returned to Indee on a wool truck. However, at Indee the workers demanded 30/- per week, and when McWhirter refused to pay this, they returned to the Twelve Mile.[12] McLeod wrote that McWhirter had promised £2, but when the workers arrived they found they were being paid at the old rate of £1.[13] Women were also now insisting on being paid. An ex-Indee worker, May, refused to work without wages when O'Neill arranged for her to help out at the Native Hospital in Port Hedland. O'Neill persuaded her to begin work pending a decision about a wage, and he recommended that the Department provide a small wage of 5/- a week.[14]

It was a new situation for O'Neill to have *marrngu* refuse employment without adequate pay. To strengthen his hand, he recommended against providing rations to 'able-bodied natives' at the Twelve Mile. Rations had initially been provided to prevent displaced *marrngu* moving about stations and causing further unrest, but it was now decided that removing the attraction of a ration depot would be the 'lesser of Two evils', enabling O'Neill to 'deliver an ultimatum' at the Twelve Mile and re-establish his authority to direct *marrngu* back into employment.[15] Constable Fletcher was instructed to cease providing rations to anyone unwilling to accept employment at prevailing rates, and to remove able-bodied people from the Twelve Mile.[16]

---

11 Coverley to the Town Clerk, Collie, and the Secretary, Goldfields District Council ALP, 17 July 1946, SROWA 1945/0800/246.
12 O'Neill to Bray, 5 July 1946, p. 1, SROWA 1945/0800/264.
13 *Workers' Star* 19 July 1946, p. 6, 'N.W. Natives Won't accept £1 wage'.
14 O'Neill to Bray, 26 May 1946, SROWA 1945/0800/144–145.
15 O'Neill to Bray, 25 June 1946, SROWA 1945/0800/202.
16 Bray to O'Neill, telegram, 28 June 1946, and Bray to Fletcher, telegram, 28 June 1946, SROWA 1945/0800/203.

This action failed to get *marrngu* back to stations, however. In early July, people at the Twelve Mile informed O'Neill of their intention to earn their own living by kangarooing and prospecting, rather than returning to station employment.[17] This group included Gordon and Joan Snowball, Donald Norman and Coombie from Indee, Ernie Mitchell and Paddy from Tabba Tabba, and Percy from Lalla Rookh, some of whom would become key players in the strike. Ernie Mitchell and Coombie would become principal leaders of the *marrngu* cooperative throughout the 1950s. Roy Mackay and Nancy from Munda Station did not join this group, but neither did they return to station employment. O'Neill believed that Mackay was still agitating for a strike and arranged for them to be sent by train to Marble Bar, where Marshall could take them in hand and make sure they remained at Moolyella.[18] Only a few *marrngu* remained at the Twelve Mile on government rations.

O'Neill was aware that there was still a possibility of further trouble when *marrngu* attended the annual races later that month, and hoped that the independent kangarooing and prospecting group would be well away from Port Hedland when *marrngu* began travelling in for the races.[19] Pastoralists shared his concern. The option of denying permission for *marrngu* to attend the races was considered, but it was feared that such an action would deepen the climate of discontentment among Aboriginal workers and cause further walk-offs.[20] Aware that races could be a flashpoint in the unrest, Bray instructed O'Neill to remain in Port Hedland for the race weekend.[21]

By early in the week leading up to the race weekend, rivers had dropped sufficiently to enable the train to operate, roads had again become passable, and station people began travelling to Port Hedland for the races. Non-Aboriginal people arrived in cars, while *marrngu* either travelled with them, on the back of station trucks, or on the train, while the few who owned cars drove their families in their own vehicles. On Tuesday 23 July, most of the fourteen Aboriginal people at Strelley were given permission to take a station vehicle to the nearest railway siding to catch the train to town, while Daisy, who worked as a cook at the homestead, remained behind to follow later with Reg and Benja Sherlock and their two daughters.[22] While whites filled the hotels and stayed with friends, *marrngu* were instructed to disembark from the

---

17   O'Neill to Bray, 5 July 1946, p. 1, SROWA 1945/0800/264.
18   O'Neill to Bray, 5 July 1946, p. 1, SROWA 1945/0800/264.
19   O'Neill to Bray, 5 July 1946, p. 2, SROWA 1945/0800/245.
20   O'Neill to Bray, 16 July 1946, SROWA 1945/0800/274.
21   Bray to O'Neill, telegram, 19 July 1946, SROWA 1945/0800/268.
22   Benja Sherlock to Kitty, 31 July 1946, Sherlock family private collection.

train outside the town and make camp at the Four Mile Well. On Wednesday, O'Neill reported that 'a fair number of natives were already gathering for the races the majority being camped at the usual place about 4 miles from the townsite'.[23] Any *marrngu* who set up camp closer to town at the Two Mile were instructed by Police Constables Les Fletcher and Tom Needle to shift out to the Four Mile. By Thursday, there were about 150 *marrngu* camped there.[24]

The races were a chance for people from the scattered station and mining communities to dress up, socialise and engage in cultural activities. The *Northern Times* detailed the costumes worn by *walypila* women at the races, the CWA ran its annual bazaar, the Tennis Club had its ball and, at a party held at the quarters of the matron of the hospital, Constable Tom Needle's wife played 'snappy dance music' and Don McWhirter and Constable Les Fletcher recited poems.[25] The Euralian residents of the town held their own entertainment, with an annual Races Ball put on by the Euralian Association, 'and we would go to the shops and buy all our long frocks and have our own dances, it was marvellous', Rose Nowers remembered.[26] For *marrngu* also, the race weekend was usually a time to dress up and socialise, plan ceremonies and marriages, and settle disputes. 'We used to get dressed up for the races in the old days', Ginger Bob recalled. But on the race weekend of 1946, few *marrngu* attended the horse races.[27]

At the Four Mile, the coming together of *marrngu* from stations and Moolyella provided an opportunity to discuss the failed strike and to plan future action. As some *marrngu* opposed the strike, it is likely that intense arguments and debates took place during that Wednesday and Thursday, but by Thursday night, 25 July, the decision had been made that those attending the races would not return to their employment when the races ended. At a large meeting, Dooley suggested that they defy police instructions to camp out of town and shift to the Two Mile on the town's outskirts. There was again, no doubt, fierce discussion about the advisability of taking such risky action, but eventually Dooley and others who supported the move were successful in persuading the group, and during the night of 25 July they shifted camp to the Two Mile, walking with their swags and billy cans and sleeping children. It was an act that took a great deal of courage. Most *marrngu* were extremely

---

23   O'Neill, patrol journal, 24 July 1946, 1946/1306/5.
24   McBeath to McDonald, 9 April 1947, SROWA 1947/0305/82–87.
25   *Northern Times*, 2 August 1946, p. 2.
26   Nowers, interviewed by Hardie, SLWA OH2701/5.
27   Ginger Bob (Palyakulayi), recorded by Anne Scrimgeour, 12 December 1993, AIATSIS collection, soundfile 'Palyakulayi 18'.

fearful of what the consequence of such an action might be – it was no small thing to disobey the police – and it took the urging and encouragement of men like Dooley, Mitchell, McKenna, and Roy and Gordon Mackay to persuade the majority to make the move. In silence, they set up camp at the Two Mile and agreed on the use of non-violent strategies to resist the pressure of intimidation that they knew would be brought to bear against them by O'Neill and the local police. Some, like Wambi Ball and his wife Daisy from Strelley Station, remained at the Four Mile, worried about the consequences of such a move. According to Donald Stuart, four other couples returned to the Four Mile the next morning to direct *marrngu* still coming in for the races to go on to the Two Mile.[28]

The decision to shift camp *en masse* in this way was a highly significant event in the development of the strike movement. John Wilson found in 1960 that the story of the shift to the Two Mile camp had taken on the flavour of stories of mythical heroes.[29] *Marrngu* discovered that the power exercised over them by the police and officers of the Native Affairs Department was not absolute and that these officers were in fact quite powerless to do anything in the face of concerted group action of this nature. O'Neill visited the camp the next day, recording in his journal simply that 'nearly all natives moved closer to Port Hedland'.[30] Both he and the police found their usual authority over Aboriginal people undermined by a stubborn refusal to be intimidated. Stern warning and threats of arrest could achieve nothing. When they tried to speak to everyone as a group, a few spokesmen responded for the rest, insisting that they had a right to remain where they were. When they tried to speak to individuals or small groups, others would close in around them, preventing them from doing so. Bluster and threats met a solid wall of resistance. The only possible course of action open to Fletcher was to arrest the main spokesmen, but with the group closing in on him when he threatened to do so, he felt vastly outnumbered. All he could do was to order *marrngu* to return to the Four Mile, and leave them.[31] *Marrngu* remained where they were, holding their position at the Two Mile the following day, when everyone else made their way to the racetrack for the first day of the races.

Despite all his years of experience as a Kimberley policeman and a Native Welfare officer, despite all his reputed expertise in 'handling the natives',

---

28 John Wilson, 'Authority and Leadership', pp. 78–80.
29 John Wilson, 'Authority and Leadership', p. 63.
30 O'Neill, patrol journal, 26 July 1946, SROWA 1946/1306/5.
31 John Wilson, 'Authority and Leadership', p. 63.

O'Neill was at a loss to know how to deal with such a situation.[32] He and Fletcher drove to the aerodrome to discuss matters with the Deputy Commissioner of Native Affairs when his plane touched down in Port Hedland en route to the Kimberley. Charles Lewis (Lew) McBeath had worked for the Department as superintendent of government settlements in the Kimberley in the 1930s, before becoming Travelling Inspector for the vast northern region in 1939, and had been appointed Deputy Commissioner in 1941. He advised O'Neill and Fletcher 'not to interfere with the natives', and said that if the situation had not improved by the time he returned from Derby he would break his southward journey and remain for a few days to investigate the position.[33]

O'Neill visited the Two Mile the following day and found that very few had obeyed Fletcher's instruction to return to the Four Mile Well. 'Natives sullen and defiant', he wrote in his journal.[34] Few *marrngu* attended the second day of races on the Monday, and on Tuesday 30 July, as non-Aboriginal station people started making their way home, those at the Two Mile remained where they were. 'No natives caught the train for Marble Bar and stations en route', O'Neill wrote. *Marrngu* told him that they would not return to work unless they were paid a flat rate of £2 a week and keep. Of about 150 *marrngu*, only seven returned to their stations.[35]

At Strelley, Benja Sherlock was dismayed at the non-return of the station's Aboriginal staff. 'Well the natives are on strike again', she wrote:

> and this time for two pounds a week!!! They all flocked to the races and when the train went up to the Bar yesterday, not one was on board!
>
> ...
>
> That swine McLeod is still in Hedland of course. He is supposed to have said that he will make the squatters weep before he has finished!! When the station people went home from the races yesterday, none of the natives would go with them! There must be about two hundred of them in there at present.[36]

---

32   Anne Scrimgeour, 'This Man's Tracks: Laurie O'Neill and Post-War Changes in Aboriginal Administration in Western Australia', *Aboriginal History*, vol. 38, 2014, pp. 39–58.
33   McBeath to Ross McDonald, 9 April 1947, p. 4, SROWA 1947/0305/85.
34   O'Neill, patrol journal, 28 July 1946, SROWA 1946/1306/5.
35   O'Neill, patrol journal, 30 July 1946, SROWA 1946/1306/6.
36   Benja Sherlock to Kitty, 31 July 1946, Sherlock family private collection.

Les Miller later said that the Aboriginal population of De Grey Station dropped from sixty to six at this time.[37] Rob Lukis remembered the effects of the non-return of workers from Port Hedland. 'I had a good gang of natives on Munda', he said:

> There were about fourteen or fifteen boys, mighty good boys too. I'd done a lot of culling and I got a good staff. If they were loyal to me, I was loyal to them. And their womenfolk, there were about thirty two on the ration just then. Some of the women used to help in the house with the ironing and washing and that kind of thing ... The shearing cut out at thirty four thousand or thirty five thousand, whatever it was we shore, somewhere thereabouts. I said to the boys, 'Now you fellows have done a mighty good job, you've worked hard seven days a week all hours, I'm sending you all in to the Twelve Mile' ... I said, 'I'm giving you all an extra weeks wages and today week I'll be sending the overseer in with a truck to collect you all, I want you to come back and help me get the sheep spread out into all their paddocks. They're all jammed up around the shed and we want to get them away from there as soon as we can. But I want you to have a spell first' ... One week later I sent in the overseer and he came back with an empty truck. McLeod had collared the lot.[38]

Marrngu later remembered the Munda truck arriving at the Two Mile to pick up the workers, with Fletcher accompanying the overseer to add weight to his demand that the Munda people return with him. The strikers sat on the ground, refusing to shift unless they were carried.[39] Lukis recalled the effects of the loss of labour on the station's production that year. 'That left four of us', he said, 'the windmill man, the overseer, a jackeroo boy and myself to get two and a half thousand sale wethers drafted up and disposed of to the butcher in Hedland':

> I would have gone for a snap lambing off-shears to get the ewes that had missed the first lambing and I used to do very well out of that,

---

37 Miller, statement to Committee Investigating Native Labour, 6 March 1952, SROWA 1952/0830/131.

38 Robert Fellowes Lukis, interviewed by Chris Jeffery, 1977, transcript, pp. 156–157, SLWA OH262. Lukis remembered this as 1947, but there is no record of people leaving Munda then. He remembered that it was two years after he had taken over management of Munda, and the confusion may have arisen because it was the second Port Hedland race meeting since he had been at Munda.

39 John Wilson, 'Authority and Leadership', p. 64.

I used to get three or four thousand lambs out of that second mating. I had to forego that because we just couldn't handle it. By the time we'd spread out the sheep it was too late, I wasn't very happy about that either.[40]

For other stations, the loss of the stockworkers at that time, with shearing over and with good recent winter rains filling the waterholes, was not so severely felt. Benja Sherlock wrote that 'just now the natives are not indispensable – after the rain things are pretty good!'[41] But if stockworkers were not entirely indispensable just at that time, for Benja herself the labour of domestic workers was. Without domestic help, the work that fell to a manager's wife was onerous indeed. 'I am so tired I can hardly sit up and my back and feet ache!!' Benja wrote the day after her domestic servant, Daisy, had failed to return:

> I've been on my feet since 6 am, and it's now 8.30 pm ... My word I curse the distance I have to travel between the house and the kitchen – I must have walked miles today – and all those cement steps up and down. The actual work is nothing, but it is trying to teach the kids, plus all the running around that is so killing ...

> The washing has piled up since our muddy weekend at the coast. I washed the boiling things this afternoon, so tomorrow will light the copper and make a day of it. Reg is going to town in the morning ... so the children and I will be utterly alone at Strelley for the first time ever! One thing all this running around should help thin me a bit![42]

Benja was cheered by news that Daisy and Wambi were planning to return to Strelley as soon as they could arrange a lift, but was aware that even if they did return, a reduction in wages to pre-shearing rates could send them away again. 'If they come back [Reg] has to make it clear that the 5/- will go, and how will they like that, poor devils?? My next letter will tell you!'[43]

In the days following the race weekend, *marrngu* remained at the Two Mile, refusing to return to their stations, and O'Neill and the police found themselves powerless to do anything about it. It must have been galling for O'Neill. He had patrolled stations throughout the area the previous year,

---

40 Lukis, interviewed by Jeffery, 1977, transcript, p. 157, SLWA OH262.
41 Benja Sherlock to Kitty, 31 July 1946, Sherlock family private collection.
42 Benja Sherlock to Kitty, 31 July 1946, Sherlock family private collection. (underlining in original).
43 Benja Sherlock to Kitty, 31 July 1946, Sherlock family private collection. (underlining in original).

warning McKenna and others against taking strike action. The Department had refrained from taking harsh action against the organisers based on his advice that Aboriginal people were not sufficiently organised to conduct a strike. In May, he had made two exhaustive and exhausting patrols gathering evidence to convict McLeod, and receiving assurances from *marrngu* that no further action would be taken. He had achieved successful convictions of McLeod, McKenna and Dooley, and yet all three were still at large. In reporting on the patrols, he had commented on the amount of travel and the long hours involved, and his feelings of extreme tiredness as a result.[44] To now be faced at the Two Mile with a stubborn intransigence and concerted refusal to obey instructions must have been extremely frustrating. I suspect that in his years of dealing with Aboriginal people he would have responded to the sort of disobedience and defiance he now faced at the Two Mile with either arrest or well-targeted and well-timed violence. I have no direct evidence for this supposition, but he had a reputation as being a very hard man. Graham Alcorn described him as 'vicious'.[45] According to Adrian Day, who some years later succeeded O'Neill as a DNA officer in Kalgoorlie, O'Neill had a friendly relationship with local police officers who boasted of using violence towards Aboriginal people. These police officers told Day 'you'll have to hit [the niggers] alright ... But hit 'em with a lump o' wood or y' jack handle first an' when they hit the deck put the boot into 'em ... That's what they understand – the boot!'[46] O'Neill's friendship with these men suggests that his own attitude and approach was not dissimilar.

But if this was the way that O'Neill would have liked to respond to the stone wall of defiance he met at the Two Mile, he knew that in this case he could not; firstly because of the tactic of overwhelming officials with the force of their numbers in a non-violent but effective show of strength, and secondly because of the level of public interest in the strike. O'Neill had received copies of the *Workers' Star* from Bray and had spent a few days in Perth at a time when the Department was coming under heavy criticism, and he knew that any response he made was under the public gaze.[47] Valued by the Department for his ability to 'control the natives', he now felt powerless. On the Wednesday following the race meeting, he wrote in his journal, 'Decided

---

44 O'Neill to Bray, 26 May 1946, p. 3, SROWA 1945/0800/145.
45 Alcorn, 'The Struggle of the Pilbara Station Hands', p. 11.
46 Adrian Day, *Wadjelas: The Memoirs of a 1950s Patrol Officer*, Hesperian Press, Carlisle, 2010, p. 44.
47 Bray to O'Neill, 2 July 1946, SROWA 1945/0800/213; McBeath to manager, MacRobertson-Miller Aviation, SROWA 1945/0800/175.

to keep away from the Native Camp pending arrival of Mr. McBeath on next day, discussed situation with various pastoralists, Father Bryan, & Const. Fletcher'.[48]

The next day, 1 August, McBeath broke his return flight from Derby to Perth to look into the situation at Port Hedland. His attempt to assert authority over those camped at the Two Mile met with the same resistance strategies that both O'Neill and Fletcher had encountered. 'It was not possible to speak, or question individual natives', he wrote, 'and if any attempt was made to single a native out many others immediately gathered close, presumably to prevent any weakening on the part of the one being interrogated'.[49] He could find no way to shift them.

Marrngu at the Two Mile faced the immediate problem of how to secure sufficient supplies of food and tobacco for 150 people. While some goods could be purchased in town, wartime rationing was still in place for essentials like tea and sugar, which could only be purchased with coupons issued by the Director of Rationing. People who had previously left the stations had been issued with coupons, but coupons for everyone else were held by their stations of residence. On 1 August, Dooley and McKenna approached Fletcher and O'Neill to inquire about obtaining their coupons and were told they would need to return to the stations if they wanted tea and sugar. Dooley and McKenna reported this to *marrngu* at the Two Mile, and the decision was made to move into town *en masse* to demand their coupons and, if necessary, enlist McLeod's assistance. The following day, *marrngu* gathered at the tennis courts in town and sent a delegation of men, including Mick Lee and McKenna, to ask McLeod to intercede on their behalf to obtain their coupons.[50] Benja Sherlock wrote that 'the whole mob had trouped into town and McLeod addressed them at the tennis courts'.[51] The deputation originally approached O'Neill and McBeath, but were referred to Fletcher as the Rationing Commission's representative in Port Hedland.[52] McLeod 'led a deputation to the police, asking for tea and sugar', Sherlock wrote. 'Fletcher refused, saying their ration was out at the stations and that they would have to get it from there'.[53]

---

48   O'Neill, patrol journal, 31 July 1946, SROWA 1946/1306/6.
49   McBeath to McDonald, 9 April 1947, p. 4, SROWA 1947/0305/85.
50   McLeod to McBeath, 23 November 1946, SROWA 1946/1416/2–3.
51   Benja Sherlock to Kitty, 6 August 1946, Sherlock family private collection.
52   McLeod to the Rationing Commission, 8 August 1946, SROWA 1946/0799/32.
53   Benja Sherlock to Kitty, 6 August 1946, Sherlock family private collection.

Fletcher repeated the information he had given Dooley and McKenna: that nothing could be done about the matter until December, when new coupons would be issued. There was nothing to stop *marrngu* going back to the stations to buy tea and sugar, he insisted.[54] He then arrested McLeod for being within five chains (100 metres) of a congregation of Aboriginal people, in breach of section 39 of the *Native Administration Act*.[55] McLeod immediately applied for bail, and a Justice of the Peace placed him on a bond of good behaviour, pending a hearing of his case on 23 August.[56] Pastoralists hoped that the new charges would see McLeod finally receive a jail sentence. 'He is out on bail again', Benja Sherlock wrote:

> The first fine has not been paid, but he has fourteen days to find that ... I can't follow it at all, but it is hoped that he goes inside this time. Whether it is true or not we don't know, but we've heard he has native blood in him, which would account for a lot of his hatred and bitterness towards the pastoralists. The man is a menace and no mistake. I wonder where it will all end.[57]

When McLeod was arrested, the *marrngu* delegation returned to the Two Mile with the news. The strikers believed that McLeod was being unfairly victimised, and, unaware that he was no longer being held, decided to demonstrate opposition to his arrest and demand his release. In a show of strength, men 'lined up like soldiers', four abreast, and marched through the streets of Port Hedland to the police station.[58] Dorothy Hewett would later write about the event in her ballad, 'Clancy and Dooley and Don McLeod':

> The young men marched down the road like thunder
> Kicked up the dust and padded it under.
> They marched into town like a whirlwind cloud
> OPEN UP THE JAIL AND LET OUT DON McLEOD.

The townspeople were disconcerted by this demonstration. It represented a further transgression of spatial constraints that underpinned settler control and Aboriginal marginalisation. 'The white women in town were getting alarmed and kept ringing the police to find out what was happening', Benja

---

54   McLeod to the Rationing Commission, 8 August 1946, SROWA 1946/0799/32.
55   McLeod to the Rationing Commission, 8 August 1946, SROWA 1946/0799/32.
56   McBeath to McDonald, 9 April 1947, p. 4, SROWA 1947/0305/85.
57   Benja Sherlock to Kitty, 6 August 1946, Sherlock family private collection.
58   John Wilson, 'Authority and Leadership', p. 65.

Sherlock wrote. 'The natives are not supposed to be in town, they should be out in the reserve'.[59]

At the police station, the marchers were told that McLeod had already been released. To make sure that this was true, the men went to the back of the station, calling out to McLeod, and then went on to look for him at the Pier Hotel, where he lived. Shops and businesses are said to have closed their doors as the men marched through the town. They found McLeod visiting the AWU union representative at the hospital, and, according to an account of the incident that McLeod gave to the *Workers' Star*, he 'asked them to disperse quietly'.[60] Fletcher told the men that 'they could not continue demonstrating, as the town women were frightened'.[61]

As with the shift into the Two Mile, the march to the police station was a significant event in the development of the strike movement, a demonstration to the authorities that *marrngu* were prepared to assert their own authority through group action. No official account of this event survives, except for a brief entry in O'Neill's work journal:

> Friday 2nd Discussed situation with Mr. McBeath & Const Fetcher & also later with Mr. McLeod & natives, some minor demonstration amongst natives & McLeod arrested by Const Fletcher. As it appeared that no useful purpose would be served by my remaining in Port Hedland I decided to leave for Roebourne & complete tableland removals. Mr. McBeath was in accordance with this plan.[62]

It is interesting that O'Neill should have left the area just as the strike was really getting underway. Was he concerned that he would react with violence? During August he toured stations in the Roebourne district, an area unaffected by the strike, removing children of mixed parentage from their families to be placed in institutions. These included two children, Amy and Fred, aged about fifteen and eleven, the son and daughter of a woman called Connie. 'Great difficulty was experienced in removing these children', O'Neill wrote, 'and it was only through the ... firmness of Sergt. McGeary that it was possible and even then the mother had to be taken also to accompany them to Roebourne'. He also wrote in his journal that he 'removed' an Aboriginal

---

59 Benja Sherlock to Kitty, 6 August 1946, Sherlock family private collection.
60 McLeod, draft autobiography, chapter 3, p. 7, Marchant Trust Collection, UWA MS118 series 1 file 13.
61 *Workers' Star*, 9 August 1946, p. 1.
62 O'Neill, patrol journal, 2 August, 1946, SROWA 1946/1306/7.

man from Millstream ration camp and took him to work on Indee Station, which was still in need of labour. This man was employed at 10/- per week, half the rate that strikers had rejected the previous month. Being 'removed' suggests that he had no choice in the matter of his placement in employment away from his own area. O'Neill did not return to Port Hedland after this patrol, but instead travelled north to Broome.[63]

On 5 August, *marrngu* decided to shift from the Two Mile, and they travelled by train to set up a camp at the Twelve Mile, much to the chagrin of Ted Richardson, owner of the adjoining Pippingarra Station, who had been complaining to the Department about the use of the Twelve Mile as a ration camp since Munda and Indee people shifted there in early May.[64] Under the leadership of Clancy McKenna and Dooley, who would still have been in prison if they had not been granted early release, the strikers began to work on ideas for obtaining independent sources of income. The following day, some of the strikers went on by train to Marble Bar to mine alluvial tin at Moolyella. Constable Marshall reported, 'I saw native Dooley (of the McLeod gang) and other natives who arrived from Port Hedland by train, they state that they intend working on tin'. Marshall wrote that he 'again warned Dooley and his mates that they were to work for their tin, & were not to collect tin or money from the other natives'.[65] About seventy *marrngu* were now at Moolyella, of whom probably only about twenty were strikers. Under Dooley's leadership, they organised themselves into family-based groups to work tin.

In the action they took in Port Hedland in late July and early August 1946, *marrngu* began to develop strategies to break down mechanisms of control that had previously kept them powerless and subservient. The complexities of their relationship with pastoralists had made it impossible to negotiate improvements in wages and living conditions when they attempted to conduct a sit-down strike on and around 1 May. Small and widely separated groups of strikers could not maintain their stand against the authority and the threats of police officers and Laurie O'Neill. To change the circumstances of their lives, *marrngu* needed to physically shift away from the stations, come together in larger groups and develop strategies to resist intimidation. The Port Hedland race meeting had provided an opportunity for them to do this. Fletcher would identify this time as the point at which he lost the ability to control the strikers. 'The natives had defied me at race time', he wrote some

---

63 O'Neill, patrol journal, August 1946, SROWA 1946/1306/8.
64 Richardson to Bray, 6 August 1946, SROWA 1938/0982/23.
65 Marshall, police patrol report, 7 August 1946, SROWA 1946/2538 v8/1.

weeks later, 'and as they are still sticking together in fairly large numbers I am not able to move them'.⁶⁶

While such disobedience by individuals and small groups carried a definite risk of punishment, *marrngu* found that the risks diminished as numbers involved in transgressions increased. They found, too, that lines drawn in the sand to ensure that Aboriginal people remained physically, socially and economically on the periphery of the settler world could be erased by the passage of many feet. With these experiences came the development of an ideology of resistance through group action.

'All got to be in one', Crow said. 'No half and half. All got to be in a one'.⁶⁷

---

66   Fletcher to Bray, 24 September 1946, SROWA 1946/0799/61.
67   Yougarla (Yakalya), recorded by Anne Scrimgeour, 21 August 1991, author's collection.

Chapter 11

'Unfortunately C of E into the Bargain'

The Arrest of Peter Hodge, August 1946

In Perth, the Committee for Defence of Native Rights was concerned to learn that McLeod had again been arrested and charged. Its secretary, Peter Hodge, decided to make a three-day trip to Port Hedland to get firsthand knowledge of the situation there. Hugh Peter Vere Hodge was an Anglican minister, born in the Western Australian wheat belt town of Kellerberrin in 1912. He was the son of Dr Theodore Hodge, who had taken up the role of resident doctor in Derby in 1920 at the age of sixty, when Peter was eight. A local character in Derby until his death in 1934, Theodore was immortalised by Ion Idriess as the Old Doc in his book *One Wet Season*, alongside fellow Derby resident Laurie O'Neill. Peter initially worked as a bank clerk before joining the ministry in 1937, and in the early 1940s was rector of the parish of Bencubbin-Nungarin in the north-eastern wheat belt. He was rector of the Wiluna-Meekatharra parish for a short period before joining the Army in 1944.[1] He had married in 1944, but his marriage did not survive his service as Army chaplain in New Guinea. Graham Alcorn wrote that he had been popular with the troops in New Guinea, known there as the Red Padre.[2]

Hodge was not long out of the Army and was working as assistant clergyman at Christ Church in the Perth suburb of Claremont when he made his visit to Port Hedland. He told the *Sunday Times* that he hoped to get full information about the situation up there following the recent arrest of McLeod.[3] Prior to his departure, Graham Alcorn applied to the Department for 200 application forms for Citizenship Rights for Hodge to take north with him, apparently

---

1   *Geraldton Guardian and Express*, 6 March 1943, p. 3.
2   Alcorn, 'The Struggle of the Pilbara Station Hands', p. 10.
3   *Sunday Times*, 11 August 1946, p. 5.

'UNFORTUNATELY C OF E INTO THE BARGAIN'

with the intention of suggesting that all the strikers evade the restrictions of the *Native Administration Act 1936* by applying for full citizenship.[4] Nothing came of this plan, however.

On the afternoon of Tuesday 13 August 1946, a week after *marrngu* had set up camp at the Twelve Mile, Peter Hodge flew to Port Hedland and stepped off the plane into the middle of a power play between McLeod and the authorities in which he became something of a sacrificial lamb. While the police and the Native Affairs Department believed that their authority could be re-established and order restored through the successful prosecution of agitators, McLeod knew that the arrest of an Anglican minister would attract criticism of the authorities and bolster public interest in the movement. He was expecting documents relating to the appeals against McKenna's and Dooley's sentences from the solicitor, Fred Curran, to arrive on the plane that day, and had arranged to pick up McKenna at the Twelve Mile to sign the documents after he had picked up Hodge from the aerodrome. He said in a court statement that he noticed Constable Needle at the aerodrome, so he was clearly aware that he and Hodge were being watched. Hodge knew that it was illegal for him to approach a group of Aboriginal people without the permission of the Protector, but McLeod told him truthfully that Fletcher was away. He failed to inform him, however, that Needle was also a Protector and could be approached for permission. As it was illegal under section 39 of the Act for them to go to the Twelve Mile, and as he was still on a good behaviour bond, McLeod had arranged to pick up McKenna some distance away from the Twelve Mile. This seemed legal enough to Hodge, and he agreed to call by the Twelve Mile with McLeod on their way into town. As they headed off from the aerodrome in McLeod's Ford utility, Needle saw them turn towards the Twelve Mile, and followed them.[5]

When McLeod and Hodge arrived to pick up McKenna, McKenna told them that a large group of people were waiting to meet Hodge in the scrub at some distance from the Twelve Mile. McLeod later claimed to have arranged this himself. 'I had an arrangement with the people to be five chains away from the camp at least', he said.[6] Hodge agreed to go on to meet everyone, and they drove through the scrub for some distance until they came to the place where *marrngu*, sitting in a semi-circle, were waiting for them. 'We had not

---

4   Bray to Coverley, 12 August 1946, SROWA 1946/0895/10.
5   Needle v. McLeod, 'Donald William McLeod', NAA A6335, 17; McLeod, interviewed by Jeffery, transcript, p. 42, SLWA OH331; *Truth*, 23 March 1947, p. 29; *West Australian*, 14 August 1946, 'Northern Natives: Two Men Arrested'.
6   McLeod, interviewed by Jeffery, transcript, p. 42, SLWA OH331.

been there five minutes before a truck approached, some men got out, and I found myself under arrest, charged with offending against section 39', Hodge said.[7] As McLeod liked to tell the story years later, with his characteristic chuckle, Hodge protested that he was a minister of the Anglican Church. Tom Needle replied, 'I don't care if you're Jesus Christ. You're under arrest'.[8]

The men were taken into the police station, charged and released on bail, with a hearing set for the following morning, as Hodge needed to return to Perth to attend Synod and had a return flight booked on the Thursday. According to Max Brown and Donald Stuart, McLeod took Hodge to meet Clancy McKenna and other *marrngu* in secret that night.

If Hodge had wondered whether he could really gain much of an insight into conditions in the north on such a lightning visit to Port Hedland, his arrest and conviction within twenty-four hours of his arrival, and the 'strange procedure' he encountered in the Port Hedland Police Court, were eye-opening, a stark illustration of the use of the justice system to support settler domination of Aboriginal people. The *Workers' Star* reported that his trial had 'exposed the law as a tool of the squatters'.[9] Hodge was permitted to say very little in his own defence. What he did manage to say – that, in approaching Aboriginal people to discuss their conditions, he had no unlawful or immoral purpose such as section 39 was designed to prevent – was left out of the transcript of the proceedings until he insisted on its inclusion.[10] He was found guilty and fined £10. He requested thirty days to pay the fine, but Fletcher demanded that no more than seven days be allowed, and this was agreed to. McLeod's hearing was set for 23 August, and he was remanded without bail and placed in the lockup. 'I'd been out on bail with Peter', he said, 'but as soon as they fined him they put me in without bail, wouldn't let me go'.[11]

That afternoon, Hodge visited the Twelve Mile with the permission and in the company of a policeman, and spoke to *marrngu* there. The refusal of town businesses to sell them tobacco was a particular hardship, they told him. McKenna told him of their plans to set up their own enterprises and said they needed a dinghy, a truck and rations to set themselves up. They also needed someone to handle their pearl shell and kangaroo skins. Hodge was impressed with McKenna's 'fine qualities of leadership and a thorough grip of

---

7   *Truth*, 23 March 1947, p. 29.
8   Personal recollection.
9   *Workers' Star*, 23 August 1946, p. 6.
10 *Workers' Star*, 23 August 1946, p. 6.
11 McLeod, interviewed by Jeffery, transcript, p. 42, SLWA OH331.

the position'. He told the *Workers' Star* that he found the people at the Twelve Mile 'strong and determined in this battle for their rights'.[12]

As well as speaking to the strikers, Hodge hoped to meet and speak with members of the broader community, and at short notice a public meeting was planned for the night of Wednesday 14 August, at the Mechanics Institute in Port Hedland. He hoped to speak to members of the local community about the injustices suffered by Aboriginal people, and to gain information about local attitudes.[13] On that day, pastoralists had planned to have a meeting at Warralong Station to formulate a united response to the strike, their previous planned meeting having been postponed due to flooding. 'It had been planned for some time', Benja Sherlock wrote, 'their first get together since the strike'. However, early that morning Alan Crawford of Tabba Tabba arrived at Strelley Station with the news:

> that a Padre Hodge was to come up from Perth and address a meeting in Hedland tonight!!! He is a Mcleod-ite, and probably an out and out Communist! I am ashamed to say that he is unfortunately C of E into the bargain.
>
> Well what a mix up. There was this meeting at Warralong, to which everyone was going from far and near, and now, this bird in town tonight, and everyone wanting to get to hear him![14]

To enable everyone to get into Port Hedland for the meeting with Hodge, the Warralong meeting was put back a day. 'Everyone was heading for town to hear the Preacher!!!' wrote Benja Sherlock that evening. She stayed home at Strelley with her children but was full of curiosity to know what was happening in town. 'My word I would love to be listening now ... No Doubt friend McLeod will be on the platform!! Gee, I bet it will be hectic'.[15]

'Friend McLeod' was not on the platform, but was sitting out the meeting in a police cell. Benja was right in thinking that the meeting was hectic, however. Had there not been a meeting planned for Warralong that day, it is likely that fewer would have learned of the meeting or been able to get into town that evening. As it was, the hall was packed. Facing an angry pastoralist and pro-pastoralist audience, Hodge was loudly derided as an ignorant busybody at best, and as 'an out and out Communist' at worst. He was initially unable

---

12   *Workers' Star*, 23 August 1946, p. 6.
13   McLeod, *How the West Was Lost*, p. 58.
14   Benja Sherlock to Kitty, 14 August 1946, Sherlock private family collection.
15   Benja Sherlock to Kitty, 14 August 1946, Sherlock private family collection.

to make himself heard over the shouting and heckling of the audience. It must have required remarkable courage to stand up before an audience of this nature, particularly as he was not a strong speaker.[16] As Hess writes, that he did so demonstrates the courage of his convictions.[17] McLeod, who heard the 'jeering and buffoonery' from his jail cell, also wrote of Hodge's courage in facing such an audience.[18]

Hodge later spoke to the *Truth* newspaper in Adelaide of the 'torrid time' he had at the meeting. The audience 'refuted completely' Aboriginal complaints of being 'underpaid, underfed, poorly clothed and without adequate sanitary and educational facilities and housing', he said. 'He was told at the meeting that 'the native had a childlike mind and would not appreciate anything that was done for him', the *Truth* article reported.

> If [the native] was given decent sanitary arrangements he would not use them. If his children were provided with proper educational facilities, it would be a waste of time. In fact, the station owners said, they would sooner be without the natives and it was the next thing to charity employing them. One white man was worth 10 blacks.[19]

The meeting was reported in the *West Australian*:

> The secretary of the Committee for the Defence of Native Rights (the Rev. Peter Hodge) addressed a representative gathering of pastoralists and townsfolk in the Mechanics Institute last night. There was continuous heckling until Mr. L. E. Taplin asked the gathering to give the speaker a hearing.
>
> Mr. Hodge was asked to explain his purpose in coming to Port Hedland and if he was in favour of the recent strike by natives, which, it was said, only served to create confusion, discontent, and dismay to all concerned. He replied that he was here to better the conditions of the natives in general.
>
> A voice: What do you know about them?
>
> Mr. Hodge said he wished to seek information from the pastoralists for his committee.

---

16 Oliphant to McLeod, 31 July 1957, SLWA 1568A/2/6.
17 Hess, 'Black and Red', p. 75.
18 McLeod, *How the West Was Lost*, p. 58.
19 *Truth*, 23 March 1947, p. 29.

> Mr. Miller (De Grey): Would you mind telling us just who comprise your committee and if there are men of standing in it?
>
> Mr. Hodge said that Dean Moore was associated with the committee, and added: Another is a man of good standing, but I cannot state his name as his employer does not like his employees to be associated with outside organisations.
>
> Mr. Miller: Then, sir, I suggest that if that man has not got the courage of his convictions he is a rat.
>
> Mr. Sherlock (Strelley Station): I consider Mr. Hodge, that you do not know what you are talking about. We are pretty straight people up here and straight speakers too. Are you or are you not in favour of the recent strike among the natives.
>
> Mr. Hodge: Yes, I am.
>
> Mr. Sherlock: In that case you are wiped off.[20]

If Hodge was given any opportunity to speak at the meeting, his views were not recorded by the *West Australian,* which focused instead on the arguments made by members of the audience. The often-repeated stories of the 'native with a gold show of his own' who 'went on strike against himself', and of the man who earned 30/- striking for 30/- were trotted out as proof that 'the majority of natives went on strike not knowing what it was all about'. The arguments that *marrngu* were happy when left alone, and that they would not know what to do with wages if they were increased, were also repeated. Ted Richardson of Pippingarra said that 'until this trouble started the natives were happy in their mode of living provided by the stations. If the natives were paid more money they would not know what to do with it, as what surplus funds they acquired they used for gambling'.

The Catholic priest Edward Bryan supported the statements of pastoralists, claiming that:

> Practically every native had two gins; the station generally employed one of them at 5/- a week, to do either the washing or the ironing, to sweep verandahs or to do other odd jobs about the homestead, but they generally only had one set job. For the employment of these two natives the station had generally to keep at least seven adults and a few children.

---

20 *West Australian*, 17 August 1946, p. 12, 'North-West Natives: Conditions on Stations'.

Rev. Robert Boulter, of the Methodist Inland Mission, also assured Hodge that 'the natives, except in isolated cases, which could be found in every walk of life, had always been well treated, and white people as well as natives had hardships to put up with through living in the North-West'. Attempts at good treatment were sometimes hampered by the actions of the putative beneficiaries, however. A scheme for taking children from Aboriginal parents for education, for example, could not be carried out in one area, Boulter said, because 'as soon as the natives heard of this they cleared out'.[21]

The Carnarvon-based *Northern Times* also provided a one-sided report on the meeting:

> The Rev Hodge was here for a very short stay last week and addressed a meeting of the Pastoralists and towns people in the Mechanics Institute which did not meet with any success on behalf of the Rev Hodge, as the Pastoralists had no time for any one who thought the natives on their stations were being ill-treated. Some very good arguments were put forward by station managers and at the close of the meeting the Rev Hodge appeared to be most frustrated, being unable to answer direct questions put forward to him. The Rev Hodge left the next day and we hope he will take the truth of the strike situation to his companions in the South.[22]

Hodge's position as a minister of religion did nothing to convince pastoralists and their supporters of his sincerity or his authority to make inquiries regarding the treatment of Aboriginal people. Rather, in the eyes of pastoralists, his presumption in questioning their good treatment of Aboriginal station residents and his support for the strike were made even more offensive by the fact of his being a clergyman. Based on her husband's account of the meeting, Benja Sherlock wrote that Hodge had been 'a pathetic object of ridicule' at the meeting. 'Reg had plenty to say and you will see his name in print! He is furious at this man lowering the dignity of the Church of England'.[23]

More scathing criticism of Hodge's involvement came from the Catholic Church's *Cathedral Chronicle*. It argued that 'in doing the bidding of Communism', the CDNR, 'one of the numerous ancillaries of the Communist Party':

---

21   *West Australian*, 17 August 1946, p. 12.
22   *Northern Times*, 23 August 1946, p. 15.
23   Benja Sherlock to Kitty, 17 August 1946, Sherlock private family collection.

would not be perfect in the order of gross deception unless there was a 'Rev' or a 'Padre' among its benighted members. Thus Padre Hodge came into the picture. If he is sincere, then his sincerity certainly outweighs his intelligence for it does not require much intelligence to discern the hand of Communism even when attired in a kid glove. If the said Padre is consumed with zeal for the welfare of the natives, then he ought to place his zeal under appropriate patronage and not under the infamous hammer and sickle which is the very antithesis of the Cross of Christ whereby men – black, white and red – are saved both in soul and body.[24]

Hodge's decision to investigate the situation in the Pilbara was also questioned by members of his own church hierarchy when he returned to Perth to attend Synod the day after the Port Hedland meeting. Archdeacon Parry asked for clarification on whether his visit to the North West had been as an official representative of the church or as a private individual. 'People in the north were concerned', he said, 'because it appeared that he had been sent officially to support striking natives'. Archbishop Le Fanu said that he had advised Hodge against making the trip, but had left it to his own discretion. Parry was 'pleased to have it made clear that he did not go as an official representative'.[25]

Meanwhile, McLeod remained behind bars at the police station in Port Hedland, awaiting the hearing set for 23 August. In an account which was probably, like Needle's Jesus Christ comment, an embellishment for the sake of a good story, McLeod said that while in jail at this time he:

> wrote down to Curran, our solicitor and said what do I do? ... He said appeal under habeas corpus act, as soon as they come in in the morning make an appeal ... so I did that, and Les Fletcher the policeman said, 'I've heard of this bloke, who is this Habeas Corpus?' So I wrote down to Curran again, and said this bloke's legally and politically illiterate, tell me again what to do? So he said tell him to look at the justice act, and he quoted a section and of course they let me go. So this was their idea, they thought if they could keep me on ice they could bust the strike, they reckoned.[26]

On 23 August, the earlier charge against McLeod of breaching section 39 when he met with *marrngu* over the issue of tea and sugar rations on 2 August

---

24   *Cathedral Chronicle*, September 1946, p. 1.
25   *West Australian*, 24 August 1946, p. 15.
26   McLeod, interviewed by Jeffery, transcript, p. 42, SLWA OH331.

was withdrawn.[27] McLeod was, however, found guilty of breaching section 39 when he visited the Twelve Mile with Hodge and sentenced to three months' imprisonment. He appealed and was released on bail awaiting his appeal.[28]

Five years, almost to the day, after Hodges 'torrid' experience at the public meeting, Bray's successor in the role of Commissioner of Native Affairs, Stanley Guise Middleton, would be treated to a similar display of northern hospitality by the residents of the town and surrounding stations, at a very similar public meeting in Port Hedland. Middleton said that he had never been so insulted as he was at the meeting he addressed in Port Hedland in August 1951.[29]

But much water would pass under the bridge before the Department would, to this extent, put itself in the firing line of pastoralists' hostility. In 1946, the DNA still supported the pastoralists' position that the industry's relationship with Aboriginal people was more about charity than exploitation. It still believed, at this time, that the prosecution of activists like McLeod and Hodge was the best means of undermining the strike movement and reasserting control over *marrngu* for their own good and for the good of the pastoral industry. But prosecution had quite different outcomes to those intended, providing a focal point for public protest, and providing test cases in which the legality of aspects of the legislative framework of control over Aboriginal people could be challenged and undermined. It also strengthened the resolve of *marrngu*, who were heartened to realise that they were not alone and that they had supporters willing to face arrest and imprisonment, just as they were. Middleton would later refer to McLeod's imprisonment 'on the frivolous charge of being within five chains of a native camp' as a near-sighted action that 'caused McLeod's stocks with the Pilbara natives to rise very high'.[30]

Despite its brevity, and the derision it occasioned, Peter Hodge's visit to Port Hedland would have lasting consequences for the movement. The eventual success of appeals against his conviction would, as we shall see, undermine the effectiveness of section 39 in preventing McLeod's direct involvement with the independent group that became established at the time of the races.

---

27 McBeath to McDonald, 9 April 1947, p. 4, SROWA 1947/0305/85; *Workers' Star*, 27 September 1946, p. 2.

28 Needle v. McLeod, 'Donald William McLeod', NAA A6335, 17; *Workers' Star*, 30 August 1946, p. 1.

29 Rodoreda, Member for Pilbara, Parliamentary Debates (Hansard), Western Australia: Legislative Assembly, 6 November 1951, p. 499.

30 Commissioner Middleton, 'Statement re Donald William McLeod, Formerly of Pilbara District', undated [March 1955], McLeod ASIO file, vol. 2, NAA A6119, 3306.

Although Hodge shifted to Adelaide the following year, he continued to talk about the experiences of his short trip to the north. In 1952, the secretary of the Victoria-based Council for Aboriginal Rights wrote to McLeod, saying that he had 'been prompted to write by a recent meeting in Adelaide with Padre H. P. V. Hodge, who told us something of what he had seen in Port Hedland during the strike a few years ago'.[31] The Council would, as a result, support and publicise the movement throughout the 1950s.

---

31   Henry Wardlaw, Secretary, Council for Aboriginal Rights, to McLeod, 4 February 1952, SLV MS 12913/1/3/282.

Chapter 12

'Start Rolling Up Swag, We Off'

Walking Off, August–December 1946

In the months following the Port Hedland races, the strike camps at the Twelve Mile and Moolyella increased in size. *Marrngu* walked away from their stations in family groups as opportunity presented itself. This was not the large, coordinated walk-off that is often described in histories of the strike, but a gradual process that took place throughout the second half of 1946, as family groups and communities made the decision to leave their stations and join the strike.

Marrngu who were still being paid at increased rates granted at the time of the 1 May strike initially returned to their stations after the Port Hedland races. At Strelley Station, Benja Sherlock, overwhelmed by the workload that fell to her without the help of her domestic servant, Daisy, waited anxiously for her return. Wambi and Daisy Ball, who had not joined the shift into the Two Mile, caught a lift back to Strelley Station on Ray Brook's truck, much to the relief of Benja Sherlock. 'Wampi and Daisy are back!!!!' she wrote:

> Oh my goodness – please God let them stay, is my fervent prayer during every waking moment ... Daisy has returned with a cold, and beyond coming up for tucker she hasn't put in an appearance! But it is still good to know that she is on the place.[1]

Sherlock's letters to her sister provide lively evidence of a dependence on the labour of Aboriginal women. With Daisy ill in the camp, Benja found herself overwhelmed with work, especially when she was informed that a *walypila* and two 'half-castes' would be staying for tea. Illustrating the racially and socially segregated hierarchy of stations, she wrote, 'Ye gods and little fishes – a hot tea to prepare for two half castes and Paddy in the kitchen, Mr Brookes and ourselves inside, and Daisy and Wampi in the camp!!'

---

1   Benja Sherlock to Kitty, 7 August 1946, Sherlock family private collection (underlining in original).

I had to leave the folding and the damping, prepare the meal, set the table and have a bath, and no Daisy to help me! Well it got done, and then came a huge wash up. I got it all scraped and stacked and the kitchen tidied, and then Reg and Mr Brooks came over and dried up for me. After that I set bread, finished folding, and then sat and talked to the men for a while – I sure was ready for bed.[2]

Daisy returned to work the following morning, to relieve Sherlock of some of her workload. 'She is excellent in the kitchen', Benja wrote with relief, 'so clean, and it was a treat to see her get things ship shape and doing the little extras that I'd had to leave'.

But Benja Sherlock knew that Daisy's return might not be permanent. Wages were still being paid at increased rates, and the Sherlocks were concerned that the couple would leave again when wages were reduced to pre-shearing levels. 'When they both know they have to drop back 5/- per week to the pre shearing rate', Benja wrote, 'they may be up and off. I feel sick at the very thought of it'.[3]

'Daisy has been wonderful', she wrote on 17 August, 'and I can't bear to think of her leaving!' The following day, Wampi was paid at the pre-shearing rates, and he and Daisy informed the Sherlocks of their intention to leave. 'I'm sorry old man', Wampi said to Reg, 'but I'll have to pull out'.[4]

Benja described receiving the news from Daisy:

> I was sewing in the dining room when I heard Daisy call, 'Are you there Missy?' In she came, with her hat on, to say goodbye. She said, 'I'm very sorry to leave you', and she was near to tears, the dear old thing. I said I was very sorry too, but I had Ann and Jane [her children] to help me, and she said, 'I'm very sorry for you Missy.' By then I was close to blubbing myself, but managed to say that perhaps they may come back when all the trouble was finished, and she agreed. I thanked her for all she had done for me, and we said goodbye.
>
> I felt the bottom had fallen out of everything. When I went over to the kitchen to see to dinner, there were their meat and veggies still in the oven and I felt too sad and depressed for words.

---

2   Benja Sherlock to Kitty, 7 August 1946, Sherlock family private collection (underlining in original).
3   Benja Sherlock to Kitty, 7 August 1946, Sherlock family private collection.
4   Benja Sherlock to Kitty, 17 August 1946, Sherlock family private collection.

> Fortunately, I had spent any spare time last week cleaning out cupboards etc, and was almost finished by Sunday. Daisy had worked like a Trojan in the kitchen, and the place was spotless, so I had a good start for being on my own. On Monday when I went to clean the copper I found she had even done that and it was gleaming! I think they must have realised they would be going and hence all the cleaning – she always had a cleaning spree before she went on pinkeye [holiday].
>
> They now belong to the strikers mob and won't be able to get a job unless they come back here poor things. Oh it is a hideous business and make no mistake. I wonder yet again when it will all end.[5]

If the exodus of Aboriginal people from stations to the strike camps seemed to contradict pastoralist representations of *marrngu* as happy and well cared for on stations, this was explained by the claim that many or most of those who left the stations did so out of the fear of physical violence from strike leaders. Les Miller, for example, claimed that a number of those who left De Grey Station did not want to go, 'but were constrained by other natives, Mitchell, Clancy McKenna and Dooley'.[6] Ted Richardson was told by *marrngu* working on Pippingarra that they had been threatened by strikers 'that when they get what they demand those boys who worked through the strike would get speared and a big belting'.[7] Tactics used by the strikers to prevent police or pastoralist pressure to return to stations also seemed to indicate that intimidation was being used to hold strikers at the strike camps. As soon as anyone approached the camp, Fletcher wrote:

> the whole crowd were called together into one solid mass, and when one began to talk, it was to the whole crowd, with Clancy, Dooley, Mulyie Tommy and Roy and Gordon McKay in the forefront, acting as spokesmen, so that when one asked a question or spoke to any boy, it was from one of these five that the answer came. I have questioned quite a few natives when it was possible to get them on their own, and almost invariably they tell of threats of violence if they do not stick to the crowd.[8]

There was certainly pressure on Aboriginal people to join the strike. As the success of their defiant action at the Port Hedland races had demonstrated,

---

5   Benja Sherlock to Kitty, 17 August 1946, Sherlock family private collection.
6   Miller, Statements to Committee Investigating Native Labour, 6 March 1952, p. 10, SROWA1952/0830/130.
7   Richardson to Bray, 6 August 1946, SROWA 1938/0982/23.
8   Fletcher to Bray, 16 August 1946, SROWA 1946/0799/37.

the group's ability to stand against the power of settler authority depended on the strength of numbers. Unanimous support from all *marrngu* in the region would have significantly boosted their position. Strikers used whatever powers of persuasion were at their disposal to convince others to join, and this included threats of punishment with a green stick. In 1952, when Pilbara Aboriginal people were again leaving station employment to join an independent mining cooperative, a departmental officer, Frank Gare, was asked to investigate persistent accusations that physical violence was being used to recruit and hold members of the group. He found no evidence to support these accusations, but did find that 'the threat of the green stick' had been used at the time of the strike. 'It's true Clancy McKenna, a very impressive man, had devised a threat – what he called the threat of the green stick', Gare said.[9] The green stick seized the imagination of some pastoralists as a symbol of savage power, and James Doherty of Pinga Station used it as the title of his pro-pastoralist and anti-Aboriginal novel. He portrayed the green stick as having ritual or 'tribal' significance:

> It had native carvings patterned along its entire length. 'Fancy sort of waddy', [Conn] commented. Ginger nodded. 'Proper Green Stick, dis one', he grinned.[10]

This belief had sufficient currency for Gare to point out that a green stick was 'simply the handiest weapon available, and [had] no other special significance'.[11]

> The green stick was simply a piece of bush, cut anywhere, just a green stick. And [McKenna] implied that he'd use this if he needed to, but in fact he never did as far as I could make out. He was a very affable sort of fellow. Not a threatening type at all although he was a big man. They used to visit stations and just talk to people and offer them an independent livelihood ... They'd say if you want to back up your mates, come and join us. If you want to be a scab and not support your mates, go back to the station. Something like that. I never ever witnessed any of this but I used to hear about it. Sort of moral suasion, I suppose you'd call it. But I was satisfied there was no real threat, no physical threat, no violence involved.[12]

---

9   Frank Ellis Gare, interviewed by Darren Foster, 1998, transcript, pp. 43–44, SLWA OH 2899.
10 Doughty, *The Green Stick*, p. 62.
11 Gare, patrol report, 15 May 1952, p. 3, SROWA 1952/0830/171.
12 Gare, interviewed by Foster, 1998, transcript, pp. 43–44, SLWA OH 2899.

The fact that many people never joined the movement suggests that threats were less influential in motivating the decision to leave stations than many pastoralists believed. Nevertheless, the explanation fitted pastoralist perceptions of station workers as childishly contented, and of the Aboriginal realm that existed beyond station boundaries as chaotic and violent. It provided pastoralists with an explanation of why *marrngu* would turn their backs on the paternalistic protection offered by station residence, to walk away from their 'station homes where they were fed and nursed and had an easy-going life that appealed to them'.[13] It enabled pastoralists to avoid the obvious conclusion presented by the exodus that their Aboriginal workers were, in fact, dissatisfied with the inequality of the relationship.

Aboriginal expressions of regret and women's tears at leaving the stations added weight to the perception that they were responding to threats of violence. When workers told their bosses they were leaving because they had to, pastoralists could only imagine that compulsion was a product of fear. Differing understandings of the word 'force' added to this perception. When *marrngu* said that the strikers were forcing them to leave, they used the word in its Aboriginal English sense to mean that they were being encouraged and felt compelled to comply. Social pressure included the strikers' strong condemnation of those who continued to work for the squatters; individuals still carried the label of 'scab' decades later.[14] Family allegiances and structures of authority and obligation within Aboriginal Law also undoubtedly operated to influence *marrngu* in their decision to join the movement. But how could *marrngu* explain social and cultural motivations to *walypila* who knew them only as 'stock boys', 'house girls' and the dependent recipients of station rations? Wampi Ball's 'I'm sorry old man but I'll have to pull out', and Daisy's tearful 'I'm very sorry to leave you' suggest divided loyalties, a reluctance to let down people they liked and who depended on their services, rather than coercion through the threat of violence.

Strikers travelled around stations urging ('forcing' in Aboriginal English terminology) *marrngu* to join the movement. Molly Williams was working as a housegirl at Mulyie Station when men from Moolyella arrived to urge them to join the strike. 'Some boys was coming from Moolyella', she remembered:

> They start strike this side, get out from station. He coming, he let us know. Alright, my husband said, 'Yes, I will'. We start strike then. We had a two old lady and a old man, mummy and daddy belong to Mulyie.

---

13 Hardie, *Nor'Westers*, p. 181.
14 John Bucknall, personal communication.

> We take that two, we went across, walking, take our swag, take our dog ... We walk across on to Shaw River, we want to catch'm train from Marble Bar between Port Hedland. We went right up to Twelve Mile.[15]

Some *marrngu* waited until the shearing was over before leaving their employment, not wanting to inconvenience station operations more than was necessary. Some informed their bosses that they were going to join the strikers, while others left without saying anything, simply failing to return to stations from holidays, for example. 'Some of the workers walked off without letting anyone know', Mac Gardiner (Pirntilkampanyaja) said. 'They pretended they were going on holiday to Moolyella'.[16]

Maggie Ginger (Nyirrarlpi) walked away from Nimingarra Station, having shifted there from Yarrie as a young married woman:

> Then we walked off. They came to see us while I was there, and we went on strike. Don McLeod and his people took us away from the stations and brought us here. We walked off the stations, all the way to Moolyella. We lived at Moolyella. I was pregnant, I carried my first child in my stomach. He was born there at Moolyella, my eldest child. That was the time.[17]

The Marble Bar races in September provided an opportunity for more people to join the strike. Many did not return to their employment when the races ended. Monty Hale's family joined the strike from Mt Edgar Station at race time. 'We watched the races on the Saturday and the Monday', he remembered:

> and then stayed in a camp on the Yukurlukurlunya creek. When the bosses came to pick everyone up to go back to work, we said, 'No, we're staying here. We're going to Moolyella and we'll live there'. Our own boss came and called us to work.
>
> 'No', we told him, 'we're staying here. That's it, we've left you. You go back, that's it'.[18]

---

15 Molly Williams (Kulyu), tape 1, recorded 13 August 1991, author's collection.
16 Gardiner (Pirntilkampanyaja), recorded by Anne Scrimgeour, 5 August 1993, AIATSIS collection, sound file 'Pirntilkampanyaja 18'.
17 Maggie Ginger (Nyirrarlpi), recorded by Anne Scrimgeour, 13 May 1993, AIATSIS collection, soundfile 'Nyirrarlpi 3'.
18 Hale, *Kurlumarniny*, p. 23.

Marrngu at Warrawagine who had been persuaded to return to work by Marshall on 30 April also left 'a few at a time' to join the strikers at Moolyella. Caroline Jula was among those who made the long journey on foot from Warrawagine to Moolyella towards the end of 1946:

> Well, we stop there, and we heard about that strike coming. Hello, old Dooley, he bin coming there. 'After, you fellas gotta strike'.
>
> We strike then, we going to Moolyella ... We bin tell'm, 'No, we want to go, we gotta follow Don'.
>
> ... 'We gotta give you little bit tucker, for road'.
>
> 'Na, we got enough, kangaroo, meat'.
>
> Start rolling up swag, that morning, Saturday, we off, and walk, Moolyella. We went walk, right up, have a dinner in the windmill, three mile windmill ... Oh, we got billy cans and blankets and all that ... Big mob, everyone! Everyone. We leave'm Warrawagine, only we leave'm four old people in Warrawagine. We went there, we make a camp in a middle, in a windmill. Boys get a kangaroo, maybe emu, and might be goanna. We finish'm all one day for supper or dinner we bin finish'm off, oh big mob. We went to Moolyella, strike. One day, when we bin sleep in the middle, in the road, we went, sleep there, morning we went in the road. We have'm dinner there, in the middle. Next morning all the big mob, big mob from Warrawagine. We went there, we see big mob here, all strike.[19]

The journey from Warrawagine to Moolyella was made longer by the need to skirt Talga Talga Station (Yirrirrinya), where pastoralist Harry Greene, chairman of the Marble Bar Road Board, would take a stockwhip to *marrngu* passing through. 'The Yirrirrinya boss had a missing arm and was hostile', Cranky said. 'He'd chase you with a stockwhip if he saw you'.[20]

'We get in Sunday, Moolyella', Jula remembered. 'We see Old Dooley there now. Oh, very crowded, you know, Moolyella. We see'm big mob, from Nullagine, from Marble Bar, from Muccan'.[21]

---

19   Jula, recorded by Anne Scrimgeour, 13 August 1991, author's collection.
20   Cranky (Kujupurra), recorded by Anne Scrimgeour, June 1993, AIATSIS collection, soundfile 'Kujupurra 4'.
21   Caroline Jula (Jula), recorded by Anne Scrimgeour, by Anne Scrimgeour, 5 November 1992, author's collection.

Her brother, Bandy Ngiyirr, joined strikers at Moolyella after returning from a cattle droving trip to Meekatharra. He and other *marrngu* drovers returned their horses to Warrawagine before leaving for Moolyella. 'That was the last trip', Cranky said. 'Bandy's mob drove them right up to Meekatharra. When he came back from that trip he came to join us at Moolyella'.[22]

Cranky (Kujupurra) and his brother Ginger decided to leave Warrawagine during the Marble Bar races in September, when they saw how many strikers had gathered at Moolyella:

> We saw them at Moolyella, and saw, phew! all the strikers there from all the different stations around about. They were all there. We went to see them, and saw the boss, Dooley, my *yaku*.[23] 'They can't hold us, after this we're walking off', we said. 'Me and my brother are walking off as soon as we get back'.[24]

Cranky's account of joining the strike displays a lack of rancour between *marrngu* and pastoralists, a genuine liking for some white bosses and a willingness to see a job completed rather than leaving their bosses in the lurch. While they were at the Marble Bar races, he and Ginger told Jim Lewis, who was now manager at Warrawagine, that they intended joining the strike, but before they did so they assisted in returning racehorses to the station:

> At the races I told Bill Sheppard and Jim Lewis, 'After the races, I'm going'.
>
> 'Oh?'
>
> We went back [to Warrawagine] after the races for a while. One morning the boss asked us, 'Well, what are you two going to do?'
>
> 'We're going. We've only come back to bring the race-horses back, but now we're going back to Moolyella'.
>
> But he was a good bloke, Bill Sheppard, and so was Jim Lewis, the manager. 'Why don't you-two fellas wait until Saturday, and get your rations before you go?'

---

22 Cranky (Kujupurra), recorded by Anne Scrimgeour, June 1993, AIATSIS collection, soundfile 'Kujupurra 4'.
23 Classificatory brother-in-law.
24 Cranky (Kujupurra), recorded by Anne Scrimgeour, June 1993, AIATSIS collection, soundfile 'Kujupurra 3'.

We did, and got rations; a little packet of sugar, about that much, and tea and tobacco. We had a packet and we cut it in half, and took half each. We had a full packet and we got half each. Then we left and headed back [to Moolyella].[25]

This lack of animosity is also evident in Cranky's account of the 100-mile journey he and Ginger made to join the strikers at Moolyella:

> I went there, Moolyella, that time we went after races, Moolyella. And we get hungry, in the middle, and tired, you know, never been walking, bin riding all the time.[26] Alright, at that Fifteen-Mile, we camped. Right, oh, late, late … We was hungry, me and my brother. Well – I see the dust coming. Oh! Mob of *kukurnjari* [sheep] coming, we'll have to wait. '*Ngaju nyungu parungu munyilamarnajanaka*'. [I'll wait for them here in the grass]. Trough was like that, and that grass, you know, I get in the grass inside. Righto, he's thirsty them sheep, all the wethers anyhow, he coming past – aah, right up trough till they was rush! coming, and all bundled up them sheep was coming, just standing right near me. I just stand up and bloody grab his leg, finish. Cut his throat, oh not far off the windmill, tree just like there, and windmill was there. Skin'm, skin'm, skin'm, finish. We take a half, liver and all them, heart, take'm and cook'm, for a feed. When we had skinned him well … tip him up other way. He's just like a dead himself, you know. Alright, we went, we went to Moolyella.
>
> And that day he went, round the windmill, Jim Lewis, he went round, he clean the trough. Right, he went, he see the crow was sitting there eating that, right, he going to have a look. 'Ah, fucking sheep, might dingo bite him'. Couldn't see. 'Only three, three leg here. One leg is gone'. Turn him round, 'Ah, oh yes, I think that two fellas bin kill it and take a half. Oh, that's all right'. [*Laughs*]
>
> After that we see him in Marble Bar.
>
> 'Oh, gidday'.
>
> 'Gidday'.
>
> 'Ah, you bin kill that sheep, at Fifteen-Mile, and take a half front leg?'

---

25   Cranky (Kujupurra), recorded by Anne Scrimgeour, June 1993, AIATSIS collection, soundfile 'Kujupurra 4'.
26   That is, they were horsemen, and not used to walking long distances.

We can't help it and, 'Yeah, we killed it'.

'Ah, that's all right'. [*Laughs*] He never got the police, no.[27]

A genial man with *maparn* powers, a big belly, long beard and ready smile, Cranky laughed as he told this story, the humour and warmth of his narrative belying his station-given name. His account provides an illustration of a claim frequently made by *marrngu* that they had no argument with pastoralists as individuals when they went on strike. On 1 May, when strikers had approached the manager of the Ironclad Hotel in Marble Bar, they told him that the strike was not against the bosses but 'for Don McLeod'.[28] Although Cranky walked off Warrawagine, he remembered the station manager fondly as a 'good bloke', painting a picture of the relationship between pastoralist and *marrngu* as amicable.

Other *marrngu* accounts describe a similar and surprising lack of animosity towards the strikers on the part of pastoralists. Caroline Jula recalled that when she walked off Warrawagine with a large group of people, Lewis simply offered to provide provisions for their long walk to Moolyella. '"We gotta give you little bit tucker, for road", he said. '"Na", the *marrngu* replied. 'We got enough, kangaroo, meat'.[29]

Reflecting O'Neill's contention that station managers were 'not at all vindictive to the natives' who left, Lewis's solicitude could perhaps be explained by a belief that Aboriginal people were as much victims in the affair as pastoralists. 'The poor things', Benja Sherlock commiserated. 'To think they should follow a swine like McLeod – it won't do them any good'.[30] Edith Miller also expressed pity. 'I could never see to this day, what sense it was', she said. 'What did they want? ... It was pitiful, really pitiful'.[31]

Believing that the strike would be short-lived, many pastoralists avoided engaging in confrontation that might exacerbate Aboriginal grievances, preferring to leave the matter in the hands of the police and O'Neill. They indicated that they were not interested in negotiating with workers whose labour they construed as essentially worthless. Consistent with the persistent pastoralist contention that they provided rations and tolerated Aboriginal

---

27 Cranky (Kujupurra), recorded by Anne Scrimgeour, 25 June 1993, author's collection.
28 Tommy Dodd, High Court appeal, D. W. McLeod v. G. R. Richards, p. 31, NAA A10074 1946/8, 9, 10.
29 Jula, recorded by Anne Scrimgeour, 13 August 1991, author's collection.
30 Benja Sherlock to Kitty, 14 August 1946, Sherlock family private collection.
31 Edith Miller, interviewed by Jamieson, 1982, transcript, p. 99, SLWA OH506.

residence on stations more for charitable than economic reasons, they feigned indifference and even support for the walk-offs. In an English version of his narrative, Cranky recalled that Lewis had asked him:

> 'What are you going to do now? You fellas going back to Moolyella?'
>
> 'Yeah, sometime, after this week'.
>
> 'Yeah, well you'll have to wait for rations. No, you can go'. And he was a good bloke, he say, 'You stick to Don McLeod. All these fellas are going to go again,[32] we'll get all the jackaroos, white men. You fellas go'.[33]

Treating Aboriginal workers as if their labour was more a burden than a benefit to stations, their labour easily replaced with more efficient non-Aboriginal labour, pastoralists sought to undermine the strike by convincing *marrngu* that they were in no position to negotiate for better wages and living conditions. They portrayed themselves, and no doubt saw themselves, as indulgent in their tolerance of dependent Aboriginal station communities.

Until now, demonstrations of solicitude had served as a key feature of labour relations on Pilbara pastoral stations, creating a familial relationship which, together with other mechanisms, had bound Aboriginal workers to stations through a sense of loyalty and kinship with pastoralist families. But kinship imposes obligations on both parties in a relationship. *Marrngu* felt that their relationship with pastoralists entitled them to expect that a request made in earnest would be granted. In 1959 and 1960, *marrngu* told John Wilson that they had felt deeply the pastoralists' refusal to give them the wage increase they asked for on 1 May. In refusing them, squatters had reneged on their obligations as something like kin. *Marrngu* 'had been "knocked back"', Wilson writes, 'not merely as individuals but collectively'.[34] The bond that had previously given *marrngu* a sense of obligation towards the stations was weakened by this collective knock-back. While many *marrngu* remained on stations to see out the shearing, they now felt able to turn their backs on pastoralists, even the 'good blokes', to join the strike camps.

Solicitude and kin-like relationships between squatter and *marrngu* were one side of the coin of labour relations in the Pilbara; police coercion was the other. Friendly or careless responses to walk-offs were often followed by calls on the police to enforce compliance to pastoral labour requirements.

---

32 That is, the other Aboriginal workers at Warrawagine were also going to leave.
33 Cranky (Kujupurra), recorded by Anne Scrimgeour, June 1993, AIATSIS collection, soundfile 'Kujupurra 3'.
34 John Wilson, 'Authority and Leadership', p. 59.

When strike action had first been attempted at Sheep Camp on 30 April, for example, Lewis had sacked those involved but called on Constable Marshall to persuade them to return to work. Three years later, in 1949, he would make a similarly insouciant response when strikers travelled to Warrawagine to remove remaining workers. According to Caroline Jula, he told the strikers, 'Alright, you fellas can take'm people in to Moolyella. That people bin sick, you can take'm away, in the river, you know'.[35] Nevertheless, as soon as the party left on the long walk back to Moolyella, Lewis telephoned the police in Marble Bar, who arrested the strikers. Again, their relationship with the police enabled pastoralists to be 'good blokes' in their dealings with *marrngu*, while the police took coercive or punitive action at their behest.

While most of those who joined the strike camps during the second half of 1946 did so voluntarily, others were evicted by pastoralists following through with their threat to 'undertake a severe cull' of non-productive station residents when the shearing was over, including less skilled and less efficient workers and non-workers. To some degree at least, pastoralists believed their own rhetoric about the value of Aboriginal labour, and their often-repeated assertion that white labour would be cheaper, more efficient and less troublesome. They thought that when the strike petered out, as they were sure it would, they could hire efficient skilled Aboriginal workers during the mustering and shearing seasons when the demand for labour was at its highest, and use non-Aboriginal labour for routine work during the rest of the year. In this way the strike could actually be exploited by pastoralists to their own advantage, enabling them to be rid of the burden of dependent Aboriginal communities while still having access to Aboriginal labour when needed. Even if higher wages were paid, pastoralists believed that their stations would be better off. However, as John Wilson has pointed out, the movement into the strike camps of important senior men evicted from stations at this time as no longer productive workers worked against the pastoralists' interests by strengthening the social and religious authority of the new communities that were becoming established in the strike camps.[36]

Expectations that the strike would peter out arose in part from a faith that colonial mechanisms would enable the police to re-establish control, but also from a confidence in the efficacy of a strategy that stations had always employed to attract and hold Aboriginal labour: pastoralist control over Aboriginal access to rations, and particularly to the addictive substances tea,

---

35   Jula, recorded by Anne Scrimgeour, 13 August 1991, author's collection.
36   John Wilson, 'Authority and Leadership'.

sugar and tobacco, which had been effective in establishing an Aboriginal labour force in northern Australia in the first place. If strikers could be denied access to alternative supplies of these goods, then pastoralist control could be reasserted. Rather than negotiate with the strikers, therefore, they chose to wait until hunger and a craving for these goods drove those they were willing to re-employ back to the security of regular station-supplied rations. Benja Sherlock wrote that the strikers:

> will have to sit on their tails until such time as hunger forces them back.
>
> The Native Department will not feed them, and no one is allowed to sell them tobacco, so I think before long the poor things will be feeling pretty sorry for themselves. We are experiencing a spell of strong easterly winds and its pretty cold, believe me, and they won't be enjoying it much. I'm sure.[37]

Pastoralists viewed *marrngu* as dependents, unable to survive without a supply of rations from either the stations or the government. According to a repeated refrain, without station rations Aboriginal people would become 'the charge of a benevolent Government, subsisting on a soul-destroying dole, contributed by the already over-burdened taxpayer'.[38] Fletcher reported in mid-August that he expected the Twelve Mile camp to break up, 'as their supply of cash must be running short now'.[39]

But while the police and pastoralists waited for hungry *marrngu* to drift back to stations, strikers found other ways to make a living. At Moolyella, tin mining had provided an alternative source of income for decades, and *marrngu* joining the strike from stations in the Marble Bar area set about acquiring knowledge and skills for what was, for many, a new form of employment. Caroline Jula, whose working life had been in domestic service at Warrawagine Station, remembered being taught to work tin by experienced Moolyella miners when she first arrived at the strike camp:

> That morning he tell us, Dooley bin tell us, we gotta work in the tin. He gotta show you, you know, we never know for tin. He bin show'm now, tin. We have a look, 'oh yeah'. Some people from Moolyella, he show'm, we have a look yandy'm, we get learn, we get'm self then.

---

37   Benja Sherlock to Kitty, 31 July 1946, Sherlock family private collection.
38   Owen C. Coppin, letter to the editor, *West Australian*, p. 3, 'NATIVES' "STRIKE": A Few Facts on the Issue'.
39   Fletcher to Bray, 16 August 1946, SROWA 1946/0799/37.

'Start Rolling Up Swag, We Off'

We get pick and shovel, we bin work there, make a, might be, you know, bag, one bag or two bag, tin. After that one, might make'm three bag or four. We sell'm then, for tucker. We get tucker, tea and sugar, tobacco.[40]

Leaders provided picks and shovels and showed newcomers where to work. 'We dug holes, square ones and long ones, really big ones', Cranky remembered:

We used the picks to dig them out. The tin was found in hard ground, with white and red soils mixed up together. We dug the dirt out into an area next to the holes which we had cleared. We spread all the wet dirt out to dry. We cut short wooden beaters and pounded the tin ore until it got really soft. We then put it into yandying dishes. We scooped up the ore in the yandying dishes and took it over to where we winnowed it, the wind blew all the dirt away until only the tin was left, falling down in a pile. That's what the men did, the women sat down and did the yandying. The separated tin ore we put into the fruit tins and meat tins. We had to use the same tins over and over again; we'd fill them up, level them off and pour them into the bag. All the tins full of ore got poured into a bag. In a good spot we could fill up over twenty fruit-tins. We got water in a dish and washed the dirt out of the ore, and spread it all out to dry on a sheet of canvas. When that process was finished, we started over again, yandying and putting the ore into fruit tins. We got the iron out of the ore with magnets, the magnets picked up all the ore and left the tin behind. And when there was no iron left we took the ore to the store run by a man with glasses called Don Thompson. He took the ore and weighed it, and gave us money for it. Then we bought stores.[41]

Supplies obtained by family groups from Don Thompson's store, the only shop on the tin field, were supplemented by meat and bush foods gathered and hunted on Sundays. Caroline Jula said:

We work right up Saturday. Right, we stop weekend, you know. Sunday, get a meat. We got a plenty dog, you know. Get some kangaroo, emu, anything. That's all we living, you know. No bullock, no sheep, you know. We get only little bit half, some, from store. Might be three dollar, might be four dollar, right we only get half, some. And bread, little bit, for living, you know, we bin living that's all …

---

40   Jula, recorded by Anne Scrimgeour, 5 November 1992, author's collection.
41   Cranky (Kujupurra), recorded by Anne Scrimgeour, 25 June 1993, translated from Nyangumarta, AIATSIS collection, soundfile 'Kujupurra 8'.

We work mob again, maybe we work right up Saturday get one bag. And we sell'm Monday. We keep'm there, you know, tucker little bit, little bit. We hold'm that tucker right up Monday, and after that one we work again for tin, for living, you know ... Sometimes we hungry, might be boys going get a kangaroo, give us.[42]

While strikers at Moolyella were able to tap into a means of subsistence already established by independent Aboriginal miners, those at the Twelve Mile needed to find new sources of income. Kangaroo skins were fetching a high price and were the main source of revenue for the strikers in the early months of the strike.[43] Gathering pearl shell along the coast was another possible source of income, but systems needed to be put in place to sell skins and shells and to purchase supplies. While these enterprises were being established, McKenna applied to the Committee for Defence of Native Rights for financial assistance for the first month. A pastoralist reported on 23 September that the CDNR was sending the strikers £25 per month, but there is no evidence that more than one such payment was made. Some *marrngu* took casual work in town to bring in some cash until the group's economic activities became established.[44]

Strikers organised themselves into work teams. Molly Williams and her husband joined a kangarooing team, initially hunting out from the Twelve Mile with the use of dogs, living mainly on kangaroo meat. 'We got a lot of dogs, I had seven', Molly said:

> Get some meat, kangaroo, do some skinning. They want a skin. I battled, every morning we going, going bush get some kangaroo, how many kangaroo might be six or four, might seven ... Right, my husband was take the skin, I take few meat for our living. Right, we get in a camp, we do some cooking, but my husband do all the packing skin. Next morning we start same again, we go and get some meat. Sometime he leave me, stay home, he going, do some cooking for him.[45]

Within a few weeks, kangaroos became more difficult to obtain around the Twelve Mile, and work teams shifted to other areas. Molly's team shifted to the coastal station of Munda, where kangaroos were more plentiful, and where they could also collect buffel grass seed for sale. 'We went to Munda

---

42 Jula, recorded by Anne Scrimgeour, 5 November 1992, author's collection.
43 *Workers' Star*, 13 September 1946, p. 5.
44 Richardson to Bray, 23 Sept 1946, SROWA 1946/0799/59.
45 Molly Williams (Kulyu), tape 2, recorded 22 October 1992, author's collection.

side now', she said, 'kangaroo shooting, grass seed. We make our own living'. While the men hunted, women gathered grass seed for sale, raking fallen seeds into piles and cleaning them by sifting out leaves and sand with mosquito nets. 'Grass seed was start for us now, we battling for grass seed and kangaroo', Molly said.

Other work teams had also shifted out from the Twelve Mile by September 1946, two teams moving to Boodarie Station to gather skins and seeds, one team shifting out to McPhees Patch to prospect and obtain kangaroo skins, and another shifting to the Shaw River on Warralong Station. A further team shifted along the coast to the old town site of Condon to gather pearl shell.[46] Any food obtained from the bush or through the sale of goods was held in common by each team, and meals for the whole team were prepared by one or two women, who took on the role of cook on a rotating basis. 'One, might two lady, do some cooking for that mob', Molly said. 'We used to have one kitchen ... nother lot team had his own kitchen'.[47] This system freed women to engage in money-making activities, especially as cooks were also able to care for young children.

But while the Twelve Mile strikers were organising independent ventures of this nature, efforts were being made to prevent them selling their produce or purchasing necessary supplies, particularly tea, sugar and tobacco. Strikers still did not have access to ration coupons to buy tea and sugar. Constable Fletcher continued to insist that, as stations held Aboriginal ration coupons and had purchased tea and sugar for their erstwhile employees, the logical solution was for strikers to purchase supplies from their former stations, at least until supplies purchased by stations were exhausted and new coupons issued. While this may have seemed a pragmatic suggestion to Fletcher, for the strikers it seemed clear that tea and sugar were again being used to draw them back to the stations. Fletcher's suggestion was unacceptable to them; their new-found strength in united action would be sorely undermined if individuals were forced to approach their old employers for supplies.

The CDNR and McLeod both applied to the Rationing Commission for ration coupons to be issued directly to the strikers. McLeod asked that 'some acceptable arrangement be made for the issuing of all rationed goods to the people who are entitled to receive them and not to their bosses who tend to use such goods as a bargaining factor'.[48] The Rationing Commission

---

46   Fletcher to McBeath, 21 September 1946, SROWA 1946/0799/54–56.
47   Molly Williams (Kulyu), tape 2, recorded 22 October 1992, author's collection.
48   McLeod to the Rationing Commission, 8 August 1946, p. 2, SROWA 1946/0799/33; *Workers' Star*, 16 August 1946, p. 1.

accepted the justice of this, writing that it 'would not like the Natives to be without tea and sugar through any fault of this office', but the Department of Native Affairs was anxious to ensure that control over access to these rationed commodities did not pass into the hands of strike leaders.[49] Commissioner Bray insisted that 'the natives are unsuitable to hold ration books' because they would not know how to use them.[50] He suggested instead, if Fletcher's recommendation was unacceptable, that Native Rationing Orders be issued by Fletcher to heads of Aboriginal families every four weeks, and:

> instructions be issued to the local storekeepers that they are not to sell goods except when each native personally signs for them, or makes his mark in the presence of a witness, and adds the address of his late place of employment.

These provisions were necessary, Bray argued, to prevent ration orders falling into the hands of strike leaders. Just as McLeod argued that station control over these commodities was being used to hold onto Aboriginal labour, so Bray believed that control over ration coupons would give strike leaders increased power to prevent workers returning to station employment. 'Unless some safeguards are imposed', he told the Rationing Commission, 'I am confident that Clancy McKenna, Dooley, McKay and other ringleaders will force natives to remain together by the exercise of pressure to surrender their ration orders'.[51] Control over rationed commodities, it seems, would guarantee control over Aboriginal people.

The system recommended by Bray to prevent strike leaders obtaining control of rationed goods was implemented in September 1946, but it was unsatisfactory to the Twelve Mile strikers.[52] The stipulation that the head of each family provide his mark or signature each month to purchase rationed goods was out of step with the strike camp arrangements for common ownership of supplies and the preparation of communal meals. By the end of October, only one striker had obtained his monthly tea and sugar ration from Alec Wyndham's Port Hedland store. Hodge petitioned the Department to reconsider these arrangements. 'Would it be possible for you to arrange for one man to collect the ration for the whole Camp?' he asked. 'Also they find it hard to pay for a

---

49 Anderson, Deputy Director Rationing Commission to Bray, 13 August 1946, SROWA 1946/0799/34.
50 Bray to Anderson, 23 August 1946, p. 1, SROWA 1946/0799/43.
51 Bray to Anderson, 23 August 1946, p. 2, SROWA 1946/0799/44.
52 Anderson to Bray, 2 September 1946, SROWA 1946/0799/ 45; Fletcher to McBeath, 26 November 1946, SROWA 1946/0799/89.

month's supply, and would appreciate if they could collect the rations weekly or fortnightly'.[53] Fletcher, however, argued that the arrangement posed no inconvenience for strikers, and that their refusal to make use of the provisions was 'in the nature of a protest against the system'. The Department therefore rejected Hodge's proposal. 'There are weaknesses in any proposal which enables one person to collect supplies for a body of people as large as the number of natives now at the Twelve Mile', Acting Commissioner McBeath wrote:

> It is not the desire of this Department to impose any hardship, particularly upon mothers with families, or aged people, by forcing them to make unnecessary or over-frequent visits to Port Hedland, but nevertheless control must be exercised to prevent unscrupulous persons from taking advantage of these natives.[54]

This refusal to acknowledge the existence of an Aboriginal organisation, or the authority of Aboriginal leaders to act on the group's behalf, was to be an ongoing source of conflict throughout the course of the strike.

Meanwhile, it was a lean time for the strikers, who lived mainly on a diet of kangaroo meat. The inability to purchase tobacco, which was also rationed, continued to cause hardship, although bush tobacco that grew in hilly country served as a less desirable substitute to keep the craving at bay to some extent. In early November, McKenna told the CDNR, 'We are still battling for tobacco, tea and sugar'.[55] Molly Williams remembered 'just living on sugarbag [bush honey] and kangaroo. When we want tobacco we get'm tobacco from the hill'.[56]

There was also an attempt to prevent the strikers becoming economically independent by pressuring businesses not to buy their produce. 'None of the regular business people will handle the shell for fear of offending the station people', Fletcher wrote in September. 'They are in difficulties in this regard'. He recommended that the Department assist the strikers by handling the strikers' produce. 'This would I know cause a lot of opposition amongst the station people', he wrote, 'but after all, our primary object is the protection of the natives themselves, whatever their occupation'.[57] The Department, already under heavy criticism from pastoralists for its inability to prevent

---

53 Hodge to McBeath, 18 November 1946, SROWA 1946/0799/82.
54 McBeath to Fletcher, 21 November 1946, SROWA 1946/0799/84.
55 *Workers' Star*, 8 November 1946, p. 5.
56 Molly Williams (Kulyu), tape 1, recorded 22 October 1992, author's collection.
57 Fletcher to McBeath, 21 September 1946, p. 2, SROWA 1946/0799/55.

the exodus from stations, was reluctant to cause further offence and chose to ignore Fletcher's suggestion.

By November, however, strikers were finding ways around the impediments set up by pastoralists and the Department. They were fortunate to have the support of Alec Wyndham, a Port Hedland store owner who was sympathetic to their cause and willing to risk the ire of station people and suffer any subsequent loss of business. He began to purchase the strikers' kangaroo skins and sell them provisions, making an arrangement for meeting Bray's stipulations for the purchase of tea and sugar without overly inconveniencing the group's activities.[58] To assist the strikers to obtain tobacco, the CDNR appealed to the Australian Tobacco Trade Distribution Committee, which decided at the end of November to provide two ounces of 'native tobacco' per week for the 208 strikers at the Twelve Mile.[59]

Clancy McKenna and Mick Lee obtained beachcombers' licences, and McLeod, who was working on the Port Hedland wharf and was already well and truly in bad odour with pastoralists, obtained a shell buyers' licence to assist the strikers by purchasing shell, which he sold on to a buyer in Carnarvon. The Department could do nothing about this, beyond demanding a monthly account of all McLeod's financial dealings with Aboriginal people. McLeod's accounts for September and November 1946, forwarded to the Department by the CDNR, show that about 1500 lbs of shell had been obtained, at a value of £200.[60] The group at the Twelve Mile was finding its feet financially. McKenna and Lee travelled between the scattered work teams in McLeod's old Ford V8 and Lee's own truck, picking up skins, seeds and shell for sale in Port Hedland, and delivering to the work camp the supplies they purchased from Wyndham's store from the proceeds of the sale.

It became clear to pastoralists, as Christmas approached, that their expectation that hunger and a craving for sugar, tea and tobacco would force chastened and submissive *marrngu* to return to meagre but regular station rations was not going to eventuate, at least as far as the Twelve Mile strikers were concerned. In construing Aboriginal people merely as dependents, they had failed to take account of Aboriginal innovation and determination to follow through with the

---

58 Jensen to McBeath, 15 May 1947, SROWA 1946/0799/99. Sugar rationing was lifted in July 1947. Although tea rationing remained in place until 1950, by 1947 there seems to have been little attempt to prevent strikers from making group purchases.

59 *Workers' Star*, 13 September 1946, p. 5; Western Australian Tobacco Trade Distribution Committee to McBeath, 27 November 1946, SROWA 1946/0799/88; *Workers' Star*, 6 December 1946, p. 5.

60 Hodge to McBeath, 4 December 1946, SROWA 1946/1416/4.

action they had begun. Nor did they take into account the ability of *marrngu* to live off the land, obtaining bush substitutes for sugar and tobacco that assisted them, perhaps, to maintain their determination. Pastoralists failed, too, to understand the importance of the southern support in enabling the Twelve Mile community to set itself up financially, particularly through the activities of Peter Hodge and the CDNR. And they failed to take account of existing cultural and family networks that formed the basis of new economic ventures.

As Christmas approached, the Department instructed Protectors of Natives throughout the state to work with local businesses to provide 'Christmas cheer' to local Aboriginal communities. Fletcher replied that in the Port Hedland district, with 'feeling locally running so high against the natives on account of the recent strike, it will be impossible to [achieve] any co-ordination of effort amongst the general public'. Instead, he wrote, he would purchase some clothing for people at the Twelve Mile, as that appeared to be their greatest need.[61]

Molly Williams remembered that everyone from the work camps returned to the Twelve Mile to celebrate Christmas. 'We all come back for Christmas now', she remembered. 'We had in a Twelve Mile. All the workers come back from every place'. The men went night shooting to obtain a supply of meat, and proceeds from the sale of skins, seeds and shell were used to buy food to be shared by everyone equally. 'What that loading ... they bring'm in a truck, got'm out, they make one, all gotta have it, all the lot, same', Molly said. Twelve Mile strikers were not dependent on settler charity for 'Christmas cheer'. 'Some old people they know how to make cakes and pudding, for Christmas', Molly remembered. 'We battle self'.[62]

There were now 173 adults and thirty-five children based in the strike camp at the Twelve Mile, and the usual Aboriginal population of about fifty at Moolyella had swelled to 200 adults and many children, with the number increasing each week, according to Marshall, 'owing to more of the station natives going on strike'.[63] 'Practically every station in this district is affected by the loss of some if not all of their natives, over the strike', Marshall wrote.[64]

Crow said that after the shearing of 1946:

---

61   Fletcher to McBeath, 4 November 1946, SROWA 1946/0799/79.
62   Molly Williams (Kulyu), tape 2, recorded 22 October 1992, author's collection.
63   Hodge to Chief Inspector, Department of Education, 14 October 1946, SROWA 1947/0594; Marshall to McBeath, 30 November 1946, SROWA 1943/0621; Marshall, patrol report, 24 November 146, SROWA 1946/2538 v8.
64   Marshall to McBeath, 29 November 1946, SROWA 1943/0621/17.

all one, two, all build up Moolyella mine. Same as Yarrie, walking, 'nother people walking to the Twelve Mile, 'nother mob going to Moolyella. Every people, all coming, every place. Munda coming, Boodarie coming, and Indee mob, Tabba ... Strelley, all the mob coming in and all build up in two place.[65]

'McLeod got us from Warrawagine, from Callewa, and we walked off those stations', Ginger Bob said:

> We went south to Moolyella and lived there. From Muccan, people went south, they walked off Yarrie, and they left only the earth at Warrawagine. We all walked off; the generation before me, I came after. They all gathered together at Moolyella. At Nimingarra only the dirt was left, at Mulyie only the dirt was left, at De Grey only the dirt was left.[66]

Pastoralist James Doughty expresses it differently in his novel *The Green Stick*, in which McLeod is represented by a sinister educated 'half-caste' named Yeller Conn. 'Aint a coon left on them places', a pastoralist growls. 'Yeller Conn's took the lot'.[67]

---

65 Yougarla (Yakalya), recorded by Anne Scrimgeour, 21 August 1991, author's collection.
66 Ginger Bob (Palyakulayi), recorded 8 December 1993, translated from Nyangumarta, AIATSIS collection, soundfile 'Palyakulayi 9'.
67 Doughty, *The Green Stick*, p. 126. A very similar comment was made by Rob Lukis, when speaking of the failure of his workers to return to Mundabullangana from the races: 'McLeod had collared the lot'. Lukis, interviewed by Jeffery, 1977, transcript, p. 157, SLWA OH262.

Chapter 13

'Far Too Strong and Cheeky'

December 1946 – February 1947

As a result of the strike, two uniquely independent Aboriginal communities were becoming established at the Twelve Mile and the Moolyella strike camps. For these to become viable, socially satisfying communities, the strikers needed to find ways to organise themselves, form productive working parties, and establish methods of selling produce and purchasing and distributing supplies. Decision-making processes and conflict resolution procedures needed to be established, either through procedures for arriving at group consensus or through a structure of authority. Means for creating group cohesion needed to be established. Existing cultural practices, kinship networks, and relationships and procedures within Aboriginal Law provided an organisational framework, but new practices and procedures were needed to meet the social and economic needs of a large group of people under persistent pressure from external forces. Caroline Jula remembered police and Native Affairs officers making frequent visits to Moolyella in an effort to return strikers to stations. 'Everybody coming, all police, all Welfare. Coming see Dooley. Coming, might be say, "You fellas got to go back might be station, some, you know, some got to work"':

> No, we not go back in a station, no, because we work there in a station, you know, no money, maybe we get a soap, and tobacco, and little bit sugar, and tea leaf. We say no, we not go back any more, strike strike, we strike in Moolyella, we got to stop, we got to work living, self.[1]

Within the new communities, men with the ability to counter such pressure took leadership roles, but senior men with religious and cultural authority within Aboriginal society were also influential, as John Wilson notes.[2] When Lew McBeath, now Acting Commissioner of Native Affairs, visited the area

---

1   Jula, recorded by Anne Scrimgeour, 5 November 1992, author's collection.
2   John Wilson, 'Authority and Leadership', pp. 57–58.

in 1947, he noted that a 'certain measure of control' had 'definitely passed over to ... elderly men', who had previously travelled 'from one station property to another, existing fairly well upon the proceeds of gambling, and also from the standing they possess as elders'. He believed that this made the situation in the Pilbara 'more involved', through the development of strike communities that provided these senior men with 'a certain amount of authority and standing'.[3] This authority influenced the organisation of strike communities.

Organisational decisions in the strike communities were also influenced by McLeod's vision for how these new, independent communities could operate. McLeod was working on the wharves in Port Hedland, awaiting the outcome of appeals against his convictions: the fines imposed in the Port Hedland Police Court in June 1946, and the three-month jail sentence he had received in August following his arrest at the Twelve Mile during Peter Hodge's visit. In October 1946, the Supreme Court of Western Australia had dismissed his appeal against these sentences, along with appeals by Hodge, McKenna and Dooley. Appeals against the Supreme Court's decision were due to be heard by the High Court of Australia in February 1947. With a three-month jail sentence hanging over his head, and under observation from the police, McLeod's meetings with *marrngu* were carried out in secret, and he later remembered creeping along under the cover of darkness, his heart in his mouth in fear of being detected by the police.[4]

When Dorothy Hewett and her husband Lloyd Davies visited Port Hedland in the summer of 1946–47, they accompanied McLeod to one of these covert meetings. As a law student, Davies was 'acutely conscious' of the damage that could be caused to his future career if he was caught by the police. He remembered creeping along the railway line with McLeod to meet strikers from the Twelve Mile:

> and losing ourselves in a thicket from which sandflies emerged in vicious droves. Deep within the mangroves there was a little clearing from the shadows of which a dozen or so Aborigines arose, including Clancy McKenna. They lit dry mangrove leaves to drive off the sandflies (not altogether successfully) and we conducted a meeting for several hours in which they discussed with us the progress of the campaign and things they needed to keep going.[5]

---

3   McBeath to McDonald, 16 May 1947, p. 2, SROWA 1947/0305/116.
4   McLeod, *How the West Was Lost*, p. 52.
5   Davies, 'Protecting Natives', p. 39.

McLeod conferred with community leaders from the Twelve Mile and also with Dooley, who made monthly trips from Moolyella to Port Hedland, according to John Wilson, to discuss matters with McLeod.[6] These meetings enabled McLeod to keep abreast of developments in the strike camps, gain information to pass on to supporters in the south, inform the strikers of the activities of the CDNR and other supporters, and suggest means for overcoming the difficulties they encountered. His influence was necessarily limited by his inability to visit the camps themselves, but terminology used by the strikers, such 'committee' to refer to the leadership of the Twelve Mile, suggests that his ideas were influential.

In September 1946, the *Workers' Star* carried an article describing the 'democratic organisation, planning and discipline' that characterised 'the 12-mile camp of native workers who have refused to go back to the stations under their former rotten conditions'. The information had probably been provided to the CDNR by McLeod, although a literate striker, Tommy Sampie, also corresponded with the Committee. While *Workers' Star* reports need to be treated with some caution, there is sufficient corroborating evidence to support its description of organisational arrangements at the Twelve Mile. Molly Williams's description of communal cooking in the work camps – 'One, might two lady, do some cooking for that mob. We used to have one kitchen' – supports the *Workers' Star* description of communal preparation of meals at the Twelve Mile, where cooking was undertaken by three cooks selected on a three-day roster system.[7] Systems were put in place for assigning other tasks. Yardmen were assigned, for example, to keep the camp clean, and carpenters constructed shelters.[8] Sanctions were established to maintain internal discipline: the *Workers' Star* reported that a prefect was selected to break up card games during working hours, and unpopular jobs such as carting water and wood were imposed as a form of punishment.[9]

Authority was in the hands of a committee made up of influential men: early in 1947, a police report referred to 'the committee men from the 12 mile', identifying the leaders as Clancy McKenna, Ernie Mitchell, Mick Lee, Adam Barker, Peter Coppin, Tommy Sampie and Harry Davis.[10] Some of these men continued to hold important and influential positions in the group during the coming years. Although Clancy McKenna would withdraw from

---

6 John Wilson, 'Authority and Leadership', p. 69.
7 Molly Williams (Kulyu), tape 2, recorded 22 October 1992, author's collection.
8 *Workers' Star*, 27 September 1946, p. 2.
9 *Workers' Star*, 13 September 1946, p. 5.
10 Mason to McBeath, 26 February 1947, SROWA 1947/0305/50.

the group in 1947, his leadership ability impressed both Peter Hodge and Dorothy Hewett during their brief meetings with him. Hodge noted that he had 'fine qualities of leadership, and a thorough grip of the position', and Hewett described him as 'a giant with the strength and resourcefulness of all good leaders'.[11] Hewett named her first son after him.[12] Ernie Mitchell, who would become the principal leader of the group during the 1950s, impressed John and Katrin Wilson with his strong but quietly efficient leadership when they met him in 1959 and 1960.[13]

Communal dining, the imposition of unpopular work tasks as a form of punishment, rostered work allocation, and efficient, well-organised and tidy camps would all become features of the group's organisation throughout the 1950s, and it is interesting to see them enumerated in the *Workers' Star* as early as September 1946. It seems likely that at this early stage these community practices were still becoming established in an evolving process that no doubt had many hiccups and much debate. Some ideas were tried and abandoned. For some weeks late in 1946, men at both the Moolyella and the Twelve Mile camps performed military-style drills each day – 'Forming fours – quick march – halt – salute, etc'.[14] Just twelve months after the end of the Second World War, this seemed an appropriate way to establish internal discipline and to display the group's unity and strength to the broader community. Railway passengers frequently observed men drilling as the train passed the Twelve Mile.[15] Military-style exercises may be a measure of the degree to which strikers felt under threat from the settler community and of their determination to resist force if necessary. By the end of the year, the practice of daily drilling was abandoned, perhaps reflecting the need to focus energy on economic activities as temperatures began to climb. That the practice was never resumed suggests that *marrngu* became confident that no direct attack would be made against them to return them to the stations.

While the group's economic enterprises overturned settler assumptions that Aboriginal people depended on either station or government rations, the effective organisation of the Twelve Mile also challenged assumptions that they needed constant paternal supervision for their own wellbeing.

---

11   *Tribune*, 6 September 1946, p. 7; Dorothy Hewett, '25 Native Children Go to Own School', *Workers' Star*, 9 May 1947.
12   Hewett, preface to Brown, *The Black Eureka*.
13   John and Katrin Wilson, recorded 22 May 2016, author's collection.
14   Marshall to McBeath, 30 November 1946, SROWA 1943/0621.
15   Marshall to McBeath, 30 November 1946, SROWA 1943/0621.

When strikers set up camp at the Twelve Mile in August, Constable Fletcher reported his concern that:

> with so many camped together, and no supervision as to cleanliness ... there will be an extensive outbreak of scabies amongst these people. I visit them at least once a week, and will continue to watch for further evidence of it, but those parties who have scattered around the country on dry-shelling expeditions are not under my supervision at all, and I have very grave doubts about what may be the state of health existing among them.
>
> When these people were on the stations, the station people generally executed considerable supervision in this regard, and to a large extent, counteracted any possibility of a serious outbreak of this sort of thing, which is, I understand, mainly a product of dirt, but now, freed from any restraint, I am afraid that the natives are not taking the care of themselves that they should.[16]

Bray agreed that 'the natives' welfare was under supervision at the Station' and that now they were 'scattered and difficult to supervise in regard to health and cleanliness'.[17] However, a month later, Fletcher wrote that, 'contrary to [his] previous expectations', the strikers at the Twelve Mile appeared to be in good health. 'The camp at the 12 mile is kept very clean now', he wrote. It was becoming 'a more or less permanent camp', with substantial spinifex sheds constructed on both sides of the creek, and a small garden planted with melons and pumpkins.[18] The Department's travelling medical inspector, Dr. L. A. Musso, also reported positively on conditions at the Twelve Mile, where there was an adequate supply of water for bathing and washing clothes. The strikers had dug three 'Army style' lavatories 'of good construction' and had built a bathroom. People lived in tents and bough shelters, and a tent with two forms and a table was being used as a school.[19] About twenty-five children at the Twelve Mile were being taught literacy and numeracy by Tommy Sampie, who had been educated at the Catholic mission school at Lombadina, on the Dampier Peninsula north of Broome. The *Workers' Star* reported in September that the community had decided that the children would have their own kitchen so that their nutritional needs could be prioritised when stores were

---

16 Fletcher to Bray, 19 August 1946, SROWA 1946/0799/39.
17 Bray to Fletcher, 22 August 1946, SROWA 1946/0799/40.
18 Fletcher to McBeath, 21 September 1946, p. 3, SROWA 1946/0799/56.
19 Medical Inspector Musso to McBeath, 2 January 1947, SROWA 1946/0799/90.

limited, and Sampie and some women cared for the children while their parents travelled out with work groups.[20] In December, a newly-appointed Inspector of Native Affairs, John Joseph (Jack) Rhatigan, described the Twelve Mile camp as one of the cleanest he had seen. 'The natives appear to be well fed', he wrote, 'and reasonably well clothed'.[21] When Dorothy Hewett and Lloyd Davies, pretending to be anthropology students, visited the Twelve Mile with the permission and in the presence of a 'protector', they were impressed by the school, the cleanliness and order of the camp, and 'the spirit of courage and initiative that prevailed there'.[22]

Conditions were more difficult at the Moolyella strike camp 200 kilometres to the south-east. Although the *Workers' Star* reported in early November, based on information provided by McLeod, that the Moolyella camp was operating along the same lines as the Twelve Mile, with a functioning committee, the camp site cleared and swept, buildings being erected and gardens set up, this was not the case.[23] Unlike the Twelve Mile, which was located on the banks of the (usually dry) Petermara Creek, where there was a well for water and trees for shade, firewood and building material, Moolyella is a barren and treeless mining area. Strikers camped close together along a dry, tin-bearing watercourse where there was no shade or water. All water for drinking and cooking was carried by bucket from a single tap at Don Thompson's store, half a mile from the camp. There was no water for bathing or washing clothes, let alone for establishing a garden, as the *Workers' Star* article claimed. Strikers also had to walk several miles to find firewood. They had no huts or tents, their only shelter being a few bushes arranged on top of stakes in the ground. Constable Marshall of Marble Bar, reporting at the end of November that people there were living under 'pretty hard conditions', was concerned that the crowded conditions and the lack of sanitation would lead to an epidemic of sickness when the rains came in the summer.[24] He recommended that the Department construct shelters, shower rooms and toilets there. Although there was a possibility that strikers would return sooner or later to station employment, there was a permanent population of about fifty *marrngu* on the tin field and Marshall felt that 'possibly they should receive some consideration'.[25]

---

20   *Workers' Star*, 27 September 1946, p. 2.
21   Rhatigan to McBeath, 27 December 1946, p. 1, SROWA 1947/0305/1.
22   *Workers' Star*, 14 February 1947, p. 6, 'Mr. Nulsen Sympathetic to Native Cause'; *Workers' Star*, 21 February 1947, p. 5, 'Nade Crown Slams Native Persecution'.
23   *Workers' Star*, 8 November 1946, p. 5, '106 Natives Set Up Co-Op Camp'.
24   Marshall, police patrol report, 28 November 1946, SROWA 1946/2538 v8.
25   Marshall to McBeath, 30 November 1946, SROWA 1943/0621.

The advantage Moolyella had over the Twelve Mile, that of having a local source of income close to where people were camped, was also a disadvantage insofar as a large number of strikers were living close together. There were benefits culturally – Monty Hale remembered that on weekends the Warrawagine ceremony belonging to Banjo Flann was performed – but crowded and harsh living conditions created social tensions.[26] Ernie Mitchell told Thompson that one cause of disputes in the camp was the discomfort experienced in being unable to bathe or wash clothes.[27] Tin mining did not bring high returns: Thompson paid 1/6 per pound for tin, and baked and sold bread at 1/- a loaf, so a pound of tin could purchase one and a half loaves of bread.[28] Marshall wrote that the strikers were in good health but were 'not over fed, as they have to work hard to win sufficient tin to pay for food'.[29] Although they were able to purchase sugar, they found that the ration was soon used up and, according to Ernie Mitchell, this caused further discontentment and disharmony in the community.[30]

There was an attempt to start a school at Moolyella, although little information exists about this. As a child, Molly Woodman was sent to Moolyella by her parents for schooling: 'My mother and father took me down to Moolyella', she said, 'and leave me there out there schooling. School used to be there, in Moolyella'.[31] According to Caroline Jula, some schooling was undertaken by brothers Roy and Gordon Mackay.[32] Moolyella lacked a committed teacher of the calibre of Tommy Sampie, however, and I have found no official reference to a school there.

Although the *Workers' Star* reported that a committee was operating at Moolyella, both *marrngu* and *walypila* invariably identified Dooley as the leader, suggesting that shared leadership arrangements were not in place there as they were at the Twelve Mile, despite the presence of men like Roy and Gordon Mackay, who had been involved in organising the strike. Dooley was a passionate and militant strike organiser, but he lacked the leadership skills of men like McKenna and Mitchell. According to John and Katrin Wilson, 'Dooley went on running strikes for the rest of his time'.[33] Dorothy

---

26   Hale, *Kurlumarniny*, p. 25.
27   Thompson to Marshall, 22 October 1946, SROWA 1943/0621/24.
28   Rhatigan to McBeath, 27 December 1946, p. 1, SROWA 1943/0621/25.
29   Marshall to McBeath, 30 November 1946, SROWA 1943/0621.
30   Thompson to Marshall, 22 October 1946, SROWA 1943/0621/24.
31   Molly Woodman, recorded by Mark Clendon, 19 October 2007, author's collection.
32   Jula, recorded by Anne Scrimgeour, 5 November 1992, author's collection.
33   John and Katrin Wilson, recorded 13 November 2014, author's collection.

Hewett wrote that McLeod also believed that Dooley was too militant.[34] At Moolyella, Dooley's energies were focused more on developing a resistance ideology among the strikers and expanding the strike than on establishing a harmonious social organisation. Donald Thompson reported to the Department of Native Affairs of frequent meetings held by the strikers, at which Dooley often spoke at length, and, according to Thompson, 'some of his words were trouble'. Thompson provided an example of Dooley's oratory:

> How to take a man you must go straight out one of you and say, you can't get no other man, you must have your law case and if you win, alright, if you lose – just your bad luck.[35]

Although the meaning of Dooley's address as paraphrased by Thompson is somewhat unclear, it suggests that Dooley was instructing strikers, most of whom had not been involved in the group action at the time of the Port Hedland races, in the strategies and ideology of resistance. Strikers were urged not to be intimidated by the threat of imprisonment that had for so long kept them fearful and subservient, but to be prepared to face court action and, if necessary, imprisonment. Being prepared to take action that risked a jail sentence would be crucial to the group's activism over the following years. In the early 1950s, the author Donald Stuart recorded the pride expressed by Monty Hale's brother, Dick McKenna (Wingoomah in Stuart's account) at having been imprisoned for his activism despite his youth. 'I been gaol, same as all them top leaders'.[36] The development of a group ideology in which imprisonment for the cause became a source of pride was to undermine police power to intimidate *marrngu* in the months and years to come.

Although Thompson generally had a good relationship with *marrngu*, he was sufficiently unnerved by the tenor of the meetings at Moolyella to feel the need to protect himself at night by sleeping outside his store with a loaded gun beside him.[37] His anxiety is an indication of the level of disagreement and discontent among the strikers and the heated nature of the debate at meetings.

By early December 1946, when temperatures were already reaching 46 °C (116 °F), the decision was made to split the camp into a number of groups and to shift to the tin-bearing areas of Tadgabanna, Mud Springs and lower Mud Springs, where there was water and shade, about three miles from

---

34   Hewett, preface to Brown, *The Black Eureka*.
35   Thompson to Marshall, 22 October 1946, SROWA 1943/0621/24.
36   Donald Stuart, *Yandy the Wind*, manuscript, NLA MS 3156/9/390.
37   Thompson to Marshall, 22 October 1946, SROWA 1943/0621/24.

Thompson's store.[38] Native Affairs Inspector Jack Rhatigan, who was stationed in Carnarvon, spent a few days in the region in December to investigate the need and feasibility of providing lavatories, showers and shelters at Moolyella, as Marshall had recommended. Since the strikers were preparing to shift camp, however, the proposal to provide facilities was dropped. 'Little can be done for them when they are moving about so much', Marshall wrote.[39] However, before the move was made, tensions in the Moolyella camp came to a head. Rhatigan noted the climate of discontent there. After speaking to 'several natives including the leader in this camp, "Dooley"', he reported that:

> I consider that McLeod's influence over the natives in this area has definitely weakened, and although I think it possible to break the strike in this area at this stage, I suggest that the matter be left over until the appeals are heard, and if the decisions are favourable, then it will be easier to finalise, than at this stage.[40]

'Favourable' decisions in the appeals to the High Court of Australia, due to be heard in February, would see McLeod imprisoned, making decisive, strike-breaking action easier to accomplish. Finalising the matter meant removing strike leaders to institutions and returning workers to stations. Marshall wrote that 'Mr. Rhatigan was quite pleased, as a result of his talk with these people, who are becoming dissatisfied with strike conditions'.[41]

It may have been Rhatigan's visit that brought matters to a head, perhaps through promises of fair treatment if strikers allowed the Department to negotiate on their behalf for better wages and conditions on stations. On the other hand, discontented strikers may simply have used the opportunity of his short visit to gain departmental support for a breakaway movement. Either way, seven strikers and two non-strikers, led by Gordon Mackay, approached Rhatigan in Marble Bar on 18 December 1946 and informed him of their intention to break away from McLeod, McKenna and Dooley and to 'follow the Government'.[42] They included men who had been – and would continue to be – staunch strikers, including Jackson, who had been drillmaster at Moolyella, and Bruce Wandarri. Mick Corbett, who worked as a yardman at the Ironclad Hotel, also attended the meeting. According to Rhatigan,

---

38 Rhatigan to McBeath, 27 December 1946, p. 1, SROWA 1943/0621/25.
39 Marshall to McBeath, 23 December 1946, SROWA 1943/0621/21.
40 Rhatigan to McBeath, 27 December 1946, SROWA 1943/0621/25–27.
41 Marshall, police patrol report, 17 December 1946, SROWA 1946/2538 v8.
42 Marshall to Bray, 23 December 1946, p. 1, SROWA 1943/0621/21.

Mackay stated that he 'now considered the strike the wrong method of gaining improved conditions for the natives', and he asked Rhatigan if he would hear him address those *marrngu* 'who also were not now in favour of the McLeod strike'. At the back of the Marble Bar Police Station, Mackay spoke to the group of defectors in the presence of Marshall and Rhatigan, and all agreed that they no longer supported the strike and 'would do all in their power to win the strikers over to their way of thinking'.[43] According to Marshall, they said that they were convinced that McLeod could do no good for them.[44]

Gordon Mackay had been an instigator of the strike movement and had been a leader and spokesman in the activism undertaken at the time of the Port Hedland races. A Nyiyapali speaker, he was born in about 1899 to Maggie Mardjuwiya and George Mackay. His father was an Aboriginal station worker who had worked for the Mackay brothers at Mundabullangana (Munda) Station and who had received an education. Both Gordon and his brother Roy were literate, possibly having attended school in Perth.[45] Gordon had a good command of English; Marshall wrote that he 'speaks very well'. Rhatigan described him as one of the strike leaders, and Marshall wrote that he was 'the real agitator type – he hails from Roy Hill way'. There seems to have been a major dispute over the direction the strike was taking; Dooley had 'made a scene', Marshall wrote, 'because he (Mackay) and others had turned McLeod down'.[46] It would be interesting to know whether 'turning McLeod down' meant that specific directions given by McLeod had been rejected by a section of the Moolyella strikers, or whether 'McLeod' had come to refer to an ideological position or an approach to the strike that was espoused by Dooley but rejected by Mackay and others. 'Turning McLeod down' may simply have referred to the decision to leave the group. Being in the group was often referred to as being 'with Don McLeod'. Marshall reported on 'a lot of ill feeling between Dooley and Mackay'. 'Mackay being educated it appears did not like taking orders from Dooley, who apart from having the gift of the

---

43 Rhatigan to Bray, 27 December 1946, p. 2, SROWA 1943/0621/26.
44 Marshall to Bray, 23 December 1946, p. 1, SROWA 1943/0621/21.
45 Norman Tindale says Mackay's mother was Nyamal and his father Kariyarra. (Tindale, journal, p. 307). Bill Day says his father was Nyamal. 'The Coffin Family of Redcliffs Station, Pilbara, Western Australia', http://www.drbilldayanthropologist.com/resources/CoffinFamilyHistory.pdf, Von Brandenstein says that Gordon Mackay had been educated in Perth. C. G. von Brandenstein and A. P. Thomas (eds.) *Taruru: Aboriginal Song Poetry of the Pilbara*, Rigby, Adelaide, 1974, p. 65.
46 Rhatigan to Bray, 27 December 1946, p. 2, SROWA 1943/0621/26; Marshall to Bray, 23 December 1946, p. 1, SROWA 1943/0621/21.

gab, is really only a bush native'.[47] While this undoubtedly oversimplifies the political situation that had developed at Moolyella, overlooking Dooley's status in the Law, for example, it suggests a level of dissatisfaction with Dooley's leadership, possibly due to his militant, anti-government stance.

Marshall and Rhatigan were heartened by this defection. 'Gordon McKay is an educated native', Rhatigan wrote, 'and can be a big assistance in combatting the McLeod influence among the other natives'. He recommended that the defection be supported by the Department through some form of remuneration to Mackay towards his keep.[48] The breakaway group obtained permission from Marshall to camp in Marble Bar, and planned to mine alluvial gold to 'keep the pot boiling' until they had sufficient numbers to return to their respective stations.[49] Although they stated their willingness to 'go with the government', their action in leaving Moolyella was not an abandonment of the strike but an attempt to steer the course of the strike towards a more proactive negotiation for wage and condition improvements and a return to station employment. Waiting until they had sufficient numbers would strengthen their hand in these negotiations. Marshall reported that they wanted 'reasonable sleeping quarters, a shade shed in which to have their meals, and to lay off in, a shower in which to wash, and the pit system lavatory, erected for them on the stations'.[50] They also wanted increased wages, but were not holding out for the universal (male) basic wage of £2 being demanded by other strikers. 'So far as wages are concerned, they want an increase', Marshall wrote, 'but Mackay does understand, and I have heard him addressing the other natives to the effect that the pastoralists cannot be expected to pay higher wages to a man that does not know his job'.[51]

At the time of the 1 May strike, Marshall had rejected any suggestion of wage increases, writing that 'if wages are raised a great expense is going to be thrown upon the Government, in feeding & clothing unemployed natives'.[52] Now, however, he was willing to listen to grievances and to concede that 'many of the natives have not been paid enough in the past'.[53] He was also now willing to speak with station managers about providing improved amenities for strikers willing to return and, despite pastoralists' claims that they were better

---

47 Marshall to Bray, 23 December 1946, p. 1, SROWA 1943/0621/21.
48 Rhatigan to Bray, 27 December 1946, p. 2, SROWA 1943/0621/26.
49 Marshall to Bray, 23 December 1946, p. 1, SROWA 1943/0621/21.
50 Marshall to Bray, 23 December 1946, p. 2, SROWA 1943/0621/22.
51 Marshall to Bray, 23 December 1946, p. 2, SROWA 1943/0621/22.
52 Marshall, police patrol report, 30 April 1946, SROWA 1943/0099 v7.
53 Marshall to Bray, 23 December 1946, p. 2, SROWA 1943/0621/22.

off without Aboriginal labour, found that Muccan Station, Corunna Downs and Meentheena Stations were all 'quite prepared to supply the accommodation as requested by the natives'.[54] In the meantime, Rhatigan contacted stations in the Port Hedland district and found that Miller at De Grey, Cullingworth at Mulyie and Lukis at Munda 'all agreed that the time has come to improve the living conditions of the natives on the stations'.[55] According to Rhatigan, Miller was willing 'to do anything within reason for the betterment of the natives on De Grey Station'.[56]

In a further attempt to strengthen their demands, Mackay wrote to the AWU:

> I beg to place before you the position of us natives up here in the nor west. We are all struggling to better our conditions both as for living & wages conditions we have as perhaps you know, come out solidly and still are out & refuse to go back to the conditions we are asked to live and work under. Your members come up here and work up here under totally different conditions. Have you made one effort to ours. You can get these bettered conditions for us and perhaps organise us a separate branch. This nor west blot could be wiped out through your organisation. We never had a leader the one that took us and we are beginning to see it has got us further into the mire.[57]

Whether the leader that was taking them 'further into the mire' was McLeod or Dooley is unclear. The letter was not sent to the AWU but was forwarded instead to the Department of Native Affairs through Constable Marshall, possibly at Marshall's suggestion.

Other strikers seem to have been unaware of this defection. In the lead-up to Christmas, some of the Moolyella people made their way to the Twelve Mile to take part in festivities, complete with puddings and cakes, planned for Christmas Day. One group of strikers set off on foot on 20 December, and on Christmas Eve a group, including Dooley, arrived in Marble Bar to take the train to the Twelve Mile.[58] That day, the defectors camped behind the police station to avoid detection.[59] Possibly taking advantage of Dooley's

---

54 Marshall to Bray, 23 December 1946, p. 2, SROWA 1943/0621/22.
55 Rhatigan to Bray, 27 December 1946, p. 2, SROWA 1943/0621/26.
56 Rhatigan, patrol report, 19 December 1946, SROWA 1947/0305/19.
57 Mackay to Secretary, Australian Workers' Union, Perth, 18 December 1946, SROWA 1943/0621/20.
58 J. M. Woods, patrol report, 22 December 1946, SROWA 1946/2538 v8.
59 Marshall to Bray, 9 January 1947, p. 1, SROWA 1947/0305/24.

absence from the area, Marshall acted quickly to have defectors returned to stations. Whether or not Marshall put pressure on these workers to return immediately is unclear; by his own account, the breakaway group approached him on Christmas Day to say that they were ready to return, and to ask if transport could be arranged.[60]

However, Marshall had previously indicated that the defectors were planning to mine gold while they built up their numbers. This plan, together with Mackay's letter to the AWU, suggests that the breakaway group hoped to establish a strong position from which to negotiate a return to station employment, and possibly form a branch of the AWU. Mackay had written that they 'refuse to go back to the conditions we are asked to live and work under', but no terms had been arranged for their return. Although some managers had given an in-principle undertaking to provide improved amenities, no definite promises had been made. Neither had there been any discussion about wages that workers were prepared to accept. Marshall had 'pointed out to Mackay and his bunch' that:

> It would be better if [a Native Affairs] Inspector could see the natives and employer together at their respective stations, where he could talk to both parties together [about wages and conditions] – Mackay was quite agreeable to this, but some of the boys wanted something definite before they returned.[61]

Yet now they were returning hurriedly without any such guarantee.

In the blistering heat of 25 December, while people at the Twelve Mile celebrated Christmas and Hewett and Davies sweltered in their hotel room in Port Hedland,[62] Marshall arranged for Yarrie Jack Coppin (Ngarlkapangu) to transport most of the defectors back to Warrawagine, the station they had left some weeks previously. A *marrngu* man who managed Warrawagine's Braeside outcamp, Yarrie Jack was planning to return there from holidays within the next two days and agreed to provide transport on his truck in return for petrol and oil, which Marshall provided.[63] Marshall also advised the managers of Muccan, Talga Talga and Mt Edgar to make arrangements to pick up workers waiting to return to their stations. On 26 December, some

---

60   Marshall to Bray, 9 January 1947, p. 2, SROWA 1947/0305/25.
61   Marshall to McBeath, 23 December 1946, p. 2, SROWA 1943/0621/22.
62   Hewett, preface to Brown, *The Black Eureka*.
63   Yarrie Jack (Jack Coppin) (Ngarlkapangu), police statements, 5 January 1947, SROWA 1947/0305/21–22; Marshall to McBeath, 9 January 1947, p. 2, SROWA 1947/0305/25.

of the defectors collected their gear from Moolyella, accompanied by a police officer to ensure that they were not interfered with by other strikers.[64] The trip out to Warrawagine was delayed, however, due to mechanical problems with Coppin's truck and the closure of Thompson's garage over Christmas. Eager to get the workers away as quickly as possible, Marshall himself took the truck's gear shift lever to the Comet mine to have it welded. By 2 January, the repairs were completed and the Warrawagine defectors prepared to set out on their return journey the following morning.[65]

Too late, however. Strikers at the Twelve Mile had been alerted to developments at Marble Bar by Mick Corbett, the yardman at the Ironclad Hotel, who had taken the train to the Twelve Mile on 31 December. Corbett's presence at the meeting with Rhatigan suggests that he supported Mackay's stance; his action in informing the Twelve Mile of the defection suggests that the breakaway movement was not going to plan, perhaps under pressure from Marshall. At a meeting at the Twelve Mile to discuss the developing situation, twelve men volunteered to take a truck to Marble Bar to bring away the defectors to prevent them undermining the strike.[66] Clancy McKenna and eleven others, including Corbett, Ronnie Captain and Teddy Allen (Mapayi), arrived at Marble Bar on the evening of 2 January.[67] A few *marrngu* had been picked up and taken to Mt Edgar and Muccan Stations that day, but twenty-one adults and five children were ready to return to Warrawagine with Yarrie Jack Coppin the next morning.[68]

---

64   J. M. Woods, police patrol report, 26 December 1946, SROWA 1946/2538 v8.
65   Marshall to McBeath, 9 January 1947, p. 2, SROWA 1947/0305/25; Yarrie Jack (Jack Coppin) (Ngarlkapangu), police statements, 5 January 1947, SROWA 1947/0305/21–22.
66   Kingsley Palmer and Clancy McKenna, *Somewhere Between Black and White: The Story of an Aboriginal Australian*, Macmillan, South Melbourne, 1978, p. 98.
67   Others involved in preventing the defection were Paddy Dean, Scotty, William of Bungalow, Rob Brown, Tommy Nungi (possibly Tommy Nangkanangka), Peter Johnson of Mulyie, Gordon Snowball and 'Big Harry' Davis of De Grey. O'Neill to McBeath, 12 February 1947, p. 1, SROWA 1947/0305/33; Yarrie Jack (Jack Coppin) (Ngarlkapangu), police statements, 5 January 1947, SROWA 1947/0305/21.
68   Marshall to McBeath, 9 January 1947, p. 2, SROWA 1947/0305/25. Yarrie Jack identified the people returning to Warrawagine as Locky and Molly; Alec; Barney; Watty; Taff and Alice; Snowy Jittermarra and three wives and one child; Charlie and his woman; Punch; Tim; Tommy; Bruce and two wives, and four children; Young Sambo; and Lucy (twenty-one adults and five children). Bruce Wandarri and Punch, who was the older brother of Caroline Jula and Sambo Bina (Yawarta-bloke), were important strikers. 'Young Sambo' may have been Sambo Bina. Watty was a brother of Cranky (Kujupurra).

Shortly after the Twelve Mile's big red truck arrived at the area near Marble Bar where the Warrawagine people were camped, Yarrie Jack Coppin pulled up in his newly-repaired truck, ready for an early morning start. He was surprised to see McKenna and the other strikers there, and to hear them tell the Warrawagine people to roll their swags and get on the truck. 'We are arresting you too', they told Coppin. 'You have to come, right or wrong'.[69] Coppin told them that he had received petrol and oil from Marshall on the understanding that he would take everyone to Warrawagine, and that he would need to sort things out with Marshall before leaving with them. He suggested that the strikers take his wife as a guarantee that he would follow later, and the strikers eventually agreed to this. In a statement for the police, Coppin said that 'all the other Warrawagine mob, got choked up, and could not talk – I think they were frightened'.[70]

Jackie Thompson, a *marrngu* man who worked at Thompson's garage, called into the Warrawagine camp that evening to see how Yarrie Jack's truck was running after its repair work. McKenna shook his hand and asked where he was working. When Thompson told him, McKenna said, 'Well, stick to it'. In a statement for the police, Thompson said he heard strikers say that they were arresting everyone so that Warrawagine would have to struggle through the shearing without labour.[71] The strikers also arrested Gordon Mackay and people camped at the town reserve.[72] Mick Corbett and others told Mackay to roll up his swag, as they were heading back to the Twelve Mile that night. Before he left, Mackay told Thompson that he 'would like to see Mr. Marshall and tell him that I am not running away, but I have to go, If I dont, the mob are going to tie me up and chuck me in the truck'.[73]

Marshall heard news of these events when Yarrie Jack Coppin arrived at the police station the following morning to explain why he was not returning workers to Warrawagine as arranged. Marshall sent an urgent telegram to

---

69 Yarrie Jack (Jack Coppin) (Ngarlkapangu), police statements, 5 January 1947, SROWA 1947/0305/21–22.
70 Yarrie Jack (Jack Coppin) (Ngarlkapangu), police statements, 5 January 1947, SROWA 1947/0305/21–22.
71 Jackie Thompson, police statement, 8 January 1947, SROWA 1947/0305/23.
72 Yarrie Jack (Jack Coppin) (Ngarlkapangu), police statements, 5 January 1947, SROWA 1947/0305/21–22.
73 Jackie Thompson, police statement, 8 January 1947, SROWA 1947/0305/23. The *walypila* names of people 'arrested' at Marble Bar were later recorded by the police as 'Punch, Taafe, Tommy, Lucky, Snowy Jittermarra, Barney, Charlie, Kenny, Waddy, Bruce, Sambo, Tom, Tommy, Alec, Tommy, Ginger, Darby, Spike, Jimmy and Lockie'. Mason to McBeath, 19 February 1947, SROWA 1947/0305/41.

Laurie O'Neill in Perth, informing him of the development and 'strongly suggesting' that he visit the area immediately to investigate.[74]

Laurie O'Neill was, at that time, Acting Commissioner of Native Affairs. At the beginning of September 1946, Commissioner Francis Bray had taken annual and long service leave as a result of illness, leading up to his retirement in April 1947, and Lew McBeath had taken on the role of Acting Commissioner in his absence.[75] O'Neill had been promoted in September to Acting Deputy Commissioner, shifting to Perth in October.[76] His role of Travelling Inspector for the northern region was to be undertaken by Jack Rhatigan, already stationed in Carnarvon, and by Thomas Emmes (Tom) Jensen, a Kimberley policeman seconded to the Department of Native Affairs, who was to be based in Derby.[77] McBeath was on leave, recovering from surgery over the Christmas–New Year period, and O'Neill was standing in for him as Commissioner, when Marshall's urgent telegram arrived on 3 January, informing him of the forced removal of the defectors from Marble Bar and urging him to fly north to investigate. The incident was considered sufficiently serious for McBeath to immediately return to work so that O'Neill could fly north, and Rhatigan, now back in his home base of Carnarvon, was instructed to accompany O'Neill back to Port Hedland.[78] McBeath thought that the twelve strikers who had removed the dissenters should be arrested and charged with breaching section 47 of the *Native Administration Act*, the section under which Dooley and McKenna had previously been charged, which prohibited the removal of natives from lawful employment.

Although the Commissioner of Police approved this course of action, Marshall thought that prosecution under section 47 was unlikely to succeed, as the workers concerned were not in employment.[79] Marshall was anxious that some form of punitive action be taken, nevertheless. Ideally, he would have liked to see the strike leaders removed under ministerial warrant. 'My reason for reporting the matter', he wrote:

---

74 Marshall to O'Neill, telegram, 3 January 1947, SROWA 1947/0305/4.
75 McBeath to Under Secretary for the NorthWest, 15 September 1946, SROWA 1946/1220/13; Coverley, Minute paper for Executive Council, undated, SROWA 1946/1220/19A.
76 O'Neill to Commissioner, 2 October 1946, SROWA 1946/1220/19.
77 McBeath to Coverley, 22 October 1946, SROWA 1946/0799/72; McBeath to Minister Coverley, 13 October 1947, SROWA 1946/1220/48.
78 McBeath to McDonald, 9 April 1947, p. 5, SROWA 1947/0305/86; Bray to Rhatigan, telegram, 6 January 1947, SROWA 1947/0305/15.
79 Bray to Marshall, telegram, 4 January 1947, SROWA 1947/0305/14; Marshall to McBeath, 9 January 1947, p. 4, SROWA 1947/0305/27.

is that I consider McKenna and gang are getting far too strong, and cheeky and dangerous, when they take on the job of arresting whole camps of natives, and carting them away at their will, and I consider that it is time something was done to prevent this.[80]

The Department had an armoury of legislation at its disposal. Section 9 of the Act allowed for the prosecution of 'any person who without the authority in writing of a protector, removes or causes any native to be removed from one district to another, or to any place beyond the State'. Although this was clearly a measure designed to protect Aboriginal people by preventing employers removing them from their own districts, it was a convenient piece of legislation for the current circumstances, since the Twelve Mile was in a different administrative district to Marble Bar.

On 5 January, Constable W. J. (Bill) Mason, a Kimberley policeman relieving in Port Hedland for ten weeks while Les Fletcher was on leave, found that those abducted from Marble Bar had not yet arrived at the Twelve Mile. He suspected that they were being kept 'bush' to prevent police intervention.[81] Although O'Neill and Rhatigan arrived in Port Hedland on 9 January, nothing could be done until the offenders returned to the Twelve Mile. In the meantime, meetings of the strikers were no doubt being carried out in a remote location, the issues being thrashed out, grievances aired, recriminations voiced and possible solutions discussed.

By 20 January, most were back at the Twelve Mile and some were out in work parties. O'Neill informed McBeath that arrangements were in hand for action to be taken against McKenna and the others.[82] 'Big Harry' Davis could not be located, but eleven others appeared in court on 31 January and 1 February to have their cases heard before Magistrate Maurice Harwood, who had, six months previously, sentenced McLeod to three months' imprisonment. O'Neill and Rhatigan were both present in court, but their involvement in gathering evidence for the prosecution disqualified them from providing defence.[83] V. L. (Wally) Lund, a Native Affairs Department employee in charge of the Port Hedland Native Hospital and a Protector of Natives, agreed with some reluctance to appear on the defendants' behalf. He was aware that defence provided in such a case was a sham while four 'protectors' – O'Neill, Rhatigan, Marshall and Mason – stood determined to achieve a prosecution.

---

80   Marshall to McBeath, 9 January 1947, p. 4, SROWA 1947/0305/27.
81   Mason to McBeath, 5 January 1947, SROWA 1947/0305/20.
82   O'Neill to McBeath, 20 January 1947, SROWA 1947/0305/20.
83   O'Neill to McBeath, 12 February 1947, p. 1, SROWA 1947/0305/33.

'Defence' involved simply lodging a plea of 'not guilty' on the defendants' behalf in accordance with departmental practice.[84] The accused were given no opportunity to speak in their own defence, and McLeod was denied permission to ask questions or address the court, although he was allowed to take notes and act as clerk to Lund, probably in preparation for an appeal.[85]

The prosecution of the eleven men was undertaken successfully by Marshall. Although the intention of section 9 was to protect Aboriginal people, Harwood's summing up illustrates the view that 'protection' meant control. 'Such mass movement of natives must be checked', he said, or the 'Department's control would be thrown into chaos':[86]

> If any person, no matter who he may be, could go along and collect natives at random and cart them around the North-West we should soon have nothing but roving bands of natives under no supervision whatever ... This kind of thing must be stopped.[87]

His statements also provide evidence of the continuing belief that the real culprit in these events was McLeod, and the accused simply his puppets:

> From my observations, from the witnesses who have given evidence, it appears that this was an organized raid and certain natives selected to carry it out and that there is a controlling organizer behind the whole event shielding himself behind these natives.[88]

Nevertheless, he believed that some of the accused 'appear intelligent and educated and it cannot be said they committed this offence without knowing they were acting wrongly ... As a warning to them and others who may contemplate any repetition of these actions they must be punished'. He sentenced all except McKenna to two weeks' imprisonment with hard labour. On account of McKenna's previous conviction, which was still subject to appeal, he imposed a two-month jail sentence with hard labour.[89]

Lund immediately gave notice of his intention to appeal McKenna's sentence.[90] O'Neill suspected that this was done 'on behalf of the Council for

---

84 O'Neill to McBeath, 12 February 1947, p. 1, SROWA 1947/0305/33; O'Neill to McBeath, 26 March 1947, SROWA 1947/0305/65.
85 O'Neill to McBeath, 12 February 1947, p. 2, SROWA 1947/0305/32.
86 Quoted in McBeath to Coverley, undated, SROWA 1946/1324.
87 Quoted in McBeath to Coverley, undated, SROWA 1946/1324.
88 Quoted in McBeath to Coverley, undated, SROWA 1946/1324.
89 Cited in McBeath to Coverley, undated, SROWA 1946/1324.
90 O'Neill to McBeath, 12 February 1947, p. 2, SROWA 1947/0305/3.

the Defence of Native Rights', as, he wrote, 'the natives admitted guilt and were prepared to plead guilty'.[91] The Department demanded an explanation from Lund. 'Please advise me immediately upon whose authority you lodged the appeal', McBeath wrote. 'You are to take no further action in respect to the appeals, except upon advice or authority of this Department'.[92]

'I appealed against what I considered a harsh and unjust sentence, for a breach of Section 9', Lund replied:

> I considered the authority vested in me as a protector of natives sufficient to justify me in taking such action, however it appears that I acted wrongly, for which I am sorry.
>
> I shall certainly take no further action in native courts unless instructed from The Commissioner.[93]

Perhaps McBeath detected a note of cynicism in Lund's apology, or perhaps his failure to follow the Department's line of opposing strike leaders was enough to raise concerns. Either way, McBeath instructed O'Neill to investigate Lund's politics. O'Neill compiled a report that was drawn in part from intelligence investigations he had carried out during the war, and partly from his experience as a departmental officer in the north. During the war, O'Neill had been attached to the Special Reserve of the WA Police force, and in this capacity had investigated allegations that Lund, serving in an Army Dental Unit in Perth, was a German sympathiser. The allegations had arisen from comments made by Lund which were interpreted as evidence that he was pro-German, 'or at least disloyal to the British Empire'. The police had found no evidence of this, but had passed their information on to the Director of Military Intelligence. O'Neill had no knowledge of any action being taken as a result. Now, he considered the question of whether Lund's action in appealing McKenna's sentence was evidence that he was a communist. 'I have heard that Mr. Lund is a sympathiser of McLeod and also that he is a Communist', he wrote:

> but I have no proof that such is the case. However, I do know that Mr. Lund has a certain admiration for McLeod, as he has informed me so himself, and I know from conversation I have had with him that he is not friendly disposed towards pastoralists in the Port Hedland district

---

91   O'Neill to McBeath, 12 February 1947, p. 2, SROWA 1947/0305/3.
92   McBeath to Lund, 27 February 1947, SROWA 1947/0305/46.
93   Lund to McBeath, 10 March 1947, SROWA 1947/0305/58.

and generally speaking does not approve of them as employers of native labour.⁹⁴

O'Neill wrote that Lund denied being a communist or being in sympathy with communism, 'and that although he admires McLeod in many ways, politically they are poles apart'.⁹⁵

As well as being critical of pastoralists' treatment of Aboriginal people, Lund and his wife Marjorie, who was matron of the Native Hospital, provided medical treatment to people at the Twelve Mile and knew more than others in the settler community about the new life that *marrngu* were making for themselves there. Marjorie Lund told Medical Inspector Musso of 'one grown-up lad' at the Twelve Mile 'who carried a spelling book with him, presumably trying to learn to spell'.⁹⁶ The Lunds' sympathetic view of the strike put them at odds with the Department's position. There was little doubt in O'Neill's mind 'that Mr. Lund does not approve of the attitude of the Department in regard to the striking natives'. Lund was 'an energetic and efficient officer', O'Neill wrote, and it was 'unfortunate that he had adopted his present attitude with regard to the native strike'. 'In his capacity of Protector of Natives and Officer-in-Charge of the Native Hospital he is in a position to further the interests and influence of McLeod should he so desire'. Although O'Neill admitted he had no proof that Lund had acted to 'further the interests and influence of McLeod', he wrote that it was 'believed by many that he has, and those opinions are held by Constable Mason and Acting Inspector Rhatigan of this Department'.⁹⁷

Despite such suspicions, the Lunds were retained in their positions in Port Hedland, perhaps due to the difficulty of finding suitable staff to replace them. No doubt a close watch was kept on their interactions with *marrngu* at the Twelve Mile, however, before their transfer to Broome eighteen months later. While O'Neill was completing his report on Lund, similar accusations were being made against another public servant stationed in Port Hedland, whose attitude towards the strike, as we shall see in Chapter 15, was considered sufficiently lenient to arouse anti-communist paranoia and victimisation.

Meanwhile, McKenna was serving a two-month sentence in the Port Hedland lockup. The CDNR would probably have appealed his sentence,

---

94   O'Neill to McBeath, 26 March 1947, p. 1, SROWA 1947/0305/65.
95   O'Neill to McBeath, 26 March 1947, p. 1, SROWA 1947/0305/65.
96   Musso to McBeath, 2 January 1947, ANU, Noel Butlin Archives Centre, Michael Hess Collection, N287, Item 1.
97   O'Neill to McBeath, 26 March 1947, p. 2, SROWA 1947/0305/66.

but believed that an appeal had been lodged by Lund and that McKenna had been released on bond awaiting the outcome.[98] Nevertheless, they and other supportive organisations in Perth took action to protest the sentences. Meetings condemned the use of the *Native Administration Act* as an anti-strike weapon, arguing that 'the section of the Act preventing the transport of natives from one district to another was intended by the Legislation to be used to protect the aborigines from unscrupulous employers, not to disrupt their own economic ventures'.[99] Dorothy Hewett, fresh from her visit to Port Hedland, spoke to audiences of her positive impressions of the Twelve Mile community.[100] She also spoke about the strikers' organisation to the Minister for Justice, Emil Nulsen, when, as part of a deputation of members of the CDNR, the Modern Women's Club and Writer's Fellowship, she urged him to have the convictions overturned.[101] Nulsen was sympathetic, stating that, if their facts were correct, the government 'should be supporting the native co-op camp at Pt Hedland and giving them all the help we are able'. Although he did not have the power to quash the convictions, he agreed that a miscarriage of justice may have occurred and promised to thoroughly investigate the matter.[102] McBeath later claimed that Nulsen refrained from taking action in the matter on his advice.[103]

The Department hoped the conviction of McKenna and the other strikers would provide an opportunity to gain the upper hand. Tom Jensen, the new Inspector of Natives for the northern region, being briefed in Perth on the situation in the Pilbara before commencing his new duties, met with O'Neill and Premier Wise to discuss strategies. They agreed that 'the natives concerned should be returned to the Marble Bar district from whence they came, and that, if necessary, warrants would be issued for their removal and detention in the Marble Bar district'. This was deemed necessary 'because of a strong suspicion that natives are being detained at the Twelve Mile against their wish'.[104] The Department was determined to counter the strikers' action in

---

98 M. Watson, Acting Secretary, CDNR, to Nulsen, 18 February 1947, SROWA 1947/0305/56.
99 *Workers' Star*, 7 February 1947, p. 5, 'Native Arrests Rouse Strong Perth Protest'; *Sunday Times*, 16 February 1947, p. 7, 'Resolution Passed at Perth Esplanade on 16/2/47', SROWA 1947/0305/56.
100 *West Australian*, 15 February 1947, p. 12; *Workers' Star*, 21 February 1947, p. 5, 'Nade Crown Slams Native Persecution'.
101 *West Australian*, 11 February 1947, p. 5.
102 *Workers' Star*, 14 February 1947, p. 6, 'Mr. Nulsen Sympathetic to Native Cause'.
103 McBeath to McDonald, 9 April 1947, p. 5, SROWA 1947/0305/86.
104 O'Neill to McBeath, 25 February 1947, SROWA 1947/0305/43.

removing and detaining people by itself taking action to remove and detain them. It was to be a reassertion of departmental authority.

O'Neill also wrote that this action was necessary 'because the congregation of natives from other districts is not desirable at Port Hedland'.[105] This was a central concern of the Department under pressure from pastoralists in a contest over access to pastoral land that was a key feature of the strike. This aspect of the history will be discussed in Chapter 19.

Shortly after the court hearing, Constable Mason was instructed to order those removed by McKenna and others to return to Marble Bar on the train. Anyone refusing to do so was to be reported to the Department with a view to removing them from the district under warrant.[106] This was easier said than done. When Mason visited the Twelve Mile, the people who had been seized by McKenna on 2 January expressed their intention of remaining where they were, despite threats by Mason that, if they refused to obey his order, warrants would be taken out for their forced removal to Moola Bulla, the government settlement in the east Kimberley that served as a detention centre for Aboriginal offenders.[107] It was a threat frequently made and frequently carried into effect as a successful means of suppressing Aboriginal dissension. The strikers at the Twelve Mile stayed where they were. On Mason's second attempt on 10 February, he 'found them more determined than ever not to return to Marble Bar'. 'In their resolution they were backed up by the other natives at the 12 mile who stated they would fight if necessary to prevent the Warrawagine boys being removed'.[108]

Tommy Sampie, one of the leaders at the Twelve Mile and the teacher at the school there, wrote to the CDNR of the encounter with Mason at the Twelve Mile on 10 February:

> The police came out this morning to have another try with the Warrawagine boys. Well he didn't know what to say at times, because some of the boys were firing words after words at him. They all told him plainly that they were not going back any more. He, of course, threatened them that Coverley and the Government wanted them to go back, and if they did not, they would be sent to Mullabulla. Before he finished saying these words all the boys said that he'd have to shift

---

105 O'Neill to McBeath, 25 February 1947, SROWA 1947/0305/43.
106 McBeath to Mason, telegram, 3 February 1947, 1947/0305/31.
107 Tommy Sampie, 'A First Hand Report on Police Persecution of Aborigines', cited by Committee for Defence of Native Rights, SROWA1943/0621/31.
108 Mason to McBeath, 10 February 1947, SROWA 1947/0305/36.

the 12 Mile and Mooleyalla up there too, because we were all one – all joined up as strikers.

Some of the boys told Mason that quite a lot of children had been sent up Moore River, taken away from their mothers, and have never been heard of.

We all just waking up to the Government laws against us. Just because our colour is black we have not the right to go where we want to.

Mason got beaten left and right, and in the finish he was laughingly telling the boys that he didn't like doing all he did.

As he was leaving the Camp he said he would be out next week again, but was told we could not wait around for him. We want to go out and do our work, instead of waiting for the police; we earn nothing for waiting. He only laughed.[109]

Seven years previously, as a Kimberley policeman, Mason had beaten an Aboriginal man unconscious because he was 'cheeky' and had given information that Mason believed was incorrect regarding the station he 'belonged to'. Now *marrngu* were openly defying his instructions, beating him 'right and left' in their replies to his threats and posturing. Although the Department held 'strong suspicions' that people from Marble Bar were being detained at the Twelve Mile against their will, their involvement in this verbal sparring with Mason suggests otherwise.[110] While threats and coercion do seem to have been used by the Twelve Mile people in conducting the 'arrests' in Marble Bar on 2 January, it would seem that most of those removed from Marble Bar now felt satisfied that their grievances could be addressed through their continued participation in the strike at the Twelve Mile, where living conditions were somewhat easier than at Moolyella and organisational structures enabled a more active participation in decision-making processes. Many of those who had been involved in the breakaway movement remained active and militant participants in the strike movement and in the cooperative movement in the 1950s.

If Mason felt himself verbally beaten by the men at the Twelve Mile during his visit on 10 February, he believed that the Department still had the means to assert control. Removal under warrant was the Department's ultimate

---

109 Quoted by Committee for Defence of Native Rights, 'A First Hand Report on Police Persecution of Aborigines', SROWA1943/0621/31.
110 O'Neill to McBeath, 25 February 1947, SROWA 1947/0305/43.

weapon. Mason had warned the strikers that they would be removed if they refused to be returned to Marble Bar, and was anxious to follow through with his threat. 'If warrants are issued for all these natives & I suggest they are', he wrote to McBeath, 'it will be necessary to have sufficient backing to execute them. The position is bad enough at present, but if the natives get away with this episode will get decidedly worse'.[111] McBeath was prepared to issue the warrants as soon as he had the full names – both *walypila* names and *marrngu* names – of the people to whom they would be issued.[112] However, with Twelve Mile people now spread out over a vast area in work parties, obtaining the names and executing the warrants became no easy task. As Mason 'anticipate[d] trouble' in executing the warrants, McBeath promised sufficient police support 'in order that the natives may be conveyed safely back to the Marble Bar District'.[113]

The plan to forcibly remove people from the Port Hedland area to Marble Bar through police action was never carried out, however. While Marshall made inquiries in the Marble Bar area to find out the names of the men seized by Clancy McKenna and the others on 2 January, the High Court of Australia overturned Peter Hodge's and Don McLeod's convictions, bringing to an end the Department's hope that McLeod would be imprisoned and that firm, decisive action could be taken to end the strike. As we shall see, the High Court's decision dramatically reduced the Department's ability to reassert its authority through punitive measures of this nature, and the plan to return the erstwhile defectors to Marble Bar was quietly dropped.

---

111 Mason to McBeath, 10 February 1947, SROWA 1947/0305/36.
112 McBeath to Mason, 13 February 1947, SROWA 1947/0305/40.
113 Mason to McBeath, 19 February 1947, SROWA 1947/0305/41–42; McBeath to Mason, 27 February 1947, SROWA 1947/0305/44.

Chapter 14

'God Help the Blackfellow'

Suppressing Dissent

The Department's inability to follow through with plans to retake control by forcibly returning strikers to Marble Bar highlights the strikers' success in gradually breaking through the strictures of settler control. *Marrngu* were breaching lines of demarcation – around towns, between districts – and getting away with it, notwithstanding the prison sentences imposed on McKenna and the ten others involved in the 'arrests' on 2 January. The significance of the strikers' refusal to return to Marble Bar when ordered to do so by Mason, and the Department's failure to enforce compliance with the order, is properly understood in the context of the continued severity with which the Department dealt with any attempt by other Aboriginal groups and individuals to step across the lines drawn in the sand or to strain against the intolerable constraints and indignities imposed upon them. This chapter examines two such incidents which may or may not have been inspired by the success of the strikers' activism, and which provide context against which the strikers' achievement in evading the heavy hand of the state's punitive colonial control can be more fully understood.

The first incident took place in the Marble Bar district at Warrawagine Station at the end of September 1946, two months after *marrngu* had defied a police order to camp at the Four Mile by setting up camp at the Two Mile, marching into Port Hedland and demanding their ration coupons and the release of McLeod from the lockup. Most of the large *marrngu* community at Warrawagine had, at this time, not yet left the station to join the strike camp at Moolyella. On the night of 30 September, Dendo Carbine returned to the Warrawagine 'native camp' from the bush and was surprised to find that his wife was not there. Carbine was a young man of about twenty-four years of age, born at Warrawagine and employed there as a stockman.[1] He was Nyamal, the traditional owner of country surrounding and including Karuwanya, or

---

1 Marshall, police patrol report, 3 October 1946, SROWA 1946/2538 v8.

Carawine Gorge, a beautiful large pool on the Oakover River.[2] Caroline Jula remembered him arriving in the camp that night:

> 'Where's my wife?'
>
> 'I don't know'. We never know. 'Maybe that whitefella got'm, might be'.[3]

Carbine may have already known or suspected that his wife had been sleeping with the *walypila* overseer, William Fredrick John (Bill) Sheppard, or he may have learned this now for the first time. Carbine's wife worked on the station as a domestic servant. Her sexual relationship with Sheppard may or may not have been consensual. At the Twelve Mile, Tommy Sampie recorded women's statements about their treatment by *walypila* men, which he compiled as the Black Book and sent to the Committee for Defence of Native Rights. Unfortunately, it no longer survives. According to Graham Alcorn, only one of the women interviewed by Sampie spoke of 'her white seducer' with affection.[4] This may not be an accurate reflection of women's willingness to engage in sexual relationships with *walypila*, as the context in which the Black Book was compiled probably made it difficult for women to admit complicity. Nevertheless, there is no doubt that sexual services were frequently demanded of Aboriginal women without their consent, almost as a component of the domestic service they provided. The practice was facilitated by the racialised and gendered designation of space on stations, which prohibited Aboriginal men from entering the *walypila* zone of the station homestead which women were required to enter to undertake their work as domestic servants.

When Dendo Carbine made the decision to confront Sheppard in his home and bring away his wife, he challenged the racial demarcation that facilitated the sexual interaction with, and exploitation of, Aboriginal women. Perhaps his decision had nothing to do with the successful challenge to settler authority being undertaken by the strikers, but it is possible that the breaking down of settler-imposed barriers gave him the courage to step across another boundary to protest the injustice of unequal treatment. Apparently unaware that Sheppard and the manager, Jim Lewis, were absent, Carbine entered the bedroom of Sheppard's house at about 10 pm that night, but instead of finding his own wife with Sheppard as he expected, he startled Sheppard's new wife, Eileen, who had been married only a few weeks. She later said that

---

2   Hale, *Kurlumarniny*, p. 279.
3   Jula, recorded by Anne Scrimgeour, 5 November 1992, author's collection.
4   Alcorn, 'The Struggle of the Pilbara Station Hands', p. 22, endnote 15.

she had heard footsteps and, looking up, saw Carbine gazing around the room. Understandably alarmed, she ran thirty metres to the station homestead and spent the night there with Jim Lewis's wife, Nancy.

The next night, 1 October, Carbine entered the Lewises' bedroom and, according to Nancy Lewis, demanded, 'Come on out, I want you'. She ordered him to leave, but he stood there and repeated, 'You come out'. He then asked for a cigarette, and, when Lewis said she had none to give him, left the house.[5]

Jim Lewis and Bill Sheppard returned to the homestead the next day, and, on being told of the incidents, immediately contacted Constable Gordon Marshall. Marshall left Marble Bar at 9 pm that night, driving through the night to arrive at Warrawagine at 6 am on 4 October.[6] Caroline Jula remembered seeing the police arrive. 'Same time we bin see'm, you know, night time you know, policeman coming. Hello? Something wrong. Somebody in trouble ... Morning now, see'm, hello, something wrong. He tell us now, "I get trouble for my woman"'.[7]

Marshall reported that Carbine had been 'sacked and paid off', but Caroline Jula's account, although unclear, suggests that he was held in the store awaiting Marshall's arrival, possibly handcuffed. Handcuffs were used by station managers to discipline Aboriginal workers; Lewis's predecessor as manager at Warrawagine, Les Miller, would punish Aboriginal men by handcuffing them and beating them with a belt.[8] Marshall took statements from Jim and Nancy Lewis and from the Sheppards, and asked Carbine to explain his actions. According to his report:

> Without any hesitation [Carbine] replied – 'I want woman'. Asked what woman, he replied, 'Mrs Belonging to Jim Lewis' – further questioned the native said 'some white man go with black woman – must be all the same, suppose I have white woman'.[9]

Marshall makes no reference in his report to Carbine's allegation that Sheppard was sleeping with his wife, although it seems unlikely that Carbine would not have mentioned this. As presented in the police report, Carbine's behaviour appears to lack motivation beyond a primitive sexual urge, a disturbing reminder of one of settler society's deepest fears: the threat posed

---

5   Marshall, police patrol report, 4 October 1946, SROWA 1946/2538 v8.
6   Marshall, police patrol report, 4 October 1946, SROWA 1946/2538 v8.
7   Jula, recorded by Anne Scrimgeour, 5 November 1992, author's collection.
8   Gardiner (Pirntilkampanyaja), recorded by Anne Scrimgeour, 29 September 1993, author's collection.
9   Marshall, police patrol report, 4 October 1946, SROWA 1946/2538 v8.

by Aboriginal male sexuality. Twelve months after the end of the war, the report entwines this fear with another fear of alien intrusion: 'He holds that he is full blood native', Marshall wrote, 'but I am of the opinion that his father was Japanese – This native has a vile face & strongly resembles a Japanese'. An impression of Carbine as a thoroughly unsavoury and unscrupulous character is heightened by Marshall's account of Carbine adding insult to injury by offering Lewis money to forget the incident. 'Here Jim you take this (offering the money) and we call it square'. When Lewis ignored him, Carbine asked Marshall several times to take the money and let him go.[10]

In offering money to Lewis to 'call it square', Carbine seems to have indicated that he had no malicious intention when he entered the *walypila* houses, but that he had done so as a form of demonstration. By treating the *walypila* women as Aboriginal women were treated, by treating *walypila* men as he himself was being treated, he was protesting the injustice inherent in an arrangement that gave *walypila* men unfettered access to Aboriginal women for sexual purposes, and which made Aboriginal men powerless to object. In offering money he was, perhaps, continuing to show Jim Lewis how it felt to be treated as he was being treated, as it seems likely that *walypila* men used money to assuage the anger of *marrngu* men: 'Here, take this and we'll call it square'.

Just as police reports were silent about the sexual violation of Aboriginal families that provoked responses of this nature, so were they silent about the use of chains in making arrests. Although Marshall's report made no reference to the fact that a chain was put around Carbine's neck when he was arrested, Caroline Jula and her brother, Sambo Bina (Yawarta-bloke), remembered that this was so. Marshall spent some time at the station looking for a skeleton that had been found by two young *walypila* jackaroos, but was unable to find it. He wrote that 'as my prisoner Wongelva [alias] Carbine was restless and could not be trusted, I had to give up the search for the time', but he does not say that Carbine was held in chains during the search and on the long trip back to Marble Bar, during which Callewa, Yarrie and Moolyella were visited.

At Marble Bar, Carbine was charged and placed in the lockup, almost certainly still wearing the neck chain.[11] His case was heard by two Justices of the Peace on 7 October. Roy Lindley, who had been a mounted policeman in the Kimberley and was still a 'Protector of Natives', entered a plea of guilty

---

10   Marshall, police patrol report, 4 October 1946, SROWA 1946/2538 v8.
11   Marshall, police patrol report, 4 October 1946, SROWA 1946/2538 v8.

on Carbine's behalf. Carbine was given no opportunity to tell the court his side of the story. He was given a sentence of six months' imprisonment with hard labour, which he served in the Roebourne jail.[12] Marshall recommended that, when he had served his term, he be removed from the district 'and taken well down south, where he might be placed as a Police Tracker'. 'His offence is regarded as very serious in these parts', Marshall wrote, '& if he is removed from the district it will have a good effect upon the other natives'. As James Doughty says in his novel *The Green Stick*:

> Any nigger that gave Kate cheek would be a plain fool. Besides, that sort of thing never happened in the north. A white woman was safe from insult by either black or white – particularly black. It would be God help the blackfellow that injured a white woman.[13]

Caroline Jula believed that Carbine had received a seven-year jail sentence, a belief that reflects the length of time that he spent away from his country and community in consequence of his action in behaving towards *walypila* as they behaved towards him. It was common practice for police and the Department of Native Affairs to extend prison sentences imposed by the courts through the imposition of much longer terms of exile, either instituted informally by assigning offenders to roles such as that of police tracker in distant parts of the state, as Marshall suggested in Carbine's case, or more formally through the issue of ministerial warrants for the removal of offenders to institutions away from their own districts. A conviction was sufficient reason for a warrant to be issued. Carbine was still away from the area in 1950, when a Native Affairs report referred to a woman working at Warralong Station whose husband had 'been banished from the country to which he belongs indefinitely as a result of becoming involved with a white woman on Warrawagine station some years ago'.[14] By 1952, he had returned to the area, however, as his name appears on a list of employees on Bonney Downs Station at that time.[15] He seems to have been 'taken well down south' as Marshall had recommended, as he spent some time in the state's south-west, where, at Roelands Mission near Bunbury, he saw Caroline Jula's beloved and only surviving little son, Colin Carlin, who

---

12 Marshall, police patrol report, 8 October 1946, SROWA 1946/2538 v8.
13 Doughty, *The Green Stick*, p. 42.
14 Native Affairs Officer Noel Hawke, patrol report, 10 March 1950, SROWA 1950/0173.
15 Native Affairs Officer Harvey Tilbrook, patrol report, 1952, SROWA 1952/0573/78.

had been removed from her care following hospital treatment in Perth just prior to the strike.[16]

The second incident to be examined in this chapter took place further south, in the state's Mid West. In early 1947, rumours that a big Aboriginal meeting was to take place near the Mid West town of Meekatharra raised concern in the Department of Native Affair as possibility having 'some bearing on the Port Hedland–Nullagine situation'.[17] Acting Commissioner Lew McBeath instructed police in Meekatharra and other northern towns to make inquiries. 'It would appear', he wrote, 'that Donald McLeod, the instigator of the Port Hedland native strike, may have had agents, either white or native, moving about on the Murchison with the object of creating industrial unrest, and arranging a strike of native station workers'.[18] Although police officers could find no evidence of the planned meeting or of any activity by an agent of McLeod, McBeath warned his officers 'not to be lulled into a sense of false security' by the lack of evidence of any potential activism. 'The Communists employ subtle methods', he warned, 'and as we know, propaganda can be circulated and organisation carried out without any official knowledge if any laxness is shown on the part of field officers'.[19]

Anxiety created by the success of the Pilbara strikers' defiant and united stance intersected with the widespread fear of subversive communist activity in the north. A determination to ensure that Aboriginal people in other parts of the state did not follow the example of the Pilbara strikers gave policemen in other parts of the state added licence to persecute and exclude Aboriginal people, particularly those already identified as not sufficiently subservient. Despite the lack of evidence that any subversive activity was taking place in the area, Constable Thomas Arthur Webb, of Mt Magnet, was quick to identify individuals he suspected of involvement in any action of this nature. Willie and Leedham Cameron were at present in his district, he wrote:

> and I should say that any trouble of the nature reported would attract these natives as they are the troublesome type and would glory in the thought of being leaders amongst the natives. This also applies to Walter CAMERON, Jack and George GILBERT who are very troublesome when the opportunity arises.[20]

---

16 Gwen Bucknall, email to author, 7 November 2011; Jula, recorded by Anne Scrimgeour, 5 November 1992, author's collection.
17 Bisley to McBeath, 17 January 1947, SROWA 1947/0285/1.
18 McBeath to Const. G. J. Barrett, 22 January 1947, SROWA 1974/0285/1.
19 McBeath to O'Neill, 11 March 1947, SROWA 1947/0285/5.
20 Webb to McBeath, 5 March 1947, SROWA 1947/0285.

The presence in Mt Magnet of 150 Aboriginal people from surrounding areas over the 1947 Easter weekend gave Webb the opportunity to demonstrate his vigilance in combating communistic influences. On Saturday night, 5 April, he noticed thirty-eight-year-old Walter Cameron and eighteen-year-old Wilfred Watson among the racegoers in the town. They had not entered the hotel but, according to Webb, were 'hanging about in the vicinity'. Webb arrested them, charged them with loitering and held them in police cells until their case was heard by a magistrate the following Monday. Released with a caution by the magistrate, Cameron told Webb that he would bring other Aboriginal people into town to protest against their arrest.[21]

Walter John Julius Cameron was born in Mullawa in 1915, the son of Charlie and Bessie Cameron, and the grandson of Scottish and Irish convicts and their Aboriginal wives.[22] His father Charlie Cameron was a well-known local identity, a sprinter in his younger days, a court interpreter and an Anglican. Charlie believed in the importance of education and fought to have his children educated at the local school in Mullewa. The family later shifted to the small centre of Yalgoo, where their acceptance within the town is indicated by a newspaper article announcing the marriage of Walter's sister in 1927. 'The marriage took place between George Curley of Woolgolong station and Miss Avy Cameron, daughter of Mr and Mrs Cameron of Yalgoo and late of Mullewa'.[23] By the 1940s, however, there was a growing antagonism towards the increasing Euralian population and their presence in towns in the region. During the war some of the towns, such as Mt Magnet, had been declared prohibited areas for Aboriginal people, and when the war ended a meeting of road boards in the region called on the Native Affairs Department to draw lines of demarcation around all regional towns and to confine all Aboriginal people in segregated reserves.[24] Wally's *walypila* ancestry did not protect him from suffering the full force of the state's draconian Native Administration legislation, and, indeed, brought about a greater degree of government intervention in his life. In 1936, when he was living in Cue, the Department tried to prevent him becoming initiated because he was classified a 'half-caste' and, as the *West Australian* reported, 'it had always been [Commissioner A. O. Neville's] policy to prevent as far as possible the interference by full-bloods with half-caste

---

21 McBeath, notes made 8 April 1946, SROWA 1947/0285.
22 Ava Curley, 'An Extraordinary Woman', *Hope Channel*, https://www.hopechannel.com/au/read/an-extraordinary-woman.
23 *Yalgoo Observer and Murchison Chronicle* (Meekatharra), 18 August 1927, p. 2.
24 *Geraldton Guardian and Express*, 27 July 1946, p. 4.

youths'.²⁵ The organisers of the ceremony, however, managed to circumvent departmental attempts to intervene, and the ceremony went ahead, although Neville believed that 'the whole affair seems to have been "hurried up," carried out as urgently as possible, and followed by a scattering of the parties concerned in all directions'.²⁶

Cameron worked as a station hand in the Murchison region, and in October 1942 enlisted in the Australian Army. He underwent training in Northam as a driver in the 5ᵗʰ Australian Ambulance Corp but, as his work as a station hand was considered essential employment in the war effort, he was returned to station work after four months.²⁷

At about 8.30 pm on 7 April 1947, the day Cameron and Watson had been released from the Mt Magnet police cell, a group of twelve men and women and some children walked defiantly along the main street of Mt Magnet. They included Cameron and Watson, Cameron's wife Esther and their daughter, his sister Avy and her husband George Curley and five of their children, and Cameron's brother Leedham and his wife Eva Harris. One of the children in the group was Leedham Cameron's son, Clarrie, who later remembered either his father or Wally Cameron tearing down a poster notifying Aboriginal people that it was an offence for them to be in the town after 6 pm. They were approached by Webb and Constable Basley from Sandstone. According to Avy Curley, the policemen followed them into a shop and one of them, a tall man, pointed over the top of her head to each of the Aboriginal men, saying, 'I want you, I want you, I want you'. Curley asked, 'What about me?' and Webb said, 'Oh yes, you can come too'.²⁸ According to Webb's account, he asked them if they were going to the pictures, and Walter Cameron and Avy Curley stepped forward as spokesmen to say that they were not going to the pictures, but had come to town to look around. Clarrie Cameron remembered Webb telling them to 'get off the street!' 'Aunty Avy and Dad and Uncle George and Uncle Wally said, "Like hell! What do you think, we're dogs, or something? Who put that up? No, we're not getting off the street. We're human beings."'²⁹

---

25   *West Australian*, 30 June 1936, p. 18; *Daily News*, 7 March 1936, p. 1.
26   Quoted in *West Australian*, 30 June 1936, p. 18.
27   ASIO file, 'Cameron, Walter John Julius', NAA B884, W90255.
28   Avy Curley, 'Mrs Avy Curley', in Colleen Glass and Archie Weller (eds.), *Us Fellas: An Anthology of Aboriginal Writing*, Artlook Books, Perth, 1987, p. 18.
29   Clarrie Cameron, interviewed by Fiona Skyring, Geraldton, 5 March 2008, quoted in Fiona Skyring, *Justice: A History of the Aboriginal Legal Service of Western Australia*, University of Western Australia Publishing, Crawley, 2001, p. 2.

Webb initially used the fact that Mt Magnet was a gazetted prohibited area as the basis on which he was ordering them to leave town, but Curley was one step ahead of him. She had had an altercation with Webb when she visited Mt Magnet from her home town of Cue the previous Christmas. Ordered out of town after sunset, she had made inquiries about the legal basis of police action on this matter, and now told Webb that she had a letter informing her that Aboriginal people could enter towns if they were employed.[30] But policemen like Webb always had more than one piece of legislation at their disposal. Whether or not the town was a prohibited area, it was illegal under the *Native Administration Act 1936* for Aboriginal people to disobey police instructions to leave town. Police needed no reason for giving such an order. Told again to leave, Curley, who had her youngest child in her arms, said they would not go home until it suited them.[31] Cameron stated that they were staying in town in protest against his earlier arrest and imprisonment, and Curley insisted that if any one of them was jailed, they would all be jailed.

Clarrie Cameron's mother, Eva Harris, did not want her children imprisoned and took them away. 'I can just remember that [Mum] grabbed us couple of boys', Clarrie said. 'She didn't want the kids being locked up'.[32] The remainder, eleven adults and six children, stood firm, the parents insisting that if they went to jail their children would go with them. Webb enlisted some *walypila* bystanders to assist him in marching the men, women and children to the police station; he claimed that violence had been avoided only by the assistance of onlookers, as 'neither the Camerons or George Gilbert are the type to allow themselves to be arrested without resisting violently when they consider the odds of a victory are in their favour'.[33] Curley also remembered that Webb 'got some white chaps off the street to march us along', but that a few non-Aboriginal bystanders gave support to the protesters.[34] 'Aunty Avy and the family, and Uncle Wally and Dad and everyone, they walked into the jail!' Clarrie said. 'And all the kids walked in with them'.[35]

---

30 Accounts differ as to the source of this letter. Curley states that she had a letter from Inspector of Police O'Brien, but Webb wrote that she had told him she had a letter from Commissioner of Native Affairs Bray. Curley, 'Mrs Avy Curley', p. 17; Webb, police report, 9 April 1947, p. 1, SROWA 1947/0285/14.

31 Skyring, *Justice*, p. 1.

32 Quoted in Skyring, *Justice*, p. 3.

33 Webb to McBeath, 9 April 1947, SROWA 1947/0285/15.

34 Curley, 'Mrs Avy Curley', p. 19; Skyring, *Justice*, p. 2.

35 Cameron, quoted in Skyring, *Justice*, p. 3.

Webb held the protesters in a police cell overnight, sending an urgent telegram to Acting Commissioner McBeath at his home to inform him that he had seventeen natives in the lockup charged with loitering. 'Trouble instigated by Walter Cameron and the Communist Party', he wrote.[36] The following morning, the prisoners refused to be taken individually to the courtroom to hear the charges laid against them and consequently had their charges read to them as a group in the courtyard, as the courtroom was too small to hold them all.[37] At 11 am, Avy Curley and Esther Cameron accepted bail to take their children home and to contact solicitors Altofer and Stow in Geraldton to defend them.[38] Webb reported that 'apparantly [sic] Altofer and Stow declined the brief to defend them as no further mention was made of Legal Assistance being obtained'.[39] According to Curley, however, she made repeated unsuccessful attempts to telephone the solicitors from the post office but was unable to get through. Years later, the postmaster told her that Webb had instructed him to block her call.[40] Webb was apparently being disingenuous when he reported to McBeath that the protesters 'were given the usual opportunity to obtain Legal Advise if they so desired'.[41]

Viewing the incident as a serious one 'inspired by some outside source', Webb arranged for the resident magistrate from Cue to travel to Mt Magnet to hear the case. All eleven charged were found guilty of loitering, and the three women were cautioned and ordered to pay costs and to return immediately to Cue. All the men except Wally Cameron received fines of either £1 or £2 with costs and were ordered to return to their home towns or places of employment, or to employment obtained for them by Webb. Webb wrote that although Avy Curley was one of the leaders of the protest, he recommended leniency, as she had a large young family. This leniency, however, did not prevent him from immediately applying to the Department to have Curley, her children and her husband removed to an institution.[42] His application was unsuccessful. Avy Curley went on to have eighteen children, becoming a passionate Christian, teacher, community

---

36 Webb to McBeath, telegram, 8 April 1946, SROWA 1947/0285/6.
37 Curley, 'Mrs. Avy Curley', p. 19.
38 Webb to McBeath, 9 April 1947, SROWA 1947/0285/6.
39 Webb to McBeath, 9 April 1947, SROWA 1947/0285/15.
40 Curley, 'Mrs. Avy Curley', p. 19.
41 Webb to McBeath, 9 April 1947, SROWA 1947/0285/15.
42 Webb, police report, 9 April 1947, SROWA 1947/0285/13.

worker and artist. In 1980 she earned a Medal of the Order of Australia for services to her community.[43]

Her brother Wally Cameron received a two-month prison sentence with hard labour for his role in the protest and was transferred to Geraldton Jail on 9 April. In passing sentence, the magistrate instructed him not to return to the Mt Magnet district when he was released.[44] As with Carbine, the formal sentence awarded by the court was viewed by the Department as just the first of a number of actions that could be taken to punish dissenters and remove them from their communities as a measure to prevent concerted Aboriginal resistance to settler domination. Formal conviction served as a justification for further punitive action. The magistrate's instructions to Cameron not to return to the district when his sentence expired was a sentence of exile, but Webb also recommended that he be removed under ministerial warrant. 'Walter CAMERON has always been a trouble maker in this district and I consider that the remainder of the Natives would be a lot more content if he were removed to a Settlement', he wrote.[45] Constable George Chedzey at Cue agreed. 'This native is looked upon as a head by the other Natives', he wrote, 'in as much as he regards himself as educated and a pugilist, and his removal from the Murchison would be an object lesson to the other Camerons'.[46]

McBeath was preparing to visit Port Hedland to find a way to reassert control there, and decided to leave the question of Cameron's removal until his return. He commended Webb for his 'firm but fair treatment', which prevented 'further developments of a nasty nature'. Cameron was 'obviously a member of the Communist Party', he wrote. 'The Communist Party may now be attempting to work direct through the native, and not in the same manner as at Port Hedland'.[47] He instructed Acting Inspectors Bisley and Martin to travel immediately to Mt Magnet to investigate the situation and to disperse all Aboriginal people to their places of employment. Although there was nothing 'industrial' in the protest, McBeath instructed the inspectors to advise Aboriginal people 'not to listen to any propaganda spread by natives or others designed to create industrial unrest'.[48]

---

43 Curley, 'An Extraordinary Woman', https://www.hopechannel.com/au/read/an-extraordinary-woman; *Australasian Record*, vol. 85, no. 48, 1980, p. 1; Alan Holman, 'Woman of Substance', *Record*, vol. 105, no. 1, 2000, pp. 8–9.
44 Webb, police report, 9 April 1947, p. 3, SROWA 1947/0285/12.
45 Webb, police report, 9 April 1947, p. 3, SROWA 1947/0285/12.
46 Chedzey to Police Inspector O'Connor, 19 April 1947, SROWA 1947/0285.
47 McBeath to McDonald, 11 April 1947, SROWA 1947/0285/16.
48 McBeath to Bisley and Martin, 9 April 1947, SROWA 1947/0285/10.

Cameron's ACP membership – he held a Communist Party Membership card no 36302 – fanned departmental fears that the successful activism of Pilbara Aboriginal people was inspiring other groups to take similar action.[49] These fears deepened in October 1947, when the vigilant Constable Webb reported that two men were travelling around the Murchison trying to recruit Aboriginal people for the Communist Party. He had no information about their appearance, but stated that they were travelling in an old model Chevrolet utility painted green and without a hood.[50] According to Graham Alcorn, the Committee for Defence of Native Rights sent Tom Bropho and the young *walypila* ex-serviceman Geoff Harcus on an organising tour to address groups in various centres throughout the state.[51] The fact that the men in the green Chevrolet mentioned having solicitor Curran working with them suggests that they may have been Bropho and Harcus.

There is no evidence that Cameron's membership of the Communist Party, the activism of the CDNR (or the Native Rights League, as it was called by mid-1947), or the example set by *marrngu* activism in Port Hedland had any impact on the decision to mount a challenge to the exclusion of Aboriginal people from Mt Magnet. In speaking and writing in later years about her leadership role in this protest, Avy Curley made no reference to any external influence. Certainly, the constraints imposed by the *Native Administration Act* and harassment by the police were enough to provoke Aboriginal people into taking defiant group action of this nature. However, an anxious desire to prevent the development of orchestrated and widely publicised activism such as that taking place in the Pilbara, along with a growing belief that communist agitation was working to achieve this in other parts of the state, may have hardened departmental responses and given greater licence to police to victimise Aboriginal people they considered insufficiently servile.

If Cameron was emboldened by his ACP membership, it provided no protection. It is likely that authorities, determined to avoid a repetition of the situation developing in the Pilbara, were vigilant in preventing him contacting potential supporters. The Native Rights League was alerted to his case by newspaper reports of the protest and his conviction, and it organised a deputation to discuss the issue with the newly-appointed Minister for

---

49   Webb to McBeath, 9 April 1947, SROWA 1947/0285/16.
50   Webb to McBeath, 6 October 1946, SROWA 1947/0285/24.
51   Alcorn, 'The Struggle of the Pilbara Station Hands', p. 4.

Native Affairs, Ross McDonald.[52] Protest was muted, however. This was probably due to a lack of information around which to develop a campaign, the small scale of the Mt. Magnet protest in relation to the action taken in the Pilbara, and the fact that, since the protest was not framed in terms of industrial action as the Pilbara action had been, unions were less interested in protesting Cameron's imprisonment than the imprisonment of Dooley and McKenna the previous year. Cameron served the full term of his two-month sentence.

On his release, Cameron returned to the Mt Magnet area to work on a station. Webb recommended that he 'be given the opportunity to rehabilitate himself' and that he be allowed to remain in the district 'providing he was industrious and of good conduct generally'. However, he warned Cameron that he would be removed to an institution if he 'foment[ed] further trouble or unrest'.[53]

Later in the year, Webb reported on rumours of further trouble planned for the race weekend of 7 to 9 November, and McBeath, in response, instructed Acting Native Affairs Inspector Martin to be in Mt Magnet at that time.[54] He told Martin to:

> interview the native Walter J. J. Cameron before the race meeting, and ascertain if he proposes to be present, and at the same time warn him that if he attempts to instigate further unrest immediate action will be taken for his removal to a Native Institution.[55]

Since the Department's file on the Mt Magnet protest ends with this instruction, there was apparently no protest action at the November race meeting. Nevertheless, some time over the next two years, Wally Cameron, and presumably his wife and daughter, were removed to the notorious Moore River settlement. In December 1949, his photo appeared in a *Daily News* article along with other photographs of Moore River people, under the heading 'The People Moore River Looks After'. Whether he had been sent there as a result of plans to organise a demonstration at the November race meeting, or for some later offence, his conviction in April would have added weight to

---

52 *Tribune*, 16 May 1947, p. 7; *Daily News*, 9 April 1947, p. 9; *West Australian*, 10 April 1947, p. 3.
53 McBeath to McDonald, undated, SROWA 1947/0285/20.
54 Webb to McBeath, 27 September 1947, SROWA 1947/0285/22; McBeath to Martin, 9 October 1947, SROWA 1947/0285/22.
55 McBeath to Martin, 9 October 1947, SROWA 1947/0285/22.

recommendations for his removal. The paternalistic tone of the article's title belied the reality that Wally Cameron was not at Moore River because he needed to be looked after, but because he had dared to challenge the restrictive racist legislation of the *Native Administration Act*. 'The settlement's windmill expert is Wally Cameron', the article states. 'He served for a while with the Light Field Ambulance in World War II and still wears the cap'.[56]

---

56   *Daily News*, 12 December 1949, p. 12.

Chapter 15

'The Hide and the Audacity to Employ Full-Blooded Natives on the Jetty'

The Politics of Racial Solidarity on the Port Hedland Waterfront, 1947

The southern campaign that provided essential support for the strike included widespread expressions of union solidarity, union condemnation of the state Labor government's response, and financial donations from unions to the Committee for Defence of Native Rights. The Labor government, in the final days of four terms in office as the 15 March election day approached, was sensitive to union criticism over the jailing of strikers. As we shall see in later chapters, the Fremantle Branch of the Seamen's Union would, in 1949, give practical support to the strikers' cause, but union support was not as 'strong and resolute' as has been claimed.[1] Anti-communism came into play, and when push came to shove, the Australian Workers' Union joined ranks with the Department of Native Affairs to oppose the strike.

The discrepancy between widely-voiced expressions of union support as opposed to practical union support for Aboriginal workers in the Pilbara during the strike was played out in early 1947, when strikers presented for work to unload the SS *Dorrigo* on the Port Hedland wharf. Don McLeod worked as a casual wharf labourer, a 'wharfie', or 'lumper' as they are called in Western Australia.[2] When wharfinger and station master Alfred (Alf) Bonham was unable to muster sufficient men to undertake the unloading on the morning of 21 January 1947, McLeod suggested that the number be made up by four men from the Twelve Mile who were in town that day to pick up three new Army surplus boats arriving on the *Dorrigo* for use in their fishing

---

1   Deborah Wilson, *Different White People*, p. 29.
2   Bonham to Secretary for Railways, 10 February 1947, p. 2, SROWA 1947/0477/7.

and pearling operations.³ Members of the Port Hedland Euralian community had been a principal source of wharf labour during the war and still made up much of Bonham's workforce; among the casual workers selected to unload the *Dorrigo* at the 8 am 'pick-up' that morning, for example, was Ernie Mitchell's nephew, Sam Mitchell, who had been working ships for the past two years.⁴ Bonham therefore had no hesitation in agreeing to engage four 'half-castes', while reminding McLeod that he was not allowed to employ 'full-bloods' as he had no permit to do so. He engaged four Twelve Mile strikers – 'fine big halfcastes', he called them – placing Tommy Monaghan to work on the jetty and Ernie Mitchell, Rob Brown and Sam Coppin, the brother of Yarrie Jack Coppin, to work on board the *Dorrigo*.⁵

Work had not progressed very far when Constable Bill Mason boarded the ship and insisted that the four strikers could not be employed without work permits.⁶ He had no legal grounds to intervene. Section 18 of the *Native Administration Act 1936*, which stipulated that employers could only engage Aboriginal people if they held a permit from the Department, made it clear that this requirement did not apply to any man:

> over twenty-one years of age who is of half blood or less than half blood descent from the original full blood inhabitants of Australia or from their full blood descendants, where such a person does not live after the manner of the original full blood inhabitants or their full blood descendants.

Although the purpose of work permit regulations was ostensibly to protect Aboriginal people from labour exploitation by enabling the Department to vet working relationships and conditions, the regulation had become an effective tool for controlling Aboriginal people by controlling their access to employment. To maintain such control, departmental officers ignored the proviso to section 18, applying work permit regulations to all Aboriginal people, except those few who had been formally granted Certificates of Exemption from the Act.⁷ The Department knew it was on legally shaky ground with regard to men of

---

3   McLeod, draft autobiography, chapter 4, p. 1, Marchant Trust Collection, UWA MS118 series 1 file 13.
4   Bonham to Secretary for Railways, 10 February 1947, p. 1, SROWA 1947/0477/6.
5   Bonham to Secretary for Railways, 10 February 1947, p. 2, SROWA 1947/0477/7.
6   Bonham to Secretary for Railways, 10 February 1947, p. 2, SROWA 1947/0477/7.
7   Section 71 of the *Native Administration Act 1905* made provision for the Minister to 'issue to any native who, in his opinion, ought not to be subject to this Act, a certificate in writing under his hand that such native is exempt from the provisions of

mixed descent, but felt confident that its interpretation of section 18 would not be challenged. Mason therefore had no qualms about boarding the *Dorrigo* and brashly informing Bonham and Captain Reynolds of the *Dorrigo* that they could not employ the four men without permits, and that permits would not be issued, as this would set a precedent.[8] Clearly, this was not a case of providing protection from exploitation but of preventing Aboriginal people, and especially the strikers, from obtaining well-paid work in town. At Mason's insistence, the men were suspended.[9]

Unloading operations came to a halt as AWU members called a stop-work meeting, refusing to work until they heard from union leadership about the eligibility of the four men to be issued with union tickets.[10] Captain Reynolds wired his employer, State Shipping Services, for instructions. 'Police and others against their employment regardless of union decision', he wrote.[11] He asked State Shipping to consult with the Department to find a way to resolve the situation. Mason, determined to prevent the strikers gaining union tickets, wired Acting Commissioner Lew McBeath, informing him of the situation and asking him to intervene in the decision. 'If tickets issued natives liable serious trouble can you assist by interviewing Golding'.[12]

There was no AWU regulation to prevent Charles (Charlie) Golding, Western Australian secretary of the AWU, from approving the granting of union tickets to the four men. Under AWU rules, Aboriginal people were eligible for membership, but acceptance of Aboriginal membership was usually left to the discretion of local union representatives.[13] In Port Hedland, members of the Euralian community had been accepted into the AWU during the war, but Euralians in Broome were still debarred and thereby denied access to well-paid employment in the town. The Department was quite happy to accept such discrimination. In 1940, Broome's coloured community had looked to the Department for support over the issue of AWU membership, asking McBeath, who was then the local Native Affairs officer, to support their efforts

---

this Act, and from and after the issue of such certificate such native shall be so exempt accordingly: But any such certificate may be revoked at any time by the Minister, and thereupon this Act shall apply to such native as if no such certificate had been issued'.

8   Bonham to Secretary for Railways, 10 February 1947, p. 2, SROWA 1947/0477/7.
9   Reynolds, Captain of the *Dorrigo* to State Shipping Service, Fremantle, telegram, undated, SROWA 1940/1194/7.
10 Mason to McBeath, telegram, 21 January 1947, SROWA 1940/1194/8.
11 Reynolds to State Shipping Service, telegram, undated [21 January 1947], SROWA 1940/1194/7.
12 Mason to McBeath, telegram, 21 January 1947, SROWA 1940/1194/8.
13 *Workers' Star*, 31 January 1947, p. 5, 'Govt's New Drive Against Natives'.

to gain tickets. Commissioner Bray had advised McBeath against interfering in union matters, insisting that, during wartime, industrial peace was more important than social justice. 'The matter should be left in the hands of the representatives', he had said. 'Cases of individual hardship will arise, but the principle of industrial peace is of paramount importance and this applies also in the circumstances of our outlook in the social amelioration of the natives'.[14] McBeath had agreed:

> Personally I would much prefer that these people should leave Broome and seek employment in the bush as station workers. Even if they were successful in obtaining a union ticket, and also their share of casual work their position would not be improved to any great extent, the more money they receive, the more they will waste, and their future will never be solved by coastal town employment.[15]

Given this history of departmental support for AWU exclusion of Aboriginal workers, McBeath now had no hesitation in contacting state secretary Charlie Golding to urge him not to approve the admission of the four strikers into his union.[16] Golding needed no encouragement. In the matter of opposition to the strike, the AWU's anti-communist stance found common ground with the Department's objective of retaining control over Aboriginal people. According to McBeath, Golding believed that:

> the whole affair had been inspired by the Communist, Donald McLeod, and because [Golding] did not favour the tactics of this individual he proposed to telegram the Union representative at Port Hedland stating that Union tickets were not to be issued to persons deemed to be natives according to the Native Administration Act.[17]

Both Mason and the AWU members in Port Hedland were also informed that Mitchell, Monaghan, Coppin and Brown could not be issued union tickets.

On receipt of telegraphic instructions from State Shipping, the AWU leadership and the Department that the four strikers were ineligible for union membership, arrangements were made for a 6 pm 'pick-up' of workers to unload the ship overnight.[18] Mason had managed to enlist the services of

---

14   Bray to McBeath, 12 December 1940, SROWA 1940/1194/5.
15   McBeath to Bray, 19 December 1940, SROWA 1940/1194/6.
16   McBeath to Coverley, 24 January 1947, SROWA 1947/0477/4.
17   McBeath to Coverley, 24 January 1947, SROWA 1947/0477/4.
18   McBeath to Mason, telegram, 21 January 1947, SROWA 1940/1194/8.

a few townspeople, but AWU members indicated that they would not work with non-unionists, and all those wanting work were asked to show their tickets.[19] While some of the men, including McLeod, were returning home to get theirs, tickets were issued to three non-unionists recruited by Mason. According to McLeod, 'the policeman persuaded the rep to issue three tickets to scabs to fill the number'. These three new members were able to sway the vote towards working the ship.[20]

Not satisfied with having prevented the strikers from gaining access to wharf employment, Mason also attempted to have other Euralian workers excluded from employment, informing Thomas Murphy that he could not work the ship because no permit had been issued and he did not have a Certificate of Exemption from the *Native Administration Act*. Murphy, a Euralian ex-serviceman with nine children, had worked as a lumper on the wharf prior to his three-year service in the armed forces, and since the war had been working in Port Hedland for the Public Works Department.[21] In no way could the permit regulations of the *Native Administration Act 1936* be said to apply in his case, but Constable Mason's manner was sufficiently officious to convince both workers and employers that he was acting within the law. Nevertheless, unionists refused to return to work without Murphy, and after protracted argument a compromise was reached, with Mason agreeing to allow Murphy to be employed, but only in the shed and not on the wharf or the ship.[22]

Few of the men who had been picked up at 8 am presented for work at the 6 pm pick-up, and the unloading proceeded overnight with a skeleton staff of less than half the required strength. The boats purchased by the strikers from Army disposal were damaged while being unloaded. 'When this crowd unloaded our boats', McLeod later wrote, 'they dropped them on an iron spike on the jetty, so they were spoiled before we could use them'. Two of the boats were repairable, but the other was damaged beyond repair.[23] Unloading was

---

19 Mason to McBeath, 22 January 1947, p. 2, SROWA 1947/0477/4; McLeod, draft autobiography, chapter 4, p. 2, Marchant Trust Collection, UWA MS118 series 1 file 13; Bonham to Secretary for Railways, 10 February 1947, p. 3, SROWA 1947/0477/8.

20 McLeod, draft autobiography, chapter 4, p. 2, Marchant Trust Collection, UWA MS118 series 1 file 13.

21 Bonham to Secretary for Railways, 10 February 1947, p. 2, SROWA 1947/0477/7.

22 Bonham to Secretary for Railways, 10 February 1947, pp. 2–3, SROWA 1947/0477/7–8.

23 McLeod, draft autobiography, chapter 4, p. 2, Marchant Trust Collection, UWA MS118 series 1 file 13.

completed at 10.30 am the following morning, and the *Dorrigo* proceeded to Broome, twelve hours behind schedule.[24]

Strike supporters in Perth, learning of the wharf dispute from McLeod, condemned Mason's actions. A meeting on the Perth Esplanade on 2 February, which denounced the arrest of Clancy McKenna and other *marrngu* for transporting people from Marble Bar to the Twelve Mile, also passed a resolution stating that 'this meeting of citizens vigorously protests against the refusal of departmental officials in Port Hedland to issue permits to Australian workers of Aboriginal descent to work on the discharging of ships on the wharf'.[25] Constable Bill Mason, however, was pleased with the outcome of his efforts. It was only through his own firm and decisive action, he claimed, that a dangerous chink in the wall of the settlers' defensive solidarity against the rising tide of defiant Aboriginal assertiveness had been successfully plugged.[26] Commissioner McBeath and Minister for Native Affairs Bob Coverley were grateful. 'Const. Mason should be thanked for his initiative in taking hold of the situation in the way he did, saving a very nasty situation', Coverley wrote.[27]

The weak point in settler solidarity that had allowed the breach to occur, according to Mason, was the officer in charge of the Port Hedland railway, Alf Bonham. 'I interviewed Mr. Bonham', Mason wrote, 'and asked why he had employed the natives and he stated he could not get other labour, which I told him was a downright lie and that I intended taking action against him'.[28]

Alf Bonham had had a thirty-six-year career with the Western Australian Railways, and had been well-liked and well respected in the various districts in which he had worked. In 1938, when promotion caused him to leave Bellevue, on Perth's eastern fringe, an article in the *Swan Express* said that, 'like the "fair lady on the horse"', Bonham and his wife had 'music wherever they go, owing to their amiable and generous dispositions'.[29] Posted to Port Hedland in 1941, he was an active member of the community, chairman of the local race club and a Freemason.[30] Now approaching retirement, he became a target of hostility arising from anti-communist paranoia and anxiety over the loss of settler control over Aboriginal people.

---

24 Mason to McBeath, 22 January 1947, p. 2, SROWA 1947/0477/4.
25 *Workers' Star*, 7 February 1947, p. 5, 'Native Arrests Rouse Strong Perth Protest'.
26 Mason to McBeath, 22 January 1947, SROWA 1947/0477/3–4.
27 Coverley to McBeath, 31 January 1947, SROWA 1947/0477/5.
28 Mason to McBeath, 22 January 1947, p. 2, SROWA 1947/0477/4.
29 *Swan Express* (Midland Junction), 2 June 1938, p. 2.
30 Bonham to Secretary for Railways, 10 February 1947, p. 4, SROWA 1947/0477/9.

'Mr. Bonham, the local S.M. is most definitely with McLeod', Mason reported to McBeath, 'and McLeod spends most of his time in Bonham's office. Bonham is a badly frightened man now but I suggest that something could be done, in his own department, to make him cease being friendly with McLeod'.[31] This information was passed on from the Minister of Railways to the Commissioner of Railways, who also received complaints about Bonham from John Donnelly, an occasional lumper and labourer who was at that time employed as a general rouseabout or cook at Indee Station. 'Your officer (i.e. Station master – come Goods Warfinger) had the hide and the audacity to employ full-blooded natives on the jetty in Port Hedland', Donnelly complained to the Railways Commissioner. He described Bonham as an 'out and out red ragger'. 'You've read of the wonderful McLeod (Nigger man), well Bonham is his mate and no bone about it':

> As you will notice, Sir, this letter is duplicated and if nothing is done on the matter of natives and MacLeod [sic] on Railways and Jetty job, I will post this letter to the Sunday Times and Mirror, and add a little more to it. (This is no threat, but mere facts).[32]

Donnelly's views had sufficient currency amongst workers that, at the pick-up for work on the *Koolinda* on 25 January, four days after the *Dorrigo* incident, a call was made for 'those men who won't work with McLeod [to] stand out'. Only two men, both Aboriginal, stood by McLeod, and he was told that AWU men would not work with him in future.[33] This decision may have been influenced by the AWU leadership's anti-communist disapproval 'of the tactics of this individual', or may simply have reflected local outrage at 'Nigger Man' McLeod's role in challenging the rigid racialised social and economic structure of the north. These views were not universally held by non-Aboriginal workers, however. On 19 February, an AWU meeting overturned the decision as unconstitutional, and voted to support Murphy and other Aboriginal members by refusing to accept Mason's edict prohibiting the employment of non-exempt Aboriginal men on the wharf. They would refuse to work if these members were not given equal opportunity for jobs.[34]

---

31   Mason to McBeath, 22 January 1947, p. 2, SROWA 1947/0477/4.
32   Donnelly to J. A. Ellis, Commissioner of Railways, 30 January 1947, SROWA 1947/0477/1.
33   Bonham to Secretary for Railways, 10 February 1947, p. 3, SROWA 1947/0477/8.
34   *Workers' Star*, 28 February 1947, p. 5, 'Port Hedland Wharfies Reject Colour Bar'.

Donnolly's letter and Mason's report condemning Bonham's action in employing Mitchell, Monaghan, Coppin and Brown convinced the Western Australian Minister for Railways, William Marshall, that Bonham should be transferred from the area. 'I have no interest in Mr Bonham's associations', he wrote:

> as I think this is a personal matter, but I do take strong exception to the action which he adopted in regard to the dispute. I feel that it would be appropriate under the circumstances that Mr Bonham be removed to a station in closer proximity to the metropolitan area, where his activities can be more closely observed than is possible at the present moment.[35]

The 'action' for which Bonham was to be transferred was the engagement of the four 'half-caste' men to fill a labour shortfall, something he had done many times during the war. The writer for the *Swan Express* may have thought that his 'amiable and generous disposition' would bring him music wherever he went, but it did not do so in Port Hedland. His crime was not that of being political, but of being apolitical in a situation in which visible, hardline opposition to the Aboriginal strike and to McLeod was expected, particularly from a government officer. Asked to provide an explanation for the information contained in Mason's report and Donnelly's letter, he wrote a detailed account of the events of 21 January, disputing Mason's version on many points. He dismissed Donnelly as a drunkard who struggled to keep a job, but expressed amazement at the hostility of Mason's report.[36] 'Constable Mason has only been here a few weeks relieving Const. Fletcher', he wrote. 'I cannot understand the tone of his correspondence. I have not had any misunderstanding with him, and fail to understand why he should write in such a vindictive manner, unless it is to make a big fellow of himself'.[37]

Both he and McLeod denied the accusation that they were friends. 'Any conversations I have had with Mr. Bonham have always been of local A.W.U. matters, as I was previously acting rep. for the local section', McLeod told the Department of Railways. 'Apart from this I have had absolutely no association with Mr. Bonham'.[38] He also refuted suggestions that Bonham was 'a member of our party':

---

35   Minister for Railways Marshall to the Commissioner of Railways Ellis, 5 February 1947, SROWA 1940/1194/12.
36   Bonham to Secretary for Railways, 6 February 1947, SROWA 1947/0477/2.
37   Bonham to Secretary for Railways, 10 February 1947, p. 1, SROWA 1947/0477/6.
38   McLeod to Secretary for Railways, 10 February 1947, SROWA 1947/0477/9.

It would be quite illogical to suggest that Mr. Bonnham [sic] is a communist for although when opportunity occurs I certainly discuss political aspects and trends, I have been unable to get a response from Mr. Bonnham nor much opportunity to do so.[39]

Bonham also denied being politically aligned with McLeod. 'I have no communist interest whatsoever, never have, and not likely to, having never been interested in the movement as what little I know of this does not appeal to me'.[40]

While the question of Bonham's suitability to remain in Port Hedland was passed back and forth between government departments in the early months of 1947, the Western Australian Railway Officers' Union and the state executive of the Australian Labor Party criticised the Minister of Railways for calling for Bonham's removal without hearing that officer's side of the story.[41] However, the Labor Government's loss at the state elections on 15 March meant that the matter was left in abeyance for some time. Meanwhile, McBeath instructed Native Affairs Inspector Tom Jensen 'to endeavour to obtain some concrete evidence of the relationship existing between Bonham and McLeod', although he knew that such evidence was unlikely to be found.[42] Nevertheless, he assured the new Minister for Native Affairs, Robert Ross (Ross) McDonald, that he knew Mason to be 'completely reliable' and recommended that Bonham be transferred.[43]

Seven years previously, when McBeath had been the Travelling Inspector of Native Affairs for the northern region, it was he who had dealt with Mason's brutal assault on an Aboriginal man at the Freney Oil Bore in the Kimberley. McBeath had been concerned that the attack indicated that Mason was 'the wrong type' for a police role that took him 'over the range' into Aboriginal country which was still sparsely settled by whites. Referring to a police massacre of Aboriginal people in the Forrest River area some years previously, he wrote that 'if he will adopt the above tactics in the presence of twenty or so

---

39   McLeod to Secretary for Railways, 10 February 1947, SROWA 1947/0477/9.
40   Bonham to Secretary for Railways, 10 February 1947, p. 4, SROWA 1947/0477/9.
41   McBeath to Coverley, 24 January 1947, SROWA 1947/0477/4; E. J. Hood, Deputy Commissioner of Railways, 19 February 1947, SROWA 1947/0477/10; J. A. Cooke, Acting General Secretary of the State Executive of the ALP to Minister for Railways Marshall, 10 March 1947, SROWA 1947/0477/12; Minister for Railways Marshall to ALP State Executive, 11 March 1947, SROWA 1947/0477/12; F. B. Bone, Acting General Secretary of the State Executive, Western Australian Railway Officers' Union, to the ALP State Executive, 26 February 1947, SROWA 1947/0477/11.
42   McBeath to McDonald, 4 June 1947, SROWA 1947/0477/13.
43   McBeath to McDonald, 4 June 1947, SROWA 1947/0477/13.

white people, then I am afraid that the Police Department is going to be faced with a similar situation to that of Forrest River Mission in the year 1926'. Nevertheless, he had recommended that the Police Department deal leniently with Mason 'to prevent the blasting of this young man's hopes and ambitions for a police career'. He was sure that Minister for the North West Coverley 'would be pleased to interest himself in this matter'. Coverley apparently had been pleased to do so. No punitive action had been taken against Mason. He was not transferred from the Kimberley, and had continued to conduct patrols 'over the range'.[44] Yet both Mason and McBeath now felt comfortable calling for Bonham to be transferred from Port Hedland for having 'the hide and the audacity' to employ Aboriginal men on the wharf.

While the question of Bonham's suitability to continue as station master and wharfinger at Port Hedland awaited the consideration of the new Minister for Native Affairs, further criticism of Bonham's conduct was made by Tom Jensen, the police officer recently seconded to the Department of Native Affairs as Inspector of Native Affairs in the north. 'The Station Master here a Mr Bonham who is responsible for the Railway has apparently reached that stage in life where his position as a responsible Officer has begun to wane', Jensen wrote. This was evident, Jensen believed, in the fact that strikers were permitted to travel without restriction on the Port Hedland to Marble Bar train. 'The fact of natives interchanging districts is a common occurrence', Jensen wrote:

> and one to my mind that is in no way conducive to the general welfare of the Native, as the main reason for travel is to break in some way the Laws of the Land per medium of direct disregard of the Native Administration Act.[45]

Aboriginal people had been using the railway for transport since the establishment of the service in 1911, and a brake van added to the train in 1938 had included a seatless compartment for Aboriginal passengers.[46] Bonham's failing, in the eyes of Jensen and others, was not that he permitted Aboriginal passengers, but that he failed to oppose the strike by prohibiting strikers from using the service. Jensen was also critical of Bonham's continued employment of McLeod. 'Apart from allowing free access as stated', Jensen wrote to McBeath:

---

44   Documents relating to the incident at Freney Oil Bore can be found in SROWA 1940/0324.
45   Jensen to McBeath, 30 April 1947, p. 4, SROWA 1947/0305/112.
46   *Western Mail*, 22 December 1938, p. 56.

he also encourages the main purge and ... cause of this trouble Don McLeod to further his preachings by giving him work that is right on the Railway property and within a couple of hundred yards of the Railway Station. This is a matter Sir that I consider you could take up with the Commissioner of Railways with a view to having these anomalies [sic] rectified.[47]

I have found no official documents to indicate that a policy was adopted of debarring strikers from using the train, but Cranky (Kujupurra) told of an incident which may have occurred at this time and which indicates that an attempted prohibition was undermined by the action of railway workers. According to Cranky, he and a group of other strikers intended taking the train from Marble Bar to the Twelve Mile but were prevented from doing so by a police officer, probably Marshall. They walked to the siding at Eginbah Tanks in the hope of being able to board the train there, but the railway guard on board had been instructed not to pick up *marrngu*:

> Right, we went Twelve Mile, and the policeman *kalungarnarra*, he didn't want us to go to Twelve Mile. He didn't let us go to Twelve Mile. He stopped the train.
>
> 'Don't pick up anyone', one gardener bloke policeman, *wurrarnajanaku* policeman [i.e. he told the guard]. *Yanayirni nganarna jinangu yanayirni* [i.e. we went on foot] right up Eginbah Tank, where the workers, railway mob was there. We camp there. Righto, train coming from Marble Bar, we chuck our blanket, and the whitefella, gardener bloke on the train, he tell us to 'Pull your blanket down'.
>
> Righto, so we, poor fellas, put us blanket down.
>
> Ah, all those workers come. 'What happen?'
>
> 'Oh this fella wouldn't take us to Twelve-Mile. He chucked us blanket down'.
>
> 'Ah'. He went see the boss.
>
> 'Alright, well tell them boys to chuck his blanket back to truck, chuck'm back'.
>
> That fella looked fucking small, whitefella.[48]

---

47 Jensen to McBeath. 30 April 1947, p. 4, SROWA 1947/0305/112.
48 Cranky (Kujupurra), recorded by Anne Scrimgeour, 25 June 1993, AIATSIS collection, soundfile 'Kujupurra 9'.

The reversal of the prohibition on strikers using the train following the intervention of the railwaymen, some of whom were probably Aboriginal, is evidence of a level of support for the strike from other workers. Practical support of this nature was patchy, however. The resolution made in February by the Port Hedland branch of the AWU to contest the edict debarring non-exempt Aboriginal people from employment on the wharf was put to the test a few months later, when a young Aboriginal man named Ronald Thompson was picked up for work loading wool on the MV *Kybra*.

Thompson was born in Geraldton of mixed-descent parents and was educated at North Perth State School. In the summer of 1946–47, he and his wife were living in Mt Magnet and came under the notice of Constable Tom Webb, the officer who was to be so vigilant in keeping Wally Cameron, Avy Curley and other Aboriginal people out of town a few months earlier. As Thompson was not employed, he was ordered by Webb to leave town. The parents of Thompson's wife, Beryl, worked at Bamboo Creek in the Marble Bar area, so the couple travelled north and Thompson worked for a while at Mt Edgar Station.[49] He later shifted to Port Hedland and stayed with Vince Clarke. Constable Fletcher, now returned from leave, reported that Thompson had 'been frequently seen in the company of D. W. McLeod'.[50] Learning on 20 June that Thompson, a 'native-in-law' as he did not have a Certificate of Exemption from the Act, had obtained work on the wharf, Fletcher threatened Bonham with prosecution if he again employed an Aboriginal man without a permit. Fletcher allowed Thompson to complete his day's work, but instructed him not to present for work the following day.[51]

McLeod brought up the matter at an AWU meeting, and, in accordance with the decision made in February, the men agreed to issue Thompson with a union ticket and, when he presented for work, to strike if he was not picked up.[52]

Thompson was one of eight men picked up to load wool when the *Kybra* was again in dock on 9 July 1947. He was put off, however, when Bonham realised who he was. Other men picked up for work that day, five Aboriginal men and McLeod, refused to work unless Thompson was reinstated. The eighth man, a *walypila* named Jim Rafferty, opposed the decision to stop work but fell in with the decision of the meeting. Fearing prosecution if he reinstated Thompson, but needing to get the *Kybra* loaded, Bonham rang

---

49   McBeath to Fletcher, 14 July 1947, SROWA 1947/0305/132–133.
50   Fletcher to McBeath, 9 July 1947, p. 1, SROWA 1947/0305/131.
51   Fletcher to McBeath, 9 July 1947, SROWA 1947/0305/131–132.
52   Fletcher to McBeath, 9 July 1947, SROWA 1947/0305/131–132.

Fletcher for assistance. Fletcher assured the striking men that Bonham would indeed be prosecuted if Thompson was engaged. It seems unlikely that the threatened prosecution would have stood up in court; Thompson was clearly covered by the proviso to section 18. The men still refused to return to work without him.[53]

Bill Hegney, state president of the AWU, was in Port Hedland that day, campaigning to be returned as the Member for Pilbara in an upcoming by-election following a tied result in the state election of 15 March.[54] Called in to break the impasse, he urged the men to refer the matter to the general secretary of the AWU, Charlie Golding, who would take the issue up with Acting Commissioner McBeath. Hegney shared Golding's anti-communist opposition to McLeod, and was no doubt aware that any instructions arising from discussions between Golding and McBeath would prioritise the maintenance of settler authority over equal employment opportunities for Aboriginal people. He urged the men to return to work without Thompson while they waited for instructions from Perth. McLeod countered this with the suggestion that, while waiting for word from Golding and McBeath, they return to work *with* Thompson, a suggestion opposed by the other non-Aboriginal unionist, Rafferty, who urged the meeting to respect Hegney's authority as AWU president and follow his advice to return to work without Thompson. Seeing no resolution to the issue, the Aboriginal workers agreed to accept Hegney's advice. McLeod bowed to the will of the majority, but criticised Rafferty as 'a crawler' for siding with Hegney and for not understanding 'the significance of the struggle'. The men returned to work without Thompson. Before Thompson left, Hegney asked to see his union ticket and tore it to pieces.[55]

Fletcher urged McBeath to take steps to prevent Thompson gaining employment on the wharf. He believed that the dispute had been created by McLeod for his own political ends, and that the Department's ability to oppose the Aboriginal strike would be weakened if Thompson was granted

---

53 Fletcher to McBeath, 9 July 1947, SROWA 1947/0305/131–132; McLeod, draft autobiography, chapter 3, pp. 7–8, Marchant Trust Collection, UWA MS118 series 1 file 13.

54 Hegney had tied with Port Hedland resident Len Taplin, who ran as an Independent. Both men had won 234 votes, but the returning officer in Marble Bar gave the casting vote to Hegney. The by-election, announced after Taplin appealed to the Court of Disputed Returns, returned Hegney to the seat.

55 Fletcher to McBeath, 9 July 1947, SROWA 1947/0305/131–132; McLeod, draft autobiography, chapter 3, p. 8, Marchant Trust Collection, UWA MS118 series 1 file 13.

AWU membership. Confident and articulate, Thompson would be a valuable asset to McLeod as an AWU member, Fletcher argued.

> There is no shortage of labour here now, and there is no need for Thompson's inclusion in the pickups. He has not been normally engaged in that class of labour, and I see no reason why he should be so now. In this district we have suffered sufficiently through the machinations of McLeod, without giving him an extra string on us.[56]

Wharf labour was the only employment available to Thompson in Port Hedland and, since only employed people were allowed to remain in town, exclusion from wharf employment meant exclusion from the town. 'If he is unable to obtain labour there, he will have to leave town', Fletcher wrote, 'and will not then be the menace he is now, but if he is allowed to work there, I shall be powerless in these matters in future'.[57]

McBeath was in full agreement. He informed Fletcher that, in accordance with the decision made by AWU leadership in collusion with the Department at the time of the January dispute, Thompson, as a 'native-in-law', was ineligible for union membership, and could not be employed on the wharf without a permit.[58]

Ron Thompson appears to have left the area, hounded from Port Hedland by Fletcher as he had been hounded from Mt Magnet by Webb. The lives of men like Thompson were entirely in the hands of the police and the Department. Permit regulations, in practice if not in law, gave police and the Department total control over the employment of Aboriginal people and, consequently, over their place of residence. As no employment could be obtained without departmental consent, low-paid or unpaid station work was often the only option available, even for people who lacked the skills and knowledge of station-born workers. Only a Certificate of Exemption from the Act could enable Thompson to gain a degree of control over his own life, but his short association with McLeod and his involvement in the 9 July dispute on the Port Hedland wharf would probably have disqualified him if he had applied for exemption. While Pilbara strikers were breaking free from settler control, the Department's determination to shore up the wall of settler resistance to their activism impacted negatively on other Aboriginal people through a hardening of police and departmental responses to any perceived challenge to its authority to control Aboriginal lives.

---

56   Fletcher to McBeath, 9 July 1947, p. 2, SROWA 1947/0305/132.
57   Fletcher to McBeath, 9 July 1947, p. 2, SROWA 1947/0305/132.
58   McBeath to Fletcher, 14 July 1947, SROWA 1947/0305/132–133.

'The Hide and the Audacity to Employ Full-Blooded Natives...'

The Port Hedland branch of the AWU had failed in its attempt to achieve greater employment opportunities for Aboriginal people. It also lacked the necessary solidarity among its rank and file to achieve a dismantling of discriminatory employment practices, particularly in the face of the closing of the ranks of the police, the Department and AWU leadership in a united determination to suppress both communist activism and Aboriginal dissent. Perhaps reflecting McLeod's frustration at his inability to achieve solid support from unionists, disagreement within the union developed into physical punches at a big pick-up of casual workers the following morning when Hegney held an AWU meeting to explain his actions of the previous day. When McLeod attempted to speak at the meeting, he and Rafferty came to blows, and were arrested by Fletcher and charged with creating a disturbance. At the hearing of the charges, McLeod pleaded not guilty and made light of the incident in presenting his own defence. An article in the *Northern Times*, entitled 'Rafferty Rules', stated that 'the cases were dealt with joyfully'. McLeod argued that, since he was a democrat and believed that everyone should have a say, 'and since the other bloke wanted a say and could only express himself with his [fists]', he had engaged him in debate. The *Northern Times* reported that 'McLeod advanced the unusual though rather logical defence that he couldn't enter into physical contest and at the same time, carry on intelligent discourse and being perplexed chose to have the fight first and do his talking afterwards'. Both men were fined £3 with 3/- costs.[59]

It was not until 24 July that Minister Ross McDonald looked into the question of Bonham's suitability to continue in the role of station master in Port Hedland. Although he considered Bonham's political views irrelevant to the issue, and although he believed that 'any man is entitled to offer for and receive and obtain employment if he is a reasonable worker and is prepared to observe the laws of the country and is not a source of trouble or loss to the community', he nevertheless agreed that Bonham should be transferred. 'Constable Mason appears to have been rightly concerned with his duty to administer the *Native Administration Act* and Regulations in relation to the employment of natives', he wrote:

> I should think that, in a town like Port Hedland, where natives are relied upon for work in the town and district and at the port, it was of importance that the provisions of the law as to employment of natives should be carefully observed.

---

59 'Rafferty Rules', *Northern Times*, 18 July 1947, p. 4; McLeod, draft autobiography, chapter 3, p. 8, Marchant Trust Collection, UWA MS118 series 1 file 13.

> It seems to me that, at Port Hedland, it would be a material part of the officer-in-charge of the Government Railways and the officer-in-charge of Police to work in close co-operation in this respect. There appears to have been an absence of this co-operation and I consider that the responsibility for this must be attributable mainly, or wholly, to the officer-in-charge of the Railways.[60]

He recommended that Bonham be shifted to another location and a more 'co-operative' officer be put in charge of the railway at Port Hedland. Bonham was not transferred, but retired four months later.[61]

The victimisation of Alf Bonham for having 'the hide and the audacity' to employ Aboriginal strikers was motivated in part by a fear of communism, but also by an imperative to maintain settler solidarity in the face of persistent efforts by Aboriginal people to push against the legislative, administrative and feudalistic mechanisms of colonial domination. In the circumstances of the strike, fear of communism wove itself around an anxiety to maintain racial barriers and added a further complication to union attempts to reconcile worker solidarity with the need to maintain a united front against Aboriginal incursion into settler physical, social and economic spaces.

But even as these events were being played out on the Port Hedland waterfront, legal challenges mounted in the courts were causing cracks to appear in the wall of settler control.

---

60   McDonald to McBeath, 24 July 1947, SROWA 1947/0477/14.
61   *Northern Times*, 21 November 1947, p. 5.

Chapter 16

'No Iron Curtain'

The High Court Appeals, March 1947

In Western Australia's struggle to maintain control over Aboriginal people, and in the strikers' struggle to maintain their independence, a great deal hinged on the outcome of the legal appeals mounted against the convictions of Dooley, Clancy McKenna, Don McLeod and Rev. Peter Hodge for breaches of Western Australia's *Native Administration Act 1936*. In early 1947, with the cases due to be heard by the High Court of Australia, the Department held its collective breath in hope that the appeals would fail and that McLeod would finally be made to serve the three-month jail sentence imposed by the magistrate in Port Hedland in August 1946. In expectation of this, the Department was poised to take advantage of McLeod's imprisonment by taking swift and decisive action to end the strike, removing 'ringleaders' to institutions in the south and returning the rest of the strikers to station employment.

McLeod had received the custodial sentence on 23 August 1946 when he and Rev. Peter Hodge were arrested for meeting *marrngu* in the scrub near the Twelve Mile, but his sentence had been held over awaiting the outcome of an appeal to Western Australia's Supreme Court. Also subject to appeal was McLeod's earlier conviction, for which he had received a fine of £50, imposed by Maurice Harwood in Port Hedland on 21 June 1946, for counselling Aboriginal people to leave their lawful service without the consent of a protector. Fred Curran, the Perth lawyer engaged by the Committee for Defence of Native Rights, obtained a judicial order granting McLeod leave to appeal to the WA Supreme Court against his prison sentence, and also granting leave for McLeod, Clancy McKenna and Dooley to appeal their convictions for enticing workers from their employment.[1] Peter Hodge's conviction for breach of section 39 of the *Native Administration Act*, for which he had been fined £10, was also up for appeal.

---

1   *Northern Times*, 23 August 1946, p. 1.

Section 39 of the Act made it was unlawful for anyone 'other than a superintendent or protector, or a person acting under the direction of a superintendent, or under a written permit of a protector, without lawful excuse':

> to enter or remain or be within or upon any place where natives are camped or where any natives may be congregated or in the course of travelling in pursuance of any native custom.
>
> Any person, save as aforesaid, who, without lawful excuse, the proof whereof shall lie with him, is found in or within five chains of any such camp shall be guilty of an offence against this Act: but no person shall be prosecuted for an offence under this section except by the direction of a Protector.

Hodge appealed his conviction on the grounds that, as secretary of the Committee for Defence of Native Rights, he had a lawful reason for meeting with Aboriginal people to investigate the conditions under which strikers were living. Since the meeting had been held at some distance from the Twelve Mile, it was also argued that he had not entered a place where natives were camped, and the natives were not congregating 'in pursuance of a native custom'.[2] In September 1946, when Judge Albert Wolff of Western Australia's Supreme Court refused to grant an order to review Hodge's conviction, Hodge applied to the Full Court of the WA Supreme Court for leave to appeal against Wolff's decision. This application was heard in mid-October by Chief Justice Sir John Dwyer and Supreme Court judge James Walker. Leave to appeal was granted and, with the application treated as the appeal itself, the appeal was dismissed.[3]

The WA Supreme Court's dismissal of Hodge's appeal centred on the semantic ambiguity inherent in the rider, appended to the first paragraph of section 39 in 1936, 'or where any natives may be congregated or in the course of travelling in pursuance of any native custom'. According to a narrow interpretation of the section, an offence was committed only if one entered an area where Aboriginal people were either travelling or congregated for ceremonial purposes. This was the interpretation that Curran insisted was the correct one. Hodge and McLeod had, however, been convicted on a *wider* interpretation of the wording of the section, according to which non-Aboriginal people were prohibited from entering a camping area, or any place where natives were congregated, or a place where they were travelling for

---

2 Hodge Peter Vere v. Needle Thomas William, NAA A10074 1947/5, p. 5; *West Australian*, 16 October 1946, p. 18, 'Cleric's Appeal'.

3 *West Australian*, 16 October 1946, p. 18, 'Cleric's Appeal'.

cultural purposes. In dismissing the appeal, Supreme Court judges Dwyer and Walker argued that it was this wider interpretation of the ambiguous section that must be applied. Their decision reinforced Western Australian settler priorities to maintain control over Aboriginal people through an effective set of legislative measures to segregate Aboriginal people from the non-Aboriginal population. To support this contention, they cited other sections of the Act which specifically prohibited Aboriginal people and non-Aboriginal people from sharing the same spaces and interacting with one another. Curran argued, on the other hand, that this wider interpretation could not have been intended by the legislators, as this would lead to a contravention of the section any time non-Aboriginal people found themselves in close proximity to two or more Aboriginal people – at a public place of entertainment, for example. The judges, however, found it entirely acceptable and consistent with Western Australia's Aboriginal policy to prohibit Aboriginal and non-Aboriginal people from sharing public spaces. If the protection of Aboriginal people required segregation from the broader community, they argued, a prohibition on non-Aboriginal people coming into contact with groups of Aboriginal people wherever they were congregated was the only logical interpretation of section 39. 'The Legislature had in mind', Walker argued:

> as the Act itself indicates, that as far as possible natives shall be kept in their native environment, and that non-native persons shall not, without express permit or lawful excuse, consort or associate or have any dealings with natives in such environment. In other words, their natural environment shall, as far as possible, be kept free of non-native persons likely by their presence there to affect prejudicially the well-being and care of the natives.[4]

'For the effective administration of the Act', he wrote, 'the wider construction and effect must be given to the language of the section'.[5]

Hodge therefore applied to the High Court of Australia for special leave to appeal the Full Court's decision.[6] Because McLeod's conviction for breach of section 39 involved a prison sentence, his appeal was before Western Australia's Court of Criminal Appeal, awaiting the High Court's decision on Hodge's case.[7]

---

4   Hodge Peter Vere v. Needle Thomas William, pp. 31–32, NAA A10074 1947/5.
5   Hodge Peter Vere v. Needle Thomas William, p. 30, NAA A10074 1947/5.
6   *West Australian*, 15 November 1946, p. 13, 'Natives' Strike'.
7   *Sunday Times*, 13 October 1946, p. 5, 'Appeals to Full Court'.

Meanwhile, Justice Wolff had also heard appeals by McLeod against his other three convictions, and by McKenna and Dooley against theirs. His reasons for dismissing the appeals indicate that racist settler attitudes were held and reinforced by the Western Australian judiciary. All five convictions were for breach of section 47 of the *Native Administration Act*, which stated that 'any person who entices or persuades a native to leave any lawful service without the consent of a protector shall be guilty of an offence against the Act'. The convictions had arisen from the activities of the three men in the lead-up to the failed strike of 1 May, and McLeod had also been convicted for attempting to arrange a meeting of delegates from stations in the aftermath of the strike. The appeals focused on the words 'to leave', the appellants arguing that the 1 May strike had not involved workers leaving stations and that organising a meeting did not constitute enticing or persuading anyone to leave employment.

In dismissing the appeals, Justice Wolff expressed views in line with mainstream understandings of the strike as engineered by McLeod among essentially passive but gullible Aboriginal people. Although McLeod's 'avowed intention was to obtain an improvement in the natives' conditions', Wolff said, he appeared to have 'a more sinister purpose'.[8] Anti-communist fears, it seems, played a part in his decision. He determined that, even if Aboriginal workers had not physically left their place of employment, they had indeed been persuaded to leave their service:

> The word 'leave' in section 47 must be construed in the light of the service, and regard must also be had to the history of the section and the psychology of the native. It is well known that the native is childlike and easily prevailed on, and he often shows a disposition, without any outside influence, to leave his employment and 'go bush', and then come back when it suits him.[9]

Wolff concluded that 'the striking of these natives with the intention of staying away indefinitely from their work until their demands were satisfied' did indeed constitute a leaving of their employment and that, when McLeod sent 'emissaries' to invite natives to a meeting, he was attempting to entice or persuade them to leave their lawful service. He dismissed all five appeals,

---

8   Wolff, judgment, p. 1, McLeod Donald William v. Richards George Ronald, NAA A10078 1946/13 pt 1.

9   Wolff, judgment, p. 2, McLeod Donald William v. Richards George Ronald, NAA A10078 1946/13 pt 1.

and Curran subsequently appealed to the High Court of Australia to review this dismissal.[10]

With these five appeals, along with Hodge's, due to be heard by the High Court of Australia on 4 March 1947, the Western Australian Department of Native Affairs planned to take full advantage of McLeod's imprisonment to bring an end to the strike. There was some fear of striker responses to McLeod's imprisonment and, to prevent the anticipated escalation of strike action and demonstrations by the strikers when McLeod was arrested, arrangements were put in place to remove strike leaders immediately the High Court decision was announced.[11] In a plan that underestimated both the grassroots nature of the strike movement and the level of outside support that the movement had attracted, the Department identified leaders destined for removal to institutions in the south. Along with Dooley and Clancy McKenna, Constable Mason had named Ernie Mitchell, Mick Lee, Adam Barker, Peter Coppin, Tommy Sampie and Big Harry Davis as leaders at the Twelve Mile.[12] With Coverley campaigning throughout the Kimberley for the upcoming state election at this critical time, McBeath brought the matter to the attention of Premier Frank Wise, acting as Minister for the North West in Coverley's absence, to ensure that warrants for the removal of the leaders could be signed as soon as it became clear that the appeals had failed.[13] As the High Court hearings approached, McBeath and Acting Deputy Commissioner Laurie O'Neill held discussions with Constable Les Fletcher, who was preparing to return to Port Hedland following ten weeks' leave, and with Tom Jensen, the policeman preparing to take up a years' secondment as the Department's Travelling Inspector in the state's north.[14]

In considering the appeals on 3 March 1947, the Full Court of the High Court of Australia, comprising Chief Justice Sir John Latham, Sir George Rich, Sir Hayden Starke, Sir Owen Dixon and Justice Williams, concurred with the WA Supreme Court's ruling regarding interpretation of the phrase 'to leave any lawful employment' and, as the Department had hoped, dismissed

---

10 Wolff, judgment, p. 3, McLeod Donald William v. Richards George Ronald, NAA A10078 1946/13 pt 1; *Daily News*, 30 October 1946, p. 8, 'Two Appeals By McLeod Fail'; *West Australian*, 7 November 1946, p. 3, 'Natives' Strike. Conviction Appeals'; *Northern Times*, 22 November 1946, p. 12, 'Natives' Strike'; *West Australian*, 15 November 1946, p. 13, 'Natives' Strike, Further Litigation'.

11 Mason to McBeath, 26 February 1947, SROWA 1947/0305/50; McBeath to Wise, SROWA 1947/0305/44.

12 Mason to McBeath, 26 February 1947, p. 2, SROWA 1947/0305/51.

13 McBeath to Wise, SROWA 1947/0305/44.

14 McBeath, note, 3 March 1947, SROWA 1947/0220/1.

the appeals against Dooley, McKenna and McLeod's convictions for 'enticing and persuading'. The game changer, however, was the High Court's judgment setting aside Hodge's conviction for entering a place where Aboriginal people were congregated. The Court decided that, despite some ambiguity in the wording, the prima facie meaning of section 39 was that the prohibition applied only to areas where Aboriginal people were camped or where they were congregated in pursuance of a cultural activity. This was the most natural interpretation of the wording of the section, Judge Owen Dixon argued, unless the mind of the reader 'be controlled by some considerations external to the precise text or unless his sensibilities to English forms of speech have been dulled'. In other words, only the overriding assumption that the intention of the Act was the complete segregation of the Aboriginal population could have led to the section being interpreted as it had been interpreted by Western Australia's Supreme Court. Dixon described as 'gratuitous' the Supreme Court's assumption 'that the Legislature in adding the words in question to the original provision, as it did in 1936, had any policy in view beyond the exclusion of strangers when natives are carrying out any tribal or native custom'.[15] This judgment was unanimous, although the conservative judge Hayden Starke was less certain than his brother judges, suspecting that the High Court's interpretation weakened the Act by altering the meaning intended by the legislature. He felt, however, that this was 'not of any great importance' as it could be easily rectified by a slight rewording of that section of the Act.[16]

While the High Court considered these issues in Melbourne, and while the Department finalised plans for the removal of strike leaders and the return of other strikers to station employment if the decision was favourable, Pilbara pastoralists came together in Perth to decide on the conditions under which strikers would be re-employed. Most pastoralists were in Perth at that time of the year, when heavy wet-season rainfall brought station work to a halt. On 3 March, two Pilbara pastoralists – the managing director of Mundabullangana Pastoral Company, Gordon Craig, and Rob Lukis, the manager of Munda Station – discussed the situation with McBeath, O'Neill, Fletcher and Jensen, and agreed that the time had come for pastoralists to approach the strikers to make an offer of wages and conditions. They arranged a meeting with all affected pastoralists in Perth at the time, planned for 5 March, when the outcome of the High Court deliberations would probably be known and a definite way forward could be agreed upon. If the High Court decision was

---

15   Dixon, judgment, Hodge Peter Vere v. Needle Thomas William, NAA 10074 1947/5.
16   Starke, judgment, Hodge Peter Vere v. Needle Thomas William, NAA 10074 1947/5.

favourable, and if McLeod and the strike leaders could be removed from the equation, the return of workers could be arranged on terms that suited pastoralists.[17]

On 4 March, a meeting of thirteen Pilbara pastoralists and the state secretary of the Pastoralists Association, H. R. C. Adkins, prepared a proposal, for discussion with the Department, of the conditions under which they were prepared to re-employ strikers. Although the *Native Administration Act* made provisions for employing Aboriginal people under agreement, such agreements were rarely entered into. Pastoralists now proposed to revert to the use of signed agreements, with the onus falling on the Department to 'take all the necessary steps to ensure that the parties to agreements faithfully carry out the conditions of such agreements'. In place of the feudalistic relationship that had existed between pastoralists and Aboriginal workers before the strike, signed agreements, policed by the Department, would ensure continued pastoralist control over poorly paid workers. The proposal did nothing to address the grievances and demands of the strikers and was clearly formulated on the assumption that the High Court judgment would enable pastoralists to again call the shots. Wages would be increased by 'up to 50%' of pre-strike rates, with a maximum of 30/- per week for musterers, a proposal well short of the universal basic wage of £2 per week demanded by the strikers. Under this arrangement, workers who had received no wages before the strike, including most women, would still be unpaid. The proposal made no mention of the provision of food and other necessities, undertaking only 'as far as practicable to stock such stores for sale at reasonable prices to native employees as are desired by them and are conducive to good health and within their capacity to purchase', suggesting that wages would not include keep. Concessions to strike demands for accommodation could not have been more equivocal, the proposal stating 'that the Department of Native Affairs be informed of employers' willingness to discuss the question of the provision of a suitable standard of accommodation for native employees'. The proposal also called on the Department to remove from stations, on request, any Aboriginal people considered by management to be 'undesirable' and to 'take steps to restrict the movement of itinerant native gamblers'. Had this proposal been adopted, Aboriginal workers would have been considerably worse off than before the strike.[18]

---

17 McBeath, note, 3 March 1947, SROWA 1947/0220/1.
18 Proposal formulated by meeting of pastoralists, Perth, 4 March 1947, SROWA 1943/0621/32–33.

The following day, 5 March, morning newspapers carried reports of the High Court's dismissal of Hodge's conviction.[19] With McLeod's appeal against his prison sentence yet to be heard, pastoralists took their proposals for discussion with the Department of Native Affairs that day with much less confidence in their ability to dictate conditions under which Aboriginal strikers would be re-employed. It was through newspaper reports that the Department first learned of the High Court determination, and the information was sufficiently concerning to prompt Commissioner Bray, still on sickness and long service leave, to send an anxious telegram to Coverley in the Kimberley town of Derby, informing him of the news.[20] It was another three weeks before the implications of the High Court decision for McLeod's prison sentence became certain, however. On 27 March, Western Australia's Court of Criminal Appeal ruled that McLeod's case involved 'exactly the same transaction and circumstances' as the Hodge case, and the same decision must therefore apply. The Court had no choice but to overturn McLeod's conviction and three-month prison sentence for breach of section 39.[21]

It was a highly significant outcome for the strike movement, putting an end to the Department's plan to remove strike leaders while McLeod was imprisoned. It was now possible for McLeod to interact more freely with the strikers, although he was still prohibited from entering Aboriginal camping or ceremonial areas. The decision effectively dismantled a key mechanism of departmental control over Aboriginal interaction with non-Aboriginal people, and the principal means by which the Department believed it could reduce McLeod's influence in the Pilbara. McBeath wrote anxiously to Coverley, overstating the implications of the decision: 'The position now is that McLeod or any other person may have access to camping natives', he wrote, 'provided they have lawful excuse and natives are not travelling in pursuance of a tribal custom'.[22]

The decision was hailed as a victory for Aboriginal people in Western Australia more generally. In a *Sunday Times* article headed 'No Iron Curtain Between White and Black Australians', Curran spoke of the undemocratic absurdity of legislation which prohibited 'a white man from talking to a group of 3 natives in the street, which were the circumstances when McLeod, on

---

19 *West Australian*, 5 March 1947, p. 12, 'Appeal Upheld. Ministers Work Among Natives'.
20 Bray to Coverley, telegram, 5 March 1947, SROWA 1947/0305/52.
21 *Daily News*, 27 March 1947, 'Don McLeod's Appeal Upheld', SROWA 1947/0305/70.
22 McBeath to Coverley, 28 March 1947, SROWA 1947/0305/74.

one occasion, was arrested'. He said the High Court decision had 'established the right of natives to have normal contact with whites on lawful matters'.[23]

The *Workers' Star* called the decision 'a milestone of progress and equality in Australian history'. 'The Committee for Defence of Native Rights, who rallied the whole Trade Union movement behind the native strike in Pt. Hedland have, by their determined and courageous fight, beaten the reactionaries to their knees', the *Workers' Star* announced triumphantly, and congratulated 'the Committee's fighting lawyer, Mr. F. Curran, for his capable handling of the case'.[24]

The court case also had implications for the Department's practice of interpreting Native Affairs legislation in accordance with its own priorities, without feeling the need to adhere strictly to the letter of the law. As we have seen, the Department, in its use of work permit regulations to control Aboriginal people by controlling their access to employment, disregarded the proviso that specifically stated that the regulation did not apply to Aboriginal men of mixed descent. While the Department continued to interpret legislation to suit its own purposes in other parts of the state, it found that in the Pilbara, for the first time, legislation needed to be applied according to the letter of the law. In September 1947, for example, Sergeant Bernie McGeary, who replaced Les Fletcher as officer in charge of the Port Hedland Police Station, found himself unable to prevent town businesses giving casual employment to 'half-caste' men. McGeary would normally have prevented Aboriginal people from working in town by threatening businesses with prosecution if they employed natives without a permit, whether or not the workers were covered by the proviso. Now he had to be sure that he had clear legal grounds for taking such action. McLeod had been making inquiries about employment for Aboriginal AWU members who were covered by the proviso, and McGeary believed he was planning to challenge the Department's across-the-board application of the regulations. McGeary feared that these short-term jobs in town were 'the thin edge of the wedge' in breaking through departmental control of Aboriginal labour, but the success of McLeod's appeal had shown that settler solidarity could not be relied on to ensure that courts interpreted legislation in such a way as to ensure the maintenance of settler control.[25] McBeath agreed with McGeary that application of permit regulations to 'half-caste' men would not stand legal challenge, and that nothing could be done to prevent the men

---

23 *Sunday Times*, 16 March 1947, p. 6, 'No Iron Curtain between White and Black Australians'.
24 *Workers' Star*, 14 March 1947, p. 2, 'Natives Win Right to Organise'.
25 McGeary to McBeath, 18 September 1947, SROWA 1947/0305/146–147.

taking jobs in town.[26] The following year, the Department again found its hands tied when McLeod threatened to take the matter to court if permit regulations were used to prevent him working with brothers Rob and Sandy Brown on a fishing operation. The Department admitted internally that 'his grounds would be sound', as the men were 'half caste'.[27] In the Pilbara, settler control and mechanisms for excluding Aboriginal people were being eroded.

---

26   McBeath to McGeary, 7 October 1947, SROWA 1947/0305/163.
27   McBeath to McDonald, 3 June 1948, SROWA 1948/0732/4a.

Chapter 17

'The Situation Is Ripe for a Complete Reorientation of Official Thinking'

Ross McDonald and Aboriginal Autonomy, April 1947

Throughout Australia in the post-war years, a growing body of thought about the nature of Aboriginality and possibilities for Aboriginal incorporation into the fabric of Australian social and economic life brought pressure for change in the administration of Aboriginal affairs. While Bob Coverley was the minister in charge, the Western Australian Department of Native Affairs held the door firmly closed against the current of new ideas, maintaining that its approach was 'grounded on years of practical experience', and not on the ideas of 'dreamers and theorists'.[1] But even while the Department digested the significance of the success of the McLeod and Hodge appeals, the state elections of 15 March 1947 brought a change of government, and the appointment of a Minister for Native Affairs who called for the door to be opened on alternative approaches in the post-war administration of Aboriginal people in the state.

After fourteen years of Labor government, the Liberal–Country Party coalition formed government in April, and eight years of Coverley's overtly pro-pastoralist ministerial oversight of Aboriginal affairs as Minister for the North West came to an end. The state's first ministry of Native Affairs was created, and barrister and King's Council Robert Ross (Ross) McDonald became its first minister. Member for West Perth in the Legislative Assembly, Ross McDonald had been leader of the Western Australian National Party from 1938, overseeing its incorporation into the Liberal Party in 1945. In 1946, he had relinquished leadership of the party to Ross McLarty, who became premier in 1947, while McDonald took on the responsibilities of Attorney General and Minister for Police and Native Affairs. His appointment

---

1   *West Australian*, 23 November 1944, p. 3.

signalled the possibility of change in the administration of Aboriginal affairs in the state. During the previous two years, he had, on a number of occasions, called for the adoption of a more constructive and nationally coordinated approach along lines being advocated by the Professor of Anthropology at Sydney University, A. P. Elkin.

In the 1940s, Elkin was a leading advocate for Aboriginal policy reform based on new understandings of the nature of human difference. Western Australia's 'protection' policy was based on the widely-held assumption that Aboriginal people were inherently and immutably different from the rest of Australia's population. Although well suited to pastoral work, they were believed to lack the mental capacity to cope with other spheres of modern life. Fair treatment involved protection through control and segregation. Alternative understandings of human difference as having social and cultural causes, rather than biological, had long been espoused within humanitarian and mission circles, but this understanding gained greater currency during the 1930s and 1940s, receiving scientific and academic affirmation. If Aboriginal disadvantage had social and cultural causes, it was argued, a new approach in Aboriginal administration was needed to address these issues and bring Aboriginal people into the fold of Australian society.

Another factor driving the impetus for change was Australia's growing population of Aboriginal people of mixed descent, for whom protection policies were felt to be inappropriate, but who remained socially and economically excluded from mainstream Australian life. Aboriginal activism across Australia was also driving change. In Western Australia, McDonald would refer to the 'growing industrial consciousness' of Aboriginal people as an imperative for reform.[2] That he did so highlights the significance of the Pilbara movement in bringing about pressure for change.

Aware of the need to formulate a new approach in Aboriginal administration, McDonald looked to the policy proposals outlined in Elkin's 1944 publication *Citizenship for the Aborigines: A National Aboriginal Policy*, as a way forward for Western Australia. In this, Elkin argued that 'the prevention of injustice and cruelty and of clash could never be realized by a policy of protection and prohibition', and urged the replacement of 'protective and really negative policy' with 'a truly positive one'.[3] His book became a blueprint for policy reform in

---

2   McDonald, Parliamentary Debates (Hansard), Western Australia: Legislative Assembly, 3 August 1949, p. 915.

3   A. P. Elkin, *Citizenship for the Aborigines: A National Aboriginal Policy*, Australasian Publishing Co., Sydney, 1944, p. 11

Western Australia as the Department prepared to move from 'protection' to a policy of 'assimilation'.

Ross McDonald had had little involvement in Aboriginal policy debate before 1944, when accusations surfaced about appalling conditions and treatment of Aboriginal people on government settlements. McDonald, then leader of the National Party and Leader of the Opposition, called for a federal Royal Commission to investigate the state of Aboriginal affairs in Western Australia and to propose changes.[4] The Western Australian Government, however, decided that the problems in Aboriginal administration were not a failure of policy but the result of a lack of funding, and, instead of a Royal Commission, asked the Commonwealth for a special grant over three years to enable the Department to undertake improvements. McLeod believed that Commonwealth funding would do nothing but strengthen the Department's ability to control and institutionalise Aboriginal people and to crush dissent. He told Elkin, 'it would be useful if the Federal Government could be encouraged to institute an inquiry on their own behalf before agreeing to advance the money which is asked for'. 'I have no hesitation', he wrote, 'in saying that if the plan as outlined by Mr Coverley is put into effect then it will be a sorry day for the natives in this state'.[5] The Federal Government, however, declined to accede to the funding request.[6]

Following the failure of McDonald's Royal Commission proposal, the Western Australian branch of the National Missionary Council planned to establish and finance its own inquiry. Since Elkin was, as his biographer notes, 'thoroughly entrenched as the expert on Aboriginal affairs', he seemed the ideal person to conduct such an inquiry.[7] Coverley initially agreed to provide information, statistics and permits to enter government reserves, and plans went ahead for Elkin and two assistants, Marie Reay and Grace Sitlington, to conduct a tour of the state in March 1946. Elkin, however, was concerned to ensure that recommendations arising from the survey would be taken up by the government.[8] He told Coverley that the survey would investigate and make recommendations as to 'whether, and how, forward steps could and,

---

4 *West Australian*, 23 November 1944, p. 3.
5 McLeod to Elkin, 26 December 1944, A. P. Elkin Papers, University of Sydney Archives, box 76, file 262.
6 'Native Affairs', *Albany Advertiser*, 15 August 1946, p. 1.
7 Tigger Wise, *The Self-Made Anthropologist: A Life of A. P. Elkin*, Allen and Unwin, North Sydney, 1985. In the early stages of planning, it was hoped that J. R. B. Love would also be involved in the inquiry.
8 A. P. Elkin, 'Australian Aboriginal and White Relations: A Personal Record', *Royal Australian Historical Studies Journal*, vol. 48, no. 3, 1962, p. 226.

perhaps in some cases, ought to be taken', and sought assurance from Coverley that his work would be 'welcomed by all concerned, and was going to be of some use'. He would need full departmental support.⁹

Coverley and Commissioner Bray became wary. They disagreed with Elkin's views on the need for policy reform. 'He has published some recent views on natives', Coverley wrote, 'but his ideas do not appeal to me, and it is doubtful whether they would be of service here, or acceptable to practical men such as station managers, and those accustomed to work with natives'.¹⁰ They saw the proposed survey as an excuse to gather evidence for further criticism of the Department. Coverley informed Elkin that, as his government was 'quite satisfied with the present administration of native affairs', the survey team would not be granted permission to enter government reserves and settlements.¹¹ Plans for the survey were dropped.

McDonald was disappointed to find that Elkin's inquiry was not going ahead, and criticised the Department for its 'failure to take advantage of the services and advice of so eminent an authority' and for failing to open the state's Aboriginal administration to the current of new ideas. 'I am keenly anxious to see the best possible brains in and outside this State and even those available outside this continent interested in the furthering of native affairs', he said. 'I think we should have a long-term policy regarding the natives for, say, the next 100 years'.¹²

McDonald's appointment as Minister for Native Affairs in April 1947, therefore, signalled a change in the Department's approach. The resignation of Francis Bray as Commissioner two weeks after McDonald took office was a further harbinger of change.¹³ Lew McBeath would almost certainly have become the new Commissioner had the Labor Party retained office; even before becoming Acting Commissioner in September 1946, he had frequently undertaken the duties of Commissioner as a result of Bray's ill health. O'Neill, too, anticipated becoming Deputy Commissioner on Bray's retirement.¹⁴ However, McDonald believed that the formulation of a long-term policy would require 'the best possible brains' and, despite McBeath's

---

9   Elkin to Coverley, 2 October 1945, SROWA 1945/0095/6.
10 Coverley, memo, undated, p. 2, SROWA 1945/0095/36.
11 Coverley to Elkin, 15 October 1945, SROWA 1945/0095/7; Coverley, memo, undated, p. 2, SROWA 1945/0095/36.
12 McDonald, Parliamentary Debates (Hansard), Western Australia: Legislative Assembly, 14 November 1946, p. 1981.
13 *Northern Times*, 2 May 1947, p. 4.
14 McBeath to McDonald, 13 October 1947, SROWA 1946/1220/48.

experience, and despite O'Neill's reputed expertise in 'handling the natives' as a Kimberley policeman and a Native Affairs Inspector, McDonald was clearly not convinced that they were the right men for the task ahead. McDonald held off appointing a new Commissioner, and McBeath and O'Neill continued in their roles in an acting capacity only. As an initial step towards reform, McDonald sought guidance from Elkin, and in July commissioned Magistrate F. E. A. (Frank) Bateman to conduct an inquiry into the current situation of Aboriginal affairs in the state and to make recommendations for departmental restructure and policy change. Elkin's influence on the direction of reform included recommendations to both McDonald and Bateman on the way forward for the Department.[15]

Meanwhile, Pilbara pastoralists lost no time in putting pressure on the new minister to prioritise their labour needs in any policy reform he might have in mind. On 2 April 1947, the day after McDonald took office, Frank Welsh, the owner of Warralong Station and Liberal Party member for North Province in the Legislative Council, met with McDonald to impress on him the urgency of taking steps to end the strike. He alerted McDonald to:

> the anxiety of the pastoralists in the Port Hedland district owing to the refusal of natives to undertake mustering on the stations. As shearing is due to commence within a very few weeks it seems possible, if the present difficulty continued, that stations would not be able to muster their sheep and would thereby be prevented from shearing, with loss to the State and personal loss to the stations.[16]

It was a clear admission that Aboriginal labour was not a burden outweighing any benefit to stations, as pastoralists had frequently claimed, but was, rather, essential to the operation of the pastoral industry. Pastoralists knew now that the strike was not going to peter out as expected, undermined by hunger, police intimidation and imprisonment. Hopes that McLeod's prison sentence would enable leaders to be removed and settler authority restored had also come to nothing. At Moolyella, *marrngu* had dispersed into working parties, camping in small groups on tin-bearing areas. About eighty strikers were based at the Twelve Mile, with other groups camped along the coast. Clancy McKenna, recently released after serving a two-month jail sentence, had a group of workers

---

15   Elkin, for example, sent McDonald reports and documents relating to the New South Wales Aborigines' Welfare Board. Acting Secretary of Aboriginal Welfare Board, Chief Secretary's Office, to McDonald, 5 November 1947; McDonald to Elkin, 1 October 1947, SROWA S3841 cons769 3.

16   McDonald, memo, 14 April 1947, SROWA 1947/0305/93.

collecting kangaroo and goat skins on De Grey Station, and another group, camped at Box Soak on Strelley Station under Ernie Mitchell's leadership, was also hunting for skins. Mick Lee and about twelve strikers were fishing and gathering mother-of-pearl shell with recently-purchased boats.[17] Despite hard times, *marrngu* had shown their determination to hold out for increased wages and better conditions.

The plan to employ non-Aboriginal station workers as a more efficient and less troublesome alternative to Aboriginal labour was proving a vain hope. A few young jackaroos had been employed from the south to replace striking workers. Constable Marshall reported in November 1946, for example, that Mulyie Station had 'lost a number of their natives through the strike, and two white lads are employed in their place'. On the neighbouring station of Warralong, the manager expressed 'the opinion that he will get better results by employing white lads' and had also employed two from the south 'to take the place of the natives that have left'.[18] However, stations found it difficult to attract sufficient numbers of white workers, and those that could be employed were unskilled and unused to the climate and conditions in the north. Just two weeks before McDonald took office, a young jackaroo, newly arrived from the south to work at Warralong, fell from his horse in the flooded Coongan River and was drowned. Without the tracking skills of Aboriginal workers, jackaroos were not effective musterers and, lacking the Aboriginal stockman's knowledge of the country, frequently became lost. In James Doughty's novel *The Green Stick,* a squatter says of stations that lost their workers, 'they're tryin' to carry on with white jackaroos from down south, at ten pounds a week an' their tucker - an' if they get out o' sight o' the homestead they get lost'.[19] Peter Coppin (Kangkushot) remembered with amusement that stations that employed boys from the south had to then employ *marrngu* to find them when they got lost. Many were only teenagers, and caring for them threw an extra burden of work on managers' wives already struggling with the lack of domestic labour.[20] For most, jackarooing was a short-term adventure. 'They are just tourists', Pilbara pastoralist David Johnston complained. 'They haven't time to learn their duties'. In contrast to the pre-strike claim that 'one white man was

---

17 Jensen to McBeath, 29 March 1947, SROWA 1947/0305/76.

18 Marshall patrol report, 10 November 1946, 1946/2538 v8.

19 Doughty, *The Green Stick,* p. 126.

20 Aubrey Alexander Hardy, statement to Committee Investigating Native Labour, p. 32, 7 May 1952, SROWA 1952/0830/94.

worth 10 blacks', Johnston stated that 'we can get white employees but their efficiency is only about 10%'.[21]

With mustering for the 1947 shearing season already underway, pastoralists finally conceded that some concession to strikers' demands would have to be granted. They hoped, however, that such concessions would be backed by the firm hand of departmental authority. Pastoralist–politician Frank Welsh urged McDonald to take immediate and decisive action to bring matters under control to enable mustering and shearing operations to be carried out. Further prosecution of McLeod was one possibility they discussed. Vince Clarke had accused McLeod of forging his (Clarke's) signature on an electoral register application, and Detective Sergeant Ron Richards, who had prosecuted McLeod for his activities in organising the strike the previous year, believed he could prove forgery. Welsh also suggested that, as McLeod was said to be working with strikers on a fishing project in their new boats, he should be prosecuted for employing Aboriginal people without a permit. He assured McDonald that, if strike leaders were removed to Moore River, other strikers would return to work.[22] A few days later, Gordon Craig, owner of Mundabullangana Station, and Bob Middleditch of Noreena Downs also met with McDonald to impress on him the urgency of taking action to return strikers to stations in time for the shearing.[23]

Under such pressure, McDonald undertook to resolve matters in the Pilbara by entering into negotiations with the strikers, something the Department had been previously unwilling to do. Acting Commissioner McBeath made plans to visit the Pilbara for this purpose, but Travelling Inspector Tom Jensen was instructed in the meantime to:

> exert your best efforts to induce the natives you are in contact with to return to their former employment. You will be quite in order in informing them that you are of the opinion that they will be granted increases in wages and better conditions than hitherto.[24]

Jensen visited the Twelve Mile on 5 April, Easter Saturday, just five days after McDonald took office. It was the first visit he had made to the camp. As most strikers were away fishing or hunting, he left instructions for everyone

---

21 *Truth*, 23 March 1947, p. 29; David Johnston, statement to Committee Investigating Native Labour, p. 11, 5 March 1952, SROWA 1952/0830/129.
22 McDonald, notes of meeting, 2 April 1947, SROWA S3841 cons769 1.
23 McDonald, note, 14 April 1947, SROWA 1947/0305/93.
24 McBeath to Jensen, 1 April 1947, SROWA 1947/0305/78.

to be present to discuss matters with him the following morning. The next day, he told a meeting of about fifty men that if they returned to work they would receive better conditions and an increase in wages. The strikers were interested. They had been on strike for eight months and this was the first time an official had approached them to negotiate a return to work in exchange for meeting wage and condition demands. They needed to be sure, however, that promises would be honoured. Their strength lay in united action, and this would be hard to maintain when they were dispersed throughout the stations. What guarantees would be given them, Clancy McKenna asked Jensen, that the promised wages and conditions would be provided if they returned? Tommy Sampie also sought assurances that ground they had won would not be undermined by a return to work. Would their organisation, the North-West Workers' Association, be recognised by the Department and government if workers returned to stations? he asked. Jensen replied that it would not, but if they returned to work under signed agreements, employers would be legally bound to provide wages and conditions agreed to by both parties. *Marrngu* had never heard of such employment agreements and were interested. Jensen told them to think the matter over, and that he would return the next morning with a book of agreement forms to explain the system more fully.[25]

The next day, Easter Monday – the day of the protest march through the main street of Mt Magnet, a thousand kilometres to the south – *marrngu* at the Twelve Mile learned more about the agreement system and expressed a willingness to negotiate with squatters to return to work under agreements to be signed by the employer, the worker and a Protector of Natives. But, just as Jensen felt that a general consensus to return to work had been reached, Sampie again raised the question of the recognition of their organisation. Not wanting the issue to obstruct the progress of his discussions, Jensen promised to put the matter before the Department. McKenna then requested that McLeod be allowed to be a fourth signatory to such agreements. It was a reasonable request. Most *marrngu* were illiterate, and Protectors of Natives had demonstrated a clear tendency to put the interests of pastoralists above those of Aboriginal workers. Jensen, however, said that this could not be done.

After discussing the matter among themselves, the strikers told Jensen that they would not return to work until their organisation was recognised. Jensen urged them to accept the agreement system on a trial basis, but McKenna insisted that:

---

25   Jensen to McBeath, 12 April 1947, SROWA 1946/1416/13–14.

'THE SITUATION IS RIPE...'

as they had stuck out for nine months, they would continue to stick out, and see what the natives still employed on the stations got in the way of better conditions and wages, and that they would carry on getting kangaroos and goats for their skins.[26]

Two large bundles of kangaroo and goat skins in the camp, recently obtained along the coast on De Grey Station by McKenna's work party, were evidence of the strikers' ability to continue holding out until their demands were met in full. Angry and frustrated, Jensen returned to Port Hedland and reported to the Department on the outcome of his efforts.[27] His previous interactions with Aboriginal people as a Kimberley policeman had involved telling, not asking, and he had had the power to ensure that his instructions were obeyed. To condescend to negotiate with Aboriginal people was concession enough, without having his offer rejected in this way. The only surviving fragment of Tommy Sampie's account of that day's meeting suggests that he may have expressed his frustration with angry threats before leaving the Twelve Mile. 'Don is the only man supporting the workers since we entered the strike', Sampie wrote after the meeting, 'and therefore we will stick to Don till we meet the bullets or anything that may happen'.[28]

On receipt of Jensen's report, and in light of urgent appeals made by Welsh and other Pilbara pastoralists, McDonald, McBeath and O'Neill met in Perth on 9 April to consider their best course of action. McDonald approved of McBeath's decision, made before he came to office, to visit the area to broker an agreement between pastoralists and strikers for a return to work. O'Neill was instructed to accompany him. The matter was considered sufficiently urgent to warrant chartering a special flight. The officers were instructed to inform strikers that the question of official recognition of the North-West Workers' organisation would be referred to the government, but that 'obviously any such request will carry less weight if it comes from a so-called organisation which is adversely affecting one of the chief industries on which the welfare of the district and the natives themselves depends'.[29] In other words, strikers would be told that if they returned to work and stopped

26   Jensen to McBeath, 12 April 1947, SROWA 1946/1416/13–14.
27   Jensen to McBeath, 12 April 1947, SROWA 1946/1416/13–14; Jensen, patrol journal, 5–7 April 1947, SROWA 1947/0127/11–12.
28   'From a written account, dated 7/3/47, by Thomas Sampey, Sect of the North-West Native Workers' Association of a meeting between Association members and the Department's Inspector at Port Hedland', quoted in *Barrier Daily Truth* (Broken Hill, NSW), 19 September 1947, p. 1, 'Rights of Aborigines'.
29   McDonald, memo, 14 April 1947, SROWA 1947/0305/93.

damaging the pastoral industry, they might have a chance of having their 'so-called' organisation recognised. If the strikers refused to return to station employment, however, McBeath would notify McDonald and 'consideration will then be given as to any further step that can be suitably taken in order to overcome the difficulty'.[30] Further steps to be considered presumably included removing leaders under ministerial warrant.

This course of action was already being urged by Jensen. He was frustrated by his inability to arrange a return to station work, blaming his failure on the intransigence of McKenna and Sampie. He recommended to McBeath that immediate application be made to McDonald for warrants to remove McKenna and Dooley, whose previous convictions for offences against the *Native Administration Act* would be sufficient grounds for their removal. He also wanted Tommy Sampie to be removed, but, as Sampie had no convictions, Jensen was uncertain 'in what light a suggestion re this native would be received'.[31] He believed that no arrangement for returning strikers to work could be achieved while McKenna, at least, remained in the area. Probably in reference to Wally Lund of the Native Hospital, under suspicion for his intention to appeal McKenna's sentence two months previously, Jensen suggested that removals should 'be effected as quietly as possible, as there appears to me to be an obvious possibility of a Departmental leak locally, and if the natives effected are made wise to what is going on that they may take [to] locating in the back country'.[32] He also wondered about the advisability of removing Ernie Mitchell, who was in charge of the Box Soak strikers' camp. He had not met Mitchell:

> but Mr. O'Neill may consider that he should be placed in the same category as those mentioned by me, and be dealt with in a similar manner. If this supposition is correct, I consider it would be the most advantageous move to make a clean sweep of the definite trouble makers all at once and clean the position up once and for all. It is my considered opinion then, that this matter can be brought to a satisfactory conclusion.[33]

There was also hope that a conviction carrying a prison sentence could be secured against McLeod, enabling the Department to establish sufficient

---

30   McDonald, memo, 14 April 1947, SROWA 1947/0305/93.
31   Jensen to McBeath, 12 April 1947, p. 2, SROWA 1946/1416/14.
32   Jensen to McBeath, 12 April 1947, p. 2, SROWA 1946/1416/14.
33   Jensen to McBeath, 12 April 1947, p. 2, SROWA 1946/1416/14.

control in time for the shearing. Jensen was given permission to hire a fishing launch to catch McLeod working with strikers in the new boats in open sea around Sandy Island and to lay charges against him for employing Aboriginal people without a permit.[34] Jensen learned, however, that the boats were registered in the names of Mick Lee and another striker, and that McLeod was not directly involved in the fishing and shelling operation. He was purchasing the strikers' pearl shell, which he sold on to a buyer in Onslow, but as he had a pearl-buyer's licence and submitted details of his financial dealings to the Department, as required by subsection 5 of section 34 of the *Native Administration Act 1936*, his financial relationship with the strikers was legal and above board.[35]

The Department still hoped that a resolution to the dispute could be achieved by discussion and negotiation, however. On 14 April 1947, two weeks after McDonald took office, McBeath flew to Port Hedland with Laurie O'Neill to find a way to break the deadlock in time for the shearing. Although most strikers were away with working parties when they visited the Twelve Mile the following day, McBeath had a long talk with Tommy Sampie, who undertook to have everyone in camp for a meeting the following morning. McBeath also had a long discussion with Clancy McKenna, who had just arrived at the Two Mile camp in Port Hedland from a firewood-gathering expedition with a party of other strikers. After months of browbeating, threats and imprisonment, senior departmental officers were, for the first time, engaging in dialogue with strike leaders. McKenna, twice imprisoned, was the reputed strongman allegedly holding strikers against their will through the threat of the green stick and was first on the list of candidates for removal to Moore River. McBeath, however, found him 'very well spoken and also intelligent' and anxious to see strikers return to station employment provided increased wages and better conditions were guaranteed.[36]

---

34   Jensen to McBeath, 29 March 1947, SROWA 1947/0305/76; Jensen to McBeath, telegram, 31 March 1947, SROWA 1947/0305/77.

35   Jensen to McBeath, 12 April 1947, p. 2, SROWA 1946/1416/14. Subsection 5 of section 34 of the Act stated that 'the Commissioner may undertake the general care, protection, and management of the property of any native, and may—
   (5) require a statement in writing from any person who has had any contractual transaction or financial dealing or dealings in property with a native of any such transaction or dealing during the period of one year preceding such requisition'.
   Alec Wyndham of Wyndham's store in Port Hedland also submitted to the Department regular accounts of the transactions he made with strikers in purchasing their kangaroo and goat skins (McBeath to McDonald, 14 April 1947, SROWA 1946/1416/15).

36   McBeath to McDonald, 28 April 1947, SROWA 1947/0305/104.

The next day, 16 April, McBeath held discussions with *marrngu* at the Twelve Mile. While Jensen had been frustrated by the role of McKenna and Sampie in his discussions of the previous week, believing they had hindered negotiations, McBeath held initial discussions with these two leaders. They told him that strikers were prepared to return to work at better rates of pay and with adequate facilities, but only on condition that their organisation was recognised by the government. McBeath agreed to recognise the North-West Workers' Association if McLeod was not involved in any way, 'either active or in any advisory capacity'. McKenna and Sampie agreed.[37] It was a significant breakthrough. An acceptance of Aboriginal corporate authority through official recognition of an Aboriginal organisation would have been a major step forward, enabling *marrngu* to return to station employment without losing the significant gains made through strike action.

When this agreement was put to a larger meeting of Twelve Mile strikers the following day, there was a general agreement to return to work under improved conditions if their organisation received government recognition. McBeath's reports on the meetings that day do not specify what arrangements were reached regarding pay and conditions, but a *Workers' Star* article, probably drawing on information provided by Sampie, claimed that strikers requested award wages, equal pay for women and an end to the permit system.[38] If these issues were indeed discussed at the meeting, it was an important advancement for women strikers, whose wages had received little consideration so far in strike demands. McBeath would not have been in a position to agree to any specific demands, but he undertook to discuss demands with employers. He later wrote that some of the strikers had 'an exaggerated idea of the value of their ability and worth as workers in this industry'.[39] Nevertheless, he felt that discussions with strikers at the Twelve Mile were proceeding well, until someone requested that McLeod be recognised as their representative and empowered to sign agreements on their behalf. To this McBeath was not prepared to agree. He told the strikers that McLeod was not considered a suitable person, and that the Department was not prepared to recognise him 'in any way whatsoever'.[40] *Marrngu* were quite firm, however, that they would not return to work unless this proposal was acceded to by the Department and government. Unable to agree to this proviso, and unable to persuade the

---

37   McBeath to McDonald, 28 April 1947, SROWA 1947/0305/104.
38   *Workers' Star*, 2 May 1947, p. 2, 'Nor-West Natives Demand Recognition'.
39   McBeath to McDonald, 16 May 1947, SROWA 1947/0305/115.
40   McBeath to McDonald, 28 April 1947, SROWA 1947/0305/104.

strikers to abandon it, McBeath advised the strikers to discuss the matter further between themselves, and told them that he would return to hear their decision later that afternoon. When he did so, they told him again that, unless McLeod was accepted as their representative and spokesman with authority to sign agreements on their behalf, they would not return to work. McBeath felt that any further discussion would be futile, and left them.[41]

Although he had failed to achieve his goal of negotiating a return to station work, McBeath's visit to the Pilbara clarified a number of points for the Department. Pastoralists and local officials had repeatedly insisted that most strikers were being kept away from stations against their will by the actions of a handful of strongmen. 'I know that a lot are very tired and would like to go back to work, but are still held by the heads', Ted Richardson of Pippingarra Station had told McBeath a few weeks previously.[42] However, neither this, nor the claim made by Welsh to McDonald that the main body of strikers would return to work if leaders were removed, seemed to borne out by the evidence of the Twelve Mile meetings of 16 April.[43] It was clear that the strike had considerable grassroots support. While most Twelve Mile strikers refused to return to work unless McLeod was accepted as their representative, some did express a willingness to accept employment, and McBeath instructed Jensen to arrange this. This did not support the contention that strikers were being held against their will.

McBeath's visit to Moolyella two days later not only reinforced this point but also made it clear that a significant number of Aboriginal people would never return to the stations. McBeath hoped to conduct similar negotiations at Moolyella to those carried out at the Twelve Mile, but most Moolyella strikers were camped in the surrounding hills in tin-bearing locations only accessible on foot. Although he, O'Neill, Marshall and Jensen made several attempts to locate working parties, including Dooley's, they were unable to do so. They were able to speak with only seven or eight Moolyella strikers, and these people expressed no interest in negotiating a return to work. They were not interested in returning to station employment, they told McBeath, even if better wages and conditions were offered.[44] Again, this evidence did not conform with claims that strikers were being prevented from returning to stations by strike leaders. Some *marrngu* enjoyed station work, were proud of

---

41   McBeath to McDonald, 28 April 1947, SROWA 1947/0305/104.
42   Richardson to McBeath, 23 March 1947, SROWA 1947/0305/69.
43   McDonald, notes of meeting with Welsh, 2 April 1947, SROWA S3841 cons769 1.
44   McBeath to McDonald, 29 April 1947, SROWA 1943/0621/35.

the knowledge and skills they brought to their tasks, both as domestic workers and stockworkers, and looked forward to a resolution of the dispute and a return to pastoral employment. This was especially the case at the Twelve Mile, where conditions had been difficult since February. Others, however, saw no reason to return to station work. Although conditions were not easy in the strike camps, many strikers, including men and women who were skilled station workers, found the freedom and independence of life in these new communities preferable to life on stations. McBeath recognised this. The strike offered a way of life that was socially satisfying and living conditions that were no worse than on many stations, and McBeath believed that many, and particularly those at Moolyella, whom he thought were 'not quite as sophisticated as the Port Hedland district people', would only be attracted back to stations by 'the inherent longing for a certain area which is usually a native trait'. 'Many of these people will never be prepared to settle down permanently in pastoral employment', he wrote.[45] In particular, he recognised that many older people, who no longer had a role to play on stations but who had authority within Aboriginal society, now had important roles within the strike communities. Before the strike, they had led a marginal existence. Older men had 'travelled from one station property to another', McBeath wrote:

> existing fairly well upon the proceeds of gambling, and also from the standing they possess as elders. From my observations of this type recently on the spot at Port Hedland, I am of the opinion that a certain measure of control has definitely passed over to these elderly men, and that because of this the general situation has become more involved. The elderly type of native is not concerned with increased wages and better living conditions, because they realise that they have no future on the stations as workers, whereas if it is possible to keep the strikers' camps in existence a reasonably good living is assured with a certain amount of authority and standing as well.[46]

The situation in the Pilbara, as it now appeared to the Department, was twofold. On the one hand, the Department needed to work with squatters to attract a sufficient number of strikers back to the stations to provide essential labour. On the other hand, it was clear now that there could be no return to the pre-strike situation in which most Aboriginal people had worked for the stations and lived in station communities. The Department faced the

---

45   McBeath to McDonald, 16 May 1947, p. 2, SROWA 1947/0305/116.
46   McBeath to McDonald, 16 May 1947, p. 2, SROWA 1947/0305/116.

question of just how to deal with the new reality of the continuing existence of a community of perhaps several hundred Aboriginal people who were no longer under pastoralist control. For McBeath, it was a question of how a new system of controls could be set in place. 'The industrial situation involving the natives at Port Hedland and Marble Bar has reached an impasse', he told McDonald. 'It is now necessary to review the position with the object of giving consideration to the welfare of the displaced natives, and their disposal'.[47] It was the old departmental approach that McBeath's successor as Commissioner would call 'dole and control'.

McDonald was looking for a new approach, however. The introduction of 'positive and forward-looking policy' offered the possibility that the Department could support, rather than oppose, the independent, self-supporting communities becoming established in the Pilbara. Indeed, the new way of life that *marrngu* were developing was not out of step with recommendations outlined by Elkin in *Citizenship for the Aborigines*. In a melding of an Enlightenment understanding of the universal right to progress towards 'civilisation' with a somewhat contradictory belief that human groups had the right to retain their own cultural distinctiveness, Elkin had recommended that, in marginal regions like the Pilbara, Aboriginal 'advancement' be undertaken, not at the individual level, but at the level of the group.[48] He proposed that Aboriginal groups find their own pathway to modernity through the 'development of self-supporting communities based on village organisation', each community developing its own unique form of civilisation, 'worked out slowly by them as a group', through the gradual adaptation and adjustment of Aboriginal religion and culture into something compatible with and resembling, but not identical to, Western civilisation.[49] The path of 'advancement' was to be in the hands of Aboriginal people themselves. Elkin had made this point to McLeod in 1944. Expressing support for McLeod's scheme for Aboriginal people to obtain their own pastoral property, Elkin wrote that Aboriginal people tended to be regarded simply as labour 'and not as individuals who should be working out their own salvation'.[50]

McDonald was cautiously prepared to view the development of community organisations at Moolyella and the Twelve Mile in this light, as 'a new pattern

---

47 McBeath to McDonald, 16 May 1947, p. 1, SROWA 1947/0305/115.
48 Cited in Russell McGregor, *Indifferent Inclusions: Aboriginal People and the Nation*, Aboriginal Studies Press, Canberra, 2011, p. 66.
49 Elkin, *Citizenship for the Aborigines*, pp. 40, 46.
50 Elkin to McLeod, 10 November 1944, A. P. Elkin Papers, University of Sydney Archives, box 76, file 262.

in native life' in which Aboriginal people were, in Elkin's terms 'working out their own salvation'. He was willing to some extent, for example, to recognise the strikers' organisation, the North-West Workers' Association, especially when this was raised as a condition for accepting station employment. Could this new social and economic organisation, he wondered, represent an 'advancement' towards civilisation? 'If they are able to live together, develop civic responsibility and a certain degree of economic independency', he told Father Bryan:

> it may indicate a growing capacity on the part of natives to take their part in the structure of society generally. Therefore, I view such camps or assemblies with interest and feel that if they can develop into something representing an advance, then it will be all to the good.[51]

McLeod encouraged the Department to view the strike communities in this light, and, as a result, to respect their autonomy. He used assimilationist understandings of human progress, very much in line with Elkin's, to urge the Department to view the strikers' organisation as evidence that Aboriginal people could find, and indeed were finding, their own path to modernity and citizenship within Australian society. The key to Aboriginal 'advancement' lay in Aboriginal hands, he argued, if they were allowed the freedom to work out their own solutions. 'The reluctance of your Dept to recognise the very real advance towards citizenship and understanding made by the natives is as puzzling to your friends as it is agrevating [sic] to the natives', he wrote to McBeath on 19 April 1947:

> Let me suggest even at this late hour despite all that has gone before that you take up the proposition as originally put forward. Recognise the natives right to organise and appoint their own representatives (their desire for this is deep seated as can be proven by even a casual visit to them) and cooperate with them to achieve a better way of life ...
>
> I really believe that the natives themselves have the remedy for their own advancement and will assist them to the full extent of my capacity against all opposition from whatever quarter it may come.
>
> The situation is ripe for a complete reorientation of official thinking.[52]

---

51 McDonald to Bryan, 9 October 1947, SROWA S3841 cons769 3.
52 McLeod to McBeath, 19 April 1947, pp. 2–3, SROWA 1947/0305/96–95.

Over the next few years, there *would* be the 'complete reorientation of official thinking' required for the Department to view the group in this light. A report produced by Ross McDonald and Frank Bateman in 1952 would describe the continued existence of the independent group as 'a new development in the history of our native population', 'a reaching out of the natives towards a higher status and greater economic independence – the expression of a racial aspiration towards social, civic and economic levels'.[53] It was a development, they would argue, that was not out of step with the policy of assimilation that was, by then, being implemented throughout the state. They would describe the movement as part of 'the historical processes of the race', not as an end in itself, but as 'part of the transitional experiences of the native population' in the process of assimilation into 'the social and economic fabric of our population'. Viewed as such, they would recommend that the group be allowed to retain its autonomy, albeit under the watchful eye of the Department.

In 1947, however, any inclination on McDonald's part to view the strikers' organisation in this light was overwhelmed by other concerns. Demands made by the strikers for the Department to recognise Aboriginal corporate authority were closely linked to the demand that McLeod be recognised as the group's representative. Despite the gentle current of attitudinal change that accompanied McDonald's accession to the ministerial role, the Department refused to give McLeod any form of official recognition. McBeath identified offences against the *Native Administration Act* as the reason for McLeod's unsuitability, but the strongest objection to McLeod was his communist ideology and affiliation. On 10 April, the day after McDonald had met with senior departmental staff to formulate strategies for dealing with the strike, and a few days before McBeath and O'Neill flew north, McBeath had shown McDonald a copy of an article in Geraldton's Catholic newspaper, the *Cathedral Chronicle*. The article reproduced a letter from McLeod, along with a vehemently anti-communist, point-by-point rebuttal by the newspaper's editor. In drawing the minister's attention to the article, McBeath referred to the protest that had taken place in Mt Magnet a few days previously 'where it's alleged that "communistic influences" are at work'.[54] Fears that the communist influences behind the Pilbara unrest were spreading to other areas in the north were underscored by McLeod's frank admission to the *Cathedral Chronicle*

---

53 'Report by Sir Ross McDonald & F. E. A. Bateman on Native Group at Marble Bar', p. 2, SLWA 5525A/2.
54 McBeath to McDonald, 10 April 1947, SROWA 1947/0329.

that 'although I personally am a communist one swallow does not make a summer', and by the *Chronicle*'s bitter denunciation of McLeod as a Soviet puppet, exploiting Aboriginal people for sinister and destructive purposes at Moscow's bidding.[55] Anti-communist anxieties overrode McDonald's concern to find a new departmental approach to the situation in the Pilbara and to recognise the potential of the new communities. The Department would not endanger the pastoral industry and the country by making concessions that vested authority in communist hands.

Pressure from Pilbara pastoralists also ensured that the Department continued to oppose the new communities, particularly at the Twelve Mile. As we shall see, the existence in their midst of a large, organised and independent Aboriginal community raised fears within the settler population and complaints at the lack of constraint that now existed over the movement and activities of the strikers. In particular, the use of pastoral leasehold land by Twelve Mile people in the pursuit of their economic activities was resented by local pastoralists, who repeatedly demanded that the community there be disbanded.

Although Elkin had recommended Aboriginal-directed change at the level of the group, this proposal was undermined by his own insistence that the expertise of non-Aboriginal anthropologists was essential in formulating strategies for Aboriginal 'advancement'. He equivocated on the question of Aboriginal capacity to adapt without the assistance and guidance of such experts. 'For all his proclamations on Aborigines developing their "own" civilised society and culture "from within"', Russell McGregor writes, 'Aboriginal autonomy was not on Elkin's agenda'.[56] As Heather Goodall has argued, the shift from 'protection' to 'assimilation' that accompanied Elkin's own involvement in Aboriginal administration in New South Wales did not result in significant changes in practice.[57] The expertise of anthropologists was prioritised over the voices of Aboriginal people themselves, and Elkin's involvement saw the continuation and rationalisation of existing practices of segregation and incarceration.[58] In Western Australia, too, non-Aboriginal expertise would

---

55   *Cathedral Chronicle*, March 1947, pp. 1–2, SROWA 1947/0329. The article gives a fascinating insight into the vehemence of anti-communist sentiment at the time within some sections of the community, and the antagonism it generated towards McLeod and the strike movement as a whole. It is reproduced in Appendix A.
56   Russell McGregor, 'Words, Wards and Citizens: A. P. Elkin and Paul Hasluck on Assimilation', *Oceania*, vol. 69, 1999, p. 252.
57   Heather Goodall, 'An Intelligent Parasite: A. P. Elkin and White Perceptions on the History of Aboriginal People in NSW', paper presented to the Australian Historical Association Conference, University of New South Wales, 1982.
58   Goodall, 'Intelligent Parasite', p. 16.

be prioritised over the voices and agency of Aboriginal people, the necessary expertise here arising, at Elkin's recommendation, from experience in native administration in Papua New Guinea. Although McDonald set in motion changes that would in time lead to departmental acceptance of the independent group as a highly significant development, in the shorter term opposition to the new communities continued.

Chapter 18

'The Feeling Locally Is Very Strong Against the Strikers'

The Strike and Settler Fear, April–August 1947

In the Pilbara, fear of McLeod's communistic agenda added to concerns about labour shortages. Pastoralists justified their refusal to have any dealings with McLeod with the statement 'We are loyal subjects and do not think he is'.[1] The general threat posed by his communist agitation and influence among Aboriginal people was menacing enough, but pastoralists felt that they and their industry were the direct target of his activities. His antagonism towards them was no secret. The widely-held belief that he had threatened to 'make the squatters weep before he was finished' probably held more than a grain of truth. The success of his legal appeal, funded by an organisation believed to be a communist front, did nothing to lessen such fears. He seemed immune to the normal legal processes that could usually be relied upon to operate in the squatters' favour.[2] Accustomed to political power and to having their needs prioritised, pastoralists were outraged at the system's inability to put a stop to activities that seemed to them to be so clearly subversive. Eight months into the strike he was still at large, and the pastoralists felt frustrated at their powerlessness. John Richardson of Pippingarra appealed to the premier to intervene for their protection. 'He has been charged 5 times in the PH courthouse and has gone to jail several times, but he seems to appeal and gets out & is now wandering about as large as life'.[3] Even their willingness to bow to strikers' demands by negotiating wage increases and improved conditions had failed to restore any level of control, either to their own hands

---

1   Edmund John Jeffries, statement to Committee Investigating Native Labour, 1952, SROWA 1952/0830/139–190.
2   Lukis, interviewed by Jeffery, 1977, transcript, p. 155, SLWA OH262.
3   J. M. Richardson to Wise, 2 October 1946, p. 3, SROWA 1946/0799/65.

or those of the Department. Already struggling under a labour shortage, they feared that McLeod might be planning other ways to damage their industry.

Frank Ellis Gare, who worked in the 1950s for the Department of Native Welfare, as it was then called, was conscious of the level of fear engendered by the strike. 'Up in the Port Hedland area', he said:

> there was an undercurrent of opposition to Don McLeod because he had led a strike in 1946 ... So there was a good deal of resentment, and there was a bit of fear about too. In Port Hedland, for instance, the whole story had become exaggerated and there were a lot of people in Port Hedland who were fearful that Don McLeod was planning an insurrection, a sort of revolution.[4]

Fear of communist subversion was not the only cause of growing anxiety in the Pilbara. There was a widespread belief that the Aboriginal population needed to be kept under strict supervision, not only for its own protection but also for the protection of the settler community. Before the strike, non-Aboriginal Pilbara residents had felt secure in the knowledge that a system of colonial control was in place to keep their community safe from Aboriginal retaliation and aggression. Repeated acts of police intimidation, made potent by the memory of the brutal acquisition of their land and labour, had kept Aboriginal people compliant and submissive. This mechanism of settler power, however, had become ineffective in the face of defiant Aboriginal activism. Imprisonment, the threat of removal, appeals to loyalty to stations and the obligations inherent in the feudalistic pastoral relationship had all failed to re-establish setter control. The strikers' defiance had exposed the weakness of settler control, and some Pilbara residents feared a violent retaliatory backlash.

Before the strike, pastoralists had resented departmental interference in their relationship with Aboriginal labour, but now they called on the Department to step in and restore settler domination. 'Surely the Dept have more control over the natives than to allow them to do just as they like and be guided by McLeod who I presume is in co-operation with the native Rights Committee', Ted Richardson growled in a letter to the Commissioner.[5] Despite talk of removing leaders and maintaining discipline, however, the Department seemed incapable of dealing with the situation. Even pastoralist concessions and negotiations carried out by senior departmental officers had failed to end

---

4 Gare, interviewed by Foster, 1998, transcript, p. 42, SLWA OH 2899.
5 Richardson to Bray, 23 September 1946, SROWA 1946/0799/59.

the strike. Now the Pilbara settler community was facing the possibility of the continuing presence in their midst of a large body of Aboriginal people who were not under pastoralist, departmental or mission control, and they felt vulnerable.

These fears seemed to be confirmed when, on the morning of 21 April, a few days after the Department refused to acknowledge McLeod as the strikers' representative, and the day after McBeath and O'Neill returned to Perth, Pilbara residents awoke to the news that overnight the woolshed on Boodarie Station had been gutted by fire, resulting in the loss of 200 sheep, and that arson was suspected. With shearing due to begin that day, 400 ewes had been penned at the shed.

Suspicion fell immediately on the strikers. At 5 am, Constable Les Fletcher and Native Affairs Inspector Tom Jensen drove to the station to investigate 'and endeavor to ascertain if any sabotage by the striking natives was in evidence'.[6] The fire had taken hold so quickly and had engulfed the shed so completely that it seemed impossible that it could have started by accident. Only arson could explain the fact that a pile of wool packs outside the shed was also burning, and the smell of kerosene was detected in the wool packs. Two empty kerosene buckets found in the shed could not be identified as belonging to the station and nobody remembered seeing them there the previous day. Since wool did not burn easily, it was thought that the sheep and the wool packs had been sprayed with kerosene before being set alight. As quickly as the fire took hold of the shearing shed, the belief that this was an atrocious act of sabotage took hold throughout the local settler population. A short report in the *West Australian* the following day emphasised the horror of the event and hinted at a link with strike:

> The anguished cries of the stricken animals was heart-rending, but the flames made rescue attempts impossible ... Mr. Hall is endeavouring to have his sheep shorn at the neighbouring Pippingarra Station. Last year the shearing was interrupted by a native strike.[7]

The fire seemed to confirm the squatters' worst fears, but it also offered hope that a firm legal response could finally impose some control through the imprisonment and removal of offenders. It was hoped that evidence of McLeod's involvement could be established. The day after the fire, Detective Sergeant Pilmer flew from Perth to carry out a thorough investigation. He

---

6   Jensen, patrol journal, 21 April 1947, SROWA 1947/0127/18.
7   *West Australian*, 22 April 1947, p. 10.

heard from Fletcher and Jensen of their suspicions of the strikers' involvement, and visited the Twelve Mile before looking into matters at Boodarie Station.

Although Jensen's role as Native Affairs Inspector was ostensibly to protect the interests of Aboriginal people, he slipped easily into the familiar policing role and worked actively with Pilmer and Fletcher to find evidence of the strikers' and McLeod's involvement.[8] When his attempt to extract information from strikers at the Twelve Mile proved unproductive, he made arrangements with one of the strikers, Munda Bobby, to be his eyes and ears among the strikers to obtain information. However, Bobby was unable to find out anything to incriminate *marrngu*. Roy Mackay, who was again working on Munda Station, was enlisted to assist in a search for tracks. No tracks were found in the vicinity of the shearing shed, but Don McWhirter of Indee Station found boot tracks about three-quarters of a mile west of the shed, along with the tracks of a truck. The strikers' boats were examined, and Sandy Brown, leader of the fishing team based at the Twelve Mile, was interviewed. Ernie Mitchell and Peter Coppin were also interviewed. Still no evidence was found to implicate the strikers.[9]

Despite the lack of evidence and the fact that investigations were still under way, the *West Australian* fanned the flames of suspicion and outrage by reporting with confidence on 24 April, three days after the fire, that it had 'been established that the fire was caused by human hands'. 'Local residents are seething with indignation at the crime. The sheep were burnt to cinders, only a few bones lying about the remains of the shed to indicate their tragic end'.[10]

At the time of the 1 May strike, Laurie O'Neill, then the district's Native Affairs Inspector, had noted the lack of animosity felt by pastoralists towards the strikers. Now, almost a year later, a growing frustration at the strikers' intransigence tipped over into open hostility. 'The feeling locally is at the moment very strong against the strikers due mainly thru the instance of the fire at the Boodarrie [sic] woolshed', Jensen wrote. 'Although no native has as yet been coupled with this atrocity in any way, public feeling is that they know more about it than they let on'. Jensen, however, now doubted that the fire was an act of sabotage perpetrated by the strikers, a view based in part on his low estimation of Aboriginal ability. 'The person or persons who were responsible for this crime were far too intelligent for an average native', he

---

8   Jensen, patrol journal, 22 April 1947, SROWA 1947/0127/19.
9   Jensen, patrol journal, 24 April 1947, SROWA 1947/0127/20.
10   *West Australian*, 24 April 1947, p. 11.

wrote, 'as the job was done too thorough for any native to have carried out'.[11] Nevertheless, the incident had caused so much tension in the area that he urged the Department to take steps to disband the strikers at the Twelve Mile. He suggested that if action was not taken by government authorities, pastoralists could take matters into their own hands:

> I conscientiously beleive [sic] that if this problem is not taken in hand in the very near future ... to counter the Communistic bug and the environs of the 12 mile camp ... this matter will ultimately end in serious trouble between the white people of this area and the Natives.[12]

With fear among the non-Aboriginal station people at a high level, police maintained a high level of visibility throughout the area. 'With the state of the native situation as it is in this district', Fletcher wrote, 'I am of the opinion that the more the Police move about the better it will be'. He thought a visible police presence was important, 'mainly for the psychological effect of a visit from Police on any natives that were contacted along the route'.[13] The decision to station a second police officer, Constable Keith Weaver, to work with Constable Marshall at Marble Bar at this time was probably a response to the level of fear arising from the Boodarie fire. Police acted to restrict Aboriginal access to firearms and bullets.[14] Strikers were denied permits to purchase rifles, and those who had rifles found themselves unable to renew their licences. Strikers found with unlicensed firearms were fined and their rifles were confiscated.[15] The sale of bullets to strikers was monitored. As hunting was essential to the strikers' survival, providing both meat for consumption and skins for sale, *marrngu* had to find ways around these restrictions. Firearms were kept hidden. According to Molly Williams (Kulyu), strikers were able to evade police surveillance with the help of storekeeper Alec Wyndham, who sold them bullets hidden in bags of flour or sugar. 'He put'm in a something, tea leaf, or sugar, inside', she said. 'Nobody know, policeman don't know'.[16]

As each station completed the shearing, bales of wool were taken to sidings along the Port Hedland to Marble Bar railway line, where they were loaded on railway wagons to be picked up by the weekly train. An indication of the

---

11   Jensen to McBeath, 30 April 1947, p. 2, SROWA 1947/0305/110.
12   Jensen to McBeath, 30 April 1947, p. 4, SROWA 1947/0305/112.
13   Fletcher to A. L. Reid, District Inspector of Police, 28 April 1947, SROWA 1939/1777 v7.
14   McDonald to Richardson, 13 June 1947, SROWA1943/0621/46.
15   *Workers' Star*, 27 June 1947, p. 5, 'Natives Refused Rifle Permits'.
16   Molly Williams (Kulyu), tape 2, recorded 22 October 1992, author's collection.

level of fear occasioned by the Boodarie woolshed fire is the request for police guards to accompany wool bales on the train to prevent destruction by the strikers. On 12 May, three weeks after the fire, Neville Flight-Smith, manager of Bungalow (Coongan) Station, contacted Constable Marshall to say that he had 240 bales of wool loaded on railway trucks at the Warralong siding ready to be picked up, and that he was afraid that strikers would burn them. He had seen a number of strikers 'hanging about Warralong siding', he said, and there was a large number of strikers camped nearby at Shaw River, the majority of whom were armed. He asked for a policeman to be on the train from Marble Bar to ensure that the wool reached the wharf safely.[17] Marshall thought this unnecessary and 'rather ridiculous'. The shearing was carried out over some months, and it would be a full-time job for the police to guard all the wool en route to Port Hedland. Once in Port Hedland, wool was stockpiled at the One Mile to await loading on a ship. 'I cannot see that the natives would burn a hundred or so bales at a siding, when they could burn many thousands of bales in the one fire, at the One Mile, if they so desired', Marshall wrote. Nevertheless, Constables Weaver and Jensen camped at Warralong siding on the night of 13 May to ensure the safety of the Bungalow wool.[18] 'The night was uneventful. 'No natives about', Weaver reported.[19]

The following day, Jensen and Weaver visited strikers camped in the area to investigate Flight-Smith's claim that they were armed. They found no firearms among strikers camped at the Shaw River, but supposed, probably correctly, that rifles had been hidden before their arrival. Weaver reported that they 'appeared to have ample food supplies, and appeared quite contented with the strike, several of the natives remarking "that they must stand by Don McLeod" and see him right'.[20] While strikers were careful to keep firearms hidden, other *marrngu* were caught in the web of the authorities' crackdown. At a windmill near the Warralong siding, officers Jensen and Weaver found Dougal Cornish with a group of strikers, his unlicensed rifle leaning against a tree. Not being a striker, he was, perhaps, less vigilant about keeping his firearm hidden. His rifle was confiscated and he was heavily fined.[21]

Fear led to a belief that the fire was lit by strikers, and the belief fanned the fear. 'I have no doubt that a feeling of tension has been engendered by

---

17 Marshall to Inspector Reid, 15 May 1947, SROWA 1946/2538 v8.
18 Marshall to Inspector Reid, 15 May 1947, SROWA 1946/2538 v8.
19 Weaver, police patrol report, 13 May 1947, SROWA 1946/2538 v8.
20 Weaver, police patrol report, 13 May 1947, SROWA 1946/2538 v8.
21 Marshall to Inspector Reid, 15 May 1947, SROWA 1946/2538 v8; *West Australian*, 17 May 1947, p. 16.

the occurrence of the fire which destroyed the Boodarie woolshed recently', McBeath told McDonald, 'and I know from my personal discussion with various people from the North that the striking natives are blamed for this atrocity'. However, after speaking to Detective Sergeant Pilmer about his findings in the north, he, too, believed that the fire had been accidental. The most likely cause appeared to be a lighted wax match, carelessly dropped beneath the batten floor of the holding pen in the woolshed. 'As you know', he wrote to McDonald:

> sheep droppings accumulate over a period of years beneath this type of floor, and owing to the dry nature of the manure ignition occurs quickly, and consequent smoldering action would, I should think, result in a gasified atmosphere admirably suited for a conflagration which resulted in the destruction of the woolshed building.[22]

Pilmer had found no evidence to lay charges against anyone for arson. At a coronial inquest into the cause of the fire held in Port Hedland in July, magistrate Maurice Harwood heard evidence of the speed with which the fire took hold of the shed, and of manager Henty Hall's conviction that such a fire could not have been accidental. Evidence of headlights seen by Mary Hall, the empty kerosene buckets, the smell of kerosene in the wool bales, the boot and tyre tracks found, was also heard. Don McWhirter of Indee Station, who had carried out investigations of his own, told the coroner that the truck belonged to Aubrey Lockyer, a member of the Port Hedland Euralian community. James McGuckin, a young *walypila* station hand, spoke of the work he had done penning the sheep the day before the fire. He had been smoking, he said, and accidentally dropped a wax match between the grating, but made sure it was out. A *walypila* station hand on Mundabullangana Station said that on the morning of the fire he had seen smoke signals along the coast about fifteen miles from Boodarie, and that he had seen them again that afternoon.

Ernie Mitchell was called as a witness to give evidence of his whereabouts and the whereabouts of other strikers on the night of the fire. Aubrey Lockyer explained that the tyre tracks left by his vehicle had been made two days before the fire, when he was looking for firewood along the Turner River. He had been fishing on the Port Hedland jetty on the night of the fire, he said, a fact corroborated by another witness.[23]

---

22 McBeath to McDonald, 16 May 1947, p. 1, SROWA 1947/0305/115.
23 *Northern Times*, 18 July 1947, p. 5.

The inquest was adjourned for a month, and further evidence heard by Magistrate Harwood on 25 August included that of the Government Analyst from Perth who gave expert evidence on the ravages of fire and likely causes of the woolshed blaze. The Boodarie wool packs had been examined in Perth and showed no evidence of flammable oil. Harwood found that the fire had started from misadventure, caused by the match that McGuckin, one of the young jackaroos employed to replace Aboriginal labour, had dropped. The magistrate found that the match had caused the accumulated sheep manure to smoulder and then burst into flame during the night.[24]

Despite this finding, non-Aboriginal Pilbara residents held firmly to their belief that the fire was an act of sabotage perpetrated by McLeod and the strikers. It seemed to the squatters that once again the legal system had failed to deliver justice. Fear of sabotage remained high. The principal theme of the 1960 novel *The Green Stick*, by Pilbara pastoralist James Doughty, is the squatters' desperate struggle against violent and brutal acts of sabotage carried out by a lawless group of Aboriginal people who had left the stations under the leadership of a sinister, educated 'half-caste' representing McLeod. Fear of the uncontrolled 'niggers', and outrage at the failure of the authorities to bring them under control, permeates the novel.

Fear of McLeod's communist agenda continued to cause his name to be linked with the Boodarie woolshed fire. Four years after the fire, for example, a report by the Commonwealth Investigation Service of the Commonwealth Police included, as evidence of McLeod's communistic activities, the statement that 'it is alleged that a wool-shed was burned down at Bullarrie Station [*sic*], Port Hedland, just prior to the commencement of shearing. It is said that McLeod may have been responsible for the fire'.[25] In 1952, Lang Hancock, at that time owner of the Nunyerry Asbestos Mine but later a Pilbara iron ore magnate, told a government inquiry that McLeod was trying to sabotage his production. 'This is the Communistic line', Hancock said. He believed that McLeod:

> always looks for an easy living and has had political aspirations. He thought he might get a nigger vote. He next joined with the Communist Party to get something for nothing. He attempted to organise natives and get their support to indulge in Communist activity.

---

24 *Northern Times*, 29 August 1947, p. 1.
25 E. Hattam, Deputy Director, South Australia, to the Deputy Director, Commonwealth Investigation Service, Perth, 3 August 1951, 'McLeod, Donald [alleged communist connected with aborigines in Western Australia]', NAA D1918, S3008.

Although it had not been proved that McLeod burned down the shearing shed at Boodarie, Hancock asserted that 'district opinion attributed this to him'.[26]

The presence in the Pilbara of a large body of Aboriginal people who were not subject to supervision was clearly a major cause for anxiety for some sections of the non-Aboriginal Pilbara population. The belief that this uncontrolled group was under the influence of a communist whose personal and political ideology was antithetical to the interests of the pastoral industry added weight to these concerns. As strikers crossed racialised lines of demarcation, further concerns were added to this fear, as their newly won freedom of movement saw anxiety turned into a contest over access to land.

---

26   L. G. Hancock, Statement to Committee Investigating Native Labour, February 1952, SROWA 1952/0830 v1/136.

Chapter 19

'The Natives Are Now Taking the Attitude They Can Camp Anywhere They Like'

Contested Ground, 1947

The issue of land was at the centre of the Pilbara movement. In the early days of the movement, *marrngu* had talked and dreamed with McLeod of a scheme to acquire their own pastoral lease on which to establish themselves as an independent community. While it was still some years before they would achieve the goal of gaining leasehold possession of a piece of their own land, strikers' actions in challenging pastoralist claims to the exclusive use of pastoral land made the issue of access to country a primary site of contestation during the strike.

The Western Australian *Land Act 1933* gave no formal recognition to the unique rights of Aboriginal people to access country covered by pastoral leases. In 1934, a proposed amendment to give Aboriginal people the right to enter any unimproved land held under pastoral lease, whether enclosed or unenclosed, 'to seek sustenance in their accustomed manner', had been opposed by Pilbara pastoralist and politician Frank Welsh of Warralong Station. Concerned about the impact of dogs on stock if Aboriginal people were 'allowed to roam at will upon land stocked with sheep', Welsh wanted to remove the provision giving Aboriginal people access to enclosed pastoral land, allowing access to unenclosed pastoral land only. This would deny them access to most pastoral land.

The Acting Minister for Lands thought this amendment unnecessary. Changes to the law would not prevent pastoralists from continuing their practice of keeping Aboriginal people off their land, he argued; Aborigines, after all, did not know the law. Welsh, however, insisted that pastoralist interests should override the rights of Aboriginal people, in law as well as in practice. As a result, the amendment only gave Aboriginal people the legal right to access unenclosed land for hunting and gathering purposes, effectively debarring them from most pastoral land.[1] In practice, limited Aboriginal access to country covered by pastoral leases was permitted by pastoralists in exchange for labour, but control over access remained in the hands of the leaseholders. Police supported pastoral interests by shifting *marrngu* from pastoral leases at the squatters' request.

Now, in the Pilbara, settler controls that restricted Aboriginal movement and access to country were being broken down by the strike. As work parties from the Twelve Mile moved across pastoral leases for their hunting, fishing and dry-shelling activities, the strike became a struggle over access to land.

The location of the Moolyella strike camp in a mining area did not cause much concern for pastoralists, but throughout the course of the strike there were persistent complaints about Aboriginal strikers living at the Twelve Mile, close to the main road and railway line. The camp was located on a forestry reserve but surrounded by rich coastal pastoral country owned by wealthy and powerful interests. Agitation from pastoralists to have strikers moved from the Twelve Mile had begun as early as June 1946, when strikers evicted from the stations for participating in the 1 May strike were placed there on rations by the Department of Native Affairs. The most persistent and strident complaints came from Alexander Edwin (Ted) Richardson of the neighbouring Pippingarra Station, who claimed that the camp was located on his lease. 'We are led to believe that you are going to establish a Depot to feed on rations natives that are unable to work ... at what is known as the 12 Mile near Pippingarra Railway Siding', he protested in a letter to Commissioner Bray. 'As this site is on our property we wish to state that we strongly object to same being established there':

> During the war period we were deprived of using same for grazing purposes a/c of the Army utilizing same for an army camp and did get some compensation for it but we would rather have been able to have had the use of the country as it is some of our best country for [lambing] ewes.[2]

Pastoralist complaints were taken seriously by the Department. Richardson was a member of a prominent pastoralist family, president of the Port Hedland Road Board and chairman of the Port Hedland committee of the Pastoralists

---

1 *West Australian*, 30 November 1934, p. 14.
2 Richardson to Bray, 24 June 1946 (incorrectly dated 1945), p. 1, SROWA 1946/0799/11.

Association, and as such carried considerable political weight. O'Neill looked for an alternative site for a ration depot that would not impinge on settler space and sensibilities. He thought an area near the Poondana railway siding could be suitable, providing there were 'no local objectors', but dropped this idea when he learned that a gang of railway fettlers was to camp there.³ No other suitable site could be found; any area that had a suitable water supply was already being used by pastoralists. He reported to Bray that the Twelve Mile was not in fact located on the Pippingarra lease, as Richardson claimed, but on common land that Richardson had been using for many years.⁴ Nevertheless, it was his job to prevent Aboriginal people from hindering pastoral operations, and he sympathised with Richardson's situation. He and Constable Fletcher moved the Twelve Mile ration depot about half a mile from the main road, where there was no possibility that *marrngu* could interfere with Pippingarra wells.⁵ Fletcher was less sympathetic to Ted Richardson's complaints, describing him as 'something of an obstructionist', who 'should not be taken too seriously'. 'Had another site been available I think we should have made use of it', he wrote:

> not because we consider it necessary, but merely to prevent Mr. Richardson from having an imaginary cause of complaint, but as no other spot is available, this one is being retained without any qualms of conscience at this end.⁶

If Richardson felt that the small ration depot had been a cause for complaint in June 1946, he found he had a lot more to worry about when 130 *marrngu* who refused to return to station work after the Port Hedland races in August 1946 set up a strike camp at the Twelve Mile. 'The position is now more serious from our point of view', he moaned:

> [They] have taken the attitude they can go where they like and stay as long as they wish ... So I would be obliged to get some word from you if anything can be done in the matter of getting them away from their present camp.⁷

---

3   O'Neill to Bray, telegram, date unclear, [June 1946], SROWA 1946/0799/15; O'Neill to Bray, 5 July 1946, p. 2, SROWA 1945/0800/245; O'Neill to Bray, telegram, 28 June 1946, SROWA 1938/0656/27.
4   O'Neill to Bray, 5 July 1946, p. 2, SROWA 1945/0800/245.
5   O'Neill to Bray, 5 July 1946, SROWA 1945/0800/246.
6   Fletcher to Bray, 8 July 1946, SROWA 1946/0799/20.
7   Richardson to Bray, 6 August 1946, SROWA 1938/0982/23.

The Indigenous population, Gillian Cowlishaw writes, is 'construed as intruding, with their disruptive and illegal practices, into the pastoralist's space'.[8] Fletcher replied to Richardson that he was 'powerless to alter the situation for the moment', but that 'as soon as any action is possible, rest assured I will take it'.[9] Bray had to admit to Richardson that the Department had lost the power to comply with pastoralist demands to move strikers from the Twelve Mile. 'It is a pity the unrest ever occurred', he wrote to Richardson. 'It has eventuated, however, and we must expect inconveniences as a result'.[10]

If squatters were frustrated by the Department's inability to prevent *marrngu* going where they liked and setting up camp where they liked, they were initially comforted by the expectation that the strike would be short-lived and spatial controls could soon be reimposed. Order would be restored and boundaries rebuilt. A month later, however, *marrngu* were still at the Twelve Mile, and Richardson was dismayed to see that they were establishing gardens and building substantial spinifex sheds on both sides of the Petermara Creek. 'The situation is becoming worse', he complained to Bray. 'It looks as [though] they intend establishing a Permanent camp'. The hope that hunger would force strikers to return to stations was fading, and Richardson expressed anxiety that lines of demarcation were being breached. 'Another thing that won't assist them to return to station work is that that some of the ... town people are allowed to give them a few days work per week and [they] wander around town as large as life'.[11]

Ted Richardson's son, John, went over the Department's head with a direct appeal for assistance to Premier Wise. 'You will be very surprised to receive a letter from me', he wrote, 'but as we can't get satisfaction anywhere else I am writing to you to see if you can oblige':

> What really worries us here is the natives having a camp at the 12 mile and no one seems to be able to shift them. Can't something be done about shifting these natives or have we pastoralists got to give the stations over to McCleod [*sic*] & his confederates which looks like what will have to be done if the Govt or some responsible body doesn't do something.[12]

---

8   Cowlishaw, *Rednecks, Eggheads and Blackfellas*, p. 95.
9   Fletcher to Bray, 16 August 1946, SROWA 1946/0799/37.
10 Bray to Richardson, 23 August 1946, SROWA 1946/0799/42.
11 Richardson to Bray, 23 September 1946, SROWA 1946/0799/59.
12 J. M. Richardson to Premier Wise, 2 October 1946, p. 3, SROWA 1946/0799/65.

Economic activities undertaken by the Twelve Mile strikers added to the pastoralists' concerns. Work parties spread out over a wide area, from Yandeyarra Station to old Condon Harbour on De Grey Station.[13] Some pastoralists were willing to allow work parties to camp and hunt on their leases. Rob Lukis, for example, was able to establish good relations with parties of strikers who hunted kangaroos and goats on Munda Station, and the strikers made sure that their activities did not interfere with pastoral operations.[14] Other squatters, however, tried to have strikers removed from their leases. In September 1946, a group of about sixty strikers began dry-shelling on the coast and set up camp at the abandoned Condon townsite. Although the townsite was not included in the De Grey lease, manager Les Miller complained that *marrngu* were 'actually wandering all over' the surrounding area, hunting kangaroos and disturbing his sheep. He called on Fletcher to shift them. Fletcher sympathised, but again found himself powerless to comply. 'One cannot blame the station people for not wanting their stock disturbed', he wrote to Bray, 'but I cannot continually be on the move after them, and even if I could, have not sufficient staff to move the natives, and nowhere to move them to anyhow', he wrote.[15]

With the strike showing no sign of petering out, and with groups of increasingly confident strikers spreading out and hunting over a wide area of pastoral country, pastoralists used their political influence to try to resolve the matter. The Port Hedland branch of the Pastoralists Association met with the local Labor Member of Parliament, Bill Hegney, to complain about *marrngu* wandering freely over their pastoral leases. They suggested that a Native Affairs Department officer be stationed in the area 'to go amongst the natives in the capacity of a friend to help them and in doing so many natives may return to their place of employment'. Hegney approached the Department to recommend this idea.[16]

Under such pressure, the Department again looked for an alternative camping site for the Twelve Mile strikers that was 'less likely to be the cause of complaint from pastoralists or other members of the community in general'.[17] Acting Commissioner McBeath instructed O'Neill to find a suitable site, 'having

---

13   Jensen to McBeath, 16 April 1948, p. 2, SROWA 1947/0305/202.
14   Jensen to McBeath, 6 May 1948, p. 2, SROWA 1947/0902/7.
15   Fletcher to Bray, 24 September 1946, SROWA 1946/0799/61.
16   A. E. Richardson, Chairman, and F. A. Leeds, Acting Secretary, Pastoralists Association Committee, Port Hedland, to Bray, 1 October 1946, SROWA 1946/0799/63; J. M. Richardson to Wise, 2 October 1946, SROWA 1946/0799/63.
17   McBeath to Fletcher, 15 October 1946, SROWA 1946/0799/68.

in mind that any spot chosen must be situated where the natives concerned are not likely to interfere with stock watering at the mills, or give cause for complaint in any other way'.[18]

O'Neill had already made a thorough and unsuccessful search for a suitable watered site not already in use. Even if such a site could be found, he knew that the strikers were no longer so submissive that they would comply with an order to relocate.[19] In other parts of the state, such control could be exercised without concern for legal niceties, but the Department knew that in the Pilbara any action taken could be challenged in a court of law. Clarity about 'the legal aspect' was important, O'Neill said, as he felt sure 'that Departmental action to shift them [would] bring about a storm of protest from certain interested parties'.[20] Aboriginal people had the legal right to camp on common land and, to make matters more difficult, inquiries revealed that Richardson had actually been illegally using the land on which the Twelve Mile was situated, never having been granted the right to use the forestry reserve for grazing purposes.[21] Although under pressure politically to shift strikers, the Department had no legal grounds for doing so. Certainly, legal means could be found within the *Native Administration Act 1936*: *marrngu* who refused to shift their camp when ordered to do so by a Protector of Natives could be prosecuted under section 40, or they could be removed to an institution under ministerial warrant, but the number of strikers involved, the strength of their organisation and the high degree of public interest in the situation led the Department to shy away from employing these options. 'Just at the moment I am not prepared to seek removals', McBeath told O'Neill.[22]

With the decline in its ability to control the strikers, the Department felt that the only suggestion it could make to pastoralists was to have offenders charged with trespass. Since the *Land Act 1933* gave Aboriginal people no special right to access enclosed pastoral country, they could be prosecuted for trespass. 'They are all amenable to the law in relation to trespass', McBeath told Les Miller:

> and if they offend in this direction then the station owners or managers must proceed in the same manner as in dealing with a white person. I realize that the situation is difficult, but at the same time this Department

---

18 McBeath to O'Neill, 15 October 1946, SROWA 1946/0799/68.
19 O'Neill to McBeath, 22 October 1946, SROWA 1946/0799/74.
20 O'Neill to McBeath, 22 October 1946, SROWA 1946/0799/74.
21 McBeath to O'Neill, 29 October 1946, SROWA 1946/0799/76.
22 McBeath to O'Neill, 29 October 1946, SROWA 1946/0799/76.

cannot control the movement of the natives who are engaged in dry shelling.²³

This was a victory of sorts for the strikers. Although deprived of their unique rights as Aboriginal people to access pastoral country, they were no longer being treated as having no legal rights at all. No longer was their freedom of movement being restricted simply because they were Aboriginal. After years of being subject to the arbitrary jurisdiction of pastoralists, police and Native Affairs officials, and to the arbitrary application of the *Native Administration Act*, their activism was giving them the same legal rights, and making them subject to the same laws, as non-Aboriginal Western Australians. This enabled strikers to find legal means of gaining access to pastoral country. In April, a working party of strikers at Poondana on Pippingarra Station was confronted by a member of the Richardson family, who demanded to know what they were doing there. The group's leader, Massey, produced a woodcutter's licence and said he was cutting firewood.²⁴ Richardson was advised by Jensen that no legal action could be taken against *marrngu* on their lease if they held woodcutters' licences, but that 'if he had particulars and facts to go on he could launch prosecutions for trespass' against the others.²⁵

In March 1947, on departmental advice and having no other option for removing strikers from his pastoral lease, Les Miller proceeded against Clancy McKenna and three other strikers for trespassing on his recently-acquired Strelley lease.²⁶ Miller told McBeath that the strikers were hunting in areas where their activities were disturbing stock, and that they had been defiant and 'insolent' when told not to hunt on those parts of the lease.²⁷ When Miller proceeded against them for trespass, the strikers accused him of victimisation and threatened to remove all labour from Strelley and from De Grey, where he was still the manager. Miller received a letter from Tommy Sampie, which read:

> I have to advise you that my association takes strong exception to your action in attempting to intimidate our members by threat of police prosecution.

---

23 McBeath to Fletcher, 15 October 1946, SROWA 1946/0799/68.
24 Jensen to McBeath, 30 April 1947, p. 1, SROWA 1947/0305/109.
25 Jensen to McBeath, 30 April 1947, p. 2, SROWA 1947/0305/110.
26 Miller to McBeath, and McBeath's reply to Miller, telegrams, 21 March 1947, SROWA 1947/0305/64.
27 McBeath to McDonald, 23 May 1947, SROWA 1947/0305/121.

We do not deny your right to prosecute in the event of a genuine breach of the law but we feel that this threat to summons Clancy McKenna and others[,] ... brought on by your known dislike for Clancy is a petty attempt to injure him[;] a personal matter. I have been asked to advise you that if you press this matter & take the case to court then in future all native labour will be withheld from those stations which you control.

When those of our friends who are still working have the chance to hear what you are proposing to do we believe that they too ... will see the danger of allowing you to continue your present policy without vigerous [*sic*] protest from them and ourselves.

So then if we do not hear from you before the 18th and the cases reach court you can take notice that as from April 18 no further native labour will be available to you.[28]

Although the letter carried Tommy Sampie's signature, the handwriting and the language style were unmistakably McLeod's, including the use of the word 'vigorous' which he frequently used in his writing and which he consistently spelled as 'vigerous'. Miller had no doubt that the writer was McLeod. When McBeath visited Port Hedland in April 1947, Miller gave him the letter 'from friend Sampey' with a note that it 'might be very useful to you'.[29] McBeath and O'Neill questioned Sampie about the letter, and when Sampie insisted that he had written it, they gave him half an hour to write a similar one. It was an unnecessary and intimidating demand, predicated on the racist and incorrect assumption that Sampie was incapable of writing such a letter. Although Sampie attempted to reproduce the letter, he was unable in the circumstances to do so, saying he felt too upset by the demand to concentrate.[30] Just what McBeath and O'Neill hoped to achieve by proving in this bullying manner that McLeod was the writer of the letter is unclear. The question of whether the letter had been written with the strikers' knowledge and consent would have been more to the point. Sampie's attempted reproduction of the original letter, retained in departmental records, indicates that he was at least aware of its contents. If the letter expressed the feelings and intentions of the strikers, then the question of who penned it seems irrelevant.

Prosecution of the four strikers for trespass went ahead, the case being held in Port Hedland on 23 May, with *marrngu* represented by Wally Lund

---

28   Sampie to Miller, 19 April 1947, SROWA 1947/0305/96, 98.
29   Miller to McBeath, 18 April 1947, SROWA 1947/0305/99.
30   McBeath to McDonald, 28 April 1947, SROWA 1947/0305/100.

of the Native Hospital and the De Grey River Pastoral Company represented by the law firm James Stone and Co. McKenna and three other strikers were found guilty of trespass and each fined 10/- with 6/- costs, with a warning from the magistrate that any further breaches would be dealt with severely.[31]

Although pastoralist complaints to the police and the Department about *marrngu* being on pastoral leases, disturbing and killing stock, continued to be made over the following decade and beyond, and although the Department and police continued to recommend prosecution for trespass, there were few such prosecutions. Despite complaints, some degree of accommodation was reached. Whether they liked it or not, pastoralists were being forced to share country with the strikers. They benefited from having kangaroo and goat numbers culled on their properties, and strikers agreed to notify station management of their movements and confine their activities to areas where they would be less likely to interfere with stock. Les Miller's wife, Edith, remembered the relationship as amicable:

> When we were at Strelley, McLeod approached my husband to ask could he send some boys out that way to catch the goats in the hills and after a while Les said, 'Yes, on one condition, that they shut the gates as they go through, and they don't do any damage round the mills'. Well he sent, I think, about five or six boys out with horses, with the instruction that they were not to damage anything round the mills, they were not to leave the gates open, and 'If you see Miller there and you can do anything to help him do it'. We never had any trouble at all.[32]

Providing evidence of pastoralist perceptions of strikers as 'boys' acting only under direction from McLeod, Edith Miller's account ignores the legal action mounted by her husband against the strikers and downplays resentment at the strikers' intrusion into the pastoralists' spaces. It does, however, give some evidence of strikers' willingness to adopt a less defiant attitude over their right to camp and hunt on pastoral leases, and of pastoralists' acceptance of the fact that, since they could no longer call on the police to remove *marrngu*, they would gain more from a cooperative relationship with strikers than from a confrontational one. While the strikers' goal of obtaining their own pastoral property was still out of reach, they were achieving a greater level of access to country.

---

31 Fletcher to McBeath, 28 May 1947, SROWA 1947/0305/126.
32 Edith Miller, interviewed by Jamieson, 1982, transcript, p. 101, SLWA OH506.

Despite some degree of accommodation, pastoralists were unnerved by the lack of control being exercised over Aboriginal movements and continued to complain that the strikers were killing and eating their stock. 'One can only assume that if they want some meat they will naturally get a sheep', Ted Richardson grumbled, 'as they are too lazy to go and get a kangaroo'.[33] Kangaroo and goat meat formed a large part of the strikers' diet, but squatters were probably right in assuming that mutton was sometimes included. Monty Hale remembered with amusement an incident that took place a decade later, when he was a member of the independent Aboriginal group that developed from the strike. One day, when he and other men were travelling on horseback, they came across *marrngu* camped at Kulykunguranya Bore. As they approached, the campers scrambled to hide the Pippingarra Station mutton they were in the process of cooking in a camp oven, but when they saw that the horsemen were their own people and not Pippingarra stockmen, they uncovered the meat and, laughing at their own panic, shared it with the newcomers.[34] The extent of stock losses that resulted from such theft was almost certainly overstated, however. In 1953, Alan White of Lalla Rookh Station wrote to Premier Bert Hawke about the loss of 900 sheep close to an area where *marrngu* members of the group were prospecting and mining. 'Although I have been unable to find anything to support the claim that they were responsible in some way for these losses', he wrote, 'I feel certain in my own mind that this is so'.[35]

It was a matter of serious concern for police officers and the Department of Native Affairs that Aboriginal people should have such unrestricted freedom of movement, and that nothing could be done to prevent it. They saw the containment of Aboriginal people and the protection of settler interests, particularly pastoral, as a major component of their role. Over and above the problem of labour shortages created by the strike was the inconvenience caused by the uncontrolled movement of strikers. Even those at Moolyella, generally seen as posing less of a problem in this regard, were causing anxiety in the settler population by their independent coming and going. The local government authority, the Marble Bar Road Board, urged Minister Ross McDonald to impose control. 'Could not something be done to confine them to a reserve well away from the white population of this

---

33 Richardson to Bray, 6 August 1946, SROWA 1938/0982/23.
34 Hale, *Kurlumarniny*, pp. 109–111.
35 White to Native Affairs Officer Noel Hawke, 21 August 1953, p. 2, SROWA 1953/0127/20.

district', the pastoralist-dominated road board asked.[36] Constable Marshall's no-nonsense approach was effective in maintaining Marble Bar as a settler space, but ensuring that such boundaries remained in place would require the assistance of a second police officer in the town. Since the strike began there had been between 150 and 200 strikers at Moolyella, Marshall wrote:

> These natives have to be kept in hand, occasionally large numbers of them have wandered into town, and wanted to take up camp within the town area, and were rather cheeky – However they departed fairly quickly from town ... Personally, I prefer working on my own when I can cope with the work, but I consider that the position is a bit touchy at the moment.[37]

As far as Native Affairs Inspector Tom Jensen was concerned, this unrestricted movement of Aboriginal people should not be tolerated. Accustomed to exercising firm and unquestioned control over Aboriginal people as a Kimberley policeman, he was outraged by the audacious manner in which Pilbara Aboriginal people were defying and undermining settler authority. Before taking up his job as Travelling Inspector, he had been briefed in Perth on the situation in the Pilbara and of the need for tact in dealing with the strikers, both because of the organised resistance strategies they used to oppose efforts to curb their freedom and because of the high level of public interest and support they attracted. But his role as a Kimberley policeman had largely focused on securing unhindered settler access to Aboriginal land for pastoral purposes, and it went against the grain of his police experience to turn a blind eye to Aboriginal intrusions into settler and pastoral spaces. The annoyance caused by strikers' unchecked ramblings all over the country as if they owned it added to his frustration at the strikers' recalcitrance in the face of the Department's attempts to negotiate a return to work. On 30 April 1947, two weeks after McBeath and O'Neill's visit to the area, and ten days after the Boodarie fire, he wrote a report to the Department arguing that, since negotiation had failed, the time had arrived for firm action to bring the strikers under control. 'During this last week the striking natives appear to have adopted an air of defiance', he wrote:

> and are apparently setting themselves out to be as much annoyance to the Pastoralist as possible ... Striking native camps are spread over a

---

36   E. F. Duncan, Secretary, Marble Bar Road Board, to McDonald, 28 May 1947, SROWA 1943/0621/39.
37   Marshall to Inspector Cowie, 3 October 1947, SROWA 1952/5174 v1.

wide area now on Pastoral properties, and this fact coupled with the travelling around the country side by scores of others per motor truck, horse back and train from Marble Bar to Hedland makes the position from the point of view of the Pastoralists in particular one of tension.[38]

He was 'well aware of the delicate position', he wrote, but felt that 'in fairness to the majority of the natives and for the natural peace in the industry', strikers had to be shifted from the Twelve Mile. He thought their refusal to take up the offer of improved employment conditions was an indication that *marrngu* had lost sight of the strike's objectives. 'They are imbued with the strike bug', he railed:

> and the knowledge that they can apparently strike and get away with it, which fact has been brought about by the intensive workings of Don McLeod over a period of years, and the bug of the strike and McLeod is that vivid in their minds that they cannot absorb any other facts at all.[39]

He understood that some of the 'half-castes among this crowd' found satisfaction in being able to 'fend for themselves and cut their own chaff as it were', and that these men would 'never return to any work as long as Kangaroo skins and goat hides hold the present high prices'. He believed, however, that the hundreds of 'full-blood' strikers who would never be capable of managing their own affairs 'in any shape or form' should not be sacrificed to the desire for independence on the part of a few 'half-castes'. 'It is quite obvious that the days of arbitration with the natives on this strike question have gone', he wrote, 'and the trouble is no closer to a satisfactory climax than it was twelve months ago'. For the protection of both the 'full-bloods' and the pastoral industry, he set out a list of recommendations to the Department to confine strikers and prevent their continued intrusion into settler spaces.

Jensen's first recommendation was to remove the strike leaders under ministerial warrant. This was the Department's go-to tool for suppressing Aboriginal dissent, but Jensen's caveat that this should be done 'if it can be carried out without a successful plea for writs of Habeus corpus being entered by some foreign body on behalf of the natives' is an indication that southern support for the strike was successfully preventing the Department from resorting to this facility in the Pilbara. The leaders identified by Jensen for removal were Clancy McKenna, Dooley, Mick Lee, Captain, Snowball,

---

38 Jensen to McBeath, 30 April 1947, pp. 1–2, SROWA 1947/0305/109–110.
39 Jensen to McBeath, 30 April 1947, p. 2, SROWA 1947/0305/110.

Gordon Snowball, Coombie, Tommy Sampie, Big Harry Davis and Ernie Mitchell.[40] Other Twelve Mile strikers, Jensen suggested, should be given the choice to return to station employment or be transferred to Moolyella, part of which would be declared a native reserve, becoming a government institution on which *marrngu* would be required to support themselves by mining tin. In effect, Moolyella would have become a concentration camp on which *marrngu* would be confined. Travel permits would be required for any *marrngu* wishing to leave the reserve, and Marble Bar and Port Hedland would be declared prohibited areas. There would be tighter restrictions on access to firearms, especially for anyone who had been involved in the strike. Although these restrictions would be irksome for 'half-castes' able to 'cut their own chaff' who were enjoying their independence, Jensen believed that the measures would provide protection for the less capable 'full-bloods'. It was a matter 'of doing the best for the most among the natives, and it will have to be appreciated that with a few of these natives it is a case of being cruel to be kind'.[41]

There is an obvious punitive tone to Jensen's suggestions. Strikers who were not prepared to accept wage and condition improvements being offered by pastoralists must be confined and controlled, he argued. The continued existence of independent Aboriginal communities sharing space with settler communities was simply not an option. 'No doubt you may consider that the aforegoing are drastic measures to put forward', he wrote to McBeath:

> but ... the days of Arbitration on this matter are gone forever in my opinion, coupled with the fact that this strike has now reached a point where the natives concerned are striking for strikings sake and without a just or reasonable cause; Greek has to meet Greek and this matter has to be adjusted under Departmental guidance and control, and not by compromises with the Communistic purge that is in evidence at the present time at the 12 mile camp. It must be readily accepted that a camp of striking natives under the control of the Department would be a far better sight than one with no ends or beginnings; no present or future such as can be witnessed at the present time in this area.
>
> I conscientiously beleive [*sic*] that if this problem is not taken in hand in the very near future and an alternative on the lines as indicated put into action to counter the Communistic bug and the environs of the 12 mile

---

40 Jensen to McBeath, 30 April 1947, pp. 2–3, SROWA 1947/0305/110–111.
41 Jensen to McBeath, 30 April 1947, p. 3, SROWA 1947/0305/111.

camp, that this matter will ultimately end in serious trouble between the white people of this area and the Natives. I concede that this is 1947 and the methods of 1947 have to be adopted, but as the Natives ... refuse to accept work at increased rates, decline to accept the fact that better conditions will be provided for them and adopt an attitude of defiance such as in this case, it is quite evident that there has to be a breaking point, and that point to my mind is not far distant. If there could be found among their present reasons for striking, one point, that could with a long stretch of imagination be termed lawful and excusable, I would be the first to assist them to achieve their object thru the good graces of yourself. But as is known to you as well as myself that the only reason expounded is they want Don McLeod, well then I say that no compromise in any way with this point can be accepted and the only solution lays in the drastic methods that I have herewith penned. I have thought this matter out from every possible angle for a solution, but cannot find any apart from drastic action that is going to be effective.[42]

McBeath thought there was considerable merit in the proposals. He had faith in Jensen's 'sincere desire to do the best for the welfare of the natives generally, with due regard to all the local circumstances', and accepted his recommendations as 'very welcome and of great interest'. It had become evident that there would be no return to the pre-strike environment of pastoralist control over resident Aboriginal station communities, maintained with the assistance of the police. While continued efforts would be made to return strikers to stations, the Department needed to find a way to impose control over those *marrngu* who did not wish to return. Establishing a native reserve at Moolyella would give the Department the legal authority, under section 12 of the *Native Administration Act 1936*, to order strikers to shift there, and the scheme would not incur additional costs for the Department, as the internees could be self-supporting. Although there were definite difficulties involved in the scheme, he recommended Jensen's proposal to the minister for his consideration.[43]

Settler anxiety at the breakdown of racialised spatial constraints, and particularly at the unrestricted intrusion of Twelve Mile strikers into settler spaces, could not be ignored by a department whose principal responsibility was to maintain control over the Aboriginal population. Repeated appeals to the Department by pastoralist Ted Richardson had to be taken seriously.

---

42 Jensen to McBeath, 30 April 1947, p. 3, SROWA 1947/0305/111-112.
43 McBeath to McDonald, 16 May 1947, SROWA 1947/0305/115-117.

The idea of shifting all strikers to Moolyella, where they would cause less annoyance to squatters and to the settler population more generally, was a solution that the Department sought to achieve by various means in the months to come. However, it was clear that any attempt to use Native Administration legislation to force *marrngu* to shift from the Twelve Mile, as Jensen suggested, would meet strong opposition from the strikers and raise a storm of protest from supporters in the south. More subtle methods were needed to impose departmental control on the Twelve Mile strikers.

Chapter 20

'The Proposal Was a Sound One in Principle'

Jack Gribble and 'Control and Supervision' of the Strikers, June – December 1947

While Minister for Native Affairs Ross McDonald was concerned to find ways to resolve pastoralist anxieties in the Pilbara, any action to be taken needed to conform to his vision for constructive policy reform in the state. In June 1947, he and Acting Commissioner McBeath conducted a tour of the north, and among those they spoke with in Port Hedland was, in his role as road board chairman, Ted Richardson, owner of Pippangarra Station and the most persistent critic of the Department's inability to control and confine the strikers.[1] The following month, McDonald commissioned Magistrate F. E. A. Bateman to conduct a full inquiry throughout the state into conditions for Aboriginal people and to make recommendations for future action. Although the Moseley Royal Commission into Aboriginal affairs in the state had been conducted as recently as 1936, McDonald defended his decision to institute a new inquiry, pointing to significant changes that had taken place in the decade since that survey had been carried out. In particular, he referred to the development of 'a new phase of the problem' in the North West, 'where in some areas, the old relations between natives and their pastoralist employers have been impaired'.[2] Bateman began his survey on 4 August, accompanied by H. A. Jones, a clerk in the Department of Native Affairs and throughout the north by the Department's Travelling Inspector, Tom Jensen.

While this survey was being conducted, McDonald attempted to bring matters under control in the Port Hedland district by appointing a special departmental officer to live at the Twelve Mile, establish personal relationships

---

1   'Visit by Minister McDonald', SROWA 1947/0500.
2   *West Australian*, 7 July 1947, p. 7.

'The Proposal Was a Sound One in Principle'

with the strikers, and influence them to adopt a more cooperative attitude. The officer would mediate between pastoralists and those strikers who wished to return to station work, but his most important role was to encourage strikers to curb their violation of settler spaces and sensibilities, particularly with regard to their intrusion on pastoral leases. 'The duties of this position', McBeath wrote, 'will entail all welfare aspects of the displaced natives in the Port Hedland and Marble Bar Districts and the general supervision of their activities in order to minimise friction with the pastoralists'.[3]

Such an appointment required someone with extensive experience in working with Aboriginal people and a demonstrated ability to gain their confidence and trust. McBeath believed he knew just the man for the job, and recommended John Wriede Bulmer (Jack) Gribble for the position. A third-generation missionary with extensive experience at the Forrest River Mission in the northern Kimberley, Jack Gribble also had experience in the Northern Territory Department of Aboriginal Affairs and, perhaps most significantly, as the WWII leader of a well-organised and well-trained Aboriginal coast watch unit on Melville Island, to the north of Darwin.[4] McBeath and Gribble had known each other in the 1920s, when McBeath ran a store in the remote northern Kimberley town of Wyndham and when Gribble ran a launch between the town and the Forrest River Mission, where he had worked as a missionary with his father, Ernest Richard Bulmer Gribble. In early July 1947, Jack Gribble was on his way back to the Forrest River Mission in search of a job when McBeath recommended him for the appointment as Special Officer with the Department at the Twelve Mile. He wired Gribble in Wyndham: 'Please stand by may be able to offer you position'. Gribble jumped at the chance: 'Standing by much appreciated'.[5] He flew to Perth for an interview and was appointed to the position on 18 July 1947.

At fifty-one years of age, Jack Gribble bore the physical and mental scars of an eventful life marked by trauma. In World War I, he had served overseas for four years in Gallipoli and France and was wounded three times, but he returned to Australia without medals, rank or eligibility for war gratuity, after being charged with 'behaving in a scandalous manner unbecoming to the character of an officer and a Gentleman' and cashiered for passing false

---

3   McBeath to Under Treasurer, 17 September 1947, SROWA 1947/0691/14.
4   See Appendix B for more information on Jack Gribble's life.
5   McBeath to Gribble, telegram, 7 July 1947; Gribble to McBeath, telegram, 10 July 1947, SROWA 1947/0691/1–2.

cheques.⁶ 'I have nothing for my services only my wounds', he later wrote.⁷ Throughout the 1920s he worked as a missionary under the authoritarian regime of his father, Ernest Gribble, at the extremely isolated Forrest River Anglican Mission in the far north of the Kimberley, suffering severe burns when petrol fumes ignited on the mission launch in 1925, killing three Aboriginal men. The following year he experienced the sudden death of his young wife. His role in leading an Aboriginal coastguard unit on Melville Island during WWII was physically and psychologically demanding. The unit's work included rescuing men from downed planes and bombed ships, often with horrific injuries and burns. Gribble suffered hunger, physical hardship and long months of social isolation, all of which took their toll on his physical and mental health. Withdrawn by the Navy from Melville Island in April 1945 suffering war neurosis, he worked for a time for the Northern Territory Native Affairs Department, but he struggled to hold down a job and was out of work when he was offered the position of Special Officer with the Western Australian Department of Native Affairs.⁸ He spent the first month of his appointment in Perth's Hollywood Repatriation Hospital to receive treatment for 'war caused disabilities'.⁹

Meanwhile, the Department continued to reassure Pilbara pastoralists that measures were being put in place to address their complaints. In doing so, they were careful not to specify the nature of the measure being taken, fearing that Gribble's chances of success could be jeopardised if McLeod and strike leaders were alerted to the purpose of this appointment before his arrival. McDonald was therefore circumspect in his responses to pastoralist complaints, assuring them that action was being taken without providing details. On 31 July 1947, Ted Richardson wrote to McDonald, blaming the Twelve Mile strikers for his station's disappointing wool clip in the recently-completed shearing, and again urging McDonald to take steps to enable Pippingarra to use the country around the Twelve Mile: 'Surely, Sir, something can be done for our

---

6   Gribble John Wriede Bulmer: Service Number – Lieutenant 1491, NAA B2455, Gribble JWB.

7   Gribble to Officer in Charge Base Records, AIF, Victoria Barracks, 10 October 1937, p. 2, NAA B2455, Gribble JWB.

8   John Morris, '"Continuing Assimilation"? A Shifting Identity for the Tiwi 1919 to the Present', PhD Thesis, University of Ballarat, 2003, p. 160; *Mirror*, 9 February 1952, p. 7, 'War Hero's Abject Appearance in Court'.

9   McBeath to Accountant, CSO, 18 September 1947, SROWA 1947/0691/15; F. K. Wallace, Medical Superintendent of the Repatriation Commission, SROWA 1947/0691/16. For a more complete account of the life of Jack Gribble, see Appendix B.

protection. If not, as I said before, we might as well get out before it is too late'.[10] In reply, McDonald referred to the difficulties involved 'in removing a settlement of natives in the circumstances obtaining and in the absence of suitable localities in the district to which they might be sent'. However, he wrote, 'I am hoping that we shall be able to take some measures shortly which may assist you in respect of the matters to which you refer'.[11] Richardson was not reassured. 'I ... regret you are unable to do anything regarding the natives camped at the 12 mile', he grumbled on 1 September. 'Surely something can be done by your Dept'.[12] The fact that this letter was filed in a folder relating to Gribble's appointment indicates that such complaints were to become the responsibility of the new Special Officer.

Gribble had been released from hospital by this time, but was still in Perth being briefed by McBeath and O'Neill about the complexities and sensitivities of the situation in the Pilbara. In reply to further reassurances from McDonald that arrangements were being made, Richardson wrote that he was 'pleased that something may be done in the near future regarding the dogs'.[13] He saw the strikers as a wasted resource. 'It seems a pity to see them all at the 12 mile camp especially the young ones growing up to be absolutely useless when they could be occupied to advantage to the pastoral industry & themselves', he wrote.[14] With Gribble preparing to leave for Port Hedland within days, McDonald replied that provisions would be in place 'by next week ... which may assist in reducing sheep losses and detriment to your flocks'.[15]

The Department kept Gribble's appointment under wraps until he could establish himself at the Twelve Mile. Bob Coverley, the former minister with responsibility for Aboriginal Affairs, got wind of the appointment and raised questions in Parliament. Was it true, he asked, that a Northern Territory Protector of Natives had been employed, and if so, what was the nature of the appointment and what special duties was he employed to fulfil? The Department revealed as little information as possible, replying that such an appointment was under consideration but had not yet been made, that it was of a temporary nature and that the officer would carry out duties as a Protector of Natives as

---

10   Richardson to McDonald, 31 July 1947, SROWA 1947/0305/137.
11   McDonald to Richardson, 5 August 1947, SROWA 1947/0305/139.
12   Richardson to McDonald, 1 September 1947, SROWA 1947/0691/12.
13   McDonald to Richardson, 9 September 1947, SROWA 1947/0691/13; Richardson to McDonald, 13 September 1947, SROWA 1947/0305/142.
14   Richardson to McDonald, 13 September 1947, SROWA 1947/0305/142.
15   McDonald to Richardson, 17 September 1947, SROWA 1947/0305/144.

assigned to him.[16] Treasury was not notified of the appointment until Gribble was due to travel north in mid-September, and even the local departmental officer, Tom Jensen, who was travelling through the Kimberley with Bateman and Jones, was not informed of the appointment. The Department saw the placement as experimental and was prepared to withdraw Gribble from the area if strikers responded negatively to his appointment.[17]

Certainly, the strikers at the Twelve Mile were demonstrating a determination to maintain their independence and group authority. As Gribble travelled north by road, conflict developed between Twelve Mile strikers and Sergeant Bernie McGeary, Les Fletcher's replacement as officer in charge of the Port Hedland Police Station. McGeary had arranged for two strikers to take work at Pardoo Station but, although the men were willing, Twelve Mile strikers decided at a meeting that employment at Pardoo should not be accepted without the promise of reasonable wages and conditions.[18] The two men told McGeary that strikers Wellington and Norman had threatened to physically restrain them if they attempted to leave.

On 23 September 1947, McGeary and Constable Needle confronted the strikers at the Twelve Mile about this. Peter Coppin remembered the occasion. There had been no altercation with the police since McKenna and others had been arrested for taking people from Marble Bar to the Twelve Mile in January. After that, 'we settle down there again for awhile', Coppin remembered:

> and then McGeary came ... By Jees, he was a rough sort of bloke ... We were having a meeting there – that was our meeting place – and McGeary come up ... and straight away he said, 'What's the cause of all this trouble?'
>
> We told him 'Oh! Nobody's causing trouble. We're just trying to fight for our rights'.
>
> We were getting poor wages and we tell him all about it: 'We can't be working all our life as cheap labour in the station'. That's what we tell him.[19]

According to McGeary's report of the incident:

---

16 Legislative Assembly, Notices and Orders of the Day for 12 August 1948, SROWA 1947/0691/6.
17 McBeath to Jensen, 31 October 1947, SROWA 1947/0305/175.
18 *Northern Times*, 3 October 1947, p. 7.
19 Read and Coppin, *Kangkushot*, p. 80.

> I interviewed a large mob of natives ... and remonstrated with them for threatening to stop any native who desired to return to any work and that nobody would be forced back to work, but they were not to stop any native who wanted to return.
>
> Ernie Mitchell, a half caste of about 45 years, who is apparently the ringleader of the 12 mile camp, spoke out loudly, 'Well, if that's the way you are going to do it, we will have another strike and cause a lot more trouble'. Most of those present loudly agreed. The situation was most threatening, although both myself and Const. Needle were armed with a revolver.[20]

McGeary was not used to having Aboriginal people forcefully asserting their rights and answering him back in this manner. His instinctive policeman's response was to threaten violence. His report does not mention that he drew his revolver on the strikers, but his reference to revolvers is telling. Peter Coppin remembered that he did so. 'I answered him', Coppin said:

> And he have a go at me then ...
>
> 'Oh, you the bloke?' He got his revolver out. He had a revolver, and he hold it in my guts, trying to bluff me.
>
> I was strong in that time – young. I wasn't scared. If he kill me, he kill me, bad luck. And, that's it. So, I said, 'All right, you can do what you like with me, take me or whatever you like'.
>
> He said, 'No. But I tell you who I'll take – Ernie Mitchell'
>
> ... He was the leader man, you see. So he took him.[21]

'I talked these natives down', McGeary reported:

> and eventually got my point so far as attention to my advice given and after some more talking I arrested Norman for using threatening words to Mirandie Mitchell on the 22nd and Ernie Mitchell for the same type of offence on the spot to me. This incident of Mitchell's could have caused a nasty situation and it is only by using much tact it was avoided.
>
> When I was leaving, a full blood Snowball shouted out we better go with you, and tried to excite the crowd to do something. I told them all

---

20   McGeary to McBeath, 24 September 1947, SROWA S3841 cons769 1.
21   Coppin, in Read and Coppin, *Kangkushot*, p. 80.

if they did anything wrong I would arrest them. They calmed down and went away and I brought the two offenders to Port Hedland.

Again, Coppin's recollection differed from the policeman's report. According to Coppin's account, strikers acted on Snowball's insistence that if one was arrested, they should all be arrested. 'As soon as he took him', Coppin said:

> bloody big mob got up and jump in his motor car! And he screamed then!
>
> Anyway, he didn't know what to do, he couldn't get away because everybody in his car. Some jumped in front of it – oh, they were doing a lot of wrong things now because they were getting very savage these people. So the old fella [Mitchell], himself, said, 'Never mind, let me go, I'll go to gaol. That will be all right, don't worry about me'. But they were all in the motor car and they can't get out; they were jumping on the car, in front, everywhere! Well they get off and he took the old fella. Took him in there to gaol …
>
> That was really the fun we had with the policeman![22]

In the Port Hedland Police Court the following day, Ernie Mitchell pleaded not guilty to the charge of disorderly conduct by using threatening words likely to lead to a breach of the peace. He was found guilty and sentenced to seven days' imprisonment.[23] Like Jensen and Marshall, and like the local police and Native Affairs officials who followed him, McGeary urged the Department to employ its strongest weapon of control to bring the strikers into line – removal under ministerial warrant. He named Ernie Mitchell, Sam and Peter Coppin, Snowball and Captain as being 'a menace to the well being and welfare of the other natives' and recommended their removal from the area. Clancy McKenna, who usually received top ranking among those put forward for removal, had taken work at Munda Station and was no longer considered a 'menace'. 'I expect Mr. Gribble here within the near future', McGeary wrote, 'and will confer with him but mob rule must be stamped out and as soon as possible'.[24]

McDonald informed the Commissioner of Police of the threatening situation that had developed at the Twelve Mile, but again held back from acting on the recommendation to remove leaders. 'I do not think we should take any action by warrant as the position stands at present and pending further

---

22   Coppin, in Read and Coppin, *Kangkushot*, p. 80.
23   *Northern Times*, 3 October 1947, p. 7.
24   McGeary to McBeath, 24 September 1947, SROWA S3841 cons769 1.

reports from Mr. Gribble', he told McBeath.[25] He hoped that Gribble would curb the militant behaviour of the strikers. He informed the Commissioner of Police on 6 October that Gribble had been appointed and would by now 'be residing at the 12 mile camp'.

'He has had a large experience with natives', he wrote:

> These assemblies of natives in what may be permanent camps is a new development and the Department feels that it should have a protector, who is an officer of the department, to keep in contact with such natives at places like the 12 mile and Moolyella near Marble Bar, in order to protect their welfare and ensure as far as possible that there is no undesirable features associated with such assemblies of natives.[26]

Departmental officers felt that were being prevented from making contact with rank and file members of the strike camps by the belligerent 'ringleaders'. Living in the area would enable Gribble to break through the negative influence and obstructionism of McLeod and the 'ringleaders' and to arrange employment for any individual willing to return to station work. He would also provide the 'benevolent supervision' assumed necessary for Aboriginal welfare, imposing order on the perceived disorder of the strike community to prevent conflict with pastoralists and bring an end to Richardson's persistent complaints.[27]

Actually, strikers were showing that they did not need the guidance and supervision of a benevolent *walypila* superintendent to run their community. Although authorities had initially expressed concern about the health effects of large groups of Aboriginal people living together without supervision, a medical inspection found that, a year into the strike, sanitary conditions at the Twelve Mile and the health of the strikers there were good, despite their poverty and lack of resources. Acting District Medical Officer with the Department of Health Frank Beamish found the health of the men to be exceptionally good, while the women, although not as fit as the men, were nevertheless healthy. Poverty meant that their diet was basic, consisting mainly of kangaroo meat, damper and tea, supplemented, as much as their limited means allowed, by tinned milk and vegetables purchased from the proceeds of skins and mining. The children received a better diet than the adults. Funds raised by the group were used by Tommy Sampie to purchase

---

25 McDonald to McBeath, 13 October 1947, SROWA 1947/0305/165.
26 McDonald to Commissioner of Police, 6 October 1947, SROWA 1947/0305/162.
27 McBeath to McDonald, 17 September 1947, SROWA 1947/0691/19.

food appropriate to the nutritional needs of children, including more milk, oatmeal, more vegetables and occasionally fruit. Beamish found the children's nutrition and health to be very good, and, according to a report in the *Workers' Star*, he congratulated Sampie on the health of the community and particularly of the children, which he thought was a credit to the settlement.[28] He was overheard to say that the Twelve Mile was a great deal cleaner than Port Hedland streets.[29] His report was sufficiently impressive for McDonald to begin speaking of the venture as an example of positive developmental change being undertaken by Aboriginal people themselves.[30]

Although Gribble was instructed to establish friendly relations with the strikers, he aligned himself with settler authority by making initial contact with *marrngu* in the company of police officers. After McGeary's lively encounter with Twelve Mile strikers the previous week, Gribble felt sure that his visit there in company with Broome-based Inspector of Police James Cowie, who was visiting Port Hedland, did 'a lot of good'.[31] On his first tour of the area, Gribble travelled with Constable Tom Needle and, when he met with strikers camping at the Shaw River siding on 30 September, he did so as a member of the triumvirate of settler power: the pastoralist, the policeman and the Native Affairs officer. By prior arrangement he and Needle were met at Shaw River by the manager of Warralong station, Beau Sainsbury, and the manager of Bungalow (Coongan) Station, Neville Flight-Smith, and, as a result of their discussion with strikers, four *marrngu* agreed to return to station employment. It seems fair to assume that some pressure was brought to bear to achieve this agreement. Four months previously, Marble Bar's Constable Keith Weaver had reported that strikers at Shaw River appeared quite contented with the strike, several remarking that they 'must stand by Don McLeod'.[32] Now, those who refused to take station work were warned against trespassing on Warralong and ordered to return to the Twelve Mile the following day. Gribble reinforced his association with settler authority by spending the night at the Warralong homestead instead of camping with the strikers. The next morning, he and Needle returned to

---

28 F. T. Beamish to Commissioner of Public Health, 25 August 1947, SROWA1943/0621/63; *Workers' Star*, 24 October 1947, p. 5, 'Health Good in Native Village'.
29 *Workers' Star*, 24 October 1947, p. 5, 'Health Good in Native Village'.
30 Myrtle Amos to McDonald, 24 April 1949, p. 3, and McDonald to Amos, 9 May 1949, SROWA S3841 cons769 1.
31 Gribble to McBeath, 28 September 1947, SROWA 1947/0305/156–158.
32 Weaver, police patrol report, 13 May 1947, SROWA 1946/2538 v8.

Shaw River to make sure that the strikers were preparing to return to the Twelve Mile as instructed, and Needle inspected their gear for firearms. That day, Gribble and Needle returned Jimmy Woodman to work at his old station of Lalla Rookh, and took another of the Shaw River strikers to work at Carlindi Station.[33]

When Gribble met the much larger group of strikers at Moolyella a few days later, the interaction was more amicable, although he again made his visit in the company of a police officer. According to Constable Weaver, Gribble told a meeting of about sixty men that he had come from Perth 'with the intention of seeing that they received better conditions if they agreed to return to work'. He was there to help them, he said, and if there was anything he could do to assist them, he would, within reason, attempt to do so. In a clear exaggeration of the length of his experience with Aboriginal people, he told the Moolyella men that he had been among natives as a missionary in the Kimberley for nearly thirty-eight years. In fact, it was his father who had been a missionary for thirty-eight years: Gribble's claim is an indication of his strong identification with his father and his family's missionary history, and is perhaps also an indication of his tenuous grip on reality.[34]

Nevertheless, the Moolyella strikers responded positively to Gribble, hopeful that their concerns would finally be taken seriously and some effort made to address them. Weaver wrote that when Gribble asked for questions, 'there was not a back-word, in stating their complaints'. They stated that their principal grievance, beyond poor wages and conditions on the stations, was 'that, if they were employed by one station, and after a while, they desired to go to another station, the manager of that station, would not employ them, because they belonged to another station'. Gribble promised to look into this practice. Strikers told Gribble that other Native Affairs officials had come and promised to arrange wage and condition improvements but had left the district and had not been seen again. Gribble assured them that he would remain in the Pilbara and would always be handy.[35]

Although hopeful that Gribble would see that their demands were met and negotiate a return to station work for those who wanted it, the Moolyella people were unwilling to make any commitments about accepting employment without first discussing the situation with strikers at the Twelve Mile. Nevertheless, Gribble was pleased with the meeting and, according to Weaver, had 'high

---

33   Needle, police patrol report, 1 October 1947, SROWA 1939/1777 v7.
34   Weaver, police patrol report, 5 October 1947, SROWA 1946/2538 v8.
35   Weaver, police patrol report, 5 October 1947, SROWA 1946/2538 v8.

hopes of being able to conclude the native strike'.[36] He was not the first official to express such confidence, and he would not be the last.

The Department remained cautiously optimistic that Gribble's appointment might achieve the results they were hoping for. 'Mr. Gribble sounds a note of optimism which I sincerely hope is not over-estimated', McBeath wrote. 'However, as he has succeeded in placing four natives back in employment his feelings may be correct'.[37] Following a short visit by Gribble to Perth in mid-October, the Department confirmed his indefinite appointment as Special Officer under Jensen's direction, reserving the right to terminate the appointment at any time.[38] Tom Jensen, due to return to the area with Bateman and Jones after their survey of the Kimberley region, was informed of the appointment and instructed to provide advice and guidance to the new officer.[39]

But the man they had appointed to impose order on the strikers was struggling to find order in the chaos of his own psyche. Daunted, perhaps, by reports of the militant independence of the Twelve Mile strikers, he never pitched his tent among them, despite repeated instructions from McBeath to do so. Instead, he lived at Port Hedland's Esplanade Hotel until his debts there became too onerous and he shifted to the Pier Hotel. He began to overindulge in alcohol and self-aggrandisement. As he set about making contacts in the town and among the pastoralists, he enjoyed the sense of his own importance as the man with the knowledge and experience of Aboriginal people necessary to restore peace, the expert called in to fix problems that nobody else could fix. He presented himself as a senior Commonwealth government official, sent to take control of Aboriginal affairs in the area, not answerable to the state's Commissioner of Native Affairs but dealing only with the minister. On the strength of his senior government position, he borrowed extensively from Port Hedland residents on various pretexts, accruing debts he could not repay. He also used government order forms, intended for vehicle expenses, to obtain further cash. As stories of drunkenness and monetary entanglements circulated, the early good impression he had created in the town quickly evaporated.[40]

---

36   Weaver, police patrol report, 5 October 1947, SROWA 1946/2538 v8.
37   McBeath to McDonald, 6 October 1947, SROWA 1947/0305/159.
38   McBeath to Gribble, 31 October 1947, SROWA 1947/0305/173.
39   McBeath to Jensen, 31 October 1947, SROWA 1947/0305/175.
40   O'Neill to McBeath, 9 December 1947, SROWA 1947/0691/84; Jensen to McBeath, 7 November 1947, SROWA 1947/0691/39–40; Jones to McBeath, 13 November 1947, SROWA 1947/0691/46.

Jensen had not yet received McBeath's letter informing him of Gribble's appointment when rumours reached him in Derby about a senior Commonwealth officer taking over his duties in the Port Hedland and Marble Bar districts.[41] When he arrived in Port Hedland with Bateman and Jones at the beginning of November, he was 'inundated' with inquiries, complaints and rumours relating to Gribble. Sergeant McGeary told him that Gribble was doing far more harm than good in the area. Jensen tried to discuss matters with Gribble, but Gribble avoided him. After some hesitation about the propriety of making complaints against a fellow officer, Jensen reported his concerns to McBeath. 'I am in total agreement with an appointment such as this especially to the Port Hedland area', he wrote:

> but I must definitely disagree with the person at present holding the position. By his every act he is bringing the Department into ridicule, and I am respectfully suggesting that this Officer be recalled to Head Office as soon as it is possible to do so, and a strong firm type of man appointed in his stead. I think under direct supervision from Head Office Sir, where every action could be watched, this man would be suitable, but in his present role, where he is more or less thrown upon his own initiative, I state very definitely that he is a total failure, and not only bringing discredit to himself but also on the Department and others such as myself.
>
> I venture to say that he is verging on being what could be styled a 'Confidence Man' and this you must agree is not what is desired anywhere in the Department and especially in the Port Hedland area, where as is well known to you the Department gets more criticism than I suppose any other area in Western Australia.[42]

Bateman and Jones, returning to Perth a few days after Jensen submitted this report, confirmed Jensen's account of Gribble's activities. Jones had no hesitation in recommending the termination of Gribble's appointment. 'Whether all the tales and rumours are true or not', Jones wrote, 'his presence in his position of trust is not doing either the Department or Mr. Gribble any good'.[43] In words reminiscent of Gribble's WWI court-martial thirty years earlier, McBeath wrote that it appeared that 'Mr. Gribble's behaviour' was 'certainly not becoming an officer of this Department', and he instructed

---

41 Jensen to McBeath, 7 November 1947, p. 1, SROWA 1947/0691/39.
42 Jensen to McBeath, 7 November 1947, p. 2, SROWA 1947/0691/40.
43 Jones to McBeath, 13 November 1947, SROWA 1947/0691/46.

Acting Deputy Commissioner Laurie O'Neill to 'proceed to either Nullagine or Port Hedland by plane as soon as possible, and investigate the position generally as far as Mr. Gribble's general behaviour and conduct is concerned'.[44]

As temperatures began to soar in the Pilbara, Jack Gribble escaped the heat of his financial entanglements in Port Hedland by travelling around the district. He engaged the services of Peter Coppin as his driver. 'My Boy ... has been one of the ring leaders of the Strike', he told O'Neill, 'but please note that he is now on my side'.[45] Coppin had not sided with Gribble, however, but took the job on the promise of payment of £2/10/- per week, with tobacco and keep. 'I was the driver for this bloody welfare bloke', Coppin said:

> Just workin' for a bit of money during the strike ... He was from the welfare, go from place to place, trying to stop the people from going on strike ... He was an old fella! He can't drive too good, that's why he had to get me to drive![46]

Coppin took the opportunity, as he travelled around stations as Gribble's driver, to encourage other *marrngu* to join the strike. Gribble had instructed him not to do so:

> He was telling me, 'Don't mention about the strike. Don't get yourself in trouble'.
>
> ...
>
> I was drivin' him around and when we get in the back of the place I was tellin' the people to go on strike! I used to tell them not to take any notice of that old bugger![47]

Gribble's activities may have precipitated further strike action, at least on one station. Many stations were now paying increased wages and providing improved conditions in an effort to attract much-needed Aboriginal labour, but were prepared to employ only a limited number of workers at these rates. Gribble may have attempted to standardise wage rates across stations at lower than the current rate to encourage stations to employ Aboriginal people in larger numbers. This would explain an incident set out in a letter sent from the Pilbara to the Native Rights League (previously the Committee for Defence of

---

44 McBeath to O'Neill, 21 November 1947, SROWA 1947/0691/50.
45 Gribble to O'Neill, 2[?] November 1947, SROWA 1947/0691/55–56.
46 Coppin, in Read and Coppin, *Kangkushot*, p. 72.
47 Coppin, in Read and Coppin, *Kangkushot*, p. 72.

Native Rights) and reprinted in the Melbourne-based journal of the Waterside Workers Federation in Australia, the *Maritime Worker*. In an account that was probably transcribed by McLeod or Sampie, a worker claimed that:

> as soon as Mr. Bateman left Port Hedland, Gribble came out to the station. When he left the manager told the boys that he had to cut down their wages and good tucker, Gribble said. He would have to cut it down same as before. He asked us would we stand that. We said we would have to consider it and bought all the tobacco and stores we could get and then pulled out and joined the strikers again. We only left one man. We would have had to buy all extra food for cash – tinned stuff, clothes, combs, soap. The women's wages would have dropped from 15/- to 7/6 and they would have had to buy all their clothes out of this and extra food too.[48]

The *Maritime Worker* article does not name the station involved in this account, but workers at Noreena Downs Station near Nullagine did stop work at this time. According to Nullagine's Constable Rowe, they had been enticed away, and threatened, by two *marrngu* men, Donald Norman and Dougal Cornish. Donald Norman was arrested and charged with 'enticement'. Rowe's telegram to McBeath, informing him of the development, concludes: 'Considerable activity revealed to keep strike movement spreading stop Gribble here'.[49]

Peter Coppin also gave an account of the incident:

> [Gribble] thought I might tell somebody, 'Eh, you'll have to pull out from here, come and join the strike'.
>
> One bloke did say that. Donald was his name. An Aborigine bloke. He went up to the station next door to Bonney Downs. He was working there ...
>
> I went up to that place now to bring Donald back to court, to Nullagine. He was telling people there to go on strike. Anybody who talk like that, well they got to go to court, they take you to court.[50]

Coppin's account suggests that Gribble himself arrested Donald Norman at Noreena Downs. Drawing on information provided by Sampie and McLeod,

---

48   *Maritime Worker* (Melbourne), 10 July 1948, p. 6.
49   Rowe to McBeath, undated, SROWA1943/0621/65.
50   Coppin, in Read and Coppin, *Kangkushot*, p. 72.

the *Workers' Star* reported that Norman and Cornish had been collecting money for the Twelve Mile school and were charged with stealing from other natives. Both were fined. McLeod told the *Workers' Star* that Gribble attended court and threatened the men with removal to the Kimberley government settlement of Moola Bulla if they repeated the offence.[51] Far from establishing friendly relations with strikers, Gribble had, like other Native Affairs officials, adopted a punitive role indistinguishable from that of the police.

It was not Jack Gribble's approach that worried the Department, however, but his financial dealings and drunkenness in Port Hedland. Arriving there on 25 November 1947, Laurie O'Neill found that reports of his misconduct were widely known. 'I feel that Mr. Gribble has performed quite a useful amount of work in the Port Hedland–Marble Bar and Nullagine districts', he wrote, 'but unfortunately the value of that work has been greatly reduced because of his conduct in Port Hedland'.[52] He wired Gribble in Nullagine with instructions to meet him in Marble Bar on 26 November. Gribble instead sent Coppin with his vehicle. 'Am sending my Boy with the car', he wrote, 'as I am not very well & feeling very tired of late more so since Noreena station came out'.[53] When the two officers met in Nullagine, Gribble admitted his debts, but was too ashamed to accompany O'Neill back to Port Hedland to settle matters. O'Neill informed him of the termination of his appointment and returned to Port Hedland with Coppin to settle as many of Gribble's debts as possible, including Coppin's wages.[54] He then collected Gribble in Nullagine and drove him back to Perth. Gribble had been in the area only two months.

The Department's hope that Gribble's influence would lead Pilbara Aboriginal people to abandon their activism and return to work on stations seems unlikely to have been successful even without his mental health problems. Drawing on his earlier experiences with Aboriginal people under his father's authoritarian mission regime and his own successful exercise of military discipline on Melville Island, Gribble had attempted to reassert settler authority over the strikers, adopting an approach in the Pilbara that differed little from that of other departmental officers who also believed they could bring an end to the strike by coercion, and who, like Gribble, failed to do so.

---

51   *Workers' Star*, 19 December 1947, p. 1, 'Natives Fined for Helping Own School'.
52   O'Neill to McBeath, 9 December 1947, SROWA 1947/0691/84.
53   Gribble to O'Neill, 28 November 1947, SROWA 1947/0691/55–56.
54   O'Neill to McBeath, 9 December 1947, SROWA 1947/0691/84.

Far from resolving pastoralist concerns about the presence of an unsupervised Aboriginal community wandering freely over pastoral land, Gribble's appointment intensified complaints, particularly from Ted Richardson. Two months after receiving assurances from McDonald that provisions would be set in place within a week to alleviate his grievances, Richardson was still waiting.[55] He was not impressed to learn that the provision promised by the Department was the appointment of Gribble. He told McDonald that Gribble had gone to Perth in mid-October 'armed with a lot of information & schemes', but that nothing had come of them. Gribble claimed to have obtained departmental agreement that compensation would be paid to Pippingarra Station for losses incurred by the strike, and Richardson had given him an account of the estimated cost of damages, but had seen nothing more of him.[56] He therefore sent the account to McDonald, estimating his losses at £1000. McBeath apologetically informed Richardson that, although the Department was 'completely sympathetic' with his situation, it could not accept any responsibility for paying compensation. He had not authorised Gribble to make any such promises, he wrote:

> This Department is willing at all times to do everything in its power to relieve the existing difficulties of the situation in the Port Hedland and Marble Bar districts, but as you know, the whole position has its complexities which intensifies the problem.[57]

Richardson's angry response highlights the squatters' belief that the role of the Department of Native Affairs was to exercise control over Aboriginal people in the interests of the pastoral industry. 'I feel that you should take some responsibility', he growled to McBeath:

> for allowing the natives to camp at the 12 mile if you have any control over them, you do not seem to show us that you have, or your sympathies are all with them & not with the pastoralists.
>
> The natives are now taking the attitude they can camp anywhere they like ...
>
> You state your Department is willing at all times to do everything in its power to relieve the existing difficulties of the situation. What has been done by your Department in the last 18 months? It does not impress us

---

55　Richardson to McDonald, 19 November 1947, SROWA 1947/0305/180.
56　Richardson to McBeath, 5 December 1947, SROWA 1947/0305/181.
57　McBeath to Richardson, 16 December 1947, SROWA 1947/0305/185.

very much that you have any power at all over them, but others seem to get things done. If McLeod orders them to go out and get gold, tin, or kangaroo skins they do so.[58]

It seemed to Richardson that departmental control over Aboriginal employment, enforced through regulations and the issue of work permits, imposed restraints on employers without imposing an equal degree of control over workers. Was it not reasonable, he asked, for those who paid for permits to expect the Department to control labour? 'You are on the Box Seat', he wrote, 'as if we did not pay for a Permit you would take us to court for employing them without, but give no assistance to us when they are causing inconvenience and damage to our Stock'.[59]

In January 1948, McBeath sent McDonald details of 'the expenses entailed in the appointment of John Gribble as a departmental Protector to exercise supervision and control over the natives in the Port Hedland, Marble Bar and Nullagine Districts'. 'Unfortunately Gribble failed to give complete satisfaction', he wrote, 'but your proposal had much to commend it, and therefore I feel was well worthy of a trial'.

'Noted', McDonald replied briefly. 'The proposal was a sound one in principle'.[60]

---

58   Richardson to McBeath, 18 December 1947, SROWA 1947/0305/186–187.
59   Richardson to McBeath, 18 December 1947, SROWA 1947/0305/186–187.
60   McBeath to McDonald, 20 January 1948, SROWA 1947/0691/80.

Chapter 21

'Imagine the Propaganda this Native Will Instil on the Younger Natives'

Schooling, 1948

In 1948, education became a focal point of settler responses to the strike. It was now clear that there could be no return to pre-strike conditions in the Pilbara and that a significant portion of the Aboriginal population in the area would never return to station employment and to the feudalistic system of controls that had existed before 1946. Reimposing control over the strikers was proving difficult indeed, and there was a growing awareness that something must be done about the children growing up in the strike community to prevent difficulties, as perceived by the settler community, continuing into the next generation. 'Something must be done to provide education', Acting Commissioner of Native Affairs Lew McBeath insisted. 'Otherwise these children will ... simply drift about the bush with their parents and develop nomadic habits and tendencies which, as you probably realize, will prevent these children from ever becoming useful citizens'.[1] His reference to the children becoming 'useful citizens' was mere cant; Aboriginal people were not citizens and the Department had no intention that they would become so. It was to make them available as useful labour that the Department turned its thoughts to schooling.

The other reason that education became a focus of settler attempts to impose order was that many strikers left the Twelve Mile in the early months of 1948, and by April the camp had become little more than a school, still being run by the indomitable Tommy Sampie. Efforts by the Department of Native Affairs to address pastoralist complaints about the Twelve Mile now became a matter of moving the school.

Tommy Sampie had begun teaching about twelve children at the Twelve Mile soon after strikers set up camp there after the Port Hedland races in

---

1   McBeath to McDonald, 16 January 1948, p. 1, SROWA 1947/0220/7.

July 1946. As a child, he had lived on a Catholic mission at Lombadina, on the Dampier Peninsula north of Broome, where he received some schooling from Irish and Scottish nuns of the Order of St John of God. He had then been sent to the nearby mission of Beagle Bay, where he was taught carpentry. Before moving south to the Pilbara, he had worked at a dairy in Broome, as a shell-opener on a pearling lugger, and as a seaman on the lighthouse tender. He had various station jobs in the Port Hedland area and was working as a cook on Munda Station when the strike began.[2] He began teaching the children under a tree at the Twelve Mile until a shelter was constructed from flattened petrol drums for use as a school. In September 1946, he asked the Committee for Defence of Native Rights (CDNA) for writing materials, primary readers, arithmetic tables, pens and ink for the children, who were, he said, eager and quick to learn.[3] A special kitchen for the school children was set up to ensure that their dietary needs were catered for.

The Committee for Defence of Native Rights provided early assistance to the school, appealing to supporters for pencils and paper and sending picture books. 'The school books have been very much appreciated', Clancy McKenna wrote in October, 'and we thank you on behalf of the school children. They are quite happy and are interested in their school lessons. Some of the children are learning fast'.[4] To assist Sampie in his work, the CDNR asked the Western Australian Department of Education (DE) to supply him with correspondence lessons, routinely supplied to isolated non-Aboriginal children, and in the longer term to provide a building for use as a school. Responses from the DE were initially positive, and the *Sunday Times*, citing CDNR secretary Peter Hodge, reported on 20 October 1946 that correspondence courses would be provided, and that consideration was being given to the provision of a building.[5]

Although supporters were impressed with the Twelve Mile school, and the DE was prepared to provide support, the Department of Native Affairs (DNA) was consistently disparaging of Sampie's efforts and ability, and initially acted to block DE support. Under continued pressure from pastoralists to close the Twelve Mile, the DNA was anxious that nothing be done to encourage strikers to remain there. Acting Commissioner McBeath was therefore alarmed to read in the *Sunday Times* that consideration was being given to building

---

2   Brown, *The Black Eureka*, pp. 167–168.
3   *Workers' Star*, 27 September 1946, p. 2.
4   *Workers' Star*, 8 November 1946, p. 5, '106 Natives Set up Co-Op Camp'.
5   *Sunday Times*, 20 October 1946, 'Moves to Assist Natives' School'.

a school. He informed the Acting Director of Education of the pastoralists' complaints and the hoped-for relocation of the strikers. 'I suggest for your consideration that no decision be reached for the establishment of a school except in consultation with this Department', he wrote.[6] The DE agreed to take no action in the matter.

Sampie continued teaching without the correspondence lessons, but in December 1946 he applied for assistance to the DE on his own behalf. His application included the names of twenty-one children aged between six and fifteen who were now attending his school. 'I am not quite certain as to what guarantees you want as far as my education is concerned', he wrote:

> but I can assure you that the parents of these native children are very keen for education and learning. Not many of us can read or write, and we all realize that we can not live full and happy lives unless there is a good state of learning among us.
>
> We are very keen to start soon and we do beg you to send us our first lessons before you close down for Christmas.[7]

Correspondence lessons had still not been provided when author and poet Dorothy Hewett visited later that month. She was impressed with the little school, describing the schoolroom, constructed from old hammered-out petrol drums and scraps of iron, as 'a tribute to the courage and initiative of 300 Aborigines'.[8] Sampie was 'stocky, earnest, with a great sense of responsibility and love towards "his kids"', she wrote, while Clancy McKenna told her of his own regret at never having had the opportunity to learn to read and write.[9] The school children stood before her 'with earnest small faces' to recite the alphabet:

> With hair slicked back and faces well scrubbed they sit down to meals at tables, use knives and forks, get all the titbits, because they are the children of the camp and as such are a precious charge.[10]

---

6   McBeath to acting Director of Education, 22 October 1946, SROWA 1947/0594.
7   Sampie to the Director, Correspondence Classes, Claremont, December 1946, SROWA 1947/0594.
8   Dorothy Hewett, '12 Mile People Hard as Steel', *Workers' Star*, 17 January 1947, p. 2.
9   Hewett, '25 Native Children go to own school, *Workers' Star*, 9 May 1947, p. 4.
10 Hewett, '12 Mile People Hard as Steel', *Workers' Star*, 17 January 1947, p. 2.

When the 1947 school year began, the CDNR made further applications to the DE for correspondence courses to be supplied.[11] The Director of Education decided that, despite the recommendation of the DNA, the possible impermanence of the Twelve Mile camp was no reason to deny the children access to the lessons. 'Though this camp may break up on the settlement of certain labour differences between the station owners and the natives', he wrote, 'there is no reason why these children should not continue their education when they go back to the stations'.[12] He gave instructions for the North West's itinerate teacher, Cedric de Passey, to visit the Twelve Mile and report on the advisability of providing DE assistance.[13]

Sampie was hopeful. He reported to the CDNR in April 1947 that, of twenty-five children attending the school, three girls and five boys were now writing and reading the Tiny Tots book. 'These eight children have learnt their times tables, sums, grammar etc', Sampie wrote. 'The other 17 smaller children are very good on their tables, days of weeks and months, money tables, all that the white schools teach in their infant classes'. He had high aspirations for his students and looked forward to the time when the girls could learn bookkeeping, accountancy, nursing and so on. He hoped that the Department of Education teacher in Port Hedland would provide assistance. 'I am going to ask the teacher to help me get a decent large school', he told the CDNR. 'I trust a little later to get a professional teacher for my school children, when they'll have passed their examinations in Port Hedland'. He would have liked to have included the Moolyella children in his school but did not have room to accommodate them. 'I hope, please God, the Education Department will build me a better school', he wrote.[14]

Sampie also wrote to the *Sunday Times* about the Twelve Mile school and its needs. Rather than publish Sampie's letter, the newspaper sought and published information on the issue from McBeath. McBeath was characteristically dismissive of the school, telling the *Sunday Times* that 'Sampie had apparently been giving the natives such elementary education as was within his powers'. One difficulty with providing a formal school, he said, was 'that it is a floating population, and possibly, if a school and teacher were provided, there would,

---

11 Hodge to Acting Director of Education, under letterhead of Committee for Defence of Native Rights, 26 February 1947, SROWA 1947/0594.
12 Director of Education to the Head Teacher, Correspondence Classes, Claremont, 10 March 1947, SROWA 1947/0594.
13 Director of Education to the Head Teacher, Correspondence Classes, Claremont, 10 March 1947, SROWA 1947/0594.
14 Hewett, '25 Native Children Go to Own School', *Workers' Star*, 9 May 1947, p. 4.

in the not too far distant future, be no children in that area to teach'.[15] His comment was disingenuous. From the DNA's point of view, it was not the possible impermanence of the Twelve Mile that was the problem, but the probability that, if a school and teacher were provided, a permanent Aboriginal community would become established there.

The Department of Education's travelling schoolteacher, Cedric de Passey, reported negatively on the school, however. He arrived in Port Hedland in April, immediately following the DNA's failed attempts to negotiate a return to station employment with the Twelve Mile strikers and when hostility towards the strikers was at its peak in the wake of the Boodarie woolshed fire. Prevailing settler attitudes and understandings of the strike strongly influenced his report, including the probability that the camp would be moved. He thought the work arrangements at the Twelve Mile, in which teams of men worked away while the women remained at the camp, were unlikely to continue, a belief based on the racist stereotype of lazy Aboriginal men dependent on their slavish wives. 'The main body of men are away working and fending for themselves', he wrote, 'which is unnatural when they have gins available'.[16]

De Passey was also critical of the school. Sampie was capable of supervising infant classes, he thought, but not twenty-four children with ages ranging from six to fourteen years. The accommodation also was inadequate, consisting of a bough and tin shed approximately fourteen foot by eight foot, with a centrally placed bench and two forms capable of seating fourteen children. The rough wooden bench allowed only eight children at a time to use it as a desk. Other children sat cramped on a seat along one wall.[17] When McBeath visited the community the previous week, he noted that Sampie was attempting to teach with the use of several badly torn picture books, probably those supplied by the CDNR months before.[18] The fact that the school was operating under these conditions is an indication both of the determination of an impoverished community to provide their children with an education, and of the school's need for material and pedagogical support.

Certainly, Sampie was aware of his need for support and understood, after speaking to de Passey, that pedagogical support, if nothing else, was to be provided. 'The teacher from the Education Department came out here, and heard what I had to say', he wrote to the CDNR. 'He promised to give me

---

15 *Sunday Times*, 27 April 1947, p. 12, 'Quiz Natives' Educational Industrial Conditions.
16 De Passey to Director of Education, 1 May 1947, p. 3, SROWA 1947/0594/44.
17 De Passey to Director of Education, 1 May 1947, pp. 1–3, SROWA 1947/0594/42–44.
18 McBeath to McDonald, 19 May 1947, SROWA 1947/0594/47.

lessons for my school the same as the white children on the stations are getting. Of course he told me the school had to have writing desks and stools, and I agreed with him'.[19] De Passey's report, on the other hand, carried a cynical tone:

> On my stating that correspondence work was impossible without bench space for all children, Sampi replied that the material to provide this space was available. However, this material was not in view, and as this school has been running for some months now, I did not place too much credence on this statement.[20]

He concluded that correspondence work could not be successfully carried out at the Twelve Mile, and he did not start the children on the courses while he was there. However, he suggested that if the Department did wish to assist the school, correspondence papers for infants could be sent to Sampie. 'Sampie seems sincere in his wish to provide education for the children', he conceded condescendingly, 'and, if supplied with the papers, may sustain the keenness until some definite move is made by the Department of Native Affairs'. He recommended, however, that no such action be taken without DNA approval.

Six years later, when *marrngu* again applied to the Department of Education for a school, the visiting superintendent of North West schools was impressed by the community's 'extreme desire for a school for their children'. 'We should be ashamed if we do not provide one', he wrote. 'They themselves are showing us the way. We can at least try to keep up with them'.[21] In 1947, however, the strikers' desire for education, demonstrated through the establishment of their own school despite a lack of resources and their own lack of education, carried no weight. Neither did their direct application to the Department of Education for support. Given that poverty and Sampie's limited education were the reasons the community asked for DE support in the first place, it seems an act of remarkable injustice for de Passey to recommend against the provision of educational assistance on the grounds that school's facilities and Sampie's level of education were inadequate.

Despite de Passey's negative report, however, the Department of Education decided, under some degree of political pressure, to trial the use of correspondence courses for the infant years at the Twelve Mile. Political pressure came from the Minister of Native Affairs, Ross McDonald.

---

19 *Workers' Star*, 6 June 1947, p. 5, 'North West Natives Tribute to Perth Committee'.
20 De Passey to Director of Education, 1 May 1947, pp. 3–4, SROWA 1947/0594/44–45.
21 William H. Rourke, District Superintendent, North West Schools, 3 November 1953, p. 3, 1952/0535/24.

Although opposed to anything that would lend permanency to the Twelve Mile, McDonald was sensitive to criticism at the lack of educational facilities there. He was aware that the DNA's disparagement of Sampie's abilities gave such criticism legitimacy. The provision of correspondence lessons would, he hoped, appease critics without creating a permanent settlement. He alerted the Minister for Education to the political expediency of taking action on the issue. 'The minister of Native Affairs (Mr. McDonald) rang me this afternoon', Minister for Education Arthur Watts told the Director of Education:

> regarding a number of native children at the 12 Mile in the Port Hedland district who are at present, it appears, being taught by some native person referred to by Mr. McDonald as 'Samby'. You are no doubt aware that there is considerable difficulty in this area with natives, and [McDonald] is anxious to remove any legitimate cause of complaint'.[22]

'All we can do for the time being', McDonald told McBeath, 'is to accept Mr. De Passey's recommendation that correspondence papers for infants be sent to Sampi'. He suggested also that some provision for better accommodation for the school could be made 'as a temporary measure without disproportionate expense until the position is clearer regarding the 12 Mile camp'.[23] No provision for better accommodation for the school, temporary or otherwise, was ever made, however. Given the Department's belief that Sampie lacked the ability even to supervise lessons at the infant level, there was cynicism in the Department's approval for lessons to be provided. It was a solution aimed at placating critics rather than a genuine attempt to support the school. 'Personally I doubt if he is capable of supervising such a course', McBeath wrote. 'However, it seems to me that something should be done to provide temporary educational facilities until some definite decision can be made in regard to the future of these people'.[24] The Department was still unable to understand that 'the future of these people' was no longer in its hands.

In June 1947, Sampie finally received, on a trial basis, four infant correspondence lessons, eight months after the CDNR first approached the Department of Education on the issue.[25] Complaints about the inadequacy of the educational facilities there continued, however. Later that year, the

---

22   Minister for Education, Arthur Watts, to Director of Education, Murray Little, SROWA 1947/0594/40.
23   McDonald to McBeath, 12 May 1947, SROWA 1947/0594/46.
24   McBeath to McDonald, 19 May 1947, SROWA 1947/0594/47.
25   Director of Education to Head Teacher, Correspondence Classes, 5 June 1947, SROWA 1947/0594/48.

State School Teachers' Union of Western Australia expressed concern at the rudimentary nature of teaching at the Twelve Mile, 'such as the use of old correspondence to teach the children by copying writing and reading'.[26] The hoped-for assistance from the Port Hedland primary school teacher never eventuated, and the *Workers' Star* continued to call for DNA assistance in the form of building material for the school and 'facilities for a trained teacher to carry still further the excellent beginning in education made by Aboriginal Thomas Sampey'.[27] Despite the lack of teaching materials and the poor and crowded conditions of his school, however, Sampie appears to have been a more capable teacher than the DNA believed, as the Department of Education found the results to be 'very fair' and decided to extend the course in 1948.[28]

One man who believed that the education provisions at the Twelve Mile were inadequate was Port Hedland's Catholic priest, Edward Bryan. Hearing rumours in early 1948 that McLeod had plans for the school, possibly involving the recruitment of a volunteer teacher from among supporters in the south, Bryan decided to step into the breach created by the failure of government departments to address the educational needs of the children. Well-liked and respected by Port Hedland's Euralian population, with whom he worked closely, Bryan was motivated by a genuine interest in educational opportunities for Aboriginal children, as well as concerns to counter what he saw as communist influences among the local population. After discussing the issue with staunchly anti-communist Bishop Gummer in Geraldton, Bryan approached the Department of Native Affairs to offer, for use as a school, a former Army hut at the Port Hedland Three Mile, currently being used as a recreation hall by the Euralian community. He also indicated that arrangements could be made for a Catholic sister to undertake the teaching. A subsidy for the school and transport for the children to and from the Twelve Mile were all that would be required from the government.[29]

The DNA hesitated. Certainly, it considered that more adequate arrangements were needed to replace the stopgap, bandaid solution of correspondence lessons under Sampie's supervision. The idea that an Aboriginal-run school could ever provide real education or be supported by government departments on an ongoing basis was never considered. While Aboriginal people wanted their children

---

26 General Secretary, State School Teachers Union of WA, to Watts, 24 October 1947, SROWA 1947/0594/52–51.
27 *Workers' Star*, 14 November 1947, p. 5, 'New Attempt to Smash Native Co-op?'
28 Director of Education, note, 15 January 1948, SROWA 1947/0594/58.
29 McBeath to McDonald, 16 January 1948, p. 1, SROWA 1947/0220/7; McDonald to Watts, 25 February 1948, SROWA 1947/0594/59–60.

to gain skills in literacy and numeracy, the main purpose of education from the DNA's point of view was to remove the perceived negative characteristics of Aboriginality and to transform Aboriginal children into 'useful citizens'.[30] Bryan's offer of a school run by Catholic sisters appealed to the Department as a form of education that would counter both the Aboriginal and communistic influences of the Twelve Mile at little government expense.

But education was also a means of control. Aboriginal people would be attracted to areas where schooling was available, and this aspect of the issue was particularly important in the Pilbara, where settler controls had been broken down. By January 1948, there were signs that *marrngu* were shifting away from the Twelve Mile, and the DNA was reluctant to support any move that might reverse this process. While not rejecting Bryan's suggestion outright, the Department decided to wait and see if the movement from the Twelve Mile continued. 'It is recognised', McBeath wrote:

> that if school facilities are provided in Hedland for the Twelve Mile children no attempt will be made by the parents to vacate the Twelve Mile camp, and thus this locality will become a permanent camping site and the existing difficulties will always be with us.[31]

Important as education may have been to counter communist influence and bring the rising generation under control, pastoralist complaints at the presence of an autonomous Aboriginal group in the Port Hedland area was still the Department's major concern.

Economic difficulties at the Twelve Mile seem to have been a major reason for its decline. Making sufficient income to keep the community fed and clothed had always been a struggle, but, as the area became hunted out and the price of skins dropped, the difficulties increased. 'The country was worked out for miles around', Donald Stuart writes in *Yandy*, 'and the dryshelling from the boats had been a failure, or at best a half-success'.[32] The summer months had always been the hardest, when rains caused the spinifex grass to grow tall, making hunting difficult. At the end of a hot December in 1947, a cyclone brought heavy rain, and another blow in February brought floods and damaged the shelters built by strikers at the Twelve Mile.[33] The Petermara Creek, on

---

30 McBeath to McDonald, 16 January 1948, p. 1, SROWA 1947/0220/7.
31 McBeath to O'Neill, 22 January 1948, SROWA1943/0621/67.
32 Stuart, *Yandy*, 1959, p. 116.
33 *Daily News*, 30 December 1947, p. 1.

the banks of which the Twelve Mile was located, became flooded.[34] Heavy rains continued throughout March and April, making the Pilbara's dirt roads impassable and river crossings, dry for most of the year, uncrossable.[35] Under these conditions, the Twelve Mile strike camp became unviable.

Tin mining at Moolyella offered an alternative means of employment for the strikers. In the early weeks of 1948 movement of strikers from the Twelve Mile saw the population there increase by fifty, bringing the number to 234 by March. Having earlier dispersed into camps at Tadgabanna, Mud Springs and lower Mud Springs, the Moolyella strikers had now returned to a central camping area about half a mile from Thompson's store, where, in the wet season of 1947–48, they sank a well and obtained a plentiful supply of good-quality water, relieving them of the need to cart water from a tap by the store. New bush shelters were constructed there, but a large community shed was, according to Jensen, awaiting completion for lack of roofing iron.[36]

Tin mining was not lucrative, but it was a stable source of income, and those shifting there from the Twelve Mile told Native Affairs Inspector Jensen that working tin provided 'a much easier living than could be obtained in the vicinity of Port Hedland'.[37] In November 1948, Don Thompson at the Moolyella store was buying £140 to £150 worth of tin per week from 250 Aboriginal miners, which equated to an income of about 12/- per week per person.[38]

A better income could be obtained by negotiated employment agreements and returning to station work, and some of those leaving the Twelve Mile chose this option instead of moving to Moolyella. Most chose to do so under formal employment agreements. According to Jensen, they asked for a wage of £2/10/- per week, from which they would purchase their own food. The preference for written agreements and for wages without keep indicates a desire on the part of *marrngu* to break away from the informal feudalistic labour relationships, based on paternalism, personal loyalty and the provision of rations in exchange for labour, that had characterised Aboriginal labour relations before the strike. Men who accepted work at Indee and Boodarie Stations in early 1948 did so at £2/10/- per week without keep, and similar conditions were obtained at Munda. In the Marble Bar region, Fred Davenport at Mt Edgar Station was paying a worker recruited from Moolyella £4 per

---

34   *Daily News*, 1 March 1948, p. 4.
35   McBeath to Sampie, 6 April 1948, SROWA 1947/0349/28.
36   Jensen to McBeath, 26 March 1948, SROWA 1943/0621/69.
37   McBeath to McDonald, 1 April 1948, SROWA 1947/0305/198.
38   Marshall to Middleton, 24 November 1948, SROWA 1943/0621/85a.

week without keep, and this was to be held up as the standard to be adopted by other stations when the dispute escalated in the following year. Jensen thought wages with keep was 'far better … from the Natives point of view and also the employer' and facilitated employment agreements along these lines. He thought Harold Chullingworth at Mulyie Station was 'easily the best employer from the point of view of wages', employing Tommy Clarke at £3 per week with keep, Teddy Allen and Jacky at £2/10/- with keep, and two others at £2 per week.[39] Significantly, some women were also now being paid, with four women employed as domestics at £1/- per week plus keep. Twenty men, women and children shifted to Mulyie in April. 'So altogether the conditions of employment are a big improvement on the past', Jensen wrote:

> and I have no doubts at all that things will work out very satisfactory … These coupled with those that have returned thru Sergeant McGeary's efforts will go a long way to bringing to a conclusion the striking atmosphere that has prevailed for so long.[40]

Despite the higher wages, the arrangement worked well for the squatters, who were selective in their choice of workers, employing only the most efficient. 'Pastoralists are fussy', Marble Bar's Constable Gordon Marshall reported, 'and will only employ the good boys'.[41]

Although the use of employment agreements was a major component of labour regulations of the *Native Administration Act 1936*, they had, until now, rarely been used in the pastoral industry. The decision to use them now was made, not by the Department or the squatters, but by *marrngu* themselves. Indeed, McBeath was worried to see agreements being used and advised Jensen against them.[42] He was afraid that written agreements would give employers the power to prosecute workers who left their jobs, and that this could result in other workers walking out in protest. The labour situation was seen as something of a balancing act. Individual workers returning to stations saw written agreements as a means of gaining a level of power in their relationship with pastoralists, but McBeath feared that written agreements would actually place too much power in the pastoralists' hands, tipping the balance and upsetting the precariously-placed house of cards that the Department felt it was slowly

---

39 Jensen to McBeath, 16 April 1948, SROWA 1947/0305/203.
40 Jensen to McBeath, 11 April 1948, SROWA 1947/0305/199.
41 Marshall to Middleton, 24 November 1948, SROWA 1943/0621/85a.
42 McBeath to Jensen, 4 May 1948, SROWA 1947/0305/208.

constructing as it facilitated the strikers' return to station work. Although McBeath claimed with some satisfaction to have always anticipated that this 'drifting back to work' of the strikers would eventually take place, *marrngu* who took station employment were not forfeiting the increased control over their own lives and the improved working conditions that had been won by two years of strike action.[43] McBeath was aware that the Department had to tread carefully to ensure that those who returned to work remained there, and feared that any action taken by pastoralists against a worker who breached an employment agreement would lead to further strike action and bring the cards tumbling down. But Jensen had no choice in the matter; many *marrngu* refused to accept employment without them.[44]

Improved living conditions were provided on some stations for workers returning to station work, although the shortage of building materials in the post-war years slowed the rate of these improvements. Mulyie Station, however, had material for building 'first class huts for the natives', according to Jensen, and the manager planned, when the shearing was over, to 'deputise some of the boys on full wages to build the huts for themselves with lavatories and showers attached'.[45] According to Molly Williams, who returned to work as a domestic servant at the adjoining Warralong Station, housing was now being provided because of the strike. 'Finish they bin hear'm strike was starting ... they give us home. You know that old house in Warralong? ... We was living there'.[46]

Political discord may have been another reason for the decline of the Twelve Mile. The development of a new social and economic organisation was inevitably a dynamic process involving competing visions of the future. McBeath cited 'petty differences' as one of the reasons people were leaving.[47] Tension between Tommy Sampie and other Twelve Mile leaders, including Ernie Mitchell, seems to have revolved around the role that Aboriginal culture and religion would play in the emerging new community. Don McLeod felt that Sampie was, in the words of *Workers' Star* editor Graham Alcorn, 'a point of disintegration of tribal culture, encouraging the young men to ape the whites'.[48] Alcorn thought that Sampie's mission education might explain this. Sampie later claimed to have fallen out with the strike community because

---

43 McBeath to McDonald, 1 April 1948, SROWA 1947/0305/198.
44 Jensen to McBeath, 30 May 1948, SROWA 1947/0305/209.
45 Jensen to McBeath, 11 April 1948, SROWA 1947/0305/199.
46 Molly Williams (Kulyu), tape 2, recorded 22 October 1992, author's collection.
47 McBeath to McDonald, 21 April 1948, SROWA/1943/0621.
48 Alcorn, 'The Struggle of the Pilbara Station Hands', p. 10.

he was 'was very strict with the Laws [he] put down for the younger generations', preventing girls from marrying and both boys and girls from 'entering tribal laws' until their education was complete at seventeen or eighteen years of age.⁴⁹ When the decision was made to shift the Twelve Mile community to Moolyella, Sampie resisted community pressure to relocate the school and remained at the Twelve Mile.⁵⁰

If McLeod considered Sampie too assimilationist in his approach, the Department of Native Affairs considered him a dangerous radical. With the Twelve Mile community diminishing around him, and under pressure to shift to Moolyella, Sampie considered leaving the area altogether. In April, he spoke to Jensen about returning to the Broome area and to his home at Lombadina. Ever fearful of Pilbara activism spreading to other areas of the state, McBeath instructed Jensen that, anxious as they were to shift Sampie from the Twelve Mile, his transfer to another district should not be facilitated by the Department. 'You must realise that Sampie is a potential menace where ever he may happen to be, because of his communistic leanings, due to the influence of McLeod', McBeath wrote:

> If his star is on the wane, I consider it more desirable to have a chastened Sampie in the area of his defeat rather than assist him to set up his abode and preach his doctrine of unrest to natives so far not influenced by this undesirable type of propaganda.⁵¹

Ernie Mitchell moved from the Twelve Mile into a leadership role at Moolyella, where he was described by pastoralists as Dooley's 'first lieutenant'.⁵² However, most of the other Twelve Mile leaders took paid employment, perhaps in part because Moolyella's large and growing population and Dooley's dominance as leader made it difficult for them to take prominent roles in decision making. Clancy McKenna was working at Munda Station, and by April 1948 Adam Barker was working at Boodarie, Ron Captain was back at Munda Station, Teddy Allen at Mulyie and Big Harry Davis had taken a job with the Port Hedland Road Board. Snowball was still at the Twelve Mile but, according to Jensen, had 'lost his punch and now [held] no sway'.

---

49   Sampie to Middleton, 7 May 1950, p. 2, SROWA 1947/0349/56.
50   De Passey to Director of Education, 5 November 1948, SROWA 1947/0594/68.
51   McBeath to Jensen, 26 April 1948, SROWA 1947/0305/205.
52   'Notes of a Deputation Which Waited on the Minister for Native Affairs on 28 March 1949', ANU, Noel Butlin Archives Centre, Michael Hess Collection, N287, Item 1.

'So it is obvious', Jensen wrote with satisfaction, 'that the elements of strike influence are scattered to the winds and all in employment'.⁵³

There were now only twenty-nine adults and twenty-seven children living at the Twelve Mile, and the only work party using it as a base was a group of thirty-five strikers hunting kangaroos and goats along the Yule River on Munda Station.⁵⁴ The DNA was relieved to see the decline of a settlement it had struggled to close for eighteen months. 'Actually it would suit this Department if the Twelve Mile camp transferred to Moolyella', McBeath wrote, 'as such a move would have the effect of centralising two very large groups, and in addition minimise the present practice of travelling about the various station properties in the Port Hedland District for the purpose of hunting kangaroos'.⁵⁵ Jensen agreed. 'Its a great pity the balance of the 12 mile natives could not be persuaded into taking up permanent residence at Molyella [sic]', he wrote. 'The position would then be centralized and better for everyone'.⁵⁶

With the Twelve Mile now little more than a school and ration depot, McBeath believed that it had 'lost most of its significance as a strikers' camp'.⁵⁷ It seemed possible that timely action could now be taken to shift the remaining residents, ridding the DNA of a persistent cause of complaint from local pastoralists. Ted Richardson of Pippingarra, still complaining about the presence of strikers on his boundary, and still critical of the Department's inaction, suggested that the camp no longer be used as a distribution point for supplying government rations to aged or infirm Aboriginal people. McDonald was willing to comply.⁵⁸ Control over the supply of rations to Aboriginal people had always been a means of controlling their movement and activities. But local officers wanted the school children to be shifted along with the ration recipients. Port Hedland's Sergeant Bernie McGeary, the officer described by Peter Coppin as 'a rough sort of bloke', was frustrated at the DNA's inability to dislodge the few remaining residents.⁵⁹ 'If you think the stopping of the rations to a few indigent natives at the 12 mile will disperse the camp you are greatly wrong, they are not the draw', he growled to McBeath. 'The children at the would-be school would be a better

---

53 Jensen to McBeath, 16 April 1948, SROWA 1947/0305/201–203.
54 Jensen to McBeath, 16 April 1948, p. 2, SROWA 1947/0305/202.
55 McBeath to O'Neill, 21 November 1947, SROWA 1947/0305/179.
56 Jensen to McBeath, 26 March 1948, SROWA 1943/0621/69.
57 McBeath to McDonald, 21 April 1948, SROWA 1943/0621.
58 McDonald to McBeath, 21 April 1948, SROWA S3841 cons769 1.
59 Read and Coppin, *Kangkushot*, p. 80.

thing to remove instead of letting the crowd play there in idleness under a rogue like Sampie'.⁶⁰ The school, he said, was a farce. 'The school to outside appearance is quite a good scheme & should be carried out in a capable manner by a qualified person', he insisted:

> Sampie is most unsuitable & is McLeod's mouthpiece in the camp. You can imagine the propaganda this native will instil on the younger natives & it will be of Communist ideas.
>
> If the children are schooled they should be schooled in the right way & it devolves on the Dept of Native Affairs or the Education Dept to do something quick.⁶¹

McGeary considered Sampie 'a bad influence on the natives' and wanted to arrest him on a charge of vagrancy. 'Sampey does not work', he wrote, '& lives on his wits as schoolteacher & I am thinking seriously of warning him & if he continues idleness vag-ing him'.⁶² McBeath agreed that Sampie had 'always been McLeod's right-hand assistant, and it is certain that the tuition he is imparting includes the principles of the Communist doctrine'.⁶³ Although he was 'allegedly conducting a school at the Twelve Mile', he was 'undoubtedly using this occupation for his own ends', McBeath wrote. Nevertheless, he recommended against taking action that would, in other parts of the state, have been taken by police as a matter of course. 'I feel that it would be most unwise to proceed against him on a charge of vagrancy', McBeath wrote:

> as he is certainly conducting a school of sorts, and I am certain that if he was charged such an action would only serve to whip up feeling against the Department and the Government, upon the grounds of victimisation, and an attempt to force the natives back to station employment. It must be borne in mind that in the main the public are not aware of the true facts concerning the industrial unrest in these districts.⁶⁴

The response of southern activists to such an action was one factor that stayed the hand of the authorities, activism of Aboriginal people in the Pilbara was another. McBeath wrote that, in his opinion, 'the result of such proceedings

---

60   McGeary to McBeath, 6 July 1948, SROWA 1948/0732/14.
61   McGeary to McBeath, 31 May 1948, SROWA 1947/0349/38.
62   McGeary to McBeath, 5 March 1948, p. 2, SROWA 1947/0305/196.
63   McBeath to McDonald, 3 June 1948, SROWA 1947/0349/39.
64   McBeath to McDonald, 1 April 1948, SROWA 1947/0305/198.

is not only doubtful but could only serve to stir the Port Hedland natives up to such a degree and further strikes would eventuate'.[65] He was soon to learn that such concerns were not unfounded.

Under pressure from both Jensen and McGeary to 'do something quick' about shifting the school from the Twelve Mile, but conscious, on the other hand, that a heavy-handed approach could undermine gains made in returning strikers to station work, McDonald and McBeath decided that the solution lay in attracting strikers away from the area by providing better schooling options elsewhere. Unlike Bryan's offer of school facilities in Port Hedland, a school at Moolyella would solve the problem of persistent pastoralist complaints by attracting the remaining Twelve Mile strikers to Moolyella for an education for their children. A school at Moolyella would also serve as a counter to supposed communistic teachings on the tin field. 'There must be some forty or fifty children at Moolyella, and in the near vicinity', McBeath wrote, 'therefore it is apparent that education is essential if Communistic influence is to be eradicated'.[66] The DNA therefore turned down Bryan's offer and urged the Department of Education to consider a school at Moolyella.[67] 'A school at Moolyella should, I think, solve the problem of the children at 12-Mile', McDonald told the Minister for Education, 'and assist in the 12-Mile camp being relinquished by natives'.[68]

The Department of Education was less than enthusiastic about Moolyella as the site for a departmental school, however. While the DNA saw a school as a means of attracting strikers to a single location to enable greater departmental control, the DE wanted controls in place before providing facilities. 'Unless a Mission [body] would undertake the establishment of a Mission among these tin workers and so establish a community in which we could establish a school and domicile a teacher', the Director of Education wrote, 'I think the difficulties in the way are great'.[69] An Aboriginal group, it seems, could only be considered a community when it was under institutional control. To provide standard educational facilities for an independent group was seen as problematic indeed.

The Department therefore considered the possibility of establishing institutional controls over the Moolyella strikers. McDonald invited the Western

---

65　McBeath to McDonald, 3 June 1948, SROWA 1947/0349/39.
66　McBeath to McDonald, 16 January 1948, p. 1, SROWA 1947/0220/7.
67　McBeath to Jensen, 11 May 1948, SROWA 1947/0349/36; McDonald to Watts, 25 February 1948, SROWA 1947/0594/59–60.
68　McDonald to Watts, 14 June 1948, SROWA 1947/0594/66.
69　Director of Education to Watts, 9 March 1948, SROWA 1947/0594/61.

Australian branch of the National Missionary Council to undertake mission work among the tin workers at Moolyella.[70] It also seemed possible that government institutional controls could gradually be put in place around the existing community. 'As a preliminary step it might be advisable to appoint some reputable person as a Protector of Natives', McBeath suggested to McDonald. He recommended Moolyella storekeeper Don Thompson, who had already established amicable relationships with *marrngu*, as the ideal person to become the DNA's representative at Moolyella and to 'exercise benevolent supervision which appears to be necessary'.[71] McDonald approved of Thompson's appointment, which McBeath felt would be 'of inestimable value to the Moolyella natives generally'.[72]

Thompson declined the honorary position, however, explaining to Marshall that the 'majority by far' of the Moolyella people were 'against the Government'. 'They do not know why', Marshall wrote, 'only they are McLeod people & must be against the Government'. If Thompson was appointed a Protector, 'he would in the eyes of these unfortunate people be classed as a Government official'.[73] McBeath replied to Marshall that 'the anti-departmental feeling possessed by the natives in this area is due to the propaganda spread by McLeod, designed obviously to place him in a strong position with these people as their only protector'.[74] Given the consistent opposition they had faced from the DNA, however, it would seem surprising indeed if strikers had been anything other than 'anti-department'.

Favouring the use of Moolyella as a central location for strikers, Jensen described the people there as 'healthy and well contented, and lack[ing] nothing, especially in the food line'. They were 'well dug in', he wrote, 'and would take a lot of moving'.[75] However, other reports indicate that the location was far from ideal as a settlement for a large population. The local government medical officer, Eric Galton Saint, reported on social and health problems, including venereal disease and malnutrition, arising from the overcrowded conditions, lack of ablution and toilet facilities, and the limited variety of

---

70 McDonald to Charles Taylor, Chairman, Native Affairs Committee, WA Branch of National Missionary Council, 20 May 1948, SROWA S3841 cons769 1.
71 McBeath to McDonald, 13 April 1948, and McDonald's response, 14 April 1948, SROWA1943/0621/70.
72 McBeath to Marshall, 19 April 1948, SROWA 1943/0621/79.
73 Marshall to McBeath, 14 June 1948, SROWA 1948/0376/10–11 (underlining in original).
74 McBeath to Marshall, 12 July 1948, SROWA 1948/0376/12.
75 Jensen to McBeath, 26 March 1948, SROWA1943/0621/69.

available food.[76] Although a good supply of water was now available in the settlement, the shortage of wood for fires and shelters was critical.[77] To obtain wood for shelters, strikers had to travel thirty kilometres. When McLeod assisted them in July 1948 by transporting wood on his truck, Marshall kept a close eye on his activities. Despite the success of Hodge's High Court appeal the previous year, McLeod could still be prosecuted under section 48 of the state's *Native Administration Act 1936* for being within five chains, or 100 metres, of an Aboriginal camp. To avoid prosecution, he had to unload wood some distance from the camp.[78]

McLeod began to participate directly in the strikers' activities at this time. He told Premier Ross McLarty in July that he intended 'taking a more active part in assisting the various groups than has been the case previously'.[79] With the economic activities of the Twelve Mile no longer viable, and with the Moolyella tin field providing a bare subsistence level of income only, he began working with the strike community to find new sources of revenue. In May 1948, he began a fishing project with Rob and Sandy Brown along the De Grey coast, with a plan to store fish in Port Hedland's newly-established freezer and then ship the frozen product to Perth.[80] Denied a work permit as an unsuitable employer of Aboriginal people, McLeod lodged an appeal against the Department's decision, as he had done successfully four years earlier, and went ahead with the fishing scheme.[81] Since Rob and Sandy Brown were classed as 'half-castes', the DNA was aware that a permit to employ them was not legally required, but was prepared to have the legislation challenged by McLeod rather than turn a blind eye to his activities.[82] The Port Hedland police made

---

76 Saint to Commissioner of Health, 6 February 1949, SROWA 1948/0732/91. Newly arrived from England when he worked in the Pilbara, Saint went on to become highly distinguished in medical research and teaching in Australia. While in the Pilbara, he was the first to alert mine management and the state Department of Health to the looming occupational health disaster posed by the mining of blue asbestos at the Pilbara town of Wittenoom. See Lenore Layman, 'Saint, Eric Galton (1918–1989)', *Australian Dictionary of Biography*, National Centre of Biography, Australian National University, http://adb.anu.edu.au/biography/saint-eric-galton-15614.
77 McLeod to Department of Education, 16 December 1948, SROWA 1947/0594/79–82.
78 Marshall, police patrol report, 1 August 1948, SROWA 1946/2538 v8.
79 McLeod to McLarty, 20 July 1948, SROWA 1948/0732/25–27.
80 McGeary to McBeath, 31 May 1948, p. 2, SROWA 1948/0732/6.
81 McBeath to McDonald, Minute attached to McGeary's of 3 June 1948, SROWA 1948/0732/4a.
82 McGeary to McBeath, 31 May 1948, pp. 1–2, SROWA 1948/0732/5a-6.

several attempts to locate his fishing operation, but gave up the effort after becoming bogged in the trackless and swampy country of the De Grey coast.[83] McGeary and Jensen were so determined to catch McLeod in the act that they chartered a light plane and spotted the fishing camp from the air, but decided that more evidence would be needed if they were to mount a successful prosecution.[84] The fishing scheme was found to be impractical, however, and was abandoned soon afterwards.[85]

Another scheme that McLeod proposed at this time was for dogging teams to cull dingoes in the White Springs, Yandeyarra and Kangan area. Dingoes had been a major cause of these stations being abandoned in 1945, and an extensive dingo cull would bring income from the government bounty on dingoes and make the country more viable as pastoral land. McLeod planned to transport teams in his old Ford V8, but was threatened with prosecution if he did so.[86] Frustrated at being constantly hounded by the police, he appealed to Premier McLarty to put a stop to the persecution. 'For some reason there has been implied locally from the Police', he wrote:

> that the various sections of the act which forbid any one without the necessary permission to go within 5 chains of a native camp and so on may be used to prevent me from taking any active part in the further assistance to native work parties if this is so I would be obliged if they would be advised of the present position ... I have had the patience to stand by and negotiate now for some three years and at all times during this period my activities have been under close scrutiny by the police so that if there is any pretence that my motives are still doubted it can only be because the Department deliberately intends to recreate the semi-slave conditions from which the natives have already revolted and if this is so I may as well be in gaol as anywhere for it is the most effective form of protest possible and will not affect the ... main issue except to make the native peoples more determined to hold out and certainly will be of little benefit to anyone.[87]

---

83   Withnell, police patrol reports, 4 July 1948, 14 July 1948, SROWA 1939/1777 v7; McGeary to McBeath, 5 July 1948, SROWA 1948/0732/12–13; McBeath to McDonald, Minute attached to McGeary's of 3 June 1948, SROWA 1948/0732/4a; McBeath to McGeary, 9 June 1948, SROWA 1948/0732/7a.
84   Jensen to McBeath, no date, SROWA 1948/0732/32.
85   McLeod to McDonald, 22 October 1948, p. 1, SROWA 1948/0732/60.
86   McLeod to McLarty, 20 July 1948, p. 1, SROWA 1948/0732/25.
87   McLeod to McLarty, 20 July 1948, pp. 2–3, SROWA 1948/0732/26–27.

Moolyella's unsuitability as the site for a settlement in the longer term, and the existence of abandoned stations along the Turner River, led McLeod to again flag the possibility that the Western Australian government could make one or more of these properties available to *marrngu* for their own use. When Premier McLarty visited Port Hedland in May 1948, McLeod presented him with a proposal for achieving this. He suggested that the government take out mortgages on the adjoining stations of Yandeyarra and Kangan, which would be vested in a committee of trustees to be appointed by Aboriginal people. This committee would service the debt and develop the properties as a permanent home for all Aboriginal people in the area. Primarily, the property would be used as the site for a school, the building for which would be constructed by the Aboriginal community. Application would then be made to the Department of Education for a teacher.[88]

McLeod felt that he received a sympathetic hearing from McLarty, who asked him to submit a written proposal for the government's consideration.[89] However, it seems unlikely that McLarty ever seriously considered the proposition. The idea that the government would facilitate Aboriginal land acquisition, respect the authority of Aboriginal people to elect a committee of trustees, or enable the development of an autonomous Aboriginal community in this way was unthinkable in 1948. Although McLeod presented the proposal as the outcome of community discussions, it is unlikely that McLarty would have viewed it as anything other than a scheme to further entrench communist influence over Aboriginal people in the area.

Much more acceptable to settler sensibilities was an alternative proposal, also relating to the abandoned Turner River stations, which was put forward at the same time by Port Hedland's Catholic priest, Edward Bryan. Critical of government department dithering on the issue of education for the children of the strikers, Bryan also spoke to McLarty in Port Hedland in May, suggesting that land be made available, not to Aboriginal people as a base for an independent community, but to the Catholic Church for use as a mission. 'As a matter of fact, at one stage I offered to supply a teacher', he wrote to the DE:

> but nobody seemed particularly interested. Anyhow this problem is being tackled just 3 years too late. These children have been allowed to stagnate

---

88 McLeod to Department of Education, 16 December 1948, SROWA 1947/0594/79–82.

89 McGeary to McBeath, 31 May 1948, p. 1, SROWA 1948/0732/5a.

in camps and no effort has been made by Government departments to help them at all.⁹⁰

The principal focus for the new mission to be established on the abandoned Turner River station of White Springs would be the education and training of Aboriginal children to counter the 'communistic' ideology of the independent group.

---

90 Bryan to Acting Director of Education, Edmondson, 29 November 1948, SROWA 1947/0594/73.

Chapter 22

'The Best Brains Available'

The Bateman Report and Restructure of the Department of Native Affairs, 1948

While Father Bryan's proposal for the White Springs Mission was taking shape, changes were underway in the administration of Aboriginal affairs in the state. The findings of the survey of Aboriginal conditions throughout the state, undertaken by Magistrate F. E. A. Bateman, were to form a framework for structural and policy change within the Department, but when this survey was delayed in early 1948, Minister for Native Affairs Ross McDonald was unwilling to wait for Bateman's report before beginning the search for a new Commissioner.[1] He looked, therefore, to A. P. Elkin's *Citizenship for the Aborigines* for guidance. This book recommended an Aboriginal administration policy that adapted to Australian conditions the approach taken in the administration of Papua and New Guinea. It should be, Elkin suggested, a 'policy of personalities'. 'Persons of the right type must be selected, given special training, and then given the power and authority to develop and work out methods', he wrote.[2]

When McDonald sought Elkin's advice on the issue, Elkin urged him to appoint a Commissioner from outside Western Australia, 'and then to back him wholeheartedly'.[3] When the position was advertised across Australia in early March 1948, Elkin encouraged two experienced administrators who had worked under Hubert Murray in Papua to apply.[4] One of these was Stanley Guise Middleton, assistant director of the Papua New Guinea Department of Native Affairs and District Services. 'Professor Elkin in Sydney ... recommended to the WA government that as a change from Neville and Co

---

1 McDonald to Public Service Commissioner, 2 March 1948, SROWA S3841 cons769 3.
2 Elkin, *Citizenship for the Aborigines,* pp. 14–15.
3 Elkin, 'Australian Aboriginal and White Relations', p. 227.
4 Draft advertisement, SROWA S3841 cons769 3; Elkin, 'Australian Aboriginal and White Relations', p. 227.

they should appoint a man who had experience with indigenous populations and had a more enlightened outlook than had existed so far', Frank Gare remembered. 'So when Stan Middleton applied for the job he was given a bit of a grilling, but he measured up and got the job'.[5] Middleton was appointed Commissioner in August 1948.

With twenty-two years experience in native administration in Papua and New Guinea, Middleton did indeed bring to the Department a new way of thinking about the present reality and the future possibilities for Western Australia's Aboriginal population. The attitudes and practices he encountered in the Department shocked him, and he wrote of the need to drag the administration 'out of the morass of apathy, neglect and prejudice into which it has been allowed to sink'.[6] From his experience in native administration under the Lieutenant Governor of Papua, Sir Hubert Murray, he brought ideas about the nature of Aboriginality and human progress that were at odds with the fundamental departmental belief in the inherent and immutable inferiority of Aboriginal people. The Department's Acting Deputy Commissioner, Laurie O'Neill, believed that Aboriginal people were 'chained to the primitive by a mental chain that [they could] never break'.[7] From Middleton's point of view, however, the chains that bound Aboriginal people were not mental but social, cultural and economic. Neither were they unbreakable. The task ahead for his restructured Department, he believed, was to break those chains and guide Aboriginal people from primitivity to modernity, from segregation and denigration to inclusion and acceptance into the social and economic life of mainstream Australian society.

During his fourteen years as Commissioner, Stan Middleton would be a vocal, eloquent and forthright advocate for the better treatment of Aboriginal people. He was often criticised, particularly in Parliament, for his outspokenness. Shocked by the racism he encountered in Western Australia, he carried out a vigorous campaign to counter the 'ignorance and prejudice' of the non-Aboriginal community. 'The problem of the half-caste is not the half-caste', he told them. 'It's you'.[8] He was also appalled at the racism enshrined in the *Native Administration Act 1936*, which he described as 'the one piece of

---

5   Gare, interviewed by Bannister, Bringing Them Home Oral History Project, 1999.
6   Middleton, Annual Report of the Commission of Native Affairs for the year ended 30th June 1950, Government Printer, Perth, 1951, p. 6.
7   Idriess, *Over the Range*, p. 25.
8   *Daily News*, 12 November 1949, p. 8, 'Yours is the Next Step in the March to Help the Half-caste'. Although the *Daily News* did not cite Middleton as the author of this article, it was almost certainly written by him.

legislation which most effectively deprives aborigines from exercising their basic civic rights, and imposes on them a heavy burden of administration, discrimination and restriction'.

Throughout his commissionership, Middleton fought against the conservatism of the Western Australian Parliament, particularly in the Legislative Council which had strong pastoralist representation, to have the legislation amended.[9] 'Whatever the intention may have been when this Act was first passed in 1905', he wrote:

> its effect on the aborigines of to-day, particularly those of the South, is calamitous. Almost universally it is regarded as being an intolerable undemocratic restriction on the personal liberty of a section of our community. We who are charged with the unpleasant duty of administering it regard it as repugnant to basic humanitarian and welfare principles, practically devoid of any common ground with the people we are trying to help and creative of more misunderstanding, dissatisfaction and abuse than any other piece of similar legislation known to the free world to-day.[10]

Despite the constraints of outdated legislation, however, structural and policy change within the Department was undertaken on the basis of recommendations made in Bateman's 'Report on Survey of Native Affairs', which was submitted in June 1948. Although far from a radical document, the report paved the way for significant change in the administration of Aboriginal affairs in Western Australia.

In the Pilbara, the system of colonial control that vested power in pastoralist hands was being broken down by the activities of the strikers. This system was premised on the belief that pastoralist beneficence in caring for resident station communities placed them in the best position to exercise paternal and protective control of people who were incapable of looking after themselves. Bateman's report signalled a shift away from official acceptance of this premise towards a belief that maintaining control over Aboriginal people in the north was a departmental responsibility. While Bateman thought that most Aboriginal people were reasonably well treated on stations, he saw the practice of allowing pastoralists to set their own rates of pay for Aboriginal workers as open to

---

9 Amendments sought by Middleton included, in the mid-1950s, an amendment to impose greater departmental control over the independent Aboriginal group in the Pilbara.

10 Middleton, 'State Legislation – and its Effect on the Aborigines', address to Rotary, 22 July 1953, reprinted in *Narrogin Observer*, 31 July 1953, p. 8.

abuse, giving rise to the level of Aboriginal dissatisfaction that had led to the strike. 'There can be no doubt that Communistic influence brought about the position', he wrote, 'but it is equally obvious that there was a certain amount of fertile soil in which to sow the Communistic seed'.[11] These conditions could have been averted, he believed, had there been greater departmental supervision of labour conditions prior to the strike:

> Their complaint is that the Department prior to the strike was disinterested in their conditions and on the rare occasions when an inspector did visit their place of employment, according to them, he spent most of his time with the manager and had little to say to them.[12]

Bateman concluded that, in order to forestall similar strikes in other parts of the state, greater departmental oversight at a local level was required. The Department had too few field staff, he argued, each with a large district to patrol. It was unrealistic to expect one field officer to maintain sufficient supervision over the vast northern district. He recommended that the size of districts be reduced and more field officers appointed. Particularly, he recommended the stationing of a field officer at Port Hedland to maintain closer supervision of that area.

Previously, the small number of departmental field officers meant that Aboriginal administration was largely undertaken by the police, acting in their designated role of 'Protectors of Natives'. Bateman considered this situation to be 'entirely wrong in principle'.[13] 'The aborigines are as a rule in fear of the police', he argued, 'and this in itself is an inherent weakness in the system'. He pointed particularly to the absurdity of one officer fulfilling the roles of both prosecutor and defender of Aboriginal people facing court. 'The objection is so obvious and so well founded as to require no further comment', Bateman wrote. Nevertheless, despite the fact that the system was 'universally condemned', he could see no satisfactory alternative to the use of police officers as Protectors throughout the state, as it was impossible to find the 'right types' outside the police force to undertake the role, and payment to non-police Protectors would have added to the cost of administration.[14] He hoped an expanded Department, employing more officers with responsibility for smaller districts, would reduce

---

11   F. E. A Bateman, Report on Survey of Native Affairs, Presented to both Houses of Parliament by His Excellency's Command, Government Printer, Perth, 1948, p. 18.
12   Bateman, Report on Survey of Native Affairs, p. 18.
13   Bateman, Report on Survey of Native Affairs, p. 35.
14   Bateman, Report on Survey of Native Affairs, p. 22.

reliance on police officers in Aboriginal administration and serve to mitigate the disadvantages of the police protector system.[15]

Policy shift from 'hard policing' to an assimilationist approach was characteristic of Aboriginal administration throughout Australia in the post-war years, but in Western Australia it was to some extent a case of making policy fit practice, at least with regard to the Pilbara. Before 1946, the Department had played little part in the lives of Aboriginal people in the north, where the pastoralists and the police exercised sufficient control. However, from the beginning of the strike, as we have seen, police intimidation was found to be no longer effective as a tool for maintaining control over the strikers, and the Department, under pressure from pastoralists, had become involved to an extent that had previously been unnecessary. Bateman noted this in his report. 'The natives maintain that until they struck they rarely saw anyone from the Department with whom to discuss their grievances', he wrote. 'When it was too late they received frequent and abortive visits from Departmental officers'.[16] In the Pilbara, responsibility for maintaining control over the Aboriginal population had already passed from the hands of pastoralists to the Department, and Bateman's recommendations were simply about formulating policy in line with this. It amounted to an official shift away from the practice of outsourcing Aboriginal administration in the north to pastoralists. Now, Bateman recommended that the Department accept responsibility for supervising pastoral labour relationships and for stipulating minimum rates of pay. For the Kimberley, he suggested the gradual introduction of wages at the rate of 2/6 or 5/- per week to each male and female worker, not in cash but by way of a credit on the station books.[17] Minimal as this pay was, it was no longer accepted that the squatters' tolerance and maintenance of resident Aboriginal communities on their pastoral leases was sufficient recompense for the labour provided.

Bateman's call for the separation of Aboriginal administration and policing included the recommendation that the practice of recruiting departmental staff from the ranks of the police force be discontinued. 'Other nations throughout the world possessing native populations have realised long ago that the problems of native administration require the best brains available', he wrote. 'Apparently that fact has not been recognised in W.A'. In a statement that clearly referred to Acting Deputy Commissioner

---

15 Bateman, Report on Survey of Native Affairs, p. 23.
16 Bateman, Report on Survey of Native Affairs, p. 18.
17 Bateman, Report on Survey of Native Affairs, p. 16.

Laurie O'Neill, he wrote that 'the practice of appointing officers outside the Native Affairs Department to field positions and then transferring them to the senior administrative positions is a most undesirable one, which should cease'.[18]

In the north, the conflation of Aboriginal administration with policing had been a key component of colonial rule. Under this regime, O'Neill's previous experience as a Kimberley policeman, and his reputation for 'knowing the natives' and how to handle them, had made him ideally suited for the role of Travelling Inspector for the northern region, and for the role of Acting Deputy Commissioner after a few years in the Department.[19] Now these qualifications were no longer considered adequate. Reflecting the influence of Elkin, who had met with Bateman during the period of his survey, the report recommended the careful selection of field officers of the 'right type', along similar lines to recruitment of patrol officers in New Guinea and the Northern Territory. A cadet system would be established: after twelve months' trial in the field, recruits would be sent to Sydney University for a short course in social anthropology, although care was to be taken to ensure that as well as academic ability they also possessed 'practical common sense'.[20]

Bateman's recommendations for enlarging and restructuring the Department was as much a response to the loss of settler control in the Pilbara as it was to the rising tide of assimilationist ideas, particularly given the belated acknowledgement that genuine grievances had motivated the strike. 'Had the Pilbara district been adequately patrolled by an inspector acting in the interests of the natives and one who had their confidence', Bateman wrote, 'it is probable that their grievances would have been discussed with their employers and a satisfactory settlement reached'.[21] Ex-policemen, he believed, could not gain the complete confidence of Aboriginal people:[22]

> Unfortunately it appears that too little notice was taken by the Department of their conditions, which in many cases required improving. Steps should be taken immediately to avoid any repetition of striking by the natives in the North-West and the North. It is essential for the

---

18 Bateman, Report on Survey of Native Affairs, pp. 35–36.
19 Scrimgeour, 'This Man's Tracks'.
20 Bateman, Report on Survey of Native Affairs, p. 35.
21 Bateman, Report on Survey of Native Affairs, p. 18.
22 Bateman, Report on Survey of Native Affairs, p. 36.

Department to know the conditions under which all natives are employed and to be in a position to insist that they receive fair treatment.[23]

Exercising adequate supervision to ensure fair treatment for Aboriginal people in the north was one means by which further acts of resistance could be averted, but Bateman was by no means advocating a softening of the Department's approach. The Department needed to retain the ability to deal firmly and decisively with Aboriginal dissent. Bateman was particularly concerned to learn from Aboriginal people in the Derby region that they were also planning to strike for better conditions. 'It only required Communistic influence to bring about the same state of affairs in Derby', Bateman wrote. 'Great vigilance should be exercised by the District Inspector to forestall any such influence and it will be necessary to adopt firm action at the first signs'.[24]

Firm action included the ongoing power to remove dissidents to institutions under ministerial warrant. Bateman noted that the Department's power to remove Aboriginal people from their districts without trial was widely criticised as open to abuse, but he nevertheless recommended that the power to do so be retained. 'Any alteration in the present procedure would be likely to result in a great deal of inconvenience and undue delay which would outweigh the present risk of injustice', he wrote.[25] Clearly, the imperative to maintain control outweighed concerns surrounding the injustice of the practice. Bateman supported departmental plans to set up an institution at Cosmo Newbery, a remote ration depot thirty miles north-east of Laverton in the state's upper south-east, as a penal settlement for repeat offenders who were 'not only a continual pest to the white population but also [had] a detrimental effect on many of the better type'.[26]

The value of Aboriginal labour to the pastoral industry was not overlooked in Bateman's report. 'This is the work for which they show a special aptitude', he wrote:

> and which at the same time admirably fits in with the economy of the State. The pastoral industry as a whole is entirely dependent on native labour and the natives should be encouraged to regard employment in the industry as their main source of employment.

---

23 Bateman, Report on Survey of Native Affairs, p. 18.
24 Bateman, Report on Survey of Native Affairs, p. 16.
25 Bateman, Report on Survey of Native Affairs, p. 38.
26 Bateman, Report on Survey of Native Affairs, p. 33.

He recommended that Aboriginal people in the pastoral regions of the state 'be trained with the object of fitting them for employment on the stations'.[27] In the Pilbara, this recommendation took shape in plans for the establishment of White Springs Mission.

In accordance with the Bateman report, Middleton set about restructuring and expanding the Department, establishing a decentralised system along the lines of the administration of Papua New Guinea. To staff the new structure, he recruited additional field officers who had had experience in native administration in Papua New Guinea, and within a year of his appointment the number of field officers in the Department would double from four to eight, with five of the eight officers being recruited from Papua New Guinea. Sydney Elliott-Smith, former resident magistrate in Papua, was appointed Deputy Commissioner and officer in charge of the northern region. Lew McBeath spent a further six months in head office handing over the reins to the new Commissioner, before being posted back to the Kimberley as superintendent of Moola Bulla Aboriginal Station, after eight years in the senior roles of Deputy Commissioner and Acting Commissioner. Laurie O'Neill relinquished his role of Acting Deputy Commissioner and was returned to the field as a District Officer. Tom Jensen, who had been seconded to Native Affairs, returned to the police force.

The Department was preparing to take a more dominant role in the north, disentangling itself from its previous complicity in a pastoralist-dominated system in which the role of its officers had converged with that of the police in supporting pastoralist power. The role of the police in Aboriginal administration was to be gradually reduced, and by 1950 Middleton would feel able to report that 'the need for the use of Police Officers as Protectors is diminishing as Departmental field officers take over more and more of the work'.[28] Predictably, pastoralists complained of the appointment of 'importations from other countries' with no experience of Western Australian Aborigines. Dave Pullen, an officer appointed from Papua as a District Officer in the Kimberley, found, however, that:

> in a short time this blatant antagonism to the introduction of new blood into Native Affairs grew much less because the better types in the community quickly appreciated the benefits to be derived from completely dissociating Native Affairs from the Police.[29]

---

27 Bateman, Report on Survey of Native Affairs, p. 35.
28 Middleton, Annual Report, 1950, p. 9.
29 Pullen, Annual Report, September 1949, p. 2, SROWA 1949/0722.

McLeod later wrote that, as a result of Bateman's report, 'the previous practice of appointing Policemen as P.N.s [Protectors of Natives] was to some extent discontinued, and their overall control over the natives was weakened'.[30] Certainly, the men recruited into the newly-created role of patrol officer saw their approach as a radical departure from earlier approaches.[31] A Western Australian patrol officer during the 1950s, Leslie Marchant, for example, criticised the *Bringing Them Home* report, which arose from an inquiry into the separation of Aboriginal children from their families, for its failure to differentiate between pre- and post-war practices, arguing that, as one of 'a new generation of young scholar-administrators spawned by the war', he had not returned home from fighting for democracy overseas 'to deny freedoms and practise genocide here'.[32]

The shift in departmental approach at this time, based on a fundamental shift in assumptions about the nature of Aboriginality and human progress, did not mean that Aboriginal people in Western Australia were no longer subject to oppressive, discriminatory and arbitrary treatment at the hands of the Department and its officials. Assumptions of social retardation and the imperative for 'advancement' could be just as destructive as assumptions of biological inferiority. Assumptions that solutions lay in the hands of non-Aboriginal administrators continued see Aboriginal people denied control over their own lives. The impact of programs and practices carried out under assimilation policy would see disruptive departmental intrusion into Aboriginal lives and the fracturing and dislocating of families and communities. Nevertheless, as Russell McGregor argues, this fundamental shift – from policies based on assumptions of Aboriginal incapacity to change, to policies based on a presumption of reformability – was far from inconsequential, despite the continuation of practices such as child removal.[33]

McDonald's predecessor, Bob Coverley, complained about the replacement of existing departmental staff with men with 'little or no knowledge of this state or of the native problems with which they will have to deal', and called

---

30   McLeod, draft autobiography, chapter 3, p. 10, Marchant Trust Collection, UWA MS118 series 1 file 11.

31   For example, Gare, interviewed by Bannister, Bringing Them Home Oral History Project, 1999.

32   Leslie R. Marchant, 'From the Diary of a Protector of Aborigines', *Quadrant*, April 2003, p. 32.

33   Russell McGregor, 'Governance, not Genocide: Aboriginal Assimilation in the Postwar Era', in A. Dirk Moses (ed.), *Genocide and Settler Society: Frontier Violence and Stolen Indigenous Children in Australian History*, Berghahn Books, New York and Oxford, 2004, p. 306.

unsuccessfully for a Select Committee to inquire into the administration of the Department.[34] In reply to these criticisms, McDonald referred to 'the new developments that have taken place in only the last few years ... the growing industrial consciousness of the natives, not only the half-castes, but the full-bloods in many areas'.[35] Elkin would describe the 'deepening and widening movement of thought and action' that drove policy changes in the middle decades of the twentieth century as a 'revolution'.[36] But another sort of revolution – Aboriginal activism within the state, and particularly in the Pilbara – was also driving change.

Changes in personnel and perspective would, in time, have a profound impact on departmental responses to the Pilbara movement. By the early 1950s, officers recruited from Papua New Guinea would come to look favourably on the movement, and the Department would, for a while, lend its cautious support. But in the shorter term the Department still struggled to deal with the situation in the Pilbara. Institutional change came slowly. During the first year of Middleton's commissionership, the Department continued to rely on old-school officials and police Protectors in the Pilbara for information, advice and action. McBeath continued to influence decision making during the second half of 1948. With an expanded staff and the ongoing power to remove miscreants to institutions, the Department had placed itself in a stronger position to monitor and address Aboriginal grievances, as Bateman had suggested, and to act quickly to suppress acts of insubordination and rebellion. But Bateman's report offered little in the way of new ideas for responding to the loss of settler control in the Pilbara. Under ongoing pressure from pastoralists, and in light of Bateman's emphasis on the pastoral industry's dependence on Aboriginal labour, the Department continued to resort to harsh, punitive and obstructive measures to curtail the activities of the strikers during the first year of Middleton's term in office. When conflict escalated in the Marble Bar area within a year of the tabling of Bateman's report, removal under ministerial warrant appeared to be the only course open to the Department, and the new administration would, as we shall see, come closer to removing strikers from the Pilbara than at any time since the strike began.

---

34 Coverley, Parliamentary Debates (Hansard), Western Australia: Legislative Assembly, 6 July 1949, p. 356; *West Australian,* 7 July 1949, 'Inquiry Sought into Native Affairs'.

35 McDonald, Parliamentary Debates (Hansard), Western Australia: Legislative Assembly, 3 August 1949, p. 915.

36 Elkin, 'Australian Aboriginal and White Relations', pp. 227–228.

Chapter 23

'Our School House Will Remain Until Bomb Blow It Apart'

Late 1948 – Early 1949

At the end of 1948, in response to repeated urging from the Department of Native Affairs, the Western Australian Department of Education (DE) was looking seriously into the possibility of establishing a school at Moolyella. Travelling schoolteacher Cedric de Passey visited the tin field in November and reported that the community there was sufficiently stable to warrant a school. He told Constable Weaver that it was likely that a technical school would be built for the children of the tin workers.[1] Despite ongoing concerns about the lack of institutional control ('as the native population is given to moving from one place to another and cannot be relied upon to stay at Moolyella') and despite the difficulty of providing teacher accommodation, the DE had decided, by the end of 1948, that there was a definite need for a school there.[2] As far as the Twelve Mile was concerned, the DE was prepared to continue to supply school teacher Tommy Sampie with correspondence lessons for as long as that camp continued to operate.[3]

McLeod advised the Department of Education against building a school at Moolyella. Tin deposits there were becoming depleted, he wrote, and would not support a large population of miners in the longer term. The lack of firewood in the area was another reason the community was unlikely to remain there. As an alternative site for a school and the one 'favoured by all native people in the Pilbara', he proposed the abandoned Yandeyarra and Kangan pastoral leases, to be acquired by Aboriginal people themselves along the lines of the

---

1 De Passey to Director of Education, 5 November 1948, SROWA 1947/0594/68; Weaver, police patrol report, 5 November 1948, 1946/2538 v8.
2 Edmondson, Acting Director of Education to Watts, Minister for Education, 16 November 1948, SROWA 1947/0594/72.
3 Edmondson, Acting Director of Education to Watts, Minister for Education, 16 November 1948, SROWA 1947/0594/72.

proposition he had put to Premier Ross McLarty. Aboriginal people would undertake to construct the school themselves, or to provide the labour if the Department was willing to supply material. 'I would be happy of the oppertunity [sic] to supply any further details you may wish to have', he wrote.

> For some time past the native peoples in this area have been eager to provide their children with the chance to gain a sound education and you could expect their wholehearted cooperation and assistance in any scheme which will provide this necessary need without prejudice to their children and without the risk of the parents loosing [sic] control of their families or having them robbed from them.[4]

Having earlier requested a school at Moolyella, the Department of Native Affairs now also advised against it. Before the Catholic Church proposed setting up a mission at White Springs Station, a school at Moolyella had been favoured by the DNA as a means of attracting strikers from the Twelve Mile and, in the longer term, preventing the ideology of a militantly independent community from being transmitted to the rising generation. In June 1948, the DNA had considered that 'urgent action [was] necessary in regard to the establishment of a school for native children at Moolyella', but within a few months and by the time a school there was being seriously considered by the Department of Education, a Catholic mission at White Springs had become the DNA's preferred approach to solving the ongoing problem of Aboriginal militancy in the Pilbara.[5] In February 1949, therefore, in reply to McLeod's recommendation that education be provided in a settlement owned and operated by Aboriginal people, the Director of Education was able to assure him that the DNA had 'the matter in hand' and had advised against proceeding with the plan for a school at Moolyella.[6]

White Springs Station, previously owned by Rob Lukis who now managed Munda Station, was one of several stations, along with Kangan, Yandeyarra and Abydos Stations, that had been abandoned in 1945 as a result of a number of factors, including dingoes. At the time of the stations' closure, McLeod had proposed that Abydos Station be made available to Aboriginal people for their own use. Abydos had since been acquired by the state government

---

[4] McLeod to Department of Education, 16 December 1948, SROWA 1947/0594/79–82.

[5] McBeath to McDonald, 3 June 1948, SROWA 1947/0349/39; McBeath to McDonald, 11 October 1948, SROWA 1947/0594/67.

[6] Edmondson, Acting Director of Education, to McLeod, 8 February 1949, SROWA 1947/0594/85.

as a research station, but the idea of using White Springs as a government institution had been floated on a number of occasions. In late 1947, rumours initiated by Jack Gribble had prompted a *Workers' Star* report warning that hundreds of strikers could be sent there:

> Natives sent there would be effectively withdrawn behind the iron curtain which surrounds other Government stations, where it is frequently alleged neglect and exploitation are their lot.
>
> If the report is correct the Minister for Native Affairs is acting in direct opposition to his own promises and is ignoring the wide public demand for a new deal for Aborigines.[7]

However, a definite plan for White Springs did not take shape until June 1948, when Port Hedland's Father Edward Bryan held discussions with his bishop in Geraldton about the availability of staff for a mission there. He travelled to Perth for further discussions on the scheme with Premier McLarty, Minister McDonald and Acting Commissioner of Native Affairs McBeath.[8] 'Something must be done if the natives are to be properly treated', he wrote, 'and if we don't want subversive influences to be acting on him [*sic*] in the same way in a few years to come. I have a definite solution to the native unrest in this area'. Schooling at White Springs was the central feature of his solution. Boys would receive elementary technical education under the supervision of Catholic brothers, 'with half-caste male monitors', and girls would be taught by nuns, 'with half-caste female monitors'.[9]

In October 1948, Bryan submitted a written proposal to the Department, undertaking to provide the necessary staff if the government would make White Springs Station available for that purpose and provide funding for the first three years of its operation. In November, while the DE was investigating the possibility of a school at Moolyella at McDonald's behest, McDonald put the White Springs proposal before the premier. 'There is an opportunity of setting up a Catholic Mission on White Springs Station', he wrote:

> which will provide for the schooling of the children in the Port Hedland–Marble Bar area (who would number probably in the vicinity of 100), provide for the care of indigent natives in the area and provide for

---

7   *Workers' Star*, 14 November 1947, p. 5, 'New Attempt to Smash Native Co-op?'
8   Jensen to McBeath, 8 June 1948, SROWA 1947/0349/37.
9   Bryan, 7 July 1948, ANU, Noel Butlin Archives Centre, Michael Hess Collection, N287, Item 1.

vocational instruction, particularly in rural pursuits, of natives both boys and girls there forming a pool of labour for the pastoral industry in those areas. It is difficult to get suitable personnel for remote institutions and the Catholic Church is prepared to find them, and of course no salaries will be involved.[10]

Estimating the cost of buildings and installations as 'something like £18,000 over two or three years', a portion of which was to be treated as a loan to the Church, McDonald concluded his proposal by reminding Premier McLarty that 'this is an area where McLeod has operated and where industrial trouble has occurred so much'.[11]

For the DNA, Bryan's scheme did indeed appear to be 'a definite solution' for restoring order and settler authority in the Pilbara in the longer term. It fitted comfortably within the new administration's assimilation agenda without creating the need for the Department to work with the strikers' organisation. The mission would offer strikers many of the benefits they had hoped to achieve through strike action but which had remained beyond their reach, including education for their children and their own community settlement with accommodation and facilities, which, Middleton claimed, 'will be [a] vast improvement on the hovels of the Twelve-Mile [and] Moolyella', on a station property they could run themselves (albeit under the benevolent supervision of mission management).[12] It would offer freedom of employment, enabling adherents to take paid work on surrounding stations without being tied to a permanent relationship with pastoralists. 'Seasonal workers will be accommodated at the [mission] station', Middleton asserted, 'and will be free to move out to shearing and other seasonal employment, and return at their will'.[13] Training in pastoral work at the mission would enable workers to realistically demand higher wages for their labour. By providing these benefits, the mission would offer a more attractive alternative to the strike camps, undermining the influence that McLeod and strike leaders wielded with their disruptive communistic doctrine. 'Anti-department' sentiment among the strikers would not stand in the way of the mission's success, as Bryan, well-known and liked by the Aboriginal community, was not associated with 'government'.

---

10   McDonald to McLarty, 29 November 1948, SROWA S3841 cons769 3.
11   McDonald to McLarty, 29 November 1948, SROWA S3841 cons769 3.
12   Middleton, responses to pamphlet 'Stop this Persecution', 9 June 1949, SROWA 1943/0621/181–184.
13   Middleton, responses to pamphlet 'Stop this Persecution', 9 June 1949, SROWA 1943/0621/181–184.

While a school at Moolyella would have had some effect in counteracting the perceived negative influences of Aboriginal culture and the supposed 'communistic' beliefs of the strike camps, children would still have lived with their families, imbibing the culture of a militantly independent Aboriginal community. On White Springs Mission, on the other hand, the dormitory system would give missionaries greater power to counter these influences.[14] The Aboriginal community itself, brought under the authority of the mission, would learn new understandings of the world to replace the ideology of independence and resistance promulgated by Dooley, Mitchell, McLeod and other strike leaders. The problem of finding an alternative site for Twelve Mile residents would be overcome, and conflict over land use and access in the Port Hedland area finally resolved. The racialised hierarchy of colonial control would be re-established, with authority vested in non-Aboriginal mission staff and judiciously delegated to selected 'half-caste monitors'.

Most importantly from the settler point of view, it was a scheme which promised to resolve the labour difficulties suffered by the local pastoral industry since the strike began. With a focus on providing Aboriginal people with the skills needed by the industry, including training girls for domestic service, it was to provide stations with a pool of labour to draw on when needed. In a manner characteristic of colonial ideology, it was a solution based on a reanalysis of the problem of labour relations in the Pilbara as one of Aboriginal deficit. Although pastoralists denigrated Aboriginal labour as more trouble than it was worth, *marrngu* were winning political and industrial benefits by withholding much-needed labour precisely because the skills and knowledge they brought to the industry were highly valuable and, indeed, irreplaceable. To develop a solution based on training Aboriginal people to qualify them for pastoral and domestic service employment was a cynical misconstruction of the actual issues.

Before the strike, pastoralists had opposed the establishment of missions in the region, believing that the mission doctrine of the brotherhood of man 'spoiled the natives', undermining and complicating an effective system of colonial domination.[15] Now that that system had been broken down by the strike, squatters embraced the White Springs solution as a means of restricting

---

14   Harvey Tilbrook, Native Affairs patrol journal, 2 April 1951, SROWA 1949/0160/199.

15   McLeod made this point a decade later in a letter to the anthropologist Peter Worsley. 'Although the pastoralists in this area in truth used to object to missions as they spoilt the Aborigines [and] turned them out as hopeless crawling hypocrites, once the strike occured they turned to Missions as a lesser of two evils'. McLeod to Worsley, 17 March 1957, Papers of Jessie Street, NLA 2683/10/240.

the uncontrolled movement and activities of Aboriginal people, while also providing a pool of trained Aboriginal labour. With the mission under the supervision of Bryan, a defender of the pastoralists' treatment of Aboriginal labour and a vocal critic of the strike, it was a scheme perfectly suited to pastoralist needs, promising to provide a readily available source of trained labour when it was needed, without the need to support workers in off-seasons or to support their dependents.[16]

While pastoralists expressed support for White Springs as a solution to their problems in the longer term, they also continued to agitate for the closure of the Twelve Mile in the short term. Although its population was now very small, and despite the fact that working parties were no longer accessing the surrounding pastoral leases for hunting, fishing and shelling activities, Ted Richardson of Pippingarra Station continued to complain to the DNA about the presence of strikers at the Twelve Mile. It was he who first raised the suggestion that the problem could be resolved by the Department declaring the area a prohibited area for Aboriginal people to camp.[17] In June 1948, his suggestion was taken up by Acting Commissioner McBeath, who referred McDonald to the relevant section of Western Australia's *Native Administration Act 1936*. 'Section 40, and particularly Regulations 107/8, were designed to deal with situations such as exists at the Twelve Mile', he wrote:

> and in view of the return to employment of many of the adult natives, and the temporary transfer of the children to the Yule river, you might be disposed to agree that the time has now arrived when the Forestry Reserve which is known as the Twelve Mile might be declared a forbidden settlement as provided for in Regulation 107 (a).[18]

That month, McDonald was pleased to inform Ted Richardson that arrangements were being made to stop the issue of government rations at the Twelve Mile and to shift old and infirm Aboriginal people to Marble Bar. 'Previously the exclusion of natives from the 12-Mile has been a matter of some difficulty', he wrote:

> because there was a considerable number there and their exclusion would only cause them to congregate in some other district where the same inconvenience might arise.

---

16 'North-West Natives, Conditions on Stations', *West Australian*, 17 August 1946, p. 12.
17 Richardson to McDonald, 22 May 1948, SROWA 1948/0732/1–3.
18 McBeath to McDonald, 4 June 1948, SROWA 1948/0732/5.

However, the position of the 12-Mile as a camping site has been the subject of discussion between myself and the Acting Commissioner for Native Affairs and it may be that some further steps can be taken which will assist the position in your district.

Richardson grumbled that shifting indigent natives was all very well but was 'of no use to us unless the area is declared non camping ground for natives'.[19] McDonald sought the views of Sergeant McGeary on the issue.[20] McGeary, unsurprisingly given his antagonism towards Sampie, supported the idea of prohibiting Aboriginal access to the forestry reserve. 'They are camped right on the road', he wrote:

> & accessible to all and sundry & where no action can be taken owing to a public road going beside the camp.
>
> ...
>
> The time now is opportune & action should be taken accordingly to rid this area of a menace.[21]

Written in October 1948, McGeary's recommendation was addressed not to Acting Commissioner McBeath, but to the newly-appointed Commissioner, Stan Middleton. When Middleton visited Port Hedland that month as part of an introductory tour of the state's north, McGeary took the opportunity of discussing with him the advantages to be gained in declaring the Twelve Mile a prohibited area.[22] Under pressure from Richardson, McDonald approved the decision, and on 3 December, Middleton declared Forestry Reserve No 70/25 a 'forbidden settlement', announcing that within a month of the publication of the notification 'such settlement shall be removed, abandoned, or pulled down and the natives of such settlement shall remove to such other part or parts of the State as have not been declared by me a forbidden settlement'.[23]

After agitating for so long for the closure of the Twelve Mile, Ted Richardson did not live to see the outcome of the declaration. He died suddenly later that month, happy, perhaps, in the belief that a solution had finally been found to

---

19 Richardson to McDonald, 14 June 1948, SROWA S3841 cons769 1.
20 McDonald to McBeath, memo, 10 June 1948, SROWA 1948/0732/9.
21 McGeary to Middleton, 4 October 1948, SROWA 1948/0732/36.
22 McBeath to McGeary, 11 October 1948, SROWA 1948/0732/37.
23 Extract from WA Government Gazette, 10 December 1948, notice dated 3 December, SROWA 1948/0732/70.

the problem of the Twelve Mile, and that Pippingarra might finally regain exclusive use of the forestry reserve.[24]

The declaration was the first decisive action taken in response to the strike under the new administration appointed to carry out the positive and forward-looking transformation of native administration in Western Australia. While Middleton took stock of the task ahead of him, many departmental decisions were still being made by McBeath, who retained the role of Deputy Commissioner during the second half of 1948. Middleton later claimed that, although instructions to Port Hedland police to close the camp were given over his signature, he had no knowledge of the circumstances and had not been involved in the decision-making process.[25] Nevertheless, there is some irony in the fact that the closure of a settlement that was, by that time, principally an Aboriginal-run school was one of the first actions taken in the Port Hedland area by an administrator whose key focus over the coming years would be the implementation of a policy of assimilation, with the education of Aboriginal children a high priority. The irony is highlighted by the fact that the day after the publication of the notice declaring the Twelve Mile a forbidden settlement, the *Daily News* carried the following report:

> Young Aborigines at a native camp near Port Hedland work unselfishly for sick white children of W.A.
>
> Members of Junior Red Cross, they trap, sew, garden and run penny concerts to raise funds for spastic children or the victims of infantile paralysis or other diseases.
>
> Like other Junior Red Cross workers in W.A. they serve with the common aim of help and kindness; of promoting good health, morality and friendship.[26]

In the spirit of the new positive approach, McBeath suggested that this effort called for a letter of appreciation from Middleton as Commissioner. To whom should it be addressed? Middleton wondered. McBeath thought that Father Bryan was probably the appropriate person.[27] Middleton accordingly wrote to Sergeant Walter Plunkett, McGeary's replacement as officer in charge of the Port Hedland Police Station, asking him to 'convey to those concerned

---

24 *Daily News*, 4 January 1949, p. 1, 'Pastoralist Dies Suddenly'.
25 Middleton to Saint, 6 September 1949, SROWA 1949/0454/95.
26 *Daily News*, 11 December 1948, p. 9.
27 McBeath and Middleton, memos, SROWA 1947/0349/42.

my thanks and congratulations for their splendid effort'.[28] Such expressions of appreciation would certainly have been withheld, however, had the DNA realised that the children involved in this 'splendid effort' were Tommy Sampie's students at the Twelve Mile school. Organising Aboriginal children to raise money for the Red Cross was commendable if carried out by a priest, but not if it was carried out by *marrngu*. Assimilation was to be a process directed by non-Aboriginal people, not undertaken by Aboriginal people themselves.

In January 1949, after some delay in having the proclamation printed, Sergeant Plunkett gave Sampie, the school children and other residents one month to dismantle the school room and other structures and to leave the Twelve Mile. 'It is not the intention of this Department to create difficulties or undue hardship upon the natives, both adult and children in residence at the Twelve Mile', Plunkett was told, 'but the location is unsatisfactory for many reasons and as these people would not transfer, or remove voluntarily it has been found necessary to invoke the provisions of the Regulations to effect the evacuation of this reserve'.[29]

Sampie wrote to the Native Rights League (formerly the CDNR) of their eviction. 'Sergeant came out to our camp & made inquiries of all the natives here', he wrote. 'When all gathered around ... Sergeant, he signed our names there in. When completed that part he told us to pull down all our houses & humpies'.[30] Strikers were advised to move their children to Moolyella and to use that as their headquarters in future, 'as their presence there does not interfere in any way with the activities of other people, and then again the adults can obtain a good living by yandying for tin when other work is not offering'.[31]

Sampie wrote a letter of protest to the DNA:

> Will you please explain. I always thought the native affair would protect us in every way and give us a home in 12 mile. After so many of our boys went back to the squatter to work for them, but now you are going to stir the whole thing up over again so dont blame us, because we are fighting for our Rightes & our childrens, we must defend our personal Rights ourselfs, if not our protectors wont do it for us, we only want our rights & freedom with liberty in our own country.

---

28   Middleton to Plunkett, 21 December 1948, SROWA 1947/0349/43.
29   Middleton to Plunkett, 20 January 1949, SROWA 1948/0732/72.
30   Sampie, incomplete letter, addressee and date missing, SROWA 1948/0732/86–87.
31   Middleton to Plunkett, 20 January 1949, SROWA 1948/0732/72.

Now Since we were born I can almost say the natives never had a home to live & enjoy himself, never, but since we went on strike, we walked into 12 mile & remained her till last Sunday we heard you our protector was closing our camp. I dont think its fair on your side to do that.

And most of our boys & girls have went back to work for the squatters but now you are causing us more trouble instead of helping us.

Five station got working, both men & women working today, and other stations will be notified in time as they are from 12 mile camp went out there, to do some work.

I thought we'd be friend with Government & squatters, but now, we got no one to help us to see we get home for our young children & ourselfs. So we might as well gave all the natives together till you find a way to protect us in a menner that will please every natives of Pilbarra district, our own Government, the Native Affairs never helped us, when we asked them to give us a home, but just went against us & fought for the squatters Rights.

If we are going to be shifted by you, where will the squatters get their cheap labors, & another thing, where can we find a home from stations if this camp is closed, so I beg you on behalf of all the Stn boys, guarantee this 12 mile camp to remain intact.[32]

'We are prepared to fight tooth and nail and never shift', Sampie told the Native Rights League. 'Our school house will remain until bomb blow it apart'.[33]

District Medical Officer Eric Saint also opposed the decision, writing to Western Australia's Commissioner of Public Health, Cecil (Mick) Cook, on 6 February of his concerns that health and social problems arising from overcrowded conditions at Moolyella would be exacerbated by the closure of the Twelve Mile. In addition to malnutrition and venereal disease, he identified the prevalence of 'vice, as distinct from the natives' normal tribal promiscuity', as one of the growing problems on the tin field. 'The presence of a well-known agitator of known Communist affiliations constitutes a perpetual threat to social stability', he added. The Twelve Mile had become an important base for Aboriginal people in transit or receiving medical treatment, who would now 'be forced to come in to the filthy encampment at the onemile, over the brow of the hill from the native hospital', which Saint considered 'dangerously

---

32 Sampie, incomplete letter, addressee and date missing, SROWA 1948/0732/86–87.
33 *Workers' Star*, 18 February 1949, p. 4, 'Dept. Threat to Native Co-op'.

close to town'. 'Also, I shall find difficulty in disposing of the aged indigent sick', he wrote:

> A large proportion of my patients are old heart failures etc. I discharge them often to the twelve mile knowing that they will be fed, and knowing that they are within easy reach if in need of further attention ... You will agree with me that this policy of herding all natives together in one slum is indefensible'.[34]

Health Commissioner Cook approached Middleton with these concerns. Moolyella had been the subject of adverse reports from Saint for some months, he wrote: 'It would be appreciated if in reaching decisions of this nature you would consider this Department's interest in the matter'.[35]

Criticism also came from the officer charged with the task of enforcing the eviction. Sergeant Plunkett made a series of visits to the Twelve Mile to discuss the closure with residents, accompanied on 10 February by Saint.[36] The following day, he wrote to Middleton expressing his opinion that, before closing the camp, a suitable alternative camping place in the same district should have been identified. 'They are born in the De Grey district and should be allowed to live in this District', he wrote. 'They would miss the sea and fishing also their natural hunting grounds'.[37] Concerned at warnings made by Twelve Mile residents that the closure would bring more workers out on strike, he sent Constable Don Withnell to travel around stations on the mail truck to make discreet inquiries into the response of station workers.

Having grown up on a Pilbara station, Withnell spoke some Nyamal, and concluded from his inquiries that if the Department followed through with the closure, there was every indication that 150 Aboriginal workers would walk off stations in protest.[38] In declaring the Twelve Mile a forbidden settlement, the DNA had acted on the assumption that the Twelve Mile was nothing more than a strike camp and a school. It may have 'lost its significance as a strikers' camp', as McBeath had noted, but the site had important cultural and religious significance of which settler society was simply unaware. Ernie Mitchell had traditional rights to the area, and there was a significant cultural

---

34   Saint to Cook, 6 February 1949, SROWA 1948/0732/91.
35   Cook to Middleton, 10 February 1949, SROWA 1948/0732/92.
36   Plunkett to Middleton, 11 February 1949, p. 1, SROWA 1948/0732/93.
37   Plunkett to Middleton, 11 February 1949, p. 1, SROWA 1948/0732/93.
38   Plunkett to Middleton, 11 February 1949, pp. 1–2, SROWA 1948/0732/93–94.

site nearby.³⁹ Men and women who took station employment at reasonable rates and conditions still regarded the Twelve Mile as a home base, a place to stay during *pingkayi* holiday periods and to hold community meetings and ceremonies. Their children attended school there. Although *marrngu* had returned to station work, they had not forfeited the power they had won as a community through strike action.

Plunkett was sufficiently concerned at Withnell's report to notify Middleton by telegram of the likelihood of further strike action. 'I do feel that the position will become serious if the natives walk off and leave the station people', he reported, 'as there has been no rain and many sheep have died and [those still alive] need constant attention by the natives employed'.⁴⁰ As soon as Middleton received Plunkett's telegram, he took action to halt the eviction, wiring Plunkett to 'withhold further action regarding transfer natives from Twelve Mile Camp and permit them remain camp for time being'.⁴¹

Middleton later described the decision to close the Twelve Mile as 'precipitate and ill-advised'.⁴² Having no local knowledge of the matter at the time, he said, he had not interfered 'until Sergeant Plunkett's telegram advising of the threat of direct action being taken by the natives was brought to my notice after Mr. McBeath's departure on leave'.⁴³ Here again is evidence of Pilbara Aboriginal activism undermining mechanisms of settler control that continued to severely impact the lives of Aboriginal people in other parts of the state. The situation was 'so fraught with serious possibilities' that Middleton decided to immediately dispatch Laurie O'Neill to Port Hedland to keep a lid on the situation.⁴⁴

On 13 February, three weeks after giving strikers the order to leave their camp, Plunkett read Middleton's telegram to Twelve Mile residents and explained that they could stay, at least for the time being.⁴⁵ 'Native Affairs Department has been forced to retreat from their attempt to shift Aborigines from their co-operative camp and school at 12 Mile, Port Hedland', the *Workers' Star* reported. '"Police Sergeant Plunkett brought out a wire from

---

39   Thanks to John and Katrin Wilson for alerting me to the cultural significance of the Twelve Mile.
40   Plunkett to Middleton, 11 February 1949, p. 3, SROWA 1948/0732/95.
41   Middleton to Plunkett, telegram, 11 February 1949, SROWA 1948/0732/97.
42   Middleton to Saint, 6 September 1949, SROWA 1949/0454/95.
43   Middleton to Saint, 6 September 1949, SROWA 1949/0454/95.
44   Middleton to McDonald, 15 February 1949, SROWA 1948/0732/96.
45   Plunkett, mileage claim, 12 February 1949, SROWA 1948/0732/111.

the Department saying the camp was not to be shifted, was to remain intact", NW Workers' Association secretary T. Sampey writes'.[46]

McLeod was apparently unaware of the DNA's retraction of the eviction order when he wrote to McDonald a few days later, criticising the Department's action. 'I am asked to forward to you advice of the following matters agreed on in general discussion by the members of the NW Workers' Co-op', he wrote:

> Despite three years of orderly negotiations in accordance with advice of Don McLeod we are no further advanced in our attempt to secure our right to a real advance towards citizenship. Since the foundation of the colony our people have had to endure the effects of slow starvation, exposure and extreme exploitation, yet, when we attempt to put a stop to such practices we are subject to a deliberate provocative campaign carried out by the police as officers of your department, obviously with the intention of intimidating us. This campaign has culminated in the attempted breaking up of the Strike Camp by declaring it a 'Prohibited Area' under the Act as from February 28th. It is clear that our orderliness has been interpreted by you as a sign of weakness and so from February 28th it is our intention to disregard the whole of this Act since in any case we are advised that it is unconstitutional in so far as it conflicts with the *Anti-Slavery Act* of 1843 passed by the Imperial Parliament. Not only were all slaves freed throughout the British Empire but a guarantee was given that never again would slavery be allowed through the Empire. We are forced to take note that the policy of your Act and similar Acts throughout the Commonwealth have had the effect of slowly murdering seven-eighths of the pro-British inhabitants of Australia during a period when the non-colored peoples increased to almost or over seven millions. This policy and the sorrow it caused was merely to provide some monetary gain to that small clique who have secured the vested interest in cheap native labor built up by the various native acts throughout the Commonwealth. In the interest of our people we demand a halt to these persecutions ... We will continue this struggle until our people throughout the Commonwealth are granted equal citizenship. Should your department attempt to use force to re-enact the conditions we object to, we will hold you responsible for any unforeseen incidents which may occur. This communication will have the effect of

---

46   *Workers' Star*, 25 February 1949, p. 4, '12 Mile School Will Remain'.

advising you that as from February 28th we repudiate your Act and will be no longer bound by it.[47]

Laurie O'Neill, no longer Acting Deputy Commissioner and assigned again to the Port Hedland area as a District Officer of the Department of Native Affairs, set about attempting once again to find an alternative site to which Twelve Mile residents could be shifted.[48] It was a quest he had made several times in 1946, and he now found, just as he had then, that all well-watered sites had been incorporated into pastoral leases. He thought it 'ridiculous' to ask stations to surrender such land for an Aboriginal settlement.[49] The DNA conceded defeat and turned its hopes on the White Springs solution. 'The 12 Mile will have to remain as a native camping place for the time being', Middleton told McDonald in early March 1949. 'I have gone into the position with Father Bryan as to White Springs last week. I will discuss with you shortly'.[50] O'Neill was instructed to contact Bryan and discuss the situation with him. 'The whole situation is bound up with the future role of White Springs', Middleton wrote, 'and it is essential, in my opinion, that we work in closest collaboration with Father Bryan henceforth in all matters affecting the interests of the Pilbarra natives'.[51]

Although the designation of Forestry Reserve 70/25 as a 'forbidden area' for Aboriginal people was not formally cancelled until 1954,[52] Aboriginal people continued using the Twelve Mile throughout the following years and decades, and pastoralists continued to agitate for its closure. In August 1949, when pastoralists again called for the enforcement of the prohibition, the move was again strenuously opposed by Dr Saint. 'The problem of striking natives is infinitely more profound than mere consideration of the geographic sites of camps', he argued:

> If they *will* strike then natural gregariousness will prompt them to infiltrate their propaganda into any alternative camp than the 12 mile, and nothing short of driving them back into the desert will answer that objection. Secondly if dogs are a menace in fact rather than in

---

47 Reprinted in the *Maritime Worker*, the official organ of the Waterside Workers Federation of Australia, printed in Melbourne. 'Conditions of Slavery for our Aborigines', 9 April 1949, p. 1.
48 O'Neill, Native Affairs patrol journal, 1 March 1949, SROWA 1949/0160/2.
49 O'Neill, Native Affairs patrol journal, 9 March 1949, SROWA 1949/0160/9–10.
50 Middleton to McDonald, 15 February 1949, SROWA 1948/0732/96.
51 Middleton to O'Neill, 9 March 1949, SROWA 1949/0160/6.
52 Extract from Government Gazette, 28 June 1954, SROWA 1948/0732/120.

theory it is surprising that the police have not been recently informed & the normal legal action taken against alleged sheep worriers or sheep stealers. For even natives, I believe, should be considered innocent until proved guilty.[53]

Sampie continued to run his small school at the Twelve Mile for some time, despite ongoing opposition from the DNA. Indeed, declaring the camp a forbidden area may not have been merely unproductive from the DNA's point of view, but counterproductive. Just prior to the closure, Twelve Mile strikers had come under strong community pressure to shift the school to Moolyella. When travelling teacher de Passey visited the tin field in November 1948, Sampie and other Twelve Mile residents were there to attend a meeting at which the issue was discussed. According to de Passey, the Twelve Mile people were reluctant to move, but were given an ultimatum and a short period of grace.[54] It is likely that, after the DNA's attempt to close the Twelve Mile, the school was permitted to remain in order to maintain a permanent Aboriginal presence there, ensuring that the camp remained available as a base for community use.

Although Sampie had dreamed of a large school developed with government support, the number of children in the tin schoolroom had reduced to only seven 'exceptionally clean and well-dressed' children when O'Neill visited in March 1949.[55] Supporters described it as a 'very fine school', and although Sampie's limited education and the community's limited resources probably meant that the school fell well short of this, it was, nevertheless, a community initiative that deserved greater respect and support from government departments than it received.[56] While government departments acknowledged the need to provide schooling for the children of the strikers, they were only prepared to investigate educational possibilities that replaced Sampie's Twelve Mile school, rather than to view the school as the foundation on which improved facilities could be provided.

The DNA continued to obstruct Sampie's efforts in petty ways. In March 1949, for example, Sampie applied to the Commonwealth Savings Bank for School Savings accounts for his students, a common practice in

---

53   Saint to Middleton, 26 August 1949, pp. 4–5, SROWA1949/0454/92–93 (underlining in original).
54   De Passey to Director of Education, 5 November 1948, SROWA 1947/0594/68.
55   O'Neill, patrol journal, 2 March 1949, SROWA 1949/0160/4.
56   Fred Curran and Frank Corser, of Curran and Corser Barristers and Solicitors, to Middleton, 21 February 1949, SROWA 1947/0349/44.

Australian schools at that time. Because Sampie and the children were Aboriginal, the bank consulted the DNA and, learning that 'the Settlement may be of only a temporary nature', requested further clarification.[57] After a long delay and on the basis of O'Neill's assessment that 'the 12 mile will not be a permanent school & anyway the children would not have money enough to save', Middleton replied in September that 'it would be useless at this stage to attempt to open Bank accounts for the children'.[58] After waiting a full six months for a response to his application, Sampie was denied permission to open savings accounts for his students.

Sampie continued teaching children at the Twelve Mile until May 1950, when he wrote to Middleton notifying him of the school's closure. 'There's been some discontent again [between] workers and myself concerning things in general and this camp', he wrote. The dispute was serious enough for Sampie to leave the strike movement entirely, taking a job as a cook at Munda Station. 'I'll never take on school teaching [again] not since the way they abused me ... I'll stand out & battle for my own personal rights'.[59] The falling out was probably at least in part the result of his attempts to persuade parents to send their children to the White Springs Mission, still in the process of being established. His dream of a large school where children received an education that prepared them for employment as accountants and nurses had long vanished, and he urged strikers to take the educational opportunity offered by the new mission.

The strike community was, however, opposed to Bryan's project. Having broken away from the authority of pastoralists, they were not about to submit themselves to the authority of the Catholic Church. In April 1949, when the mission was still in the very early stages of its establishment, Bryan invited Twelve Mile residents to shift there to commence a garden and to act as caretakers.[60] O'Neill found the strikers to be 'interested but somewhat suspicious'.[61] According to John Wilson, a large meeting was held after one of Bryan's visits to the Twelve Mile, at which Dooley spoke strongly against the mission. Dooley argued that Bryan 'was jealous of McLeod, and pointed

---

57 Barnett, Superintendent of the Commonwealth Savings Bank, Perth, to McBeath, 3 March 1949, SROWA 1947/0349/47.
58 Note, unsigned and undated, SROWA 1947/0349/52; Middleton to J. E. Ranford, for Superintendent of the Commonwealth Bank of Australia, 9 September 1949, SROWA 1947/0349/53.
59 Sampie to Middleton, 7 May 1950, p. 3, SROWA 1947/0349/57.
60 O'Neill, patrol journal, 12 March 1949, SROWA 1949/0160/22.
61 O'Neill, patrol journal, 5 April 1949, SROWA 1949/0160/18.

out that whereas Father Bryan had been in the district for seven years, he had only just begun to introduce the Mission'. *Marrngu* 'could run their own strike and gain their own freedom', Dooley insisted.[62] Daisy Bindi, who would join the movement in 1952, later expressed a similar sentiment. When a police officer told her that Father Bryan was the 'only man doin' something for blackfellers', she replied, 'Father Bryan, he's orright ... but he start too late. He's only taking Don McLeod's dust'.[63]

Strikers wanted education for their children but were deeply fearful of having their children removed. When de Passey visited Moolyella in November 1948, he found it difficult to obtain much information on the children; the community, he said, were 'not wonderfully co-operative', fearing he had come to take their children away. Families were still mourning the loss of children who had been removed before the strike. They had been told that children were being taken away to be educated: 'Oh, they'll learn to read and write, and come back, they'll help you then, once they've learned to read and write'. 'We waited for the children', Mac Gardiner said, 'but they'd gone for good, they'd taken them away for good'.[64] Now, much as the strikers wanted access to the skills in literacy and numeracy essential for their survival as an independent community, the bitter experience of pre-strike removals meant that they would not accept schooling options in which they did not retain control over their children.

'The workers have always wanted their own school here', Sampie told Middleton in 1950:

> but as it is closed I'd like to see especially this kiddies who have already been going to school here, to White Springs ... but these people objected to Fr Bryan & they wont send their childrens to Marble Bar. I really don't know what school will the children go to.[65]

In reply, the DNA's new Senior District Officer assured Sampie that the children would be well cared for at the new mission. 'I want to thank you too', he added, 'for the very great interest you have shown towards their welfare over the past few years'.[66] After four years of DNA denigration and opposition to Sampie's efforts, it was too little, too late.

---

62 John Wilson, 'Authority and Leadership', p. 75.
63 Stuart, *Yandy the Wind*, manuscript, NLA MS 3156 folder 9, p. 409.
64 Gardiner (Pirntilkampanyaja), recorded by Anne Scrimgeour, 5 August 1993, AIATSIS collection, sound file 'Pirntilkampanyaja 15'.
65 Sampie to Middleton, 7 May 1950, p. 3, SROWA 1947/0349/57.
66 Sydney Elliott-Smith to Sampie, 9 May 1950, SROWA 1947/0349/59.

Chapter 24

'Plenty of Police and Plenty of Jails'

Civil Disobedience, March–May 1949

For Commissioner Middleton, the debacle of the attempted closure of the Twelve Mile was 'exemplary of the danger of trying to settle these distant problems from Perth' and reinforced his belief in the importance of creating a decentralised system of administration.[1] It seemed essential that decisions of this nature not be made in Perth, a thousand miles to the south, but be made on the ground, by experienced officers with knowledge of all the pertinent facts and the implications of departmental responses. With Laurie O'Neill now stationed in Port Hedland, Middleton hoped that more appropriate responses would be forthcoming as issues arose. But the Department of Native Affairs still had no clear strategy for dealing with the situation in the Pilbara. In part, this was a reflection of conflicting priorities. A statement made by Middleton at a meeting with representatives of the Pastoralists Association in Perth in early 1949 highlights these conflicting priorities. In the north, the aims of the new administration were, Middleton told pastoralists, 'to short-circuit certain elements interested in native labour in the North and to benefit the natives as well as the industry'.[2] Finding solutions to the situation in the Pilbara that would oppose the supposed communistic influences in the area, remove McLeod from the equation, improve the lives of Aboriginal people *and* meet the labour needs of the pastoral industry was never going to be easy. The White Springs solution promised to tick all these boxes, but this was still some way from becoming established. In the meantime, the Department's continued reliance on officers drawn, like O'Neill, from the police force, together with an ongoing reluctance to engage positively with the strikers as an organised group, or to accept McLeod's intentions as anything other than subversive and

---

1   Middleton to McDonald, 21 March 1949, SROWA 1943/0621.
2   Notes of Conference between representatives of the Pastoral Association and Middleton, 7 February 1949, SROWA 1950/0488/1.

dangerous, ensured that departmental responses remained ineffective and counterproductive. When the issue of Aboriginal group authority came to a head in the first half of 1949, the new administration reached for the old repressive weapons of control.

Throughout the early months of 1949, most strikers continued working tin at Moolyella until alternative and more profitable sources of income could be established. Prospecting groups set out to search for new fields to relieve the overcrowded conditions at Moolyella. Young Monty Hale (Minyjun), for example, went out with a prospecting party led by Jimmy Uridja (Juwikarayirti) to look for gold in the Warrawoona hills, thirty kilometres south-east of Marble Bar.[3] Some of the strikers shifted to an area ninety kilometres to the south-west, to work tin in the creek beds of the Cooglegong tin field. McLeod periodically exchanged their tin for food and other necessities. While he had previously assisted the strikers by purchasing pearl shell and had been involved to some extent in attempts to establish fishing projects on the coast, this was the beginning of his involvement with *marrngu* in mining. Strikers at Cooglegong worked in family groups as they did at Moolyella, and were supplied according to the amount of tin they produced, at least in theory. In practice, inefficient work groups were supported by other workers. Without organisational systems in place to foster efficient work practices, this arrangement was found to be unsatisfactory, and in later mining enterprises *marrngu* would organise themselves along different, more cooperative lines.[4]

The overcrowded conditions at Moolyella could also be relieved by arranging for some *marrngu* to return to work on stations offering reasonable rates of pay and conditions. Leaders at Moolyella insisted that prospective employers approach them to negotiate wages and conditions before engaging workers. Fred Davenport of Mt Edgar Station had done so, discussing his labour needs with leaders at Moolyella and engaging workers with their approval.[5] Davenport was unusual among pastoralists in maintaining a positive relationship with the strikers and a willingness to cooperate with them. He was also willing to deal with McLeod, something most other pastoralists refused to do.[6] McLeod

---

3 Hale, *Kurlumarniny*, p. 65.
4 McLeod, draft autobiography, chapter 4, p. 1, Marchant Trust Collection, UWA MS118 series 1 file 13.
5 Moojing (Jackson), court statement, Court proceedings before Magistrate Hogg, Marble Bar, 25 March 1949, p. 7, SROWA 1943/0621/114.
6 *Workers' Star*, 10 June 1949, p. 7, 'Wool Ban Threat Cheers Natives'.

later wrote in his draft autobiography that 'everybody bar Freddy Davenport was against me. He strongly backed me up (and still does)'.[7]

Pastoralists resented striker demands that the leadership be consulted before any employment agreement was made with individual workers. As far as they were concerned, if individual strikers wished to return to stations and were willing to accept pay and conditions being offered, then no-one else had the right to prevent them taking the work. This issue came to a head in 1949, when a young striker, Cocky Brine (or Brown) (Purnungurrara), accepted work on Corunna Downs Station without the permission of strike leaders.

According to Aboriginal memory of the event, Cocky was hijacked by Corunna Downs manager, Keith Bligh, who grabbed the young man when he attended the Saturday night open-air picture show in Marble Bar. It appears from court evidence, however, and seems more likely, that Cocky went voluntarily with Bligh. Before Christmas 1948, he had approached Bligh to ask if there was any work available for him on his old station, Corunna Downs, which he described as his 'proper country'.[8] Bligh had no work for him at that time of the year, but promised to contact him when workers were needed. On 7 March he spoke to Cocky in Marble Bar at the Returned Service League Sports Day, which included special races for Aboriginal people, and told him that work was now available if he wanted it. Bligh arranged to pick him up from the Marble Bar creek after the weekly picture show that night. Cocky asked strike leaders for permission to take the job, but permission was denied. Nevertheless, he met with Bligh after the picture show as arranged, returned with him to Corunna, and began working there the next morning.

The strikers were angered by Cocky's decision to leave furtively at night, and by Bligh's action in engaging him in this way. They considered that Cocky had sneaked back to the station and that Bligh had deliberately avoided negotiating a fair work agreement for him. 'If the squatters come to talk to us at Moolyella it is alright', one of the strike leaders, Jackson, explained at a court hearing. 'Moolyella boys not free to get a job on a station if he wants it unless mob agrees ... Mob will agree if conditions are satisfactory. As long as squatter got house bathrooms and tucker on table'.[9] Jackson said that the

---

7 McLeod, draft autobiography, chapter 3, p. 10, Marchant Trust Collection, UWA MS118 series 1 file 13.
8 Cocky (Purnungurrara), Court proceedings, 25 March 1949, p. 2, SROWA 1943/0621/119.
9 'Mob' is the Aboriginal English term for a group.

only employment agreement that had been made was with Fred Davenport at Mt Edgar Station, who had employed Sambo after discussing his wages and conditions with the Moolyella strikers.[10] Sambo was being paid £4 per week, and bought his own food.[11]

To discipline Cocky and prevent him undermining the strike effort, Jackson and ten other men volunteered to bring him away from Corunna Downs. At 7 am on 14 March, a week after Cocky began work, the men arrived on foot at Corunna Downs and told Bligh they had come to get Cocky. Jackson told Bligh that he had no right to employ Cocky without first approaching Dooley.[12] Bligh replied that it was a free country and that a worker had the right to take whatever work was being offered. Jackson retorted that it did not seem like a free country to him.[13] Cocky, understandably intimidated by the arrival of the Moolyella men, agreed to return with them, and the men formed two lines and marched him away between them.[14]

Bligh immediately telephoned Constable Tom Jensen, who had been returned to the police force from the Department of Native Affairs and who was, just at that time, in Marble Bar relieving Gordon Marshall, who was on leave. Marshall might have taken a different approach to dealing with the removal of Cocky, but Jensen considered the action on the part of the strikers very serious, and made the decision to arrest the eleven men. They were arrested at Moolyella, charged with enticing native workers from lawful employment in breach of section 48 (previously section 47) of the *Native Administration Act*, and remanded in custody for eight days.[15] Given the seriousness of the matter in Jensen's eyes, it was agreed that the matter should be heard by a magistrate rather than the local Justices of the Peace.[16]

In response to the arrests, the strikers decided to retaliate by withdrawing Bligh's other Aboriginal worker from Corunna Downs. Joe had been a striker but had taken station work three months earlier. On 22 March, when seven men arrived at Corunna Downs to take him away, he stated that he did not wish to return to Moolyella. Bligh ordered the strikers off the station,

---

10   Jackson, Court proceedings, 25 March 1949, p. 7, SROWA1943/0621/114.
11   Jensen to Middleton, 16 April 1948, p. 3, SROWA 1947/0305/203.
12   Bligh, Court proceedings, 25 March 1949, p. 3, SROWA 1943/0621/118.
13   Jackson, Court proceedings, 25 March 1949, p. 6, SROWA 1943/0621/115.
14   O'Neill to Middleton, 29 March 1949, p. 1, SROWA 1943/0621/213; Bligh, Court proceedings, 25 March 1949, p. 3, SROWA 1943/0621/118.
15   Jensen to Middleton, 16 March 1949, SROWA 1943/0621/91; O'Neill to Middleton, 7 July 1949, SROWA 1949/0454/35–36; Jensen to Middleton, 21 March 1949, SROWA 1943/0621/92.
16   Jensen to Middleton, 16 March 1949, SROWA 1943/0621/91.

threatening to call the police when they refused to leave without Joe. 'We are not frightened for bloody Police', the spokesman, Henry, asserted. 'We will wait for them'. Two of the strikers left before Jensen arrived, but five held their ground and were arrested, initially on 'enticement' charges in breach of section 48 of the *Native Administration Act*. Since no-one had actually been enticed from their employment, however, the charge was later changed to entering a place for an illegal purpose in breach of section 66 of the *Police Act 1892*.[17] Sixteen men were now in custody, and Jensen wired Middleton about the escalating situation. 'Very serious position here', he wrote, 'recurrence general strike threatened'. He suggested that O'Neill be sent immediately from Port Hedland to 'endeavor [to] appease ringleaders'.[18]

Middleton wired instructions to O'Neill, telling him to proceed immediately from Port Hedland to Marble Bar to 'endeavour [to] pacify ringleaders without condoning lawlessness'.[19] He approved of Jensen's decision to arrest and charge the Moolyella men, hoping that it would 'have the effect of causing the natives to at least pause in their unlawful, obviously inspired, behaviour'.[20] He had no doubt that events were being orchestrated by McLeod. McDonald agreed. McLeod's declaration, made in response to the attempted closure of the Twelve Mile, that strikers would no longer comply with Native Administration legislation, was clearly at the bottom of the disturbance, McDonald believed.[21] To deal with the situation, and in line with the new decentralised administrative system being adopted by the Department, O'Neill was given district executive powers to act on his own initiative, with authority to use his local knowledge to make decisions without reference to Perth. Middleton felt that matters could best be handled locally now that O'Neill was there to provide the 'effective district representation' which was 'of vital importance'.[22] Jensen was instructed to refer directly to O'Neill as the local representative of the Department.[23] This authority would soon be withdrawn, however.

As O'Neill and Port Hedland's Constable Don Withnell proceeded to Marble Bar on a chartered plane on the morning of 23 March, the *Daily News* carried the alarmist headline 'Police Rushed to Native Troubles'. 'Trouble

---

17 O'Neill to Middleton, 29 March 1949, p. 2, SROWA 1943/0621/124.
18 Jensen to Middleton, 22 March 1949, SROWA1943/0621/99.
19 Middleton to O'Neill, 22 March 1949, SROWA1943/0621/100.
20 Middleton to McDonald, 21 March 1949, SROWA 1943/0621.
21 McDonald, note, 22 March 1949, SROWA 1943/0621.
22 Middleton to O'Neill, urgent telegram, 22 March 1949, SROWA1943/0621/100.
23 Middleton to Jensen, telegram, 22 March 1949, SROWA 1943/0621/98.

among the natives which has caused local residents and employers much concern is stated to be a continuance of allegedly inspired discontent in the north'.[24]

Pastoralists, police and the Department saw the trial of the sixteen strikers as an opportunity to challenge the attempted establishment of Aboriginal corporate authority in the area. It would be a test case, Jensen wrote:

> as to whether the Communistic minded elements among the Natives at Molyella are going to control the employment of Natives on Stations, or whether the Natives willing to accept Pastoral work – such as this Native did – will be freely permitted to do so.[25]

Ironically, given the restrictions imposed on Aboriginal freedom throughout the state, authorities couched the issue as one of individual freedom. Jensen and O'Neill agreed with Keith Bligh's comment to Jackson about workers in a free country having the right to take any employment offered. Cocky had gone to Corunna of his own free will, Jensen argued, was quite happy working there, and had a right to continue to do so without interference from Dooley or from the committee of leaders at Moolyella. He referred to Dooley as 'the local Commissar of the Molyella Comintern'.[26] At a meeting of fifty or sixty men at Moolyella, O'Neill 'endeavour[ed] to explain to the natives that as they themselves were not being interfered with at Molyella and were being treated as free agents they should be prepared to allow other natives to accept Station or other employment as they wished'. 'Dooley uses the word "scab" freely', O'Neill wrote:

> and is obviously trying to control the employment of others although he is too cunning to take any direct action himself but prefers to incite others to do his dirty work and I have little doubt he is supported and advised by McLeod in this regard, I think I made an impression on the majority but not with Dooley who is a rabid supporter of McLeod.[27]

The next day, 25 March 1949, a large number of Moolyella strikers, together with pastoralists and their Aboriginal employees, gathered at the imposing stone buildings of the Marble Bar Police courthouse to hear the charges brought against all sixteen men.[28] Magistrate Keith Hogg, who travelled from

---

24 *Daily News*, 25 March 1949, p. 10.
25 Jensen to Middleton, 16 March 1949, SROWA 1943/0621/91.
26 Jensen to Middleton, 16 March 1949, SROWA 1943/0621/91.
27 O'Neill to Middleton, 29 March 1949, SROWA 1943/0621/123–125.
28 O'Neill to Middleton, 29 March 1949, p. 1, SROWA 1943/0621/123.

Carnarvon for the hearing, refused McLeod's application to represent the men on the ground that O'Neill, as an officer of the Department of Native Affairs, was present as their representative. No consideration was given in the hearing to the men's right as workers to bargain collectively for employment conditions, or the right of an Aboriginal group to establish its own authority. It would not have occurred to O'Neill to advocate for such rights; according to his way of thinking, the development of a strong Aboriginal political or industrial organisation was the last thing needed for peace in the area or the welfare of Aboriginal people themselves. Aboriginal interests could best be served, he believed, by persuading them not to interfere with station workers, and he had no doubt that imposing jail sentences for offenders was the best way to achieve this. Having told strikers that every man had the right to negotiate his own work agreement, he expected the magistrate to reinforce his message. In accordance with departmental practice, he pleaded not guilty on the men's behalf, but provided no defence, asking questions of witnesses that did nothing more than reinforce the prosecution's case. All the accused were found guilty.[29]

McLeod later wrote to Minister Ross McDonald about the hearing and the lack of justice accorded to Aboriginal people at trials such as this. He warned McDonald that departmental reports received in Perth might not accurately reflect the real attitude and behaviour of the northern field officers who wrote them. 'I can appreciate how difficult it must be for one situated a thousand miles from here and having only reports to go on to arrive at a sound conclusion', he wrote, 'particularly when those whose duty it is to present reports have an axe to grind and are not wholly controlled by the Dept'.

> I have often thought what a difference it should make if you or someone in whom you have confidence could sit in incognito and watch the travesty of justice which takes place at various hearings up here when the evidence is manufactured on which the enumerable natives have been convicted during the last three years.[30]

Aware of McDonald's desire for reform in Aboriginal administration, he added:

> The greatest obstacle to the progressive improvement of opportunities and conditions of our native population lies in the minds of those whose duty it is to carry out the policy decided upon by yourself and your

---

29 Court proceedings, 25 March 1949, p. 3, SROWA 1943/0621/118.
30 McLeod to McDonald, 6 April 1949, p. 2, SROWA 1943/0621/129.

departmental advisors and while they persist in the present negative attitude and the obvious belief that because the native has ... been born black he is mentally deficient and devoid of the normal processes of thought, so long will the sum of money large or small set aside for the department be wasted.[31]

Magistrate Hogg set down the sentences the following day. Warning the men that serious action would be taken if these unlawful acts were repeated, he imposed a three-month sentence on Jackson and two-month sentences on twelve others.[32] The case against one of the men accused of entering Corunna Downs on the second occasion was dismissed as unproven, while nineteen-year-old Tommy was cautioned and seventeen-year-old Bob had his case dismissed because of his youth.[33]

Outside the courthouse, a large crowd of Aboriginal people questioned O'Neill about the implications of the convictions, particularly on the charge of entering Corunna Downs Station unlawfully. Joe, the worker who a few days previously had resisted removal from Corunna Downs by a party of strikers, stated that, in protest at the sentences imposed on the men, he was no longer willing to undertake station work, particularly as Bligh had threatened to shoot any Moolyella native who entered his property.[34] Was it now the case, he asked, that station workers could no longer be visited by family members from the strike camp? O'Neill took the opportunity to reinforce restrictions on Aboriginal access to pastoral leases. There was no objection to strikers visiting family, he assured the gathering, provided that they were orderly, that visits were at reasonable times, and 'wherever possible they should first advise the Marble Bar Police of their intention so that if necessary he could contact the Station owner or manager concerned and obtain his O.K'. Bligh said that they could visit family as long as they did not come in a big party and only stayed one night.[35]

Dooley then spoke to the gathering in what O'Neill described as 'a tirade of propaganda directed against the "squatters" as he terms them and also the Dept'. Although O'Neill's role at the hearing had ostensibly been to defend the accused, and although Middleton had instructed him to try to appease the ringleaders, the only way he knew to respond to such demonstrations of

---

31 McLeod to McDonald, 6 April 1949, pp. 2–3, SROWA 1943/0621/129–128.
32 *West Australian*, 28 March 1949, p. 17, 'Aborigines Cross the Law'.
33 Court proceedings, 25 March 1949, p. 7, SROWA 1943/0621/114.
34 McLeod to McDonald, 6 April 1949, p. 4, SROWA 1943/0621/130.
35 O'Neill to Middleton, 29 March 1949, p. 3, SROWA 1943/0621/125.

Aboriginal anger and defiance was to forcefully threaten legal action. 'I then shut him up', he later reported to Middleton:

> and told him that by his interference he was only causing trouble for the other natives and not helping them and that if the natives did not abide by the laws of the country but continued to obey mob law as expounded by himself they would continue to be in conflict with the law.[36]

Dooley would not be shouted down and took up the challenge. 'Dooley replied that there was plenty of boys ready to go to Jail and he could get another Hundred if necessary', O'Neill wrote. 'I then told him that there was also plenty of Police and plenty of Jails to accommodate them, the mob then dispersed'.[37]

McLeod wrote to McDonald about the altercation that took place outside the courthouse:

> It would be interesting to hear what useful purpose Inspector L O'Neil [sic] hoped to achieve by his light hearted threat that any further action would result in the gaoling of those involved and his confirmation in the same jovial manner when Dooley accepted the dare on behalf of a hundred or several hundred of his friends. Not only will it not profit the Dept to have several hundred men in gaol but this action will obviously snowball until every native in the district becomes involved.[38]

McLeod also thought that McDonald would be surprised at the attitudes expressed by departmental representatives if he was to sit in incognito at 'a meeting of Pastoralists where the native question comes up for discussion'. 'If you had any previous doubts', he told the minister, 'such an experience would convince you in whose interests the natives have been administered'.[39] In particular, he was speaking of a meeting of pastoralists held in Marble Bar on 26 March, the day the strikers received their sentences, to discuss concerns about the 'native situation'. It was convened by Keith Bligh, who was clearly unnerved by confrontations with two parties of strikers on his station and disappointed that jail sentences imposed that day had not been more substantial. The country was no longer safe for white women and children, he insisted, if natives were allowed to do as they liked without consequence, apart from

---

36   O'Neill to Middleton, 29 March 1949, p. 3, SROWA 1943/0621/124.
37   O'Neill to Middleton, 29 March 1949, p. 3, SROWA 1943/0621/125.
38   McLeod to McDonald, 6 April 1949, pp. 4–5, SROWA 1943/0621/130–129a.
39   McLeod to McDonald, 6 April 1949, SROWA 1943/0621/127–130.

short terms of imprisonment. He called on those present to write letters to the Ministers of the Police and Native Affairs to demand an increased police presence in the area, and suggested that this demand be supported by the Pastoralists Association at the state level.

While many of those attending the meeting found Bligh's position alarmist, they expressed concern at the impact of the latest developments on their access to Aboriginal labour. Many had become reconciled to the fact that to employ Aboriginal labour they now had to pay higher wages than formerly and to make moves towards providing living, dining and ablution facilities, and were prepared to do so. But, while they conceded that Aboriginal workers had the right to ask for reasonable conditions, they were determined to resist any move that increased the authority of strike leaders. According to Laurie O'Neill, who attended the meeting:

> it was generally resolved that ... all reasonable demands for conditions and wages be granted at the discretion of the individual employer and that any difference of opinion if it could not be settled between the parties with the assistance of the protector could only be adjusted by the employer making other arrangements for labour.
>
> The general opinion was that the demands of the natives were not unreasonable and that if they were worth employing at all they were worth the conditions and wages usually asked for, the only aspect considered unreasonable was the demand of the Molyella [*sic*] leaders that no native should be allowed to accept employment without their approval, it was generally agreed that employers should retain the right to engage labour as required wherever they could contact the natives, either by going to Molyella or on the roads streets or in the bush wherever they might meet them, and that if there were any breeches of law and order the matter should be reported to the Police for the necessary action.[40]

This resolve was motivated by both political and racial anxieties. Two years earlier, the question of Aboriginal group authority had been a sticking-point in negotiations between the Department and strikers at the Twelve Mile, especially when *marrngu* insisted that McLeod be recognised as their representative. Pastoralists believed that negotiating with strike leaders for labour would play into communist hands by giving McLeod control of an essential resource. But racial anxieties also contributed to the refusal of the Department

---

40 O'Neill to Middleton, 29 March 1949, p. 3, SROWA 1943/0621/125.

and pastoralists to give way on this point. Pastoralist control over Aboriginal people in the region had already been seriously undermined by the strike and they feared that their authority and access to Aboriginal labour would be further eroded if they conceded Aboriginal group authority by agreeing to negotiate with Aboriginal leaders. For some years, this would become something of a code of honour among pastoralists, who sought to shore up their position through concerted action in much the same way as *marrngu* were doing. In 1952, a pastoralist admitted that he might be forced, through the need for Aboriginal labour, to apply to McLeod for workers, although to do so would put him 'at variance with other pastoralists'.[41] To some extent, the prestige of the squatters was at stake in this affair. Pastoralists occupied the top rung of the social hierarchy in the north. They held power through their prominence on road boards and as Justices of the Peace, and through the influence of the Pastoralists Association. Their power and status were being challenged by the strike, however. One of the new recruits to the Department noted in July 1949 that non-pastoral Pilbara residents blamed squatters for failing to resolve the dispute with *marrngu* because they 'refused to even talk with McLeod or to try to find out what he was agitating for. In other words, they thought that they would lose "prestige" if they evinced other than a savage interest in him'.[42] For pastoralists to attract Aboriginal workers by increasing wages and improving conditions was one thing, but to go cap in hand to Dooley or McLeod to engage labour, however much that labour was needed, was a bridge too far.

Some squatters felt that more decisive action was needed to curb the strikers' activities. Reflecting pastoralist anxiety at the growing militancy of the strikers, the *Sunday Times* carried an article about the meeting of 26 March under the heading 'Native Position Worries Them'. This article reported that 'many station owners expect the native position in this district to become serious, with a grim outlook for some stations employing native labour now that mustering and shearing time is approaching'.[43] Carnarvon's *Northern Times* ran the same article a few days later, with the added line that 'although the meeting was well attended it is believed that little satisfaction was obtained'.[44]

---

41 David Johnston, Statement to Committee Investigating Native Labour, 5 March 1952, p. 11, SROWA 1952/0830 v1/129.
42 Pullen, Native Affairs patrol report, 30 June 1949, SROWA 1949/0456.
43 *Sunday Times*, 27 March 1949, 'Native Position Worries Them'.
44 *Northern Times*, 31 March 1949, p. 1.

Two days after the meeting, a deputation made up of Pilbara pastoralists Bob Middleditch and Ted Jeffries, together with pastoralist–politician Mervyn Forrest, met with Ross McDonald and Stan Middleton in Perth to call for firmer action to be taken to pull strike leaders into line. Two- and three-month terms of imprisonment were no deterrent, Middleditch insisted, amounting to nothing more than 'a "pink-eye" [holiday] at the Government expense'. With the approach of another shearing season, they said, harsher penalties were needed to curb the strikers' lawlessness and prevent further disruption to the industry. Unless McDonald used his ministerial power to remove ringleaders, they would continue to 'keep the natives in a state of foment' and would work to ensure the failure of the Department's planned solution to the situation, the White Springs Mission. They named Dooley, his 'first lieutenant' Ernie Mitchell, and '2nd lieutenant' Jackson as the three men whose removal would ensure that shearing could proceed unhindered. They also identified Tommy Sampie as 'a bad man'.[45]

Removal under warrant appeared to be the only course of action open to McDonald and Middleton to prevent further actions of this nature. Bateman's report had offered little in the way of recommendations on how the Department might respond to defiant activism in the Pilbara. The plan to establish a mission at White Springs was in line with Bateman's recommendation regarding the provision of training for pastoral employment, but it was not a solution to lawlessness in the shorter term. Bateman had, however, recommended that the Department retain the power to remove miscreants to institutions, and supported the use of the remote Aboriginal ration depot of Cosmo Newbery as a departmental institution for 'native delinquents'. It seemed that the time had indeed come to end the unrest and the disruption to station labour by removing troublemakers. McDonald and Middleton agreed to have the thirteen convicted men removed to Cosmo Newbery at the expiration of their sentences as a salutary lesson to other strikers that such lawlessness would not be tolerated. Middleditch and Jeffries promised on their part to say nothing of this plan in the meantime, and returned north with a wink and a nod to other pastoralists that the Department had agreed to take the matter in hand as soon as the men had served their sentences.[46] Middleton, meanwhile, made initial moves for the men's removal, informing the superintendent of Cosmo Newbery by telegram on 4 April 1949 of the 'propose[d] transference

---

45   Notes of a Deputation which waited on the Minister for Native Affairs, 28 March 1949, SROWA S3841 cons769 3.
46   Middleditch to McDonald, 14 May 1949, SROWA S3841 cons769 3.

native prisoners ex Marble Bar to Cosmo Newberry', and inquiring 'can you accommodate'.[47]

In the Pilbara, two weeks of uneasy peace followed the sentencing of the thirteen strikers. At a large meeting at Moolyella on Sunday 27 March, the day after the sentences were passed, *marrngu* discussed the trial and convictions, and considered the challenge thrown out by Dooley that they would respond to repression by filling the jails with strikers. Jensen learned from a striker named Johnson that the meeting had decided to ignore Dooley's call for civil disobedience action as 'only causing trouble'.[48] Strikers were obviously selective about the information they gave to police officers, but Johnson's statement and his decision to take work at Lalla Rookh Station suggest that Dooley's response was not unanimously accepted by strikers at Moolyella, and that considerable discussion was underway during that time.

Nevertheless, at meetings held that Sunday, the decision was made to escalate strike action and to send out parties of volunteers to bring more workers away from stations. 'Old Dooley bin talk about, "What about we got to get a more people from the stations?"', Caroline Jula remembered. Strikers put extra effort into tin production to purchase additional food and tobacco for the volunteers. 'Alright, all boys, make a tin, make a little bit money and tobacco for that boys for road, you know?' Caroline Jula said. 'We bin talk about on Sunday morning'.[49] Efforts were made to enlist the support of *marrngu* in the Port Hedland area, with individuals moving around *marrngu* station communities to encourage workers to strike or demand higher wages.[50]

O'Neill, however, was confident that the imprisonment of the thirteen strikers had brought the unrest to an end. He felt that the best approach was to avoid paying undue attention to the strikers at Moolyella, and turned his attention instead to assisting Father Bryan in repairing old station buildings at White Springs.[51] Drawing on a press release provided by Middleton, the *Daily News* stated, under the heading 'Marble Bar Quiet Now', that the situation had been brought under control.[52] The Sydney-based *Smith's Weekly* was less certain that the trouble was over, however. An article headed

---

47 Middleton to Donegan, Superintendent of Cosmo Newbery, 4 April 1949, SROWA 1943/0621/26.
48 O'Neill to Middleton, 29 March 1949, SROWA1943/0621/213–215.
49 Jula, tape 1, recorded by Anne Scrimgeour, 13 August 1991, author's collection.
50 O'Neill, Native Affairs patrol journal, 7 April 1949, SROWA 1949/0160/19–20.
51 O'Neill to Middleton, 29 March 1949, p. 3, SROWA 1943/0621/125; O'Neill, patrol journal, 30 March – 4 April 1949, SROWA 1949/0160/17–18.
52 *Daily News*, 6 April 1949, p. 14.

'Red Cunning Fools Abos', probably written by Ion Idriess, reported that although authorities had the situation under reasonable control, short-term jail sentences would not mean the end of the trouble while others were free 'to carry on the mischief-making under the inspiration and with the under-cover backing of the Communists'. 'There are plenty to carry on with the insidious work of un-settling the natives, who, left to themselves, would be happy to continue the conditions under which they are employed by the pastoralists', the article claimed.

> Native Affairs Department is fortunate to have on its staff Inspector Laurie O'Neill, who has been selected to re-establish control in the area of disaffection. O'Neill served many years with the North-west Police Force, and none knows the native, or the native mind, better. The Reds respect O'Neill as an adversary whose influence will go a long way toward countering their campaign.[53]

Whatever respect the 'Reds' may have had for O'Neill, many of the strikers were prepared to put themselves on the line to challenge his authority. During the first week of April, Dooley called for volunteers to begin the process of filling the jails. 'Alright, we want all the strong men', Dooley said. 'We stand out then', Crow remembered.[54] Thirty men volunteered to join a raiding party for Meentheena and Warrawagine under the leadership of Punch (Yulpina). 'All boys want to go Warrawagine and Meentheena', Punch's sister, Caroline Jula, said, 'get'm more people from stations'.[55] The size of the party suggests that the primary purpose was not to encourage station workers to join the strike, but was, rather, a strategy of mass civil disobedience. 'We knew we would be arrested', Punch's brother Sambo Bina said, but 'Dooley said – Never mind, we'll fill up their jails'.[56]

'Alright, that morning boys roll their swag and go', Caroline Jula said, 'going to Meentheena'.[57] They set off on foot with four packhorses and were joined on their way by strikers Brumby, Bruce and Willalang and their wives.[58] Arriving at Meentheena Station on the evening of 7 April, the party spent the night at the 'native camp' talking to people there. In the morning, workers

---

53 *Smith's Weekly*, 9 April 1949, p. 3. Ion Idriess, who wrote for the *Weekly* under the name of Gouger, had travelled with O'Neill on patrol in the Kimberley in the 1930s.
54 Yougarla (Yakalya), recorded by Anne Scrimgeour, 21 August 1991, author's collection.
55 Jula, recorded by Anne Scrimgeour, 13 August 1991, author's collection.
56 Sambo Bina, in Williams and Noakes, *How the West Was Lost*.
57 Jula, recorded by Anne Scrimgeour, 13 August 1991, author's collection.
58 Stuart, *Yandy*, 1959, p. 120.

told the *walypila* boss, Charlie Blair, that strikers had come to take them to Moolyella. According to Blair's account of the incident, Punch told the workers, 'There are many of us and only a few of you'. Blair said he ordered the mob to leave his property, stating that he was 'prepared to protect his boys'. They left, 'muttering to themselves', Blair said.[59] However, Max Brown claims in *The Black Eureka* that the reason strikers took no-one away from Meentheena was that an old man there, one of Clancy McKenna's uncles, was dying.[60] The party then set out for the long walk to Warrawagine.

At Warrawagine, where there had once been a large *marrngu* community of over 100 people, there were now only seventeen, many of whom were older, non-working people. Mac Gardiner and his family were still working there, having never joined the strike. 'We stayed there', he said in Nyangumarta, 'and they came back again to get us. This time they came in earnest to get all the station workers. Thirty-three *marrngu* came up from the south'.[61] As at Meentheena, the Moolyella party spent the night in discussion with the community there, urging them to leave the station and join the strike. 'And my brother, big brother, he bin boss for them', Caroline Jula recalled. 'Ah he bin talk about, people, "We got to take you fellas this morning"'.[62] Having for three years resisted community and family pressure to join the strike, the Warrawagine people were probably somewhat nonplussed by the arrival of so large a contingent of strikers to take them away, and they agreed to leave with them in the morning. Bill Sheppard, previously overseer but now manager of Warrawagine, claimed that they only agreed to leave because they were in fear of their lives, but this was surely an exaggeration; they had cultural and kinship links with the strikers. Some of the visiting strikers were ex-Warrawagine people, including Punch.[63] During the night, *marrngu* prepared themselves for what they would say to Sheppard in the morning. 'Tomorrow morning we coming, what we got to say [is], "We got to go with this mob"'.[64]

The following morning, Sheppard refused to attend a meeting at the native camp, but was approached by *marrngu* at the station kitchen. 'Alright, we coming early', Crow remembered. 'Bill Sheppard was manager then … We coming there':

---

59   *Daily News*, 21 April 1949, p. 2.
60   Brown, *The Black Eureka*, p. 198; Stuart, *Yandy*, 1959, p. 120.
61   Jula, recorded by Anne Scrimgeour, 13 August 1991, author's collection.
62   Jula, recorded by Anne Scrimgeour, 13 August 1991, author's collection.
63   *Daily News*, 21 April 1949, p. 2.
64   Yougarla (Yakalya), recorded by Anne Scrimgeour, 21 August 1991, author's collection.

- Gooday.

- Gooday everyone.

- Gooday.

- Where you going?

- We aftering these people.

- Why you going aftering this mob?

Punch told Sheppard that they were taking all seventeen station residents to Moolyella:

Squatter-bloke say – You want to go with this mob?

- Yes.

According to evidence given at the subsequent court case, Warrawagine people cited poor wages and working conditions as their reason for leaving. A stockman named Roy (probably Roy Dobey, or Toby) told Sheppard that they were leaving because they were paid only a small wage and only bread and meat was provided for meals.[65] Mac Gardiner remembered that Sheppard had argued with them about leaving, 'but we said no, we've only got humpies to live in'.[66] Aboriginal oral history accounts claim that the Warrawagine people were not only willing but determined to leave, telling Sheppard, 'We bin waiting for this mob, we got to go. All got to be in one way, no scab. We got to following this mob'.[67] This contention is supported by the fact that, although Warrawagine workers were returned to the station by the police following this incident, they walked off again a few weeks later.

Caroline Jula understood that Sheppard had in fact requested that non-working station residents be taken to Moolyella. 'Alright, you fellas can take'm people in to Moolyella. That people bin sick, you can take'm away, in the river'.[68] However, happy as he may have been to have non-working people taken off his hands, Sheppard would struggle in the following months to secure the Aboriginal labour he needed for mustering and shearing operations.[69]

---

65 *West Australian*, 22 April 1949, p. 5, 'Natives in Court'.
66 Gardiner (Pirntilkampanyaja), recorded by Anne Scrimgeour, 5 August 1993, AIATSIS collection, sound file 'Pirntilkampanyaja 18'.
67 Yougarla (Yakalya), recorded by Anne Scrimgeour, 21 August 1991, author's collection.
68 Jula, recorded by Anne Scrimgeour, 13 August 1991, author's collection.
69 Constable Chipper, police patrol journal, 17 June 1949, SROWA 1946/2538 v8.

As the forty-seven *marrngu*, including elderly people, set off with their swags and billy cans for the long journey back to Moolyella, Sheppard used pedal radio to inform the Marble Bar police that all his workers had been removed and were headed on foot towards Callewa Station. The Marble Bar police hoped to be able to intercept the party before they caused any further disturbance to station labour, but realised that a large vehicle would be needed to bring in so many people. When Constable Don Withnell and Constable Vern Chipper set out later that morning, therefore, they did so in a semi-trailer truck driven by Charles McMillan, and camped that night at Callewa.[70] Since the party had not been seen at Callewa, the officers and Bill Sheppard left the truck at Sheep Camp (Pintunya), where the road crosses the De Grey River, and drove in Sheppard's vehicle between the Oakover and Nullagine Rivers, searching for tracks. They cut the tracks about two miles from Warrawagine and followed about ten miles back along the dry bed of the Nullagine River until they came to a place called Milinganinya by *marrngu*, where they found the party camped.

'We saw the police arriving from the east', Mac Gardiner remembered. 'There were two policemen and the white station boss from Warrawagine. They confronted us in the river'.[71]

Having successfully located the party, the officers now faced the problem of making the arrests. Bill Marney recalled that Chipper and Withnell took two bags of chains from the car and demanded, 'Who's the boss in this mob?'

'No one boss here', the strikers answered, 'we all the same'.

'No, you must got somebody here?'[72]

As well as refusing to identify leaders, the strikers refused to give their names. The officers brought out their chains. 'They said – see these two bags? And on saying this they threw down two bags with chains and handcuffs. They put chains around the neck of Yulypina and his father's father'.[73] When Chipper threw the chain around Punch's neck, the strikers threw it off. He threw it around the neck of the next man, Punch's classificatory grandfather,

---

70 Withnell, police patrol report, 13 April 1949, SROWA 1946/2538 v8.
71 Gardiner (Pirntilkampanyaja), recorded by Anne Scrimgeour, 5 August 1993, AIATSIS collection, sound file 'Pirntilkampanyaja 18'.
72 Bill Marney, in Williams and Noakes, *How the West Was Lost*.
73 Gardiner (Pirntilkampanyaja), recorded by Anne Scrimgeour, 5 August 1993, AIATSIS collection, sound file 'Pirntilkampanyaja 18'.

and again the strikers threw it to the ground. Vastly outnumbered and conscious, no doubt, of the isolation of the location, the officers were finding their old intimidatory tactics unsuccessful, and became uneasy at the strikers' defiant attitude. They drew their revolvers and levelled them at the strikers. 'He pulled a revolver out of his pocket', Mac Gardiner remembered. 'Then we all jumped up and crowded around the policeman, crying out, 'Drop your gun!'[74]

According to Bill Marney, the men shouted, 'Drop your guns – please! We're not animals, we're human beings'.[75]

Neither officer had much experience of the resistance tactics adopted by *marrngu* during the strike, and they were startled when the men closed in around them. This was a strategy commonly used by strikers as a tactic of non-violent resistance against anyone threatening violence. The officers later claimed that the strikers were on the point of attacking them when they surged forward as a group. 'When effecting the arrest of the 16 natives for refusing name they were going to attack Const Chipper & myself & surged forward to do so & it was necessary for us to show revolvers in order to stem them'.[76] The claim that police had used their weapons to repel an attack by strikers at Milinganinya was still being made two years later. At a public meeting held by Middleton in Port Hedland in 1951, Constable Tom Jensen used the incident to illustrate his claim that the movement was 'definitely subversive'. 'In the bed of a river near Warrawagine', he said, two police officers 'were attacked by natives with the result they had to draw their rifles to keep the natives back. Luckily they were carrying rifles'.[77]

Chipper again attempted to place a chain around a striker's neck, and this time he managed to lock it. 'As soon as it was locked we agreed to be arrested quietly', Bill Marney recalled.[78] 'So then he put a long chain around all our necks', Mac Gardiner recalled, 'and he put handcuffs on others. He shackled the *marrngu* together in pairs. The two policemen took us away from Milinganinya'.[79]

---

74 Gardiner (Pirntilkampanyaja), recorded by Anne Scrimgeour, 5 August 1993, AIATSIS collection, sound file 'Pirntilkampanyaja 18'.
75 Marney, in Williams and Noakes, *How the West Was Lost*.
76 Withnell, police patrol report, 13 April 1949, SROWA 1946/2538 v8.
77 'Meeting re Native Affairs in the Pilbarra District, Held at Port Hedland', 19 August 1951, p. 6, SROWA1952/0830 v1/38.
78 Marney, in Williams and Noakes, *How the West Was Lost*.
79 Gardiner (Pirntilkampanyaja), recorded by Anne Scrimgeour, 5 August 1993, AIATSIS collection, sound file 'Pirntilkampanyaja 18'.

Thirty-two men were arrested, twenty-two chained together in two long chains, and ten handcuffed together. 'Put'm in the neck, yeah, he had a long long chain', Caroline Jula remembered. 'That one my brother ... he was leader, he talk us, for everybody, you know. Yeah well that brother bin head of all people in that long chain. That brother bin go, nother cousin coming behind, Solomon's brother, that two boss'.[80] The strikers and the men and women who had left Warrawagine were walked for twelve miles along the Nullagine and De Grey Rivers back to where the semi-trailer was waiting for them. 'They led us away on foot', Mac Gardiner said in Nyangumarta:

> The rest of us station workers were to be witnesses. We walked all the way to Ngampurrupurrunya, the junction of the two rivers, and we had a drink of water there where the two rivers join up together, the Ngalangkanya and the Papurrunya. The Ngalangkanya, that's the Nullagine River, and Papurrunya is the Oakover. After we'd had a drink we climbed up the bank on the north side ... That's where we saw that truck, the semi-trailer. We climbed on it and went to Callewa, and from Callewa we went on to Yarrie where we had supper. They took us straight to the jail at Marble Bar.[81]

The men were placed in the police lockup, still in chains and handcuffs, although O'Neill, who had flown to Marble Bar in response to the further trouble, later told Middleton that chains had been removed before the men were locked up. Billy Thomas recalled the indignity of having to go to the toilet while chained or handcuffed to other men. 'Policeman not satisfied he had people locked up', he said. 'He should have take the chain or something off, give them a bit of a chance. He was really using blackfellas as animal, that day'.[82]

The men were placed in the lockup just before midnight on 14 April, the night before Good Friday. They were charged with entering a property for illegal purposes in breach of section 66 subsection 8 of the *Police Act 1892*, and with enticing Aboriginal workers away from lawful employment, in contravention of section 48 (previously section 47) of the *Native Administration Act 1936*. Some were also charged with failing to provide names and addresses

---

80   Jula, recorded by Anne Scrimgeour, 13 August 1991, author's collection.
81   Gardiner (Pirntilkampanyaja), recorded by Anne Scrimgeour, 5 August 1993, AIATSIS collection, sound file 'Pirntilkampanyaja 18'.
82   Thomas (Pitpit), in Williams and Noakes, *How the West Was Lost*.

when asked to do so by a police officer, in contravention of section 50 of the *Police Act*.[83]

O'Neill had been in Port Hedland when this further action by the strikers took place. On learning of the new disturbances, he made arrangements to return to Marble Bar, wiring Middleton of his intention.[84] But the Department was beginning to fear that O'Neill's ex-policeman's approach was exacerbating the situation rather than settling it. Having recently seen McLeod's account of O'Neill's threat that there were 'plenty of Police and plenty of Jails', Middleton was alarmed at the news of further unrest and warned O'Neill not to confuse his role with that of the police. 'It will no doubt be apparent to you', he wrote:

> that an important aspect of the native situation in the Pilbara District at this stage is propaganda to counter that of McLeod and his native henchmen; also that where Police action is required it will not be in the best interests of this Department to appear in a role which may be mistaken for that of assistance to the Police or otherwise than that involved in true protectorship of the natives themselves.[85]

However, 'true protectorship of the natives themselves' did not preclude the removal of the main agitators to a remote institution, and Middleton felt that, with this latest outbreak of trouble, it was timely that O'Neill should be made aware of the planned removals. By making a distinction between the role of the Native Affairs officer and that of the police, Middleton said, he did not mean:

> that we should in any way condone breaches of law and order. To the contrary, it may be necessary to indirectly assist the Police in maintaining law and order in that district by removing the more violent ringleaders under warrant from the district altogether. This, for the time being, is for your information only, but I want you to know of it in case you are called on in the near future to submit certain recommendations.[86]

With the men held in the lockup over Easter, strikers at Moolyella received a message that they needed tobacco. Caroline Jula remembered:

---

83 O'Neill to Middleton, telegram, 20 April 1949, SROWA1943/0621/136.
84 O'Neill to Middleton, telegram, 12 April 1949, SROWA 1943/0621/132.
85 Middleton to O'Neill, 14 April 1949, SROWA 1943/0621/133.
86 Middleton to O'Neill, 14 April 1949, SROWA1943/0621/133.

He went there, night, Marble Bar, he sent word ... for girls, all them ask'm to coming, all the wives coming, bring'm tobacco, matches, cigarette paper. That night, Saturday, we went Marble Bar, we give'm, you know, husbands, bring'm tobacco.

McLeod hoped to secure the services of a Perth lawyer, Thomas John Hughes, to defend the men, but he could do nothing about this over the Easter long weekend. Instead, he wrote to trade unions to seek their support. 'In order that the opportunity should be given for organised workers generally to express their opinion in support of this unique struggle', he wrote:

> the strike committee have decided to place a black ban on all wool throughout the state produced on stations & farms where native workers are employed under the present slave act and to call on all workers to unite with them to confirm this action and to make the ban thorough & complete.
>
> I have been asked to contact as many workers as possible especially those unions where members would generally handle wool and appeal to them to support this ban and to campaign with others in their district to widen the knowledge of the background of this action.
>
> I ask that this matter be discussed by your members at the earliest possible date so that the struggle can be taken up shortly. I am sure that each of you as unionists cannot but be proud of the splendid effort which has been sustained by the native workers for three hard and bitter years, and as a reward and to encourage them further will join with them and make your voices heard in their defence.[87]

Although remand was set at eight days, the police tried to organise Justices of the Peace to hear the case on 19 April, the Tuesday after Easter, as the police cell was not designed to hold so many people.[88] Only one Justice of the Peace was available, however, and arrangements were made for Magistrate Hogg to hear the cases on the Thursday. With little time to prepare their defence, McLeod tried to find out the charges laid against the men, but O'Neill refused to give him this information, referring him to the Clerk of Courts.[89] Learning from the Clerk of Courts that the cases would not be heard before Friday, McLeod wired Hughes to arrange for him to

---

87   McLeod to Hurd, 14 April 1949, SLWA 5121A.
88   O'Neill to Middleton, telegram, 19 April 1949, SROWA 1943/0621/134.
89   O'Neill, patrol report, 19 April 1949, SROWA 1949/0160/24–25.

fly north to provide defence.⁹⁰ However, Hogg arrived on Wednesday, and the hearing went ahead the following day.⁹¹ O'Neill claimed that he asked the accused if they wished to wait for legal assistance, and, after discussing the matter among themselves, the men replied that they wished to proceed with the hearing.⁹²

The case attracted keen interest throughout the district. The *Daily News* reported that it was having a negative effect on shearing, as 'most natives left their employment to attend the trial'. In a statement that was no doubt an exaggeration, but that nevertheless suggests that the strikers' activism had tapped into racial fears in the settler community, the report also claimed that a further cause of disruption to the shearing was the fact that 'many station owners have been afraid to leave their families and homesteads unattended while doing the mustering'.⁹³

When the court hearing began on 21 April, McLeod handed the magistrate a letter requesting an adjournment to enable legal assistance to be obtained. O'Neill, however, stated that the accused had advised him that they 'wanted to get it over' and, when Punch confirmed this, the hearing went ahead. By the lunch break, all thirty-two men had been found guilty on the charge of 'enticement'.⁹⁴

On the resumption of the trial that afternoon, O'Neill stated that the accused men had requested an adjournment to obtain legal counsel. Contrary to his usual approach, O'Neill insisted that this request be complied with, despite Constable Jensen's adamant objection on the ground that the cells were overcrowded and lavatory facilities totally inadequate for thirty-two prisoners.⁹⁵ O'Neill's insistence that the hearing not proceed until legal counsel had been obtained is an interesting shift in his usually punitive approach. In *The Black Eureka*, Max Brown explained O'Neill's change of heart as arising from fear of the criticism that would fall on the Department when news got out that the men had been arrested at gunpoint.⁹⁶ His advocacy for the men's right to obtain legal counsel may also have been the result of Middleton's exhortation for him not to confuse his role with that of the

---

90   McLeod to Hurd, 15 May 1949, p. 2, SLWA 5121A.
91   O'Neill, patrol journal, 19 April 1949, SROWA 1949/0160/24.
92   O'Neill, patrol journal, 21 April 1949, SROWA 1949/0160/26.
93   *Daily News*, 22 April 1949, p. 4, 'Natives Leave Jobs to Watch Trial'.
94   O'Neill, patrol journal, 21 April 1949, SROWA 1949/0160/26–27; *Daily News*, 21 April 1949, p. 2; *West Australian*, 22 April 1949, p. 5, 'Natives in Court'.
95   O'Neill, journal, 21 April 1949, SROWA 1949/0160/26–27.
96   Brown, *The Black Eureka*, p. 201.

police and to work for 'the true protectorship of the natives'. Jensen was so adamant that he could not continue to hold the men in the police cell that he threatened to drop the two charges on which convictions had not been recorded – that is, the charges of withholding names and addresses and of entering property for unlawful purposes – rather than have the hearing adjourned.[97]

The hearing proceeded, but, according to McLeod, the men refused to give evidence unless he (McLeod) was allowed to act in their interest. Hogg agreed to allow remand until 18 May if McLeod could produce a telegram from Hughes by 10 am the next day, indicating that he could definitely attend on that date. Hogg then called a halt to proceedings for the day, with sentences still to be set for the charge on which the men had already been found guilty.[98]

McLeod received a wire the next morning, Saturday 23 April, confirming Hughes's intention to defend the men on 18 May, but, when the hearing resumed, Hogg told the court that it was too late to grant a further period of remand as he had already handed down a finding on one of the charges. The accused had previously stated their wish to proceed with the trial, Hogg said, and they had made no previous request for legal aid. There had been plenty of time prior to the trial to obtain legal aid, and if legal aid was to be engaged, it should have been engaged through the Inspector of Natives, who represented the Commissioner. McLeod had no standing in the court, he said; the accused were ably represented by O'Neill.[99]

The hearing therefore went ahead, although the accused, according to McLeod, refused to answer questions or give evidence unless McLeod was permitted to speak for them. The charges of withholding names and addresses were dropped, but all the men were found guilty on the charge of entering property for unlawful purposes. Punch was sentenced to three months' imprisonment, and twenty-nine others received two-month sentences. Having warned strikers during the previous trial that any similar offences would attract severe punishment, Hogg told the accused that the lightness of the sentences should not be taken as a sign of weakness, but that he was 'aware that they had only been pawns for others'.[100] Mac Gardiner remembered the magistrate asking, 'Has anybody got anything more to say?' Then, he said:

---

97 *West Australian*, 22 April 1949, p. 5, 'Natives in Court'; Brown, *The Black Eureka*, pp. 201–202.
98 McLeod to Hurd, 15 May 1949, pp. 2–3, SLWA 5121A.
99 *West Australian*, 23 April 1949, p. 15, 'Gaol for Natives'.
100 *West Australian*, 23 April 1949, p. 15, 'Gaol for Natives'.

that old man who lives over in the west, Mirlpanga, they call him by his *walypila* name Jack Gardiner, old Jack Gardiner ... said that they were all talking wrong. Then they all went to jail, some to Port Hedland, some to Roebourne, some to Marble Bar'.[101]

Two youths were not sentenced, and were instead placed in employment on Meentheena Station by the police.[102]

McLeod reported that the strikers were required to provide food, clothing and tobacco for the men held in prison. 'Under what section of the Native Affairs Act can the authorities demand that the Moolyalla native workers provide clothing, tobacco, and toilet necessities for those in jail', he wondered. In reference to the thirteen men imprisoned in March, the *Workers' Star* quoted him as saying:

> on demand [the strikers] provided 13 pairs of trousers, 13 shirts, 13 mirrors, 13 combs, 2lbs tobacco, one dozen soap, one dozen hair oil in case their interned fellow workers would be without. But they provided them under protest. It should be reasonable to expect the Department to make restitution for this flagrant imposition.[103]

Caroline Jula remembered having to work hard producing tin to provide provisions for the imprisoned men. 'And girls we working in tin, in Moolyella', she said:

> We do'm little bit tucker ... we working. All the girls working. Making money little bit, little bit tucker, bit tea, sugar or cigarette paper, matches. We get clothes, you know, for boys.[104]

With forty-three strikers now imprisoned, Middleton was anxious to prevent further lawlessness by removing the instigators to Cosmo Newbery. He reminded O'Neill to identify the ringleaders whose removal would be most effective in stemming the unrest. His belief that this was now the most appropriate course of action was reinforced by a visit he received from the Marble Bar policeman Gordon Marshall, who was about to return north from leave, and who was concerned to learn of the degree to which the situation had deteriorated in his absence. Calling on Middleton in Perth while the trial

---

101 Gardiner (Pirntilkampanyaja), recorded by Anne Scrimgeour, 5 August 1993, AIATSIS collection, sound file 'Pirntilkampanyaja 18'.
102 O'Neill, patrol journal, 22 April 1949, SROWA 1949/0160/28–29.
103 *Workers' Star*, 22 April 1949, p. 5, 'Flagrant Imposition on Jailed Aborigines'.
104 Jula, recorded by Anne Scrimgeour, 13 August 1991, author's collection.

was still underway in Marble Bar, Marshall argued strongly for the removal of the ringleaders, assuring the Commissioner that Aboriginal labour would be an ongoing problem for stations while strike leaders remained in the area. The threat of imprisonment, which had once served as an effective means of control, had lost its potency among the strikers, he said. Imprisonment had even become a badge of honour, evidence of a willingness to stand up for the cause, and the jailing of strikers was likely to compound the problem, by bringing further workers into the strike in sympathy.[105]

Middleton passed these recommendations on to Minister McDonald. Marshall's 'opinion and recommendation where native matters in the Marble Bar area are concerned', he wrote, 'are of great value because he is generally recognised as being an authority on the subject, in addition to being a good friend and advocate of the natives'. He thought the matter called for 'an urgent decision and prompt action' from the Department.[106]

But McDonald was having second thoughts about this course of action. He had responded sympathetically to pastoralist calls for agitators to be sent to Cosmo Newbery, but the strikers' activism made him think again about the advisability of taking such a step. He had given Bob Middleditch and Ted Jeffries to understand that the thirteen men convicted in March would be removed to an institution at the expiration of their sentences, but if he was to follow through with this policy he would now have forty-three warrants to sign when the prison sentences had been served. If terms of local imprisonment led strikers to break the law in such numbers, what would be their response to the indefinite removal of their leaders? he wondered. Despite Marshall's expertise and local knowledge, and despite the need to bring the situation under control in the Pilbara, McDonald was wary of inflaming the situation by taking steps that would spark further protest action, extending and entrenching the problem and bringing national and international criticism.[107]

The practice of removing Aboriginal people to institutions under warrant was already subject to public scrutiny. Two months earlier, the Anti-Slavery Society in London had written to McDonald asking, among other things, what action had been taken to amend the *Native Administration Act* to ensure that Aboriginal people were not removed to an institution except under a Court Order, as suggested (although not recommended) in the Bateman report.[108]

---

105 Middleton to McDonald, 21 April 1949, SROWA 1943/0621/139.
106 Middleton to McDonald, 21 April 1949, SROWA 1943/0621/139.
107 McDonald to Middleditch, 19 May 1949, SROWA S3841 cons769 3.
108 Greenridge, Anti-Slavery Society, to McDonald, 18 March 1949, SROWA S3841 cons769 3. The following month, the Narrogin Native Welfare Committee, which

Given the militancy of the strikers and the level of public interest, McDonald decided that the danger of removing strikers was too great for the Department to take action without further investigation. The day after Marshall's visit he asked Middleton to travel to the Pilbara to personally investigate the situation and advise on the wisdom of removing agitators.[109]

Middleton flew north on 27 April and spent four days in the area, speaking with strikers, prisoners and members of the settler community and looking over the preparations underway for a mission at White Springs.[110] McLeod took the opportunity to approach him, at the suggestion of solicitor T. J. Hughes, to ask him to lodge an appeal on behalf of the thirty men most recently convicted. Middleton declined to do so, telling McLeod that the men had broken the law and must suffer the consequences.[111] Nevertheless, during his visit Middleton backed away from a determination to take more punitive action against the strikers, returning to the established departmental position that *marrngu* were innocent victims of McLeod's machinations. Middleton spoke to strikers, both in prisons and at Moolyella, about new policies being developed by the Department, of plans to increase field staff so that more continuous contact could be maintained, and of plans to develop White Springs as an education centre, particularly for teaching trades and skills to qualify them for employment in the pastoral industry. These discussions led Middleton to view the strikers as innocent pawns in McLeod's political game. 'Subversive influence', similar to the 'Communist influence' that had been at work in 1946, was at the bottom of the unrest, he wrote. After his visit, he felt sure that the situation was 'now more likely to return to a satisfactory basis and the natives are looking forward to the closer contact which the Department hopes to maintain with them'.[112] McDonald now felt confident to respond to expressions of concern at the treatment of strikers with assurances that Middleton had 'explained the position to the natives in a

---

had been established at the end of 1946 to address Aboriginal justice and welfare issues in the Narrogin area of the state's south-west, asked to be immediately informed by the Department whenever an Aboriginal person was being committed to an institution. Doney to McDonald, 12 May 1949, SROWA S3841 cons769 3.

109 McDonald, note to Middleton, 23 April 1949, SROWA 1943/0621/139.
110 O'Neill, patrol journal, 27 and 29 April, SROWA 1949/0160/31–32.
111 McLeod to Hurd, 15 May 1949, p. 4, SLWA 5121A.
112 Middleton, press statement, 6 May 1949, SROWA S3841 cons769 3; *West Australian*, 7 May 1949, p. 13, 'Subversive Influence'.

satisfactory way' and that there was now 'much less likelihood of a recurrence of these incidents'.[113]

It seems simplistic for Middleton to have believed that the conflict could be so easily resolved. His belief that 'the great majority of them' had 'now come to a realization that they acted wrongly in interfering with the lawful employment on the pastoral properties' echoes similar statements made by police and Native Affairs officers when reassured by *marrngu*, in the aftermath of the failed 1 May strike, that they now knew they had acted wrongly in attempting to strike. It suggests that Middleton was taken in by the strikers' polite reception and the 'dumb blackfellow' stance they adopted when spoken to as if they were children. The expectation that a few reassuring and fatherly words from him was all that was needed to convince the strikers to change their behaviour suggests a perception of Aboriginal people as essentially childlike, responding to 'subversive influences' without a clear understanding of the reason for their actions or their consequences. All that was needed, it seemed, was for the strikers to have the matter carefully explained to them. It seems overly-optimistic, too, given the opposition that strikers had experienced and the anti-government attitude identified by Don Thompson, for Middleton to believe that that strikers would look forward to closer contact with the Department. And since strikers had, for three years, been resisting pressure to return to station employment, it seems naïve of Middleton to believe that they would welcome a scheme to provide training in station work.

Still, it is possible that the strikers welcomed the Commissioner's visit. Perhaps his manner in speaking to them differed sufficiently from the manner adopted by officers like O'Neill and Jensen for his visit to suggest the possibility of a new kind of relationship with the Department. Perhaps Middleton encountered a genuine openness on the part of the strikers to engage with the Department if the Department was, in turn, willing to change its attitude towards them. Certainly, the strikers demonstrated this willingness three months later, when another senior officer of the Department offered to set the relationship on a more respectful footing.

Perhaps Middleton found that the strikers were not the dangerous radicals he had come to expect, but rather reasonable people who listened to what he had to say, replying with respect and dignity. Whatever the reason, plans to remove strike leaders to Cosmo Newbery were dropped. If McLeod, for his own financial or political gain, was stirring up unrest in the Pilbara by inciting

---

113   McDonald to Vic Johnson, Minister for the Interior, 12 May 1949, SROWA S3841 cons769 3.

the strikers to travel out to stations and take away workers, then imprisoning them was simply playing into his hands. The Department was back at the drawing board, looking for a way to end the unrest.

The strikers' campaign to fill the jails was undertaken to support their call for the recognition of corporate authority, expressed as a demand for collective negotiations in labour agreements and the right to exercise internal authority and discipline. The demand for recognition of, and respect for, Indigenous corporate authority is an ongoing feature of the struggle for Aboriginal rights in Australia. In 1949, it was also an issue sufficiently familiar to the labour movement to prompt union activism in response to the arrests. As the strike reached its third anniversary, the threat of union activism in support of the strike would increase pressure on the Department to find alternatives to incarceration and removal to resolve the dispute.

Chapter 25

'And Justice and Common Sense Would Prevail'

April–July 1949

On 26 April, the day before Middleton flew north for his visit to the Pilbara, a stop-work meeting of the Fremantle branch of the Seamen's Union passed a resolution protesting against the imprisonment of the Pilbara strikers and resolving to impose a ban on the transportation of all wool from stations 'where the slave conditions apply that brought about the present strike' unless the convicted men were released. The meeting also called on the union's federal executive to donate a sum of £100 'to the strike committee to ensure the wives and children are fed, while these workers are in prison'.[1]

This resolution to impose a ban on wool shipments if prisoners were not released was forwarded to both the Western Australian Minister for Native Affairs, Ross McDonald, and to the federal Minister for the Interior, Vic Johnson, by Fremantle Branch secretary Ron Hurd, a communist who had fought with the International Brigade in the Spanish Civil War and who was always prepared, according to the *Workers' Star*, 'to call a spade a spade and a fascist a fascist'.[2] Over the following weeks, Hurd repeatedly urged the Western Australian government and the Department to release the imprisoned strikers, warning them that a ban would be implemented if persecution of the strikers did not cease.

With wool prices at their peak, McDonald was anxious to avert a ban that could damage the state's economy and draw censure on the Department from the powerful pastoral lobby. The threatened ban by a union with strong links to the Australian Communist Party also fed concerns that the imprisonment of strikers was playing into communist hands. Accounts of the imprisonment

---

1   Hurd to McBeath, 28 April 1949, SROWA1943/0621/162.
2   Hurd to McBeath, 28 April 1949, SROWA1943/0621/162; *Workers' Star*, 3 December 1937, p. 1.

of large numbers of strikers, and the use of guns and chains in making the arrests, received double-page coverage in the *Workers' Star*, and front-page coverage in the Melbourne-based *Maritime Worker* and the Sydney-based *Tribune*. While Middleton was in the north, the *Workers' Star* carried an article on the Seamen's Union's threat to ban the shipment of wool from 'slave stations', and the fifteenth state conference of the ACP hailed:

> the courageous three-year-old struggle of the Pilbarra Aborigines for economic independence, for education for their children and for an end to the slave conditions of the stations as an historic landmark in the struggle of their people for emancipation.

The conference condemned:

> the despicable and cowardly action of the McLarty Government in jailing 43 able bodied members of the native co-operative for the 'crime' of inducing fellow workers to strike in an attempt to smash the co-operative before the shearing season starts and to slash the better wages and conditions won on many stations as a result of strike action.[3]

It called on trade unions:

> and all democrats to take the most vigorous action in support of the Pilbarra Aborigines, to force the release of the imprisoned men, full award rates for all native station hands, full freedom and assistance to the Aborigines to develop their own economic ventures, and the provision of educational facilities for their children.[4]

The Native Rights and Welfare League produced a pamphlet to publicise and protest the imprisonment of the strikers. Bearing the imprint 'a communist publication', the pamphlet fed concerns that communists were exploiting the situation in the Pilbara for their own political gain. Under the heading 'Stop the Persecution! Aboriginal Strikers Arrested at Gun Point, Chained, Jailed', it set out in some detail the history of the strike and the latest developments, drawn largely on information supplied by McLeod. It called on readers to raise the issue with their unions and other organisations, to write to members of Parliament, the premier and McDonald, to organise deputations, and to

---

3   *Workers' Star*, 29 April 1949, p. 3, 'Seamen Threaten Ban on Slave Stations Wool if NW Natives Not Freed'.

4   *Workers' Star*, 29 April 1949, p. 3, 'Seamen Threaten Ban on Slave Stations Wool if NW Natives Not Freed'.

support the black ban on wool. Readers were urged to demand the release of the jailed workers, the abandonment of 'White Springs concentration camp plans', the extension of the 'Mt Edgar Agreement' to all stations, and the recognition of Don McLeod as the natives' spokesman and negotiator of all agreements. Drawing on a union model of strike action as undertaken by male breadwinners with wives and children to support, the pamphlet expressed concern at the burden placed on the tin-mining cooperative at Moolyella, which had to feed and clothe the dependents of forty-three men while they were in prison, and called for donations to support them. It criticised Middleton for raising 'the Red bogey' in response to the strike.[5]

Circulated to churches, trade unions, and social and welfare groups, including interstate and international organisations, and distributed door to door in at least one Perth suburb, the pamphlet generated letters of protest to McDonald.[6] To assist McDonald in answering concerns raised, Middleton provided pointed and angry rebuttals of the pamphlet's 'numerous distortions of fact, half-truths, and deliberately misleading statements'. He pointed to inaccuracies, such as the assertion that 75 per cent of the wages of Aboriginal workers could be deducted by the Department and redirected to projects such as White Springs, and he challenged the pamphlet's portrayal of the situation as involving male breadwinners with wives and children to support, along with the description of the Moolyella community as a cooperative. But his most vitriolic responses were directed towards the championing of McLeod, whom he accused of exploiting the strikers for personal and political gain. He was angry that the situation should itself be exploited as propaganda for the ACP.[7]

To counter the claims made in the circular, McDonald published a series of articles in the *West Australian*.[8] He referred in correspondence to:

---

5   Circular letter from Gilbert Foxcroft, President of the Society of Friends, Catherine Lockwood, Secretary, Modern Women's Club, and Francis Amos, Hon Treasurer of the Native Rights and Welfare League, to 'Churches, Trade Unions, Social and Wolfare [sic] Organisations', SROWA 1949/0454/48; Middleton to McDonald, 9 June 1949, SROWA 1943/0621/181–184.
6   Middleton to McDonald, 9 June 1949, SROWA 1943/0621/181; Western Australian Housewives' Association to McDonald, 10 June 1949, and McDonald to E. K. Fletcher, Australian Women's Charter Committee, 13 June 1949, SROWA S3841 cons769 3.
7   Middleton to McDonald, 9 June 1949, SROWA 1943/0621/181–184. Middleton's responses make interesting reading, and can be accessed in full at https://pilbarastrike.org/content/middleton-disputes-communist-publicity-about-strikers%E2%80%99-imprisonment
8   McDonald to W. P. Pidgeon, Liberal Club of the University of Western Australia, 12 July 1949, SROWA 1949/0454/57.

the unrest occasioned in the Marble Bar district by a man called McLeod who, if not a Communist, is closely allied with Communist activities and who is feeding them with misleading information which has been the subject of a fair amount of propaganda by circular, in the *Workers' Star* and otherwise.[9]

Interstate and overseas circulation of the Native Rights and Welfare League's pamphlet brought a wider focus on the treatment of Aboriginal people in Western Australia. The image of Aboriginal prisoners in chains in Fitzroy Crossing was reproduced in overseas publications. In 1946, the imprisonment of Clancy McKenna and Dooley had come to national and international attention, and now, three years later, the imprisonment of large numbers of Aboriginal men attracted similar concern. The association of chains with slavery, together with the fact that many Aboriginal workers were unpaid, gave rise to national and international accusations of slavery in Western Australia. In July 1949, questions were raised in federal Parliament by Independent Labor Senator Doris Blackburn about the use of chains in making the arrests. Minister for the Interior Vic Johnson thought that such reports had to be exaggerated, as 'the natives of that area are a civilised community', and he was 'confident that there would be no necessity to resort to the chaining of them'.[10] Nevertheless, he made inquiries of his counterpart in Western Australia, causing Middleton in turn to question O'Neill about the use of chains in arresting the strikers, and to publicly defend their use in these circumstances.

Just prior to the Pilbara arrests, the practice of walking prisoners long distances in chains in remote areas of Western Australia had been raised by the London-based Anti-Slavery Society in a letter to Premier McLarty, no doubt prompted by reports made to the Society by Mary Bennett. In October 1949, the *Sydney Morning Herald* reported on the Anti-Slavery Society's concern and on McLarty's defence of the practice. The following day, the NSW Labor Senator Donald Grant, referring both to the Anti-Slavery Society's inquiry and to criticism of Australia's treatment of Aboriginal people made in the UNO by Soviet Foreign Minister Andrey Vyshinsky, called on the federal government to stop the barbarity of Aboriginal prisoners being taken in chains over long distances for trial in Western Australia. According to the *West Australian*, Grant 'said that for many months photographs had been appearing in periodicals overseas depicting Western Australia aborigines in chains'.[11]

---

9   McDonald to A. H. Malloch, 8 July 1949, SROWA S3841 cons769 3.
10 Extract from Hansard, 1 July 1949, SROWA 1949/0454/50.
11 *West Australian*, 26 October 1949, p. 8.

Although the Commonwealth government lacked the power to intervene in state administration of Aboriginal affairs, it expressed grave concern 'about anything said abroad that would reflect on Australia's good name'. Perth's *Daily News* was confident that such criticism was unfounded. 'Western Australia was the subject of unpleasant notoriety abroad because of the allegations that our aborigines were enslaved and that native prisoners were loaded with chains', an article stated. 'Neither charge has any substantial foundation'.[12] Nevertheless, Middleton chafed at being placed in the position of having to defend the treatment of prisoners in the north.[13]

Criticised over the chaining and imprisonment of strikers on the one hand, the Department was facing criticism from the police and pastoralists on the other for not dealing with strikers severely enough. When twelve of the thirteen strikers convicted in March returned to Moolyella in mid-May, having served their two-month sentences, Bob Middleditch, the owner of Noreena Downs Station, complained to McDonald about his failure to follow through on his promise to have them removed to Cosmo Newbery. Middleditch urged the minister to at least arrange for the removal of Jackson, who was still serving his sentence in Roebourne. McDonald replied that:

> in the circumstances ... it would not be wise to remove natives from the district under warrant and there is always the possibility that propaganda can be used that such natives have been made martyrs and the removal of the natives might be utilised to bring about an extent of the unrest that might be far more widespread and difficult to cope with than had previously happened.[14]

With the threatened wool ban and communist prominence in protests over the imprisonment of strikers feeding perceptions of the strike as the weak point in the state's defences against communism, the Department felt it had a fine line to walk, needing to mount strong opposition to communist agitation on the one hand, but not play into communist hands by imprisoning or removing strikers on the other.

Rumours of plans to remove leaders and convicted men to institutions reached the ears of strikers, and throughout May and June 1949 the situation in the Pilbara remained tense.[15] Despite assurances given to Middleton that

---

12 *Daily News*, 2 November 1949, p. 4.
13 *West Australian*, 26 October 1949, p. 8.
14 McDonald to Middleditch, 19 May 1949, SROWA S3841 cons769 3.
15 *Workers' Star*, 13 May 1949, p. 2.

no further disruption would be made to station labour, strikers continued to move around stations, encouraging workers to protest against the prison sentences and planned removals. In the Port Hedland area, *marrngu* who had returned to station work under labour agreements were reluctant to participate in the protests, and a planned meeting at the Twelve Mile to discuss responses failed to eventuate. Tommy Sampie assured O'Neill that they wished only for a quiet life.[16] Some strikers wanted to express their support for the protests but were unwilling to leave their stations to attend meetings while the shearing was underway.[17]

Strikers were also attempting to enlist the support of workers further south in the Nullagine area, where stations had been largely unaffected by the strike.[18] Constable Rowe travelled around the district, warning station owners that a 'mob of Moolyella natives were touring the district intimidating the station boys to strike'. He told Middleditch that strike agitators had visited two stations in the area and were heading towards his own station of Noreena Downs.[19] Middleditch wrote angrily to McDonald, blaming the unrest on the Department's failure to remove offenders to Cosmo Newbery as promised. Most of his 'boys' were happy and contented and wanted nothing to do with McLeod's mob', he wrote:

> The older boys say – 'if they bring green stick we giveim spear'. If my boys are getting the worst of it, I am going to chip in & will not use either spear or stick.
>
> If any tragedy occurs here you and your Mr Middleton can say you just did not understand and did not want to.[20]

McDonald was sympathetic, but strongly cautioned against the use of violence:

> It is necessary for me to say with the utmost emphasis that any use of force other than is essential to protect oneself from justifiable apprehension of bodily harm should not under any circumstances be entertained. Any person using force, unless for necessary protection, must accept full

---

16 O'Neill to Middleton, 17 May 1949, p. 2, SROWA 1943/0621/171; O'Neill, patrol journal, 10 May 1949, SROWA 1949/0160/36–37.
17 O'Neill to Middleton, 17 May 1949, p. 2, SROWA 1943/0621/171.
18 O'Neill, patrol journal, 10 June 1949, SROWA 1949/0160/49.
19 Middleditch to McDonald, 12 June 49. SROWA 1949/769/v3.
20 Middleditch to McDonald, 12 June 1949, SROWA S3841 cons769 3.

responsibility before the law and cannot pass that responsibility to the Native Affairs Department or anybody else.

The Department and I myself have been and are giving most anxious thought to the situation in order to safeguard the interests of the natives from influences which are being brought to bear upon them to their detriment, and at the same time to give all appropriate assistance to the pastoral industry in connection with the services to pastoralists from native labour which have been secured under fair and reasonable industrial conditions.[21]

While strikers were attempting to stir station workers into taking protest action, McLeod urged the Seamen's Union to follow through with a ban on wool shipments from Pilbara stations. 'I am convinced & I am sure you too will agree that a complete ban on the transport of all wool is amply justified', he wrote:

for it will be only by such action that we will be able to bring home to the Govt & the Dept sharply that the time has at last arrived when organised workers are determined to take action to remove the stain of the retention of slave labour in this country'.[22]

Only Mt Edgar and Limestone Stations were clean, he told Seamen's Union secretary Ron Hurd.[23] Fred Davenport of Mt Edgar Station had been willing to approach strike leaders for workers, taking on a striker at £4 per week without keep and providing adequate housing and ablution facilities. George Mallett of Limestone Station had apparently approached McLeod to negotiate for workers, although he later denied doing so. The wage scale that McLeod claimed to have set down for employment on Limestone Station was £3 for general station hands, £3 for horse breakers plus 30/- a horse and 7/6 for shoeing, £4/10/- for windmill men, £1 for elderly men and female domestic servants, and £1/10/- for youths, rising 10/- each six months to adult wages after eighteen months. These wages were to include keep, valued at £2 per week, with workers having the option of drawing the £2 and keeping themselves. Contract work (fencing, well sinking, firewood cutting) was to be paid at the same rates paid to non-Aboriginal workers. Accommodation and ablution facilities were also to be provided. These rates were well above the 30/- originally demanded for all male workers, with wages for women now being included, albeit still at a low rate

---

21   McDonald to Middleditch, undated, SROWA S3841 cons769 3.
22   McLeod to Hurd, 17 May 1949, pp. 2–3, SLWA 5121A.
23   McLeod to Hurd, 29 May 1949, SLWA 5121A.

and still below the rate originally demanded for men.[24] No written agreement had been made, and Mallett denied having entered into one. McLeod, on the other hand, claimed that Mallett had been forced to approach him for workers and that 'if this does not constitute an agreement then I am not concerned whether I have an agreement with Limestone or not'.[25] McLeod's identification of Mt Edgar and Limestone, both in the Marble Bar area, as 'clean' was less a reflection of the wages and conditions offered on these stations than the fact that managers had been willing to recognise the authority of the strikers' organisation by approaching either himself or strike leaders when they needed workers.

Middleton replied to the threat of a wool ban by dismissing the union's concerns, assuring Hurd that Aboriginal people in the Pilbara were not on strike, that workers had been taken unwillingly from their jobs and that a competent senior officer of the Department was in the area to watch over their interests. He emphasised settler fears at the strikers' activities. 'I feel sure your members will appreciate', Middleton wrote to Hurd:

> that the sudden entry of a large body of natives on an isolated station property where possibly the station-owner may be absent and his wife and family the only white persons present, must be a source of concern to pastoralists where, as was the case here, employees of the station were obliged to leave the station through intimidation.[26]

Hurd in turn dismissed Middleton's reassurances and persisted in urging the government to release the strikers. He wrote to Premier Ross McLarty, alerting him to the gravity of the situation and the reality of the ban threat. 'We appreciate the inconvenience that the imposition of a wool ban would create', he wrote, 'and consequently it is only as a last resort that we would implement same, but we are adamant that unless justice is done to the people concerned in this instance we will apply same'.[27] On 26 May, the *West Australian* carried a small article about the threatened ban.[28]

The Department hoped that the Seamen's Union would hold off imposing the ban long enough for most of the imprisoned strikers to have served out their sentences, thus removing the union's principal reason for taking action.

---

24 *Workers' Star*, 1 July 1949, p. 8.
25 McLeod to Hurd, 20 July 1949, p. 2, SLWA 5121A.
26 Middleton to Hurd, 12 May 1949, SROWA 1943/0621/164.
27 Hurd to McLarty, 10 June 1949, SROWA S3841 cons769 3.
28 *West Australian*, 26 May 1949, p. 6, 'Wool Ban Mooted'.

When twenty-nine of the thirty men imprisoned in April were released in mid-June, it seemed that the threat might really be averted. On 16 June, having learned that the prisoners had returned to Moolyella, McDonald released a warning against the Native Rights and Welfare League pamphlet, assuring the public that financial support for the strikers was unnecessary and that only one striker now remained behind bars. A few days later, he advised Premier McLarty to reply to Hurd's letter with the assurance that all but one of the strikers had been released.[29]

The last thing the government needed now was for more strikers to be arrested. O'Neill was active in the Pilbara trying to keep the situation under control.[30] Strikers were said to be moving around stations talking to working people. These agitators included songman Banjo Flann, who was travelling around with two or three other strikers on horseback. On Bonney Downs, where the movement had begun in discussions between McLeod, Kitchener and the other *Milangka* men six years earlier, workers told the manager that they intended to join the strike, but after a visit from Constable Rowe they decided to continue working. At Warrie Station, the threat of strike action resulted in pay increases.[31]

At Warrawagine Station, Mac Gardiner and other workers also announced their intention to leave. These workers had left the station two months previously, taken away by the thirty-three strikers who were subsequently arrested in the dry bed of the Nullagine River on their way to Moolyella. Some of the workers, including Mac Gardiner, had been taken with the chained prisoners on the semi-trailer to Marble Bar as witnesses at the trial. Before returning to Warrawagine, they had asked the manager, Bill Sheppard, for a wage increase of 10/- per week. Although Sheppard refused, they decided to return to work to complete the shearing and then leave. Now, they informed Sheppard that, when the shearing was over at the end of the week, they would leave the station and join the strike community at Moolyella. Sheppard followed the usual pastoralist practice of calling on the police to enforce Aboriginal worker compliance, and, on 17 June, Constable Chipper and Laurie O'Neill made the journey out to Warrawagine to carry out the request, just as, three years earlier, Gordon Marshall had successfully prevented *marrngu* from carrying out the planned strike of 1 May.[32]

---

29 McDonald to McLarty, 20 June 1949, ANU, Noel Butlin Archives Centre, Michael Hess Collection, N287, Item 1.
30 O'Neill, journal, 10 and 19 June 1949, SROWA1949/0160/49, 51.
31 O'Neill to Middleton, 21 June 1949, 1949/0454/8–9.
32 O'Neill, journal, 17 June 1949, SROWA 1949/0160/51.

But *marrngu* were no longer so easily intimidated. As Mac Gardiner expressed it:

> Well I got used to that man ... we pull out from the station. Alright, we're not listening – even the squatter, we're not listening, we're going. 'We're getting nothing from you, we're doing a good job for you, no wages'. We're still going, anybody, Welfare, policemen, we tell them, squatters. We was that strong!³³

In the face of the workers' refusal to be pressured back to work, Sheppard agreed to pay the 10/- wage increase, and appealed to their sense of loyalty to Warrawagine as their place of birth. 'Mr Shepherd [*sic*] reminded the natives that many of them had been on Warrawagine all their lives', O'Neill wrote, 'and that there was still another shearing to do this year for which they were now mustering (Warrawagine is a large property and has two shearings a year). Nothing either he or I could say would make any difference'.³⁴ Chipper reported that, in spite of O'Neill's efforts 'they had definitely made up their minds to leave'.³⁵ All the Warrawagine people, including elderly men and women, left the station that day and joined the strikers at Moolyella. O'Neill felt that Sheppard had acted unwisely in not granting the 10/- pay rise when the workers had asked for it two months earlier, particularly as he was now prepared to do so under threat of strike action and 'therefore he must consider that the natives are worth the extra money'.³⁶ It was a marked change in attitude since the strike had begun; three years earlier, the idea that Aboriginal labour had value, or that workers should be paid the wage increases they demanded, had been ridiculed by O'Neill. After three years of strike, it was finally being conceded that the issue would not be resolved until Aboriginal people received reasonable wages and living conditions.

Three days later, on 20 June, a party of ten strikers visited Bob Middleditch's station of Noreena Downs in the Nullagine area and took away four young workers, including Snowy Jittermarra. Speaking of the incident decades later, when he was a leader of a community that looked back with enormous pride on the events of the 1940s, Snowy claimed to have called on the strikers to come and get them. 'Alright, I call the mob, "We want some people come up

---

33 Gardiner (Pirntilkampanyaja), recorded by Anne Scrimgeour, 29 September 1993, author's collection.
34 O'Neill to Middleton, 21 June 1949, p. 2, SROWA 1949/0454/9.
35 Chipper, police patrol report, 17 June 1949, SROWA 1946/2538 v8.
36 O'Neill to Middleton, 21 June 1949, p. 2, SROWA 1949/0454/9.

and pick us up'".[37] This seems unlikely, however. Had they really wished to join the strike, workers could have left Noreena Downs without having a party of strikers come to get them. Indeed, McLeod states in his draft autobiography that 'this was the first time the natives had attempted to high-jack people'.[38] The principal object to fill the jails, rather than to expand the strike. 'I was ready to take off big mustering now', Snowy remembered, 'I was the head stockman. Anyhow we made a strike, we come off from the station, we walk out from the station, we walk out right up to Nullagine, and the police caught us'.[39]

Making no attempt to avoid arrest, the strikers camped on the native reserve at Nullagine. Just as the Department was hoping that the release of imprisoned strikers would remove the Seamen's Union's main criticism and so avert the threatened wool ban, and just as McLarty prepared to advise Hurd that only one striker remained behind bars, Constable Rowe arrived at the Nullagine reserve and used chains to effect the arrest of ten more strikers.[40] 'Three man in the handcuff and seven man was in the one chain', Snowy remembered.[41] Because Nullagine lacked the facilities to hold them, the men were transported, in the back of a utility and still in chains, to the lockup in Marble Bar, charged with enticing workers from lawful employment.[42]

In Marble Bar, Constable Marshall had no hesitation in laying the blame for the further unrest at the door of the Department of Native Affairs for its failure to take his advice to remove strikers to Cosmo Newbery. There was a feeling in the Pilbara that the Department's reluctance to take this step arose from a level of sympathy with the strikers' cause within the new administration. 'The Dept of Native Affairs could remedy this position by removing several of the native ringleaders, well away from the district', Marshall grumbled to his senior officer in Broome, 'but it appears that this course of action is considered by the powers that be, to be too serious a step

---

37 Jittermarra (Maruntu), recorded by Anne Scrimgeour, 5 August 1993, author's collection.
38 McLeod, draft autobiography, chapter 3, p. 14, Marchant Trust Collection, UWA MS118 series 1 file 13.
39 Jittermarra (Maruntu), recorded by Anne Scrimgeour, 5 August 1993, author's collection.
40 O'Neill to Middleton, 21 June 1949, p. 1, SROWA 1949/0454/8; O'Neill to Middleton, 7 July 1949, SROWA 1949/0454/35; Chipper, police patrol report, 21 June 1949, SROWA 1946/2538 v8.
41 Jittermarra (Maruntu), recorded by Anne Scrimgeour, 5 August 1993, author's collection.
42 O'Neill's report, 7 July 1949, SROWA 1949/0454/35.

to take'.⁴³ He suggested that a detective sergeant be sent quietly to the area to obtain evidence to convict McLeod, who, he wrote, 'is at the bottom of all the unrest amongst the natives, & McLeod has strong backing by the Communist Party, as is well known'.⁴⁴

Noreena Downs pastoralist Bob Middleditch also blamed the loss of his workers on the Department's 'weak-kneed attitude' in dealing with Aboriginal lawbreakers. He accused the Department of double-dealing, by feigning support for pastoralists while colluding with the strikers to achieve better wages and working conditions. He complained bitterly to McDonald about the removal of his four young workers, carried out while he was away from the station. 'In my absence, my old boys did not produce their spears', he wrote:

> so the operation went off very well from McLeod's, I daresay also Mr. Middleton's, point of view. It will take a lot to drag me away from the place again until some of these agitators are taken or blown away.⁴⁵

He believed he had been targeted by the strikers for having called for the removal of lawbreakers, and suspected the Department of passing this information to McLeod. 'I am not squealing', he wrote. 'I suppose I have been looking for it. I understand [McLeod] knew all about my interview with you before I returned from Perth'.⁴⁶

O'Neill had no doubt that prison sentences would be imposed on the ten men now held in the Marble Bar lockup. 'I can not see that anything can be done other than to let the law take its course where an offence has been committed, and wherever possible visit Stations where trouble is expected before it actually happens', he wrote to Middleton.⁴⁷ In other words, nothing could be done but to continue policing the area. Middleton and McDonald, however, convinced now that the arrest of strikers was simply inflaming the situation and playing into communist hands, were alarmed by the further arrests. Middleton sent an urgent telegram to O'Neill instructing him to avoid prosecution if possible. Three months earlier he had authorised O'Neill to use his own judgement in dealing with the developing situation, but now he

---

43   Marshall to Inspector Triat, 21 June 1949, SROWA 1946/2538 v8.
44   Marshall to Inspector Triat, 21 June 1949, SROWA 1946/2538 v8.
45   Middleditch to McDonald, 20 June 1949, SROWA S3841 cons769 3.
46   Middleditch to McDonald, 20 June 1949, SROWA S3841 cons769 3.
47   O'Neill to Middleton, 21 June 1949, p. 2, SROWA 1949/0454/9.

prepared, for the second time in two months, to make an urgent trip north to try to bring matters under control.[48]

Meanwhile, McDonald also took action to try to defuse the situation. With punitive action only worsening matters, the only course of action seemed to be to remove the communists' main weapon of influence in the area: Aboriginal dissatisfaction with wages and conditions on stations. On 21 June 1949, the day he received news about the new arrests, McDonald wrote to the Pastoralists Association, urging them to take action on this front. He enclosed a copy of the Native Rights and Welfare League circular. 'You will see that McLeod claims the initiative in getting better conditions for the natives', he wrote, 'although this claim is not borne out by facts':

> It is preferable that the initiative in these matters should be with the pastoralists and with the Native Affairs Department. A great deal of propaganda is being laid by McLeod regarding conditions of native employment on stations which appear in the Communist paper, the *Workers' Star*, and in one part of the city printed leaflets on the subject, containing many misrepresentations, were delivered from door to door.
>
> I hope that it will be possible to continue the discussions between your Association and the Department of Native Affairs so that any pretext for misrepresentation of the position may be avoided.[49]

It was an important shift in focus, brought about by the strikers' campaign to fill the jails and the Department's determination not to let communists get the upper hand. Until now, pastoralists had been calling on the Department to fix the situation in the Pilbara and were sneeringly critical of its failure to do so. Now the ball was thrown back in their court. As long as Aboriginal people had genuine complaints about wages and conditions, the Department asserted, unrest in the area would continue. Middleton planned to hold a meeting with pastoralists in the Pilbara, presumably with a view to impressing them with the need to set a scale of wages for Aboriginal workers.[50]

Government fears that the new arrests would cause the seamen to follow through with their resolve to impose a wool ban proved to be well founded. On 24 June, Hurd advised the General Secretary of the Seamen's Union in Sydney that, although most of the imprisoned strikers had now been released,

---

48 Middleton to O'Neill, urgent telegram, 21 June 1949, SROWA 1949/0454/1.
49 McDonald to H. R. C. Adkin of the Pastoralists Association, 21 June 1949, SROWA S3841 cons769 3.
50 Middleton to Hogg, telegram, 24 June 1949, SROWA 1949/0454/13.

more had been arrested and were being held on remand, and plans to ban wool shipments were going ahead.[51] The next day, the union representative on the SS *Dorrigo*, in Wyndham but heading south towards Port Hedland, informed Hurd by telegram that the crew was willing to support any union decision regarding the imposition of a ban.[52] In Fremantle, a 'most enthusiastic' stop-work meeting of seamen voted on 28 June for its immediate implementation. Hurd informed the *Dorrigo* of the union decision, which was, he said, 'of terrific importance, with repercussions far beyond Pt Hedland and Fremantle as this is [the] first industrial action of any union to assist abos'.[53] Since the loading of wool was undertaken by shore-based lumpers (or wharfies) as well as by the ship-based seamen, implementation of the ban in Port Hedland would depend on the cooperation of the local lumpers, who were members of the AWU, and Hurd wrote urgently to appeal for their support. With the *Dorrigo* due to arrive in Port Hedland in three or four days' time, Hurd also informed McLeod that the ban was instituted, and asked that he or a representative be on the wharf to identify wool from blacklisted stations.[54]

On the day the Seamen's Union voted to proceed with the ban, Bob Coverley, the former minister with responsibility for Aboriginal affairs, raised questions in Parliament about unrest in the Pilbara, to which McDonald replied that 'the same influence, with communistic affiliations, which became active industrially in the Port Hedland district in 1945–46 is now being manifested in the Marble Bar area'.[55] On the other side of the continent, coal miners in New South Wales stopped work that day in a strike that was believed to be communist-driven, leading the federal Leader of the Opposition, Bob Menzies, to ask, 'Who is in charge of the country?' This question was picked up by Western Australia's *Daily News* in a report on Seaman's Union decision. 'For some time' the *Daily News* article claimed, 'communist agents have been working to prove the fitness of our aborigines for the full rights of citizenship by introducing them to Marxian theory, and persuading them that they have chains to cast off'. The writer believed, however, that 'those who teach the natives whiteman's ways and secure for them whiteman's wages are not their true friends', since 'money is a curse

---

51   Hurd to E. V. Elliott, 24 June 1949, SLWA 5121A.
52   Seamen's Union Delegate, SS *Dorrigo*, to Hurd, telegram, 25 June 1949, SLWA 5121A.
53   Hurd to Seamen's Union Delegate, SS *Dorrigo*, 28 June 1949, SLWA 5121A.
54   Hurd to McLeod, 28 June 1949, SLWA 5121A.
55   Coverley, Parliamentary Debates (Hansard), Western Australia: Legislative Assembly, 28 June 1949, p. 213.

to those aborigines who can get easily to a town and of little value to those who have no means of spending it':

> Obviously the decision of the Fremantle Seamen's Union is more a blow at the pastoralist capitalists than evidence of solicitude for aboriginal welfare.
>
> It is another instance of Communist-inspired usurpation of the authority of elected government – like banning certain exports and blacklisting foreign ships.
>
> Well may Mr. Menzies ask 'Who is in charge of this country?'[56]

News that the wool ban was being implemented led Middleton to change his plan to visit the Pilbara, presumably in the belief that he could more effectively deal with developments as they arose by remaining in Perth. In his place, he sent the Department's new senior administrative officer in charge of the northern region, Sydney Elliott-Smith, recently arrived from Papua, where he had been a resident magistrate before the war, and where, during the war, he had commanded the 1st Papuan Infantry Battalion. Elliott-Smith flew to Port Hedland on 30 June 1949, 'with the task', he wrote, 'of dealing with McLeod'.[57] En route, he held discussions in Carnarvon with Magistrate Keith Hogg, due to hear the cases in Marble Bar on 6 July, to press on him the Department's concern to prevent further convictions.[58] Another Native Affairs officer, Dave Pullen, an old friend of Middleton's and newly recruited from Papua as district officer for the west Kimberley, drove south from his base in Derby to accompany Elliott-Smith on his tour of the Pilbara. The visit to the area of these two officers in July 1949 would see a significant, although short-lived, breakthrough in the relationship between the strikers and the Department.

Also travelling southwards down the Western Australian coast towards Port Hedland was the SS *Dorrigo*, crewed by men prepared to impose their union's ban on wool from Port Hedland. While Elliott-Smith held discussions with Magistrate Hogg, *Dorrigo* seamen sent an urgent telegram to Hurd asking him to fly to Port Hedland to advise them in the upcoming dispute on the Port Hedland wharf. The situation was, they said, very unsatisfactory. AWU lumpers in Port Hedland had indicated their willingness to load the wool

---

56   *Daily News*, 29 June 1949, p. 4.
57   Elliott-Smith to Middleton, 2 March 1950, p. 1, SROWA1949/0454/109.
58   Elliott-Smith, patrol journal, 30 June 1949, SROWA 1949/0488/36.

that was waiting on the wharf, and the ship's master had threatened to log (or fine) all crew members who refused to assist.[59] However, as Hurd prepared to fly north, the master of the *Dorrigo* decided to avoid an extended stand-off and the ship bypassed Port Hedland, leaving wool bales waiting on the wharf.[60]

On 1 July, Elliott-Smith and Pullen held discussions with the small community of strikers still living at the Twelve Mile. Elliott-Smith was a Tasmanian and, despite a reputation in Papua as a man who knew 'more about the natives than most people', this was his first encounter with Aboriginal people.[61] 'My first impressions on original contact with the aborigine are favourable', he wrote. 'A good humoured fellow, easy to get along with, but I should like to see the other side of him before offering any firm opinion'.[62] He advised the Twelve Mile community not to listen to idle advice, as this would only bring them into conflict with the law and bring discredit upon themselves. Instead, they should bring all their problems to their friends, the Department of Native Affairs. They should be perfectly straight with the Department, he told them, and the Department would do likewise with them. Elliott-Smith and Pullen then discussed the situation with Sergeant Plunkett, O'Neill, Bryan and storekeeper and strike supporter Alec Wyndham, before attending a Euralian Club social and discussing matters with members of the Euralian community.[63]

After meeting with pastoralists on stations en route, the officers arrived in Marble Bar on 4 July, expecting to find a letter from McDonald setting out the grounds on which the defence of the ten accused strikers was to be conducted. McDonald's letter, however, had been lost in a fatal air crash at Perth's Guildford airport on the morning of 2 July. Middleton sent a precis by telegram, informing Elliott-Smith of McDonald's instructions that, if the men were found guilty, the Department's view, that they were acting without understanding as tools of 'outside influences', should be taken into account in imposing penalties.[64] After discussing matters with the accused men, however,

---

59 Seamen's Union Delegate, SS *Dorrigo*, to Hurd, urgent telegram, 30 June 1949, SLWA 5121A.
60 Seamen's Union Delegate, SS *Dorrigo*, to Hurd, telegram, 1 July 1949, SLWA 5121A.
61 *Sydney Morning Herald*, 23 March 1943, p. 4.
62 Elliott-Smith, patrol journal, 1 July 1949, p. 2, SROWA 1949/0488/34.
63 Elliott-Smith, patrol journal, 1 July 1949, p. 2, SROWA 1949/0488/34.
64 Middleton to Elliott-Smith, urgent telegram, 4 July 1949, SROWA 1949/0454/31–32.

Elliott-Smith was convinced that there was no case against them, and became determined to argue for an acquittal.

On their first day in Marble Bar, Elliott-Smith and Pullen, accompanied by O'Neill, spoke to strikers at Moolyella. Spokesmen Dooley and Jerry told them that they had been promised better working conditions over the years by various officers of the Department, and were simply asking that these promises be honoured. Their chief demand, they told the officers, was a wage scale of 30/- to £3/10/- per week. Since they needed to purchase clothing from these wages, Pullen considered this 'far from being an unreasonable demand'.[65]

After meeting *marrngu* at Moolyella, the officers met with McLeod, together with Fred Davenport of Mt Edgar Station and George Mallett of Limestone Station. Although their purpose was to challenge McLeod's claim to have made labour agreements with these two stations, the meeting was significant. McLeod wrote in 1994 that:

> it was the first and last time that any official of the Department of Native Affairs was willing to speak to me as a spokesman of the Beneficial Owners of Western Australia. At all other times, this Department and its successors have treated me as if I were public enemy number one.[66]

Although it certainly was not the last time that the Department would recognise McLeod's role as a representative of the Aboriginal group, it was the first time since he visited Commissioner Bray in 1943 that departmental officers were prepared to include him in discussions. Both Davenport and Mallett denied having signed any agreement with the North-West Workers' Association. According to Elliott-Smith, 'both categoricly [sic] denied that any such agreement existed'.[67] Elliott-Smith challenged McLeod on his authority to negotiate wages on behalf of Aboriginal people. He told McLeod 'he could not, under any circumstances, be considered a representative of the natives in dealings they may have with the Government or anybody else'.[68] McLeod replied that, as far as he was concerned, he had simply been involved in negotiations between workers and employers, and the Department had nothing to do with the matter.

Despite their insistence that McLeod had no standing with the Department, Elliott-Smith and Pullen met with him again later that day and heard his

---

65 Pullen, patrol report, 4 July 1949, SROWA 1949/0456/23.
66 McLeod, *How the West Was Lost*, p. 62.
67 Elliott-Smith, patrol journal, 4 July 1949, SROWA 1949/0488/35.
68 Elliott-Smith, patrol journal, 4 July 1949, SROWA 1949/0488/35.

views on Western Australia's unjust treatment of Aboriginal people, past and present. McLeod told them of the state's action in reneging on the commitment, made in exchange for self-government and enshrined as section 70 of the Constitution, to expend £5000 or 1 per cent of consolidated revenue for the benefit of Aboriginal people. The story of the Western Australian government's cynical and self-interested betrayal of Aboriginal people in repealing section 70, opening the way to continued mistreatment and exploitation, was a story that McLeod would repeat, and continue to repeat for another half century, to anyone who would listen. 'I hammered Eliot Smith [sic], Pullen and the two squatters, until sundown', he wrote:

> reviewing the 70th section of the old const. and how we'd got control of these people etc. and how we had only set up an adjunct of the police department to control them, and the Dept's. shocking attitude to the natives ... I pointed out generally that natives know us only by our sins.[69]

Pullen was impressed by McLeod's erudition and passion. He 'showed considerable moral courage', he wrote, 'and stuck to his guns. Has as a vast knowledge of the activities of the Department in the past'.[70] 'He does not appear to be the double-dyed villain that people try to make out'.[71]

The next day, 5 July, the officers again held talks with strikers at Moolyella, listening to their grievances and urging them to accept the Department's undertaking to change its approach and to genuinely work to improve the circumstances of their lives, particularly regarding their demands for improved wages and conditions on stations. The court hearing would be a test of the Department's sincerity.[72]

At 9 am on 6 July, strikers crowded into Marble Bar's solid stone courtroom to hear the cases of the ten men arrested in Nullagine for removing Snowy Jittermarra and three other young workers from Noreena Downs Station. 'We filed into court', McLeod wrote, 'keenly interested to see what would happen'.[73] According to Pullen, Nullagine's Constable Tom Rowe presented a poor case.[74] Police officers rarely needed to worry about making a strong case to convict Aboriginal people, as conviction was usually a foregone conclusion.

---

69 McLeod draft autobiography, chapter 3, p. 13, Marchant Trust Collection, UWA MS118 series 1 file 13.
70 Pullen, extract of journal, 4 July 1949, SROWA 1949/0454/61.
71 Pullen, patrol report, 4 July 1949, SROWA 1949/0456/23.
72 Elliott-Smith, patrol journal, 5 July 1949, SROWA 1949/0488/35.
73 McLeod, *How the West Was Lost*, p. 62.
74 Pullen, extract from journal 49/50, 20 June to 10 July 1949, SROWA 1949/0454/61.

Now the reverse was the case, and Rowe no doubt felt it pointless to put forward a strong case when those in authority were clearly determined to ensure the men's release. 'Elliot-Smith rose after the prosecution had completed its case', McLeod wrote:

> and argued that there was no case to answer. He and the magistrate bandied words about for some time before agreeing that technically a case had been established. Indeed it had been: the thirteen [sic] accused had been quite blatant in the manner they hijacked the Noreena Downs Station mob! However the magistrate agreed to let them go on the rising of the court on the grounds that they had already been jailed and chained for over a week.[75]

Hogg found the cases to be proven but, since there was no evidence that intimidation had been used, the cases were dismissed under section 669 of the Criminal Code, which gave him the option, when extenuating circumstances made it inexpedient to do so, to refrain from lodging convictions against first offenders.[76] McLeod had the impression that the matter had been worked out beforehand.[77]

On the stony red dirt outside the courthouse, the atmosphere following the hearing of 6 July was very different from that which had pertained following the trial, three months earlier, of the men who had removed Cocky and attempted to remove Joe from Corunna Downs. Then, *marrngu* had expressed anger at the lack of justice they received in court. Now, there was a sense of jubilation that change was finally taking place. 'Outside the Court', Pullen wrote, 'Mr. McLeod came up to me and said it was a welcome change to find such an honest atmosphere in a Court where natives were being charged'. Remarkably, given the Department's persistent view of McLeod as a dangerous subversive, Pullen added, 'I am inclined to like this man'.[78] Both Pullen and McLeod noted the strikers' pleasure at seeing *marrngu* treated with greater respect and accorded justice in court. Pullen wrote that they 'seemed very pleased with the result of the case'.[79] 'The natives were very satisfied with [Elliott-Smith's] success', McLeod wrote. 'And all of us, that is to say, the

---

75 McLeod, *How the West Was Lost*, p. 62.
76 O'Neill, patrol journal, 6 July 1949, SROWA 1949/0160/55; Elliott-Smith, patrol journal, 6 July 1949, SROWA 1949/0488/33, 66.
77 McLeod, *How the West Was Lost*, p. 62.
78 Pullen, extract of journal, 20 June 1949 to 10 July 1949, SROWA 1949/0454/61.
79 Pullen, patrol report, 4 July 1949, p. 2, SROWA 1949/0456/24.

natives and myself, Elliot-Smith, Hogg, O'Neill and Mr. Buckingham their driver all met together at Moolyella in a very friendly spirit'.[80]

Elliott-Smith, due to undertake a tour of the Kimberley, asked strikers to refrain from any further disturbance of station labour for three or four months, to give him time to prove that he was as good as his word in undertaking to have their grievances taken seriously. 'Mr. Elliot-Smith was able to assure the natives that from now on they could expect the full sympathy of the Dept.', McLeod wrote, 'and justice and common sense would prevail in dealing with their problems providing that they were prepared to let bygones be bygones. They all agreed'.[81] According to Pullen, McLeod said that if the officers proved as sincere as they seemed to be, he was prepared to step out of the picture. 'He thought that the 3 or 4 months asked for was a fair time for a trial period', Pullen wrote. 'The natives also agreed to this'.[82] Elliott-Smith wrote that:

> McLeod and Dooley give me unqualified assurance that no further action would in any way be taken to prejudice the situation during my absence, or for a further four months, until such time as I was able to go into the matter thoroughly and with complete understanding of the situation, as it affected the whole of the native labour throughout the North-West.[83]

'And the party broke up', McLeod remembered, 'amid congratulations and rejoicing'.[84]

The agreement made between strikers and departmental officials at Moolyella that day was a highly significant development in the strike movement. It represented a recognition of the strikers' right to be consulted and to enter into agreements *as a group*. McLeod was, for the first time, included these discussions. McLeod's recognition as a representative and spokesman of the strikers had been a sticking-point in earlier negotiations, and although Elliott-Smith reiterated the Department's position that McLeod could not be officially recognised, his inclusion represented a growing acceptance that

---

80   McLeod, draft autobiography, chapter 3, p. 14, Marchant Trust Collection, UWA MS118 series 1 file 13.
81   McLeod, draft autobiography, chapter 3, p. 14, Marchant Trust Collection, UWA MS118 series 1 file 13.
82   Pullen, patrol report, 4 July 1949, SROWA 1949/0456.
83   Elliott-Smith, patrol journal, 13 August 1949, SROWA 1949/0488/25.
84   McLeod, draft autobiography, chapter 3, p. 14, Marchant Trust Collection, UWA MS118 series 1 file 13.

he could be part of a solution and not merely (in the Department's eyes) the cause of a problem. Pullen was openly admiring of McLeod's point of view, and Elliott-Smith was at least willing to view his advocacy as an important antidote to the racist attitudes he encountered on his visit to the Pilbara, although any respect he had for McLeod was tempered by his perception of him as a communist. The officers had accepted assurances given by both the strikers and McLeod that no further protest action would be taken for four months to give Elliott-Smith the time he needed to implement the new wage scale. In return for these assurances, the strikers' demand of a wage scale of 30/- to 70/- was accepted as the basis of negotiation with pastoralists, and Elliott-Smith had undertaken to ensure that stations stepped up to the mark and paid these wages. He had demonstrated his sincerity by securing the release of the ten strikers.

The Moolyella agreement included a further remarkable concession on the part of the Department. The strikers agreed to work towards a new and more positive relationship with the Department, but insisted that this could not be achieved while Laurie O'Neill remained its local representative. As a further demonstration of his determination to address striker grievances and reshape race relations in the Pilbara, Elliott-Smith responded to this demand by removing O'Neill from the district as the Department's representative.

Elliott-Smith's visit to the Pilbara at this time was his first encounter with racist settler attitudes to Aboriginal people, an encounter he described as 'not a very pretty experience'. He found 'bitterness and in some cases outright and outspoken hatred, almost amounting to "Jim Crowism", intolerance, lack of appreciation and really an amazing ignorance of the subject, except perhaps in a queer negative way'.[85] 'The attitude was something one had to experience to believe', he later wrote, 'and could be described as nothing short of primitive'.[86] O'Neill, on the other hand, having grown up in the southern goldfields town of Kalgoorlie and having worked as a policeman and Native Affairs Inspector throughout the north, was very much at home in the settler culture that Elliott-Smith found so disturbing, accepting and expressing prevailing racist attitudes without question. Officers like O'Neill were liked by pastoralists and had once been valued by the Department precisely because their views conformed with prevailing settler attitudes in the north. They were remembered by the protagonist of the pro-pastoralist novel *The Green Stick* as 'bluff, practical men, highly educated in the ways of blackfellows, if little

---

85 Elliott-Smith to Middleton, 2 March 1950, p. 1, SROWA 1949/0454/109.
86 Elliott-Smith to Middleton, 2 March 1950, p. 3, SROWA 1949/0454/111.

else'.[87] O'Neill had once described Aboriginal people as being 'chained to the primitive by a mental chain [they could] never break', but it was his attitudes that were now considered primitive. 'Unfortunately', Elliott-Smith wrote, 'our cause has not been helped by the attitude of certain of our officers and even men in a much higher category, if my information is correct'.[88] His information probably came from a number of sources, but the strikers and McLeod left him in no doubt that solutions would never be found while officers like O'Neill remained in the Department. McLeod described the Department of Native Affairs as simply an adjunct of the Police Department, designed to maintain control. According to Pullen, McLeod:

> asserted that if the Dept. had done its job in the past, the necessity for him to champion the natives cause would not have arisen. He was very emphatice [sic], however, that none of the old school should remain in or be sent to this District. The natives themselves went further than that and actually named the officers.[89]

The strikers' agreement to refrain from militant action to give the Department time to prove its sincerity was conditional on having no 'old school' officers remain in the district. Pullen wrote that 'once again they mentioned the names of officers in whom they had lost confidence'.[90]

O'Neill was immediately instructed to shift to Port Hedland and from there to return to Perth to attend to his Public Service appeal against his demotion and loss of salary within the Department. 'It is my intention', Elliott-Smith wrote, 'to leave this place free as a test of the sincerity of both McLeod and the native people during my visit to the North'.[91] At the beginning of the strike three years earlier, when O'Neill had received the urgent call to proceed to the Pilbara to deal with 'McLeod's insidious, anti fascist communistic activities', he could never have imagined that the time would come when he would be relocated from the district in response to Aboriginal expressions of dissatisfaction with his attitude and behaviour towards them. Just six months earlier, returned to the district to deal with the fallout from the attempted closure of the Twelve Mile, he had been given decision-making authority as a district officer, in accordance with Middleton's plans for a decentralised

---

87   Doughty, *The Green Stick*, p. 178.
88   Elliott-Smith to Middleton, 2 March 1950, p. 1, SROWA1949/0454/109.
89   Pullen, patrol report, 4 July 1949, SROWA 1949/0456.
90   Pullen, patrol report, 6 July 1949, SROWA 1949/0456.
91   Elliott-Smith, patrol journal, 7 July 1949, SROWA 1949/0488/33.

administration. In April, three months before he left the area, he had been asked to identify strikers whose removal to Cosmo Newbery would be most effective in restoring order in the Pilbara. Now it was he who was being removed. Following an unsuccessful Public Service appeal, he was posted to his home town of Kalgoorlie. 'All them old hand's 've been slung out on their necks', a pastoralist in *The Green Stick* laments. 'There's a lot o' new young galahs been stuck in their places, kids that never seen a coon in their lives before hardly'.[92] Two years later, further demoted to assistant district officer under one of the 'new young galahs' with experience in native administration in Papua New Guinea, and shortly after the death of a much-loved brother, O'Neill took his own life.[93]

It was not just the different perspective of new departmental officers that led them to heed the concerns of strikers, however. The civil disobedience action of the strikers in filling jails and rendering the threat of imprisonment ineffective as a tool of colonial control was forcing the Department to bring the situation under control by addressing striker grievances instead of punishing offenders. Anti-communism was also at play. The wool ban by a communist-dominated union heightened fears that communists were exploiting Aboriginal inequality and dissatisfaction to damage the state's economy and promote their own ideology. While punitive action had only exacerbated the strikers' grievances and unrest, giving unions grounds for militancy, the Department hoped it could frustrate the communists' agenda by improving its relationship with strikers and addressing their concerns. Elliott-Smith's active defence of the accused men in court, which convinced the strikers of his sincerity in promising fairer treatment, was driven to a large extent by the need to ensure that the Seamen's Union had no grounds for banning the shipment of wool. The day after the Marble Bar court hearings, McDonald suggested that Premier McLarty could finally answer the Seamen's Union with the reply that 'no natives are now in gaol in connection with the incidents at Marble Bar. The Government is unable to countenance the unjustifiable action taken by you to the prejudice of a section of the wool industry of the State'.[94]

By now, however, the wool ban had begun. As Elliott-Smith and Pullen headed up the coast road to undertake a tour of the Kimberley, the *Kybra*, with its crew of Seamen's Union members, travelled northward towards Port Hedland, where 950 bales of wool were awaiting shipment to Fremantle.

---

92   Doughty, *The Green Stick*, p. 126.
93   Scrimgeour, 'This Man's Tracks'.
94   McDonald to McLarty, 7 July 1949, SROWA S3841 cons769 3.

Chapter 26

'How Politics Enter into This'

The Seamen's Union Ban, July 1949

As the strike reached the end of its third year, it must have seemed to McLeod that everything was finally coming together. For the first time since he applied to Commissioner Bray for appointment as an honorary Protector of Natives in 1945, the Department was including him in discussions with *marrngu* and demonstrating a genuine willingness to address striker grievances. The dismissal of the charges brought against the ten strikers and the removal of O'Neill from the area at the strikers' request indicated that *marrngu* were winning significant improvements in authority and status. At the same time, the union movement was finally paying more than lip service in support of the strike, something that McLeod had long been pressing for. Seamen's Union's ban on the shipment of Pilbara wool promised to significantly strengthen his and the strikers' position in negotiations with the pastoralists and the Department.

The situation must have presented him with a quandary, however. He and the strikers had undertaken to leave station labour undisturbed for three or four months to enable Elliott-Smith to find his feet in his new position and prove that the Department really was prepared to cooperate. Neither Elliott-Smith's nor Pullen's reports, nor McLeod's account, indicate that the wool ban was raised in these discussions, but if it was not discussed it was surely the elephant in the room. O'Neill believed that the Moolyella agreement made it unlikely that McLeod would involve himself in the union's action.[1] Elliott-Smith, too, appears to have been confident that he had a gentleman's agreement with McLeod with respect to the wool ban, referring to the 'unqualified assurance' given by McLeod and Dooley 'that no further action would in any way be taken to prejudice the situation' during his absence in the Kimberley. But McLeod now embarked on a course of action that would

---

1   O'Neill, patrol journal, 13 July 1949, SROWA 1949/0160/57.

completely undermine the gains that the strikers had won in their relationship with the Department.

When McLeod wired the *Workers' Star*, in time for their issue of 15 July 1949, to inform them that Elliott-Smith had secured the release of the ten strikers, he could also have wired news of this development to Hurd, asking him, in accordance with the Moolyella agreement, to call off the wool ban.[2] But, having finally secured the active involvement of the union movement, McLeod was apparently unwilling to pass up the additional leverage provided by the seamen's willingness to throw their weight behind the strikers. Allowing the wool ban to go ahead could significantly strengthen his and the strikers' hand in future negotiations by demonstrating to the government the power of its union backing. At the same time, it would provide an opportunity for him to demonstrate his good intentions to the Department by interceding to bring the ban to an end. Instead of asking the seamen to call off the ban, therefore, McLeod headed to Port Hedland to comply with Hurd's request that he be present to identify 'black' wool to be left on the wharf as opposed to that coming from 'clean' stations, which could be loaded.[3]

Arriving in Port Hedland on 10 July 1949, a few days after the Moolyella meeting, McLeod found the SS *Dulverton* in port. Speaking to crewmen on board, he found them supportive but not involved in the ban, as their ship was heading north and not picking up wool.[4] He also found that AWU organiser Jack Walsh was in town to persuade local members not to support the ban. According to O'Neill, who was in town for a week prior to his return to Perth, Walsh informed local AWU members that the ban was unconstitutional and not authorised by their union.[5] He urged them to ignore the ban and to load wool on the *Kybra* when she arrived that weekend, with or without the assistance of the seamen.[6] AWU state secretary Charlie Golding also sent instructions to the local men to ignore the ban.[7] The determination of the AWU leadership to undermine the ban was driven in part by its anti-communist opposition to the militant and communist-dominated Seamen's Union, but, given the history of cooperation between the union and the Department of Native Affairs, it is likely that

---

2   *Workers' Star*, 15 July 1949, p. 6, 'Native Workers Freed After Wool Ban'.
3   Hurd to McLeod, 28 June 1949, SLWA 5121A.
4   McLeod, 'Report on AWU Scabbing on Wool Ban Occasion', 1949, SLWA 5121A.
5   O'Neill, patrol journal, 9 July 1949, SROWA 1949/0160/56.
6   McLeod to Hurd, urgent telegram, 11 July 1949, SLWA 5121A.
7   *Workers' Star*, 15 July 1949, p. 6, 'Native Workers Freed After Wool Ban'.

Golding was also acting in response to a request from the Department to use his influence to undermine the ban. On 11 July, McLeod wired Hurd, informing him that the AWU leadership was working to persuade Port Hedland lumpers to load wool.[8]

With the support of the Port Hedland AWU lumpers unlikely, there seemed little chance that the Seamen's ban would be successful. The crewmen's employer, State Shipping Services, had declared the ban illegal and threatened to fine, or log, seamen for each day they refused to load wool.[9] The *Kybra* was an older ship with an older crew, and the *Dulverton* seamen doubted that they were sufficiently militant to hold out against AWU and employer opposition.[10] When local AWU members voted by a small minority to load black wool on the *Kybra*, due in port on 16 July, McLeod feared the seamen's action would fail.[11] A successful ban would have strengthened his bargaining position, but if the AWU loaded the wool his position would be lost. He therefore decided to make what capital he could out of the situation by immediately demanding a concession from Elliott-Smith in return for ending the ban. On 14 July, he sent a wire to Elliott-Smith in the Kimberley town of Fitzroy Crossing, later abbreviated in notes of the dispute made by Hurd:

> Due to intervention local AWU in attempt to break black ban on wool, real possibility S.S.S. [State Shipping Service] disloc. indef. & all coast & shipping eventually involved. As actual rates pay only material point difference between us, am hopeful seamen may consider lifting ban time being if Mt Edgar – Limestone rates accepted general application allow further discussions proceed.[12]

He also wired Hurd, informing him that he was:

> endeavouring locate Elliott Smith suggesting he agree Edgar–Limestone rates have general application commissioner has power enforce desired rates ... If affirmative would you recommend temporary lifting ban allow further discussion prevent general dislocation.[13]

---

8   McLeod to Hurd, urgent telegram, 11 July 1949, SLWA 5121A.
9   Owen, Manager of State Shipping Service, to Hurd, 5 July 1949, SLWA 5121A.
10 McLeod, draft autobiography, chapter 3, p. 14, Marchant Trust Collection, UWA MS118 series 1 file 13.
11 Hurd to Seamen's Union Members, MV *Kybra*, 14 July 1949, SLWA 5121A.
12 McLeod, 'Report on AWU Scabbing on Wool Ban Occasion', 1949, p. 3, SLWA 5121A.
13 McLeod to Hurd, urgent telegram, 14 July 1949, SLWA 5121A.

Hurd replied in the affirmative, but by Saturday 16 July, when the *Kybra* came into port, McLeod had not yet received a reply from Elliott-Smith.[14] McLeod boarded the *Kybra* to discuss the situation with the crew, but was ordered off and, at the request of the ship's captain, a police officer was stationed on the gangplank to prevent him reboarding.[15] An AWU meeting agreed to work the *Kybra*, 'winches, storage, & all', but, after discussions with the Seamen's delegate, AWU members agreed not to load unless the *Kybra* crew manned the winches.[16] McLeod wrote that, despite this agreement, the AWU men 'turned to' when called for work on Sunday.[17] The seamen were each logged, or fined, £1 on Saturday and £5 on Sunday.[18] McLeod paid a Sunday opening fee at the post office and again wired Elliott-Smith, informing him that the threatened dispute had developed, and that the Seamen's Union was prepared to consider a temporary lifting of the ban if he guaranteed that the Mt Edgar – Limestone rates would be applied generally.[19] He received the hoped-for reply from Elliott-Smith:

> Your telegram just received stop assure union Limestone Mt Edgar rates basis of future rates general application your area stop telegram much appreciated not able answer earlier.[20]

Elliott-Smith later justified his decision to make this guarantee, writing that he did so 'only in the interests of the community and the industry'.[21] Having been appointed Senior Administrative Officer in charge of the state's north, he was confident that he had the authority to make such a concession. He may or may not have been aware of the wage scale which, according to McLeod, had been agreed to by the management of Mt Edgar and Limestone, but the strikers at Moolyella had made clear their demand for a minimum of 30/- per week for stockmen to a maximum of 75/- for skilled workers. Elliott-Smith believed not only that the strikers' demand was justified, but

---

14 McLeod to Hurd, telegram, 16 July 1949, SLWA 5121A.
15 O'Neill, patrol journal, 16 July 1949, SROWA 1949/0160/58.
16 Union Delegate, MV *Kybra*, to Hurd, urgent telegram, SLWA 5121A.
17 McLeod, 'Report on AWU Scabbing on Wool Ban Occasion', 1949, p. 4, SLWA 5121A.
18 McLeod, 'Report on AWU Scabbing on Wool Ban Occasion', 1949, pp. 3–4, SLWA 5121A.
19 McLeod, draft autobiography, chapter 3, p. 15, Marchant Trust Collection, UWA MS118 series 1 file 13.
20 McLeod to Hurd, 17 July 1949, SLWA 5121A.
21 Elliott-Smith to Middleton, 14 August 1949, SROWA1949/0454/84.

that paying workers at this rate was essential if unrest in the Pilbara was ever going to be resolved. 'Frankly, the natives' claim for wages are reasonable and fully justified', he later wrote, *'they will have to be met'*. Many workers were already receiving wages with this margin, and during his visit to the Pilbara he had begun discussions to encourage more stations to pay wages at these rates.[22] Given that these negotiations were already underway, agreeing that Mt Edgar and Limestone rates would form the basis of further discussion seemed a small concession to make to ensure the continued shipment of Pilbara wool. On receipt of Elliott-Smith's telegram, McLeod wired Hurd with news of his response.[23]

On the morning of Monday 18 July, the seamen on the *Kybra* again refused to man the winches and were again logged.[24] O'Neill wrote that 'no finality [had been] reached regarding the loading of wool'.[25] In Fremantle, Hurd sought and received an assurance from the shipping company that fines imposed on the seamen would be rescinded if the ban was lifted, and a union meeting of seamen from the *Dorrigo*, the only ship in Fremantle at the time, agreed to lift the ban on the basis of Elliott-Smith's undertaking.[26] Hurd wired both the *Kybra* and McLeod with this information, and McLeod wired Elliott-Smith that the dispute was resolved on the basis of his guarantee.[27] By the afternoon of 18 July, the ban had been lifted.[28] The loading of wool commenced, and the following day the *Kybra* set sail on her return trip to Fremantle with 950 bales of Pilbara wool.[29] The *Northern Times* reported that she had been held up by the seamen's ban for three days, but a short article in the *West Australian* stated that the *Kybra* 'had been delayed for about twenty-four hours while negotiations were in progress ... Apart from the slight delay to the *Kybra* no other shipping was affected'.[30]

---

22   Elliott-Smith to Middleton, 14 August 1949, SROWA1949/0454/84 (emphasis in original).
23   McLeod to Hurd, 17 July 1949, SLWA 5121A.
24   Fowers, Acting Delegate, MV *Kybra*, to Hurd, urgent telegram, 17 July 1949, SLWA 5121A.
25   O'Neill, journal, 18 July 1949, SROWA 1949/0160/59.
26   Hurd to Owen, Manager of State Shipping Service, 18 July 1949, SLWA 5121A.
27   Hurd to Seamen's Union Delegate, MV *Kybra* and Hurd to McLeod, 17 July 1949; McLeod, 'Report on AWU Scabbing on Wool Ban Occasion', 1949, SLWA 5121A.
28   O'Neill, journal, 18 July 1949, SROWA 1949/0160/59.
29   Seamen's Union Delegate, MV *Kybra*, to Hurd, telegram, 18 July 1949, SLWA 5121A; *Northern Times*, 21 July 1949, p. 7.
30   *West Australian*, 19 July 1949, p. 10, 'North-West Wool'.

Hurd's telegram to McLeod informing him of the lifting of the ban included the request 'write me immediately if O.K. publicise Elliott-Smith agreement'. McLeod replied, 'Yes, go ahead'.[31] It was a miscalculation on McLeod's part. If he thought that publicising Elliott-Smith's concession would serve to consolidate the agreement, he underestimated the strength of the pastoral lobby and anti-communist sentiment among those who held power in the state. An article in the *Workers' Star* on 22 July 1949, which cited Elliott-Smith's telegram and claimed victory for the Aboriginal strikers, caused consternation in Perth.[32] Bob Coverley, minister in charge of Native Affairs in the former Labor Government, sent a clipping of the *Workers' Star* article to McDonald with a note demanding, 'Would like to know if this statement is true and what are the real circumstances'.[33] The Department was criticised for negotiating a wage scale with McLeod without consulting the Pastoralists Association. Middleton made urgent attempts to contact Elliott-Smith. 'Considerable alarm caused by article *Workers' Star* indicating departmental recognition McLeod as natives representative and spokesman', he wired on 27 July. 'Have officially refuted same stop McLeod unacceptable this role and no agreement for scale wages or otherwise should be concluded with him or natives without approval minister and self'.[34]

Still touring the Kimberley, Elliott-Smith did not receive this telegram until he returned to Port Hedland two weeks later, when he also received a further anxious telegram sent from Middleton on 8 August alerting him to the political sensitivity of the situation. 'Minister directs no scale wages be finalized without approval himself and pastoralists association', he instructed.[35] When Elliott-Smith arrived in Marble Bar on 14 August, he received yet another urgent telegram from Middleton, this one in code, urging caution in his dealings with McLeod. Decoded, the telegram read:

> AWU secretary perturbed and annoyed report in 'Star' which wrote that you and communist in agreement stop they and pastoralists disapprove his views and labourites previously threw him out stop exercise caution.[36]

---

31 McLeod to Hurd, telegram, 18 July 1949, SLWA 5121A.
32 *Workers' Star*, 22 July 1949, p. 8, 'Seamen's Solidarity Wool Ban Wins Victory for Aboriginal Workers'.
33 Coverley to McDonald, undated note, SROWA S3841 cons769 3.
34 Middleton to Elliott-Smith, telegram, 27 July 1949, SROWA 1949/0454/73.
35 Middleton to Elliott-Smith, 8 August 1949, SROWA 1947/0220/9.
36 Middleton to Elliott-Smith, urgent coded telegram, 12 August 1949, SROWA 1949/0454/79.

Elliott-Smith, new to the state and its political power structure, was taken by surprise. Until he received Middleton's correspondence, he had been confident that his intervention in the district was bearing fruit. The wool ban had been successfully ended, no further action had been taken by strikers to disrupt station labour, and plans were in place for further discussions with pastoralists to secure an agreement for better wages and conditions for Aboriginal workers. A few days earlier, he had wired Middleton that 'satisfactory conclusion to recent upset anticipated'.[37] Now he was surprised to see that his efforts had aroused a storm of criticism in Perth. His telegraphic reply to Middleton expressed his frustration. Sent in code, its translation, worded no doubt somewhat differently from the wording Elliott-Smith would have chosen, reads, 'This communist is mad and lies greatly stop tell the AWU this stop letter being forwarded by air mail stop it will explain'.[38]

He was anxious to counter the impression that he had been prepared to negotiate directly with McLeod. 'I had no idea such an extraordinary rumour had been placed in circulation', he wrote:

> Had I known this you would have most certainly been placed in possession of the facts at once.
>
> I am sure you will accept my personal regrets in this connection.
>
> For your own information and that of the Minister, I <u>have not, at any time</u>:
>
> (a) recognised Mc Cleod [sic] as a representative of the natives or their spokesman – quite the reverse – I met the fellow and listened to his views but always in the presence of pastoralists, natives and D. O. Pullen, where my own standing in the matter was plainly and even brutally, conveyed to him
>
> (b) laid down any scale of wages nor do I intend to do so until a full consultation with all interested has taken place – however, in this connection an interim settlement is imperative and this was being organised in consultation with the resident pastoralists throughout this area who, at this juncture, are proving most co-operative and reasonable.
>
> I did communicate with McCleod in connection with the wool ban on shipments in the vessel *Kybra* and then only in the interests of the

---

37 Elliott-Smith to Middleton, telegram, 11 August 1949, SROWA 1949/0488/14.
38 Elliott-Smith to Middleton, 14 August 1949, SROWA 1949/0454/80.

community and the industry and subsequent to the receipt of a telegram from him.[39]

As a result of concerns being expressed in Perth, and no longer accompanied by the more open-minded Dave Pullen, Elliott-Smith now backed away from his earlier willingness to negotiate directly with strike leaders and McLeod. The positive way he had responded to McLeod's telegram four weeks previously, guaranteeing that Mt Edgar and Limestone rates would form the basis of future negotiation and expressing appreciation of McLeod's action in making contact, suggests that he believed that McLeod's efforts in Port Hedland had been directed towards bringing an end to the ban. Middleton's correspondence convinced him otherwise. Middleton had no doubt that McLeod had worked to ensure the successful implementation of the ban rather than to find a way to end it. He referred to McLeod's activities in Port Hedland at the time of the wool ban as evidence of his subversive intentions. McLeod had travelled to Port Hedland with the express purpose of contacting the seamen, Middleton wrote, and had been seen to board the *Dulverton* and the *Kybra*.[40] Elliott-Smith now viewed McLeod's intervention in this light. Since his own intervention in the Pilbara had been primarily to prevent communists making political mileage from Aboriginal discontent and activism, it was particularly galling to have his concession trumpeted in the communist press as a union victory. He now considered McLeod's behaviour to be duplicitous, directly contravening the agreement made at Moolyella. 'McLeod and Dooley give me unqualified assurance that no further action would in any way be taken to prejudice the situation during my absence, or for a further four months', he wrote to Middleton. 'This guarantee both he and his minions have clearly broken and negotiations can no longer continue'.[41]

His meeting with strikers at Moolyella on this second visit to the region, therefore, had none of the bonhomie and optimism of the earlier meetings. No longer willing to negotiate with strikers, Elliott-Smith laid down the terms of their relationship with the Department when he met with over 200 strikers at Moolyella on 18 August 1949. 'I reiterated', he wrote:

---

39   Elliott-Smith to Middleton, 14 August 1949, SROWA 1949/0454/80 (underlining in original).

40   Middleton to Secretary, University Branch of ALP, 23 August 1949, SROWA 1949/0454/65.

41   Elliott-Smith, patrol journal, 13 August 1949, p. 12, SROWA 1949/0488/25.

(1) That McLeod was not and could not be accepted as their representative or spokesman

(2) That he had no standing either in the eyes of the Government or anyone else.

(3) That they must and could elect their own representative from amongst their own people

(4) That arbitration in relation to conditions and wages concerning their employment would only take place on the station upon which the natives were employed.

(5) That they must have confidence in the Department as now constituted. That I would have them supplied with:—

   (a) a football

   (b) a set of boxing gloves as they had requested.

(6) That no further strike action should be taken or could be tolerated.[42]

Elliott-Smith was still prepared to negotiate with pastoralists for the wage scale of 30/- to 70/- demanded by the strikers, and which they again stated as their primary demand, but his belief that their agreement had been broken meant that he was no longer willing to have them participate in negotiations as a group. Earlier indications that they would be accorded greater respect as a community were now replaced with a clear intimation that no such group authority would be recognised. Negotiations would only be undertaken between individual workers and employers once *marrngu* had already returned to station work. Orderly and compliant behaviour on the part of the strikers would be rewarded, not with a respectful acceptance of their right to exist and to make decisions as a group, but with a football and a set of boxing gloves. The authority of their leaders would not be accepted. Elliott-Smith dismissed Dooley's leadership as lacking both agency and rationality. 'The black-fellow appears to be completely unreasonable in his outlook and clearly led by influence not necessarily for his good', he wrote.[43]

McLeod was not at the Moolyella meeting on 18 August, although Elliott-Smith claimed to have sent messages inviting him to attend. Claiming to have been laid up with a ricked back, McLeod wrote to Pullen wondering at

---

42   Elliott-Smith, patrol journal, 18 August 1949, p. 14, SROWA 1949/0488/23.
43   Elliott-Smith, patrol journal, 13 August 1949, p. 13, SROWA 1949/0488/24.

Elliott-Smith's failure to make contact while he was in Marble Bar, particularly in view of his own success in lifting the wool ban 'to enable discussions to proceed in a better atmosphere'. He was most anxious to see Elliott-Smith, he wrote on the day of that officer's departure from the area, as there were several matters that needed his attention:

> It is possible, of course, that his views may have been changed for him and his avoiding me is a matter of deliberate policy. I have some knowledge of how politics enter into this, as, no doubt, you too will find in due course. Should this be so, it will put an entirely different aspect on the whole business, for in this case it will mean that the old policy of double dealing is to apply and if this is so I shall have reluctantly to make an unqualified withdrawal of all previous promises of support and secure the desired improvements in our own way as opportunities occur.[44]

Elliott-Smith dismissed this letter as an example of McLeod's twisted political machinations. While Dave Pullen had warmed to McLeod, finding him sincere, well informed and holding views in line with the new approach being adopted by the Department, Elliott-Smith was scathingly critical. McLeod was 'vain in the extreme', Elliott-Smith wrote:

> completely unscrupulous, and utterly insincere. In my opinion, his motives are entirely personal and possibly political and I am sure that he is exploiting the tin workers for his own benefit. Unfortunately for the moment, proof of this is not forthcoming.
>
> Until McLeod is removed or in some other way made ineffective, he will continue to be a source of infection and a menace to the well-being of the native people he dominates.[45]

Although the Department had come to accept the need to address Aboriginal grievances in the Pilbara, it still believed that to restore order it was necessary to counter McLeod's seditious influence. 'McLeod is the main influence, or has been in the Pilbara area', Elliott-Smith wrote:

> and has caused the Department considerable embarrassment for a long time – although he is not officially connected with the Communist Party, he has imbibed its doctrine and certainly preaches it ... He

---

44   Pullen to Middleton, 24 August 1949, SROWA 1949/0454/88.
45   Elliott-Smith, patrol report, 2 September 1949, SROWA 1949/0488/66.

detests the Department, constituted authority and hates the Roman Catholic Church.[46]

McLeod's anti-establishment doctrine had been able to take root in the fertile soil of Aboriginal discontent, Elliott-Smith believed, because the Department had failed to provide the necessary leadership to guide Aboriginal people along more peaceful paths towards social advancement. 'Logical and sane leadership' must now be employed to convince Aboriginal people that their aspirations could more successfully be achieved by placing their faith in the Department than by taking the 'communistic' path of defiant independence along which McLeod was leading them.[47] Improvements in Aboriginal status and conditions were necessary and, indeed, urgent, but these must be achieved, not through revolution, but through social evolution under departmental direction. The Department would lead Aboriginal people towards assimilation into the Australian community through the evolutionary stage of disciplined, paid labour.[48] 'Irreparable harm will be done', Elliott-Smith asserted, 'not only to the native question itself, but to the pastoral industry they serve, unless this administration does give the required lead'.[49]

Elliott-Smith had no further interaction with McLeod or with the strikers as a group. Lack of suitable housing in Broome meant that he was never able to adequately fulfil the role of Senior Administrative Officer for the northern region, and he was instead based in Perth as Deputy Commissioner until his resignation in February 1951, when he returned to New Guinea. He had little direct involvement in the Pilbara following his visits of July and August 1949, and what involvement he did have during 1950 was focused on assimilationist efforts being made towards the social inclusion of mixed-descent people in Marble Bar. Engaging in dialogue with McLeod or with the strikers was no longer seen as the way forward. 'I think with McLeod, as well as with his native adherents, that the best policy is to completely ignore them', Elliott-Smith wrote:

> By that I do not mean that we should slacken our efforts to offset any influence he may still weild [sic], but that our dealings with him or about him should in no way be ostentatious and give he or anyone connected with him the notoriety they so badly seek.[50]

---

46 Elliott-Smith to Middleton, 2 March 1950, p. 2, SROWA1949/0454/110.
47 Elliott-Smith to Middleton, 2 March 1950, p. 1, SROWA1949/0454/109.
48 Cowlishaw, *Rednecks, Eggheads and Blackfellas*, p. 121.
49 Elliott-Smith to Middleton, 2 March 1950, p. 1, SROWA 1949/0454/109.
50 Elliott-Smith, 'Summary of Visit to Pilbara, 18–27 March 1950', 4 April 1950, SROWA 1950/0119/22.

This reversion by the Department to its old position of opposing the movement, rather than working with it, may not have occurred had McLeod resisted the temptation to agree to the publication of Elliott-Smith's concession as evidence of union success in winning wage and condition improvements for Aboriginal workers. Under fire from the pastoralist lobby and the AWU, the Department was forced to deny the charge that one of its officers was making concessions to communists. Shortly after Elliott-Smith's return to Perth, questions regarding his agreement with McLeod were raised in the state's Legislative Assembly by Labor Member for Boulder and AWU official Cecil (Charlie) Oliver. Had Elliott-Smith negotiated any agreement with McLeod, Oliver asked, and had McDonald authorised departmental officers to negotiate wage rates and conditions of employment with McLeod? To both questions, McDonald answered in the negative.[51]

The kind of public exposure that had previously operated to the strikers' advantage by ensuring some level of restraint in government responses had in this case worked to their disadvantage, causing them to lose ground in their relationship with the Department. The Seamen's Union's activism itself had not been unproductive; the Department's more conciliatory attitude towards the strikers had been partly motivated by an imperative to prevent disruption to the pastoral industry and stop communists making political mileage from the strike. Its impact had already been felt by the time the *Kybra* berthed at Port Hedland on 16 July. The ban had contributed to the Department's determination to prevent further imprisonment and to its willingness to enter into genuine discussion with strikers, even to the point of removing O'Neill from the district. But McLeod's decision to allow the communist press to publicise Elliott-Smith's concession resulted in the Department again closing the door on genuine dialogue with the strikers. The strikers' significant achievement in reaching an agreement with a departmental officer that recognised their right to organise and to negotiate as a group had been lost.

---

51 McDonald, Parliamentary Debates (Hansard), Western Australia: Legislative Assembly, 23 August 1949, p. 1323.

Chapter 27

'In Their Struggle for Self Determination'

The End of the Strike, September 1949–1950

For *marrngu*, the sudden cooling of the relationship with the Department, and the stand-off between Elliott-Smith and McLeod just one month after the optimistic rapprochement of the previous month, must have been puzzling. In the weeks following Elliott-Smith's second visit to the area there seems to have been discussion and debate among strikers about the way forward. McLeod may have been prepared to break off negotiations and to 'secure the desired improvements in our own way', but for many strikers the political storm created by the wool ban must have seemed extraneous to the agreement they themselves had made with Elliott-Smith, under which it seemed that their concerns were finally being heard and treated with respect. Their own wage demands, clearly and repeatedly articulated to departmental officers, were not the Limestone–Mt Edgar rates that were the subject of the wool ban and Elliott-Smith's telegraphic concession, but rather the more moderate demand of 30/- to 70/- per week. This Elliott-Smith had agreed to secure for them, demonstrating his sincerity by securing the acquittal of the ten strikers, and in return for this undertaking, they had they taken no further action to disturb station labour. There was no reason for *marrngu* to believe that this arrangement, and the hope that strike objectives would finally be achieved, did not still stand.

In early September 1949, *marrngu* from across the region took the opportunity presented by the annual Marble Bar races to hold meetings to discuss the future direction of the movement. A major topic of discussion seems to have been the question of whether to accept Elliott-Smith's assurances that their demands would be met, or whether to continue to 'secure the desired improvements in our own way', as McLeod now advocated. Some may have been critical of McLeod for undermining their agreement with Elliott-Smith. Constable Marshall reported that about 400 Aboriginal people were attending the meetings, and that debate for and against McLeod was taking place. As they were asking for Elliott-Smith, presumably to clarify matters relating to their arrangements with him, Marshall recommended his urgent attendance.[1] Elliott-Smith was unavailable, however.[2] Noel Hawke, the officer preparing to replace O'Neill as the Department's representative in the district, flew up from Perth and spent a few days there while the meetings were being held, but Elliott-Smith's failure to attend must have caused *marrngu* to wonder if the Department was not simply reverting to type after all.[3]

Nevertheless, many strikers were prepared to place their trust in the Department and to look to its officers to negotiate wage and condition improvements. Individual employment contracts were negotiated between workers and employers on stations rather than at Moolyella. In November, the new manager of Warrawagine Station, Ron Johnson, visited Moolyella to arrange for the return of workers who had left in June over the previous manager's refusal to increase wages by 10/- per week. Workers now agreed to return, but, before doing so, striker Roy Dobey arranged for Moolyella storekeeper Don Thompson to wire Elliott-Smith in Perth of their intention. 'We are returning expecting yourself or Mr Hawke to come along at your earliest convenience and fix our contracts with the Station Manager', he wrote.[4]

Marrngu had walked off Warrawagine Station in June 1949 when their request for a 10/- wage increase to £2/10/- had been refused, but by early 1950, all male workers there were receiving £3 per week, with the exception of an eighteen-year-old, who was receiving £2.[5] Native Affairs reports make no mention of pay rates for women at Warrawagine, who were possibly still undertaking domestic service without payment. The £3 per week wage for men may have been for the services of both themselves and their wives. Nevertheless, the wage increases for male workers were significant. In 1946, most had been unpaid, and the wages of skilled workers were well below the £3 now being paid. Bruce Wandarri, who had worked as a blacksmith, had received only 12/- per week, from which he had to purchase his own tobacco and clothing for himself and his children.[6]

---

1 Marshall to Middleton, telegram, 8 September 1949, SROWA 1949/0454/96.
2 Middleton to Marshall, telegram, 8 September 1949, SROWA 1949/0454/97.
3 Middleton to Marshall, telegram, 8 September 1949, SROWA 1949/0454/97; Hawke, Native Affairs journal, 8–16 September 1949, SROWA 1949/0160/62–64.
4 Roy Dobey ('per D. T.') to Elliott-Smith, telegram, 21 November 1949, SROWA 1949/0454/100.
5 Hawke, Native Affairs patrol journal, 24 February 1950, SROWA 1950/0173.
6 Marshall to McBeath, 23 December 1946, p. 2, SROWA 1943/0621/22.

Dobey wrote to Elliott-Smith, expressing satisfaction at their employment conditions. 'Re the work at Warrawagine, everything seems to be going along satisfactorily', he wrote:

> and we are satisfied with the wages and food and are looking forward to our two houses from south arriving. We have a kitchen of our own and a new stove is on order and should be along soon, and we have a bough shed to dine under or in. The only thing not quite right is the housing but we think Ron Johnson is doing his very best to get that for us and we believe he is doing his very best in every way.[7]

Middleton was heartened by this evidence of striker confidence in the Department. He forwarded Dobey's letters to the state's new Minister for Native Affairs, Herbert Parker. 'In view of the criticism and abuse that has been levelled at this Department in the past over the arrest and imprisonment of the native "strikers" in the Pilbara District', he wrote, 'and the emphatic refusal of the Moolyella natives to co-operate with Mr. O'Neill and other Departmental officers in any way, it is refreshing to see the very evident change of feeling towards the Department exemplified by the two letters'.[8]

By the early months of 1950, a significant number of strikers had taken employment, and labour shortages on stations had eased considerably. Elliott-Smith was happy to state that:

> without exception, Stations in the Pilbara District are now fully staffed with native labour and are being paid in accordance with the rates they themselves requested during my visit in August of last year. Housing conditions, amenities and sanitation are being greatly improved and I would say that generally speaking they are content and reasonably happy with their lot.[9]

Although labour shortages had not been resolved to quite the extent that Elliott-Smith claimed, Middleton was relieved to learn that the strike was drawing to an end. 'The improvement in the industrial situation', he wrote, was 'undoubtedly due to the efforts of Officers of the Department' and 'some very useful "anti-McLeod" propaganda' carried out by Elliott-Smith

---

7   Dobey to Elliott-Smith, 12 December 1949, SROWA 1949/0454/103.
8   Middleton to Minister Parker, 14 December 1949, SROWA1949/0454/105.
9   Elliott-Smith, 'Summary of Visit to Pilbara, 18–27 March 1950', 4 April 1950, SROWA 1950/0119/22.

throughout the district.[10] He passed news of the Department's success to local newspapers, and the following day the *West Australian* carried an article under the headline 'Native Station Hands Return to Their Former Jobs'. 'A white man – alleged in 1946 to be a Communist – had persuaded the natives to leave their employment', the article read, but following the intervention of departmental officials 'most of the original strikers had returned to work and there appeared to be a general drifting back of natives to stations'.[11] After four years of losing battles against the strikers, the Department felt that it was finally winning the war.

But the victors of the strike were the *marrngu*. They were not 'drifting back' to stations, but many were choosing to negotiate a return to station employment. Although the right to bargain collectively was still denied them, they had, through strike action, earned the right to negotiate as individuals the conditions under which they would accept work. Dobey's letters are evidence that the accord established between Elliott-Smith and strikers in July 1949 had not been entirely broken, at least as far as *marrngu* were concerned. Many were willing to honour their undertaking and to look to the Department to represent their interests in their relationship with pastoralists. And the Department was willing to negotiate wages and conditions according to striker demands. To obtain workers, employers now needed to convince the Department of their willingness to pay wages in line with these demands. Pastoralists who were slow to raise wages and improve conditions found labour difficult to obtain.[12] In April 1950, the manager of Bungalow (Coongan) Station applied to Hawke for additional Aboriginal workers. 'Nil available', Hawke wrote, 'and in any case I have stations offering better living conditions listed who have vacancies for additional boys'.[13]

Pastoralists could no longer claim that providing station rations and tolerating an Aboriginal presence on their pastoral leases was sufficient recompense for the labour they received. The pre-strike claim that such labour was of little value, tolerated out of kindness rather than need, had been successfully challenged by the strike. 'If little payment for work is slavery then a mild form of slavery did exist in the North west up to a few years ago', the manager of Corunna Downs Station, Keith Bligh, admitted to the *West Australian* in November 1949. But:

---

10 Middleton to Parker, 14 March 1950, SROWA 1950/0173.
11 *West Australian*, 15 March 1950, p. 16.
12 Hawke, extract of patrol report no. 2 of 1949/50, 22 February to 4 March 1950, SROWA 1949/0454/07.
13 Hawke, patrol journal, 24 April 1950, SROWA 1949/0160/90.

as far as the Pilbara district was concerned slavery did not exist now. In recent years wages had been increased and the living conditions of the native considerably improved. Admittedly, [Bligh] added, this was largely because the pastoralists had realised how difficult it would be to work their properties without native labour.[14]

While prepared to admit the value of Aboriginal labour, Bligh was quick to insist that this realisation was not the result of the strike. 'It must be understood that most of the natives were satisfied and happy with their conditions' he added:

> but unfortunately a Communist minority had debarred numbers of willing workers from carrying on with their jobs ... There were certain elements in the cities who made it their hobby to take up the cudgels of the native but a native was still a native and ... on entirely different lines from any other nationality, creed, sect or colour. Under these conditions ... the native is perfectly content to carry on with his job on an employee–employer basis provided he has no further interference from subversive Communist elements.[15]

Despite the restatement of racist understandings of the immutable otherness of Aboriginal people, expressed as 'the native is still a native', and elsewhere in the article as 'the native is still a blackfellow', Bligh's reference to Aboriginal satisfaction with the 'employee–employer basis' of labour relations was an admission that Aboriginal workers were employees and not mendicants who did a little work in return for squatter charity. It was a significant outcome of the strike. 'Pastoralists, although well aware of the fact, must continue to be made aware of the extremely valuable asset they have in northern native labour', Elliott-Smith wrote. 'The time has long past when the employer of native labour, and I speak now of the Pilbara District, may treat them as of no account'.[16]

Marrngu had demanded that their contribution to the pastoral industry be recognised and adequately rewarded. They insisted on having signed employment agreements to place their relationship with pastoralists on a more equitable and more respectful footing. The preference of many workers to negotiate wages without keep suggests a desire to break away from the rationing relationship that had underpinned labour relations before the strike.

---

14 *Northern Times*, 3 November 1949, p. 4, 'North-West Natives'.
15 *Northern Times*, 3 November 1949, p. 4, 'North-West Natives'.
16 Elliott-Smith to Middleton, 2 March 1950, p. 2, SROWA 1949/0454/110.

They had demanded, and achieved, a relationship with pastoralists that no longer involved police coercion. Pastoralists now had to attract workers with competitive wages and living conditions, rather than depend on the police to ensure worker compliance. *Marrngu* were no longer tied to a particular station to the extent that they had been before 1946, having gained greater freedom to move between stations, or between station labour and other forms of work such as mining. The squatters' unwritten law of never employing Aboriginal people who 'belonged' to another station was no longer adhered to; Elliott-Smith noted 'the keen competition among pastoralists and other employers for the services of skilled men. They are prepared to pay top wages for these'.[17]

To some extent, squattocratic rule in the Pilbara had been broken down. Before the strike, the Department had been anxious to support pastoralist authority and keep government interference in pastoral labour relations to a minimum, fearing that pastoralists would follow through with their threat of expelling Aboriginal communities from stations if the burden of supporting them became too great. When *marrngu* left the stations and established their own communities, squatters had called on the Department to intervene to restore control, and were quick to complain when their labour needs were not met. The Department had accepted criticism for the ongoing unrest and responsibility for its resolution. But the pastoralists' authority had been undermined by the strike. The Department now pointed to the squatters' failure to use their influence over Aboriginal people to prevent the strike happening in the first place. 'After all the Department's control in those days was remote', Elliott-Smith wrote, 'and it was indeed unfortunate that ... unified action could not have been taken and so possibly obviated all the subsequent unpleasantness'.[18] The squatters' failure to pay for Aboriginal labour according to its true value, and to provide adequate living conditions, had created the conditions that led to the strike, the Department asserted. It was now up to employers to resolve the situation in the Pilbara. They must 'strive voluntarily', Elliott-Smith wrote, 'to achieve and maintain a standard of conditions that must inevitably offset any inspired influence that may arise'.[19] And the Department was there to ensure that they did so. 'Employers [in the Pilbara] are keen to see improvements take place in the pastoral industry, with regard to native labour', Elliott-Smith wrote, 'but

---

17 Elliott-Smith, 'Summary of Visit to Pilbara, 18–27 March 1950 and 4 April 1950', SROWA 1950/0119/22.
18 Elliott-Smith to Middleton, 10 March 1950, SROWA 1950/0488/6–7.
19 Elliott-Smith to Middleton, 2 March 1950, p. 2, SROWA 1949/0454/110.

they need leadership'.[20] Pastoralists as well as *marrngu* were to be guided along an evolutionary road to reform.

It would be a few years yet before the Department was willing to use the term 'exploitation' in this regard, but that time would come. 'The plain truth', Middleton was to write in late 1953:

> is that the pastoralists and other employers in the Port Hedland district are now reaping the benefit of their own exploitation, neglect and bad treatment of natives in the past, and instead of acknowledging their own guilt they are trying to lay it at the door of this Department.[21]

The strike also created pressure for change in pastoral labour relations in other parts of the state. The activism of Pilbara Aboriginal people stood as a warning to pastoralists in other districts that similar action could be taken elsewhere if Aboriginal labour conditions were not improved. On his tour of the Kimberley in 1949, Elliott-Smith urged pastoralists to anticipate the kind of unrest occurring in the Pilbara and to take steps to forestall such action by improving conditions for Aboriginal people on their stations.[22] Forwarding Elliott-Smith's report to the Pastoralists Association in September 1949, Middleton called for a conference between the Department and pastoralists on 'the question of the early introduction of a scheme for the payment of wages where not already paid, and such other matters as are rapidly becoming contentious and embarrassing throughout the North'.[23] Referring to the strike movement as 'McLeod', Elliott-Smith wrote that 'it cannot be denied that he has played a leading part in making the State aware of the necessity for reform in native employment conditions'.[24]

Through strike action, *marrngu* had achieved a presence and a status in relation to the settler community that they had not previously enjoyed. Hawke warned *marrngu* that, in continuing their civil disobedience activities, they were 'not advancing their own status among the community', but the opposite was the case.[25] While their social, cultural and religious world still remained hidden from most non-Aboriginal people, *marrngu* had stepped

---

20 Elliott-Smith, patrol report, 1 September 1949, p. 4, SROWA 1949/0488/63.
21 Middleton to Minister for Native Affairs Hegney, 1 December 1953, p. 2, SROWA 1953/0127/79.
22 Elliott-Smith, patrol report, 1 September 1949, p. 3, SROWA 1949/0488/64.
23 Middleton to Secretary, Pastoralists Association, 16 September 1949, SROWA 1947/0220/11.
24 Elliott-Smith, patrol report, 1 September 1949, p. 2, SROWA 1949/0488/65.
25 Hawke to Elliott-Smith, 19 July 1950, SROWA 1949/0454/119.

'In Their Struggle for Self Determination'

out of the shadows and made themselves visible. In the parlance of the squatters, they were no longer 'the niggers in the creek'. Lines of demarcation that had kept them socially and economically excluded had been erased by three years of sustained activism. Their actions had created awareness in the settler community of their existence as men and women striving to make better lives for themselves and their children, belying the widely-asserted claim that a low level of social or biological development made them ideally suited and perfectly happy to live powerless and impoverished lives as low-paid or unpaid station workers. Early fears of unruly and disruptive behaviour by a large, uncontrolled group of Aboriginal people had proven to be unfounded; while squatters continued to complain of their activities, other members of the settler community found the strikers to be peaceful and law-abiding. Many were impressed by the order and cleanliness of the Twelve Mile camp. The arrest in chains of large numbers of men struck non-Aboriginal Pilbara residents as unnecessarily heavy-handed, and the way the cards were stacked against them when they appeared before the magistrate highlighted the injustice of a system in which their 'protectors' were also their prosecutors.

When Dave Pullen visited Port Hedland in July 1949, he heard many expressions of concern at the poor treatment and lack of justice accorded to Aboriginal people arising from the close alliance between the Department and the police. 'The opinions rarely varied', Pullen wrote:

> The townspeople blamed the Dept. for the trouble that has arisen because of the errors of the past and because Native Affairs Officers usually moved about in company with the police. The pastoralists also came in for criticism inasmuch that they refused to even talk with McLeod or to try to find out what he was agitating for.[26]

McLeod himself noted a growing level of awareness in the Pilbara. 'It is of interest', he wrote in April 1949, when thirty-three men were arrested:

> that this present campaign of persecution of native workers has aroused considerable adverse criticism amongst local residents and shows that at last there is becoming evident signs that we can expect some support at least in future and may be able to build up a solid movement locally in support of the natives in their struggle for self determination.[27]

---

26 Pullen, patrol report, 30 June 1949, SROWA 1949/0456.
27 Quoted in *Maritime Worker*, 30 April 1949, p. 3, 'The Persecution of Native Workers!'

Elliott-Smith also noted that the strike had created an awareness in the Pilbara of the issue of Aboriginal rights. For all his disparagement of McLeod, he admitted that 'McLeod, though a periodic headache to the Department, has done more than any other source to make the Pilbara District native conscious'.[28] Certainly McLeod was vocal in speaking of the issues and influential in the developing ideology of the strikers, but it was the actions over three years of several hundred men and women that had been most effective in bringing to the public consciousness the inequities and injustices that impacted their lives.

Through their activism, *marrngu* had also reshaped their relationship with the police. 'They were the boss for us', Billy Thomas said when recalling their sense of powerlessness in dealings with the police before the strike. But *marrngu* would no longer be cowed. They had stood together in the face of threats and bluster, insisting that if one of their number was imprisoned, they should all be imprisoned. Their willingness to risk arrest and imprisonment was making them free. They knew now that the powers of the police and the courts were not absolute but were circumscribed by law. If threatened with arrest, they now asked under what law they were to be arrested. Although still subject to the discriminatory *Native Administration Act 1936*, they now had access to knowledge about their legal rights and were prepared to stand up for these in court. The strike had brought public scrutiny that was creating pressure for a more just, and less arbitrary, application of the law, at least with regard to Aboriginal people involved in the movement. There was growing pressure to discontinue the practice of using chains on Aboriginal prisoners. The practice of the killing of dogs in dawn raids on Aboriginal camps continued, but this would be successfully challenged by *marrngu* in 1951.

The gradual process of disentangled policing from the administration of Aboriginal affairs in the north was also brought about in part by the activities of the strikers. Responses to the strike, both by the police in the role as Protectors of Natives and by departmental representatives who were ex-policemen, had proved ineffective. That the strikers were able to achieve the removal of Laurie O'Neill from the district is a clear indication of their influence in bringing about the shift away from hard policing in Aboriginal administration. The answer to the situation in the Pilbara was 'not prosecution nor persecution', Elliott-Smith wrote, 'but constant personal attention by a competent officer of the Department to the problem and counter propaganda applied similarly'.[29]

---

28 Elliott-Smith to Middleton, 2 March 1950, SROWA1949/0454/109–111.
29 Elliott-Smith, patrol report, 1 September 1949, p. 1, SROWA 1949/0488/66.

'IN THEIR STRUGGLE FOR SELF DETERMINATION'

The Department believed that its counter propaganda was having a positive effect in undermining the strike movement. By early 1950, only fifty strikers were still working tin at Moolyella. Elliott-Smith was pleased. 'There is a definite breaking up of the native factions at Marble Bar', he wrote, 'clearly brought about by the Department's added interest and the helpful attitude of the better type of white people'.[30] Hawke was only prepared to say that the movement was 'possibly on the wane'.[31] Elliott-Smith sought clarification. 'There appears to be a clear indication that there is a split-up of natives throughout the District', he wrote to Hawke, 'but it is not clear from your report as to whether there has been a wholesale return of natives to pastoral employment. I should be glad of some information of this, if you can supply it'.[32]

In fact, the return to pastoral employment was not as 'wholesale' as Elliott-Smith hoped. Not everyone who left Moolyella at this time took work on stations. Now that they had gained confidence and increased status in the community, some chose to continue to live independently. Cranky shifted from Moolyella to Munda Station to join a group of ten people, including Paddy Dean and strike leader Coombie, gathering buffel grass seed, which they transported for sale in Port Hedland on Coombie's truck.[33] Mining offered another source of income. About fifty strikers from Moolyella were working with McLeod in the Pilgangoora mining area, extracting columbite, tin and tantalite, using the yandy in the process of separating the ore. 'I started off with 25 in the first place and took them to Pilgangoora', McLeod told an inquiry in 1952:

> The 25 consisted of men, women and a few children. They came from Moolyella. We started a prospecting campaign in this district. We got some production of tin, tantalite, columbite and some gold. We built the camp up to 75 before long, including women and children. We then went through the district producing and prospecting as we went.[34]

This mining venture exposed McLeod to the risk of prosecution for breach of employment permit regulations or section 39 of the *Native Administration*

---

30 Elliott-Smith to Middleton, 2 March 1950, SROWA 1949/0454/109–111.
31 Hawke, patrol report no. 2 of 1949/1950, 22 February to 4 March 1950, SROWA 1949/0454/7.
32 Elliott-Smith to Hawke, 24 February 1950, SROWA 1950/0173.
33 Hawke, patrol report no. 2 of 1950/1951, 2 August to 8 September 1950, SROWA 1950/0741/11.
34 McLeod, statement to Committee Investigating Native Labour, February–March 1952, p. 14, SROWA1952/0830/112.

Act 1936. Plans and movements were kept under wraps. 'Although the natives when I first visited Moolyella informed me that quite a few of their number had moved to the Pilgangoora area', Hawke wrote, 'they were very non-commital when inquiries were made as to the reason for the move or the mode of transport, and no tangible evidence was obtained'.[35]

In fact, McLeod was transporting people in his old Ford V8, doing so secretly at night. 'At that time McLeod would come in stealthily to take us away', Maggie Ginger (Nyirrarlpi) remembered:[36]

> We had all gathered together at Moolyella ... McLeod had to come in secretly at night to pick us up. He took us all the way to Pilgangoora. That place was full of all us *marrngu* now. We stayed there while some others went to Blue Bar. He brought us all there, one lot at a time.
>
> He can't see'm, that's the proper dark way he gotta go, pick us. We bin stop Moolyella ... He can't see'm policeman, no. He gotta go dark way. We tell'm now – *Oh, he coming*. All going, we bin go Pilgangoora, cart all the people. Nother mob Blue Bar, big mob ... Nother mob going Cooglegong.[37]

Hawke's report of movement from Moolyella to the Blue Bar and Mosquito Creek (Minyminy) mining area was welcomed by Elliott-Smith as evidence that the Department's opposition to the movement was bearing fruit. 'Break-up!' he wrote. 'Good'.[38] Certainly, the movement had declined in numbers, but it was not fading away under the guidance of the Department's positive leadership as Elliott-Smith thought. Rather, it was finding another direction. Numbers involved were initially small. With stations now paying wages in line with striker demands, and in light of the agreement made with Elliott-Smith, many *marrngu* were unconvinced that this mining venture with McLeod was the best way forward for the movement. By mid-1950, however, the decision was made to trial the mining venture and to reassess the position the following year at meetings held during the Marble Bar races. One of Elliott-Smith's 'better type of white people' reported in June that *marrngu* at Moolyella had 'now reached a very awkward stage where

---

35 Hawke to Middleton, 1 March 1950, SROWA 1949/0454/113.
36 Maggie Ginger (Nyirrarlpi), recorded by Anne Scrimgeour, 19 May 1993, translated from Nyangumarta, AIATSIS collection, soundfile 'Nyirrarlpi 19'.
37 Maggie Ginger (Nyirrarlpi), recorded by Anne Scrimgeour, 19 May 1993, author's collection.
38 Hawke, patrol report no. 1 of 1949/1950, 21 February 1950, p. 5, SROWA 1950/0173.

the majority are of the opinion that, "We may as well give McLeod a go until race-time etc"'.[39]

By August, everyone had left Moolyella, and Sampie's school at the Twelve Mile was closed. Hawke reported that there had been:

> a general exodus of natives from this area to the Cooglegong bent on tin mining for McLeod. Information has it that the natives are going to give McLeod a trial to Race Meeting time in September next, and will then decide whether they will continue.[40]

By the end of 1950, there were 200 men and women involved in the mining venture.[41] McLeod's knowledge of minerals and markets, together with the extensive knowledge of Country and highly developed powers of observation that *marrngu* brought to the venture, would be a recipe for mining success. Valuable discoveries of tanto-columbite and wolfram, extracted using hand tools and yandies, would bring large profits. In 1951, six years after *marrngu* struck for 30/- per week, their mining venture would earn £500,000, equivalent to $2 million today. Their dream of having legal possession, in *walypila* terms, of their own piece of land as a community base – a dream first imagined in early discussions between Kitchener, Clancy McKenna and McLeod in 1944 and which had taken hold at the 1945 race-time meetings at the Port Hedland Four Mile – would be realised with the purchase from mining profits of Yandeyarra and two other stations.

At meetings held during the Marble Bar races in September 1951, at the end of the trial period of 'giving McLeod a go', *marrngu* would decide that the mining venture was indeed the way forward for the movement. Men and women from across the region, including most of those who had returned to station employment, would again leave their workplaces to take part. By 1952, more than 700 people would be involved, more than at any time during the strike, living and working in shifting mining camps set up across a wide area of the Pilbara, with both men and women engaging in mining. White Springs Mission, once seen as a solution to the problems in the Pilbara, would fail to attract adherents and would be abandoned. From the strike would grow a confident, autonomous and, for a few years at least, prosperous Indigenous social and economic organisation developed by *marrngu* on the

---

39 Eileen Thompson to Elliott-Smith, 27 June 1950, p. 2, SROWA 1950/0088/24.
40 Hawke, extract of patrol report 1950/51 (otherwise undated), SROWA 1949/0454/126; Hawke to Middleton, 1 August 1950, SROWA 1949/0454/124–125.
41 Boyland, District Inspector of Mines, to State Mining Engineer, 14 November 1950, SROWA 1950/0096/12.

foundation of the continuation and adaptation of Aboriginal social, cultural and religious mores.

The formation of this community was a highly significant outcome of the strike. It would be built on the ideology of non-violent and proudly assertive independence, forged in the crucible of the strike movement from a melding of McLeod's socialist dreams with their own aspirations, determination and vision, strengthened by the ongoing maintenance of Aboriginal Law, culture and language. In the early years of the 1950s, their right to exist as a community with authority to make decisions as a community would finally be recognised and respected. But the history of the movement in the 1950s, its remarkable successes and its struggles and disappointments, is another story.

Appendix A

Cathedral Chronicle

Cathedral Chronicle, **March 1947, pp. 1–2**

COMMUNISTS AND THE NORTH-WEST NATIVES. Don McLeod's letter answered. It will be recalled that the 'Cathedral Chronicle' in its August and September issues of last year dealt at length with the strike and unrest among the North-West natives in so far as they were the result of communistic agitation and inspiration. It was also pointed out that the 'Committee for the Defence of Native Rights' was just another stunt to advance the interests of the Communist Party at the expense of the Natives. We are now in receipt of a letter purporting to come from Mr. Don McLeod which charges the 'Chronicle' with gross distortion of the facts. Mr. McLeod was the central figure in the strike and was convicted under Section 47 of the Native Administration Act.

We publish in full the letter (signed on behalf of Don McLeod per???? *a second party whose initials are indecipherable*) and add our comments after each paragraph.

It was with interest that I read a copy of your September Chronicle and the prominence you gave to the activities of the North-West Natives.

> Comment:– You should keep on reading the 'Chronicle' for in this way you will learn something of the treachery of the Communist Party, of which you profess to be a member. Remember, however, that you are very small fry in the Party's scheme of things. When it suits its purpose it will dump or liquidate you and your equals. It has happened to greater than you. Incidentally, we gave prominence to the activities of communists among the natives and not 'to the activities of the North-West Natives' as you so naively remark.

Letter continues:– It is a pity your sources of information are so unreliable, for it is evident that your interest in the matter is profound.

Comment:– It is a pity we understand Communism so well for otherwise you would get away with quite a lot. Unlike you and other puppets of the Communist Party, we understand Communism. And understanding it, we are able to detect its presence even when it tries to shield itself with a barrage of crocodile tears for the unfortunate natives. You would recognise that as deduction, a mental process with which you must surely be acquainted, for are not all Communists passionately devoted to the culture of the mind? As you remark, our interest in this matter is profound. And why wouldn't it? In the first place we are desperately concerned to defend the natives against communistic aggression and exploitation. They are honest people and quite possibly believe you when you say you want to emancipate them. But we know that communistic emancipation is slavery of the vilest kind. Then again, our profound interest for the natives and their activities has many concrete expressions. You must surely have heard of Catholic missionaries; you know those people, men and women, whom communists delight in butchering as the opportunity arises. There are such people here in Australia, even under your own eyes, who are devoting their lives (not their tongues) to the welfare of the natives and half-castes. Did you ever hear of New Norcia? Did you ever hear of Drysdale Mission? Did you ever hear of Beagle Bay Mission? Did you ever hear of Wandering Brook Mission? Did you ever hear of the Leper Colony at Derby, in the charge of the famous St. John of God Sisters? Those Catholic Missions are but a few of the many throughout Australia and there are more to come. So you see we are profoundly interested in the natives and our interest is very practical indeed. How many armchair reformers in the 'Committee for the Defence of Native Rights' would sacrifice their lives to the care of natives afflicted with the dread disease of leprosy. Would they sit in a bus or train beside a native? Do not answer. We know how they would shrivel like an asp leaf at the very thought of such contact: 'Distance lends enchantment to the scene' and all that.

Letter continues:– I am enclosing herewith a copy of the pamphlet printed by the 'Committee for the Defence of Native Rights' which will give you a true version of the facts. It is obviously impossible to do justice to any case when the argument, as in this case, rests on false premises. I refer to the reprint of the 'West Australian' article, which is obviously a gross distortion.

Comment:– Having read the pamphlet we are more convinced than ever that the strike among the natives was the result of communist agitation,

Appendix A

and that the so-called Committee for the Defence of Native Rights is a puppet show. It tells us that the natives met in July 1945, at Port Hedland to discuss their deplorable condition and that they requested you (Mr. D. W. McLeod) to represent them in their demands for better conditions. As a fairy tale that would be quite good. But it's too good to be true. How amazing that the natives should have picked upon a communist to represent them: Did you, by any chance, whisper into their ear that you were the man for the job? Don't you see, the pamphlet does tell us how the natives picked on you. And there in lies the sting. But it is quite in keeping with the tactics of Communism to associate with any move that will bring prestige to the Communist Party. Do not forget, of course, that you left it in writing that all these natives were potential communists: That came out in your trial. You did not write that all these natives were so many people who could be raised to the standard of the white man. No, they were all potential communists and as such, of immense use to the interests of the Communist Party.

Letter Continues:– Had I the opportunity of attending the meeting referred to in this article, I would have been able to refute many of the deliberate mis-statements and particularly Father Bryan, if the 'West' account is a true version of his contribution. I am referring to the alleged hangers-on, whom the squatters are supposed to support in order to secure the services of a man and his wife.

Comment:– Had you been at the meeting, perhaps you would have answered the questions which the Rev. Mr. Hodge, Secretary of the Committee for the Defence of Native Rights, refused to answer. He would not divulge all the names of those who made up the Committee. Why? Had these people no caste in the eyes of the public? Were they too closely associated with the Communist Party? We smell a rat and a Red one: Being neither the appointed nor the self-appointed spokesman for the squatters we have no obligation to defend them against your charge. Their statements were supported by people who are not squatters, but who spoke as independent witnesses and from first-hand knowledge. You are not an independent witness, for, being a communist, you have an axe to grind, and unless you grind it, it will fall on your own neck. As for the other members of the Committee, they know no more about the natives than the natives know about them. And that is nothing! In singling out Father Bryan for special contradiction, you prove yourself a true hireling of Moscow. A Catholic priest is always big game for the communists, more especially when he has the standing that Father Bryan has among the natives and half-castes of the North-West. A Catholic priest spells disaster for communism. It is not for nothing that communists detest the Catholic Church and its priests. The Church stands for human freedom within the framework of morality. Communism stands for human slavery, ignoring all morality. Think for a moment of Archbishop Stepinac, Tito's victim. In the eyes of communists, every Catholic priest is an Archbishop Stepinac, and is represented as an 'enemy of the people'. In the North-West communists would represent Father Bryan and every other priest as an enemy of the native, although the exact opposite is true. As we shall see, Father Bryan's statement at the meeting in question is slavishly true, but is represented as false by communists because it gives the lie to their propaganda.

Letter continues:– At the present time there are, out from Port Hedland, some 208 native strikers, the subject of this controversy. Of this number 105 are able bodied workers, 77 are women, 21 are children of school age, and five children under school age. It will at once be seen that instead of each man having two wives and several dependents, the proportions are less than one dependent both wife and child to each male worker.

Comment:– In challenging Father Bryan's statement re 'hangers-on' as you are pleased to call them, you give a census of the strikers at the present camp out of Port Hedland, appealing to that as the normal state of affairs. But that is not so. Father Bryan was not talking about natives as gathered together in your native strike camp, but as they are when dispersed throughout the stations on which they work. The following statistics from a few of the stations bear out Father Bryan's statement and dispose of your challenge.

'Hangers-On'

On DeGrey Station, shearing time, 1946, there were 62 natives, of whom 32 were men, 24 women and 6 children. The average number of men who worked and were paid per month was 22, whilst the average number of women who worked with pay was 12. Thus, to employ 34 natives another 28 had to be kept. Of the 34 employed, 9 averaged about 2 hours work per day. These 28 'hangers-on' as you call them, lived on the station and received clothes and rations.

Appendix A

Two Wives and Four Children

On Mulyie Station there is a native who has two wives and four children. One of the wives does odd jobs whilst the second wife and four children are housed, fed and clothed.

Five Work but Sixteen Kept

Yarrie Station keeps and feeds 16 natives in return for the work of 5. One of the men who is quite useless has two wives and three children. One of the wives works whilst the other and the children are pure liabilities on the station. Here is a case where 5 people are kept on the strength of the work of one woman!

On Munda Station a native, Snowball by name, has two wives and five children. In this instance Snowball is employed whilst his two wives and children are maintained. Occasionally the two wives do odd jobs but as there are twelve other women employed on the station there is little or nothing for them to do.

Rations

The following system of rationing obtains at De Grey Station. When going for a pinki (holiday) the natives are given rations to cover the period they intend to be away. If they remain on the station they can at all times receive rations for the asking. As a general rule if a native is put off for slack time or rain he is rationed. On the other hand, if he goes pinki when it is most inconvenient for the manager he is given a week's ration but is expected to pay for further supplies. Most of the smaller stations including Pardoo and Mulyie ration the natives (i.e. feed them) all the time they are off whether they are sent for pinki or ask for one. All aged hands incapable of work get their rations every Sunday. Women with young babies do not work but yet they are fed and clothed. The rations per head consist of 10lbs flour, 2 lbs. sugar, one pannikin of tea, baking powder, soap and tobacco.

Cost of Feed

It is estimated that the actual cost of feeding a native is about 15/6 per week. The cost of meat is not included in this. The average number of sheep killed per day for native rations is one and a half.

Clothes

The cost at De Grey Station at last shearing was just under £200. Each native received a rug and cardigan, the women received in addition dress and handkerchiefs and the men shirt and trousers. Up to 1943 the men received a full tweed suit when war shortages made the practice impossible of continuation. At Christmas women and children receive an issue of clothes and a billycan. Men and boys who are not employed are issued with clothes about four times a year, whilst boots and hats are supplied as often as required.

Medical

In addition to the foregoing expenses the Station has to pay £1 per head per annum into the medical contributory scheme whereby all natives receive free medical attention.

Who is Guilty of Distortion

The foregoing statistics from a few stations make it abundantly clear that Father Bryan's statement 'that on the whole the natives were well and fairly treated' was no distortion of facts. By no stretch of the imagination can their lot be described as slavery as the communists say. Father Bryan did not suggest that these conditions were absolutely ideal or incapable of improvement. He was speaking to a motion which in effect stated that the natives were the slaves of the squatters, being underpaid, underfed, and under clothed. On the evidence of their own senses both Father Bryan and Rev. Mr. Boulter, of the Methodist Inland Mission, rebutted this communistic calumny. As missionaries meeting the natives and observing their mode of existence on the stations these gentlemen are in a better position to gather facts than the armchair reformers of the Committee for the Defence of Native Rights. 'Metropolitan Squatters' whose pet hobby seems to be to assail the characters of the men in the outback who are doing a good job for the country. It is simply rot of the most stupid kind to think that the native is going to be uplifted by higher wages. Assuming that higher wages is the solution to the problem and that the native is educated to the use of money, who is going to employ him in his present state of 'civilisation'. Through no fault of their own they lack that initiative which is required of any worker; excepting as stockmen, they are unskilled in every other branch of work. And for this

Appendix A

reason they require the constant supervision of an overseer. The higher wage agitation inspired by the communists can only have one of three effects: Stations will not employ natives, or they will employ only such as can work, dismissing all followers, or keeping workers and followers on as at present and deduct the cost of maintaining the drones from the wages of the workers. No matter how we slew these alternatives the natives are going to be the losers! But the communists will be happy for they will have achieved their objective – discontent among the natives there by rendering them vulnerable to communistic propaganda.

Letter continues:– Had I not been in jail (bail was disallowed) I could have been present at this meeting, and put an altogether different complexion on the picture, which in a rue light is seen to be the case where the squatters are fighting to retain the services of the slave labour against the opposition of an enlightened public.

Comment:– fortunate for you that you live in a free country and not one run on communistic lines for otherwise you would not be in gaol but in a concentration camp or in a quick-lime grave! You were in gaol awaiting bail not because you criticised the law (which brings dire penalties in communistic counties) but because you broke it. There is a difference, as you can see, and it is the distinguishing mark between totalitarianism and democracy, between injustice and justice, between slavery and freedom, between Communism and democratic methods if you acted in Russia or any of its puppet States in Eastern Europe as you acted in this state you would not be in gaol but in a state of liquidation; you would not be awaiting a fair trial for such a thing is not allowed by Communism! No doubt you would put a different complexion on the picture, but we guess it would be Red. From the report of the public meeting it was by no means obvious that 'the squatters were fighting to retain the services of their slave labour'. They were there to defend themselves against unscrupulous people who are carrying on a campaign of character assassination in accordance with the highest ideals of Communism. The institution of slavery exists to-day only in the Soviet Union and such countries as have been forcibly incorporated into it since the war. Into the unspeakable system of communistic slavery you would entice the unfortunate natives and half-castes. Compared with that their condition under the squatters is heavenly indeed.

And what of the 'enlightened public' of which you speak? Poor Rip Van Winkle! Asleep so long and just wakening up to the fact that there is a native problem. What is your enlightened public (you refer, of course, to the Committee for the Defence of Native Rights) doing to uplift the native? Passing resolutions! Cheap, isn't it? Demanding higher wages for the native, so long as someone else pays it! Crying out for better clothes for the Australian native, but sending sheep skins to Russia! Collecting money in aid of the Committee for the Defence of Native Rights and spending it in repeated appeals to have convictions against a communist squashed! Now, let us be practical. Why not approach all such as are on your committee with a view to adopt some or all of these enslaved natives. The Catholic Church and other organisations do adopt hundreds of natives into their institutions to uplift them, to educate them in mind and body, to teach them trades, etc. If your metropolitan friends of the said Committee open up their houses to these less fortunate of their countrymen then we might attribute a little sincerity to them. Acts speak louder than words. Even if the Government refused the necessary permission, the gesture would still be appreciated.

It is also noted that your pamphlet lists many organisations such as the Geraldton Municipal Council, the Geraldton Lumper's Union, the Eureka Youth League (Commo.) and the Hands off Indonesia Committee (also Commo.). Approach these bodies for something more practical than resolutions to emancipate the natives from the squatter slavery. Municipal Councils could draft so many natives into their municipalities providing work and housing for them. We do not think, however, that many of the individual councillors would smile on this plan. It is like a dream to us that here in Geraldton some time ago a councillor whose ideas fairly represent the opinions of his fellows, approached the Minister for Education to segregate the natives and half-castes in the State School. To which the Minister replied in the negative stating that these people fought side by side with the white Australians in the last war! Perhaps the Lumpers' Union would give lumpers' tickets to a number of natives thus affording them an opportunity to earn in one day on the wharves as much as they would earn for a week on the station. The political organisation could make grants of money to the natives rather than send their money as at present to Moscow. 'Action this Day' was Churchill's war-time motto, and armchair reformers couldn't do better than adopt it towards the natives. But 'distance lends enchantment to the scene!'

Appendix A

Letter Continues:— If you peruse the pamphlet already referred to, I am sure you will give equal space to rebutting the false claim made in your September issue.

> Comment:— the only claim made by the 'Chronicle' was that the real issue was 'Communism at work among the natives' and that Communists were only using the grievances, just or otherwise of the natives to further their own ends. Far from changing our opinions your pamphlet only reinforces them.

Letter Continues:— Although I personally am a communist, one swallow does not make a summer, and by the same token, because a few communists are included in that body of citizens who are out to secure justice for our natives, it cannot be held that the whole campaign is a communist plot as alleged in your report. Indeed it would be strange if such a committee did not include among its members a few Communists. Being vanguard fighters in the struggle of the workers to secure social justice in Australia, and the struggle of native workers being a just cause, it is only natural to expect some of our party to be in the movement.

> Comment:— True enough, one swallow does not make a summer, but it is nonetheless a sign of the times! But there is a big difference between one swallow and one communist. A swallow cannot disguise itself as a dove of peace whereas a communist can, or at least he thinks he can. It is part of the game, isn't it? Deception is the warp and woof of Communism. Australian unions suffer to-day and industry is in a state of chaos, because unsuspecting unionists view the presence of communists with the disregard which a weather expert might attach to the presence of a solitary swallow. Being on the Committee for the Defence of Native Rights is not a reflection on you or your comrades who are only carrying out your orders to white-ant every possible organisation. But it is a reflection on the committee that it tolerates communists and suffers them to hold important positions on it. If the Committee is ignorant of the sinister designs of communists then it is not fit to exist. If, on the other hand, it is aware of these things and still tolerates communists as it does then it deserves neither the support or the respect of discerning people. It is our opinion that the Committee is just another ancillary of the Communist Party. If we are wrong how do you explain the presence of so many communists holding leading positions on the Committee. For instance the President of the Committee is one Dr. A. Jolly who has been nominated by the Communist Party to contest the Guildford seat in the

coming State elections! Other members of the committee are actively associated with such communist subsidiaries as the Hands off Indonesia Committee! And you, on your own admission are a Communist. You are the central figure, even if you later turn out to be the scapegoat for those whose names cannot be divulged. According to the Secretary, Rev. Mr. Hodge, some members do not wish to have their name made known. It would be putting it very mildly to say the Committee has a strong communist bias.

In explanation of the presence of communists on the committee you say that it is quite natural, as communists are vanguard fighters in the struggle of the workers. This is the biggest fairy tale of all! Lenin is a better authority on communism than you or your comrades. He tells us how communists are to support the workers: 'As a hangman's rope supports its victim!' You cannot deny this. The servant is not above his master. And history proves the truth of Lenin's statement. Communism betrays the workers. It substitutes the slavery of State Capitalism (Communism) for private capitalism. In Russia where the doctrine of Communism is realised the workers are slaves. Mr. Moloney, a former Australian Minister to Russia, has exploded with a vengeance the myth of the 'Workers' paradise'. The condition of the Soviet worker is infinitely worse than the condition of the Australian worker in the days of the depression. Strikes are illegal in Russia. Trade Unions are simply state police bodies which see that the worker keeps his back bent. When absence from work does not bring worse penalties it brings starvation, for the absentee worker is deprived of his rations, as also are his dependents … These are the improved conditions which the Communists would give Australians, black and white, should ever you get into power! In the meantime, communists simply hitch their waggon to the just cause of the worker. And when the worker gains his victory you snatch it from him and land him into the clutches of the Red Monster to be reduced to a state of slavery worse than the first.

Letter Continued:– So far as the international matters are concerned with which your article concludes this matter is also a similar distortion, and is based on opinions about facts and not on facts, and because of this hardly warrants reply.

Comment:– Our article concluded by pointing out the hypocrisy of the Committee for the Defence of Native Rights in sending a resolution to U.N.O. demanding it to take steps against Australia to see that it grants

Appendix A

the Four Freedoms of the Atlantic Charter to the natives. Fancy that coming from a clique which owes allegiance to Moscow, especially in view of the fact that Moscow was alone in opposing Australia's demand for a Charter of Human Rights for the people of all the world. This is no distortion, and you know it. It is a grim, cruel, stark reality which millions of European people know to-day to their dire distress. Why is Moscow opposed to the Charter of Human Rights? Because it denies that men are human! It treats men as mere chattels of the State to be used for the State's aggressive and expansionist policy and afterwards it throws them on the rubbish dump when they become non-productive. That is Communism. That is the future you hold up your sleeve for the native.

Letter Continued:– if in future you circularise your sources of information asking them to give unbiassed and true records of the proceedings which are reported to you for publication, I am sure that you will find as a consequence the prestige of your journal would be enhanced considerably instead of as at present you leave yourself open to attack for bias and distortion. Yours faithfully, Don McLeod, per??? (*a second party whose initials are indecipherable*)

Concluding Comment:– When the 'Chronicle' wins the esteem of communists it will be time for it to examine its conscience. If your party had its way every Catholic paper would be suppressed as they are suppressed in all communistic-dominated countries. The fact that you accuse us of bias and distortion does not prove the truth of your assertion. We have given facts and figures; we have analysed the composition of your 'Committee for the Defence of Native Rights' and found that it is dangerously overcharged with 'red corpuscles'; we have exploded the myth that communists are in the vanguard of the struggle of the worker; we have shown how the workers are treated under Communism; finally we conclude that Communism has nothing to offer humanity, white or black, but total slavery of the mind and body.

We shall end on the note with which we embarked on this topic last August. 'It is not our business to make apologies for the employers of half-castes or natives, or to pretend that the present conditions of native labor are necessarily ideal. But we do know that the native will not benefit by adopting the tactics towards their employers urged upon them by the communists'. The editor.

Appendix B

Jack Gribble

John Wriede Bulmer (Jack) Gribble was eighteen years old and studying for the ministry when he enlisted to serve in WWI, landing at Gallipoli on 7 May 1915, six days after the initial landing. He was evacuated three months later with a gunshot wound to the eye and abdominal injuries, and he returned to rejoin his unit a month before the evacuation, on 15 November. He then served in France and was wounded for a second time in Pozières in July 1916. He returned to France as a second lieutenant, and was wounded a third time in April 1917, receiving a serious arm injury that remained an ongoing disability. He was declared unfit for active service and then served in Italy, conducting troops in transit.

On his return to London to receive new orders in April 1918, he was court-martialled for being absent without leave, although he insisted that he had not been in hiding but had been, as instructed, standing by to receive further orders. He believed that he was fit to return to active service and was hoping to be returned to France. In September, he was accused of passing false cheques for cash and vehicle hire and, charged with 'behaving in a scandalous manner unbecoming to the character of an officer and a Gentleman', he was deprived of his seniority and war medals and, on 25 January 1919, was cashiered.[1] He was returned to Australia after four years of overseas service without medals, rank or eligibility for war gratuity. He felt this injustice deeply. In 1937 and 1938, after the birth of his daughter, he attempted to have his war medals returned to him, 'if only for my young child to cherish & to know that I have … served my country in the Great War', he wrote. 'I have nothing for my services only my wounds'.[2]

Gribble did not return to theological studies at the end of the war. Instead, he joined his father, Ernest Richard Bulmer (Ernie) Gribble, at the extremely isolated Forrest River Anglican Mission in the far north of the Kimberley, near the tiny, remote town of Wyndham. His father had begun mission work

---

1   Gribble John Wriede Bulmer: Service Number – Lieutenant 1491, NAA B2455, Gribble JWB.
2   Gribble to Officer in Charge Base Records, AIF, Victoria Barracks, 10 October 1937, p. 2, NAA B2455, Gribble JWB.

Appendix B

in 1886 when he assisted his own father, Jack's grandfather, John Brown Gribble, to establish a mission on Western Australia's Gascoyne River, in the Murchison district south of the Pilbara. The project was abandoned the following year, after John Brown Gribble launched fierce accusations against local pastoralists over their treatment of Aboriginal people in the region. John Gribble senior then established Yarrabah Mission near Cairns in Northern Queensland, with the assistance of his son Ernie, who took over its management when his father died. Jack was born in Cairns, but moved to Gosford, on the central coast of New South Wales, when his parents separated. His father Ernie returned to Western Australia in 1913 to take charge of the fledgling Forrest River Mission, and Jack worked with him there throughout the 1920s.[3]

In 1925, the year he married fellow mission worker Edith Kent, Jack Gribble was working on the mission launch in Wyndham when petrol fumes ignited, causing an explosion. Three Aboriginal men were killed, and Jack suffered severe burns.[4] The following year, he and Edith had several months' furlough in Edith's home state of South Australia, where Jack preached at various churches throughout the state and lectured widely on the mission.[5] Two months after their return to Forrest River, while Jack was in Wyndham with the new launch, Edith became ill and died within two days, before her husband was able to get back.[6]

In 1927, Ernie Gribble accused police officers of committing a massacre of Aboriginal people in the vicinity of the mission, and Jack, who was highly critical of the treatment and exploitation of Aboriginal people in the north of Western Australia, was involved as a witness in a Royal Commission that investigated the allegations.[7] During the hearing in Perth in 1928, Jack came to know Gweneth Barrett, who returned with him to Forrest River as

---

[3] 'Gribble, John Brown (1847–1893)', *Australian Dictionary of Biography*, National Centre of Biography, Australian National University, http://adb.anu.edu.au/biography/gribble-john-brown-3668/text5727, published first in hardcopy 1972; Christine Halse, 'Gribble, Ernest Richard Bulmer (Ernie) (1868–1957)', *Australian Dictionary of Biography*, National Centre of Biography, Australian National University, http://adb.anu.edu.au/biography/gribble-ernest-richard-bulmer-ernie-10367/text18363, published first in hardcopy 1996; see Christine Halse, *A Terribly Wild Man*, Allen and Unwin, Crows Nest, 2002.

[4] *News* (Adelaide), 21 May 1926, p. 4; *West Australian*, 19 October 1925, p. 6.

[5] *Recorder* (Port Pirie, SA), 18 February 1926, p. 4.

[6] *Capricornian* (Rockhampton), 31 March 1927, p. 9; *News* (Adelaide), 11 June 1926, p. 7, and 21 May 1926, p. 4; *Register* (Adelaide), 22 February 1926, p. 10.

[7] See Neville Green, *The Forrest River Massacres*, Fremantle Arts Centre Press, Fremantle, 1995.

a missionary and as his second wife.[8] Travelling back and forth to Wyndham in the launch for supplies, Gribble would have come to know Lew McBeath, who was at the time storekeeper at Wyndham.[9]

In November 1928, Jack's father left the mission and returned to Queensland, after the Australian Board of Missions received a report from A. P. Elkin, who was undertaking anthropological field research in the Kimberley, that was critical of Ernie Gribble's harsh and autocratic management.[10] The Australian Board of Missions found it difficult to secure the services of a permanent superintendent to replace Ernie and, after the six-month temporary appointment of a clergyman from the south, Jack was placed in charge of the mission until a permanent superintendent could be appointed. His term as manager was short-lived: he was absent from the mission for some months due to ill health and was dismissed when other staff made accusations against him and appealed to the Chief Protector for Aborigines, A. O. Neville, to have him removed. Gribble in turn accused his accusers of the sexual abuse of children at the mission.[11] The Gribbles shifted south, and for the next few years they engaged in farming on their property 'Gweneth Vale', at Tenterden near Mt Barker in the south-west of Western Australia.[12]

When WWII began, Gribble was back at Forrest River for a short period with a job as boatman on the mission launch, but too much had changed in the decade since his father's autocratic management for him to remain long. According to Neville Green, the sight of neglected gardens that had once been highly productive was enough to convince Gribble that he could not continue working there.[13] Instead, he took a job with the Northern Territory Native Affairs Department, working to maintain Darwin as a settler space by ensuring that only those Aboriginal people who serviced settler needs remained within its boundaries.[14] Aboriginal people thought he was a policeman, as he moved around Aboriginal camps removing anyone who was not employed in the

---

8   Neville Green, *Triumphs and Tragedies: Oombulgurri, an Australian Aboriginal Community*, Hesperian Press, Carlisle, pp. 52–53; *Mirror* (Perth), 9 February 1952, p. 7.
9   *West Australian*, 27 November 1929, p. 11.
10 Biskup, *Not Slaves*, 1973, pp. 128–129; Green, *Triumphs and Tragedies*, pp. 53–54.
11 Biskup, *Not Slaves*, p. 129.
12 Gribble to Officer in Charge Base Records, AIF, Victoria Barracks, 10 October 1937, p. 2, NAA B2455, Gribble JWB.
13 Green, *Triumphs and Tragedies*, pp. 92–93.
14 Jeremy Long, *The Go-Betweens: Patrol Officers in Aboriginal Affairs Administration in the Northern Territory 1936–74*, North Australia Research Unit, Australian National University, 1992, p. 37.

Appendix B

town.[15] To deal with the problem of repeat offenders, and especially those who came frequently before the court for alcohol and opium offences, he established a departmental settlement for 'incorrigibles' at Garden Point on Melville Island, which he later moved to Snake Bay on the island's north coast, now called Milikapiti.[16] It was there that, as a special lieutenant of the Royal Australian Navy Volunteer Reserve (RANVR), he led an official naval unit, made up of 'incorrigibles' and Melville Islanders, which undertook coast watch and rescue duties.[17] The first arrest of a Japanese soldier on Australian soil was made by a Melville Islander, Matthias Ulungura.[18]

Observers were impressed by the energy and dedication of Gribble's unit. 'His natives are a credit to him', Native Affairs patrol officer Bill Harney wrote. 'They are all well drilled (Army fashion) ... Some of the native people of this Department sent to him from Darwin (noted incorrigibles) have stood by him all through and all intend to remain, "Longa Mr. Gribble".'[19] Gribble developed a high regard for the men who formed the Snake Bay patrol, writing of 'their sincere loyalty and their very fine courage'.[20] After the war, he tried to draw public attention to the service that Aboriginal people had rendered during the war. Australia's failure to recognise and reward members of the Snake Bay Patrol for their war service mirrored the lack of recognition he had received for his own services in the previous war, and he felt the injustice of this. 'They saved 39 lives for which they have received no commendation', he wrote.[21] He believed that Australia owed them a debt of gratitude.[22]

---

15 *Northern Standard* (Darwin), 9 April 1940, p. 10.
16 Lt. John Gribble, *Beverley Times*, 9 April 1953, p. 2; Long, *The Go-Between*, p. 37; Morris, '"Continuing Assimilation"?', p. 146.
17 *Mirror*, 14 June 1952, p. 5, 'Sad Saga of a War Hero Who Can't Land Civil Job'; Morris, '"Continuing Assimilation"?', pp. 153–156.
18 Morris, '"Continuing Assimilation"?', p. 146; *Daily News*, 25 July 1945, p. 9, 'Native Captured First Enemy Here'.
19 Harney to Director of Native Affairs, 6 April 1944, 'Report on J. B. Gribble's Old Government Settlement, Snake Bay', Patrol Officer W. E. Harney Patrols & Reports, NAA F1 1944/275/42.
20 *Beverley Times*, 26 February 1953, p. 3.
21 *Daily News*, 2 October 1945, p. 4.
22 *Daily News*, 28 July 1945, p. 6; Raymond Bowers, 'Black Garrison of Melville Island', *Sunday Times*, 2 September 1945, p. 3. Members of the Snake Bay Patrol were not paid during the war, and did not become eligible for the award of service medals and ex-gratia payments in recognition of their service until 1962. John Perryman, 'A Brief History of Indigenous Service to the RAN', *A Naval Salute: Celebrating the Centenary of the Royal Australian Navy 1911–2011*, p. 24, http://www.navy.gov.au/sites/default/files/documents/A_Naval_Salute_music_program.pdf.

His wartime years on Melville Island were physically and psychologically demanding for a man now in his mid-forties. He suffered hunger, physical hardship and long months of social isolation. The unit's work included rescuing men from downed planes and bombed ships, often with horrific injuries and burns. Gribble later said the remains of men from the bombed wreck of the 'Don Isldro' was a sight he would never forget. 'Surely the men of the British Empire will never again tolerate anything like this', he wrote. 'I feel sure the people in our cities do not realise the horrors of bombing from the air, unless they have experienced and seen the results and the long trail of destruction it leaves behind it'.[23]

Perhaps determined to atone for the misdemeanour that had marred his previous war record, Gribble undertook long and arduous patrols. According to one story, he received an instruction to report to a senior naval officer in Darwin and, having no other means of transport, travelled to the mainland with three members of his unit in a thirteen-foot dinghy with a 3-horsepower engine. Shabby and unshaven, he was arrested as a spy until his identity could be established. When he told his superior officer that he had made the trip in a dinghy, the officer looked at him for a few seconds and said, 'I didn't bloody-well ask you to swim across'.[24]

The isolation, deprivation and physical demands of his role took their toll on his physical and mental health. He was withdrawn by the Navy from Melville Island in April 1945 suffering war neurosis, now known as post-traumatic stress disorder.[25] 'This Officer was hardworking', his naval officer's report of January 1945 states, 'and, until recently, carried out his duties cheerfully and promptly, but is now not very reliable and appears very excitable and forgetful'. The report adds that he was 'very competent with natives and holds their confidence'.[26]

Jack Gribble spent 1945 in Perth, but returned to the Northern Territory with his wife and daughter in 1946 to work for the Native Affairs Department as supervisor of the newly established Aboriginal compound at the old RAAF camp at Berrimah. In February 1947, he resigned to take employment with Qantas Empire Airways. A few days later, Aboriginal domestic and

---

23 *Beverley Times*, 26 February 1953, p. 3.
24 *Daily News*, 25 July 1945, p. 9; *Mirror*, 14 June 1952, p. 5.
25 Morris '"Continuing Assimilation?"', p. 160; *Mirror*, 9 February 1952, p. 7, 'War Hero's Abject Appearance in Court'.
26 Captain Baldwin, RAN, 20 January 1945, 'Special Report to Accompany my NT Ship HMAS Melville, Period of Report 1.2.44 to 21.1.45', 'Officers (RANVR) Personal Record – John Wriede Bulmer Gribble', NAA A3978 Gribble JWB.

Appendix B

municipal workers in Darwin staged a twenty-four-hour strike, reported to be the first Aboriginal strike in the Northern Territory. Many of those involved, including strike committee leader Tommy Play-up-Jimmy, were from Melville and Bathurst Islands.[27] In addition to demanding higher pay, working conditions equal to those of non-Aboriginal workers, and an end to the practice of paying a portion of their wages into a trust account,[28] they demanded that Gribble be returned as superintendent of Berrimah. Although the strikers dropped this demand when authorities explained that Gribble had resigned voluntarily, it is an indication of the high regard in which he was held.[29] The communist press reported that the Darwin workers had been inspired to take strike action by the activism of Aboriginal people in the Pilbara.[30]

Gribble's job with Qantas was short-lived, and he was attempting to find work back at the Forrest River Mission when he was offered the position of special officer with the Western Australian Department of Native Affairs in mid-1949. His dismissal from the Department after just two months in the Pilbara weighed heavily upon him. He was unable to face McBeath. 'I feel it very hard to write to you let alone coming to see you', he wrote:

> and I really cannot face the office after having failed in my work ... My work and life has now failed and must accept your verdict and seek another job @ once ...
>
> I am more than sorry for my wife & child, how can I face them I do not know ... Really my present health is causing me concern, as my nerves are bad.[31]

In a statement that reflects the degree to which he carried the burden of his family's missionary history, he wrote:

> My work among natives for so long seems to me to have come to an end, and the work of my late grandfather and my Father will be spoilt.[32]

---

27 Douglas Lockwood, 'Native Claims Rights', *Mail* (Adelaide), 8 February 1947, p. 2; *Tribune*, 11 February 1947, p. 7.

28 *News* (Adelaide), 3 February 1947, p. 1; Tom Wright, 'Fight for Aborigines', *Communist Review*, April 1947, report to Australian Communist Party central committee meeting, 14–16 February 1947.

29 *News* (Adelaide), 3 February 1947, p. 1.

30 *Workers' Star*, 21 February 1947, p. 4.

31 Gribble to McBeath, 7 December 1947, p. 5, SROWA 1947/0691/62.

32 Gribble to McBeath, 7 December 1947, p. 5, SROWA 1947/0691/62.

The following week, he wrote to McBeath:

> I have made a vow not to touch drink again and lead a life that I had led when I first met you some years ago. My nerves in the past has failed me and I don't feel myself at all, I just want to be with my family and daily seek their forgiveness for my past.[33]

Four years later, Perth Criminal Court tried to reconcile Jack Gribble's past history and war record with the 'the dazed, mumbling, shuffling, helpless man' who was half-carried onto the dock to plead guilty to a charge of bigamy. It seemed to the judge that this 'shambling wreck of humanity' should have been receiving treatment in Hollywood Repatriation Hospital.[34]

---

33   Gribble to McBeath, 14 December 1947, SROWA 1947/0691/unnumbered.
34   *Mirror*, 9 February 1952, p. 7.

Character List

Alcorn, Graham: Editor of the Communist Party newspaper, the *Workers' Star*.

Bateman, F. E. A.: Magistrate commissioned in 1947 to conduct a survey of Aboriginal Affairs in Western Australia. His report was tabled in 1948.

Bligh, Keith: Manager, Corunna Downs Station.

Bob, Ginger (Palyakulayi) (*Purungu*): A Mangarla speaker.

Bonham, Alfred (Alf): Port Hedland wharfinger and station master.

Bray, Francis Illingworth: Western Australian Commissioner of Native Affairs, 1940–47.

Bryan, Edward: Catholic priest at Port Hedland.

Captain, Ron: Aboriginal strike organiser.

Carbine, Dendo: Aboriginal employee of Warrawagine Station.

Chipper, Vern: Police constable at Marble Bar, 1949.

Clarke, Lawrence (Pop): Founder and secretary of the Port Hedland Euralian Association.

Cocky Brine (or Brown) (Purnungurrara): Striker who took work on Corunna Downs in March 1949.

Coppin, Jack (Yarrie Jack, or Ngarlkapangu): Half-brother of Peter Coppin and overseer of Warrawagine Station's Braeside outcamp. A non-striker.

Coppin, Peter (Kangkushot) (*Purungu*): Striker, and a leader at the Twelve Mile.

Coverley, Aubrey Augustus Michael (Bob): Minister for the North West, with responsibility for Aboriginal affairs, 1939–47 (Labor).

Cranky (Kujupurru) (*Purungu*): Striker who left Warrawagine Station in 1946.

Crawford, Alan: Owner-manager of Tabba Tabba Station.

Curran, Fred: Lawyer engaged by the Committee for Defence of Native Rights (CDNR) to provide legal defence for strikers and their supporters.

Dooley (Dooley Binbin) (Winyirin or Yurlpuly) (*Milangka*): Aboriginal strike organiser and leader at Moolyella throughout the strike.

Elkin, A. P.: Professor of Anthropology at Sydney University.

Elliott-Smith, Sydney: Deputy Commissioner of Native Affairs and officer in charge of the northern region, from July 1949.

Fletcher, Les: Police constable at Port Hedland, 1945 – July 1947.

Gallop, Doug and Thora: Part owners and managers of Bonney Downs Station, and friends of McLeod. Following Doug's death in 1945, it was rumoured that Thora and McLeod might marry.

Gardiner, Mac (Pirntilkampanyaja) (*Milangka*): Aboriginal worker at Warrawagine. A non-striker for most of the strike, he was taken away by a party of strikers in April 1949, but was returned to Warrawagine by the police. Joined the strike in June 1949 when wage demands were not met.

Ginger, Maggie (Nyirrarlpi) (*Milangka*): Domestic worker who walked away from Nimingarra Station, shifting to Moolyella.

Gribble, John Wriede Bulmer (Jack): Special officer of the Department of Native Affairs (DNA), appointed to deal with the strike, July–December 1947.

Hale, Monty (Minyjun) (*Panaka*): Striker who joined the strike at Moolyella from Mt Edgar Station in 1946.

Hegney, William (Bill): Labor Member for Pilbara in the Western Australian Legislative Assembly 1939–50. Also a member of the state executive of the Australian Workers' Union (AWU).

Hewett, Dorothy: Writer and journalist for the communist newspaper the *Workers' Star*, Hewett and her husband Lloyd Davies visited the strikers in the summer of 1946–47.

Hodge, Hugh Peter Vere (Peter): Anglican minister and secretary of the CDNR.

Hogg, Keith: Resident magistrate based at Carnarvon.

Hurd, Ron: Secretary, Fremantle Branch of Seamen's Union.

Jensen, Thomas Emmes (Tom): Travelling Inspector of Native Affairs for the northern region of Western Australia, based in Derby, seconded from the police force in April 1947, and returned to the police force December 1948. Police constable in Marble Bar, relieving Gordon Marshall, December 1948 – April 1949.

Jittermarra, Snowy (Maruntu) (*Panaka*): Non-striker for most of the strike, taken away from Noreena Downs Station in 1949 by other strikers.

CHARACTER LIST

Jolly, Alexander Thomas Hicks (Alec): President of the CDNR. A communist.

Jones, H. A.: Clerk in the DNA who accompanied Bateman on his tour of Western Australia, 1947–48.

Jula, Caroline (Jula) (*Milangka*): Aboriginal domestic servant at Warrawagine Station, who joined the strike at Moolyella in 1946.

Kitchener: Aboriginal organiser of the strike, who played an important part in the early instigation of the strike but was himself a non-striker.

Lee, Mick: Strike leader at the Twelve Mile.

Lewis, G. A. (Jim): Manager at Warrawagine Station, 1944–49.

Lund, V. L. (Wally): Native Affairs Department employee in charge of the Port Hedland Native Hospital.

Mackay, Gordon: Striker who led a breakaway movement in December 1947.

Mackay, Roy: Aboriginal strike organiser.

Marshall, Gordon: Police constable at Marble Bar throughout the strike.

Mason, W. J. (Bill): Police constable relieving in Port Hedland in January–March 1947 while Les Fletcher was on leave.

McBeath, Charles: Deputy Commissioner of Native Affairs, 1941–47.: Acting Commissioner of Native Affairs, April 1947 – August 1948.

McDonald, Robert Ross (Ross): Western Australian Minister for Native Affairs, April 1947 – October 1949.

McGeary, Bernie: Police sergeant at Port Hedland, July 1947–48.

McKenna, Clancy (Warntupungkarna) (*Purungu*): Aboriginal strike organiser and a leader at the Twelve Mile until 1947.

McLarty, Duncan Ross (Ross): Western Australian Liberal Premier, April 1947 – February 1953.

McLeod, Donald William (Don) (Ngarnka, Ngarnkawaru, or Mirta) (*Milangka*): Non-Aboriginal strike organiser.

Middleditch, Robert (Bob): Owner-manager of Noreena Downs Station.

Middleton, Stanley Guise (Stan): Commissioner of Native Affairs from August 1948.

Miller, Les and Edith: Managers of Warrawagine Station, 1924–44 and De Grey Station, 1944–48. Owner-managers of Strelley Station from 1948.

Mitchell, Ernie (Putungaja) (*Karimarra*): Strike leader at the Twelve Mile 1946–48, and a leader at Moolyella 1948–49.

Needle, Tom: Police constable at Port Hedland, 1946–47.

O'Neill, Laurence (Laurie): Travelling Inspector of Native Affairs for Northern Region 1941 – September 1946. Stationed in Perth as Acting Deputy Commissioner of Native Affairs, September 1946 – August 1948. Returned to Pilbara as District Officer of Native Affairs, February–July 1949.

Plunkett, Walter: Police sergeant at Port Hedland, December 1948–49.

Rhatigan, John Joseph (Jack): Native Affairs Inspector for the Gascoyne and Ashburton districts, based in Carnarvon, late 1946 to mid-1949.

Richards, G. R. (Ron): Police detective sergeant who carried out investigations against McLeod in May and June 1946. He was known to communists as 'the Black Snake'.

Richardson, A. E. (Ted): Owner-manager of Pippingarra Station.

Sampie, Thomas (Tommy): Strike leader at the Twelve Mile and teacher at the strikers' school there. (This spelling of Sampie's surname is in accordance with his own signature and is agreed to by his niece, Sheila Sampie).

Sheppard, W. F. J. (Bill): Non-Aboriginal overseer at Warrawagine Station.

Sherlock, Reg and **Benja**: Managers of Strelley Station in 1946.

Thomas, Billy (Pitpit) (*Panaka*): Striker who walked off Bonney Downs Station.

Thompson, Don: Non-Aboriginal owner of the store at Moolyella.

Weaver, Keith: Second police constable at Marble Bar, 1947–48.

Welsh, Frank: Owner of Warralong Station and Liberal Party member for North Province in the Legislative Council.

Williams, Molly (Kulyu) (*Purungu*): Domestic servant at Mulyie Station who joined the strike at the Twelve Mile in 1946.

Wise, Frank: Western Australian Labor Premier, July 1945 – April 1947.

Wyndam, Alec: Port Hedland store owner and supporter of the strike.

Yougarla, Crow (Yakalya) (*Panaka*): Striker who joined the strike from Yarrie Station.

Bibliography

Archival Material

National Archives of Australia (NAA)
Cameron, Walter John Julius, B884, W90255.
GRIBBLE John Wriede Bulmer: Service Number – Lieutenant 1491; B2455, Gribble JWB.
Patrol Officer WE Harney, Patrols & Reports, F1 1944/275.
Hodge Peter Vere versus Needle Thomas William, A10074 1947/5.
Donald William MCLEOD, A6335, 17.
McLeod, Donald [alleged communist connected with Aborigines in Western Australia], D1918, S3008.
McLEOD Donald William versus RICHARDS George Ronald, A10074 1947/8, 9, 10.
MCLEOD, Donald William – Volume 1, A6126, 1188.
McLeod Donald William v. Richards George Ronald, A10078 1946/13 Part 2.
McLeod Donald William versus Richards George Ronald, NAA A10078 1946/13 Part 1.
Officers (RANVR) Personal Record – John Wriede Bulmer Gribble, A3978 Gribble JWB.
Submission by the Nomads Group of Aborigines to the Federal Cabinet, Commonwealth of Australia, 1973, p. 6, A4252, 49.

South Australian Museum
Tindale, Norman, journal, 'University of Adelaide and University of California Anthropological Expedition, 1952–1954', South Australian Museum, AA 338/1/19/1.

University of Western Australian (UWA)
Marchant Trust Collection, MS118 series 1.

National Library of Australia (NLA)
Papers of Jessie Street, MS 2683.
Stuart, Donald, *Yandy the Wind*, manuscript, MS 3156 folder 9.

Australian National University, Noel Butlin Archives Centre
Michael Hess Collection, N287, Item 1.

State Library of Western Australia (SLWA)
MN 1034, Papers of John and Roma Gilchrist, ACC 3255A.
MN 1444, Papers of Don McLeod, ACC 1568A, 5121A, 5525A.
MN 1843, Papers of Joan Williams, ACC 5425A.

University of Sydney
A.P. Elkin Papers.

State Library of Victoria (SLV)
Records of the Council for Aboriginal Rights, MS 12913.

State Records Office, Western Australia (SROWA)
S3841 cons769 1 – Minister's correspondence file – Native Affairs.
S3841 cons769 3 – Minister's correspondence file – Native Affairs.
S2030 cons7198 1937/0432 – Mulyie Station – Native Matters.
S2030 cons993 1938/0656 – Reserve for Natives – Poondano.

S2030 cons1667 1938/0982 – Native Matters – Pippingarra Station.
S2030 cons7198 1939/1226 – Native Matters – Warragine Station – 1. General Correspondence. 2. Reports.
S76 cons430 1939/1777 v7 – Port Hedland – Patrol Journals.
S2030 cons993 1940/0324 – Alleged Assault of Native by Constable Mason.
S2030 cons993 1940/1194 – Industrial – Australian Workers' Union – Membership of Natives.
S2030 cons993 1941/0763 – Education of Natives – Port Hedland.
S1691 cons1498 1941/1107 – O'NEILL, Mr L. (Inspector of Natives).
S2030 cons993 1942/0919 – Port Hedland – 1. Proposed Evacuation of Natives. 2. Suggested Declaration of a Prohibited Area.
S76 cons430 1943/0099 v7 – Marble Bar – Police Patrol Journals.
S2030 cons993 1943/0102 – Natives – North/West Areas.
S2030 cons993 1943/0441 – Port Hedland – Marble Bar – Employment of Natives by Government Railways.
S2030 cons993 1943/0460 – Half Castes of Port Hedland – Employment of.
S2030 cons993 1943/0621 – Moolyella – Native Matters.
S2030 cons993 1943/0685 – Anti-Fascist League.
S2030 cons993 1943/0796 – Port Hedland Euralian Assoc.
S2030 cons993 1944/0077 – Communist Party – Native Policy.
S2030 cons993 1944/0162 – Application to Employ Natives by D. W. McLeod of Bonny Downs Stations, Marble Bar.
S2030 cons993 1944/0394 – Application to Lease Land, Port Hedland by D. W. McLeod.
S2030 cons993 1945/0800 – D. W. McLeod Port Hedland – Appointment as Protector of Natives.
S36 cons5761 1946/150/46 – D. W. McLeod – Re Strike of Native Workers, Pt. Hedland District.
S2030 cons993 1946/0799 – Twelve Mile Camp – Port Hedland.
S2030 cons993 1946/0895 – Committee for 'Native Defence Rights'.
S1691 cons1498 1946/1220 – O'NEILL, L.
S2030 cons993 1946/1306 – Journal – NW Inspector M. L O'Neill.
S2030 cons1667 1946/1324 – Native Matters – Marble Bar.
S2030 cons993 1946/1416 – D. W. McLeod Port Hedland – Purchase of Pearl Shell.
S76 cons430 1946/2538 v8 – Marble Bar – Police Patrol Journals.
S2030 cons993 1947/0127 – NW Inspector (Mr T. E. Jansen) – Journal.
S2030 cons993 1947/0220 – Port Hedland and Marble Bar Districts – Employment and Conditions of Natives on Stations.
S2030 cons993 1947/0285 – Reports of Unrest Amongst Natives along Murchison Railway.
S2030 cons993 1947/0305 – D. W. McLeod Port Hedland – Breaches and Unrest.
S2030 cons993 1947/0329 – Communists and the North West Natives.
S2030 cons993 1947/0349 – 12-Mile Camp – Port Hedland & Mooyella Camp.
S2030 cons993 1947/0477 – Mr A. C. Bonham – Station Master Port Hedland.
S2030 cons993 1947/0500 – Visit of Hon Minister and Acting Commissioner for Native Affairs to NW and Kimberley – June 1947.
S24 cons1497 1947/0594 – Port Hedland 12 mile camp – Establishing of School for Natives.
S2030 cons993 1947/0691 – Appointment of Dr John Gribble for Special Duties in the Department of Native Affairs.
S2030 cons7198 1947/0902 – Mundabullangana Station. – Employment, Living and General Conditions – Reports and Statistics re.
S2030 cons993 1948/0732 – D. W. McLeod Port Hedland – Unrest Amongst Natives.
S2030 cons993 1949/0160 – Port Hedland District – Inspector of Natives – Journal (1 & 2).
S2030 cons993 1949/0454 – Industrial – Unrest Amongst Natives in the Pilbara District.
S2030 cons993 1949/0456 – West Kimberley District Officer, Derby – Patrol Reports.
S2030 cons993 1949/0488 – Visit of Assistant Deputy Commissioner (Mrs [sic] S. Elliot-Smith) to the North West.
S2030 cons993 1949/0722 – District Officers and Travelling Inspectors – Annual Reports.
S2030 cons993 1950/0088 – Marble Bar – Native Welfare Committee.
S20 cons964 1950/0096 – McLeod D. W. M. C. 221 Pilbara (3 m S E of Pitgangoora) for Columbite, Tantalite and Tin.

488

S2030 cons993 1950/0119 – Outstations – Visits and Inspections by Deputy Commissioner of Native Welfare.
S2030 cons993 1950/0173 – Pilbara – Port Hedland – Patrol Reports.
S2030 cons1667 1950/0488 – Pastoralists Association – Discussion re. Native Matters – Miscellaneous Reports re.
S2030 cons993 1950/0741 – Pilbara District – Marble Bar. Patrol Reports.
S2030 cons993 1951/0161 – Outstations – Visits and Inspections by Commissioner of Native Affairs.
S2030 cons993 1952/0573 – Pilbara District – Marble Bar – Patrol Reports.
S20 cons3390 1952/0830 v1 – Committee of Inquiry – Use of Native Labour by D. W. McLeod and Associates.
S76 cons430 1952/5174 v1 – Marble Bar – Police Protection at.
S2030 cons993 1953/0127 – Pilbara District – Natives Co-operative Movement.

Oral Histories

Bob, Ginger (Palyakulayi), recorded by Anne Scrimgeour, 30 September 1993, translated from Nyangumarta by Barbara Hale and Mark Clendon, AIATSIS collection, 'Palyakulayi 1'.
Bob, Ginger (Palyakulayi), recorded by Anne Scrimgeour, 5 October 1993, translated from Nyangumarta by Barbara Hale and Mark Clendon, AIATSIS collection, 'Palyakulayi 4'.
Bob, Ginger (Palyakulayi), recorded by Anne Scrimgeour, 8 December 1993, translated from Nyangumarta by Barbara Hale and Mark Clendon, AIATSIS collection, 'Palyakulayi 9'.
Bob, Ginger (Palyakulayi), recorded by Anne Scrimgeour, 12 December 1993, translated from Nyangumarta by Barbara Hale and Mark Clendon, AIATSIS collection, 'Palyakulayi 18'.
Clarke, Vincent Fredrick, interviewed by Anne Bloemen, 1996, SLWA OH3608/2.
Cocky, Solomon, recorded by Anne Scrimgeour, 15 May 1991, author's collection.
Cranky (Kujupurra), recorded by Anne Scrimgeour at Warrawagine, 1991, author's collection.
Cranky (Kujupurra), recorded by Anne Scrimgeour, June 1993, translated from Nyangumarta by Barbara Hale and Mark Clendon, AIATSIS collection, soundfiles 'Kujupurra 3' and 'Kujupurra 4'.
Cranky (Kujupurra), recorded by Anne Scrimgeour, 25 June 1993, author's collection.
Cranky (Kujupurra), recorded by Anne Scrimgeour, 25 June 1993, translated from Nyangumarta, AIATSIS collection, 'Kujupurra 8' and 'Kujupurra 9'.
Gardiner, Mac (Pirntilkampanyaja), recorded by Anne Scrimgeour, 5 August 1993, author's collection.
Gardiner, Mac (Pirntilkampanyaja), recorded by Anne Scrimgeour, 5 August 1993, translated by Barbara Hale and Mark Clendon, AIATSIS collection, soundfiles 'Pirntilkampanyaja 1', 'Pirntilkampanyaja 15' and 'Pirntilkampanyaja 18'.
Gardiner, Mac (Pirntilkampanyaja), recorded by Anne Scrimgeour, 29 September 1993, author's collection.
Gare, Frank Ellis, interviewed by Darren Foster, 1998, SLWA OH 2899.
Gare Frank Ellis, interviewed by W. J. E. Bannister, Bringing Them Home Oral History Project, 1999, http://www.nla.gov.au/nla.oh-vn1379490.
Ginger, Maggie (Nyirrarlpi), recorded by Anne Scrimgeour, 13 May 1993, author's collection.
Ginger, Maggie (Nyirrarlpi), recorded by Anne Scrimgeour, 13 May 1993, translated from Nyangumarta by Barbara Hale and Mark Clendon, AIATSIS collection, soundfile 'Nyirrarlpi 3'.
Ginger, Maggie (Nyirrarlpi), recorded by Anne Scrimgeour, 19 May 1993, author's collection.
Ginger, Maggie (Nyirrarlpi), recorded by Anne Scrimgeour, 19 May 1993, translated from Nyangumarta by Barbara Hale and Mark Clendon, AIATSIS collection, soundfile 'Nyirrarlpi 19'.
Ginger, Maggie (Nyirrarlpi), recorded 15 June 1993, translated by Barbara Hale and Mark Clendon, AIATSIS collection, soundfile 'Nyirrarlpi 27'.
Jittermarra, Snowy (Maruntu), recorded by Anne Scrimgeour, 5 August 1993, author's collection.
Jula, Caroline (Jula), recorded by Anne Scrimgeour, 13 August 1991, author's collection.
Jula, Caroline (Jula), recorded by Anne Scrimgeour, 5 November 1992, author's collection.
Lukis, Robert Fellowes, interviewed by Chris Jeffery, 1977, SLWA OH262.
McLeod, Don, interviewed by John Clements, 1975, SLWA OH4005/3.

McLeod, Don, interviewed by Chris Jeffery, 1978, SLWA OH331.
McLeod, Don, interviewed by David Carlton, 1996, SLWA OH2739.
Miller, Edith, interviewed by Ronda Jamieson, 1982, transcript, SLWA OH506.
Nowers, Rose, interviewed by Jenny Hardie, undated, SLWA OH2701/5.
Thomas, Billy (Pitpit), addressing school children on a field trip to Wantilurr (Skull Springs), recorded by Anne Scrimgeour, 21 September 1992, translated from Nyangumarta by Barbara Hale and Mark Clendon, AIATSIS collection, soundfile 'Pitpit Talking to Kids'.
Thomas, Billy (Pitpit), recorded by Anne Scrimgeour, 6 October 1993, author's collection.
Thomas, Billy (Pitpit), recorded by Anne Scrimgeour, 6 October 1993, translated from Nyangumarta by Barbara Hale and Mark Clendon, AIATSIS collection, soundfile 'Pitpit 1'.
Welsh, Frank (Bidge), interviewed by Anne Bloemen, 1995, SLWA OH2689/42.
Williams, Joan, interviewed by Susan Hartley, interviews with members of the WA Communist Party, 1997, SLWA OH3989.
Williams, Molly (Kulyu), tape 1, Woodstock Station, 13 August 1991, author's collection.
Williams, Molly (Kulyu), tape 2, recorded by Anne Scrimgeour, Woodstock Station, 22 October 1992, author's collection
Wilson, John and Katrin, recorded by Anne Scrimgeour, Fremantle, 13 November 2014.
Wilson, John and Katrin, recorded by Anne Scrimgeour, Fremantle, 22 May 2016, author's collection.
Wilson, John and Katrin, recorded by Anne Scrimgeour, Fremantle, 25 May 2016, author's collection.
Woodman, Molly, recorded by Mark Clendon, 19 October 2007, author's collection.
Yougarla Crow (Yakalya), recorded by Anne Scrimgeour, 21 August 1991, author's collection.

Private Papers

Letters to Kitty, Sherlock family private collection.

Reports

Annual Report of the Commission of Native Affairs for the year ended 30th June 1950, Government Printer, Perth, 1951.

Annual Report of the Commission of Native Affairs for the year ended 30th June 1951, Government Printer, Perth, 1953.

Bateman, F. E. A., Report on Survey of Native Affairs, Government Printer, Perth, 1948.

Parliamentary Debates

Western Australian Parliamentary Debates (Hansard).

Newspapers

Newspapers listed below were national publications unless indicated otherwise.

Albany Advertiser.
Argus (Melbourne).
Australasian Record.
Australian Town and Country Journal.
Barrier Daily Truth (Broken Hill).
Beverley Times (Western Australia).
Bruce Rock Post and Corrigin and Narembeen Guardian (Western Australia).
Capricornian (Rockhampton, Queensland).
Cathedral Chronicle (Geraldton).
Communist Review.
Daily News (Perth).
Fremantle Districts Sentinel.

Geraldton Guardian.
Geraldton Guardian and Express.
Herald (Fremantle).
Mail (Adelaide).
Maritime Worker (Melbourne).
Mikurrunya (Strelley community newsletter).
Mirror (Perth).
Narrogin Observer (Western Australia).
News (Adelaide).
Northern Standard (Darwin).
Northern Times (Carnarvon, Western Australia).
Recorder (Port Pirie, South Australia).
Register (Adelaide).
Smith's Weekly (Sydney).
South Western Advertiser (Western Australia).
Sunday Times (Western Australia).
Swan Express (Midland Junction).
Tribune.
Truth (Adelaide).
Voice (Hobart).
West Australian.
Western Mail (Western Australia).
Westralian Worker.
Workers' Star (Western Australia).
Yalgoo Observer and Murchison Chronicle (Meekatharra).

Books, Articles and Theses

Adam Smith, Patsy, *No Tribesman*, Rigby, Adelaide, 1971.
Alcorn, Graham, 'The Struggle of the Pilbara Station Hands for Decent Living Standards and Human Rights', with forward and notes by Max Brown.
Allen, Margaret, 'The Brothers Up North and the Sisters Down South: The Mackay Family and the Frontier', *Hecate*, vol. 27, no. 2, 2001, pp. 7–31.
Anthony, Thalia, 'Criminal Justice and Transgression on Northern Australian Cattle Stations', in Ingereth Macfarlane and Mark Hannah (eds.), *Transgressions: Critical Australian Indigenous Histories*, Aboriginal History Monograph 16, ANU E Press, 2007, pp. 35–60.
Anthony, Thalia, 'Labour Relations on Northern Cattle Stations: Feudal Exploration and Accommodation', University of Sydney Law School, Legal Studies Research Paper 07/43, 2007.
Berndt, Ronald M., and Catherine H. Berndt, *End of an Era: Aboriginal Labour in the Northern Territory*, Australian Institute of Aboriginal Studies, Canberra, 1987.
Biskup, Peter, *Not Slaves, Not Citizens: The Aboriginal Problem in Western Australia 1898–1954*, University of Queensland Press, St. Lucia, 1973.
Bridge, Peter J., *Fighting the Kimberley: The Three Australian Corps Kimberley Guerilla Warfare Group 1942–1943*, Hesperian Press, Carlisle, 2011.
Brown, Max, *The Black Eureka*, Australasian Book Society, Sydney, 1976.
Bucknall, John, 'Commentary to Extracts Taken from Letters Authored by Reg and Benja Sherlock', unpublished paper, 2010.
Bucknall, John, 'Jacob Oberdoo (Minyjun) c. 1920s – 1989 (First Draft)', unpublished paper.
Bunbury, Tim, *It's Not the Money It's the Land: Aboriginal Stockmen and the Equal Wages Case*, Fremantle Arts Centre Press, North Fremantle, 2002.
Butler, Raymond J. T., 'Education, the State and the Indigenous Minority: A Case Study from Western Australia', Master of Education Thesis, Murdoch University, 1985.
Clohesy, Lachlan, 'Fighting the Enemy Within: Anti-Communism and Aboriginal Affairs', *History Australia*, vol. 8, no. 2, 2011, pp. 128–152.
Cowlishaw, Gillian, *Rednecks, Eggheads and Blackfellas: A Study of Racial Power and Intimacy in Australia*, Allen and Unwin, St Leonards, 1999.

Curley, Avy, 'Mrs Avy Curley', in Colleen Glass and Archie Weller (eds.), *Us Fellas: An Anthology of Aboriginal Writing*, Artlook Books, Perth, 1987, pp. 17–25.
Curthoys, Ann, and Jeremy Martens, 'Serious Collisions: Settlers, Indigenous People and Imperial Policy in Western Australia and Natal', *Journal of Australian Colonial History*, vol. 15, 2013, pp. 122–144.
Davies, Lloyd, 'Protecting Natives? The Law and the 1946 Aboriginal Pastoral Worker's Strike', *Papers in Labour History*, vol. 1, 1988, pp. 31–42.
Day, Adrian, *Wadjelas: The Memoirs of a 1950s Patrol Officer*, Hesperian Press, Carlisle, 2010.
Doughty, James, *The Green Stick*, Collins, London, 1960.
Drake-Brockman, Judith, *Wongi Wongi*, Hesperian Press, Victoria Park, 2001.
Elkin, A. P., 'Australian Aboriginal and White Relations: A Personal Record', *Royal Australian Historical Society Journal*, vol. 48, no. 3, 1962, pp. 208–230.
Elkin, A. P., *Citizenship for the Aborigines: A National Aboriginal Policy*, Australasian Publishing Co., Sydney, 1944.
Elkins, Stanley, *Slavery: A Problem in American Institutional and Intellectual Life*, University of Chicago Press, Chicago, 1959.
Goodall, Heather, 'An Intelligent Parasite: A. P. Elkin and White Perceptions on the History of Aboriginal People in NSW', paper presented to the Australian Historical Association Conference, University of New South Wales, 1982.
Green, Neville, 'From Princes to Paupers: The Struggle for Control of Aborigines in Western Australia 1887–1898', *Early Days: Journal of the West Australian Historical Society*, vol. 11, no. 4, 1998, pp. 446–462.
Green, Neville, *The Forrest River Massacres*, Fremantle Arts Centre Press, Fremantle, 1995.
Green, Neville, *Triumphs and Tragedies: Oombulgurri, an Australian Aboriginal Community*, Hesperian Press, Carlisle, 2011.
Hale, Monty, *Kurlumarniny: We Come from the Desert*, Aboriginal Studies Press, Canberra, 2012.
Hall, Robert A., *The Black Diggers: Aborigines and Torres Strait Islanders in the Second World War*, Aboriginal Studies Press, Canberra, 1997 (electronic edition).
Halse, Christine, *A Terribly Wild Man*, Allen and Unwin, Crows Nest, 2002.
Hardie, Jenny, *Nor' Westers of the Pilbara Breed*, Hesperian Press, Carlisle, 1988.
Hasluck, Paul, *Shades of Darkness: Aboriginal Affairs 1925–1965*, Melbourne University Press, Carlton, 1988.
Hess, Michael, 'Black and Red: The Pilbara Pastoral Workers' Strike, 1946', *Aboriginal History*, vol. 18, no. 1, 1994, pp. 65–83.
Hewett, Dorothy, *Wild Card, an Autobiography, 1923–1958*, McPhee Gribble, South Yarra, Vic, 1990.
Hokari, Minoru, 'From Wattie Creek to Wattie Creek: An Oral History Approach to the Gurindji Walk-off', *Aboriginal History*, vol. 24, 2000, pp. 98–116.
Holman, Alan, 'Woman of Substance', *Record*, vol. 105, no. 1, 12 August 2000, pp. 8–9.
Holthouse, Edward, *One Life's Journey*, Hesperian Press, Carlisle, 1987.
Idriess, Ion, *Over the Range: Sunshine and Shadow in the Kimberleys*, Angus and Robertson, Sydney, 1937.
Jebb, Mary Anne, *Blood, Sweat and Welfare: A History of White Bosses and Aboriginal Pastoral Workers*, University of Western Australia Press, Crawley, 2002.
Johnston, Peter W., 'The Repeals of Section 70 of the Western Australian Constitution Act 1889: Aborigines and Governmental Breach of Trust', *Western Australian Law Review*, vol. 19, 1989, pp. 318–351.
Kinnane, Steven, *Shadow Lines*, Fremantle Arts Centre Press, Fremantle, 2003.
Long, Jeremy, *The Go-Betweens: Patrol Officers in Aboriginal Affairs Administration in the Northern Territory 1936–74*, North Australia Research Unit, Australian National University, 1992.
Lutze, E. C., 'Donald McLeod Before Skull Springs: The Origins of his Radicalism', BA (Honours) Thesis, University of Western Australia, 1984.
Lydon, Jane, and Ann Curthoys (eds.), *Governing Western Australian Aboriginal People: Section 70 of WA's 1889 Constitution, Studies in Western Australian History*, vol. 30, 2016.
Marchant, Leslie R., 'From the Diary of a Protector of Aborigines', *Quadrant*, April 2003, pp. 32–34.
McGrath, Ann, *Born in the Cattle: Aborigines in Cattle Country*, Allen and Unwin, Sydney, London and Boston, 1987.

Bibliography

McGregor, Russell, 'Governance, not Genocide: Aboriginal Assimilation in the Postwar Era', in A. Dirk Moses (ed.), *Genocide and Settler Society: Frontier Violence and Stolen Indigenous Children in Australian History*, Berghahn Books, New York and Oxford, 2004, pp. 290–311.

McGregor, Russell, *Indifferent Inclusions: Aboriginal People and the Nation*, Aboriginal Studies Press, Canberra, 2011.

McGregor, Russell, 'Words, Wards and Citizens: A. P. Elkin and Paul Hasluck on Assimilation', *Oceania*, vol. 69, no. 4, 1999, pp. 243–259.

McKnight, David, *Australia's Spies and their Secrets*, Allen and Unwin, St Leonards, 1994.

McLeod, D. W., *How the West Was Lost: The Native Question in the Development of Western Australia*, Don McLeod, Port Hedland, WA, 1984.

Monteath, Peter, and Valerie Munt, *Red Professor: The Cold War life of Fred Rose*, Wakefield Press, Mile End, 2015.

Morgan, Sally, *Wanamurraganya: The Story of Jack McPhee*, Fremantle Arts Centre Press, Fremantle, 1989.

Morris, John, '"Continuing Assimilation"? A Shifting Identity for the Tiwi 1919 to the Present', PhD Thesis, University of Ballarat, 2003.

Morrow, E., *The Law Provides*, Herbert Jenkins Ltd, London, 1937 (facsimile edition, Hesperian Press, Carlisle, 1984).

Muecke, Stephen, 'Don McLeod's Law: The Genesis of the Aboriginal Concept of the Strike', in Russell West-Pavlov and Jennifer Wawrzinek, *Frontier Skirmishes, Literary and Cultural Debates in Australia after 1992*, Winter Verlag, Heidelberg, 2010, pp. 71-79

Nettelbeck, Amanda, and Robert Foster, 'Food and Governance on the Frontiers of Colonial Australia and Canada's North West Territories', *Aboriginal History*, vol. 36, 2012, pp. 21–41.

Niall, Brenda, *True North: The Story of Mary and Elizabeth Durack*, Text Publishing Company, Melbourne, 2013.

Oliver, Bobbie, and W. S. Latter, 'Spooks, Spies and Subversives! The Wartime Security Service', in Jenny Gregory (ed.), *On the Homefront: Western Australia and World War II*, University of Western Australia Press, Nedlands, 1996, pp. 176–85.

Ostenfeld, Shane, 'The Pilbara Dispute', BA (Honours) Thesis, University of Sydney, 1991.

Owen, Chris, *Every Mother's Son is Guilty: Policing the Kimberley Frontier of Western Australia 1882–1905*, University of Western Australia Publishing, Crawley, 2016.

Palmer, Kingsley, and Clancy McKenna, *Somewhere Between Black and White: The Story of an Aboriginal Australian*, Macmillan, South Melbourne, 1978.

Preaud, Martin, 'Country, Law and Culture', PhD Thesis, James Cook University, 2009.

Read, Jolly, and Peter Coppin, *Kangkushot: The Life of Nyamal Lawman Peter Coppin*, Aboriginal Studies Press, Canberra, 1999.

Rose, Deborah Bird, *Hidden Histories: Black Stories from Victoria River Downs, Humbert River and Wave Hill Stations*, Aboriginal Studies Press, Canberra, 1991.

Rowse, Tim, *White Flour, White Power: From Rations to Citizenship in Central Australia*, Cambridge University Press, Cambridge, New York and Melbourne, 1998.

Scrimgeour, Anne, 'This Man's Tracks: Laurie O'Neill and Post-War Changes in Aboriginal Administration in Western Australia', *Aboriginal History*, vol. 38, 2014, pp. 39–58.

Skyring, Fiona, *Justice: A History of the Aboriginal Legal Service of Western Australia*, University of Western Australia Publishing, Crawley, 2001.

Stuart, Donald, *Yandy*, Georgian House, Melbourne, 1959.

Swain, Tony, *A Place for Strangers*, Cambridge University Press, Cambridge, 1993.

von Brandenstein, C. G., and A. P. Thomas (eds.), *Taruru: Aboriginal Song Poetry of the Pilbara*, Rigby, Adelaide, 1974.

Williams, Justina, *Anger and Love*, Fremantle Arts Centre Press, South Fremantle, 1993.

Wilson, Deborah, *Different White People: Radical Activism for Aboriginal Rights 1946–1972*, University of Western Australia Publishing, Crawley, 2015.

Wilson, John, 'Authority and Leadership' in a "New Style" Aboriginal Community', Masters Thesis, University of Western Australia, 1961.

Wilson, Katrin, 'The Allocation of Sex Roles in Social and Economic Affairs in a "New Syle" Australian Aboriginal Community, Pindan, Western Australia', Master of Science Thesis, University of Western Australia, 1961.

Wise, Tigger, *The Self-Made Anthropologist: A Life of A. P. Elkin*, Allen and Unwin, North Sydney, 1985.
Wyatt-Brown, Bertram, 'The Mask of Obedience: Male Slave Psychology in the Old South', *The American Historical Review*, vol. 93, no. 5, 1988, pp. 1228–1252.

Film

Williams, Heather, and David Noakes, *How the West Was Lost: The Story of the 1946 Aboriginal Pastoral Workers' Strike*, directed by David Noakes, Friends Film Productions and Market Street Films Ltd, Perth, 1987, DVD.

Online Sources

Curley, Avy, 'An Extraordinary Woman', 2009, *Hope Channel*,
https://www.hopechannel.com/au/read/an-extraordinary-woman, accessed 24 February 2019.

Day, Bill, 'Coffin Family of Redcliffs Station, Pilbara, Western Australia',
http://www.drbilldayanthropologist.com/resources/CoffinFamilyHistory.pdf, accessed 29 May 2017.

'Gribble, John Brown (1847–1893)', *Australian Dictionary of Biography*, National Centre of Biography, Australian National University,
http://adb.anu.edu.au/biography/gribble-john-brown-3668/text5727, published first in hardcopy 1972, accessed 23 November 2017.

Halse, Christine, 'Gribble, Ernest Richard Bulmer (Ernie) (1868–1957)', *Australian Dictionary of Biography*, National Centre of Biography, Australian National University,
http://adb.anu.edu.au/biography/gribble-ernest-richard-bulmer-ernie-10367, published first in hardcopy 1996, accessed 23 November 2017.

Layman, Lenore, 'Saint, Eric Galton (1918–1989)', *Australian Dictionary of Biography*, National Centre of Biography, Australian National University,
http://adb.anu.edu.au/biography/saint-eric-galton-15614, published first in hardcopy 2012, accessed 24 February 2019.

Perryman, John, 'A Brief History of Indigenous Service to the RAN', *A Naval Salute: Celebrating the Centenary of the Royal Australian Navy 1911–2011*, p. 24,
http://www.navy.gov.au/sites/default/files/documents/A_Naval_Salute_music_program.pdf, accessed 28 July 2019.

Wikipedia, '1946 Pilbara Strike', *Wikipedia the Free Encyclopedia*,
http://en.wikipedia.org/wiki/1946_Pilbara_strike, accessed 28 July 2019.

Index

101 North Australia Field Security 51–2

Aboriginal administration
  Bateman inquiry and report 297, 364–9, 400, 413
  call for Royal Commission into 283
  Elkin inquiry 283–4
  role of police in 365–7, 369–70, 389, 438, 459, 460
  see also Department of Native Affairs (DNA)
Aboriginal autonomy 295–7, 298–9
Aboriginal corporate authority
  assertion in dispute at Corunna Downs 391–3
  call for recognition of 416
  demand for recognition of McLeod as representative 288, 292–3, 398, 436–7
  refusal of DNA to recognition of McLeod as representative 433
  recognised by some station managers 424
  trial of strikers as challenge to 394–6
Aboriginal culture
  and access to country 26
  authority of older men recognized in strike camps 219, 293–4
  pastoralists' blindness to richness of 36, 92
  in Riverline Country 7
  see also Aboriginal Law
Aboriginal difference, racist understandings of 47, 132–3
Aboriginal labour
  disparagement of workers as lazy and incompetent 16–17
  domestic workers 17–18, 110, 351, 177, 179, 196–8
  employment agreements 10, 277, 350–2, 453
  exclusion from award 13
  forced labour. *see* forced Aboriginal labour
  importance for pastoral industry 11, 285–7, 368–9, 455–6
  lack of freedom to move between stations 24–5
  police support for pastoralist control over 22–6, 111
  purported cost to pastoralists 12–16, 18–20, 191
  wages and conditions in Pilbara 13, 121
  work permit system 10, 56–7, 60–1, 64–5
Aboriginal labour relations
  fabric of 38

marrngu resentment at inequality of treatment 39–42, 76–7, 200
  move to employee--employer basis 456–7
  pastoralists' control over 11
  reluctance of DNA to regulate 19
  throughout WA 458
Aboriginal Law, McLeod's exposure to and appreciation of 97–9
Aboriginal League of NSW 155
Aboriginal policy
  assimilation policy 282–3, 298, 370
  Communist Party policy 59, 99, 106, 147
  pressure for reform 282–5
  protection policy 10, 282
Aboriginal rights, awareness of issue in Pilbara 460
Aboriginal rights movement
  anti-communism in 64–5
  role of communists in 167
Aboriginal women
  impact of withdrawal of domestic labour 110, 177, 179, 196–8
  participation in strike 110
  payment for domestic service 351
  sexual exploitation of 241–4
Aboriginality, new understandings of 47, 281, 363
Aborigines Act 1905 20
Aborigines Department 9–10
Aborigines Protection Board 9
Abydos Station 38, 84, 85, 86, 96, 373–4
access to country
  accommodation reached between pastoralists and strikers 317
  actions against strikers for trespass 315–17
  conflicts over 27
  enclosed pastoral country 314
  legal means of gaining 315
  pastoralists control over residence on pastoral leases 111
  during *pingkayi* 26
  restrictions on access to pastoral leases 396
ACP. *see* Australian Communist Party
Adkins, H.R.C. 277
AFL. *see* Anti-Fascist League
Alcorn, Graham 69, 79, 106, 120–1, 146, 152, 155, 169, 186, 252, 352
Alcorn, Joy 155, 169
Alcorn, Wilson 151
Allen, Teddy 83, 351, 353
Allen, Tommy 82

495

ALP. *see* Australian Labor Party
anthropologists 298
Anti-Fascist League (AFL)
   on Aboriginal issues 58–9, 62
   foundation 48–9
   Marble Bar branch 49
   Port Hedland branch 61, 63–4
Anti-Slavery Society (London) 156, 413, 420
ASIO. *see* Australian Security Intelligence Organisation
assimilation policy 282–3, 298, 370
Australian Army, proposed internment camps for Aboriginal people 55–6
Australian Communist Party (ACP) 10, 64
   banning of 48
   campaign to support Pilbara strike 146–9, 155, 169–70
   on imprisonment of strikers 418
   policy on Aborigines 59, 99, 106, 147
   portrayed as instigator of strike 165
Australian Labor Party (ALP) 64
   call for amendments to *Native Administration Act* 157
   on release of Dooley and McKenna 161
Australian Security Intelligence Organisation (ASIO), report on McLeod 141
Australian Tobacco Trade Distribution Committee 214
Australian Workers' Union (AWU) 64
   anti-communism 255, 258, 441
   Broome branch 257–8
   membership of Aboriginal people 257
   Port Hedland branch 257, 261, 266, 269
   and wool ban 430, 441–3
AWU. *see* Australian Workers' Union

Balfour Downs Station 6
Ball, Daisy 176, 196–8, 200
Ball, Murphy 126
Ball, Wambi 105, 122, 123, 176, 196, 197, 200
Barker, Adam 219, 275, 353
Barramine Station 3–4, 6
Bateman, F. E. A. 335, 285, 324
Bateman Report 297, 364–9, 400, 413
Baxter, Charles 11
Beamish, Frank 331
Beazley, Kim (Snr) 154
Beeby, Edward 48, 49, 63
Bendhu Station 9
Bennet, Mary Montgomery 156, 157, 420
Bina, Sambo 402
Bindi, Daisy 388
Bisley, John 50–1, 52, 53, 54
The Black Eureka (Brown) 69, 403, 410

Blackburn, Doris 420
Blair, Charlie 403
Bligh, Keith 391–2, 396, 397–8, 455–6
Bob, Ginger (Palyakulayi) (*Purungu*) 175
   initiation 7, 91–2
   on interaction with gold miners 45
   migration to Riverline Country 2, 5
   on walk offs from stations 216
Bonham, Alfred (Alf) 255, 260–1, 262–3, 264, 266–7, 269–70
Bonney Downs Station 66, 73, 74–5, 93, 118–19, 245, 425
Boodarie Station 105, 126, 211
   return of workers under employment agreements 350
   woolshed fire 302–4, 305–8
Boulter, Robert 192
Braeside, Peter 31
Bray, Francis Illingworth 20, 56, 61, 63
   on Aboriginal mental capability 133
   on arrest of McKenna 135
   on consequences of May Day strike 142–3
   denial of work permit for McLeod 74
   on eligibility of Aboriginal people for AWU membership 258
   opposition to evacuation of Aborigines from North-West coastal areas 55, 56
   proclaiming of Port Hedland as prohibited area 53–4
   on prosecution of McLeod 144
   on public protest over imprisonment of strikers 165–6
   on rations for strikers 211
   resignation 284
   response to letters of protest 166–7
   response to May Day strike 128
Brine (or Brown), Cocky (Purnungurrara) 390–2
Bringing Them Home Report 370
Bropho, Tommy Nyinda 152, 157, 252
Brown, Max 69, 403, 410
Brown, Rob 256, 258, 358
Brown, Sandy 303, 358
Bryan, Edward 432
   on cost of Aboriginal labour 13, 191
   and Euralian community 50, 64, 65, 87–8
   invitations to strikers to move to White Springs 387–8
   proposal for Catholic Mission at White Springs 360–1, 374–5
   proposal for Catholic school in Port Hedland 348–9, 356
buffel grass seed, gathering of 210–11, 461
Bungalow (Coongan) Station. *see* Coongan Station
Bungalow, Billy 104, 124

INDEX

Callewa Station 114, 116–17, 125–6
Cameron, Avy. *see* Curley (née Cameron), Avy
Cameron, Bessie 247
Cameron, Charlie 247
Cameron, Clarrie 248, 249
Cameron, Esther 248, 250
Cameron, Leedham 246, 248
Cameron, Walter
　background 247–8
　Communist Party membership 251–2
　initial arrest for loitering 247
　initiation 247–8
　police view of 246
　protest against initial charge of loitering 248–50
　removal to Moore River 253–4
　second arrest and imprisonment for loitering 251
Cameron, Willie 246
Canning Stock Route 2, 3
Captain, Ron 82, 89, 100–2, 230, 353
Carbine, Dendo 241–6
Carlin, Colin 245–6
Carlindi Station 105, 124, 136
Cathedral Chronicle 297–8
　on Hodge as dupe of communists 192–3
　response to letter from McLeod 465–75
CDNR. *see* Committee for Defence of Native Rights
Chedzey, George 251
Chifley, Ben 156
children
　numbers on pastoral stations 14
　removal of children of mixed descent 31–3, 245–6, 388
Chipper, Vern 405–7
Chipperfield, Charles 53, 54, 56–7, 61–2, 64, 425, 426
Chullingworth, Harold 351
Citizenship for the Aborigines (Elkin) 216, 282–3, 295, 362
Clarke, Helena 50
Clarke, Lawrence (Pop) 49–50, 54, 61, 64, 88, 129
Clarke, Tommy 83, 351
Clarke, Vince 88, 287
Clarke family 49, 52–3, 54, 61
Cocky, Solomon (Ngalyarrkiny) 2
Cocky Brine (or Brown) (Purnungurrara)
Coffin, Jack 57, 96
columbite extraction 461
Committee for Defence of Native Rights (CDNR)
　appeal against convictions of Dooley and McKenna 162
　appeal to United Nations 155–6
　assistance for strikers 210, 214

assistance for Twelve Mile school 342
　criticisms of 164
　election of permanent committee 152
　legal defence for McLeod 149
　misrepresentation as communist organisation 167–8
　protest against treatment of McKenna and Dooley 149, 151–6
　protest against use of *Native Administration Act* as anti-strike weapon 236–7
　Provisional Committee 149, 151–2
　renaming of organisation 169
　withdrawal of communist members 169
Commonwealth Police, Commonwealth Investigation Service 307
Commonwealth Powers Act 1943 11
Communist Party. *see* Australian Communist Party
Conochie, Edith 147
Coobie 174
Cooglegong tin field 390
Cook, Cecil (Mick) 382
Coolbaroo Club 50
Coongan Station 13, 31, 104, 117, 124–5, 455
Coppin, Jack (Yarrie Jack, or Ngarlkapangu) 82
Coppin, Owen 18, 19
Coppin, Peter (Kangkushot) (*Purungu*) 82, 96, 97, 126, 219, 275, 303
　on conflict between McGreary and strikers 328–30
　as driver for Gribble 336
　on Gribble at Noreena Downs 337
　on non-Aboriginal jackaroos 286
　playing the 'dumb blackfellow' 138–9
　on prevention of workers leaving pastoral stations 24–5
　on social distance 34
Coppin, Sam 14, 256, 258
Coppin, Yarrie Jack (Ngarlkapangu) 113, 115, 229–30, 231
Corbett, Mick 225, 230, 231
Cornish, Dougal 89, 101, 104–5, 126, 337–8
Corunna Downs RAAF airbase 44, 66, 73
Corunna Downs Station 65, 228
　arrest of Moolyella strikers 392–3
　dispute over negotiation of wages and conditions 390–2
　paid to release Aboriginal workers 14
Cosmo Newbery 400–1, 412, 415
Council for Aboriginal Rights 195
Court of Criminal Appeal, Western Australia, overturning of McLeod's conviction and prison sentence 278
Coverley, Aubrey Augustus Michael (Bob) 61, 63, 260, 264, 327, 370–1, 430, 445
　on Aboriginal workers 21

497

on CDNR as communist organisation 168–9
on cost of Aboriginal labour 13
as Minister for the North West 20–1
pro-pastoralist approach 281
and proposed inquiry by Elkin 283–4
on protection of Aborigines 20
on release of Dooley and McKenna 161
segregated toilets for school in Port Hedland 50
on unregulated use of Aboriginal labour 20
Cowie, James 332
Craig, Gordon 276, 287
Craig, Les 12
Cranky (Kujupurru) (*Purungu*)
  friendship with Peter Miller 37, 38
  on Harry Greene 202
  journey to Moolyella 204
  lack of wages 13
  living independently 461
  on mealtimes at Warrawagine 39
  on prevention of strikers using trains 265
  on sharing of rations 15
  strike on 29 April 1946 112–13, 115
  on tin mining 209
  walk-off from Warrawagine 203–4
Crawford, Alan 122, 123, 189
Criminal Code, section 669 435
Curley (née Cameron), Avy 247, 248–51, 252
Curley, George 247, 248
Curran, Fred 149, 151, 157, 160, 252, 272, 273, 275, 279

Dann family 49
Davenport, Fred 390–1, 392, 423, 424, 433
Davies, Lloyd 167, 169, 218, 222
Davis, Harry 219, 233, 275, 353
DE. *see* Department of Education
De Grey River 1
De Grey River Pastoral Company 19
De Grey Station 33, 105
  on 1 May 1946 117
  acceptance of temporary 5/- wage increase 117, 121
  decision by workers to forego extra wages 171
  domestic workers demand for wages 110
  extent of work done by *marrngu* 1
  living conditions for workers 228
  loss of workers 177
  strike by workers on 26 April 1946 109
  walk-offs by workers 198
de Passey, Cedric 344, 345–6, 372, 388
Department of Education
  correspondence lessons for Twelve Mile school 342–4, 346–8, 372

de Passey's report on Twelve Mile school 344, 345–6
proposed school at Moolyella 356, 372–3
Department of Native Affairs 123, 282, 297, 453
  assimilation policy 50–1, 169, 450
  attempt to resolve Pilbara dispute by discussion and negotiation 287–9, 291–5
  attempt to return Moolyella defectors to Marble Bar 237–40
  campaign to counter criticism of its response to strike 162–4
  concerns over links between Aboriginal people and AFL 61–6
  conflicting priorities 389–90
  control over Aboriginal employment 10, 56, 65, 256–7, 268, 279–80
  counter propaganda 460–1
  and education of children in strike camps 341, 342–3, 356, 373, 376, 386–7
  employment of ex-policemen as Native Affairs officers 22–3
  establishment 10
  Gribble's appointment as Special Officer 325, 327–8, 334, 335–6, 338, 340
  interpretation of Native Affairs legislation 279–80
  negotiation of employment contracts 453–4, 455, 456–7, 458
  opposition to wartime internment camps for non-working Aboriginal people 55–6
  plans to remove strike leaders following High Court decision 275, 278
  prevention of initiation of 'half-castes' 247–8
  prohibited areas for Aboriginal people 53, 247
  proposed native reserve at Moolyella 322–3
  proposed support for self-supporting communities 295–8
  prosecution of McLeod 131–2, 135–6, 151
  on rations for strikers 212–13
  on reasons for May Day strike action 141–2
  reduction of control over Aboriginal interaction with non-Aboriginal people 278–9
  refusal to recognise McLeod as strikers' representative 288, 292–3, 436–7, 447–8
  refusal to negotiate with strikers 447–8, 450–1
  on release of Dooley and McKenna 162
  reluctance to disrupt pastoral labour relations 19, 457
  removal of Aboriginal people from home country and community 90, 245, 368, 400, 413–14, 422
  removal of children of mixed descent 31–3

removal of 'old school' officers from Pilbara 437–8
structural and policy change 364, 369–71
support for Aboriginal workers strike in Pilbara 456–7
support for segregation 50–1
Twelve Mile declared as prohibited area 377–9
on wage scale for pastoral workers 445
on White Springs Mission 373, 375–6, 385
see also Bray, Francis Illingworth; McBeath, Charles; Middleton, Stanley Guise (Stan); Neville, A.O.; O'Neill, Laurence (Laurie)
dingoes 359
Dixon, Owen 275, 276
DNA. *see* Department of Native Affairs
Dobey, Roy 453, 454, 455
Dodd, Tommy 126, 141, 151, 158, 159
dog culls, dawn raids by police on *marrngu* camps 27–9
domestic workers 351
Donnelly, John 261
Dooley (Dooley Binbin) (Winyirin or Yurlpuly) (*Milangka*) 69, 290
arrest, conviction and imprisonment 134–6, 143, 145, 146
call for mass civil disobedience 396–7, 401, 402
conflict with Gordon Mackay 226–7
on deductions from wages 14
dismissal of appeals against conviction 218, 274, 275–6
leadership of Moolyella camp 223–4, 400
meetings with McLeod 219
and Moolyella agreement 447
move to Twelve Mile camp 184
opposition to White Springs Mission 387–8
on origins of strike movement 94
and race-day demonstrations 175–6, 181
release from prison 161–2
role in strike movement 93, 101, 102–5, 128
as witness in trial of McLeod 158
Dorrigo, SS 444
dispute over unloading of 255–60
and wool ban 430, 431–2
Doughty, James 199, 216, 245
Drake-Brockman, Judith 38
Dulverton, SS 441, 442, 447
'dumb blackfellow' strategy 137–9, 415
Duncan, Ken 103, 128, 158, 159
Durack, Elizabeth 38
Durack, Mary 38, 59, 78–9
Durack, Michael 34
Dwyer, John 272, 273

Eginbah Station 104, 125, 126
Elkin, A. P. 79, 281, 282, 283–4, 285, 295, 298, 362, 371
Elliott-Smith, Sydney 369
agreement with strikers 436–8
assimilationist views 450
background 431
criticism of DNA 449
defence of strikers 432–3, 435, 439
discussions with Hogg 431
discussions with Moolyella strikers 433, 447–8
discussions with Twelve Mile strikers 432
failure to attend Marble Bar meeting with strikers 453
guarantee regarding wage rates in return for end to wool ban 442–5, 446–7
on improved employment conditions on stations 454
meetings with McLeod 433–4
on racist settler attitudes to Aboriginal people 437, 438
view of Dooley 448
view of McLeod 437, 447, 449–50
employment agreements, between employers and Aboriginal workers 10
equality 45–6
Ethel Creek Station 48
Euralian Association
affiliation with Anti-Fascist League 61, 64–5
annual Races Ball 175
establishment and role 49–50
and Marble Bar convention 87–9
protest over native passes 54, 58, 60
protest over work permits 56–7, 60–1, 64–5
Euralian community, Port Hedland
AWU membership amongst 257
contribution to war effort 51, 52, 63
social status 49–51
as source of wharf labour 256
surveillance during war 52–3, 56–7
Evatt, H.V. 156

Fenton, Alec 47, 69
Flann, Banjo 425
Fletcher, Les 175, 275
arrest of McLeod 182
attempts to quash strike idea 90
discussions with strikers 122–3
on employment of Thompson on wharf 267–8
and Four Mile camp meeting 83
investigation of Boodarie woolshed fire 302–3
loss of ability to control strikers 184–5
on ration coupons for strikers 211, 213
refusal to distribute ration coupons to strikers 181–2

on tactics used to hold strikers at strike camps 198
as witness in trial of McLeod 160
Flight-Smith, Neville 124, 305, 332
Forrest River Anglican mission 325, 326
Forrest River massacre 239
Four Mile meetings 82–5, 94, 96, 97
Fox, A.C. 166
Foxcraft, Gilbert 152, 167
Fremantle Branch of Seamen's Union. *see* Seamen's Union, Fremantle Branch
Fremantle Districts Sentinel 59

Gallop, Doug 66, 75, 94
Gallop, Thora 66, 75, 94, 118
Gardiner, Mac (Pirntilkampanyaja) (*Milangka*)
 on arrest of strikers 405, 406, 407
 arrival at Barrmine Station from desert 5
 on beating of workers 27
 birth 3–4
 lack of wages 13
 on removal of children 32, 388
 settlement at Warrawagine Station 6
 strike on 29 April 1946 116
 walk off from Warrawagine 425, 426
 on walk-offs by workers 201
Gare, Frank 199, 301
Gilbert, George 246, 249
Gilbert, Jack 246
Ginger, Maggie (Nyirrarlpi) (*Milangka*)
 hidden from police as a child 33
 on Lang Coppin 37
 on mining in Pilgangoora area 462
 on walk-off from Nimingarra 201
Golding, Charles 257, 258, 267, 441
Grant, Don 420
Great Sandy Desert
 migration of Aboriginal people to Riverline Country 2–7
 settler violence 2–3
The Green Stick (Doughty) 23, 24, 25, 27, 35, 114, 199, 216, 245, 247, 286, 307, 437, 439
Greene, Harry 86, 202
Greenwood, Irene 152
Gribble, Ernest Richard Bulmer 325, 326
Gribble, John Wriede Bulmer (Jack)
 appointment as DNA Special Officer at Twelfve Mile 325, 327–8, 331
 association with settler authority 332
 background 325–6, 476–82
 as cause of further strike action 336–8
 first tour of area 332–3
 misconduct 334, 338, 339
 termination of appointment 338
 visit to Moolyella 333–4
Groves, Bert 155

Hale, Monty (Minyjun) (*Panaka*) 318, 390
 on dawn dog cull raid 28
 on life at Moolyeal 223
 move to Mt Edgar Station 30–1
 on move to strike camp 201
Hall, Henty 306
Hall, Mary 306
Hancock, Lang 307–8
Harcus, Geoff 252
Harris, Eva 248, 249
Harwood, Maurice 158, 160, 233, 234, 306, 307
Hasluck, Paul 156
Hawke, Noel 453, 455, 458, 461, 462
Hegney, William (Bill) 61, 64, 157
 anti-communism opposition to McLeod 267
 RAAF airbase 65
 response to May Day strike 132
 on striking workers 140
Hewett, Dorothy 106, 147, 155, 170, 218, 220, 222, 224, 237, 343
High Court of Australia
 dismissal of appeals by McLeod, McKenna and Dooley 275–6
 setting aside of Hodge's conviction 28, 240, 271, 276
Hillside Station 125–6
Hodge, Hugh Peter Vere (Peter) 169, 194, 275
 appeal against conviction dismissed by Supreme Court 218, 272–3
 arrest and trial 187–8
 background 186
 on McKenna's leadership qualities 220
 portrayal as dupe of communist manipulation 167
 at public meeting in Port Hedland 189–93
 on rations for strikers 212–13
 as secretary of CDNR 149, 152, 186
 setting aside of conviction by High Court 240, 271, 276, 278
 trip to Port Hedland following second arrest of McLeod 186–7, 194–5
 visit to Twelve Mile camp 188–9
Hodge, Theodore 186
Hogg, Keith 394–5, 396, 409, 410, 411, 431, 435
Holthouse, Edward 24, 26–7
Hughes, Thomas John 409, 411
human rights 45–6
Hurd, Ron 417, 424, 429–30, 442–3, 444, 445

Idriess, Ion 90, 133, 186, 402
Indee Station 88, 119, 129, 131, 173, 184, 350
internment camps 55–6

Index

Jackson 126, 151, 158, 159, 225, 391-2, 422
Jeffries, Edmund 126, 400
Jensen, Thomas Emmes (Tom) 237, 264-5, 275, 305, 369, 406, 411
  on Aboriginal corporate authority 393
  attempt to persuade strikers to return to stations 287-9, 290
  complaints about Gribble 335
  and dispute on Corunna Downs 392-3
  on employment agreements 351
  investigation of Boodarie woolshed fire 302-4
  on living conditions at Moolyella 357
  recommendations to curtail Aboriginal freedom of movement 319-22
Jittermarra, Snowy (Maruntu) (*Panaka*) 2
  on inequality of treatment 41-2
  on lack of shelter 40
  on origins of strike movement 76-7
  on settler violence 8
  on use of police to return workers to stations 29-30
  walk off from Noreena Downs 426-7, 434
Johnson, Vic 420
Johnston, David 286-7
Jolly, Alexander Thomas Hicks (Alec) 148, 149, 152, 165
Jones, H. A. 324, 335
Jula, Caroline (Jula) (*Milangka*) 217
  on chaining of Aboriginal people 407
  friendship with Patsy Miller 37
  as housegirl at Warrawagine Station 17-18
  on journey to Moolyella 202-3
  on learning to work tin 208-9
  on mass civil disobedience 401, 402
  physical punishment of 27
  on rations 39, 40
  removal of son 245-6
  walk-off from Warrawagine 205
Julurru cult 96, 97

Kangan Station 360, 372, 373
Kariyarra people 1, 8
Kelly, Cecil 52
Kitchener 85, 102, 108
  employment by McLeod 73
  friendship with McLeod 48, 66
  reputation 48
  role in strike movement 48, 82, 89, 118-19
  as witness in trial of McLeod 151, 158, 159
Kybra, MV 175, 441, 442, 443, 444, 447, 451

Lalla Rookh Station 104, 126
Land Act 1933 309-10, 314
Latham, John 275
League of Coloured Peoples 156
Lee, Mick 110-11, 117, 181, 214, 219, 275, 286
Leeds, F.A. 135
Leeper, Valentine 79
Lefroy, Langlois 164
legal assistance, denied to Aboriginal people on trial 250, 409-11
Leslie, Hugh 133
Lewis, G. A. (Jim) 113, 114, 115, 203, 204-5, 207, 243
Lewis, Nancy 243
Limestone Station 127, 423-4
Lindley, Roy 244
Lockyer, Aubrey 306
Lockyer, Edgar 48, 57, 61
Lockyer, George 159
Lockyer, Willie 126
Lukis, Rob 110-11, 178, 228, 276, 313, 373
Lund, Marjorie 236
Lund, V. L. (Wally) 233-6, 290, 316

Mackay, Gordon 176, 223
  arrest by strikers 231
  background 226
  conflict with Dooley 226-7
  leadership of breakaway movement 225-30
Mackay, Nancy 111, 117, 174
Mackay, Roy 82, 159, 174, 176, 223, 303
  background 226
  eviction following refusal to work 110-11
  strike on 30 April 1946 117
  support for land scheme 85
  support for May Day strike 105
Mallet, George 423, 424, 433
Mandora Station 134
Mangarla people 2, 5
Mann, James 164
Marble Bar convention 87-9
Marble Bar native reserve, eviction of striking workers 127-8
Marble Bar races 201
Marchant, Leslie 370
Marney, Bill 405, 406
marrngu 175, 293-4
  assertion of authority through group action 183, 184-5
  exclusion from settler social spaces 35-6
  imprisonment for cause as source of pride 224
  incorporation of Aboriginal people from Great Sandy Desert 2-7
  interaction with servicemen during war 44-5
  interaction with miners 45
  knowledge of legal rights 24, 460
  as labour force on stations in Riverline Country 1-2
  maintenance of religious and cultural practices and connection with Country 18

meaning of word 'force' 200
meaning of word 'strike' 140
presence and status in relation to settler community 458–60
pressure to join strike 198–200
purchase of stations 463
negotiations for return to station employment 455
relationship with pastoralists. *see* pastoralist–*marrngu* relationship
relationship with police 460
restricted access to firearms and bullets 304, 305
strategy of playing the 'dumb blackfellow' 137–9
treatment in court 435
Marshall, Gordon
　on abduction of defectors 231, 232–3
　on breakaway group 226, 227
　criticism of DNA 427
　eviction of striking workers from native reserve 127–8
　fictional portrayal of 23–4
　gathering of evidence against McLeod 147
　on influence of Anti-Fascist League 62–3
　on lack of sanitation at Moolyella 222
　planned return of defectors to stations 229–30
　removal of children of mixed descent 31, 32
　on removal of strike ringleaders 412–13, 427
　response to strike at Warrawagine Station 114–17
　suppression of May Day strike 124–6
　surveillance of McKenna 101
　threats against striking workers 115–16
　on workers' reasons for strike action 140–1
Marshall, William 262
Mason, W. J. (Bill)
　and abduction of defectors from Moolyella 233
　attempt to remove strikers at Twelve Mile 238–40
　condemnation of Bonham 260–1, 262
　exclusion of Euralian workers from employment 259
　prevention of strikers working on wharf 256, 258–9, 260
　violent assault on Aboriginal man 137, 239, 263–4
mass civil disobedience 397, 401, 402–16, 439
May Day strike 117
　30/- wage demand 120–1, 122–3, 153
　action by town workers and miners 126–8, 141
　competing objectives 123
　difficulty of adhering to plan 119–20

difficulty of coordinating action 124
expected duration 104
extent of intention to participate 119–20, 125–6
imprisonment of organisers 134–6
planned action 118–19
police questioning of workers in aftermath 136–40
principal demands 121–2
prior sporadic strike action 109–17
response of DNA to 131–2
sporadic strike action during first week of May 128
suppression by police patrols 124–6
weakened by compromises 123–4
McBeath, Charles Lewis (Lew) 152, 177, 181, 213, 237, 253, 275
　on abduction of defectors 232
　attempt to break deadlock in time for shearing 291–5
　bullying of Sampie 316
　on employment of Thompson on wharf 268
　on eligibility of Aboriginal people for AWU membership 258
　on employer agreements 351–2
　fears of subversive communist influence on Aboriginal people 246, 251, 253
　on leadership at strike camps 217–18
　on Mason's assault of Aboriginal man 263–4
　overlooked for position of Commissioner 284–5
　on Sampie as dangerous radical 353, 355
　as superintendent of Moola Bulla 369
　on Twelve Mile school 344–5, 347
McCrae, - (Constable) 25, 28
McDonald, Robert Ross (Ross) 253, 263, 269–70
　background 281
　as first Minister of Native Affairs 281–2, 283
　on Native Rights and Welfare League pamphlet 419–20, 425
　on need for inquiry into Aboriginal administration 183, 184
　negotiations with strikers 287
　pressure on DE to support Twelve Mile school 346–7
　on removal of strike ringleaders 413, 422
　tour of the north in June 1947 324
　on Twelve Mile as prohibited area 377–8
　on use of violence against strikers 422–3
　on wages and conditions on stations 429
McGeary, Bernie 279, 328–30, 378
McGregor, Don 124
McGuckin, James 306, 307

Index

McKenna, Clancy (Warntupungkarna) (*Purungu*) 45, 176, 187
  arrest, conviction and imprisonment for breach of s 47 134–6, 144, 145, 146, 161–2
  arrest, trial and imprisonment for breach of s 9 233–4, 236–7
  background 75
  beachcombers licence 214
  on deductions from wages 14
  dismissal of appeals against conviction for breach of s 47 218, 274, 275–6
  and Four Mile camp meeting 82
  and initiation of Ginger Bob 7, 91–2
  on land scheme for Aboriginal people 84
  leadership qualities 219–20
  leadership role at Twelve Mile 285–6, 290, 291, 292
  move to Twelve Mile camp 184
  on origins of strike movement 94
  prevention of defectors returning to Warrawagine 230–3
  prosecution for trespass 315, 317
  and race-day demonstrations 181
  relationship with McLeod 75–6, 78, 84
  role in strike movement 75–6, 82, 89, 103–4, 105, 128, 134
  and 'threat of the green stick' 199
  threatened with legal action and removal from district 101–2
  as witness in trial of McLeod 158–9
  work at Munda Station 330
McKenna, Dick 224
McLarty, Duncan Ross (Ross) 358, 359, 360, 420
McLeod, Donald William (Don) (Ngarnka, Ngarnkawaru, or Mirta) 107, 278
  on Aboriginal 'advancement' 296
  on Aboriginal Law 97–9
  account of May Day strike 128
  advocacy for regional development 80–1
  advocacy for rights of Euralian community in Port Hedland 57–66, 73
  and Anti-Fascist League 49, 58–9, 61, 63–4, 73, 78
  arrest and trial for breach of s 47 144–5, 146, 149–50, 157–61
  arrests and trials for breach of s 39 182–3, 188–9, 193–4
  assistance for strikers 214, 358–9, 390, 461–3
  authority within Aboriginal Law 72, 96, 98
  banned from entry to Corunna Downs airbase 73
  and Boodarie woolshed fire 303, 307–8
  campaign to support Pilbara strike 156–7
  campaigning for public support for strike 106–9
  Communist Party connections 79, 106
  Communist Party membership 106–7, 164–5
  conviction and prison sentence for breach of s 39 overturned 278
  dismissal of appeals against conviction for breach of s 47 218, 274, 275–6
  and dispute over employment of non-exempt Aboriginal people on wharf 266–8, 269
  and dispute over employment of strikers on wharf 255–60
  early life 46–7
  electoral candidacy for Progressive Labor 78
  ending of wool ban in return for guarantee regarding wage rates 442–5, 449
  on eviction of Twelve Mile residents 384–5
  financial relationship with strikers 291
  Four Mile camp meeting 82–5
  friendship with Kitchener 48, 66
  on imprisonment of strikers 417–18
  influences on 47–8, 58, 65
  on lack of justice in trials of Aboriginal people 395–6
  on mass civil disobedience 397
  meetings with Elliott-Smith and Pullen 433–4
  meetings with strike camp leaders 218–19
  mining venture in Pilgangoora area 461–3
  One Mile reserve meeting 93
  pearl-buyer's licence 290
  permit to employ Aboriginal workers 73–5, 81, 93
  persecution by police 358–9
  under police surveillance 101
  political activism for Aboriginal rights issues 57
  on principle demands of May Day strike 121–3
  on relationship with Alf Bonham 262–3
  relationship with Thora Gallop 94, 98
  release on bail 151
  request for appointment as a Protector of Natives 81–2, 85
  request for appointment as honorary Inspector of Natives 102, 106, 108
  role in strike movement 77–8, 79, 86, 94–5, 132, 149
  schemes to acquire land for Aboriginal people 59, 71, 79–80, 85, 86, 360, 372–3
  settler fear of his communist agenda 300–1

and Skull Springs meeting 67–73, 93–4, 97–9
support for Aboriginal social, economic and political equality 49
support for Communist Party 78
and trial of thirty-two strikers 409–12
McPhee, Bidgie 36, 38
McPhee, Jack 52, 77–8
McPhee, Rory 36, 83, 104
McWhirter, Don 173, 175, 303
Meentheena Station 228, 402–3
Menzies, Robert 168, 430
Methodist Inland Mission 192
Middleditch, Robert (Bob) 287, 400, 421, 422, 426, 428
Middleton, Stanley Guise (Stan) 194
  appointment as Commissioner of Native Affairs 362–3
  declaration of Twelve Mile as probited area 378–9, 383
  discussion with strikers over new DNA policies 414–15
  on Elliott's guarantee to McLeod 445
  on improvement in industrial situation 454–5
  on Native Rights and Welfare League pamphlet 419
  on proposed wool ban by Seamen's Union 424
  on racism in Western Australia 363–4
  on removal of strikers to Cosmo Newbery 411–12, 413–14
  on strikers as victims of McLeod's machinations 414
  warning to O'Neill over his approach 408
Miles, George 159
Miles, J.B. 107
Miller, Edith
  on Aboriginal people as childlike 30
  friendship with Bidgie McPhee 38
  interference in removal of children 32–3
  on organisational capacity of Aboriginal people 92
  on payment of domestic workers 110
  on physical punishment of workers 27
  pity for strikers 205
  respect felt for 38
  on striker's lack of understanding of their actions 141
  on Twelve Mile work parties 317
Miller, Les 177
  on improving living conditions at stations 228
  interference in removal of children 32–3
  on intimidation of workers by strikers 198
  on intrusions by Twelve Mile work parties 313
  physical punishment of workers 27, 243
  proceedings against strikers for trespassing 315–17
  at public meeting in Port Hedland 191
  response to strike by workers 109, 111
Miller, Patsy 37
Miller, Peter 37, 38
Mining Act 1904 80
mining as source of income for *marrngu*
  columbite extraction 461, 463
  profits from 463
  tantalite extraction 461, 463
  tin mining 6, 30, 184, 208–9, 223, 285, 350, 390, 461, 463
  wolfram 463
Mitchell, Ernie (Putungaja) (*Karimarra*) 105
  arrest for using threatening words 328–30
  and Boodarie woolshed fire 303, 306
  'dumb blackfellow' strategy 138–40
  employment on wharf 256–60
  ineligibility for AWU membership 258
  leadership role at Moolyella 353, 400
  leadership role at Twelve Mile 176, 219–20, 286, 290, 330
  move to Twelve Mile camp 124, 171, 174
  wages at Tabba Tabba 122, 123
Mitchell, James 161
Mitchell, Sam 83, 256
Modern Women's Club 108, 152, 237
Monaghan, Tommy 256, 258
Moola Bulla Aboriginal Station 100, 238, 338, 369
Moolyella 119, 128, 174
  agreement between strikers and DNA officials 436–8, 440–1, 447–8, 452, 455
  breakaway movement 225–30
  food supplies 209–10
  leadership arrangements 223–4, 353
  living conditions 222, 224–5, 357–8, 381, 390
  location 310
  McBeath's visit 293–4
  negotiation of wages and conditions on stations 390–2
  and Pilgangoora mining venture 461–2
  population of camp 196, 215, 222, 319, 350, 463
  school 223, 372
  tin mining 6, 30, 184, 208–9, 223, 285, 350, 390, 461
  visits by police and Native Affairs officers 217, 225
Moore, Robert Henry 152, 167, 168
Moore River settlement 32, 152, 239, 253–4, 287, 291
Morden, Mary 152
Morrow, Edgar 27–8

Moseley Royal Commission in Aboriginal affairs 324
Mt Edgar Station, return of defectors 229, 230
Mt Magnet
  prohibited areas for Aboriginal people 247, 249
  protest against imprisonment for loitering 248–53, 297
Muccan Station 24
  living conditions for workers 228
  removal of children of mixed descent 33
  return of defectors 229, 230
  suppression of strike action by police 125
Mulyie Station 125, 286
  Ettrick outcamp 29
  living conditions for workers 228, 352
  ownership of 19
  provision for indigent residents 15–16
  wages paid 351
  walk-offs by workers 200–1
Mundabullangana Pastoral Company 276
Mundabullangana Station 89, 105
  on 1 May 1946 117
  access by Twelve Mile work parties 313
  eviction of striking workers 111, 119
  living conditions for workers 228
  loss of workers 177–8
  return of workers under employment agreements 350
  strike by workers on 30 April 1946 110–11
Murphy, Thomas 259
Murray, Hubert 362, 363
Musso, L.A. 221

Nangananga, Tommy (Manapurjta) 134
National Council for Civil Liberties (London) 156
National Missionary Council 283, 357
Native (Citizenship Rights) Act 1944 64–5
Native Administration Act 1936 10, 65, 413, 460
  Certificates of Exemption 256, 259, 268
  employment agreements 351
  labour conditions imposed on Aboriginal people 160
  police power to order Aboriginal people to leave town 249
  racism enshrined in 363–4
  regulation 81A--C 150
  regulations 107/8 377
  section 9 233
  section 12 90, 322
  section 18 256–7, 267
  section 18(1) 56
  section 26 24
  section 34(5) 291
  section 39 81, 135, 187, 271, 272–3, 461–2
  section 40 377
  section 47 134, 154, 161, 232, 274, 392, 407
  section 48 358, 392, 393, 407
  work permit regulations 256, 268
Native Rights and Welfare League 169, 418–20
Native Rights League 169, 252–3, 336
Needle, Tom 175, 328, 332–3
Neville, A.O. 15, 20, 247, 248
Ngarla people 1, 8
Ngiyirr, Bandy 203
Nimingarra Station 201
non-violent resistance 176, 180, 181, 406
Noreena Downs Station 2, 93, 337, 426–7, 434
Norman, Donald 174, 337–8
North 151
Northover, Paddy 127, 159
North-West and Kimberley Advancement Association 87, 93–4, 131–2
North-West Workers' Association, recognition of 288, 289–90, 292
Nowers, Rose 50, 51, 54, 55, 65, 175
Nullagine 118, 142
Nullagine Progress Association 81, 87, 88
Nulsen, Emil 157, 161, 237
Nyamal people 1, 8
Nyangumarta language 1
Nyangumarta people 2
Nyiyaparli people 1, 8

One Wet Season (Idriess) 216
O'Neill, Laurence (Laurie) 51–2, 89, 117, 275, 367, 369
  on Aboriginal biological inferiority 133, 140, 438
  arrest and prosecution of McKenna 134
  bullying of Sampie 316
  on conditions for Aboriginal station workers 159–60
  confusion over role 408
  enforcement of Aboriginal worker compliance 425, 428–9
  executive powers to act on his own initiative 393
  gathering of evidence against McLeod 147, 151
  investigation of Gribble 338
  investigation of Lund 235–6
  on legal assistance for strikers on trial 410
  on likelihood of a strike 90, 100
  on McLeod as possible pastoralist 94
  on needs and wants of Aboriginal station workers 142
  opposition to provision of rations at Twelve Mile 172–3

overlooked for position of Commissioner 284–5
patrol of stations in aftermath of strikes 134–6
powerlessness in face of race-day demonstrations 179–81
on reasons for strike action 139–40
removal from office 437–9
removal of children of mixed descent 183
reputation 180, 402
response to abduction of defectors 232, 233
response to *marrngu* resistance 176–7
search for site to house Twelve Mile residents 385
suicide 439
threats made to strike organisers 100–1
and trial following Corunna Downs dispute 393–7
as witness in trial of McLeod 159–60

Paanju, Jack 3–4
Pardoo Station 105
Parker, Herbert 454
pastoral industry
   impact of Second World War 44, 45, 55–6
   importance of Aboriginal labour 11, 18, 285–7, 368–9, 455–6
pastoral leases
   Aboriginal access to. *see* access to country 309
   pastoralist control over Aboriginal residence on 111
pastoral stations
   Aboriginal people sent away during low season 18
   control over access to country 26–7
   control over rations 207–8
   evictions of non-productive station residents 207
   forced Aboriginal labour 4, 9
   holiday time/*pingkayi* 18, 24–5
   importance of domestic labour 18
   as key sites of colonial governance 11
   labour shortages due to strike 285–7, 454
   living conditions for Aboriginal workers 352
   non-Aboriginal labour 286–7
   physical punishment of workers 27
   proposed conditions for re-employment of strikers 276–7, 278
   provision for children resident on 14
   provision for indigent residents 14–16
   purported cost of Aboriginal labour 12–16, 18–20
   removal of children of mixed descent 31–3, 461
   social separation of *marrngu* 33–6

stock losses resulting from theft by strikers 318
systems to prevent workers from leaving 24–6
workers responses to unfair treatment 29
pastoralist-*marrngu* relationship
   demonstrations of solicitude 18, 30, 33, 205
   duplicitous nature of 31
   friendships 37–8
   hostility towards strikers 303
   kinship and loyalty 33, 37, 206
   lack of animosity towards strikers 204–6
   limited power of *marrngu*
   paternalism 29–31
   and removal of children 31–3
   social distance 33–7
pastoralists
   blindness to richness of Aboriginal culture 36, 92
   demand for harsher penalties against strikers 400
   fear of McLeod's communistic agenda 300–1
   meeting over 'native situation' 397–8, 399
   power and prestige challenged by strike 399
Pastoralists Association 85, 92, 132, 135, 158, 277, 313, 389, 399, 429, 445
paternalistic benevolence, and Aboriginal people as childlike 30–1
pearling industry, forced Aboriginal labour 8–9
Pilbara settler community 292–3
   anxiety over freedom of movement of Aboriginal people 318–19, 322
   belief that McLeod behind woolshed fire 303, 307–8
   fear of violent retaliatory backlash by Aboriginal people 301–2
Pindan Pty Ltd 138–9
pingkayi (holiday time) 18, 25–6
Pippingarra Station 198, 310–11
   acceptance of temporary 5/- wage increase 117
   presence of Twelve Mile working parties 315
   strike by workers on 30 April 1946 109–10
   walk-offs by workers 172, 198
Plunkett, Walter 382, 383, 432
police
   appointed as Protectors of Natives 23
   chaining of Aboriginal prisoners 405–7, 417–18, 420, 421, 427
   coercion and arrests of strikers 206–7
   dawn dog cull raids 27–9
   increased visibility throughout Pilbara 304

INDEX

role in Aboriginal administration 365–7, 369–70, 389, 438, 459, 460
support for pastoralist control over Aboriginal labour 22–6, 111
suppression of strike action 124–6
surveillance of McLeod's activities 74
Police Act 1892
  section 50 408
  section 66 393
  section 66(8) 407
Port Hedland
  attempts to prevent sexual contact between soldiers and Aboriginal women 53
  breaking down of racial segregation 50–1
  demonstrations during race week. *see* race-time demonstrations
  Euralian community. *see* Euralian community, Port Hedland
  exclusion of Aboriginal people without native pass 53–5
  as prohibited area for Aboriginal people 53
  war effort 51, 52
Port Hedland wharf, dispute over employment of strikers 255–60
Prichard, Katharine Susannah 59, 79, 106, 108, 146, 148, 149, 152
protection, recasting of concept 11–12
protective legislation 10
Protectors of Natives
  police appointed as 23
  work permits issued to employers 10
Pullen, Dave 14–15, 447, 448
  on allliance between DNA and police 459
  discussions with Moolyella strikers 433
  discussions with Twelve Mile strikers 432
  meetings with McLeod 433–4
  on Rowe's case against strikers 434–5
  tour of Pilbara 431
  view of McLeod 434, 435, 437, 449
Punch (Yulpina) 402, 403, 404, 411

RAAF. *see* Royal Australian Air Force
rabbit-proof fence 5
race-time demonstrations 201
  attempt to secure food supplies 181–2
  march to police station to demand McLeod's release 182–3
  marrngu instructed to camp at the Four Mile Well 174–5
  non-violent resistance 176, 180, 181
  refusal of *marrngu* to return to work 177–9
  shifting of camp to Two mile 175–7
railways, prevention of strikers using trains 264–6
Rationing Commission 211–12
rations
  access controlled by pastoralists 207–8

essential items excluded from 13–14
paucity and poor quality of 39–40
provision in return for labour 10–11
for residents at Twelve Mile 211–13
Reay, Mary 283
regional development for North West
  Marble Bar convention 87–8
  McLeod's advocacy for 80–1, 87–9
  Whim Creek convention 87
Rhatigan, John Joseph (Jack) 222, 233
  on breakaway group 225–6, 227
  on conditions at Moolyella 225
Rich, George 275
Richards, G. R. (Ron) 144, 147, 151, 152, 160, 287
Richardson, A. E. (Ted)
  claim that workers were forced to strike 198, 293
  claims strikers stealing his stock 318
  complaints about Twelve Mile camp 184, 310–12, 326–7, 354, 377, 378
  on costs of Aboriginal labour 19
  criticism of DNA for not controlling strikers 324, 327, 339–40
  death 378
  illegal use of land at site of Twelve Mile 314
  increases wages during shearing 109–10
  on increasing payment of Aboriginal workers 191
  reduction of wages following shearing 172
Richardson, John 300–1, 312
Robinson, Vivian 31
Rose, Frederick (Fred) 49, 59, 148
Rowe, Tom 422, 427, 434–5
Roy Hill Station 47–8, 129
Royal Australian Air Force, base at Corruna Downs 44, 66, 73

Sainsbury, Beau 332
Saint, Eric Galton 357–8, 381–2, 385–6
samboism 137–8
Sampie, Thomas (Tommy) 400, 422
  Black Book 242
  leadership role at Twelve Mile 219, 275, 290, 292
  on removal of children 32
  on resistance against police 238
  response to eviction of Twelve Mile residents 380–1
  as school teacher at Twelve Mile 221, 222, 341–8, 354–5, 386–7, 388
  tensions with other Twelve Mile leaders 37, 352–3
  and tresspass action against strikers 315–16
Seamen's Union, Fremantle Branch 255
  ending of wool ban 442–5

507

financial support for strikers 417
impact of wool ban 451
implementation of ban 430–1, 439, 441–3
plan to impose wool ban 417, 418, 429–30
protest against imprisonment of Pilbara strikers 417
Seaton, Leonard 151
Second World War
Aboriginal coastguard unit on Melville Island 325, 326
Aboriginal people in north seen as security threat 51–2, 55–6
and development of Aboriginal activism 43–4
enlistment of Euralians rejected 52–3
impact on rise of liberal ideas 48
and Pilbara Strike 43–5
settler violence
in Great Sandy Desert 2–3
in Riverline Country 8–9
Sheppard, Eileen 242–3
Sheppard, W. F. J. (Bill) 115, 203, 242, 243, 403–5, 425–6
Sherlock, Ann 38
Sherlock, Benja 38, 181
on Hodge's visit to Port Hedland 189, 192
on lack of rations available to strikers 207
on loss of domestic servant 177, 179, 196–8
on loss of station workers 172, 177
on McLeod 161, 182–3
pity for strikers 205
Sherlock, Reg 38, 92, 122, 123, 161, 191, 192
Simdan 138
Sitlington, Grace 283
Skull Springs meeting
discussion of strike idea 75
marrngu accounts of 68–9, 93
McLeod's account of 67–73, 93–4
nature of 96
timing of 95–6
Slavery Abolition Act 1883 (UK) 160
Snowball 320, 329, 330, 353
Snowball, Gordon 173, 174, 321
Snowball, Joan 173, 174
southern support for strike movement
campaign by McLeod to attract 106–9, 146
CDNR campaign 149, 151–7
Communist Party campaign 146–9
Native Rights and Welfare League pamphlet 419–20, 425
protest over imprisonment of McKenna and Dooley and arrest of McLeod 146
protests against refusal of union tickets for strikers 260
undermined by anti-communism 169
union support for 255
Starke, Hayden 275, 276

State School Teachers' Union of Western Australia 348
State Shipping Services 257
stike camps, organisation and leadership 217–19
Strelley Station 22, 38, 105
acceptance of temporary 5/- wage increase 123
loss of domestic workers 179, 196–8
May Day strike 122–3
reasons for strike 136–7
trespass by Twelve Mile work party 315–17
walk-offs by workers 172, 177, 196–8
strike camps
McLeod's meetings with leaders 217–18
preference of some residents to never return to stations 293–5
recognition of authority of older men 219, 293–4
see also Moolyella; Twelve Mile
strike movement
breakaway group 225–30
conflict over access to land. *see* access to country
corporate authority. *see* Aboriginal corporate authority
distribution of calendars 103–5
encouragement of workers to join strike 422–3
Four Mile meetings 82–5, 94
funds collected towards acquiring a station property 88
future direction 452–3
impetus for strike action 94–5
leaders selected to organise strike 82–3
as manifestation of religious movement 96–7
Marble Bar meeting 103
marrngu accounts of origin of 75
May Day strike 1946. *see* May Day strike
meetings during *pingkayi* time 1945-46 92–3
Nullagine One Mile reserve meeting 93
and organisational capacity of *marrgnu* 91–2
pastoralists response to 91, 92
police threats against organisers 100–2
race-time demonstrations. *see* race-time demonstrations
regrouping after May Day strike 134
setting of strike date 92
southern support for. *see* southern support for strike movement
spreading of strike idea by *marrngu* organisers 88
strategy 86
strike demands 292, 437, 452

tactics. *see* tactics employed by strike movement
Twelve Mile meeting planned for 25 May 149–50
union support for 255
see also North-West Workers' Association
Stuart, Donald 69, 224
submissive obedience 137–8
Supreme Court of Western Australia, dismissal of appeals by McLeod, McKenna and Dooley 218, 274

Tabba Tabba Station 105
  acceptance of temporary 5/- wage increase 123
  loss of workers 171
  May Day strike 122–3
  reasons for strike action 136–7, 139–40
  tactics employed by strike movement
    'dumb blackfellow' strategy 137–9, 415
    mass civil disobedience 393, 397, 401, 402–16, 439
    non-violent resistance 176, 180, 181, 406
Talga Talga Station 86, 202
tantalite extraction 461
Taplin, Len 51
Thomas, Billy (Pitpit) (*Panaka*) 4, 5, 460
  on inequality of treatment 40–1
  on origins of strike movement 76–7, 95
  on police coercion to ensure return after *pingkayi* 25–6
  on reasons for strike 41
Thompson, Don 209, 224, 350, 357, 415, 453
Thompson, Jackie 231
Thompson, Ronald 266–8
Thornton, Ernie 78
tin mining 6, 30, 184, 208–9, 223, 285, 350, 390, 461, 463
tobacco 3–4
trade unions
  support for Aboriginal workers strike in Pilbara 255, 266, 440–1
  see also names of unions
Tribune 155
Turner, George 103, 105, 159
Twelve Mile 293–4
  abducted defectors resist return to Marble Bar 237–40
  acceptance of employment agreements 350
  access to rations and supplies 172–3, 211–13, 354
  authority and leadership 219–20
  Christmas celebrations 215, 228
  cultural and religious significance of site 383–4
  declared prohibited area 377–9, 385–6
  decline of 349–50, 352–4

economic difficulties 349–50
economic enterprises 189, 210–11, 213–14, 220, 285–6, 313
eviction of residents 380–4
living conditions 221–2, 331–2
location 310–11
McBeath's visit 291–3
meeting planned for May 25 1946 134
military-style drills 220
organisational arrangements 219–20
pastoralist demands that camp be moved 310–15
political discord 352–3
population of camp 196, 215, 285, 341, 349
relocation of many to Moolyella 350
residents intention to earn own living 174
sanitary conditions 331
school 221, 341–8, 353, 379–8, 386–7, 463
strikers move to 119, 129–30
visit by Hodge 189
Two Mile camp
  attempt to secure food supplies 181–2
  defiance of police over where to camp 175–7
  march to police station to demand McLeod's release 182–3
  move to Twelve Mile camp 184
  refusal of *marrngu* to return to work 177–9

United Nations Organisation (UNO) 153, 155-155 155–6
Uridja, Jimmy (Juwikarayirti) 390

VDC. *see* Volunteer Defence Corp
violence against *marrngu*
  constant threat of 27–9
  by early settlers. *see* settler violence
  by police 137, 180, 239, 263–4
Volunteer Defence Corp 51, 55–6, 58
Vyshinsky, Andrey 420

Walker, James 272, 273
Wallal Station 25, 134
Wallareenya Station 129
Walsh, Jack 441
Wandarri, Bruce 13, 14, 225, 453
Wandarri, Harry 3, 5
Warnman people 2, 3
Warralong Station 37, 104, 211, 286
  living conditions for workers 352
  marrngu refusal to work 86
  reticence of workers to join strike action 126
  return of some workers 332
Warrawagine Station
  arrival of people from desert 6
  marrngu initially driven away from station 5
  mealtime segregation 39

raiding party 403–5
ration distribution 13–14, 15, 40
removal of children of mixed descent 31, 32
return of workers for better employment conditions 453–4
sexual exploitation of Aboriginal women 241–4
strike by workers on 29 April 1946 112–16, 117, 207
wages paid 453
walk-offs by workers 202–5, 403–5, 425–6, 453
Warrie Station, pay increases 425
Watson, Wilfred 247
Watts, Arthur 347
Weaver, Keith 304, 305, 332
Webb, Thomas Arthur 246–7, 248–51, 252, 253, 266
Welsh, Frank (Bidge) 37, 285, 287, 293, 309
West Australian 157, 163–4, 190–1, 303
Western Australia
  calls for Commonwealth control over administration of Aboriginal people 153
  conditions of self-government 9, 60
  international accusations of slavery 420–1
  racism 363–4, 439
Western Australian Constitution, section 70 9, 60, 70, 434
Western Australian Nurses Association 154–5
Western Desert Language-speaking people 3
Western Desert people 2
Whim Creek regional development convention 87
White, Alan 318
White Springs Mission 362, 369, 463
  DNA support for 373, 375–6
  opposition of strike community to 387–8
  pastoralist support for 376–7
  proposed school 32
White Springs Station 175, 361, 373–4
Williams, Dudley 275
Williams, Joan 106, 107, 120, 147, 160

Williams, Molly (Kulyu) (*Purungu*) 140, 305, 352
  on communal cooking 211, 219
  at Ettrick outcamp 29
  on rations 39
  on walking off station 200–1
  work on kangarooing team 210–11
Wilson, Deborah 96, 219
Wilson, John 34, 45, 68, 69, 82, 96, 98, 138–9, 149, 169, 176, 206, 207, 217, 219, 220, 223, 387
Wilson, Katrin 68, 69, 98, 102, 138–9, 220, 223
Wise, Frank 163
  defence of *Native Administration Act* 154
  on native welfare and working conditions 154–5
  response to letters of protest 166–7
Withnell, Don 382–3, 393, 405–6
Wolff, Albert 272, 274
women
  murrngu women. *see* Aboriginal women
Women's Christian Temperance League 152, 154
Women's National Missionary Council 152
Woodman, Jimmy 83, 104, 333
Woodman, Molly 223
Woodman, Tommy 83
Workers' Star 69, 79, 81, 106, 108, 109, 146, 147, 150–1, 155, 162, 163, 164, 219, 279, 348, 445
World Federation of Trade Unions 156
Wright, Tom 59, 157
Wyndham, Alec 214, 305, 432

Yabarla, Paddy 171–2
Yandeyarra Station 96, 111, 360, 372, 373, 463
Yandy (Stuart) 69, 103, 143, 349
Yarrie Station 18, 19, 117
Yougarla, Crow (Yakalya) (*Panaka*), strike on 29 April 1946 113, 114–15
Yule River 1